TORT LAW FOR LEGAL ASSISTANTS

LINDA L. EDWARDS AND J. STANLEY EDWARDS

TORT LAW FOR LEGAL ASSISTANTS

LINDA L. EDWARDS, J.D.
Phoenix College

J. STANLEY EDWARDS, J.D.

WEST PUBLISHING COMPANY
St. Paul   New York   Los Angeles   San Francisco

DEDICATION

To our parents,
Audrey and Louis Dixon
and Esther and William Dean,
for their love and support
and to Teddy and his friends
for the inspiration they provided.

Copyediting: Sheryl Rose
Indexing: Terry Casey
Composition: Parkwood Composition

About the Cover
The photograph on the cover shows the doors leading into the Great Hall of the Supreme Court of the United States. These doors were created in the 1930's by John Donnelly, Jr. for the Supreme Court Commission. They are made of bronze and weigh 13 tons. The eight illustrations on the doors portray significant events and people in the evolution of law through history. Beginning with the upper right and continuing clockwise: Supreme Court Justices Marshall and Storey, Lord Coke and James I, Statute of Westminister, the signing of the Magna Carta, the Shield of Achilles, Preactors Edict, Julian and the Scholar, the creation of the Justinian Code. Collection of the Supreme Court of the United States.

WEST'S COMMITMENT TO THE ENVIRONMENT
In 1906, West Publishing Company began recycling materials left over from the production of books. This began a tradition of efficient and responsible use of resources. Today, up to 95 percent of our legal books and 70% of our college texts are printed on recycled, acid-free stock. West also recycles nearly 22 million pounds of scrap paper annually—the equivalent of 181,717 trees. Since the 1960's, West has devised ways to capture and recycle waste inks, solvents, oils, and vapors created in the printing process. We also recycle plastics of all kinds, wood, glass, corrugated cardboard, and batteries, and have eliminated the use of styrofoam book packaging. We at West are proud of the longevity and the scope of our commitment to our environment.

Printed in the United States of America

99 98 97 96 95 94 93 8 7 6 5 4 3 2 1

Library of Congress Cataloging-in-Publication Data

Edwards, Linda L.
Tort law for legal assistants / Linda L. Edwards, J. Stanley Edwards.
p. cm.
Includes index.
ISBN 0-314-93447-2 (hard)
1. Torts—United States. I. Edwards, J. Stanley. II. Title.
KF1250.Z9E38 1992
346.7303—dc20 91-42152
[347.3063] CIP 

TABLE OF CONTENTS

PREFACE

Down-to-earth explanations and practical application of tort law concepts relevant to legal assistants are the trademark of this text. Legalese is avoided and simplicity in both language and organization is sought. The edited cases that are included were selected because they were well-written and offer particularly enlightening explanations of the case law in a specific area or, in some instances, because they provide uniquely entertaining reading.

Most chapters begin with a hypothetical situation designed to stimulate the reader's interest and to give an overview of the basic principles presented in the chapter. A common scenario links together chapters five through ten (dealing with negligence) and an application section in each of these chapters shows the reader how to put the principles within that chapter into practice. A summary at the end of each chapter encapsulates the essential concepts into an easily reviewable format. Practical procedural skills, such as summarizing depositions, drafting and answering interrogatories, preparing trial exhibits, and organizing personal injury files, are highlighted in the Practice Pointers section. The Tort Teasers that conclude each chapter pose questions and present actual cases that give readers the opportunity to integrate and apply the concepts they have been exposed to.

To assist instructors in their classroom preparation, an Instructor's Manual is available, which contains questions suggested for classroom discussion, exam questions, edited versions of the cases cited in the Tort Teasers, and answers to the questions posed in the Tort Teasers. A Student Study Guide also supplements the text, allowing students to become actively involved in the learning process and focusing them on key concepts. Sample forms are included so that students can get an idea of what the documents mentioned throughout the text actually look like.

Special thanks go to our typists, Mary Insera, Sue Davis, and Julie Konizeski, who dedicated so much of their time and energy to see this project through to completion. We are very indebted to those students who served as "guinea pigs" during the production process and helped review the manuscript. Their comments and observations helped make this a "user friendly" text. We gratefully acknowledge the aid of our production editor, Beth Kennedy, and our acquisitions editor, Elizabeth Hannan, whose expertise and cordiality greatly facilitated the creation of the text. We also wish to acknowledge the following reviewers whose helpful suggestions and supportive advice so greatly enriched our work.

Stacey Barone
Adelphi University

Cindy Coker
Florence-Darlington Technical College

John DeLio
Central Pennsylvania Business School

Marshall Dyer
Rogers State College

Dolores Grissom
Samford University

Susan Harrell
University of West Florida

Jean Hellman
Loyola University

Debbie Howard
University of Evansville

Jane Kaplan
New York City Technical College

Paul Marsella
Salem State College

Chanda Miller
Des Moines Area Community College

Dave Pardys
William Rainey Harper College

Leo Villalobos
El Paso Community College

We wish you a stimulating and enjoyable journey through the captivating world of tort law!

TORT LAW FOR LEGAL ASSISTANTS

LINDA L. EDWARDS AND J. STANLEY EDWARDS

PART I INTRODUCTION

INTRODUCTION

CHAPTER OBJECTIVES

In this chapter you will learn to:

- Define a tort and distinguish between a tort and a crime as well as a tort and a contract.
- Trace the evolution of tort law.
- Recognize the philosophical principles and arguments underpinning tort law.

You come home one evening to find that one of your children has been bitten by your next-door neighbor's dog, who was safely secured behind his fence when your child, contrary to your instruction, entered the yard to retrieve a wayward ball. Your neighbor took every precaution of isolating the dog, short of locking the fence. Should the neighbor be held liable?

Someone in your family contracts a deadly disease whose cause can be traced to chemical contaminants found in toxic wastes dumped by the city in which you live. The city dumped the wastes several decades before the area became residential and, at the time, was totally ignorant of the long-term effects. Should the city be held liable?

You allow your grandfather, whom you know has imbibed more than his usual two shots, to drive and he injures someone. Should you be held responsible?

Someone trespasses and falls in a hole on your property. Should you be held liable?

Your daughter finally succeeds in becoming a famous actress. Without her permission, a magazine publishes nude photographs of her. Should she be able to sue for invasion of privacy?

Your son is wrongfully detained because a storekeeper suspects him of shoplifting. Should he be able to sue the store for the emotional distress he endures?

Should the attorney that you work for be held liable for your negligent acts?

Should you be held liable for the intentional torts of your children?

You have been burglarized on several occasions and, in a desperate attempt to protect your property, you set up a mechanical protective device. Should you be held liable if a would-be burglar is seriously injured by the device?

These questions, which illustrate the broad scope of human concerns that fall under tort law, will be examined in this text. Tort law is an intriguing area of the law that covers virtually every aspect of human endeavor. It not only governs the conduct of many in our society but also reflects our attitudes toward living itself. Within the parameters of tort law can be discovered many of the philosophical underpinnings of our society.

BACKGROUND

It has been said that tort liability is like a tax that makes products and services more costly to all and ultimately unaffordable to some. This "tax," it is argued, has put some gynecologists out of business, prohibited the sale of certain drugs, and severely hampered municipalities and other governmental bodies in their delivery of services. (See P. Huber, *Liability,* 1988 for a discussion of this issue.)

Advocates of expanded tort liability see tort law as the knight in shining armor, duly anointed to protect the interests of the consumer. In their perception, manufacturers and those who deliver services are better able than consumers to predict and prevent potential accidents. The burden of injury, they reason, should be borne by those who create risks rather than by those who fall prey to them. The philosophical and political debates on the issue of risk allocation have gained new significance in one of the most recent developments in tort law—product liability.

WHAT IS A TORT?

But what is this thing we call a "tort"? Although the term has evaded concrete definition, it has been described as a civil wrong for which the victim receives a remedy in the form of damages (Table 1–1). Included under this heading are intentional torts (assault, battery, and false imprisonment are some examples), negligence (acts committed without intent but in violation of a reasonable person standard), and strict liability (acts committed with no intent at all).

REASONABLENESS OF CONDUCT

The common threat interweaving all torts is the notion that socially unreasonable conduct should be penalized and those who are its victims should be compensated. Of course, determining what is unreasonable is a formidable task since reasonableness, like beauty, is in the eyes of the beholder. The

TABLE 1.1 Definition of a Tort

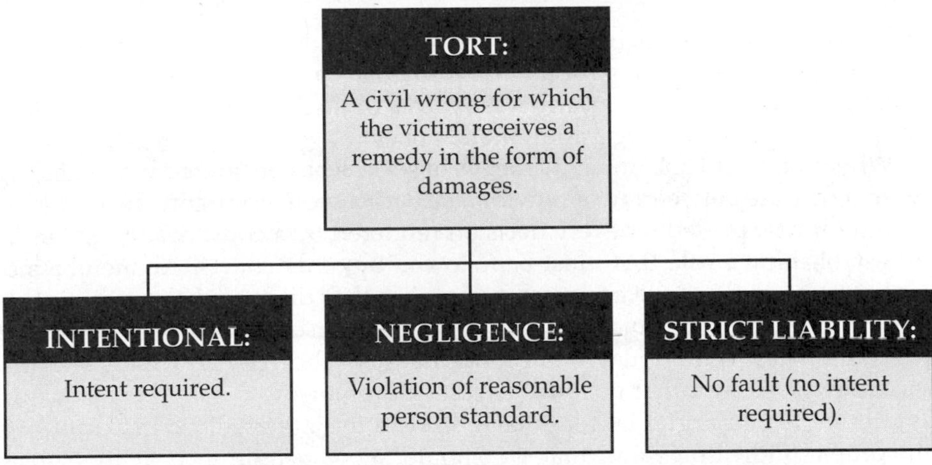

overall goal in defining "reasonableness" is to balance the plaintiff's need for protection against the defendant's claim of freedom to pursue his own ends. But how does one determine reasonableness of conduct? Should one take into consideration, for example, the parties' religious beliefs, their physical disabilities, or their emotional idiosyncracies?

To get a feeling for where you stand on this issue of reasonableness, consider the following. You are sitting as a juror on a case in which the plaintiff, a devoutly religious Catholic woman, was severely injured by the negligent driving of the defendant. The plaintiff was pregnant at the time of her injury and was told that because of the serious pelvic injury she sustained she would be in grave danger if she carried her baby to term. Because of her intense aversion to abortion she chose to deliver the baby and died in the process.

Do you think the defendant should be required to compensate the plaintiff's family for her death? How would you determine the reasonableness of the plaintiff's conduct? Would you require her to conform to the conduct of the "average" person or would you compare her conduct to that of a reasonable person holding her beliefs? These are just some examples of the types of questions with which jurors and courts must grapple in their struggle to assign fault and apportion damages equitably.

Sometimes the reasonableness of the defendant's conduct is not at issue because of the far-reaching social consequences of his or her actions. In the area of product liability, for example, even those manufacturers and sellers who act reasonably are held liable to plaintiffs injured by their products. This is done in the name of protecting society. By holding manufacturers and sellers responsible for all such losses, the argument is made, consumers will be better protected and sellers and manufacturers will be more conscientious in the delivery of their services and products. Similarly, one who innocently defames another will be held liable despite his benign intent. The victim's reputation is irreparably tarnished no matter how reasonable the defamer's conduct, it is reasoned, and so compensation is required.

PUBLIC POLICY

Tort law often goes beyond recompensing individuals and considers, more broadly, the interests of society. These interests are often referred to by the courts as **public policy** concerns. The ideals of justice, fairness, and equality dominate discussions regarding public policy.

Why, you might ask, must the needs of society be considered when dealing with a dispute between two individuals? Because our common law system is based on case precedent every decision rendered by a court has the potential of establishing a rule that must be followed by other courts. All members of society, therefore, have an interest in seeing that disputes between litigants are resolved in such a manner that the principles set forth in that process of resolution are fair and just for all concerned. For the very principles set forth today will be those that govern the cases of tomorrow.

Others would argue that we have become too paternalistic in our efforts to protect individuals and that we should allow people to bear the consequences of their decisions. After all, they point out, the process of living comes with no guarantees and the assurance of safety is too high a price to pay for freedom.

In addition to this philosophical concern, there is reluctance to burden a defendant, particularly an industry, with all losses for fear of financial ruin. As a result, new technological developments may be inhibited or become financially prohibitive.

This problem of distribution of losses continues to haunt those who would seek an equitable balance between the needs of plaintiffs and defendants. You must decide the proper solution to this controversy. Suffice it to say that whichever philosophical trail you choose to follow will predetermine your resolution of many cases.

MORALITY OF CONDUCT

Is the morality of a defendant's conduct relevant in tort law? Although personal morality may be subject to variation, tort law borrows heavily from a sense of public morality. It can be said that, at least in certain cases, we all have a sense of what is universally regarded as right and wrong. Tort law generally reflects that sense.

There are circumstances, however, in which a defendant can be held liable even though he or she has violated no moral code. One who, for example, trespasses on the land of another in the reasonable belief that it is his own land is still liable for trespass. With the increasing popularity of no-fault torts, such as strict liability, we appear to be moving away from a need to cast moral judgment on a defendant's conduct. On the other hand, tort law does not deal with all blatantly immoral acts. While it may be morally reprehensible, for example, to allow a stranger to die when you could save her, in most circumstances you will have committed no tort.

"SLIPPERY SLOPE" ARGUMENTS

Another concern that has affected the development of tort law is the consideration of the effect of a ruling on future case law. Courts are often hesitant to crack open a legal door in a particular case for fear of creating a "flood of litigation," an occurrence they are ever on the alert to avoid. For that reason, some types of flagrant misdeeds go unavenged in tort law. Relatively trivial concerns must also go by the wayside in an effort to protect the courts. Many of our most grievous hurts are inflicted in the context of interpersonal relationships and yet most of these must go without redress. Lovers are jilted, children are verbally belittled by parents, friends are "used," and so on. Yet the law cannot become enmeshed in these psychically damaging events if the legal system is to avoid an administrative nightmare created by an onslaught of cases. Clearly, not all human wrong can be remedied. It is the province of the courts to decide which shall and shall not be eligible for litigation.

Perhaps you have heard of the **"slippery slope" argument**, which means, essentially, that allowance of an argument in one case will allow application of that same argument in innumerable other cases. The metaphor is used to show that once you take the first step, it is too easy to fall down the slippery slope to the bottom of the hill, presumably into a morass of undesirable outcomes. The slippery slope argument is, in essence, an administrative concern. A court fears that if it finds negligence on behalf of the sympathetic plaintiff before it, hundreds of thousand of similarly situated individuals or those whose situations are analogous to the case will also seek redress.

Keep in mind that while courts are to focus on the long term in making their decisions, they sometimes are understandably sympathetic to the plight of the individuals before them. In such cases they often render decisions that meet the short-term goals of justice but that prove untenable over the long run. Justice, you will soon discover, is an illusory goal that often eludes capture by even the most conscientious judge.

CREATION OF CASE LAW

Tort law is largely a product of the common law, which involves case-by-case decision making by the courts. This decision-making process is affected, to some degree, by statutes, which the courts are mandated to follow unless statutory gaps exist that leave a court with unanswered questions. Some statutes, such as the wrongful death and survival acts, directly address issues that arise in the context of tort law. Others, such as certain criminal statutes, serve as guidelines to the courts in establishing policy. A statute, for example, that makes it a misdemeanor to drive while under the influence of alcohol sets forth the standard of care expected of drivers. A driver having a blood alcohol level in excess of the statutory limit would be considered to have breached the duty of care he owed to those around him.

Another guideline that courts use in formulating their holdings is the Restatement of the Law of Torts. The Restatement was compiled by eminent legal scholars and practitioners in an attempt to provide lawyers and judges with black-letter principles (legal principles generally accepted by the legal community) of tort law. Adopted in many jurisdictions, the Restatement is frequently cited in court opinions.

Although criticized for creating the impression of uniformity in the law where there is none, the Restatement is, nevertheless, a frequently used guide through the maze of tort law decisions. For this reason, the Restatement is often cited throughout this text. Keep in mind, however, that your state may not have adopted the Restatement position. Consult the case law in your state when dealing with a specific case.

RELATIONSHIP BETWEEN TORT LAW AND OTHER AREAS OF THE LAW

TORTS vs. CRIMES

How does a tort differ from a crime? Although the two share several similarities, they differ in terms of the interests affected, the remedy granted, and some of the procedural mechanisms used (see Table 1–2). A crime is consid-

TABLE 1.2 Torts vs. Crimes and Torts vs. Contracts

	TORTS	CRIMES
PURPOSE	Compensation	Punishment
STANDARD OF PROOF	Preponderance of Evidence	Beyond a Reasonable Doubt
INTERESTS VIOLATED	Individual's Interest	Society's Interest
PROCEDURAL RULES	Civil Rules	Criminal Rules

	TORTS	CONTRACTS
DUTIES ASSIGNED	Imposed by Law	By Parties' Consent
OBLIGATIONS MADE TO	Society in General	Specific Individuals

ered an offense against society while a tort is an offense against another individual or group of individuals. The purpose of prosecuting someone who has committed a crime is to vindicate the interests of society by punishing the offender. The purpose of suing in tort, on the other hand, is to compensate the victim.

Although the primary purpose of criminal law is punishment and the primary purpose of tort law is compensation, there is some overlap between the two. Compensation of a crime victim (known as restitution) is frequently used by the courts as part of an offender's sentence. By the same token, punitive damages, which are intended to punish the tortfeasor (one who has committed a tort), are used in certain circumstances in tort law. Despite this overlap, the primary functions of criminal law and tort law remain distinct.

Moreover, the rules of civil procedure are used in tort cases while the rules of criminal procedure are used in criminal cases. Also, the plaintiff's burden of proof in a tort case is by a preponderance of the evidence while the state's burden of proof in a criminal case is beyond a reasonable doubt. The rules of evidence applicable in criminal cases vary, to some degree, from those applicable in civil cases.

Many acts may be both a crime against the state and a tort against the individual. If a drunk driver, for example, is involved in a vehicular accident, she may be charged with a criminal offense as well as sued by the injured parties for negligence. For this reason those charged with criminal offenses often plead nolo contendere (no contest). If they were to plead guilty, their admission of guilt could be used against them in a subsequent civil trial whereas a plea of nolo contendere could not. This is true, however, only if the issue tried in the criminal case is also relevant to some aspect of the tort action. Because of the lower standard of proof in a civil case, the plaintiff in a tort case will have an easier time establishing liability than the state will have proving guilt.

TORTS vs. CONTRACTS

Tort law differs from contract law in terms of the voluntariness of entering into an agreement. When two or more parties create a contract, they each agree to give up something in return for receiving some benefit. In a contract action the parties have voluntarily and knowingly assumed duties or obligations to others. In tort law, by contrast, duties are imposed by the law without the express consent or awareness of those involved (Table 1–2). If a guest is injured on a landowner's premises, the landowner is liable, not because he expressly contracted to prevent injury to the guest, but because the law imposes certain obligations on him by virtue of being a landowner.

Just as with criminal law, however, there is an overlap between tort law and contract law. Certain tort duties may coincide with those duties set forth in a contract, for example, so that if a party fails to live up to its obligations, an action may lie in either tort or contract. Additionally, some quasi-contractual obligations (such as the obligation to act in "good faith") are imposed by law without the consent of the parties, just as in tort law.

One other distinction between contract and tort law is that in contract law obligations are made to specific individuals whereas in tort law duties are owed to people in general. In tort law one is bound to act as a reasonable person toward all other persons but in contract law one is bound in contract only to certain chosen individuals. This distinction is not completely valid, however, in that tort law principles impose special duties in some cases because of the relationship one has with another. An employer, for example, owes duties of care to her employees that she does not owe to other persons.

You will find as you pursue your study of torts that this area of law overlaps with most other areas of law. Therefore, you will frequently find yourself referring to knowledge that you have gained from the study of property law, constitutional law, criminal law, contract law, corporate law and so on.

BRIEF HISTORY OF TORT LAW

If this is the point in most textbooks where you skip ahead, try to persevere. You might be surprised at how interesting the evolution of tort law really is (Table 1–3).

In barbaric societies the only "law" that seemed to control group behavior had its roots in the blood feud. The protocol of the blood feud required that the clan go to war against any outsider who inflicted harm on a clan member, thereby dishonoring the clan as a whole. Atonement for the humiliation suffered by the victim's kin seemed the primary goal. When the law first assumed a more civilized veneer, the remedies created served as substitutes for the feuding process, and thus emerged the concept of monetary compensation.

Early in Anglo-Saxon history, individuals were assigned a monetary value based principally on their rank. Money instead of blood was offered as a salve for injured clan pride. Compensation was directed toward the clan rather than the individual and awards were distributed proportionately among the

TABLE 1.3

EVOLUTION OF TORT LAW
Blood feud (no fault)
Action in trespass (no fault) (Vi et armis) (Direct use of force)
Trespass on the case (wrongful intent or negligence) (No force or indirect injury)
Negligence (fault required)
Strict liability (no fault)

injured person's relatives. There was no distinction between crimes and torts. Furthermore, there seemed to be no concern regarding issues of fault or blameworthiness. Even the most remote causal connection was sufficient to justify the imposition of punishment.

Interestingly enough, during this same time period vengeance was exacted on whatever was determined to be the immediate cause of death, even if it were an animal or inanimate object. The offending object, be it a horse or a sword, might be turned over to the victim or the victim's family to be used as they saw fit, or delivered to the king.

ACTION IN TRESPASS

Exactly how the **action in trespass**, which emerged sometime in the middle of the thirteenth century, evolved out of this cauldron of vengeance is unclear. This action, which was basically of a criminal nature, dealt with serious and forcible breaches of peace. One of its requirements was the showing of force and arms, referred to as *vi et armis*. Notice the procedural remnants of that cause of action that appear in the whimsically written case of *Tricoli v. Centalanza.*

The plaintiff had to allege that the defendant had used force directly on his person or property; thus, the term *vi et armis* appeared in every writ of trespass as a matter of course. No further showing of blameworthiness or fault on the part of the defendant was necessary. As time went on, however, even mild, innocuous physical contact was sufficient for the plaintiff to prevail in a trespass action and the pleading of *vi et armis* became a mere technical device.

Tricoli v. Centalanza et al.
(Supreme Court of New Jersey. Oct. 8, 1924.)

MINTURN, J. "Run away, Maestro Juan, I am going to kill you." Such was the ferocious threat that disturbed the atmosphere, not of prehistoric Mexico, where upon desolate plains the savage coyote still bays at the moon, not yet of classic Verona, where dramatic memories of the houses of Montague and Capulet still linger to entrance the romantic wayfarer, but from the undiluted atmosphere of Bloomfield avenue, where it winds its attractive course through the prim rococo shades of modern Montclair, which upon the day succeeding Christmas in 1923 sat like Roma immortalis upon its seven hills, and from its throne of beauty contemplated with serene satisfaction the peace and tranquillity of the modern world.

The Maestro, however, with true chivalric disdain, refused to retreat, but determined at all hazards, like Horatius, to hold the bridge, or rather the stoop, upon which he stood. Like a true Roman, inoculated with the maximum percentage of American patriotism, he turned defiantly to the oncoming house of Centalanza, and proclaimed in the bellicose language of the day "you too son of a gun."

In the day of the Montague and Capulet aristocratic rapier and swords defended the honor of their respective houses; but in this day of popular progress the Maestro and the Centalanza sought only the plebeian defense of fists and a shovel. As a result of a triangular contest, the physician testified that the Maestro was battered "from head to buttocks"—a distribution of punishment, it may be observed, which, while it may not be entirely aesthetic in its selection of a locum tenens, was to say the least equitably administered and distributed. Indeed, so much was the Maestro battered that his daily toil lost him for 12 days, and the trial court estimated that this loss, together with his pain and suffering, and the aggravation of the trespass, entitled him to receive from the house of Centalanza $240.

[1, 2] The latter, however, has appealed, and alleges that the Maestro proved no substantial cause of action against them. But the learned trial court, upon this contested state of facts, concluded, and we think properly, that there was an issue of fact thus presented, since the suit was for assault and battery in the nature of trespass vi et armis. But the defendants Centalanza insist that two distinct encounters took place, one by both defendants, and the other by one only, and they ask: How can such a physical contretemps be admeasured, so as to impose upon each member of the house of Centalanza his fair share of compensation for his physical contribution to the melee? The inquiry possesses its latent difficulties, but, since it is an admitted rule of law that the court will not distribute the damages between tort-feasors, upon any theory of equitable admeasurement, the house of Centalanza obviously must bear the entire loss, without seeking a partition thereof. "Ex Turpi causa oritur non actio."

[3] Indeed, it would prove to be a rare feat of judicial acumen, were the court to attempt to give due credit to Donato Centalanza for the the prowess he displayed in his fistic endeavors, and to assess to Raffale Centalanza his mead of financial contribution for the dexterity with which he wielded his handy implement of excavation. It is doubtful, even in these days of the mystic prize ring, whether such a metaphysical test may be included among the accredited mental accomplishments of a quasi militant judiciary, which, while it occasionally indulges in a caustic punch, still strenuously endeavors to maintain the proverbial respectability and regal poise of its ancestral prototype. In such a situation we are not inclined to impose this extraordinary and novel field of jurisdiction upon our inferior courts. The occurrence of trespass vi et armis, confers upon the trial court the right to assess exemplary damages as smart money and this the trial court properly did under the circumstances of the case.

[4] It is contended, however, that the actual damage sustained by the Maestro was inconsequential, and that the rule, "de minimis non curat lex," applies. It must be obvious, however, that damage which to the attending physician seemed to penetrate the Maestro "from head to buttocks" may seem trivial to us as noncombatants, but to the Maestro it manifestly seemed otherwise, and doubtless punctured his corpus, as well as his sensibilities. Indeed, he well might declare in the language of the gallant Mercutio of Verona, concerning the extent of his wound: "it is not as wide as a church door, or as deep as a well, but 'twill serve."

The judgment will be affirmed.

TRESPASS ON THE CASE

The action in trespass was highly restrictive in that it precluded recovery by those who could show no use or only indirect use of force by the defendant. A companion form of action known as **trespass on the case** arose to allow recovery in the absence of force or in those cases where an injury was inflicted indirectly. A plaintiff who was injured when the defendant wielded a plank of wood against him could pursue an action in trespass to redress his injuries while a plaintiff who tripped over that same piece of wood left carelessly in her path by the defendant had to resort to a trespass on the case.

While damage to the plaintiff was implied in an action in trespass, the plaintiff was required to show injury and damage. Trespass on the case actions demanded proof of the defendant's wrongful intent or negligence whereas an action in trespass required no showing of fault. Trespass on the case was frequently used as a means of recovering for breach of a legal duty grounded on custom. Those who served the public, such as innkeepers, were frequently the defendants in such cases.

NEGLIGENCE

The development of public transportation seems to have had a profound influence on the evolution of tort law. As the courts were faced with more traffic-related cases, they came to the realization that decisions mechanically rendered in favor of victims under the trespass theory (which merely required the showing of direct force) would have a prohibitive effect on the use of highways. Under this approach, few could afford to risk traveling on the highways and losing their fortunes as a result of accident. Thus, the idea of negligence emerged as a compromise. Travelers were granted some measure of protection from liability as long as they drove in such a manner that they reduced the risk of accidents.

The rise of negligence as a cause of action coincided with the disintegration of actions in trespass and trespass on the case, although negligence ultimately assumed many of the characteristics of a trespass on the case action. The distinction between trespass and trespass on the case has basically disappeared except in those states where some trace of the distinction has been retained through common law pleadings. One vestige of the distinction that continues to hang on, however, is the necessity of proving damages. Those torts that trace their ancestry back to trespass require no proof of actual damages; those that trace back to trespass on the case do require such proof. Although reminders of these dinosaurs of tort law emerge occasionally, they have for the most part been replaced by the modern torts that are the subject of this text.

COMING FULL CIRCLE

This brief overview of the development of tort law demonstrates the cyclical evolution of our attitude toward the notion of fault. Strict liability (no fault) reigned supreme during early Anglo-Saxon law and was evident in the action in trespass. Only in actions on the case did the notion of duty and neglect arise. Now, as we near the beginning of the twenty-first century, strict liability has once again assumed importance in our legal system. More and more modern courts are assigning liability even where there is no showing of fault.

As you study this text consider what you think the purpose of the law should be. Should society bear the cost of losses suffered by individuals or should that responsibility be shifted to the individual? What role should fault play in tort law? Once you have formulated your position, see how consistent you are as you read the cases interspersed throughout the text.

CLASSIFICATION OF TORTS

Today torts are divided into three categories, depending on the nature of the defendant's conduct: intentional torts, negligence, and strict liability. By far the most common is negligence. The bulk of personal injury practice centers around automobile accident cases, "slip and fall" cases, and other types of cases in which someone failed to use reasonable care. Strict liability is found to a lesser degree, usually in the context of product liability. Intentional torts are rarely encountered in practice.

The organization of this text reflects the relative importance of each of these tort classifications. While considerable coverage is devoted to negligence and related topics relatively little consideration is given to intentional torts. Although intentional torts are conceptually easier to comprehend than negligence, negligence is addressed first because paralegals must have a solid foundation in negligence when they begin practicing even if their understanding of intention is a bit superficial.

We will divide our discussion into three separate areas, but you should be aware that many torts may be based on any one of the three types of conduct. Misrepresentation, for example, can be committed intentionally, negligently, or with no fault (strict liability), as can defamation. Malpractice is a tort based on negligence. Bad faith is primarily an intentional tort. But many other causes of action are hybrids that defy precise classification. Rather than trying to pigeonhole all torts into neat categories, recognize that some distinctions are blurred.

SUMMARY

A tort can be defined as a civil wrong for which the victim receives compensation in the form of damages. The feeling that socially unreasonable conduct should be penalized underlies tort law and much of the case law is focused on determining what constitutes unreasonable conduct. In some cases, however, reasonableness is not an issue because the goal is to protect society no matter how reasonable the conduct.

Public policy concerns prevail throughout tort law. These concerns center primarily around the ideals of justice, fairness, and equality. One of the philosophical dilemmas that permeates tort law is how much weight should be placed on the needs of society when resolving disputes between individuals. In balancing these needs, courts frequently resort to slippery slope arguments to justify their refusal to grant relief to sympathetic plaintiffs.

Tort law is largely a product of common law although statutes are, in some instances, relied on. The courts frequently look to the Restatement of the Law of Torts in formulating the law.

Although similar in some ways to crimes, torts differ in terms of purpose, burden of proof, and procedural rules. Many acts are considered both a crime and a tort. Torts differ from contracts in that the duties assigned according to tort law are those imposed by law while those assigned in the context of contracts are by virtue of the party's consent. Furthermore, in contract law obligations are assumed toward specific individuals whereas tort law assumes that obligations are owed to society as a whole.

The origin of tort law can be traced back to the blood feud. When the concept of monetary compensation emerged, it was directed toward the clan rather than the individual. The action in trespass, which evolved in the thirteenth century, required proof that the defendant used force directly on the plaintiff or his property. The plaintiff did not, however, have to prove fault on the part of the defendant. In contrast, trespass on the case allowed recovery even when the defendant did not use force or inflicted injury indirectly. Proof of damages and the defendant's wrongful intent or negligence were, however, required in a trespass on the case action. The concept of negligence developed along with the evolution of public transportation. At the same time, actions in trespass and trespass on the case fell into disfavor and ultimately disappeared. Strict liability has now assumed an important role in tort law and is evidence of its cyclical evolution, in that the law began with no fault (action in trespass) and has now culminated in no fault.

TORT TEASERS

As indicated in this chapter the issue of risk allocation is a troublesome matter that the courts and legal scholars have grappled with over the years. To help clarify the questions related to risk allocation consider a hypothetical situation in which a manufacturer of aspirin fails to warn consumers that aspirin should not be given to children suffering from flulike symptoms. A four-year-old child contracts Reyes Syndrome after being given aspirin for the flu. Write out all the reasons supporting your belief that the manufacturer either should or should not be held liable for the child's damages. Be sure to include in your discussion public policy arguments that you think are relevant.

KEY TERMS

Action in trespass (*vi et armis*)
Early cause of action involving serious, forcible breaches of peace that evolved to encompass even minor physical contact; no showing of fault was required.

Public policy
Consideration by judges of the effects of proposed legal principle on society as a whole.

Slippery slope argument
Argument that once you take a first step in allowing something in one instance you are in danger of falling down the "slippery slope" into a bottomless pit of circumstances requiring comparable treatment.

Trespass on the case
Early cause of action involving injuries inflicted indirectly and requiring some showing of fault.

OVERVIEW OF A TORT CASE

CHAPTER OBJECTIVES

In this chapter you will be given a procedural overview of a tort case and will learn the terminology associated with:

- The initiation of a complaint and a response to that complaint.
- The conducting of the discovery process.
- The preparation for trial.
- The conducting of a trial.
- The implementation of posttrial procedures.

OVERVIEW OF A TORT CASE

After leaving work on Friday afternoon, Hanna drove to Happy Valley Bank to cash her paycheck. Leaving the bank, as she prepared to enter Sunshine Avenue, the street on which the bank is located, she came to a complete stop and looked into the mirror provided by the bank to see if there was any oncoming traffic. The bank found it necessary to install this mirror because customers experienced so much difficulty in seeing any oncoming cars. The curved shape of the street obstructed their view. As fate would have it, rain from earlier that afternoon had caused the mirror to fog over. Consequently, Hanna did not see the car being driven by Fred and pulled out directly in front of his car. Fred, being unable to stop in time, rammed into Hanna's car, causing her to spin around and collide with the car being driven by Sunny, who was proceeding in the opposite direction. Fred and Sunny sustained only minor injuries in the accident but Hanna received a broken leg and a concussion. As a result, Hanna was out of work for a month.

FIGURE 2.1

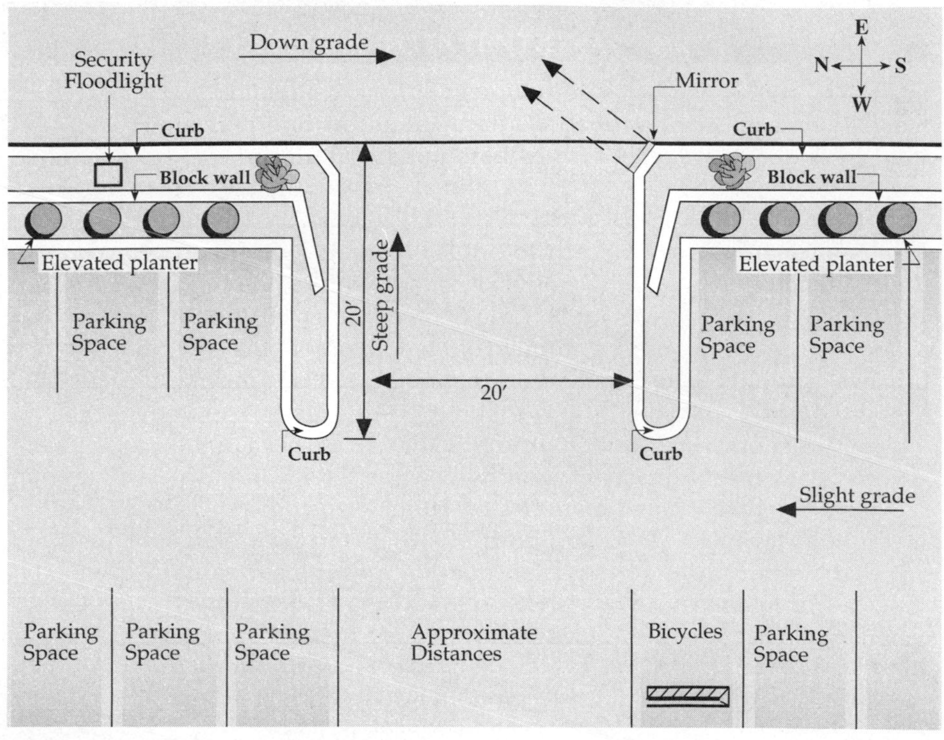

Hanna relates these events to an attorney and then tells her that she wants to sue the bank, who Hanna believes was the ultimate cause of her accident. Hanna is aware that Fred and Sunny may sue her for the property damage and physical injuries they incurred. Let us walk through the likely chain of events that will occur as Hanna enters the legal world.

INITIATING A COMPLAINT

First, the attorney must ascertain whether the legal elements of a negligence claim have been met. Did the bank have a duty to maintain the mirror in a safe condition and, if so, did the bank breach that duty by allowing the mirror to fog over? The attorney must also determine whether the mirror was, in fact, the cause of the accident and whether Hanna sustained monetary and other damages as a result of the accident.

To address these questions the attorney will need to find out several things. Who owns the mirror? Who is responsible for the maintenance of the mirror? Who owns the bank? Does the bank have any agreements with the city regarding the maintenance of the mirror? Is the design of the street itself defective? Was Hanna negligent in her use of the mirror? Were there any witnesses to the accident? Does the extent of Hanna's money damages warrant a lawsuit?

TABLE 2.1

OVERVIEW OF A CASE	
INITIATING A COMPLAINT	•Interview •Investigation •Filing complaint
DEFENDANT'S RESPONSE	•Answer •File counterclaim or cross-claim •File motions •Default
DISCOVERY	•Interrogatories •Depositions •Requests for admissions •Requests for production of documents •Requests for medical or psychological exam •Motions to compel and for protective order •Motions for summary judgment
PRE-TRIAL PROCEDURES	•Pre-trial conference •Motions in limine •Opening statements •Direct and cross examination
TRIAL	•Voir dire (challenges for cause and peremptory challenges) •Opening statements •Direct and cross examination •Motion for directed verdict •Closing arguments •General or special verdict
POST-TRIAL PROCEDURES	•Motion for new trial •JNOV •Appeal and cross-appeal

After conducting her investigation, if the attorney concludes that Hanna does have a viable claim, she will send a **demand letter** to Happy Valley Bank. In this letter she will explain why she believes the bank is liable, she will detail the extent of her client's damages, and she will put forth a demand for settlement of the case. If she cannot negotiate a settlement she will initiate the case by filing a **complaint** (FRCP 8(a)).[1]

1. Reference to the Federal Rules of Civil Procedure is made throughout this text.

A complaint has four basic elements. First, a complaint must state that the court has jurisdiction, i.e., the authority to hear the case. The attorney must show, for example, that she has met any residence or amount-in-controversy requirements of the court. The plaintiff has the right to choose the court within which to file her complaint so long as she meets the jurisdictional requirements of that court.

Second, the complaint must list the parties to the action. In this case Hanna would be the plaintiff and Happy Valley Bank the defendant.

Third, the complaint must provide a brief summary of each of the elements of the case along with the basic facts that will be used to prove each element. Hanna's attorney must allege that Happy Valley Bank had a duty to maintain the mirror in a safe condition, that it breached that duty, that as a result of the breach Hanna was injured, and that she sustained monetary damages. The degree of factual detail required in this part of the complaint is dictated by the procedural rules of the particular state in which the complaint is being filed (check the Rules of Civil Procedure in your state).

Finally, the complaint must specify the relief being sought by the plaintiff. In Hanna's case she will be asking for compensation for her hospital and medical bills, her lost salary, as well as additional monies for the pain and suffering she endured. In some states a verification must be submitted along with the complaint. The **verification** is an affidavit indicating that the plaintiff has read the complaint and that, to the best of his or her knowledge, it is true. The Rules of Civil Procedure in Hanna's state will determine how defendant Happy Valley Bank should be served with the complaint, where the complaint should be filed, and who may serve it.

DEFENDANT'S RESPONSE

Once Happy Valley Bank has been served, it has several options. If the bank does nothing, Hanna can get a **default judgment** in which the court would resolve the case in Hanna's favor because of Happy Valley Bank's lack of opposition (FRCP 55). Such a default judgment would normally be set aside if the defendant could show it had a good reason for failing to act.

Defendant Happy Valley Bank could choose to file an **answer** (FRCP 8(b)). In so doing it would admit those allegations in Hanna's complaint it thought

TABLE 2.2 Elements of a Complaint

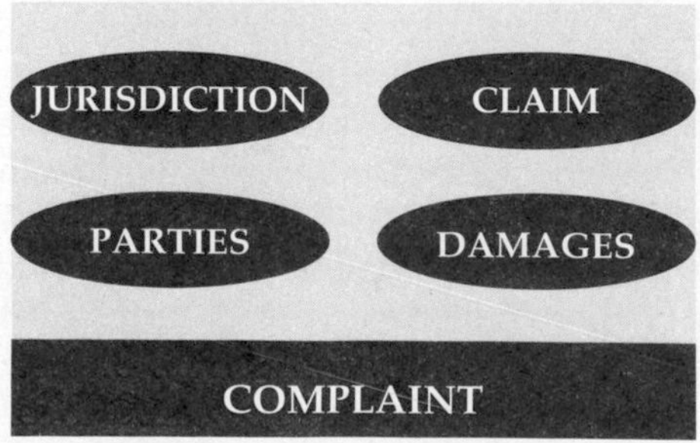

to be true, deny those with which it disagreed, and indicate lack of sufficient knowledge for those allegations requiring further investigation. At the same time the defendant could raise any affirmative defenses it might have, such as contributory negligence. An **affirmative defense** is any defense that the party asserting it must affirmatively prove or, in other words, for which it bears the burden of proof (FRCP 8(d)). So if Happy Valley Bank asserted that Hanna's negligence was the cause of her damages (thus using contributory negligence as an affirmative defense), it would have the burden of proving that negligence.

The defendant may at this time also raise any counterclaims or crossclaims. A **counterclaim** is a claim raised by the defendant against the plaintiff, while a **crossclaim** is a claim raised against a co-party. For example, if Fred sued Hanna and Happy Valley Bank to recover for his injuries and property damage, Hanna could raise a counterclaim against Fred alleging he was contributorily negligent and a crossclaim against Happy Valley Bank alleging negligence.

At the same time Happy Valley Bank answers Hanna's complaint it could file a *motion* (FRCP 12). Motions can be filed alleging, among other things, a lack of jurisdiction over the person or subject matter, improper venue, insufficiency of process, or failure to state a claim upon which relief can be granted. The most important of these is a motion for failure to state a claim upon which relief can be granted, which is referred to in some states as a motion for dismissal or a **demurrer**. By filing such a motion the defendant, in essence, is asserting that the plaintiff has failed to state a legally necessary element of the cause of action. If, for example, Happy Valley Bank did not own the mirror and had no legally recognizable duty to maintain it, the element of duty would be unfulfilled. If that were the case, Happy Valley Bank could file a motion alleging that Hanna failed to state a claim upon which relief can be granted. By granting the motion, the court would dismiss the case.

DISCOVERY

If the case were not dismissed in these early stages of the process, it would move into the **discovery** phase (FRCP 26). The theory underlying discovery is that the more each side finds out about the other side's case, the more likely that the parties will be able to settle the case and the final outcome will be an equitable one. Discovery can be compared to a game of poker. In this game each party tries to gain as much information as possible about the opposing side's position and, at the same time, reveal as little information as possible about its own position. Admittedly the stakes in litigation are often higher than those in poker, but the strategies employed are remarkably similar. It is fair to say that most cases today are won or lost in the discovery process. And since legal assistants play a major role in this process, you must become adept at creating and manipulating the tools of discovery.

There are five basic types of discovery: (1) interrogatories, (2) depositions, (3) requests for admission, (4) requests for production of documents, and (5) requests for medical and psychological examinations.

Interrogatories are written questions submitted to the opposing party which that party must answer in writing and under oath (FRCP 33). Interrogatories are a relatively inexpensive way of soliciting basic objective information. Hanna's counsel, for example, will want to use interrogatories to find out the names, addresses, and duties of the employees of Happy Valley Bank who maintain the mirror as well as information regarding Happy Valley Bank's relationship to the owner of the property on which the bank is located. Interrogatories are limited in usefulness because they are usually answered by or with the assistance of opposing counsel, whose aim is typically to provide as little information as possible.

A **deposition**, on the other hand, is an oral examination of a witness under oath (FRCP 27–32). Since depositions are considerably more time-consuming and more expensive than interrogatories, attorneys carefully select those whom they want to depose. At a deposition, deposing counsel not only will be able to pursue lines of questioning more thoroughly than by using interrogatories, but also will be able to assess how a jury will respond to the deponent. A court reporter, present during the deposition, prepares a transcript of everything that is said. The transcript can then be introduced at trial. For that reason an attorney may opt to depose a witness whose testimony she wants to use at trial if she believes that witness will not appear for the trial. Counsel can also use the witness' statements made during the deposition to impeach (discredit) his testimony at trial.

Happy Valley Bank's counsel would most likely want to depose Hanna in order to elicit detailed information from her about what she did before the accident as well as to assess her probable demeanor before a jury. This kind of information would be pertinent to counsel not only in mapping a trial strategy but in considering the advisability of settlement.

Requests for admission are simply requests by one party asking that the other party admit certain facts (FRCP 36). If Hanna's attorney, for example, ascertained that the bank did in fact own, install, and maintain the mirror, she would want the bank to admit those facts. Once a party admits a fact, that matter is conclusively established and cannot be argued at trial. Under the Federal Rules and the rules in many states if a party fails to respond to requests for admissions, those matters are deemed admitted.

Documents vital to a case that are in the possession of the opposing party can be obtained via a **request for production of documents** (FRCP 34). Hanna's attorney will want to review any maintenance records pertaining to the maintenance of the mirror and defense counsel will want to examine Hanna's hospital and medical records. Both can do so by filing a request for production of documents. Because Hanna has put her medical condition at issue in this case, Happy Valley Bank's counsel will also want to select a physician to examine Hanna in order to get a second opinion about the seriousness of her injuries. This can be done through a **request for medical examination** (FRCP 35).

During the pretrial discovery process both parties can make discovery-related motions as well as motions for summary judgment. Discovery-related motions include motions to compel and motions for protective orders. A **motion to compel** is appropriate when the opposing party refuses to reveal discoverable material (FRCP 37). A **motion for a protective order**, on the other hand, prevents discovery of information that is privileged and, therefore, not discoverable (FRCP 26(c)).

During the discovery process a party may glean sufficient information to determine that there is no material fact at issue and that a court could render a decision as a matter of law without having to go to trial. In such case the party will file a **motion for summary judgment**, requesting that the court enter a judgment on its behalf, thus dispensing with the need for a trial (FRCP 56). A party can also request a partial summary judgment which, in effect, eliminates particular issues. If Hanna's attorney filed a motion for a partial summary judgment and the court determined, as a matter of law, that Happy Valley Bank had a duty to maintain the mirror in a safe condition and that it breached that duty, then the only remaining issue to resolve would be the extent of Hanna's injuries and whether Happy Valley Bank was the proximate and actual cause of Hanna's injuries.

To rebut a motion for summary judgment the opponent must show that a genuine factual dispute exists and that a trial will be necessary to resolve that dispute. The mere allegation that a factual dispute exists is, however, insufficient. Using answers from interrogatories, deposition answers, and affidavits, the opposing party must show that he can controvert the facts alleged by the other side.

PRETRIAL PROCEDURES

If the parties cannot resolve the dispute during the discovery process, the case will proceed toward trial. Most courts require a **pretrial conference** to clarify the issues and defenses for trial, to establish the witnesses and exhibits that will be used at trial, and to promote settlement (FRCP 16). How vehemently the judge pushes for settlement depends on his or her philosophical bent. Statistics tell us, however, that most cases settle at or before the pretrial conference.

Before trial the parties will once again have an opportunity to move for dismissal as well as to make motions *in limine.* The purpose of a **motion *in limine*** is to resolve evidentiary questions so that they need not be brought up before the jury. In that way only evidence that is relevant and not unduly prejudicial will be presented. For example, if Hanna's attorney wanted to introduce testimony that Happy Valley Bank had instituted a new procedure for maintenance of the mirror subsequent to Hanna's accident, Happy Valley Bank's attorney would want to make a motion *in limine* to prevent that testimony. The generally prevailing argument, by the way, is that a motion such as this should be granted since admission of this type of evidence would inhibit defendants from taking measures to remove dangerous conditions.

TRIAL

If Hanna's case goes to trial, she will have the opportunity to decide between a **bench trial** (trial before a judge) and a jury trial (FRCP 39). In a jury trial all factual issues are resolved by the jury while all legal issues are resolved by the judge. In a bench trial the judge decides both factual and legal issues. Whether to opt for a jury trial or a bench trial is a strategical decision although case law does limit the right to a jury in certain types of cases.

Jury selection is conducted through a process known as ***voir dire,*** which consists of a series of questions asked of potential jurors by the trial judge or the attorneys, depending on local practice (FRCP 47). A party who wants to excuse a particular juror and can show that the juror has already formed a judgment as to how the case should be decided or for some reason is unable to decide the case impartially may use a **challenge for cause** (FRCP 47 (c)). On the other hand, the party who wants to dismiss a particular juror and cannot allege bias may remove the juror using a **peremptory challenge** (FRCP 47(e)). No reason need be given for a peremptory challenge.

While an attorney has an unlimited number of challenges for cause, he or she has a limited number of peremptory challenges (the specific number being dependent on local practices). Hanna's attorney might want to use her peremptory challenges to eliminate those jurors engaged in a particular occupation if research has shown that members of that profession are generally reluctant to compensate plaintiffs generously. She will also want to excuse those people that instinct or observation tell her will be unsympathetic to her client's plight.

When the trial begins Hanna's counsel will be given an opportunity to make *opening statements*. She will probably give an overview of the basic elements of her case, introduce the parties and witnesses that will be involved in the trial, and in general set the tone and theme of her case. Opening statements are not considered part of the evidence, but they are extremely important, especially in light of the research that shows that the majority of jurors decide the outcome of the case during opening statements and do not change their minds after hearing the testimony. Since Hanna has the burden of proving each element of her case by a *preponderance of the evidence* (that each element is more likely than not), she will be given the opportunity not only to begin the trial with opening statements but to end the trial by making the final statement in closing arguments.

The evidence in any civil case consists of witness testimony and exhibits. On *direct examination* questions are posed by the counsel calling the witness; *cross-examination* is conducted by opposing counsel. The function of cross-examination is to impeach (discredit) testimony given by the witness during direct examination. This process continues through redirect and recross-examination and so on until counsel exhaust all their questions.

During the course of the trial counsel may object to questions being asked or evidence being presented. The trial court will rule on the admissibility of evidence using the Rules of Evidence appropriate for that court. If the court sustains (grants) an objection to a question, that question cannot be asked but if the court overrules (denies) an objection, that question can be asked.

After Hanna's counsel rests, counsel for Happy Valley Bank will probably move for a **directed verdict**, arguing that Hanna failed to meet the requisite burden of proof on all the elements of her case (FRCP 50). Such motions, while frequently made, are commonly denied but if a motion for a directed verdict is granted, the case, in essence, is dismissed. Hanna's counsel will make a similar motion if Happy Valley Bank presents evidence regarding an affirmative defense. At the close of Happy Valley Bank's case, Hanna will be given an opportunity to present rebuttal evidence, which is used to refute evidence presented by the defendant.

Since Hanna has the burden of proof, her counsel will be given the opportunity to present the first *closing argument*. In this argument Hanna's attorney will summarize the facts of the case, showing how the evidence established each of the legal elements. Using the theme established in her opening statements, she will use her most persuasive rhetoric to convince the jury that Hanna should prevail and that generous damages should be awarded. Counsel for Happy Valley Bank will do likewise in his closing arguments and then Hanna's attorney will close with a rebuttal argument.

Finally, in a process known as **charging the jury**, the judge will instruct the jury on the rules of law to be applied (FRCP 50). In some states standard jury instructions are used. In others attorneys draft proposed instructions for the judge's consideration and, in a conference conducted outside the earshot of the jury, argue which instructions should be adopted. Much attention is given to the adoption of jury instructions and counsel are given an opportunity to object to any instructions the judge gives or fails to give. Jury instructions are important because objections to these instructions are typically the fundamental components of an appeal.

The jury will then be asked to render either a general or special verdict (FRCP 49). In Hanna's case a **general verdict** would require the jury to decide if Happy Valley Bank was liable for Hanna's injuries and to determine what damages should be awarded. If a **special verdict** were requested, the jury would be required to answer special interrogatories and the judge would have to determine the prevailing party after reviewing the jury's answers. In a case tried before a judge alone, the attorneys may be required to submit trial briefs in which they present the applicable law and show how it would apply to the facts of the particular case.

POSTTRIAL

If Hanna loses she can make a *motion for a new trial*, arguing that errors were committed during the trial (FRCP 59). Or she can move for a **judgment notwithstanding the verdict (JNOV)**, arguing that the verdict reached was contrary to the evidence and law (FRCP 50(b)). Such motions are generally contingent on counsel making appropriate objections during the trial; if counsel fails to do so, these procedural remedies will be denied. Hanna could also *appeal* (see Federal Rules of Appellate Procedure) the decision to a higher court and if Happy Valley Bank were unhappy with part of the outcome at the trial level, it could file a *cross-appeal*. Once a final judgment was entered, however, and all appeals were completed, the issues litigated would be ***res judicata***, in that they could not be relitigated at a later time. The philosophy underlying this rule is that litigation must ultimately come to an end and cannot be allowed to go on forever.

EMPHASIS ON DISCOVERY THROUGHOUT THIS TEXT

Although this overview of a civil case is certainly not exhaustive, lacking many of the subroutes parties can pursue in litigation, it does give you a framework within which to analyze tort problems. Examples will be provided throughout the text of typical discovery tools and you will be encouraged to consider the information presented in each chapter in the context of how it could be applied in discovery. Keep the importance of discovery foremost in your mind as you work through this book. And remember that a key contribution paralegals can make to the litigation team lies in their ability to create, manipulate, and organize discovery tools.

SUMMARY

To initiate a tort claim, the plaintiff must file a complaint. This complaint must state the basis for the court's jurisdiction, the parties to the action, the elements of the case, and the relief being sought. The defendant may then file an answer admitting or denying allegations in the plaintiff's complaint and raising any affirmative defenses. The defendant may also bring a counterclaim against the plaintiff or a crossclaim against a co-party. Additionally, he or she may file a motion alleging, for example, that the plaintiff failed to state a claim upon which relief can be granted.

In the discovery phase both parties try to find out as much as possible about the other side's case while revealing as little as possible about their own. Interrogatories, depositions, requests for admission, request for production of documents, and requests for medical and psychological examinations are the most frequently used tools of discovery. A party may also file a motion for summary judgment if no material fact is arguably at issue.

A case that cannot be resolved during the discovery process moves on to trial. Before trial, most courts require the parties to attend a pretrial conference and to resolve evidentiary questions by making motions *in limine.* At the trial the parties are allowed to select jurors through a process of *voir dire,* dismissing jurors on the basis of either a challenge for cause or peremptory challenge. At trial the plaintiff has the burden of proving each element of his or her case by a preponderance of the evidence. Both counsel are given the opportunity to introduce their cases by making opening statements, to elicit testimony through direct examination, and to impeach witnesses through cross-examination. Motions for directed verdict are generally made after opposing counsel has presented his or her case. After both counsel have given closing arguments, the judge charges the jury. The jury is then asked to render either a general or special verdict, the latter of which requires the answering of special interrogatories.

Subsequent to trial, a party can move for a new trial or a judgment notwithstanding the verdict. Appeals and cross-appeals can also be filed but once a final judgment is entered and all appeals are completed, the issues litigated are considered *res judicata.*

TORT TEASERS

Make a flowchart of the events and activities leading up to trial, those events that occur at trial, and those events that occur subsequent to trial. Which of these events do you think you will be most involved in as a legal assistant?

KEY TERMS

Affirmative defense
Any defense that a party asserts for which it bears the burden of proof.

Answer
A pleading in which the defendant responds to the plaintiff's complaint.

Bench trial
Trial before a judge.

Challenge for cause
Request to remove a potential juror because of his or her alleged inability to decide the case impartially.

Charging the jury
Process in which the judge instructs the jury in rules of law they are to apply.

Complaint
An initial pleading filed on behalf of the plaintiff whose purpose is to provide the defendant with the material elements of the plaintiff's demand.

Counterclaim
A claim presented by a defendant in opposition to the plaintiff's claim.

Crossclaim
A claim brought by a defendant against a co-defendant in the same action.

Default judgment
Judgment entered due to lack of opposition on behalf of opposing party.

Demand letter
A letter detailing a client's damages and setting forth the reasons for her demand.

Demurrer
Motion for dismissal based on a defect in the form or content of a complaint.

Deposition
Oral examination of a witness under oath.

■ **Directed verdict**
Request that the case be dismissed because of the opposing party's failure to meet the requisite burden of proof.

■ **Discovery**
Process that parties engage in in order to find out as much as possible about the other side's case.

■ **General verdict**
Verdict in which a jury decides issues of liability and damages.

■ **Interrogatories**
Written questions submitted to the opposing party which that party must answer in writing and under oath.

■ **JNOV (Judgment Notwithstanding the Verdict)**
Motion arguing that the verdict reached was contrary to the evidence and the law.

■ **Motion for protective order**
Motion that protects a party from having to disclose privileged information.

■ **Motion for summary judgment**
Motion requesting that the court enter a judgment on the party's behalf because there is no material fact at issue.

■ **Motion *in limine***
Motion to prevent evidence from being presented to the jury.

■ **Motion to compel**
Motion compelling the opposing party to comply with request for discovery.

■ **Peremptory challenge**
Request to remove a potential juror for no articulated reason.

■ **Pretrial conference**
Conference involving the judge and parties at which issues and procedures for the trial are clarified and efforts are made at settlement.

■ ***Res judicata***
Legal principle that requires that issues litigated cannot be relitigated at a later time.

■ **Request for admissions**
Request by one party asking the other party to admit certain facts.

■ **Request for medical examination**
Request that the opposing party be examined by a physician chosen by the party making the request.

■ **Request for production of documents**
Request for document in possession of the opposing party.

■ **Special verdict**
Verdict in which the jury is required to answer special interrogatories, which the judge must review in order to determine who the prevailing party is.

■ **Verification**
Affidavit indicating plaintiff has read the complaint and to the best of his or her knowledge believes it to be true.

■ ***Voir dire***
Process of jury selection involving the use of challenges for cause and peremptory challenges.

3 READING, BRIEFING, AND ANALYZING CASE LAW

CHAPTER OBJECTIVES

In this chapter you will learn to:

- Read cases.
- Brief cases.
- Analyze cases using the IRAC method.

READING CASE LAW

Reading your first court opinion can be a somewhat intimidating experience. A few simple rules will guide you through this process and will make studying court opinions the exciting experience that it should be. In any opinion you need to identify the following: (1) procedural history, (2) issues, (3) facts, (4) rationale, and (5) holding.

We will use *Isaacs v. Powell* to illustrate each of these elements. Please skim through the opinion to get a feeling for what the case is about and then we will examine each of the elements separately. A brief overview of the case is in order to assist you in pulling out the key ideas. The defendants are being sued by the plaintiffs for injuries inflicted by the defendants' monkey. Two issues are before the court. First, should the owner or keeper of a chimpanzee be held strictly liable for harm caused by the chimpanzee? Second, even if the defendants are strictly liable should the plaintiff be precluded from recovering if he (plaintiff) is the sole cause of his injuries? The court answers both questions in the affirmative, citing legal authority and using logic to justify its conclusions.

Scott ISAACS, a minor, by his father and natural guardian, Howard Isaacs, Appellant v. Lester M. POWELL and Arlyss R. Powell, doing business as Monkeytown, U.S.A., Appellees. No. 71-683 District Court of Appeal of Florida, Second District Oct. 4, 1972 Rehearing Denied Nov. 13, 1972.

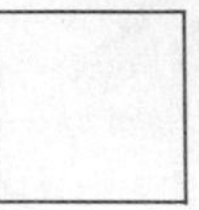

McNAULTY, Judge.

This is a case of first impression in Florida. The question posed is whether Florida should adopt the general rule that the owner or keeper of a wild animal, in this case a chimpanzee, is liable to one injured by such animal under the strict liability doctrine, i.e., regardless of negligence on his part, or whether his liability should be predicated on his fault or negligence.[1]

Plaintiff-appellant Scott Isaacs was two years and seven months old at the times material herein. His father had taken him to defendants-appellees' monkey farm where, upon purchasing an admission ticket, and as was usual and encouraged by appellees, he also purchased some food to feed the animals. While Scott was feeding a chimpanzee named Valerie she grabbed his arm and inflicted serious injury.

The exact details of how Valerie was able to grab Scott's arm are in dispute. Appellees contend that Scott's father lifted the boy above reasonably sufficient protective barriers to within Valerie's reach, while appellants counter that the barriers and other protective measures were insufficient. But in any case, appellants do not now, nor did they below, rely on any fault of appellees. Rather, they rely solely on the aforesaid generally accepted strict or, as it is sometimes called, absolute liability doctrine under which negligence or fault on the part of the owner or keeper of an animal ferae naturae is irrelevant. Appellees, on the other hand, suggest that we should adopt the emerging, though yet minority, view that liability should depend upon negligence, i.e., a breach of the duty of care reasonably called for taking into account the nature and specie of the animal involved. We will consider this aspect of the problem first and will hereinafter discuss available defenses under the theory we adopt.

The trial judge apparently agreed with the appellees that fault or negligence on the part of the owners of a wild animal must be shown.

[T]he trial judge asked the jury to decide whether Scott was injured through the fault of defendants-appellees and/or through the fault of his father. The jury returned a verdict for the defendants; but obviously, it's impossible for us to determine whether . . . the jury so found because they were unable to find fault on defendants' part, or whether they so found because they believed the cause of Scott's injury to be the fault of the father. If, of course, we adopt the negligence theory of liability there would be no error in submitting both issues to the jury. But we are of the view that the older and general rule of strict liability, which obviates the issue of the owner's negligence, is more suited to the fast growing, populous and activity-oriented society of Florida. Indeed, our society imposes more than enough risks upon its members now,

1. Although the precise question has never been decided in Florida, our sister court in the third district recognized the general rule in dictum while deciding that the bees involved in that case were not wild animals and thus the rule of negligence applied regardless. *Ferreira v. D'Asaro* (Fla. App. 1963), 152. So.2d 736.

and we are reluctant to encourage the addition of one more particularly when that one more is increasingly contributed by those who, for profit, would exercise their "right" to harbor wild animals and increase exposure to the dangers thereof by luring advertising. Prosser puts it this way:

". . . [Liability] has been thought to rest on the basis of negligence in keeping the animal at all; but this does not coincide with the modern analysis of negligence as conduct which is unreasonable in view of the risk, since it may not be an unreasonable thing to keep a tiger in a zoo. It is rather an instance of the strict responsibility placed upon those who, even with proper care expose the community to the risk of a very dangerous thing. While one or two jurisdictions insist that there is no liability without some negligence in keeping the animal, by far the greater number impose strict liability."

Additionally, we observe that Florida has enacted Sec. 767.04, F.S.A.,[5] relating to dogs, which abrogates the permissive "one bite" rule of the common law. That rule posited that an owner of a dog is liable to one bitten by such dog only if he is chargeable with "scienter," i.e., prior knowledge of the action therefor was predicated on the negligence of the owner in failing to take proper precautions with knowledge of the dog's vicious propensities. Our statute, however, has in effect imposed strict liability on a dog owner (from which he can absolve himself only by complying with the warning proviso of the statute). It would result in a curious anomaly, then, if we were to adopt the negligence concept as a basis for liability of an owner or keeper of a tiger, while Sec. 767.04, supra, imposes potential strict liability upon him if he should trade the tiger for a dog. We are compelled to adopt, therefore, the strict liability rule in these cases.

Concerning, now, available defenses under this rule we share the view, and emphasize, that "strict or absolute liability" does not mean the owner or keeper of a wild animal is an absolute insurer in the sense that he is liable regardless of any fault on the part of the victim. Moreover, we do not think it means he is liable notwithstanding an intervening, efficient independent fault which solely causes the result, as was possibly the case here if fault on the part of Scott's father were the sole efficient cause.

As to the fault of the victim himself, since the owner or keeper of a wild animal is held to a rigorous rule of liability on account of the danger inherent in harboring such animal, it has generally been held that the owner ought not be relieved from such liability by slight negligence or want of ordinary care on the part of the person injured. The latter's acts must be such as would establish that, with knowledge of the danger, he voluntarily brought the calamity upon himself. This general rule supports the Restatement of Torts, Sec. 515, which we now adopt and set forth as follows:

"(1) A plaintiff is not barred from recovery by his failure to exercise reasonable care to observe the propinquity of a wild animal or an abnormally dangerous domestic animal or to avoid harm to his person, land or chattels threatened by it.

(2) A plaintiff is barred from recovery by intentionally and unreasonably subjecting himself to the risk that a wild animal or an abnormally dangerous

5. This section provides in pertinent part: "The owners of any dog which shall bite any person, while such person is on or in a public place, or lawfully on or in a private place, including the property of the owner of such dogs, shall be liable for such damages as may be suffered by persons bitten, regardless of the former viciousness of such dog or the owner's knowledge of such viciousness . . . Provided, however, no owner of any dog shall be liable for any damages to any person or his property when such person shall mischievously or carelessly provoke or aggravate the dog inflicting such damage; nor shall any such owner be so liable if at the time of any such injury he had displayed in a prominent place on his premises a sign easily readable including the words 'Bad Dog.' "

domestic animal will do harm to his person, land or chattels."

With regard to an intervening fault bringing about the result we have no hesitancy in expanding the foregoing rule to include as a defense the willful or intentional fault of a third party provided such fault is of itself an efficient cause and is the sole cause. If a jury were to decide in this case, therefore, that the sole efficient cause of Scott's injury was the intentional assumption of the apparent risks on the part of the boy's father and his placing of the boy within reach of the danger, it would be a defense available to appellees. Clearly, though, this defense would be related only to causation and is not dependent upon any theory of imputation of the father's fault to the son, which is not irrelevant in view of the extent of strict liability in these cases and the limited defenses available thereunder.

The judgment is reversed and the cause is remanded for a new trial on the theory of strict liability, and the defenses thereto, as enunciated above.

Reversed.

PROCEDURAL HISTORY

Although the *procedural history* in this particular opinion is scattered throughout the opinion, we can ascertain from the caption that the opinion is being rendered by the District Court of Appeals of Florida, District 2, and that a rehearing before the appellate court was denied. In paragraph 2 we learn that the **appellant**, i.e., the appealing party, is Isaacs and in the fifth paragraph we find that the jury returned a verdict for the defendants. The court informs us in the first paragraph that this is a **case of first impression** in Florida; in other words, this is the first time that this particular question has been faced by this court.

ISSUE

In paragraph 1 the court clearly states that the first *issue* is whether the owner or keeper of a wild animal should be liable to one injured by such animal under the strict liability doctrine or whether his or her liability should be predicated on negligence. Be forewarned that not all courts are this forthright in setting forth the issues so clearly. Often you will have to comb through the opinion to determine the issue. In some cases the court will not state the issue explicitly and you will have to infer it from the discussion of the rules.

FACTS

Paragraphs 2 and 3 of the opinion discuss the substantive (as opposed to procedural) facts of the opinion. *Substantive facts* pertain to the events experienced by the litigants; *procedural facts* refer to the steps taken by the parties to resolve their dispute within the legal process. Notice that the parties are in dispute as to how the chimpanzee was able to grab the plaintiff's arm but do appear to agree on the rest of the facts.

RATIONALE

In setting forth its *rationale* the court looks to the majority rule, cited by Prosser. That rule is: "[S]trict responsibility [is] placed upon those who, even with proper care, expose the community to the risk of a very dangerous thing."

The court also cites a Florida statute that imposes strict liability on dog owners. Then the court reasons that, in light of the statute imposing strict liability on dog owners, it cannot logically adopt a negligence standard for owners of wild animals. The court also relies on a public policy argument that members of society should not be exposed to any unnecessary additional risks, especially when that risk is contributed by one who profits from exposing others to wild animals through the use of "luring advertising."

HOLDING

The court's **holding** is stated succinctly at the end of paragraph 6 in which the court states that it has decided to adopt the strict liability rule. Note that the court clued you in to its ultimate holding in paragraph 5, where it said, "But we are of the view that the older and general rule of strict liability, which obviates the issue of the owner's negligence, is more suited to the fast growing, populace and activity-oriented society of Florida."

DICTUM

It is important to distinguish a dictum from a holding. **Dictum** is not necessary to the case and does not carry the weight of a holding. Dictum involves issues that are not before the court and have not been argued by the parties. For example, in *Issacs* if the court had discussed how the outcome might have differed had the offending animal been a goat rather than a chimpanzee, that discussion would be classified as dictum and would have no precedential value. A holding may be considered **binding authority** (authority that the court must follow) while dictum is considered **persuasive authority** (authority that the court may or may not follow).

SECOND ISSUE AND RATIONALE

The next issue the court addresses is whether the defendant is entitled to any defenses. The court then cites and adopts the rules set forth by the Restatement of Torts. Under the Restatement a plaintiff is not barred from recovery by failure to exercise reasonable care but is barred from recovery by intentionally and unreasonably subjecting himself or herself to the risk posed by a wild animal. Reasoning that the foregoing rules apply to the intentional fault of a third party, the court concludes that the jury must decide if the sole cause of the plaintiff's injury was his father's actions. If the jury were to determine that the boy's father was the sole cause of his injury, the defendant would be absolved of all liability.

Note that the judgment of the trial court is reversed and the case is remanded (sent back) to the trial court for a new trial. The new trial must be conducted in accordance with the appellate court's decisions regarding the application of strict liability as well as its discussion pertaining to the appropriate defenses.

CONCURRING AND DISSENTING OPINIONS

Typically, not all members of the appellate court will agree. It is common for some members of the court to write a concurring or a dissenting opinion. A *concurring opinion* is written by a judge who agrees with the result but would use a different rule in reaching that result or who would analyze the issue in a different manner. A *dissenting opinion* is written by a judge who disagrees with the outcome and, typically, disagrees with the analysis of his or her colleagues.

BRIEFING CASES

As you read a case, you will find it helpful to summarize the important elements so that you can refer to them later without having to read the entire case again. This is called **briefing** a case and it incorporates the elements that were discussed above. Although case briefing may seem extremely time-consuming at first, you will find it most helpful when you are doing legal research. Therefore, it is to your advantage to become efficient and skillful in briefing cases.

The key elements of a case brief (shown in Table 3–1) are:

■ *Procedural history*—a brief note entailing how the case arose with reference to the appellate court.

■ *Facts*—substantive facts necessary to the court's holdings on the issues. All relevant facts should be included. Facts are relevant if they are pertinent to the outcome of the case. When unsure if you should include a fact, ask yourself if the court could have arrived at a different conclusion if that fact had been different. If the answer is yes, include the fact.

■ *Issues*—questions presented in the context of the substantive facts of the specific case. State the issue as narrowly and concretely as possible to maximize the benefit you will gain from using the brief for future reference.

■ *Holding*—decision rendered by the court as applied to the facts specific to the case. Like the issue, the holding should be narrow and concrete.

■ *Rationale*—court's application of statutes and/or case law to the facts of the case and the reasoning used by the court in reaching its decision.

SAMPLE

ISAACS v. POWELL

Procedural History: Jury rendered verdict for defendants; plaintiffs appealed.

Facts: Plaintiff, who was two years and seven months at the time of the incident, was taken by his father to Defendant's monkey farm. Plaintiff and

TABLE 3.1

BRIEFING A CASE	ANALYZING CASE LAW
Briefing a case: summarizing the important elements. • Procedural history • Facts • Issue(s) • Holding(s) • Rationale	Analyzing case law: applying holdings of other cases to facts in your case. • Issue(s) • Rule(s) • Analysis / application • Conclusion(s)

his father were encouraged by Defendant to feed the animals. While Plaintiff was feeding a chimpanzee, the chimpanzee grabbed his arm and inflicted serious physical injury. The parties are in disagreement as to exactly how the chimpanzee was able to grab Plaintiff's arm, i.e., whether Plaintiff's father or Defendants were negligent.

Issues:

Issue No. 1: Should the owner or keeper of a wild animal (specifically a chimpanzee) be held strictly liable to one injured by such animal or should his liability be based on negligence?

Holding No. 1: The owner or keeper of a wild animal, such as a chimpanzee, is strictly liable to one injured by such animal.

Rationale No. 1: The risk for injury caused by wild animals should be borne by those who harbor them and not by society at large. Those who expose the community to the risk of a dangerous thing should be held strictly liable even though they used proper care. Furthermore, logic dictates that owners or keepers of wild animals should be held strictly liable since Florida statute mandates that dog owners are strictly liable for injuries inflicted by their animals.

Issue No. 2: Should the owner or keeper of a wild animal be held strictly liable regardless of any fault on the part of the victim?

Holding No. 2: An owner or keeper of a wild animal is strictly liable if the victim was not the sole cause of his own injuries.

Rationale No. 2: A plaintiff who intentionally and unreasonably subjects himself to the risk posed by a wild animal should be barred from recovery since he voluntarily brought his injuries upon himself. On the other hand, owners should not be relieved from liability due to the plaintiff's failure to exercise reasonable care in dealing with wild animals.

TORT TEASERS

Brief *Weiner v. Ash* using the sample brief above as a model.

33 Ariz. Adv. Rep. 48
IN THE COURT OF APPEALS
STATE OF ARIZONA
DIVISION TWO

Jeffrey A. WEINER and Barbara S. Weiner, husband and wife; and Merton B. Weiner and Jean Weiner, husband and wife,

Plaintiffs/Appellees,

v.

Steven Perry ASH and Christine L. Ash, husband and wife,

Defendants/Appellants

No. 2 CA-CV 88-0326
DEPARTMENT A

FILED: April 25, 1989

LIVERMORE, Presiding Judge.

This is an appeal from the judgment of the trial court awarding $250,000 in damages for future fear, anxiety, and emotional distress. The award arises out of an incident in which appellant Steven Ash shot at the appellees, wounding Jeffrey Weiner and causing Merton Weiner to suffer cardiac problems. Ash was tried criminally but was found not guilty by reason of insanity. In the ensuing civil action the court found, among other things, 1) that Ash suffers from paranoid schizophrenia which is currently in remission or controlled by drugs and therapy, 2) that he has a history of schizo-affective mental illness and failure to take prescribed medication to control the illness, and 3) the failure to take the medication is a significant problem in the care, treatment, management, and control of the illness. The Weiners were awarded damages for past and future, medical bills, past and future pain, suffering and disability, and past emotional distress and anxiety. They were also awarded $250,000 for future emotional distress and anxiety, but only if Ash failed to comply with the court's orders that he continue to take prescribed medications and undergo psychotherapy and random periodic urinalysis to determine the level of anti-psychotic medication in his bloodstream. In a prior appeal, we reversed the conditional award for future damages, holding:

> There is ample evidence of continuing fear by the plaintiffs that defendant, if he stops taking his medication, will again suffer a paranoid delusion about plaintiffs and will again seek to kill them. But it is also clear from the findings that in the trial judge's view no compensable future damage will occur if defendant does not again deteriorate mentally. The judgment, therefore, cannot be affirmed on the basis that it is an actual award of compensation for probable future damages.

Weiner v. Ash, 157 Ariz. 232, 234–35, 756 P.2d 329, 331–32 (App. 1988). This case was remanded for an award of presently proven future damages. On remand judgment was entered in favor of the Weiners in the amount of $250,000 "for future fear, anxiety and emotional distress." This appeal followed.

At issue is whether the Weiners are entitled to damages for their fear that if Ash fails to take the prescribed medication he will again seek to kill them. Ash argues first that the award impermissibly compensates the Weiners for fear of a second, separate tort unrelated to the first. We disagree. The Weiners are not being compensated for a possible future attack by Ash. They are being compensated for the present fear of a possible future attack, a fear that clearly arises from the shooting incident and resulting physical injuries. See *Lavelle v. Owens-Corning Fiberglas Corporation*, 30 Ohio Misc. 2d 11, 507 N.E.2d 476(1987).

Although there are no cases directly on point from this jurisdiction, a number of cases from other jurisdictions have held such fears to be compensable. In *Hardin v. Munchies Food Store*, 521 So.2d 1200 (La.App.1988), the court found that the general damages awarded the victim of an assault was inadequate to compensate her for fright and distress emanating from the attack, including a continuing fear of men and phobia of entering crowds of people. In *Reardon v. Department of Mental Health*, 157 Mich. App. 505, 403 N.W.2d 582, rev'd on other grounds, *Reardon v. State*, 130 Mich. 398, 424 N.W.2d 248(1988), the court upheld an award of damages to a sexual assault victim whose damages included worry about recurrence of the assault, fear of strangers, and a distrust of men. In *Barry v. City of Monroe*, 439 So.2d 465 (La.App. 1983), the plaintiff suffered epileptic seizures after colliding with a support column. Finding that further seizures had been prevented by medication, the court nevertheless permitted an award of damages for the fear of future seizures, noting that "[w]hile mere speculation of such an event cannot provide the basis for an award, the anxiety produced by the possibility of another seizure is one of the compensable items we include in the award." 439 So.2d at 468.

Ash next argues that the event the Weiners fear is too remote and speculative to be compensable. See *Howard v. Mt. Sinai Hospital, Inc.*, 63 Wis.2d 515, 217 N.W.2d 383(1974). The reason the trial court gave for making the initial award contingent on continued treatment was "to alleviate any reasonable basis for future mental distress." Implicit in the second award, however, is the trial court's belief that given Ash's past history of failing to take prescribed medication and the court's inability to coerce him to do so, the possibility that Ash would again experience paranoid delusion and attack the Weiners was not so remote and speculative that the fear of such an attack was uncompensable. The record supports this conclusion.

Finally, noting that recovery in tort is limited to the results of tortious conduct, Ash argues that any fear the Weiners may have of a future attack results from Ash's condition, not from his tortious conduct. We find this argument unpersuasive. Tortious behavior is always the product of the tortfeasor's character. Fear of future behavior arises both from the past attack and what it demonstrates about that character. To deny recovery for present fear clearly arising from past tortious conduct on the ground that it rests in part on fear of the tortfeasor's character would be to deny a very real element of the harm initially caused.

Affirmed.

JOSEPH M. LIVERMORE, Presiding Judge

CONCURRING:

JAMES D. HATHAWAY, Judge

LAWRENCE HOWARD, Judge

ANALYZING CASE LAW

Once you have read and briefed the cases applicable to any issue you are researching, you must then compare those cases to the facts of your particular case. Are the facts of your case so different from the facts of the cases you researched that those cases can be distinguished and therefore are not helpful? Or are those cases analogous to your case so that you can apply the legal rules set forth in those cases to your case? This is the process of case analysis.

Analyzing case law requires you to think like a lawyer. And lawyers do think in a unique way. In their first year of law school students are encouraged to adopt a highly structured approach to problem solving. If you want to penetrate the legal mind, you too must adopt this thinking pattern.

Some legal scholars refer to the mode of analysis used by lawyers as **IRAC**. Although many lawyers are unfamiliar with this acronym, by virtue of graduating from law school they have assimilated this means of thinking into their practice. IRAC represents the four steps in legal analysis: (1) identifying the *issue;* (2) stating the applicable legal *rule;* (3) *applying* the rule to the applicable facts or *analyzing* using the applicable rules; (4) drawing a *conclusion*.

Because tort law revolves primarily around the application of case law and not the application of statutes and ordinances, we will use the application of case law to illustrate IRAC. Recall *Issacs v. Powell,* which was discussed earlier in this chapter. Now suppose you have a client who was bitten by a rattlesnake after sticking his hand in an unlocked box of snakes on public display at Defendant's service station. Defendant argues that your client should be barred from recovery because he was negligent in sticking his hand in a box of snakes. Your client, however, claims that he was unaware of the dangers involved when he stuck his hand in the box.

ISSUE

The issue in this case is whether a plaintiff who sticks his hand in a box of snakes is barred from recovery for the injuries he sustains when he is bitten. Notice that the issue is narrow in that it is restricted to the facts at hand. It is not phrased in a more general fashion, such as asking whether a plaintiff who is negligent is barred from recovery for the injuries he sustains.

RULE

The rule established in *Issacs v. Powell* is adopted from the Restatement of Torts, Sec. 515. Under the Restatement a plaintiff who simply fails to use reasonable care in dealing with wild animals is not barred from recovery but a plaintiff who intentionally and unreasonably subjects himself to the risk posed by a wild animal is barred from recovery. In many cases several rules are applicable and the courts are then faced with the task of harmonizing all the rules in their analyses.

APPLICATION/ANALYSIS

When applying the rule in this case, you will first want to ask yourself if your client was merely negligent in his behavior or if he acted so unreasonably as to preclude his recovery. As an advocate for your client, you would want to argue that your client was unaware of the danger posed by the snakes. Perhaps he was unaware that they were rattlesnakes or perhaps he was unaware that rattlesnakes are dangerous. You would contend that even though he failed to use reasonable care he did not intentionally and unreasonably subject himself to danger. Notice that in making this argument you are using the terminology and phraseology set forth in the rule (e.g., failing to use "reasonable care" and not "intentionally and unreasonably subjecting himself" to danger). But you are doing so in the context of the facts of your case. Recognize that Defendant will likely argue that anyone who sticks his hand into a container holding snakes is, by definition, unreasonable.

At this point you might be wondering if you should argue both sides of this issue or if you should simply argue the position most favorable for your client. The answer to this question depends on what your role is and to whom you are making the argument. If your supervising attorney has asked you to write a memorandum advising her whether your firm should take on this individual as a client, you should make the attorney aware of the arguments on both sides of the issue. Similarly, if this were an issue on an exam or classroom assignment, most likely you would want to raise all the possible arguments. If, on the other hand, you were writing a persuasive memorandum to the judge to convince the judge of the soundness of the plaintiff's position, you would argue as forcefully as possible that the plaintiff should prevail. In such case you would allow the defendant to make the counterarguments.

Another factor you will want to consider in your analysis is whether any factual differences exist between the reference case and your case. In *Issacs,* for example, the offending animal was a chimpanzee while the animal in your case is a rattlesnake. Is that a relevant distinction? Could the defendant argue that anyone who initiates contact with a rattlesnake is inherently unreasonable whereas someone feeding a chimpanzee is not? Another factual difference is that the plaintiff in *Issacs* was feeding the animal whereas the plaintiff in your case stuck his hand in and, arguably, baited the animal. Should it make any difference that the plaintiff in *Issacs* was a minor while your client is an adult? In making your analysis you would want to determine whether these differences are relevant differences, i.e., differences that could result in a court distinguishing your case from *Issacs.*

The thoroughness of an analysis and the creativity used in conducting an analysis is what separates the average student from the excellent student and the competent paralegal from the outstanding paralegal. Novices at legal analysis tend to skirt over the analysis, looking at only the most obvious points and often jumping to a conclusion. This is called *conclusory writing* and should be avoided. For example, if you were to conclude that your client is in the same position as the plaintiff in *Issacs* without ever contemplating the factors discussed above, your analysis would be considered conclusory. The unpleasant result of such an analysis is that you frequently overlook arguments your opponent will raise and, therefore, fail to take action to rebut those arguments.

CONCLUSION

Once you have completed your analysis you will have to arrive at a conclusion. This is sometimes difficult because of all the ambiguities you raised in your analysis. Legal novices often shy away from drawing conclusions but it must be done. Your conclusion is your suggestion as to how you think the issue should be or will be resolved in light of the various factors considered in your analyses. In this case you might conclude that a court will follow *Issacs* despite the factual differences and will allow your client to recover if a jury determines that he acted negligently but not unreasonably. On the other hand, you might conclude that anyone sticking his hand in a box of snakes is, as a matter of law, unreasonable and that a court would not allow such a case to come before a jury.

At this point you might be weaseling, saying that you simply do not have enough facts to draw a conclusion. You still must formulate a conclusion, indicating the facts you are lacking and how the nature of those facts will affect the resolution of the issue. In your snake case you might want to find out if your client had any idea that he was putting his hand into a box of snakes and if he had any recognition of the reputation enjoyed by rattlesnakes. The answer to those questions would affect your conclusion. But remember, whether you have been asked to write a legal memorandum or answer an exam question, you must draw a conclusion (albeit a tentative one) even if you do not have all the facts.

SUMMARY

Reading any court opinion requires the identification of the procedural history, issues, facts, rationale, and holding. Although some opinions clearly identify these components, others will require the reader to use some discernment. Dictum must be distinguished from the holding as it is considered persuasive but not binding authority.

Briefing cases, while time-consuming, is extremely helpful in doing legal research. Typically, a brief consists of the procedural history, facts, issues, holding, and rationale of the court.

Deciding whether case law is relevant to the issue at hand involves the process of legal analysis, which can be facilitated using the IRAC method. This method requires the identification of the pertinent issues and rules of law, the application of those rules to the facts at hand, and the drawing of a conclusion. Except when the purpose is to persuade, legal analysis requires the consideration of both sides of an issue, i.e., the making of an argument and a counterargument. Conclusory analysis should be avoided. Ultimately, however, a conclusion must be drawn even if ambiguities in the problem make it difficult to do so.

TORT TEASERS

Wanda was raped by Roger while they were on a date. At his criminal trial Roger was acquitted. Wanda has come to your firm because she wants to sue him for her medical bills and the emotional distress and anxiety she has suffered and continues to suffer. Among other things, Wanda fears dating anyone for fear that she will be raped and she also fears that Roger, who is now receiving psychiatric care, will try to kill her if he ever stops taking his medication, which seems to control his outbursts of rage against women. Wanda wants to be compensated for her past and future emotional distress. Assume *Weiner v. Ash* is the only applicable case in your jurisdiction. Write a legal memorandum to your supervising attorney, telling her what you think your chances of success are for recovering for Wanda's future emotional distress. Use IRAC to organize your memorandum.

KEY TERMS

■ **Appellant**
One who appeals a decision made by a lower court.

■ **Binding authority**
Legal authority that a court must follow.

■ **Briefing**
Summarizing the key elements of a case, including the procedural history, facts, issues, legal rules, holdings, and rationale.

■ **Case of first impression**
First case heard within a particular jurisdiction regarding a specific point of law.

■ **Dictum**
Discussion in a court opinion not related to the issues actually before the court.

■ **Holding**
Appellate court's decision.

■ **IRAC**
Steps involved in legal analysis: identifying the issue (I), identifying the applicable rules (R), applying the rules (A), and drawing a conclusion (C).

■ **Persuasive authority**
Authority that a court may consider but which it is not legally bound to follow.

4 INTERVIEWING

CHAPTER OBJECTIVES

In this chapter you will learn how to:

- Set the stage for an interview.
- Gather background information about a client and pertinent information about the client's problem.
- Interview and work with a police officer.
- Interview a lay witness.

Johnny and Susie are lovers. Johnny has just bought a new red Corvette and, of course, he wants to impress Susie with his acquisition so he picks her up at her house to take her to a very expensive French restaurant. While enroute he enters the intersection at Seventh Avenue and Primrose Lane at the same time that Harriet, driving to the weekly meeting of the local Library Preservation Society in her fourteen-year-old Chrysler, turns in front of him. Neither sees the other vehicle until a few split seconds before impact. No one is permanently injured but the Corvette suffers extensive damage and Harriet's car, although relatively unscathed, needs minor repairs. Within a month of the accident Johnny comes into your office with Susie in tow. Your supervising attorney asks you to interview them. What do you do?

POTENTIAL CONFLICT OF INTEREST

Suppose that as you escort Johnny and Susie into your office Johnny impulsively blurts out that the investigating officer and two of the witnesses are liars and are out to get him. In this spontaneous diatribe he further alleges that Harriet was drunk and that three witnesses will testify that the other two witnesses are lying when they said Johnny ran a red light. Without taking

FIGURE 4.1 Diagram of Accident

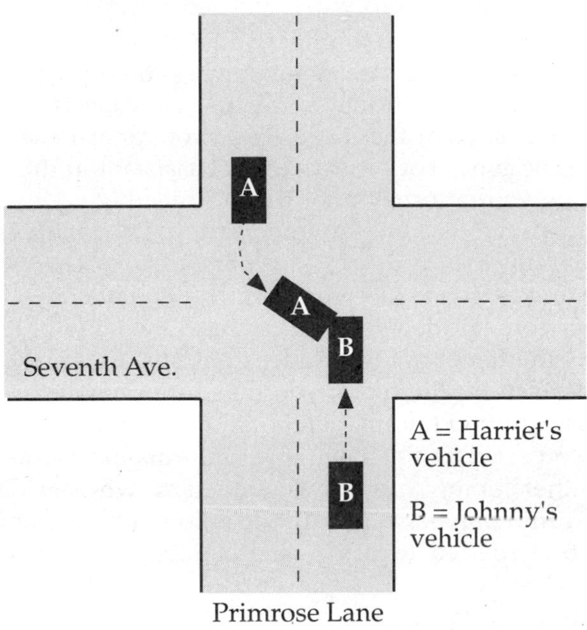

a breath he assures you that the witnesses are also prepared to testify that the officer was incorrect when he concluded that Johnny was speeding at the time of the accident.

Having heard this capsulized version of Johnny's defense you are now alerted to the potential conflict that may exist between Johnny and Susie. Susie, if she were injured, may have to name Johnny in her suit since he may have been wholly or partially to blame for her injuries. Caution and conservatism are now your best attributes. You should either get assistance from your supervising attorney to guide you according to your firm's policy or take the risk that further investigation of this potential conflict may preclude the firm from representing either Johnny or Susie.

Be forewarned that Susie is likely to protest that she could never consider suing Johnny because it was all Harriet's fault. Also, Susie herself saw that the light was green and that Johnny was not speeding. Do not be pacified by this assertion. Before getting any information from Susie or even discussing the case further with the two of them together, you must determine whether Susie's claim is so inconsistent with Johnny's that they need separate representation.

If you conclude that Susie's and Johnny's claims are so at odds that they cannot be represented by the same attorney, you must advise Susie accordingly and then ask her to wait in the reception area. Note that Susie and not Johnny is asked to leave because it is Johnny who made statements to you with respect to the case. Since Susie has said nothing at this point your firm can still represent Johnny. Susie, however, needs to seek alternate counsel.

SETTING THE STAGE

Typically your first contact with Johnny will be after he has spoken with the attorney who will handle the case. Interviewing Johnny will be far easier if he has already met with the attorney since the basic cause(s) of action already will have been determined by the attorney and you can narrow your questions to those particular claims. Your role as a legal assistant in this case will have been explained by your attorney prior to your meeting with Johnny. Nevertheless, it is imperative that Johnny understands from the onset what your duties and limitations are.

If you are the first person to talk with Johnny, remember that in the opening moments of your conversation you will establish the tenor of his relationship with your firm. Whether or not he decides to use the firm may be determined by this initial contact. Furthermore, you must not only obtain essential biographical and background information but also ascertain the potential claims he may have. You need to glean sufficient information so that the attorney can decide whether Johnny has a cause of action, whether the claim is the type your firm would pursue, and, if not, to whom Johnny might be referred. You may also be expected to field some of Johnny's questions regarding his case.

Before you start asking questions, you should try to establish a rapport with Johnny so that he will feel free to speak openly and frankly to you about his case. Remember that you may need to ask very personal questions about, for example, injuries sustained, emotional damage, sexual dysfunction, and scarring. Such information is not easily revealed to friends, let alone complete strangers, so you must put Johnny at ease if you are going to elicit such sensitive disclosures.

At the outset, you should impress upon Johnny that anything he says to you is privileged and that that privilege is just as applicable to conversations he has with you as it is to conversations he has with the attorney. Also advise him that the privilege is applicable even if he and the firm do not enter into a contractual relationship. Try to interview him in the privacy of an office or relatively small room. Your assurances regarding the confidentiality of the information he gives you will have little meaning if strangers pass through while you are interviewing him.

You can help create a relaxed environment by the way in which you arrange the furniture. Relegating Johnny to a low-backed reception chair while you stare at him from behind a palatial desk, seated in an imposing high-backed chair, will not promote trusting, uninhibited communication. You can appear more approachable if you position your chair alongside his. Be careful, however, that you do not get so close that you make him feel uncomfortable by "invading his space."

You can also offer him a cup of coffee, glass of water, or some soda to help break the ice. Devoting a few minutes to small talk will give him an opportunity to get used to you and his surroundings. Taking time to create a comfortable setting will be time well spent and will certainly reap more benefits than immediately bombarding him with questions.

HOW TO ASK AND HOW TO LISTEN

Once you have succeeded in relaxing Johnny, you should try to determine as soon as possible why he came to the office. Although he may be unable to articulate the precise legal basis of his concern, he can probably convey the general nature of his claim, i.e., personal injury, trespass, nuisance, slander, and so on. Of course, regardless of what he believes the claim to be, the facts as they unfold may not support his claim as he perceives it or may support additional claims that will become apparent when subject to appropriate legal analysis.

Rather than asking for directed responses at the beginning of an interview, allowing a client to give a free-flowing narrative of his or her version of what happened is often better. Therefore, you might start by letting Johnny tell his side of the story. Then you can follow up with more directed questions in order to fill in the gaps and clarify any points of confusion you might have. You might consider structuring these follow-up questions using the five W's demanded of a good journalist—who, what, where, when, and why. Who are the key actors involved? What did they do? Where and when did they do it? Why did they do it? Making sure you can answer these key questions will minimize your chances of forgetting to ask relevant questions.

Using notes and prepared questions to organize your thinking will be helpful if you know in general what you will be discussing with Johnny. You can use your notes to refresh your memory about key points you want to explore. Do not, however, become so dependent on your notes that you are unable to deviate in any way. Be flexible; adapt your questions to Johnny's statements. Do not fail to hear what Johnny is telling you. Free yourself of any preconceived notions and be willing to explore avenues that you had not previously considered.

Most importantly, *listen* carefully to Johnny. Pay attention to the details. Note any omissions in his story. Be aware of his body language and the pace, volume, and pitch of his speech. These subtle clues may reveal more than his verbal communication. When you think you have gathered all the pertinent information, summarize what you think he has said to you. You may be surprised at how many discrepancies exist between what you think you heard and what he thinks he said.

An awareness of basic human nature comes in handy when conducting interviews. Some people will provide you with only the sketchiest of details. They will treat each piece of information you extract from them as if it were some kind of valuable ore. Others will inundate you with details, digressing into so many subplots of their story that you will begin to lose sight of their central theme. Some will reexperience the emotional trauma of the events and will become so distraught they will be unable to recount what happened to them.

Although you must distance yourself emotionally enough to be objective regarding the legal claims, you must remain sensitive to the emotional needs and psychological defenses of those you interview. A certain amount of detachment is necessary to do your job but divorcing yourself from your own humanity is neither necessary nor desirable. You must develop your own means of cajoling information from the reclusive, channeling the storytellers, and reassuring the distressed. And you must do this as you are clinically evaluating their potential causes of action—a formidable task!

Remember that interviewing is a two-way street. Just as you are assessing Johnny, so he is assessing you. Be conscious of the messages you are sending. Are you acting bored? Incredulous? Impatient? Condescending? You must communicate a sense of receptivity and warmth if you want him to trust you and cooperate with you fully.

GATHERING BACKGROUND INFORMATION

In almost all cases you need to obtain relatively detailed background information. For example, suppose a minor is involved in the case. The nonclient parent may be the primary custodial parent and the one who has actual authority to institute litigation on behalf of the minor. If a shared custody agreement exists providing that the parents are jointly responsible for decisions made on behalf of the child, one parent alone may be unable to select the child's attorney. You may find yourself in an embarrassing situation if you involve your employer in litigation only to find out that your client is not authorized to institute the suit. Consequently, obtain relatively detailed background information, including residential address, marriages, children, employment history, medical history, and the like. In any tort case, but especially in a personal injury case such as Johnny's, this information is essential.

Any tort case also requires that a complete insurance profile be constructed. First, determine if Johnny has automobile insurance for the vehicle and, if so, whether it provides medical payments and collision coverage. If he has such coverage, assure Johnny that, except for the deductible, the collision coverage will repair his new Corvette. The medical payments coverage, as you should point out, will help pay for his medical expenses as well as Susie's, even if she subsequently submits a claim against him. Note that if Johnny were a pedestrian or a bicyclist who had been injured in an accident involving a motor vehicle, some coverage would be available from his homeowner's policy.

Review any applicable insurance policies *very, very* thoroughly in the context of state statutes and court decisions. Be particularly concerned with the enforceability of clauses in the policies. The mere fact that an insurance policy appears to deny coverage does not mean that that provision is necessarily enforceable. We will discuss this problem in Chapter 22.

Obtain basic information from Johnny, such as his date of birth, Social Security number, the addresses of his residence and place of employment, the identity of his insurance carrier and, to the extent known, his coverage and its limits. Then ask for detailed information regarding the nature and extent of his injuries. If his injuries could potentially interfere with his relationships with third parties, such as parents, children, and perhaps even brothers and sisters, consider the possibility of filing a separate loss of consortium claim against Harriet.

Inquire about Johnny's prior medical history. Who is his family physician? What injuries or diseases has he had? What physical examinations has he had, including those for obtaining employment, for school attendance, or for other activities? This information is important since Johnny's medical history prior to the accident may have a significant impact on the amount of damages he will be entitled to receive.

Find out if Johnny was taken to an emergency room and, if so, whether he was taken by ambulance or if he drove himself. Identify Johnny's treating physicians, if any, since the accident and find out how many times he has seen them and for what reasons. Note whether Johnny has been unable to work or has been able to do only those jobs characterized as "light duty." In many instances, an injury does not prevent the client from working but may preclude him or her from working in certain activities or force the client to forego certain benefits, such as overtime.

You also need to determine the nature and extent of the damages to Johnny's vehicle. Depending on your firm's policy, you may become involved in assisting Johnny with his property damage claim.

SCENE OF THE ACCIDENT

When you first ask Johnny to describe the accident he may want to relate what happened in a conclusory fashion. He may say, for example, "I was obeying the law and this drunk turned in front of me on a green light." Let him ventilate. Once he has done that you need to piece together the chain of events leading up to the accident and to verify the validity of the facts he has given you. Suppose, for example, that Johnny tells you that the accident occurred at 8:00 P.M. on Saturday evening, April 9, one month ago. You need to confirm that April 9 was a Saturday. Later, if your firm accepts this case, you will need to ascertain the weather and road conditions at the time of the accident. For example, was there any construction? Was the road made of dirt, granite, asphalt, or concrete? How many lanes of traffic were there in each direction?

In piecing together the events that preceded the accident you will need to take Johnny back to the time he woke up that morning. What time did he get up? Where had he been the night before? Did he have breakfast? What did he do prior to the accident? Did he have lunch? Did he have anything to drink during the afternoon? Was he with friends who could confirm his whereabouts and activities? Did he have a good night's sleep or was he overtired? Did he have dinner Saturday evening? Did he go to Susie's to pick her up or was she with him to begin with? Do they live together? Did he have anything to drink prior to the accident?

You will also want to question Johnny regarding his new Corvette. Had he had it for a long time? Was he accustomed to driving it? Had he had prior traffic violations? Were his headlights on? Was the car functioning properly? What was he doing prior to the accident? Was he talking to Susie? Was he looking forward or to the left or right? Did he see Harriet before she made the turn? Did he see Harriet making the turn? What evasive actions did either

Johnny or Harriet make prior to the collision? You will want to find out how much traffic was on Primrose Lane and on Seventh Avenue that night at 8:00 P.M. How well lit was the intersection? Were Harriet's headlights on? Had Harriet turned on her turn signal? Did Harriet appear to hesitate and then speed up or did she make the left-hand turn as though there was no oncoming traffic? Were Johnny and Susie wearing seat belts? Was Harriet wearing a seat belt?

Then you need to zero in on what happened at the scene of the accident. Does Johnny recall slamming on the brakes and hearing any sounds associated with skidding tires? Did the brakes of the Corvette lock up? Where exactly was the point of impact? Could Johnny or Susie get out of the vehicle immediately after the accident? Were they coherent? Was anyone cut? Was blood evident anywhere? Did the vehicle itself remain secure, i.e., did the seats break their mountings or did the backs collapse? How much damage was done to Harriet's old Chrysler? Who was the first person on the scene? Did Johnny, Susie, or Harriet speak to that person? Did Johnny or Susie speak to Harriet? Did they speak to any of the other witnesses? Where were the other witnesses at the time of the accident? Did any of them almost collide with Harriet or Johnny? Did any of them actually collide with either? Were there any other accidents that occurred as a result of the collision between Harriet and Johnny?

Since Johnny indicated that an officer eventually came to the scene, you should determine what law enforcement agency the officer worked for. Did Johnny speak to the officer? What was the nature of their conversation? What was Johnny's attitude at the time, i.e., was he angry, subdued, crying, in pain? Did the officer speak with Susie or Harriet? Does Johnny know whether the officer spoke with any of the other witnesses and, if so, which ones? Did the officer make any measurements at the scene of the accident that Johnny is aware of?

Johnny made several allegations during his earlier soliloquy. Now you need to follow up on those. Johnny indicated to you that Harriet was drunk. How does he know that? Did he speak with Harriet or smell her breath? Did the officer indicate that he was citing Harriet for driving under the influence? Johnny indicated that the officer cited him for speeding. Did the officer tell him the basis for making that determination? Johnny also stated that other witnesses said he ran a red light. Was he cited for running a red light? Where were those alleged witnesses when they saw Johnny run the red light? In which direction were they facing?

DISCOVERING THE WEAKNESSES

As you conduct the interview do not become so wrapped up in the tale that is being told that you fail to notice any time gaps or apparent inconsistent statements. The appropriate time to discover any problems with your case is when you first become involved, not after a great deal of time, money, and effort have been expended in pursuit of the claim. Remember that not everyone who is involved in an automobile accident is entitled to compensation, and even if a victim is entitled to compensation it may well be that problems with respect to liability, i.e., who was at fault and to what extent, will discourage the firm from representing that person. Someone with $100,000 worth of injuries, for example, who is 99 percent responsible for those injuries has a $1,000 case, not a $100,000 case (in a comparative negligence state). The recoverable damages would not justify a firm's investment in such a case.

STATUTE OF LIMITATIONS PROBLEMS

Clients often "sit" on their claims for some time before acting on them and when they do finally get around to pursuing their claims they may be barred because the statute of limitations has expired. Be aware of the appropriate statute and act in a timely fashion, both to protect the client's claim and to protect your firm from being sued for malpractice for inadequate representation. If the expiration of the statutory time period were imminent in Johnny's case, the attorney might opt to draft a bare-bones complaint naming Johnny as his own attorney. This would prevent the attorney from having to evaluate the case too hastily and would still protect the interests of all involved. If the client serves as his or her own attorney no paperwork will have to be filled out for substitution of attorney if your firm decides to decline representation.

INVESTIGATING OFFICER INTERVIEW

Having determined Johnny's side of the story, you must now interview the third parties involved to find out their recollections of the events. The first person to start with is the investigating officer. Although in most cases the officer has no personal firsthand information other than the measurements taken, he or she may have talked to some of the witnesses. In some states the actual investigation with respect to skid marks, point of impact, estimated speed of travel, and so forth is left to civilian employees of the police department. Therefore, you must determine which individuals actually investigated the accident scene and what their training, job classification, and responsibilities were.

Should your jurisdiction be one of those in which the police officer does the actual investigation, including making measurements and interviewing witnesses, interview the officer as soon as possible. The notion that police officers can recall specific details of every investigation they conduct by simply reviewing their notes is an erroneous one. Remember, they are involved in numerous incidents on a daily basis and substantial time has usually passed between the accident in question and your interview. Nothing is as important as fresh, firsthand information.

Any attempt to interview the investigating officer should begin with the Police Liaison Unit. This unit, which exists in one form or another in most jurisdictions, is primarily involved in ensuring that the officers involved in a criminal case are aware of the events that are occurring and the times when they must appear in court. You can also use this unit to make arrangements to interview the officer about the strictly civil portions of an incident. Since it may often be possible for the officers to be paid for the time involved in meeting and discussing the case with you, it is imperative, at the outset at least, to work with the Police Liaison's office. Certainly officers will be far happier talking with you if they know they are getting paid or being given release time for the time spent with you, rather than receiving only the standard jurisdictional witness fee.

Additionally, since police officers frequently encounter attorneys in an adversarial context, they are often prepared to do battle. Therefore, make sure you are well prepared for the interview. Do not create the impression of wasting the officer's time with irrelevant or nonsensical questions. When you interview a police officer you should have a detailed outline of your questions.

Prior to interviewing the officer, mentally retrace the events leading up to, during, and after the accident in as much detail as possible, noting the names of any witnesses that you are aware of. Using precise questions will not only enhance your credibility with the officer but will also greatly reduce the amount of time necessary to complete the interview.

If departmental procedures allow it and the officer has no objections, tape record the interview. Transcribe the interview as soon as possible and send it to the officer, asking him or her to make appropriate corrections. Let the officer know about this procedure at the beginning of the interview if you intend to tape it.

Never "talk down" to an officer or try to contradict him or her. Establishing a good rapport will serve you well later in the case whereas being patronizing will result in an adversarial rather than a cooperative relationship. You should maintain control of the interview and strive to earn the officer's respect but you must do so without sacrificing his or her ego. You will undoubtedly encounter the arrogant officer who will test your capacity to control your tongue. Before you succumb to the temptation to engage in a verbal repartee, remember that an officer who dislikes your style of questioning could become a liability rather than an asset to your case. Prudence is often the wisest course of action.

All basic background information, such as time on the force, experience in accident investigation, and training, is important. Focus, however, on the information contained in the report the officer prepared. Determine what information in the report came from the officer's firsthand observations at the accident scene, which information came from witnesses the officer deemed credible, and which information the officer rejected because he or she thought the witnesses were not credible.

The officer writing the report may not have interviewed some of the witnesses, so you need to ascertain which officers spoke to which witnesses and, if necessary, interview each of those officers. You need to find out, for example, if there was a backup unit that assisted the investigating officer and if those officers talked to witnesses, if statements were taken by any other officers, and if measurements were made by a different officer or by a civilian accident investigator. You need to get the names of these individuals and establish the relevance of the information they may have to offer to determine if you should also interview them.

At this juncture you must determine whether the officer has any independent recollection of the accident. Then you must distinguish what the officer knows by virtue of independent recollection versus what he or she remembers by reviewing the police report and other documents that you brought to the interview. Knowing when and where to give information to the officer comes from experience and intuition. What you should do will vary on a case by case and officer by officer basis.

LAY WITNESS INTERVIEWS

As soon as possible after the incident and, hopefully, prior to being spoken to by the adverse party, contact all lay witnesses. Many people are very concerned about the perceived hazards of having to testify in court and you should do everything possible to allay their fears. It is not unusual for someone to "not recall" an event to ensure that her testimony will not be required. Meeting the person at his or her home after work or for lunch can make a reluctant witness feel more comfortable and less "put out" than requesting the person come to your office.

Once you know whether the witness will either support or negate your client's position, you will need to decide whether to tape record the interview, assuming the witness will allow it. If the witness's recollections are supportive of your client's position, you might want to provide a copy of the tape to opposing counsel in the hope of speeding up settlement. Note, however, that the presence of a tape recorder makes many people very uncomfortable and may therefore be counterproductive. If you opt to record the interview, be sure the witness feels comfortable and at ease before starting. Be forewarned that several evidentiary obstacles must be hurdled before tape-recorded statements can be used in court, even for impeachment purposes.

Once again, you must explain at the beginning of an interview who you are, why you want to talk to the witness, and what the potential ramifications of talking with you could be. You should also advise witnesses that the opposing parties' attorney or legal assistant may also want to interview them. Any attempts to influence the testimony of witnesses or to discourage them from speaking with opposing counsel could, and should, result in your being fired. Such overt attempts to influence witnesses could also, in many jurisdictions, result in criminal charges being filed against you.

Typically one begins questioning by allowing the witness to give a free-flowing narrative of the events he or she observed. Note that the ability to make these observations depends on conditions at the time of the incident. For example, the witness may be wearing glasses at the time of the interview but that does not mean that as she observed the events she had her glasses on. Her observations may therefore be suspect.

Try to pinpoint the exact location of the witness at the time the events occurred to determine whether the observation was possible. It is not uncommon for witnesses to make materially false statements and be honestly unaware of their falsity. For example, a driver who was behind a vehicle that was involved in an accident may state that he saw the driver of the other vehicle lose physical control of the automobile. In reality, all he could see was the back of the other driver's head. If later he saw paramedics remove somebody from the driver's seat of the vehicle, he would assume, quite logically, that the person he observed being removed from the driver's side of the car was the person he had observed driving the car, which is not necessarily true. Consequently, his statement regarding the driver's identity could be honest but false.

What if the witness is hostile and alleges, for example, that the accident was all your client's fault and that he should be punished for what he did? In such a case you will have to summon all of your interpersonal skills to get an in-depth and accurate interview. Pin down a hostile witness with as many specific facts and details as possible. You need to find out exactly where the witness was standing, what she was doing, who was at the scene, what they were wearing, who was doing what to whom, and so on. If nothing else, by restricting the witness to exacting factual details she may be more easily impeached at a later date should other witnesses or physical evidence conflict with her statements.

Witnesses may ask to review the transcription of the tape recording, obtain a copy of the tape, or review your notes. Be aware of your firm's policy in this regard. In most instances there would be no problem in allowing a witness to review the transcribed interview or taking a copy of the actual tape recording itself. Problems arise, however, if the tape recording or its transcription is discoverable when in the hands of the witness but not discoverable when in the possession of one of the party's attorneys. It may be prudent to advise witnesses that the tape recording or its transcription is available for review at the attorney's office but legal procedural rules prohibit a copy being given to them.

Do not assume that only personal, firsthand information is of any value. A witness may be able to provide you with useful information that leads to legally admissible evidence. She may, for example, advise you that a photographer from one of the local newspapers took photographs of the scene, that other individuals in the vicinity observed the accident, or that she was accompanied by friends whose names are not on the police report. This information might allow you to obtain additional collaborative evidence to support your client's story or to impeach the recollections of a hostile witness.

Finally, and most importantly, always be gracious. An interview is not the place for aggressive, hard-hitting questions. Witnesses do not have to talk to you. If you irritate them, they may terminate the interview. You cannot afford to burn bridges at the initial stages of an investigation only to find out later that the witness you alienated is the one you most need.

SUMMARY

Explain to the client at the beginning of any interview that you are a legal assistant, not an attorney, and delineate your responsibilities. The opening moments of your conversation will establish the tenor of your relationship. Therefore, you must make sure the client feels free to speak openly and frankly to you. Social amenities should be observed and everything should be done to create as comfortable an environment as possible.

Interview questions can be structured around the five W's—who, what, where, when and why. Use notes and anticipated questions to organize your thinking but do not depend on them to the extent that you ignore the client's responses. An understanding of human nature will facilitate your interviews of "difficult" clients but in all cases you need to pay attention to what the client says with his body and voice inflections in addition to the words he utters.

Allow the client first to describe the events leading up to his injuries. Then ask him specific, detailed questions that will allow you to assemble a more complete picture of what happened. Later you will want to confirm some of the details but during the initial interview you should be attentive to any time gaps or apparent inconsistent statements. You will also need to gather considerable background information on the client, such as medical history and extent of insurance coverage.

If the case involves the police, you will want to interview the investigating officer as soon as possible. Determine the nature of the officer's role in the investigation. Prepare your questions in advance and, if departmental procedures allow and the officer is willing, tape record the interview. Try to establish a cooperative relationship with the officer; never patronize or argue with an officer. After obtaining background information about the officer, such as experience and time on the force, determine what information in the report came from firsthand, personal observation and which came from witnesses. Find out if statements were taken or measurements were made by other officers or civilian investigators and get the names of those individuals.

Witnesses are often concerned about getting involved. Therefore, you must make every effort to make a witness feel comfortable talking to you. Explain who you are and what you want and also advise the witness that she will probably be contacted by the opposing side. If you can gain the witness's confidence and if you determine that her recollections support your client's position, you will want to consider tape recording your conversation.

Typically, you should begin your questioning by allowing the witness to give a chronological explanation of the events observed. While you are listening note any factors that might give less credence to the observations. If the witness is hostile you will want to pin her down with as many specific details as possible. Always be alert to soliciting any useful information that the witness can give, which may lead to legally admissible evidence. Above all, be gracious toward the witness.

PRACTICE POINTERS

Below are examples of questions you would likely ask when interviewing a potential client regarding a possible personal injury claim. Review this list and make sure you can see the relevance of each question.

CLIENT INTERVIEW CHECKLIST

Name: ____________________
Birth name: ____________________
Address: ____________________
Telephone number: ____________________

Continued on next page

PRACTICE POINTERS—Continued

Employer: ______________________________
Occupation: ______________________________
Employer address: ______________________________
Employer telephone number: ______________________________
Age: ______________________________
Birthdate: ______________________________
Birthplace: ______________________________
Social Security number: ______________________________
Driver's license number: ______________________ State: ________
Name of spouse: ______________________________
Spouse's employer: ______________________________
Spouse's occupation: ______________________________
Address of spouse's employer: ______________________________
Telephone number: ______________________________
Names of children: ______________________________
Ages of children: ______________________________
Names of children living with you now: ______________________________

Description of injuries received: ______________________________

Names of medical providers who treated you (ambulance, hospitals, doctors, physical therapists, etc.) ______________________________

Names of medical providers currently providing treatment: ______________________________

Information regarding prior injuries or accidents: ______________________________

Names of witnesses: ______________________________
Addresses of witnesses: ______________________________

Statements made by witnesses: ______________________________

Loss of wages due to injury: ______________________________

IF VEHICLE ACCIDENT ASK THE FOLLOWING QUESTIONS AS WELL:
Time of accident: ______________________________
Location of accident: ______________________________

Make, model, and year of vehicle client was driving: ______________________________

License plate of client's vehicle: ______________________________
Name, address, and telephone number of passengers in client's vehicle at time of accident: ______________________________

PRACTICE POINTERS—Continued

Use of seat belts/carbelt: ____________________
Name, address, and telephone of driver of defendant's vehicle:
____
____

Make, model, and year of defendant's vehicle: ____________________
____

License plate of defendant's vehicle: ____________________
Name, address, and telephone number of passengers in defendant's vehicle:
____
____

Condition of defendant driver: ____________________
Statements made by defendant to client: ____________________
____

Weather and road conditions at time of accident: ____________________
____

Traffic signs and signals in effect: ____________________
Obstructions to view of either driver: ____________________
Whether vehicles' lights were on or off: ____________________
Defective equipment on vehicles: ____________________
Description of how accident occurred (in as much detail as possible): ____________________
____

Diagram of accident scene: ____________________
Traffic violations charged by police: ____________________
Whether police report was filed: ____________________
Whether photographs were taken: ____________________
Damages sustained by vehicle: ____________________
____

Estimation of cost of repairs: ____________________
Name and address of client's insurance company: ____________________
____

Policy number: ____________________
Extent of coverage provided: ____________________
____

Name and address of defendant's insurance company: ____________________
____

Policy number: ____________________
Extent of coverage provided: ____________________
____

Information regarding other insurance coverage (such as worker's compensation, disability, etc.): ____________________
____

Whether client has been contacted by anyone concerning the accident:
____
____

TORT TEASERS

1. Recalling the scenario given at the beginning of this chapter, draw up a list of questions that you would ask Susie if she decided to file a claim against Johnny. You can assume that their relationship has cooled since the accident so that this will not be a "friendly" suit.

2. Assuming that Johnny is willing to be interviewed, how would you question him now that he is a "hostile" party?

3. What strategy would you use in interviewing Harriet?

4. Draw up a list of questions that you would want to ask the police officer who investigated the accident involving Harriet and Johnny.

5. Draw up a list of questions you would want to ask a witness who was driving immediately behind Johnny at the time of the accident.

NEGLIGENCE: AN OVERVIEW

CHAPTER OBJECTIVES

In this chapter you will learn to:

- Recognize the elements of negligence, which include duty, breach of duty, causation, and damages.
- Recognize the concepts of negligence *per se*, *res ipsa loquitur*, and objective versus subjective standards.
- Classify damages.
- Appreciate the mechanics of proving a case in terms of burdens of proof and functions of the judge and jury.

One beautiful summer afternoon Jonathan and Teddy, both age six, were engaged in a particularly rollicking game of football in the backyard of Teddy's house. In an effort to emulate the quarterback hero of his fantasies, Jonathan took aim at Teddy and catapulted the ball into the air. Unfortunately, his aim was off and the ball landed in the backyard of Teddy's neighbors, Mr. and Mrs. Baxter. The Baxter backyard was surrounded by a six-foot wooden fence. Undeterred by this obstacle between him and his ball, Teddy attempted unsuccessfully to scale the fence. Jonathan, who was two months older than Teddy and, therefore, proportionately wiser, suggested that they try the gate to the yard.

Teddy knew that the Baxters always kept the gate locked and he also remembered that he had been warned repeatedly by both the Baxters and his parents that he should never enter the Baxter yard without supervision. Jonathan urged him to try the gate anyway but Teddy was hesitant. Other than his parents' and the Baxters' admonitions, he was circumspect about entering the yard because of the presence of Gertrude, the Baxters' German shepherd. Gertrude and Teddy had a somewhat strained relationship because Teddy, in some of his less enlightened moments, had taken a certain perverse pleasure in provoking Gertrude into a barking frenzy by teasing her through the gate. He was reluctant to test her capacity for forgiveness, but, egged on by Jonathan, he tried the gate latch and found, much to his surprise, that it was unlocked. Hesitantly, he opened the gate and peered inside. With Gertrude nowhere in sight he bolted across the yard to retrieve the ball.

Gertrude, her hearing somewhat impaired by advanced age, was deeply immersed in canine daydreams and was oblivious to Teddy's activities. Because of this Teddy might have escaped undetected if he hadn't stubbed his toe on a sprinkler and let out a loud yell. The slumbering Gertrude, awakened by Teddy's cries, sprang to her feet. Somewhat disoriented but drawing on her instincts as a guard dog, Gertrude leaped off the porch in the direction of the unknown intruder. When she was within lunging distance of the now-panicked Teddy, vague memories of loathing filtered into Gertrude's consciousness as she began to recall the many indignations she had endured as a result of Teddy's tormenting.

Goaded by these memories, as well as her instinctual drive to protect her domain, Gertrude took aim for the hapless Teddy. When Teddy felt Gertrude grab hold of one of his pant legs he screamed in terror and tried desperately to kick Gertrude away. Incensed by the pummeling she received from Teddy, Gertrude plunged her teeth deeper, piercing Teddy's flesh. Teddy's continual thrashing about only made Gertrude more determined to maintain her viselike grip on Teddy's leg.

Meanwhile, Jonathan, who was a spectator to this whole drama, valiantly attempted to rescue his friend by pelting Gertrude with rocks he found in the Baxters' driveway. Unfortunately, the sting of the rocks further enraged Gertrude and, not realizing their source, she reinforced her grip on Teddy's leg.

Drawn by Jonathan's pleas for help and Teddy's screams of terror, a passerby, Mr. Dooright, came running into the Baxters' backyard. Immediately sizing up the situation, Mr. Dooright began kicking at Gertrude with all his might to induce her to release Teddy. Gertrude, stunned by his blows, let loose of Teddy to attack the object that was causing her pain. Seizing this opportunity to escape, Teddy dragged himself toward the gate and Jonathan pulled him to the safety of the driveway.

The courageous Mr. Dooright now pitted his wits against 120 pounds of wrath. Gertrude, enraged by the kicks she had received, lashed out wildly and caught Mr. Dooright's right hand. Pummeling Gertrude's head with his free arm, Mr. Dooright struggled desperately to free his hand from Gertrude's jaws.

The duo might have continued this struggle until one of them collapsed from exhaustion but, as fate would have it, Mr. Baxter arrived home early from work. As he drove in and caught sight of the fracas taking place in his backyard, he vaulted out of his car, yelling at Gertrude as he ran. When her master's commands finally penetrated her consciousness, Gertrude released her prey.

But the damage had already been wrought. Both Teddy and Mr. Dooright were bleeding profusely from their wounds and Teddy, his attention no longer diverted by the combat between Mr. Dooright and Gertrude, was beginning to become painfully aware of the full extent of his injuries. Both Mr. Dooright and Teddy sustained serious injuries from their battles with Gertrude.

Teddy would bear emotional as well as physical scars as a result of his encounter with Gertrude. In the future he would experience a phobic disorder connected to dogs to the extent that the approach of any dog in his direction would trigger an anxiety attack. Mr. Dooright, a longtime animal lover and therefore more sympathetic to Gertrude's acts, would experience no emotional reactions from his trauma but would have to suffer the long-term consequences of his heroic efforts. He would endure several operations to repair the damage to his hand and would never gain full control of his hand again. As a result, his career as a much-heralded concert pianist would come to an untimely end and he would be relegated forever to the humble life of a piano teacher.

DEFINITION OF NEGLIGENCE

We will use the facts of this scenario throughout this and the next five chapters to illustrate the fundamental elements of negligence. Negligence involves conduct that creates an unreasonable risk of harm for another. It can be contrasted with an intentional tort, such as assault, where the tortfeasor's mental state must be such that the tortfeasor is aware of or actually intends that a certain result will occur. The mental state of a negligent tortfeasor is irrelevant.

There are four elements of negligence (see Table 5–1), each of which will be discussed in detail in subsequent chapters. These elements are as follows:

1. *Duty:* A legal duty requiring the tortfeasor to conform to a certain standard of conduct in order to protect others from unreasonable risk of harm (Chapter 6).
2. *Breach of duty:* A failure of the tortfeasor to conform his or her conduct to the standard required (Chapter 7).
3. *Causation:* A causal connection between the tortfeasor's conduct and the resulting injury (Chapter 8).
4. *Damages:* The actual loss or damages resulting from the tortfeasor's conduct (Chapter 9).

Let us look briefly at each of these elements and see how they apply to the Gertrude/Teddy scenario.

DUTY

The notion of *duty* arises out of the legal obligations that result from our relationships with others. Parents, for example, owe a duty of care to their children; airline companies and their employees owe a duty of care to their passengers. The nature of this duty varies depending on the nature of the

TABLE 5.1 Elements of Negligence

DUTY	BREACH OF DUTY	CAUSATION	DAMAGES
•Did the defendant, as a result of his relationship to the plaintiff, owe the plaintiff a duty of care?	•Did the defendant conduct himself as a reasonable person would have under similar circumstances?	•Was the defendant's conduct the actual cause of the plaintiff's injuries? (actual cause) •Was it reasonably foreseeable that the defendant's conduct would cause the plaintiff's injuries? (proximate cause)	•Did the plaintiff suffer compensable injuries as a result of the defendant's conduct?

relationship. Landowners owe a different duty of care to trespassers than they do to those whom they invite on their premises. In some cases the tortfeasor may owe a duty of care to those with whom he has no direct contact, such as third parties that he could reasonably anticipate being injured by his conduct. A tavern owner, for example, could owe a duty of care to those injured by intoxicated patrons whom the tavern owner recognizes as being so intoxicated as to constitute a danger to those about him.

BREACH OF DUTY

As a practical matter, the key issue that arises in most negligence cases is not whether the defendant owed a duty of care to the plaintiff but whether she breached that duty. A key question that must be answered when dealing with **breach of duty** is whether the defendant conducted herself as a reasonable person would have under similar circumstances.

OBJECTIVE VS. SUBJECTIVE STANDARD

In making this determination the courts use what is referred to as an **objective standard**. Under this standard the defendant's actions are compared to those of a hypothetical "reasonable person." In contrast, under a **subjective standard** one asks whether the tortfeasor herself believes she acted reasonably.

Suppose, for example, a woman believes that she is about to be burglarized and, fearing for her own safety, shoots a would-be burglar. Using an objective standard one would ask whether the woman acted as a reasonable person would in that same situation. Using a subjective standard one would question whether the woman herself believed that she acted in a reasonable fashion.

The difference in outcome resulting from using two different standards is most evident if the woman in question were unusually fearful of being attacked.

Suppose the woman, having been burglarized several times in the past, became hysterical when she saw a man's outline in her window and shot him through the window before he made any actual attempt to enter her home. Under an objective standard her actions probably would not qualify as reasonable. A reasonable person in those circumstances most likely would have waited to ascertain whether the individual outside the window actually posed a threat. From a reasonable person's standpoint, it would have been just as likely that the person was a solicitor or a friend as a burglar. Under a subjective standard, however, the only question would be whether the woman herself in fact believed that her life was in danger.

Even under an objective standard, however, the physical characteristics of the tortfeasor are taken into consideration. A defendant who is blind, for example, is held to the standard of care expected of people similarly impaired and not to the standard of care of sighted persons. The circumstances in which the defendant acts are also taken into consideration. The rescuer who responds in an emergency situation is not held to the same standard of care as one who acts under less demanding conditions.

PROFESSIONALS

Those blessed with a higher degree of knowledge, skill, or experience are held to a higher standard of care than the ordinary reasonable person. Since police officers, for example, have received training and presumably have experience in the handling of firearms, they are held to a higher standard of care when they discharge their weapons than the average person. Police officers are held to a "reasonable police officer" standard rather than a reasonable person standard. Therefore, a civilian might be justified under the reasonable person standard in taking another's life whereas a police officer under equivalent circumstances might not be. Specialists in a particular field are held to an even higher standard. A police officer trained as a hostage negotiator, for instance, is held to a higher standard of care in a hostage situation than the average police officer.

NEGLIGENCE *PER SE*

In some cases statutes will determine the reasonable standard of care. Statutes that set forth safety standards, for example, in essence define minimal standards of reasonable conduct. Violation of those statutes will be treated as **negligence *per se*** (negligence in itself). A traffic ordinance mandating a speed of fifteen miles per hour in school crossing zones sets forth the standard of conduct expected of a reasonable driver in a school crossing zone. A driver who injures someone in the crossing zone as a result of violating the ordinance is negligent *per se*. In other words, the driver's negligence is presumed. Note that several factors limit this general rule; they will be discussed in Chapter 7.

RES IPSA LOQUITUR

In some cases the plaintiff is unable to prove the defendant's negligence because she is unable to gain access to information regarding the defendant's conduct. In such cases the plaintiff can rely on the doctrine known as ***res ipsa loquitur***, which means "the thing speaks for itself." In order to utilize this doctrine, the plaintiff must show: (1) the event that injured the plaintiff was one that does not ordinarily happen except through negligence; (2) the instrument that caused the plaintiff's injury was under the exclusive control of the defendant; and (3) the plaintiff's injuries were not due to his own actions. In some courts, the plaintiff must further show that the explanation underlying the events that occurred is more readily accessible to the defendant than to the plaintiff.

A plaintiff injured in a modern-day airplane crash could use this doctrine to allow the jury to infer that negligence was more than likely the cause of the crash. Notice how the elements mentioned above are applicable to such a case. (1) Airplane crashes do not normally occur except through negligence. (2) Planes are under the exclusive control of the defendant airline company. (3) The plaintiff in such instances does not ordinarily contribute to the cause of the crash. (4) Finally, the defendant airline company is generally more capable of assessing the cause of the accident than the plaintiff.

CAUSATION

ACTUAL CAUSE

The third element the plaintiff must prove is causation. Causation is divided into two categories: actual cause and proximate cause. **Actual cause**, or causation in fact, is a factual question that asks whether the defendant's conduct was the actual, factual cause of the plaintiff's injuries. Actual causation is not generally a legal problem unless there are multiple causes of the plaintiff's injuries. Suppose, for example, three different assailants throw rocks at the plaintiff. Only one of the rocks hits its mark, causing the plaintiff to sustain a serious eye injury. The question in this case would be which of the three assailants actually caused the plaintiff's injury. In the event of concurrent causes, as illustrated in this example, the courts generally find that each of the events was a cause of the injury, thereby forcing the defendants to apportion the damages. Further discussion of proof of actual cause is found in Chapter 8.

PROXIMATE CAUSE

Proximate cause, referred to by some writers as "legal cause," revolves around the issue of foreseeability. The concept arises from the notion that even the most negligent defendant should not be responsible for consequences that are too remotely connected to his or her conduct. Suppose the plaintiff is knifed by the defendant and is hospitalized for his injuries. If the plaintiff refuses medical treatment, contracts gangrene, and dies from wounds that, under the ordinary course of treatment, would have been minimal, should the defendant be held responsible for his death? In other words, was the defendant in this case the proximate cause of the plaintiff's death or was the plaintiff's death due to some intervening factor, namely, the plaintiff's decision to reject medical care?

Another example of a situation in which proximate cause is an issue is one in which the plaintiff dies as a result of an injury that, if sustained by an ordinary person, would have resulted in only minor injuries. In these "eggshell skull" cases, so-called because the plaintiff has a skull of eggshell thinness, the rule often expressed by the courts is that the defendant should "take his plaintiff as he finds him."

The issue of foreseeability also arises in what is sometimes referred to as the "unforeseeable plaintiff" problem. The question in this case is whether the defendant's conduct posed any foreseeable risk of harm to the plaintiff. Suppose the defendant's conduct is unquestionably negligent in reference to a third party but the plaintiff, rather than the third party, is injured as a result of the defendant's conduct. Should the defendant be held liable for the plaintiff's injury even if she did not act negligently in reference to the plaintiff?

That question was posed in one of the most famous American tort cases, *Palsgraf v. Long Island R.R. Company,* 162 N.E. 99 (N.Y. 1928). The defendant in that case negligently caused a passenger to drop a package of fireworks, which, through a series of bizarre events, caused injury to the plaintiff. Although the defendant was undeniably negligent toward the passenger, at issue was whether such negligence could give rise to liability to the plaintiff. The court, in a decision written by Judge Cardozo, held that the defendant was not liable because the plaintiff was not a foreseeable plaintiff. Judge Andrews, in his dissent, argued that the defendant owed a duty of care to everyone in society to protect them from unnecessary danger. Everyone, he said, has a duty to refrain from any acts that unreasonably threaten the safety of others.

FORESEEABILITY OR DUTY OF CARE?

The question of foreseeability is often phrased in terms of duty of care. As a result, the elements of proximate cause and duty are often interwoven in a court's analysis. The majority in *Palsgraf* phrased the question of liability in terms of whether the defendants had a duty of care to the plaintiff. In essence, this question is the same as asking whether the plaintiff is a foreseeable plaintiff, i.e., one to whom the defendant's conduct poses a foreseeable risk. This and other interesting issues arise under the subject of proximate cause and will be discussed in great detail in Chapter 8.

DAMAGES

The final issue that must be addressed in any tort case is one of damages. Damages can be classified using a variety of labels, but we will lump all damages into one of three categories: compensatory damages, nominal damages, and punitive damages (see Table 5–2). **Compensatory damages**, as the name implies, are designed to compensate the plaintiff for her actual loss or injury. Compensatory damages can be further divided into two subcategories, general damages and special damages.

General damages are those damages that typically result from the kind of conduct the defendant engaged in. Monetary compensation for the loss of a leg resulting from a traffic accident falls into the category of general damages. Compensation for the plaintiff's pain and suffering resulting from her injuries is also classified as general damages.

Special damages, on the other hand, are specifically tied to the plaintiff. Damages resulting from loss of earnings and medical expenses are examples of special damages.

Nominal damages are awarded when the plaintiff has proved to the jury's satisfaction that a tort was committed but has not been able to prove that any

TABLE 5.2 Classification of Damages

PUNITIVE	COMPENSATORY	NOMINAL
• Designed to punish the defendant.	• **General** Compensation for damages antipicated as a result of conduct defendant engaged in. • **Special** Compensation for damages specially tied to plaintiff.	• Awarded when tort was committed but no actual loss occurred.

actual loss occurred. Nominal damages are not allowed in negligence actions because the plaintiff must prove the existence of an actual loss in a negligence case.

Punitive damages are designed to punish the defendant. Unlike compensatory damages, the purpose of punitive damages is not to make the plaintiff whole but to deter future, undesirable conduct of the defendant and similarly situated individuals. Punitive damages are reserved for those situations in which the defendant acted with particular ill-will toward the plaintiff or in conscious disregard for the well-being of others. Pure negligence by itself will not support the award of punitive damages.

The computation of damages is a highly complex process and will be dealt with only at an elementary level in this text. We will discuss the classification and computation of damages in Chapter 9.

FUNCTION OF JUDGE AND JURY

It might be advisable at this point to mention the role of the judge and the jury in a negligence case. The judge, as you probably know, decides all questions of law, while the jury is the finder of fact. In a negligence claim the judge determines as a matter of law what the defendant's duty was to the plaintiff. So in a suit by a plaintiff who was a social guest of a defendant, the court will instruct the jury regarding the duty of care owed by the defendant to a social guest. Based on that instruction, the jury will determine whether the defendant breached that duty of care.

If, however, the judge decides that reasonable people could not differ in their decision as to whether the defendant breached his duty of care, she will instruct the jury as to the finding of fact they must make. By making such an instruction the judge, in essence, takes the case out of the jury's hands. If the judge decides that, as a matter of law, the plaintiff failed to prove one of the elements of his case, the judge may remove the case from the jury by directing a verdict.

Therefore, even though the jury is considered the finder of facts, it may do so only when the facts are such that reasonable people could differ as to the nature of those facts. If a case does go to the jury, the jury determines whether the defendant breached his duty of care to the plaintiff, if he did so in such a way that proximately caused the plaintiff's injuries, and what damages the plaintiff is entitled to receive.

As you might recall from some of your other law-related classes, the plaintiff in a civil case bears two burdens of proof: the burden of production and the burden of persuasion. The **burden of production** requires the plaintiff to come forward with sufficient evidence to avoid a directed verdict. He must show in a negligence claim, therefore, that the defendant owed a duty of care to the plaintiff, that he breached that duty, that the plaintiff suffered an injury and that the defendant's negligence was the proximate cause of that injury. In some states if the plaintiff can invoke the doctrine of *res ipsa loquitur,* the burden of production will shift to the defendant, who will be presumed negligent unless he can offer some rebuttal evidence. Ordinarily, however, at the end of the plaintiff's case, the defendant will usually move for a directed verdict, in essence requesting the court to declare that the plaintiff failed to meet the burden of production.

If the plaintiff manages to hurdle the evidentiary obstacle of the burden of production, he must then meet the **burden of persuasion** by convincing the jury that it is more likely than not that the plaintiff's injuries were due to the defendant's negligence. In other words, he must prove his case by a preponderance of the evidence. In quantitative terms this means that the plaintiff must convince the jury that there is more than a 50 percent chance that the defendant caused his injuries.

The burden of persuasion generally rests on the plaintiff throughout the case but, in a few jurisdictions, the courts have shifted this burden to the defendant in cases involving the doctrine of *res ipsa loquitur.* In other words, in those jurisdictions once the plaintiff establishes the elements of *res ipsa loquitur,* the burden of persuasion shifts and the defendant must prove by a preponderance of the evidence that he was not negligent.

APPLICATION

Let us now examine the basic elements of a negligence claim in the context of the hypothetical confrontation involving Gertrude, Teddy, and Mr. Dooright. If Teddy and Mr. Dooright decided to sue the Baxters for their damages, they would have to prove by a preponderance of the evidence that the Baxters owed them a duty of care, that they breached that duty, that they sustained injuries, and that the Baxters' negligence was the proximate and actual cause of their injuries.

The first question that we would have to answer if we represented the Baxters is whether they owed any duty of care to the two people who trespassed on their property. We would also want to find out whether the duty of care owed to Mr. Dooright was different from that owed to Teddy, in light of the fact that Mr. Dooright's presence at the scene was directly linked to his commendable efforts to rescue a boy who was only a stranger to him.

Once we determined what, if any, standard of care the Baxters owed to Teddy and Mr. Dooright, we would have to ascertain whether they breached that duty in their failure to lock their gate on the occasion of Gertrude's attack. We would want to find out if there were any applicable statutes, the violation of which would make the Baxters negligent *per se*. We would also want to research case law in our jurisdiction to determine what precautions the courts thought were necessary for dog owners to take to protect others from being victimized by their pets.

We would also have to resolve whether the defendants' negligence was the actual and proximate cause of the plaintiff's injuries. While there is no doubt that Gertrude was the actual cause of Teddy's and Mr. Dooright's injuries, proximate cause could be disputed. The Baxters, for example, might argue that Mr. Dooright would not have been injured had he not blindly dived in to rescue Teddy and that it was, in fact, his own gross negligence in carrying out his rescue mission that caused his injuries.

Causation is not to be confused with the defenses of contributory and comparative negligence, either of which is likely to be raised by the Baxters. Note that proximate cause is one of the elements of negligence for which the plaintiff bears an affirmative burden of proof. Contributory or comparative negligence, on the other hand, must be raised by the defendant. The argument made by one who raises the defense of contributory negligence is that even though the defendant was negligent, the plaintiff's own negligence contributed to his injuries to the extent that he should be barred from recovering. If a defendant successfully raises the defense of comparative negligence, the plaintiff's recovery will be reduced in proportion to his own negligence. Defenses to negligence will be covered in Chapter 10.

Although it would be relatively straightforward to prove that Teddy and Mr. Dooright sustained injuries as a result of Gertrude's attack, we would need to go to considerable effort to compute the value of the appropriate damages. In essence, we would have to quantify the extent of emotional harm that Teddy sustained as well as the physical scarring he suffered. With both parties we would have to assign a numerical value to the pain and suffering they endured as a result of their traumatic experiences. In addition to assessing medical expenses we would need to project the potential lost earnings suffered by Mr. Dooright. Assigning a value to the loss of limbs, bodily disfigurement, or emotional pain and suffering may seem cold and calculating, but must be done so that some quantifiable amount of damages can be suggested to the jury.

SUMMARY

Any conduct that creates an unreasonable risk of harm for another is called negligence. The mental state of a negligent tortfeasor is irrelevant in that he or she need not intend nor be aware that the conduct will result in a particular consequence. Negligence consists of four elements: duty, breach of duty, causation, and damage.

The duty of care depends on the relationship between the plaintiff and the defendant. In some cases the tortfeasor may even owe a duty of care to one with whom he or she has had no direct contact.

PRACTICE POINTERS

As a practical matter the attorneys representing Teddy and Mr. Dooright, after having conducted their preliminary investigations, will contact the insurance adjustor representing the Baxters' insurance carrier and attempt to settle the case as soon as possible. In their ensuing conversations both sides will attempt to represent the facts known to them at that time in a light that best supports their position. The purpose of settlement, of course, is to avoid litigation, which is both expensive and burdensome to all involved. Most cases are, in fact, settled before trial but it is advantageous to both sides to resolve disputes before entering into the costly discovery process.

At some point in this preliminary negotiation process the attorneys for Teddy and Mr. Dooright will write a demand letter to the insurance carrier. In this demand letter they will set forth the elements of the tort they claim the defendant committed and they will also spell out the damages to which their client is entitled as a result of the defendant's actions. Figure 5–1 is an example of a demand letter that might be written in this case.

FIGURE 5.1 Demand Letter

Digger Odell
Attorney at Law
62 Happy Trail
Gotcha, AZ 85034

Ms. Agnes Pain, Esq.
Happy Days Insurance Company
298 Refusal Way
Why, AZ 85602

Dear Ms. Pain:

I represent Teddy Jones with respect to the incident that occured between Teddy Jones and your insured, Mr. & Mrs. Stephen Baxter. The attack occurred on June 6, 1990. Teddy was severely mauled by the Baxter's German sheperd, Gertrude. Gertrude attacked Teddy by seizing his right leg and inflicting serious physical injury. Teddy's injuries would have been even worse, and perhaps even fatal, had he not been rescued by a passerby. Teddy was only six years old and did nothing to provoke the attack.

The severity of the tissue damage caused by Gertrude's mauling necessitated surgical repair. Two surgical operations plus ongoing medical care resulted in total medical costs of over twenty-five thousand dollars ($25,000.00). Despite having received excellent medical care, Teddy must endure permanent and extensive scarring.

Continued on next page

PRACTICE POINTERS—Continued

The emotional scars, however, run much deeper. Teddy now suffers from a severe panic disorder which was propitiated by Gertrude's savageness. This disorder is triggered by the sight of any dog. Although he has received extensive psychiatric counselling to control this disorder, he continues to have an uncontrollable fear of dogs. This disorder is extemely debilitating to Teddy and has caused him extensive mental pain and anguish as well as much embarrassment. He continues to be fearful of walking the streets alone and absolutely refuses to ride his bicycle for fear of being chased by a dog. Teddy's psychiatrist feels that over time and with the use of drug therapy, Teddy will eventually be able to function relatively normally but that he will most likely retain an abnormal fear of dogs for life.

Teddy's counselling fees amount to twelve thousand one hundred dollars ($12,100.00) as of this date. His treating psychiatrist, Dr. Harmony, estimates that he will have to spend at least another two years in counselling, with an additional cost of fifteen thousand dollars ($15,000.00).

Although the extensive pain and suffering already experienced by Teddy, as well as the pain and suffering it can be anticipated he will suffer, cannot be justly quantified with only a monetary award, we demand the sum of one hundred thousand dollars ($100,000.00) in compensation to settle Teddy's claim. Failure to pay this amount will result in our immediately filing suit against your insured.

I expect prompt payment of our very reasonable settlement proposal. If the funds demanded are not paid within ten (10) days from the date of this letter, I will assume this settlement proposal is unacceptable to you and this offer will be deemed withdrawn. I am enclosing copies of all of Teddy's medical records and billings as well as narratives from Teddy's treating physicians.

Sincerely,

Digger Odell, Esq.

In determining whether the defendant breached the duty of care, the question asked is whether the defendant conducted himself or herself as a reasonable person would have under similar circumstances. An objective standard is used in assessing the defendant's conduct. Some physical characteristics of the defendant, however, are taken into consideration, as are the circumstances in which the defendant acted. Those with a higher degree of knowledge, skill, or experience than the ordinary person are held to a higher standard of care. A defendant who violates a statute may be considered negligent *per se*. If the plaintiff is unable to prove the defendant's negligence because he or she lacks access to information regarding the defendant's conduct, the plaintiff may be able to rely on the doctrine of *res ipsa loquitur*.

The plaintiff must also prove actual cause and proximate cause. The defendant must be the actual, factual cause of the plaintiff's injuries. If there are concurrent or multiple causes of the plaintiff's injuries, the courts will generally find that each of the defendants was the actual cause of the plaintiff's injuries, forcing the defendants to apportion the damages.

Proximate cause, on the other hand, revolves around the issue of foreseeability. The question is whether the consequence of the conduct are so remote that the defendant should not be held responsible for his or her actions. If the plaintiff's injuries are really caused by some intervening factor other than the defendant's negligence, the defendant will be excused from liability. The question that often arises under the issue of proximate cause is whether the plaintiff was a foreseeable plaintiff. Under the "eggshell skull" rule a defendant is required to "take his plaintiff as he finds him."

The final issue is that of damages. The three categories of damages are compensatory damages, nominal damages, and punitive damages. Compensatory damages can be divided into two subcategories of general and special damages. General damages are those damages that typically result from the kind of conduct the defendant engaged in and include compensation for pain and suffering. Special damages are more specifically tied to the plaintiff and include compensation for medical expenses. Nominal damages are awarded if the jury is convinced of the defendant's liability but not of the occurrence of any actual loss. Punitive damages are designed to punish the defendant.

Questions of law are decided by the judge; factual questions are resolved by the jury. In certain circumstances the judge has the right to instruct the jury as to the finding of fact it must make. If the plaintiff fails to bear the burden of production, he or she faces a directed verdict imposed by the judge. The plaintiff also bears the burden of persuasion.

TORT TEASERS

What do you think would be the key issue in each of the following cases:

1. Defendant negligently runs into Plaintiff with his taxicab. Plaintiff, an alcoholic, dies from delirium tremens, a condition associated with alcoholism but whose development was hastened by the accident. *McCahill v. New York Transportation Co.*, 94 N.E. 616 (N.Y. 1911).

2. Plaintiff is a passenger in a car driven by Defendant. Defendant runs into a tree, resulting in injuries to Plaintiff. Defendant renders no aid to Plaintiff and Plaintiff claims this lack of assistance aggravated her injuries. *Tubbs v. Argus*, 225 N.E. 2d 841 (Ind. 1967).

3. Defendant ophthalmologists routinely administer eye exams to Plaintiff over a period of years but never test her for glaucoma. When Plaintiff is 32 years old she contracts glaucoma. Because the chances of any one under the age of 40 contracting glaucoma is 1:25,000, the test is not routinely given to those under the age of 40. *Helling v. Carey*, 519 P. 2d 981 (Wash. 1974).

4. Plaintiff experiences numbness, weakness, and pain in her left arm after having surgery that does not involve her left arm. Her expert testifies that this condition does not usually occur in the absence of negligence. Defendant doctors vehemently maintain that nothing unusual occurred during surgery. *Marrero v. Goldsmith*, 486 So.2d 538 (Fla. 1986).

KEY TERMS

■ **Actual cause**
Cause in fact of Plaintiff's injuries.

■ **Breach of duty**
Failure to conform to the required standard of care.

■ **Burden of persuasion**
Burden of proving the elements of a case by preponderance of the evidence.

■ **Burden of production**
Burden of producing sufficient evidence to avoid a directed verdict.

■ **Compensatory damages**
Damages designed to compensate the plaintiff; consist of both general and special damages.

■ **General damages**
Compensatory damages that can generally be anticipated to result from the type of conduct the defendant engaged in.

■ **Negligence *per se***
Presumed negligence that arises from the unexcused violation of a statute.

■ **Nominal damages**
Damages awarded when liability is shown but no actual damages are proved.

■ **Objective standard**
Comparison of a defendant's conduct to that of a reasonable person.

■ **Proximate cause**
Legal cause of plaintiff's injuries; emphasis is on the concept of foreseeability.

■ **Punitive damages**
Damages designed to punish the defendant (also referred to as exemplary damages).

■ ***Res ipsa loquitur***
Doctrine plaintiff can turn to in proving negligence when it is difficult to obtain information about the defendant's conduct.

■ **Special damages**
Compensatory damages specifically linked to the plaintiff.

■ **Subjective standard**
Use of the defendant's own subjective perceptions to determine whether the defendant behaved reasonably.

6 NEGLIGENCE: DUTY

CHAPTER OBJECTIVES

In this chapter you will learn to:

- Describe the standard of care expected of a possessor of land toward those who enter her land.
- Describe the standard of care that arises out of certain special relationships (e.g., employer-employee) and special situations (e.g., rendering emergency care).
- Describe the standard of care expected of landlords, tenants, and sellers of land.
- Recognize the concepts of vicarious liability and the family purpose doctrine.

One of the first questions that the attorneys representing Teddy and Mr. Dooright in our hypothetical case will have to consider is the question of duty. Did the Baxters owe a duty of care to one who trespassed on their land? Did they owe a different duty of care to a child than to an adult? Did they owe a higher duty of care to a rescuer than they did to an ordinary trespasser?

OVERVIEW OF DUTY

In any negligence claim, the concept of duty raises the question of whether the defendant is under any obligation to act for the benefit of the plaintiff. In general terms, the defendant's duty is to act reasonably. In other words, the defendant must exercise the degree of care that any reasonable person would exercise under similar circumstances. You will notice when you read cases that most courts spend relatively little time addressing the question of duty but, instead, jump directly into an analysis of breach of duty. Nevertheless, for educational purposes we need to explore the concept of duty in some depth.

The relationship between individuals determines the duty owed. An owner of land, for example, owes a different duty of care to a trespasser than to someone invited on the premises. A landlord owes a different standard of care to someone injured on the premises than does a tenant.

Generally, a legal obligation exists only when a direct relationship between the defendant and the plaintiff exists. A duty to the plaintiff may also arise, however, if a relationship exists between the defendant and a third party whose negligence causes injury to the plaintiff. For example, a defendant who loans her automobile to someone who is intoxicated and who injures others could, under certain conditions, be found liable for the injuries caused by the intoxicated individual.

In this chapter we will examine the duty of care owed by possessors of land and the duty of care arising out of special relationships, such as landlord-tenant, seller-buyer and lessor-lessee. We will also touch lightly on the issue of vicarious liability (although that subject will be discussed in greater detail in Chapter 18) and will consider how that doctrine affects employers and car owners.

POSSESSORS OF LAND

Throughout this chapter we will refer to "possessors" and not owners of land. The possessor, not the landowner, was the focus of protection under the common law. The purpose of limiting the liability of possessors was to encourage full utilization of the land, unhampered by burdensome legal obligations to others. For that reason it was the tenant, not the landlord, who was generally designed to benefit from the common law rules.

Under the common law the duty of care owed by a possessor was determined by the class into which the plaintiff fell (see Fig. 6.1). The three classes of plaintiffs were trespassers, licensees, and invitees. A trespasser was one who had no right to be on the defendant's land, a licensee was one who came on the land as a social guest and hence with the owner's consent, and an invitee was one who came on the land with a business purpose. The owner owed the highest duty of care to the invitee and the lowest duty of care to the trespasser. Note that while most courts continue to apply these classifications, the differences between the classes have blurred over time. Some courts have abandoned these distinctions altogether.

TRESPASSERS

Early common law established the principle that possessors of land could not deliberately set traps or spring guns with the intent of injuring a trespasser.

FIGURE 6.1 Duties of Possessor of Land

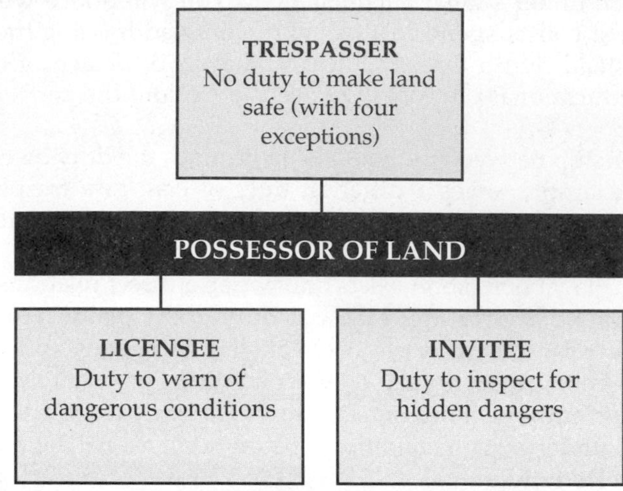

From this principle evolved the rule that possessors of land must refrain from willful and wanton negligence in regard to trespassers.

In general, a possessor owes no duty of care to a trespasser to make the land safe or to protect the trespasser in any way. If the possessor is pursuing dangerous activities on the property, he or she need not warn the trespasser of such dangers nor avoid carrying on such activities (Restatement (Second) of Torts Sec. 333). There are four exceptions, however, to this general rule (see Table 6–1). Some duty of care is owed where the plaintiffs are (1) trespassing children, (2) individuals known to be trespassers, (3) rescuing someone in danger as a result of the defendant possessor's negligence, or (4) trespassing on a very limited portion of the possessor's land. We will discuss each of these exceptions in more depth in the following sections.

ATTRACTIVE NUISANCE

The notion that children who are trespassers should be entitled to greater protection than adults evolved from the **attractive nuisance** doctrine. Under this doctrine a possessor is liable if he or she maintains a dangerous condition on the land that induces children to enter the premises because it is an enticing item on which to play. A construction site might be considered an attractive nuisance. It is usually replete with lumber, ladders, and other items that make wonderful props for fertile imaginations.

Under the Restatement, a possessor can be found liable to a trespassing child if the following conditions are met (Restatement (Second) of Torts Sec. 339):

- The possessor has reason to know that the condition is on a place on the land where children are likely to trespass.
- The possessor must have reason to know of the condition and to know that it poses an unreasonable risk of serious injury or death to trespassing children.
- Because of their youth, the children must not have discovered the condition or realized the danger posed by coming into the area made dangerous by the condition.

TABLE 6.1 Exceptions to No Duty Rule for Trespassers

ATTRACTIVE NUISANCE	RESCUERS	KNOWN TRESPASSER	LIMITED TRESPASS
•Knows children are likely to trespass. •Knows condition poses unreasonable risk of injury to children. •Child is unaware of danger posed by condition. •Benefit in maintaining condition is slight compared to risk posed. •Possessor fails to use reason-able care to protect children.	•Possessor negligently causes harm to person or property. •Harm must be imminent, real, and require immediate action.	•Possessor is aware of trespasser. •Possessor is aware of dangerous condition.	•Trespasser uses only limited portion of land.

- The benefit to the possessor in maintaining the condition in its dangerous form must be slight in comparison to the risk posed to the children.
- The possessor must fail to use reasonable care to eliminate the danger or to protect the children.

Suppose a two-year-old child, left unattended for approximately ten minutes, wanders into a neighbor's backyard, falls in the pool, and drowns. Assume the backyard is inadequately fenced and that the owner is aware that on previous occasions children have climbed over the fence into the backyard. Does the swimming pool meet the criteria of an attractive nuisance as set forth in the Restatement? Yes. The owner knows that children are likely to trespass since he is aware they had trespassed in the past. A swimming pool certainly poses an unreasonable risk of serious injury or death to very young children since they are not usually fully cognizant of the danger posed. The owner has failed to use reasonable care by failing to provide adequate fencing. Any benefit the owner gains from not expending the money to install safe fencing is slight when weighed against the risk of injury posed to trespassing children.

The age, experience, and intelligence of the child may determine whether the attractive nuisance doctrine applies. The question is whether the child is able to appreciate the risk of the condition involved. Even a relatively young child may be expected to understand the risk of drowning or the risk of falling from a great height. If the defendant can show that the injured child, because of her experience or intelligence, was aware of and appreciated the danger, even if other children of her age might not have been so appreciative, the child will be barred from recovery.

If the condition causing the injury is a "natural" rather than an "artificial" condition, the courts are less likely to allow the child to recover. The reasoning seems to be that a natural condition such as a lake is prohibitively expensive to protect children from and is one with which children are more likely to be familiar with the risk involved. The distinction, however, between a natural and an artificial condition is a stilted one and should not be relied on as the sole basis for denying liability.

The bottom line for possessors is that they must take reasonable measures to prevent harm to children. This does not mean that they need to make their premises "childproof." Nor does it mean they are required to inspect for dangerous conditions of which they would otherwise have been unaware. Posting a warning may in many instances be sufficient.

RESCUE DOCTRINE

Under the rescue doctrine anyone who negligently causes harm to a person or property may be liable to one who is injured in an effort to rescue the imperiled person or property. The rationale is that the rescuer would not have been injured were it not for the negligence of the tortfeasor. This doctrine prevents a plaintiff from being found contributorily negligent for voluntarily placing herself in a dangerous situation in order to save another. Often dubbed the "danger invites rescue" doctrine, it stems from an opinion written by Judge Cardozo: "Danger invites rescue. . . . The wrong that imperils life is a wrong to the imperiled victim; it is wrong also to his rescuer" *(Wagner v. International Ry. Co.,* 133 N.E. 437(N.Y. 1921).

The rescue doctrine is warranted only where the threatened danger is both imminent and real and requires immediate action if the victim is to be saved. If the defendant's conduct is neither negligent nor intentionally tortious, the doctrine is inapplicable.

KNOWN TRESPASSERS

Another exception to the general rule regarding trespassers involves those trespassers of whom the possessor is aware. Once a possessor knows that a particular person is trespassing on her property, she owes a duty of reasonable care to that person. This duty clearly applies when the danger to the trespasser arises out of something the possessor has done, such as excavate her land. The nature of the duty is less clear, however, when the condition is a natural one. (According to the Restatement (Second) of Torts Sec. 337, comment b, the duty to exercise reasonable care should still apply when the condition is natural.)

The justification given for the imposition of this duty is that the possessor's continuing tolerance of the trespass constitutes an implied permission to use the land. Thus, the trespasser is elevated to the status of a licensee. As a practical matter, however, defendants often do not attempt to thwart trespassing because to do so would be expensive and probably unproductive. Imagine the futility of a railroad company spending time and money trying to deter trespassers from using its tracks. Nevertheless, possessors have been shifted from a position of complete exemption from liability to a more moderate position of limited liability when dealing with known trespassers.

LIMITED TRESPASS
Possessors of land also owe a limited duty of care to frequent trespassers who use only a very limited area of their land. Suppose a farmer knows of a well-worn path across the edge of his property created by children taking a shortcut to school. In such a case he would be expected to anticipate the traversing by these children and would be required to use reasonable care in his activities for their protection.

LICENSEES

A **licensee** is one step up from a trespasser. She has the possessor's consent to be on the property but does not have a business purpose for being there. Most licensees are social guests. The duty a possessor owes to a licensee is to warn her of any dangerous conditions if the possessor is aware of that condition and should reasonably anticipate that the licensee may not discover it. Suppose your dinner guest, for example, trips on a toy left unattended by one of your children. If you failed to warn your guest of the presence of the toy and the lighting conditions were such that he could not reasonably be expected to see it, you could be held liable for his injuries.

The possessor is, however, under no duty to inspect for unknown dangers when dealing with a licensee. As with trespassers, the courts are more likely to find a higher duty of care if the possessor is carrying out activities on the land than if the danger arises out of some natural condition on the land.

Social guests in an automobile are due the same standard of care as are licensees on land. Unless there is a statute to the contrary, most courts have held that the guest is owed no duty of inspection. Therefore, if the owner of a vehicle fails to inspect the car's brakes, which ultimately fail and cause injuries to the guest, the owner will not be liable for his failure to inspect.

INVITEES

Invitees are those persons invited by the possessor onto her land to conduct business. Under the majority position invitees also include those members of the public who come onto the property for the purpose for which the property is being used and do so with the intent of doing business. A visitor in a national park and someone using a public golf course are both considered invitees. Someone entering a bank to get change or entering a public amusement park on a free pass or using a telephone provided for the public is also an invitee.

Even if the plaintiff is not engaged in business at the time of his injury, he is considered an invitee so long as he has a general business relationship with the possessor. In *Campbell v. Weathers,* 111 P.2d 72 (Kan. 1941) the plaintiff had been a longstanding customer of the defendant, who operated a lunch counter and cigar stand in an office building. After standing next to the cigar stand for several minutes, the plaintiff used the toilet in the back of the building. On the way he fell into an open trap door in the dark hallway. The defendant argued that the plaintiff was not an invitee since he had made no purchases on the day of his injury and because the toilet was intended for the defendant's employees and not the general public. The court classified the plaintiff as an invitee and pointed out that anyone who goes into a store with the intent of doing business at the present or in the future is an invitee. The court noted that many people shop for hours without making any purchases. Could they be denied invitee status in light of the fact that owners implicitly invite them for their potential business purpose? The *Campbell* court thought not.

A social guest does not rise to the status of an invitee even by performing an incidental service for her host, such as repairing a broken faucet. The host must gain some type of economic benefit before the guest can be considered an invitee. By the same token, a salesperson making an unsolicited call to a private home is not an invitee unless she is invited in (Restatement (Second) of Torts Sec. 332, comment b). On the other hand, a salesperson who calls on a business where she reasonably believes that door-to-door salespeople are typically received is considered an invitee.

LOSING INVITEE STATUS

An invitee may become a licensee or trespasser if she goes to parts of the premises that extend beyond her invitation. So long as the visitor reasonably believes that the premises are open to the public, however, she will be treated as an invitee even if, unknown to her, the possessor intends that the area is to be off limits to the general public. On the other hand, even if a visitor receives explicit authorization from the possessor to go onto a private portion of the premises, she will lose her invitee status if she enters purely for her own benefit. In one such case a customer who came to a store with the intent of shopping was given permission, in her search for a particular saleswoman, to enter an alteration room reserved for employees. When she entered the room she fell down a stairway. The court held that she was a licensee because she entered the room for her own benefit and without invitation by the owner (although she had its permission to enter). As a licensee she was required to take the premises as she found them (*Lerman Brothers v. Lewis,* 126 S.W.2d 461 (1939)).

Compare this case with *Campbell v. Weathers,* where the plaintiff retained his invitee status because he entered an area that reasonably appeared to him to be open to the public. Reasonable belief of the plaintiff appears to be the operative fact that the courts focus on in these cases.

An invitee also loses her status if she stays on the premises for a longer period of time than is reasonably necessary to conduct her business. Once her purpose becomes social rather than business she becomes a licensee.

NATURE OF DUTY TO INVITEE

A possessor owes a higher duty of care to an invitee than he does to either a licensee or trespasser. Most importantly, he has a duty to inspect his premises for hidden dangers when dealing with invitees. Although he has no duty to ferret out all hidden dangers, he must use reasonable care in making his inspection (Restatement (Second) of Torts Sec. 343). He may even be liable for a dangerous condition resulting from faulty construction or design even if the condition existed before he came into possession of the property.

The definition of "reasonable care" varies depending on the use of the premises. The possessor of a shopping mall, who may readily anticipate the passage of thousands of customers, is held to a higher duty of inspection than the owner of a private home who invites an insurance salesperson in for the purpose of discussing coverage. In some cases the use of a warning of a dangerous condition will meet the requirements of "reasonable care" but in other situations affirmative action will be required. If a store owner knows, for example, that customers will be distracted by goods on display and probably will not notice a sign warning them of danger, then a warning will not be sufficient (Restatement (Second) of Torts Sec. 343A, illustration 2).

Even if an invitee is aware of and appreciates the danger involved, the possessor may be obligated to take reasonable steps to reduce the danger. In *Wilk v. Georges,* 514 P.2d 877 (Ore. 1973), the plaintiff and her husband were shopping for Christmas trees in a nursery operated by the defendant. On the day of the plaintiff's visit it had been raining and the walkways, put together using planks, were slippery and dangerous. The defendant had posted a sign that read:

> Please watch where you are going. This is a nursery where plants grow. There is four seasons: summer and winter, cold and hot, rain, icey spots. Flower petals always falling on the floor, leaves always on the floor.
>
> We are dealing with nature and we are hoping for the best. We are not responsible for anyone get hurt on the premises.
>
> Thank you.

The court found that the defendant should have anticipated an unreasonable risk of harm to the plaintiff despite the posted signs. The defendant, according to the court, had an obligation to take reasonable steps to prevent the harm that occurred to the plaintiff.

In some cases reasonable care may require the possessor to exercise control over third persons. As a tavern owner, for example, he may be obligated to prevent his patrons from becoming so intoxicated they cause injury to others. This will be discussed more in the section dealing with special relationships later in this chapter.

COMMON LAW DISTINCTIONS TODAY

It is interesting to note that several states have rejected the rigid distinction between invitee, licensee, and trespasser and have instead adopted a "reasonable person" standard of liability. Some states have abolished the invitee/licensee distinction but have continued to apply the old rules of liability regarding trespassers. The majority, however, continue to adhere to the common law classifications.

OUTSIDE THE POSSESSOR'S PROPERTY

The reasons underlying the limitations on landowner liability are less persuasive when the dangerous condition affects those outside the possessor's property. Possessors are generally found liable for conditions that pose an unreasonable risk of harm to persons outside the premises (Restatement (Second) of Torts Sec. 364–365). This is particularly true where the hazardous condition is artificially created by the possessor. Artificial conditions include man-made structures, additions to the land, such as trees, and alterations to the land, such as excavations. If a possessor of land, for example, alters the condition of the premises so that the normal course of surface water is altered and it flows out onto a highway, she may be held liable for injuries caused by her negligence. Courts are less likely to impose liability, however, if the offending object is something like a telephone pole or mailbox, which are necessities and are also above-ground objects.

On the other hand, if the hazardous condition is a natural one, the possessor is under no duty to remove it or protect others from it even if it poses an unreasonable danger of harm to people outside the property (Restatement (Second) of Torts Sec. 363(1)). This general rule becomes more complicated when dealing with trees. In urban and suburban areas the courts have obligated possessors to prevent trees from exposing people outside the premises to an unreasonable risk of harm. They have also required the removal of rotten trees and have imposed an affirmative duty to inspect to discover potential defects in trees. In rural areas no duty to remove rotten trees or to inspect for defects has been imposed. Some modern courts have rejected the rural/urban distinction in the case of fallen trees and have held possessors to a reasonable care standard.

SPECIAL RELATIONSHIPS

OVERVIEW

Under the common law a defendant has no legal obligation to aid a plaintiff in distress unless a special relationship exists between the plaintiff and the defendant. This rule applies even though the defendant could assist the plaintiff without causing any harm to himself. The extent to which this doctrine can be taken is illustrated dramatically in *Yania v. Bigan,* 155 A.2d 343 (Pa. 1959). In this case the defendant enticed his friend to jump into a trench containing eight to ten feet of water and then refused to rescue his friend when it became obvious he was drowning. The court found that the defendant was not liable for his friend's death even though he could have easily saved him. For obvious reasons this doctrine has been subject to scathing criticism by legal commentators and seems to be unique to Anglo/American law.

When a special relationship exists between the plaintiff and defendant liability will be found for failure to act (see Table 6–2). Examples of such special relationships are those between husband and wife, parent and child, jailor and prisoner, teacher and pupil, innkeeper and guest, and common carrier and passenger. Common carriers such as airline, railroad, and bus companies have a duty to protect their passengers. A bus company may be liable, for example, if a brawl breaks out on a bus, resulting in injury to several passengers, and the bus driver does nothing to intervene. An employer also has a duty to protect employees from those dangers from which they are not able to protect themselves. Such duty is limited to situations within the scope and course of the employees' responsibilities.

In some situations a special relationship may exist even between a university and a student. A court is likely to impose a duty of care on a university, for

TABLE 6.2

SPECIAL RELATIONSHIPS CREATING DUTY OF CARE	
Parent	Child
Husband	Wife
Teacher	Pupil
Jailor	Prisoner
Common Carrier	Passenger
Employer	Employee
University	Student
Possessor of Land	Licensee/Invitee
Innkeeper	Guest
Rescuer	Victim

DEFENDANT'S RELATIONSHIP WITH THIRD PARTY CREATING DUTY OF CARE TO PLAINTIFF	
Attorney	Client
Doctor	Patient
Guardian	Mentally Ill Person
Tavern Owner	Intoxicated Patron
Car Owner	Intoxicated Driver

example, when the harm involved is that of a physical nature, such as a criminal attack. A court is most unlikely, however, to hold a university responsible for the private affairs of its students, particularly when the harm that occurs is of a moral nature.

DEFENDANT'S RELATIONSHIP WITH THIRD PARTIES

In some cases the duty of care owed by the defendant to the plaintiff arises out of a special relationship the defendant has with a third party. For instance, the guardian of a mentally ill patient who is potentially dangerous may be held liable for injuries inflicted by his dangerous charge.

The obligation to control a third party becomes particularly problematic when the relationship between the defendant and the third party is that of attorney–client or doctor–patient. In the controversial case of *Tarasoff v. Regents of University of California*, 529 P.2d 553 (Cal. 1974), a patient told his psychotherapist that he intended to kill the plaintiff (whom he did, in fact, kill). The court held that the defendant psychotherapist had a duty to warn the plaintiff of the patient's intentions if a reasonable person in those circumstances would have done so. Admittedly, the doctor–patient privilege was inapplicable in this case since disclosure was necessary to prevent threatened danger. Nevertheless, the *Tarasoff* holding blurs the line between professionals' obligation to protect others and their need to promote open communication between themselves and their clients.

An area in which the defendant's relationship with a negligent third party is becoming increasingly significant involves those situations in which the third party is intoxicated. A defendant who loans her vehicle to an intoxicated person, for example, may be liable for injuries caused by that person. Similarly, a tavern owner who sells liquor to an obviously intoxicated patron may be liable for injuries inflicted as a result of the patron's negligence. An increasing number of states are extending such liability to social hosts, especially those hosts who violate statutes prohibiting the sale of liquor to minors. As the public becomes more conscious of the potential dangers associated with the immoderate consumption of alcohol (and other drugs), the courts appear to be more inclined to elevate the standard of care to which providers of alcohol are held.

EMERGENCY ASSISTANCE

Duty also arises out of the special relationship that is created when a defendant begins to render assistance to a person in need. Once assistance is begun it must be administered using reasonable care. Every reasonable means possible must be utilized to keep the plaintiff safe. Part of the rationale underlying this rule is that once a party has begun helping another, others will be less likely to provide aid themselves. Also, if the defendant discontinues aid or gives it in an unreasonable manner, the plaintiff is essentially in a worse position than had the defendant done nothing at all.

One hospital, for example, was found liable for the injuries sustained by a child who was turned away and whose condition was worsened as a result (*Wilmington General Hospital v. Manlove,* 174 A.2d 135 (Del. 1961). The court reasoned that by maintaining an emergency ward the hospital had in effect induced the plaintiff to forego other forms of medical assistance. Thus, the hospital was liable for the injuries it had created by the delay it had indirectly caused.

In another example the defendant was found liable even though it had no legal duty to protect the plaintiff. In this case the defendant railroad company established a watchman at a street crossing to warn drivers of approaching trains. When the watchman failed to give a warning and a driver, who was aware of the practice and relied on it in crossing the track, was injured, the defendant was found liable (*Erie R. R. Co. v. Stuart,* 40 F.2d 855 (6th Cir. 1930)). Once the defendant undertook to protect drivers, the court reasoned, it induced reliance and was therefore liable when it discontinued its practice.

Some modern courts have allowed a plaintiff who relied on a defendant's promise to recover even if the defendant made no overt act of assisting the plaintiff. In one case the sheriff's department was found liable for failing to live up to its promise to warn the plaintiff's wife when a dangerous prisoner, whom she had assisted in having arrested, was released. Shortly after his release he killed her. By inducing the plaintiff's wife to rely on its promise to warn her, the defendant was held liable even though it had done nothing overtly to assist her (*Morgan v. County of Yuba,* 41 Cal. Rptr. 508 (1964)).

LANDLORD/TENANT LIABILITY

Under the common law the reason for limiting a possessor's liability was to promote the possessor's right to use the land to its fullest potential with minimal interference from others. Therefore, protection was given to the actual possessor of the land and not the abstract legal owner. As a result of this principle a tenant who is in possession of the property is entitled to the protection of the common law rules. In addition, members of the tenant's household, as well as those in his employ or working the land for him as independent contractors, are also entitled to the protection of the common law rules. A landlord, on the other hand, was relieved of liability under the traditional common law once she surrendered possession of her property to the tenant.

TENANT'S DUTIES

A tenant is held to the same duty of inspection in reference to invitees as is a landowner. Consequently, a tenant is liable for the injuries to an invitee resulting from a defect that could have been discovered using reasonable care even if the tenant did not in fact discover it. This liability does not extend, however, to common areas such as elevators, stairways, and corridors if the building is an office building or a dwelling with multiple tenants.

LANDLORD'S DUTIES

The general rule of nonliability of landlords has been significantly altered today due to modern social policy concerns. A landlord is liable, for example, to the tenant and to the tenant's invitees and licensees for those dangers that the landlord knows or should know about and that the tenant has no reason to know about (Restatement (Second) of Torts Sec. 358). Most courts do not interpret this as requiring the landlord to inspect the premises. The thrust of this rule is to protect the tenant from hidden dangers of which the landlord is aware or should reasonably anticipate. The landlord has a higher duty if he has reason to believe that the tenant is planning on holding the premises open to the public. In such cases the landlord has an affirmative duty to inspect the premises to find and repair any damages.

What happens if the landlord contracts with the tenant to keep the premises in good repair? Certainly the tenant can sue for breach of contract if the landlord fails to make timely repairs. The question is, however, whether the tenant can sue in tort as well. The majority of courts allow a tort claim to anyone injured as a result of the landlord's breach of his covenant to repair. In such a case the plaintiff must show that the landlord failed to use reasonable care in performing his contractual duties. The landlord, of course, must be given a reasonable time to correct a condition once he has been notified of it.

Even if a landlord has no contractual duty to perform repairs, once he begins performance he must do so reasonably. If he initiates repairs and then fails to complete them, he in effect makes the situation worse because tenants are implicitly led to believe that the dangerous condition no longer exists. In such a case anyone on the premises with the tenant's consent who is injured by the landlord's negligence will be allowed to recover against the landlord. However, if the tenant is aware that the repairs were incomplete or were done in a negligent manner, the tenant and not the landlord will be held liable. If the landlord hires an independent contractor to carry out the repairs he will usually be held liable for the contractor's negligence. The reasoning is that a landlord cannot delegate his responsibility to a third party.

Does a landlord have a duty to take security precautions to make the premises as safe as possible for tenants? Such a duty was imposed in the landmark

TABLE 6.3

TENANT'S DUTIES	LANDLORD'S DUTIES
•Same duties as possessor of land. •Duty does not extend to common areas.	•Liable for dangers he knows or should know about and tenant has no reason to know about. •Duty to inspect for dangers where landlord knows property is to be held open to public. •Must use reasonable care if he contracts with tenant to keep premises in good repair. •If landlord begins to make repairs he must perform reasonably. •In some cases has duty to take security precautions to protect enants from criminal activity.

decision *Kline v. 1500 Massachusetts Avenue Apartment Corp.* 439 F2d 477 (D.D.C. 1970). Note in reading this case the analogy the court draws between the duty of innkeepers to protect their guests from attacks and the duty owed by landlords to protect their tenants.

Sarah B. KLINE, Appellant, v.
1500 MASSACHUSETTS AVENUE APARTMENT CORPORATION et al. No. 23401.
United States Court of Appeals, District of Columbia Circuit.
Argued April 10, 1970. Decided Aug. 6, 1970.
Petition for Rehearing Denied Sept. 8, 1970.

WILKEY, Circuit Judge:

The appellee apartment corporation states that there is "only one issue presented for review * * * whether a duty should be placed on a landlord to take steps to protect tenants from foreseeable criminal acts committed by third parties". The District Court as a matter of law held that there is no such duty. We find that there is, and that in the circumstances here the applicable standard of care was breached. We therefore reverse and remand to the District Court for the determination of damages for the appellant.

I

The appellant, Sarah B. Kline, sustained serious injuries when she was criminally assaulted and robbed at approximately 10:15 in the evening by an intruder in the common hallway of an apartment house at 1500 Massachusetts Avenue. This facility, into which the appellant Kline moved in October 1959, is a large apartment building with approximately 585 individual apartment units. It has a main entrance on Massachusetts Avenue, with side entrances on both 15th and 16th Streets. At the time the appellant first signed a lease a doorman was on duty at the main entrance twenty-four hours a day, and at least one employee at all times manned a desk in the lobby from which all persons using the elevators could be observed. The 15th Street door adjoined the entrance to a parking garage used by both the tenants and the public. Two garage attendants were stationed at this dual entranceway; the duties of each being arranged so that one of them always was in position to observe those entering either the apartment building or the garage. The 16th Street entrance was unattended during the day but was locked after 9:00 P.M.

By mid-1966, however, the main entrance had no doorman, the desk in the lobby was left unattended much of the time, the 15th Street entrance was generally unguarded due to a decrease in garage personnel, and the 16th Street entrance was often left unlocked all night. The entrances were allowed to be thus unguarded in the face of an increasing number of assaults, larcenies, and robberies being perpetrated against the tenants in and from the common hallways of the apartment building. These facts were undisputed and were supported by a detailed chronological listing of offenses admitted into evidence. The landlord had notice of these crimes and had in fact been urged by appellant Kline herself prior to the events leading to the instant appeal to take steps to secure the building.[3]

Shortly after 10:00 P.M. on November 17, 1966, Miss Kline was assaulted and robbed just outside her apartment on the first floor above the street level of this 585 unit apartment building. This occurred only two months after Leona Sullivan, another female tenant, had been similarly attacked in the same commonway.

II

At the outset we note that of the crimes of violence, robbery, and assault which had been occurring with mounting frequency on the premises at 1500 Massachusetts Avenue, the assaults on Miss Kline and Miss Sullivan took place in the hallways of the building, which were under the exclusive control of the appellee landlord. Even in those crimes of robbery or assault committed in individual apartments, the intruders of necessity had to gain entrance through the common entry and passageways.[4] These premises fronted on three heavily traveled streets, and had multiple entrances. The risk to be guarded against therefore was the risk of unauthorized entrance into the apartment house by intruders bent upon some crime of violence or theft.

3. Appellant Kline testified that one could hardly fail to notice the police cars about the building after each reported crime. She further testified that in 1966, before her assault, she herself had discussed the crime situation with Miss Bloom, the landlord's agent at the premises, and had asked her 'why they didn't do something about securing the building'. Moreover, the record contains twenty police reports of crimes occurring in the building in the year 1966, showing that in several instances these crimes were an almost daily occurrence. Such reports in themselves constitute constructive notice to the landlord.

4. The plaintiff testified that she had returned to her apartment after leaving work at 10:00 P.M. We are in agreement with the trial court that her assailant was an intruder. . . .

That such intruders did enter apartments from the hallways is substantiated by the Police reports which appear in the Record. In a number of instances doors are described as having been forced; in another instance, a tenant surprised a man standing in his front hallway; and there are still more instances of female tenants being awakened in the early morning hours to find an intruder entering their front doors. We also take notice of the fact that this apartment building is of the high rise type, with no easily accessible means of entry on the floors above the street level except by the hallways.

While the apartment lessees themselves could take some steps to guard against this risk by installing extra heavy locks and other security devices on the doors and windows of their respective apartments, yet this risk in the greater part could only be guarded against by the landlord. No individual tenant had it within his power to take measures to guard the garage entranceways, to provide scrutiny at the main entrance of the building, to patrol the common hallways and elevators, to set up any kind of a security alarm system in the building, to provide additional locking devices on the main doors, to provide a system of announcement for authorized visitors only, to close the garage doors at appropriate hours, and to see that the entrance was manned at all times.

The risk of criminal assault and robbery on a tenant in the common hallways of the building was thus entirely predictable; that same risk had been occurring with increasing frequency over a period of several months immediately prior to the incident giving rise to this case; it was a risk whose prevention or minimization was almost entirely within the power of the landlord; and the risk materialized in the assault and robbery of appellant on November 17, 1966.

III

In this jurisdiction, certain duties have been assigned to the landlord because of his *control* of common hallways, lobbies, stairwells, etc., used by all tenants in multiple dwelling units. This Court in Levine v. Katz, 132 U.S.App.D.C. 173, 174, 407 F.2d 303, 304 (1968), pointed out that:

> It has long been well settled in this jurisdiction that, where a landlord leases separate portions of property and reserves under his own control the halls, stairs, or other parts of the property for use in common by all tenants, he has a duty to all those on the premises of legal right to use ordinary care and diligence to maintain the retained parts in a reasonably safe condition.

While Levine v. Katz dealt with a physical defect in the building leading to plaintiff's injury, the rationale as applied to predictable criminal acts by third parties is the same. The duty is the landlord's because by his control of the areas of common use and common danger he is the only party who has the *power* to make the necessary repairs or to provide the necessary protection.

As a general rule, a private person does not have a duty to protect another from a criminal attack by a third person. We recognize that this rule has sometimes in the past been applied in landlord-tenant law, even by this court. Among the reasons for the application of this rule to landlords are: judicial reluctance to tamper with the traditional common law concept of the landlord-tenant relationship; the notion that the act of a third person in committing an intentional tort or crime is a superseding cause of the harm to another resulting therefrom; the oftentimes difficult problem of determining foreseeability of criminal acts; the vagueness of the standard which the landlord must meet; the economic consequences of the imposition of the duty; and conflict with the public policy allocating the duty of protecting citizens from criminal acts to the government rather than the private sector.

But the rationale of this very broad general rule falters when it is applied to the conditions of modern day urban apartment living, particularly in the circumstances of this case. The rationale of the general rule exonerating a third party from any duty to protect another from a criminal attack has no applicability to the landlord-tenant relationship in multiple dwelling houses. The landlord is no insurer of his tenants' safety, but he certainly is no bystander. And where, as here, the landlord has notice of repeated criminal assaults and robberies, has notice that these crimes occurred in the portion of the premises exclusively within his control, has every reason to expect like crimes to happen again, and has the exclusive power to take preventive action, it does not seem unfair to place upon the landlord a duty to take those steps which are within his power to minimize the predictable risk to his tenants.

This court has recently had occasion to review landlord-tenant law as applied to multiple family urban dwellings. In Javins v. First National Realty Corporation, the traditional analysis of a lease as being a conveyance of an interest in land—with all the medieval connotations this often brings—was reappraised, and found lacking in several respects. This court noted that the value of the lease to the modern apartment dweller is that it gives him "a well known package of goods and services—a package which includes not merely walls and ceilings, but also adequate heat, light and ventilation, serviceable plumbing facilities, *secure windows and doors,* proper sanitation, and proper maintenance." It does not give him the land itself, and to the tenant as a practical matter this is supremely unimportant. Speaking for the court, Judge Wright then went on to state, "In our judgment the trend toward treating leases as contracts is wise and well considered. Our holding in this case reflects a belief that leases of urban dwelling units should be interpreted and construed like any other contract."

Treating the modern day urban lease as a contract, this court in *Javins, supra,* recognized, among other things, that repair of the leased premises in a multiple dwelling unit may require access to equipment in areas in the control of the landlord, and skills which no urban tenant possesses. Accordingly, this court delineated the landlord's duty to repair as including continued maintenance of the rented apartment throughout the term of the lease, rightfully placing the duty to maintain the premises upon the party to the lease contract having the capacity to do so, based upon an implied warranty of habitability.

In the case at bar we place the duty of taking protective measures guarding the entire premises and the areas peculiarly under the landlord's control against the perpetration of criminal acts upon the landlord, the party to the lease contract who has the effective capacity to perform these necessary acts.

As a footnote to *Javins, supra,* Judge Wright, in clearing away some of the legal underbrush from medieval common law obscuring the modern landlord-tenant relationship, referred to an innkeeper's liability in comparison with that of the landlord to his tenant. "Even the old common law courts responded with a different rule for a landlord-tenant relationship which did not conform to the model of the usual agrarian lease. Much more substantial obligations were placed upon the keepers of inns (the only multiple dwelling houses known to the common law)."

Specifically, innkeepers have been held liable for assaults which have been committed upon their guests by third parties, if they have breached a duty which is imposed by reason of the inkeeper-guest relationship. By this duty, the innkeeper is generally bound to exercise reasonable care to protect the guest from abuse or molestation from third parties, be they innkeeper's employees, fellow guests, or intruders, if the attack could, or in the exercise of reasonable care, should have been anticipated.

Liability in the innkeeper-guest relationship is based as a matter of law either upon the innkeeper's supervision, care, or control of the premises, or by reason of a contract which some courts have implied from the entrustment by the guest of his personal comfort and safety to the innkeeper. In the latter analysis, the contract is held to give the guest the right to expect a standard of treatment at the hands of the innkeeper which includes an obligation on the part of the latter to exercise reasonable care in protecting the guest.

Other relationships in which similar duties have been imposed include landowner-invitee, businessman-patron, employer-employee, school district-pupil, hospital-patient, and carrier-passenger. In all, the theory of liability is essentially the same: that since the ability of one of the parties to provide for his own protection has been limited in some way by his submission to the control of the other, a duty should be imposed upon the one possessing control (and thus the power to act) to take reasonable precautions to protect the other one from assaults by third parties which, at least, could reasonably have been anticipated. However, there is no liability normally imposed upon the one having the power to act if the violence is sudden and unexpected provided that the source of the violence is not an employee of the one in control.

We are aware of various cases in other jurisdictions following a different line of reasoning, conceiving of the landlord and tenant relationship along more traditional common law lines, and on varying fact situations reaching a different result from that we reach here. Typical of these is a much cited (although only a 4–3) decision of the Supreme Court of New Jersey, Goldberg v. Housing Authority of Newark, *supra* relied on by appellee landlord here. There the court said:

> Everyone can foresee the commission of crime virtually anywhere and at any time. If foreseeability itself gave rise to a duty to provide "police" protection for others, every residential curtilage, every shop, every store, every manufacturing plant would have to be patrolled by the private arm of the owner. And since hijacking and attack upon occupants of motor vehicles are also foreseeable, it would be the duty of every motorist to provide armed protection for his passengers and the property of others. Of course, none of this is at all palatable.

This language seems to indicate that the court was using the word *foreseeable* interchangeably with the word *possible*. In that context, the statement is quite correct. It would be folly to impose liability for mere possibilities. But we must reach the question of liability for attacks which are foreseeable in the sense that they are *probable* and *predictable*. Thus, the United States Supreme Court, in Lillie v. Thompson encountered no difficulty in finding that the defendant-employer was liable to the employee because it "was aware of conditions which created a likelihood" of criminal attack.

In the instant case, the landlord had notice, both actual and constructive, that the tenants were being subjected to crimes against their persons and their property in and from the common hallways. For the period just prior to the time of the assault upon appellant Kline the record contains unrefuted evidence that the apartment building was undergoing a rising wave of crime. Under these conditions, we can only conclude that the landlord here "was aware of conditions which created a likelihood" (actually, almost a certainty) that further criminal attacks upon tenants would occur.

Upon consideration of all pertinent factors, we find that there is a duty of protection owed by the landlord to the tenant in an urban multiple unit apartment dwelling.

Summarizing our analysis, we find that this duty of protection arises, first of all, from the logic of the situation itself. If we were answering without the benefit of any prior precedent the issue as posed by the appellee landlord here, "whether a duty should be placed on a landlord to take steps to protect tenants from foreseeable criminal acts committed by third parties," we should have no hesitancy in answering it affirmatively, at least on the basis of the facts of this case.

As between tenant and landlord, the landlord is the only one in the position to take the necessary acts of protection required. He is not an insurer, but he is obligated to minimize the risk to his tenants. Not only as between landlord and tenant is the landlord best equipped to guard against the predictable risk of intruders, but even as between landlord and the police power of government, the landlord is in the best position to take the necessary protective measures. Municipal police cannot patrol the entryways and the hallways, the garages and the basements of private multiple unit apartment dwellings. They are neither equipped, manned, nor empowered to do so. In the area of the predictable risk which materialized in this case, only the landlord could have taken measures which might have prevented the injuries suffered by appellant.

We note that in the fight against crime the police are not expected to do it all; every segment of society has obligations to aid in law enforcement and to minimize the opportunities for crime. The average citizen is ceaselessly warned to remove keys from automobiles and, in this jurisdiction, may be liable in tort for any injury caused in the operation of his car by a thief if he fails to do so, notwithstanding the intervening criminal act of the thief, a third party. . . . In addition, auto manufacturers are persuaded to install special locking devices and buzzer alarms, and real estate developers, residential communities, and industrial areas are asked to install especially bright lights to deter the criminally inclined. It is only just that the obligations of landlords in their sphere be acknowledged and enforced.

Secondly, . . . there is implied in the contract between landlord and tenant an obligation on the landlord to provide those protective measures which are within his reasonable capacity. Here the protective measures which were in effect in October 1959 when appellant first signed a lease were drastically reduced. She continued after the expiration of the first term of the lease on a month to month tenancy. As this court pointed out in *Javins, supra,* "Since the lessees continue to pay the same rent, they were entitled to expect that the landlord would continue to keep the premises in their beginning condition during the lease term. It is precisely such expectations that the law now recognizes as deserving of formal, legal protection."

Thirdly, if we reach back to seek the precedents of common law, on the question of whether there exists or does not exist a duty on the owner of the premises to provide protection against criminal acts by third parties, the most analogous relationship to that of the modern day urban apartment house dweller is not that of a landlord and tenant, but that of innkeeper and guest. We can also consider other relationships, cited above, in which an analogous duty has been found to exist.

IV

We now turn to the standard of care which should be applied in judging if the landlord has fulfilled his duty of protection to the tenant. Although in many cases the language speaks as if the standard of care itself varies, in the last analysis the standard of care is the same—reasonable care in all the circumstances. The specific measures to achieve this standard vary with the individual circumstances. It may be impossible to describe in detail for all situations of landlord-tenant relationships, and evidence of custom amongst landlords of the same class of building may play a significant role in determining if the standard has been met.

In the case at bar, appellant's repeated efforts to introduce evidence as to the standard of protection commonly provided in apartment buildings of the same character and class as 1500 Massachusetts Avenue at the time of the assault upon Miss Kline were invariably frustrated by the objections of opposing counsel and the impatience of the trial judge. At one point during appellant's futile attempts, the judge commented with respect to the degree of proof required to show a custom: "I think the old proverb that one swallow does not make a summer applies. If you can get 100 swallows, you say this must be summertime."

Later, but still during appellant's efforts on this point, the judge commented to opposing counsel,

> [M]ay I remind you that it is very dangerous to win a case by excluding the

other side's testimony because the Court of Appeals might say that testimony should have been admitted even though you might have won the case with the testimony in.

Appellant then attempted to offer evidence of individual apartment houses with which she was familiar. The trial judge became impatient with the swallow by swallow approach, and needled by opposing counsel's objections, disregarded his own admonition and cut short appellant's efforts in this direction. The record as to custom is thus unsatisfactory, but its deficiencies are directly chargeable to defendant's counsel and the trial judge, not appellant.

We therefore hold in this case that the applicable standard of care in providing protection for the tenant is that standard which this landlord himself was employing in October 1959 when the appellant became a resident on the premises at 1500 Massachusetts Avenue. The tenant was led to expect that she could rely upon this degree of protection. While we do not say that the precise measures for security which were then in vogue should have been kept up (e.g., the number of people at the main entrances might have been reduced if a tenant-controlled intercom-automatic latch system had been installed in the common entryways), we do hold that the same relative degree of security should have been maintained.

The appellant tenant was entitled to performance by the landlord measured by this standard of protection whether the landlord's obligation be viewed as grounded in contract or in tort. As we have pointed out, this standard of protection was implied as an obligation of the lease contract from the beginning. Likewise, on a tort basis, this standard of protection may be taken as that commonly provided in apartments of this character and type in this community, and this is a reasonable standard of care on which to judge the conduct of the landlord here.

V

Given this duty of protection, and the standard of care as defined, it is clear that the appellee landlord breached its duty toward the appellant tenant here.[24] The

24. In an apparent attempt to show that, regardless of the amount of care exercised, the landlord here could not possibly have prevented an assault such as that which had befallen the plaintiff, the following cross examination of Miss Kline was undertaken:

Q. Is it also correct that this apartment building also houses office apartments?

A. As the years went by they were putting more and more offices into the building, yes, sir.

Q. What type of offices would they be?

A. Well, I understood they were supposed to be professional offices because I tried to get my name listed once.

Q. Irrespective of whether you tried to get your name listed or not, did you observe the offices?

A. Yes, I worked for some of them.

Q. What type of organizations had their offices there?

A. Manufacturing representatives; there was a lawyer's office, maybe two; there were some engineers; there were some tour salesmen. That is all I can think of right now.

Q. So that there would be then in the course of a normal day clients going in and out of the lawyers' offices or customers going in and out of the other type offices, would that be correct?

A. Yes.

Q. And they would be able to walk in even if there was a doorman there?

A. Yes.

Q. And one would only speculate as to whether or not anyone could ever leave or not leave, isn't that also correct?

A. What do you mean, speculate if one could leave or not leave?

To which the trial court commented:

THE COURT: Well, we assume the general public would come into any office building or in any big apartment house.

* * * * *

THE COURT: The point is though that an intruder who commits this kind of an assault is apt to act a little different from the rest of the public although it does not always follow, you never know. Of course an intruder is not likely to come in through a public entrance either.

To this we add our own comment that it is unlikely in any case that a patron of one

risk of criminal assault and robbery on any tenant was clearly predictable, a risk of which the appellee landlord had specific notice, a risk which became reality with increasing frequency, and this risk materialized on the very premises peculiarly under the control, and therefore the protection, of the landlord to the injury of the appellant tenant. The question then for the District Court becomes one of damages only. To us the liability is clear.

Having said this, it would be well to state what is *not* said by this decision. We do not hold that the landlord is by any means an insurer of the safety of his tenants. His duty is to take those measures of protection which are within his power and capacity to take, and which can reasonably be expected to mitigate the risk of intruders assaulting and robbing tenants. The landlord is not expected to provide protection commonly owed by a municipal police department; but as illustrated in this case, he is obligated to protect those parts of his premises which are not usually subject to periodic patrol and inspection by the municipal police. We do not say that every multiple unit apartment house in the District of Columbia should have those same measures of protection which 1500 Massachusetts Avenue enjoyed in 1959, nor do we say that 1500 Massachusetts avenue should have precisely those same measures in effect at the present time. Alternative and more up-to-date methods may be equally or even more effective.

Granted, the discharge of this duty of protection by landlords will cause, in many instances, the expenditure of large sums for additional equipment and services, and granted, the cost will be ultimately passed on to the tenant in the form of increased rents. This prospect, in itself, however, is no deterrent to our acknowledging and giving force to the duty, since without protection the tenant already pays in losses from theft, physical assault and increased insurance premiums.

The landlord is entirely justified in passing on the cost of increased protective measures to his tenants, but the rationale of compelling the landlord to do it in the first place is that he is the only one who is in a position to take the necessary protective measures for overall protection of the premises, which he owns in whole and rents in part to individual tenants.

Reversed and remanded to the District Court for the determination of damages.

of the businesses, even if disposed to criminal conduct, would have waited for five hours after the usual closing time to perpetrate his crime—especially one of a violent nature. Further, although it is not essential to our decision in this case, we point out that it is not at all clear that a landlord who permits a portion of his premises to be used for business purposes and the remainder for apartments would be free from liability to a tenant injured by the criminal act of a lingering patron of one of the businesses. If the risk of such injury is foreseeable, then the landlord may be liable for failing to take reasonable measures to protect his tenant from it.

We note parenthetically that no argument regarding any change in the character of the building or its tenants was pursued on appeal.

SELLERS OF LAND

In general, a seller of land is released from tort liability once she turns over the property to the buyer. If, however, the seller fails to disclose a dangerous condition of which she is or should be aware and which she should realize that the buyer will not discover, she will be liable to anyone injured as a result of that condition (Restatement (Second) of Torts Sec. 353). Her liability ceases when the buyer has a "reasonable opportunity" to find and correct the defect, even if the buyer does not in fact discover it (Restatement (Second) of Torts Sec. 353(2)). If the seller hides the defect or intentionally misleads the buyer into not looking for it, the seller's liability will continue until the buyer actually discovers the condition and has a reasonable time to correct it.

If the seller of a house is also its builder, some courts hold the seller liable for any injuries caused by defects in the house. The courts in such cases analogize to product liability cases, where both negligence and strict liability theories are utilized. See Chapter 14 for a discussion of liability in this area.

UNBORN CHILDREN

An area that has been subject to considerable controversy of late is whether a duty of care is owed to an unborn child. Suppose a defendant assaults a pregnant woman, recklessly injuring the fetus and causing defects that manifest physically when the child is born. Under the common law the child could not recover for its injuries. Modern courts have reversed this no-duty rule and have allowed recovery in most instances where a causal link between the defendant's act and the fetus' injury can be proven.

Considerable controversy continues to stem around the question of whether a wrongful death action can be brought if a fetus is stillborn as a result of its injuries. The Restatement suggests that recovery should not be allowed "unless the applicable wrongful death statute so provides" (Restatement (Second) of Torts Sec. 869(2)). The courts are divided on this issue although more courts allow recovery than deny it.

VICARIOUS LIABILITY

Under the principle of **vicarious liability** a defendant may be liable for the tortious acts of another even though he is not at fault. An employer is vicariously liable for the tortious acts of her employees under the doctrine of *respondeat superior*. Vicarious liability also arises under the "family purpose" doctrine. Since these doctrines impose a duty of care on people who are not directly at fault, we will discuss them in this chapter even though they will be discussed in greater depth in other chapters.

Respondeat superior means, literally, "Let the superior respond." Under this doctrine the employer is liable for any torts committed by an employee during the scope and furtherance of his employment. An employer can escape liability if she can prove that the employee was acting on his own behalf and not the employer's when he committed the tortious act. Suppose an employee is instructed to use a vehicle to run an errand for his employer but, in the course of running the errand, he deviates substantially from his route to see his girlfriend. If the employee negligently causes a vehicular accident upon leaving his girlfriend's house, his employer will be absolved of liability because the employee was acting outside the scope of his employment.

The rationale underpinning this doctrine is that employers, rather than employees, should bear the expense of any accidents resulting from doing business. Such expense, it is reasoned, should be considered part of the price of doing business. The bottom line is that an employer owes a duty of care to any plaintiff injured by an employee acting in the scope and furtherance of his duties as an employee.

The **"family purpose" doctrine** holds the owner of a car vicariously liable for the torts committed by those members of his household whom he allows to drive his car. If a father loans his car to his daughter and she negligently injures someone, the father will be vicariously liable for his daughter's negligence. Some states have extended this liability by statute and have provided that the owner of an automobile is vicariously liable for the negligence of anyone who uses his car with his permission.

APPLICATION

In the case involving Teddy, Mr. Dooright, and Gertrude several questions come to mind in reference to duty. Did the Baxters, for example, owe any duty of care to Teddy, who was a trespasser on their land? To answer that question Teddy's attorney will have to determine if Teddy was a known trespasser. Also she will want to consider whether Gertrude is an "attractive nuisance." In answering this question she will have to ask whether the Baxters had reason to know that children were likely to trespass in their backyard and whether Gertrude posed an unreasonable risk of injury to trespassing children. Most importantly, she will have to argue that the Baxters failed to use reasonable care in protecting children from Gertrude by failing to keep the gate locked. She will also have to be able to prove that Teddy was not aware of the danger posed by Gertrude and that children of his age, intelligence, and experience would not have perceived the danger.

Another question to be addressed is whether the Baxters owed any duty of care to Mr. Dooright. At first it may appear that Mr. Dooright was a trespasser; however, since he entered the land with the express purpose of rescuing another, he would not be considered a trespasser. Consequently, Teddy's attorney would have to research the standard of care accorded rescuers under the case law in her state.

Mr. Baxter did, in fact, have a duty to assist Mr. Dooright once he saw him being attacked by Gertrude. Remember that while generally there is no duty to render assistance to one in need, an exception exists when the danger has been created by the defendant's own conduct or by an instrument under his control. In this case, since Gertrude was legally under Mr. Baxter's control, Mr. Baxter had a duty to aid Mr. Dooright.

SUMMARY

The first question that arises in any negligence case is one of duty. Generally, a defendant is expected to exercise the same degree of care that any reasonable person would use under similar circumstances. The nature of the relationship

PRACTICE POINTERS

Early in a case both parties will attempt to eliminate as many factual disputes as feasible. One way to do this is to serve the other side with requests for admissions. The party drafting the admission request writes the questions narrowly so that she can pinpoint as precisely as possible the position of the opposing party. The party responding to such a request makes as few admissions as possible and looks for any reason to justify a response of denial.

The requests for admissions that follow are illustrative of the type of requests that would be submitted by Teddy's attorney to the Baxters' attorney.

DIGGER ODELL
62 Happy Trail
Gotcha, Arizona 85034
843-5285
State Bar No. 0063928

Attorney for Plaintiff

IN THE SUPERIOR COURT OF THE STATE OF ARIZONA

IN AND FOR THE COUNTY OF MARICOPA

TEDDY JONES, a minor and MARY JONES, as guardian ad litem	)	
Plaintiff,	)	No. CV 90-32567
vs.	)	PLAINTIFF'S REQUEST FOR ADMISSIONS TO DEFENDANT
FRED BAXTER and ROSE BAXTER, Husband & Wife,	)	
Defendants.	)	

Plaintiff, Teddy Jones, a minor, and MARY JONES, as guardian ad litem, by and through counsel undersigned, request that Defendants, Fred and Rose Baxter, pursuant to the Rules of Civil Procedure, either admit or deny the following:

ADMISSION NO. 1

Admit that Defendants own a German shepherd dog known as Gertrude.

Admit _____ Deny _____

Continued on next page

PRACTICE POINTERS—Continued

ADMISSION NO. 2

Admit that Defendants maintain a German shepherd dog in a yard surrounded by a six-foot wooden fence.

Admit _____ Deny _____

ADMISSION NO. 3

Admit that between the hours of 3:00 P.M. and 4:00 P.M. on June 6, 1990, Defendants' German shepherd dog was in Defendants' backyard.

Admit _____ Deny _____

ADMISSION NO. 4

Admit that between the hours of 3:00 P.M. and 4:00 P.M. on June 6, 1990, Defendants' German shepherd dog was unsupervised.

Admit _____ Deny _____

ADMISSION NO. 5

Admit that is was Defendants' habit when not at home to lock the gate entering into Defendants' backyard.

Admit _____ Deny _____

ADMISSION NO. 6

Admit that on June 6, 1990 between the hours of 3:00 P.M. and 4:00 P.M. the gate entering into Defendants' backyard was unlocked.

Admit _____ Deny _____

ADMISSION NO. 7

Admit that Teddy Jones lives next door to Defendants.

Admit _____ Deny _____

ADMISSION NO. 8

Admit that Teddy Jones had on occasions prior to June 6, 1990, entered Defendants' backyard with Defendants' permission.

Admit _____ Deny _____

ADMISSION NO. 9.

Admit that Defendant was aware that prior to June 6, 1990, Defendants' German shepherd dog, Gertrude, would bark at and threaten to attack anyone who entered Defendants' yard without Defendants' being present.

Admit _____ Deny _____

ADMISSION NO. 10

Admit that Defendants' German shepherd dog, Gertrude, has bitten people other than Teddy Jones.

Admit _____ Deny _____

between the defendant and the plaintiff is important in determining the duty owed.

The duty owed by possessors of land to those on their land depends on the latter's status as either a trespasser, licensee, or invitee. No duty of care is owed to a trespasser to make the land safe or to protect the trespasser in any way. There are four exceptions, however, to this general rule. Some duty of care is owed to trespassing children, to rescuers, to known trespassers, and to those trespassers using only a very limited portion of the possessor's land. A possessor has the duty to warn a licensee of any dangerous conditions of which the possessor is aware and should reasonably anticipate that the licensee will not discover. Invitees are owed the highest duty of care. A possessor has a duty to inspect her premises for hidden dangers when dealing with invitees. Possessors may be liable for those conditions that pose an unreasonable risk of harm to persons outside their premises, especially if the hazardous condition was artificially created by the possessor.

In Anglo/American law people generally have no obligation to assist others in danger. However, when a special relationship exists between plaintiff and defendant, liability may be found for failure to act. A duty of care may also arise out of a special relationship between the defendant and a third party. Those who render aid to others in need establish a temporary special relationship. Once they initiate assistance they have an obligation to use every reasonable means possible to keep the plaintiff safe.

In the special relationship of the landlord and tenant, the tenant is the one entitled to the protection of the common law rules. Although the landlord generally escaped liability under the common law once he transferred possession to the tenant, today he is liable for failure to keep premises in good repair and is liable for those dangers that he knows or should know about and about which the tenant has no reason to know.

Like landlords, sellers of land are released from tort liability once they turn the property over to the buyers. However, if a seller fails to disclose a dangerous condition of which he is or should be aware and which he should realize that the buyer will not discover, he will be liable for any injuries resulting from that dangerous condition.

Under the common law children could not recover for injuries sustained by them while *in utero.* Modern courts are more inclined to allow recovery.

The doctrine of *respondeat superior* and the family purpose doctrine are examples of vicarious liability, in which the defendant is liable for the tortious acts of another even though she was not at fault. The doctrine of *respondeat superior* pertains primarily to employers while the family purpose doctrine applies to car owners who allow members of their household to drive.

TORT TEASERS

In each of the following cases determine the duty of care owed by the defendant to the plaintiff.

1. Plaintiff, a sixteen-year-old boy, is visiting the home of a friend when he notices a cat at the top of a utility pole in a neighboring yard. He climbs the pole, in part to rescue the cat and in part to see if he can climb the pole. When he arrives at the top of the pole he receives an electric shock and falls, sustaining injuries. *Brown v. Arizona Public Service Company,* 55 Ariz. Adv. Rep. 38 (1990).

2. Plaintiff, who is a pedestrian walking by a baseball park, is hit on the head by a foul ball hit by one of the players. Plaintiff sues Defendant, the owner of the baseball park, for her injuries. *Salevan v. Willington Park, Inc.,* 72 A.2d 239 (Del. 1950).

3. Plaintiff, who was shopping in Defendant's store, is bitten by Defendant's cat. Defendant promises to lock up the cat for fourteen days so that he can be tested for rabies. Defendant fails to live up to his promise and the cat disappears for a month, requiring Plaintiff to undergo a series of painful rabies shots. After Plaintiff completes the treatment the cat returns in perfect health. *Marsalis v. La Salle,* 90 S.2d 120 (La. 1957).

4. Plaintiff and Defendant are officers of a Masonic lodge. Plaintiff comes to Defendant's house to discuss lodge business. Defendant's mentally ill son stabs Plaintiff while he is in the home. Although Defendant is aware that his son committed some violent acts approximately ten years prior to this incident, he has no knowledge at the time of this incident that his son is likely to be violent to Plaintiff or anyone else. *Barmore v. Elmore,* 403 N.E.2d 1355 (Ill. App.Ct. 1980).

KEY TERMS

■ **Attractive nuisance**
Dangerous condition on the defendant's property that is likely to induce children to trespass.

■ **Family purpose doctrine**
Doctrine that makes the owner of a car liable for the tortious acts of family members committed while driving.

■ **Invitee**
Person invited by possessor of land onto her property for the purpose of conducting business.

■ **Licensee**
Person who has possessor's consent to be present on land.

■ ***Respondeat superior* doctrine**
Doctrine that makes employer liable for the tortious acts of employees committed in the scope and furtherance of their employment.

■ **Vicarious liability**
Liability for the tortious acts of others.

NEGLIGENCE: BREACH OF DUTY

CHAPTER OBJECTIVES

In this chapter you will learn to:

- Identify the criteria used to assess the reasonableness of a person's conduct.
- Distinguish between objective and subjective standards.
- Use the Learned Hand formula.
- Apply the concepts of negligence *per se* and *res ipsa loquitur*.

If it can be established that the Baxters owed a duty of care to Teddy and to Mr. Dooright, the next question is whether they breached that duty. Since the duty required in most instances is to use reasonable care, that duty is breached by engaging in unreasonable conduct. Did the Baxters exercise the precautions expected of a reasonable person in their maintenance of Gertrude? Was she adequately confined for a dog of her size and temperament? Did the Baxters create an unreasonable risk of harm for Teddy and other children by failing to latch the lock on their gate?

WHAT IS REASONABLE CONDUCT?

A defendant's conduct must be evaluated at the time of the plaintiff's injury. "Monday-morning quarterbacking" is not allowed. What is important is how reasonable people would perceive the defendant's acts at the time they occurred. The plaintiff, consequently, is not permitted to use the self-serving argument that he or she was injured as a direct result of the defendant's conduct and, therefore, the defendant must have been unreasonable.

The question boils down to what a reasonable person would have done under similar circumstances. The characteristics of the proverbial "reasonable

> **"REASONABLE PERSON" DEFINED**
>
> It is impossible to travel anywhere or to travel for long in that confusing forest of learned judgments which constitutes the Common Law of England without encountering the Reasonable Man . . . The Reasonable Man is always thinking of others; prudence is his guide, and "Safety First," if I may borrow a contemporary catchword, is his rule of life. All solid virtues are his, save only that peculiar quality by which the affection of other men is won . . . While any given example of his behavior must command our admiration, which taken in the mass his acts create a very different set of impressions. He is one who invariably looks where he is going, and is careful to examine the immediate foreground before he executes a leap or a bound; who neither star-gazes nor is lost in meditation when approaching trap doors or the margin of a dock; who records in every case upon the counter-foils of checks such ample details as are desirable, scrupulously substitutes the word "Order" for the word "Bearer," crosses the instrument "a/c Payee only" and registers the package in which it is dispatched; who never mounts a moving omnibus and does not alight from any car while the train is in motion; who investigates exhaustively the bona fides of every mendicant before distributing alms, and will inform himself of the history and habits of a dog before administering a caress; who believes no gossip, nor repeats it, without firm basis for believing it to be true; who never drives his ball till those in front of him have definitely vacated the putting-green which is his own objective; who never from one year's end to another makes an excessive demand upon his wife, his neighbors, his servants, his ox, or his ass . . . Devoid, in short, of any human weakness, with not one single saving vice, sans prejudice, procrastination, ill-nature, avarice, and absence of mind, as careful for his own safety as he is for that of others, this excellent but odious character stands like a monument in our courts of Justice, vainly appealing to his fellow-citizens to order their lives after his own example. (79 Ariz. Adv. Rep. at 20, quoting from A. P. Herbert, *Uncommon Law* (1955).)

person" will be discussed shortly. (For a tongue-in-cheek depiction of the characteristics of the reasonable person read the " 'Reasonable Person' Defined" as quoted from *Newman v. Maricopa County*.) But first we must consider how our reasonable person decides what to do in a predicament. We can assume that any reasonable person will avoid creating an unreasonable risk of harm for others. The tough question is how he or she calculates such risks and avoids actions that create unreasonable risks.

LEARNED HAND FORMULA

Judge Learned Hand, an influential jurist who is well known for his pragmatic approach to the resolution of this problem, advocated a type of cost/benefit analysis (see Figure 7–1). The judge asked the court to consider the probability that harm would occur as a result of the defendant's conduct *(P)*, the gravity of the potential harm *(L)*, and the burden of precautions that would have to

FIGURE 7.1 Learned Hand Formula

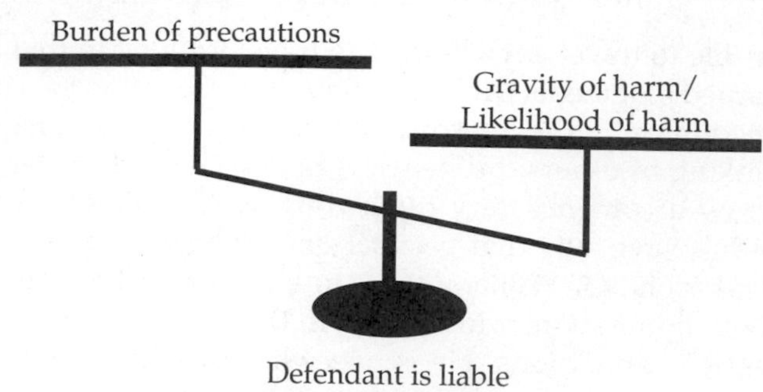

be borne by the defendant to avoid the possible risk *(B)*. He reduced these considerations into a formula and concluded that a defendant breached his duty if:

$$P \times L > B$$

In other words, according to this equation the defendant would be liable if the probability of harm occurring *(P)* multiplied by the gravity of such harm *(L)* exceeded the defendant's burden of taking precautions to avoid the harm *(B)*.

In considering *B*, the burden of precautions, the courts not only look at the cost involved in taking precautions, but also look at the social utility of the defendant's conduct. What is the social value of the defendant's conduct? If society would be better served by allowing all defendants in the defendant's position to act as he or she did, the courts are less likely to require the defendant to alter that course of conduct.

APPLICATION OF LEARNED HAND FORMULA

Let us apply this equation to a hypothetical problem. Suppose an automobile manufacturer discovers a defect in the design of its automobile, which under certain circumstances has the potential of creating harm to the occupants of the vehicle. Will the manufacturer be acting unreasonably if it fails to alter this defective design?

In answering that question, one would have to calculate the statistical likelihood that accidents resulting in injury to a vehicle's occupants would occur. Next, one would have to consider the gravity of the types of injuries that would most likely occur as well as the burden to the manufacturer of altering the design. Suppose it can be anticipated that 100 of those vehicles having this defect will be involved in serious accidents within one year and those accidents will result in injuries costing an average of \$1 million in medical expenses. If altering the design would cost the manufacturer \$1 million, the manufacturer would be obligated to make the alteration since 100 × \$1 million > \$1 million.

Notice that under the Learned Hand formula, the more serious the potential injury that could be incurred, the less probable its occurrence must be before the defendant will be obligated to guard against the anticipated injury. Suppose, for example, the risk of injury were less than 20 percent and yet the type of injury likely to occur was death or serious physical injury. The court would be more likely to find the defendant negligent for failure to redesign the vehicle under those circumstances than if there were a 40 percent chance of an accident but the anticipated injuries were relatively minor.

In assigning a value to *B* the courts would not only calculate the cost of altering the design but would consider the social consequences of not requiring similarly situated defendants to alter their comparably defective designs. If consumers could no longer afford a redesigned vehicle, the new design would have little social utility. Suppose the court in our hypothetical case concludes that the cost of redesigning the vehicle would be prohibitive and that the likelihood and gravity of injuries resulting from the defect would be relatively slight. The court would then conclude that the defendant manufacturer had not breached its duty of care to its consumers. Note, however, that the plaintiffs in such cases could still opt for strict liability and warranty causes of action (both of which are discussed in Chapter 14, Product Liability).

RESTATEMENT POSITION

The Restatement (Second) of Torts Sec. 291 basically incorporates the Learned Hand formula and states that an act is negligent if "the risk is of such magnitude as to outweigh what the law regards as the utility of the act or of the particular manner in which it is done." The following factors are considered in determining the utility of the defendant's conduct:

a. "the social value which the law attaches to the interest which is to be advanced or protected by the conduct;
b. "the extent of the chance that this interest will be advanced or protected by the particular course of conduct;
c. "the extent of the chance that such interest can be adequately advanced or protected by another less dangerous course of conduct." (Restatement (Second) of Torts Sec. 292)

The factors to be considered in determining the magnitude of the risk are:

a. "the social value which the law attaches to the interests which are imperiled;
b. "the extent of the chance that the actor's conduct will cause an invasion of any interest of the other or of one of the class of which the other is a member;
c. "the extent of the harm likely to be caused to the interests imperiled;
d. "the number of persons whose interest are likely to be invaded if the risk takes effect in harm." (Restatement (Second) of Torts Sec. 293)

REASONABLE PERSON STANDARD—OBJECTIVE V. SUBJECTIVE

In assessing whether the defendant imposed an unreasonable risk of harm to others, his or her conduct is compared to that of a reasonable person (see Figure 7–2). In essence, the question put before a jury in a negligence case is whether a reasonable person of ordinary prudence standing in the defendant's shoes would have done the same thing the defendant did. Phrasing the question this way requires the use of an objective standard, in that the defendant's conduct is compared to that of a hypothetical reasonable person.

FIGURE 7.2 Factors Taken Into Consideration in Determining Reasonableness

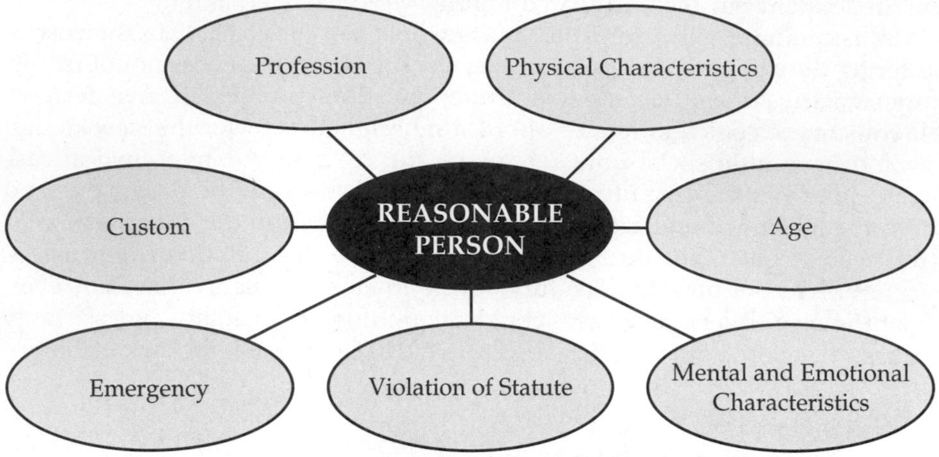

By contrast, if a subjective standard were used, the question would be whether the defendant believed that he or she behaved in a reasonable manner. Under a subjective standard the reasonableness of one's acts vary depending on one's perception.

Let us illustrate the difference in outcome of these two standards by using a hypothetical problem. Suppose a driver pulled out in front of oncoming traffic, causing an accident. The driver had poor depth perception and was unable to accurately estimate the distance between himself and other vehicles. If an objective standard were used, one would ask whether a reasonable driver of ordinary prudence would have pulled out in front of the traffic. If the driver did not conform to that reasonable standard, his conduct would be considered negligent. On the other hand, under a subjective standard, one would ask whether the driver himself perceived if there were any risks. If he did not, he would be deemed to have used reasonable care and, hence, would not be negligent.

From this example you can probably deduce why the objective and not the subjective standard is used in most instances in tort law. To reduce the uncertainty in our legal system and to maximize safety to members of society, the peculiar frailties and idiosyncracies of defendants generally are not taken into consideration in assessing the reasonableness of their conduct. With few exceptions, then, in tort law we use an objective standard.

DEFENDANTS WITH SPECIAL CHARACTERISTICS

Special allowances are not made for those defendants who are emotionally unstable or who are of substandard intelligence. The Restatement (Second) of Torts maintains this position even for persons whose intelligence is so low that they are not even aware that their conduct creates any danger. The majority rule is, however, at odds with the Restatement and does not impose liability where there is an extreme mental deficiency. An intoxicated person is held to the standard of a reasonable sober person (Restatement (Second) of Torts Sec. 283C, comment d).

Even insane people are generally held to a reasonable person standard, although some courts are beginning to deviate from that standard when the insane person is unable to understand or avoid the danger. Two policy considerations are used to justify this apparently harsh rule. One is that the allowance of an insanity defense would lead to fraudulent claims of insanity in an effort to avoid liability. The second is that where injury results from an interaction between two innocent persons, the one causing the injury should bear the consequences.

In considering the attributes of the reasonable person the physical characteristics of the defendant are taken into consideration. A blind person, for example, is held to the standard of a reasonable blind person. Such a person may be expected to use a cane, a seeing eye dog, or some other form of assistance to make her way through town. If such a person fails to use any form of assistance and sues the city for injuries resulting from falling into a depression in the sidewalk, she may be precluded from recovering because of her own negligence.

This rule applies to known physical conditions. A defendant who suffers a heart attack while driving and has an accident will not be found negligent because he lost control of his car. If, however, he had had several previous heart attacks, he might be found to be negligent merely because he was driving a car (Restatement (Second) of Torts Sec. 283C, comment c).

CHILDREN

Children are not held to the standard of care expected of an adult but instead are held to the standard of a "reasonable person of like age, intelligence, and experience under like circumstances" (Restatement (Second) of Torts Sec. 283A). This is somewhat of a subjective standard since the intelligence and experience of the child, both of which are relative, are taken into consideration. Therefore, a ten-year-old child of above-average intelligence is held to a higher standard of conduct than a ten-year-old child of below-average intelligence.

Children are held to an adult standard when they engage in potentially dangerous activities that are normally reserved for adults. A child who drives a car is held to the standard of care expected of a reasonable adult driver. The courts are split as far as the standard of care to be applied when children engage in dangerous activities that are not necessarily pursued only by adults. For example, should a child that goes hunting be held to the standard of care of a child or an adult? Some courts reason that because we can reasonably anticipate that children will engage in this activity, they should be held to a standard of care of other children. Others emphasize the inherent dangerousness of the activity and hold children to an adult standard.

EMERGENCIES

In addition to considering the age and unique characteristics of the defendant, the courts also look at the circumstances in which the defendant was operating. In an emergency, for example, people are not expected to act with the same rational and calm consideration that one would expect in a less stressful situation. But even in an emergency a defendant is expected to act reasonably and if he does not, he can be found liable for his actions. For example, in the process of rendering emergency medical assistance a person who takes no reasonable precautions in moving the victim from one position to another may be found negligent for any injuries he causes. A case that is illustrative (in content, not form) of the analysis employed by the courts in emergency situations is *Cordas v. Peerless Transportation Company*, 27 N.Y.S.2d 198 (1941). The court's whimsical presentation of the facts makes this a particularly entertaining opinion to read.

Cordas v. Peerless Transp. Co.
27 N.Y.S.2d 198

CARLIN, Justice.

This case presents the ordinary man—that problem child of the law—in a most bizarre setting. As a lowly chauffeur in defendant's employ he became in a trice the protagonist in a breath-bating drama with a denouement almost tragic. It appears that a man, whose identity it would be indelicate to divulge was feloniously relieved of his portable goods by two nondescript highwaymen in an alley near 26th Street and Third Avenue, Manhattan; they induced him to relinquish his possessions by a strong argument ad hominem couched in the convincing cant of the criminal and pressed at the point of a most persuasive pistol. Laden with their loot, but not thereby impeded, they took an abrupt departure and he, shuffling off the coil of that discretion which enmeshed him in the alley, quickly gave chase through 26th Street toward 2d Avenue, whither they were resorting "with expedition swift as thought" for most obvious reasons. Somewhere on that thoroughfare of escape they indulged the strategem of separation ostensibly to disconcert their pursuer and allay the ardor of his pursuit. He then centered on for capture the man with the pistol whom he saw board defendant's taxicab, which quickly veered south toward 25th Street on 2d Avenue where he saw the chauffeur jump out while the cab, still in motion, continued toward 24th Street; after the chauffeur relieved himself of the cumbersome burden of his fare the latter also is said to have similarly departed from the cab before it reached 24th Street. The chauffeur's story is substantially the same except that he states that his uninvited guest boarded the cab at 25th Street while it was at a standstill waiting for a less colorful fare; that his "passenger" immediately advised him "to stand not upon the order of his going but to go at once" and added finality to his command by an appropriate gesture with a pistol addressed to his sacro iliac. The chauffeur in reluctant acquiescence proceeded about fifteen feet, when his hair, like unto the quills of the fretful porcupine, was made to stand on end by the hue and cry of the man despoiled accompanied by a clamourous concourse of the law-abiding which paced him as he ran; the concatenation of "stop thief", to which the patter of persistent feet did maddingly beat time, rang in his ears as the pursuing posse all the while gained on the receding cab with its quarry therein contained.

The hold-up man sensing his insecurity suggested to the chauffeur that in the event there was the slightest lapse in obedience to his curt command that he, the chauffeur, would suffer the loss of his brains, a prospect as horrible to an humble chauffeur as it undoubtedly would be to one of the intelligentsia. The chauffeur apprehensive of certain dissolution from either Scylla, the pursuers, or Charybdis, the pursued, quickly threw his car out of first speed in which he was proceeding, pulled on the emergency, jammed on his brakes and, although he thinks the motor was still running, swung open the door to his left and jumped out of his car. He confesses that the only act that smacked of intelligence was that by which he jammed the brakes in order to throw off balance the hold-up man who was half-standing and half-sitting with his pistol menacingly poised. Thus abandoning his car and passenger the chauffeur sped toward 26th Street and then turned to look; he saw the cab proceeding south toward 24th Street where it mounted the sidewalk. The plaintiff-mother and her two infant children were there injured by the cab which, at the time, appeared to be also minus its passenger who, it appears, was apprehended in the cellar of a local hospital where he was pointed out to a police officer by a remnant of the posse, hereinbefore mentioned. He did not appear at the trial. The three aforesaid plaintiffs and the husband-father sue the defendant for damages predicating their respective causes of action upon the contention that the chauffeur was negligent in abandoning the cab under the aforesaid circumstances. Fortunately the injuries sustained were comparatively slight.

. . . In Steinbrenner v. M. W. Forney Co., [cite omitted] it is said, "The test of actionable negligence is what reasonably prudent men would have done under the same circumstances"; Connell v. New York Central & Hudson River Railroad Co. [cite omitted] holds that actionable negligence must be predicated upon "a breach of duty to the plaintiff. Negligence is 'not absolute or intrinsic,' but 'is always relevant to some circumstances of time, place or person.' " In slight paraphrase of the world's first bard it may be truly observed that the expedition of the chauffeur's violent love of his own security outran the pauser, reason, when he was suddenly confronted with unusual emergency which "took his reason prisoner". The learned attorney for the plaintiffs concedes that the chauffeur acted in an emergency but claims a right to recovery upon the following proposition taken verbatim from his brief: "It is respectfully submitted that the value of the interests of the public at large to be immune from being injured by a dangerous instrumentality such as a car unattended while in motion is very superior to the right of a driver of a motor vehicle to abandon same while it is in motion even when acting under the belief that his life is in danger and by abandoning same he will save his life." To hold thus under the facts adduced herein would be tantamount to a repeal by implication of the primal law of nature written in indelible characters upon the fleshy tablets of sentient creation by the Almighty Law-giver, "the supernal Judge who sits on high". There are those who stem the turbulent current for bubble fame, or who bridge the yawning chasm with a leap for the leap's sake or who "outstare the sternest eyes that look, outbrave the heart most daring on the earth, pluck the young sucking cubs from the she-bear, yea, mock the lion when he roars for prey" to win a fair lady and these are the admiration of the generality of men; but they are made of sterner stuff than the ordinary man upon whom the law places no duty of emulation. The law would indeed be fond if it imposed upon the ordinary man the obligation to so demean himself when suddenly confronted with a danger, not of his creation, disregarding the likelihood that such a contingency may darken the intellect and palsy the will of the common legion of the earth, the fraternity of ordinary men,—whose acts or omissions under certain conditions or circumstances make the yardstick by which the law measures culpability or innocence, negligence or care. If a person is placed in a sudden peril from which death might ensue, the law does not impel another to the rescue of the person endangered nor does it condemn him for his unmoral failure to rescue when he can; this is in recognition of the immutable law written in frail flesh. Returning to our chauffeur. If the philosophic Horatio and the martial companions of his watch were "distilled almost to jelly with the act of fear" when they beheld "in the dead vast and middle of the night" the disembodied spirit of Hamlet's father stalk majestically by "with a countenance more in sorrow than in anger" was not the chauffeur, though unacquainted with the example of these eminent men-at-arms, more amply justified in his fearsome reactions when he was more palpably confronted by a thing of flesh and blood bearing in its hand an engine of destruction which depended for its lethal purpose upon the quiver of a hair? When Macbeth was cross-examined by Macduff as to any reason he could advance for his sudden despatch of Duncan's grooms he said in plausible answer "Who can be wise, amazed, temperate and furious, loyal and neutral, in a moment? No man". Macbeth did not by a "tricksy word" thereby stand justified as he criminally created the emergency from which he sought escape by indulgence in added felonies to divert suspicion to the innocent. However, his words may be wrested to the advantage of the defendant's chauffeur whose acts cannot be legally construed as the proximate cause of plaintiff's injuries, however regrettable, unless nature's first law is arbitrarily disregarded. * * * 'The law presumes that *an act or omission done or neglected under the influence of pressing danger was done or neglected involuntarily.*' It is there said that this rule seems to be founded upon the maxim that self-preservation is the first law of nature, and that, where it is a question whether one of two men shall suffer, each is justified in doing the best he can for himself." Laidlaw v. Sage [cite omitted] (Italics ours.) Kolanka v. Erie Railroad Co. [cite omitted] says: "The law in this state does not hold one in an emergency to the exercise of that mature judgment required of him under circumstances where he has an opportunity for deliberate action. He is not required to exercise unerring judgment, which would be expected of him, were he not confronted with an emergency requiring prompt action". The circumstances provide the foil by which the act is brought into relief to determine whether it is or is not negligent. If under normal circumstances an act is done which might be considered negligent it does not follow as a corollary that a similar act is negligent if performed by a person acting under an emergency, not of his own making, in which he suddenly is faced with a patent danger with a moment left to adopt a means of extrication. The chauffeur—the ordinary man in this case—acted in a split second in a most harrowing experience. To call him negligent would be to brand him coward; the court does not do so in spite of what those swaggering heroes, "whose valor plucks dead lions by the beard", may bluster to the contrary. The court is loathe to see the plaintiffs go without recovery even though their damages were slight, but cannot hold the defendant liable upon the facts adduced at the trial. Motions, upon which decision was reserved, to dismiss the complaint are granted with exceptions to plaintiffs. Judgment for defendant against plaintiffs dismissing their complaint upon the merits.

In some situations the reasonable person will be expected to anticipate the actions of others. A driver making her way down a residential street where children are playing will be expected to anticipate that children may run into the street. She will be expected to exercise special care to guard against their carelessness. A reasonable person is not, on the other hand, expected to anticipate the crimes or intentional torts of another unless her relationship with that person is such that she should reasonably anticipate such behavior.

CUSTOM

Custom may also be considered in determining reasonable care. Courts will look at the standard practices of a trade or community in assessing the reasonableness of the defendant's conduct. Adherence to custom is persuasive evidence of the reasonableness of conduct but is not necessarily conclusive. It is possible, although not likely, that a court might conclude that an entire industry is negligent if it fails to adopt certain safety precautions.

PROFESSIONS

A defendant who possesses a higher degree of knowledge or skill as a result of training or experience will be held to a higher standard of care. Lawyers, doctors, accountants, and police officers, among others, are held to the standard of care commonly exercised by members in good standing of their profession (Restatement (Second) of Torts Sec. 299A). A medical doctor who administers first aid to someone injured on the street is held to a higher standard of care than someone lacking that training. Professionals who have specialized in a particular area are held to a specialist's standard of care, which exceeds that of the minimal standard of care expected of other members of the profession.

The standard of care applied to professionals is an objective one. Therefore, the question in malpractice cases is whether the professional met the standard of care expected by members of the profession. Relative inexperience is not taken into consideration. Novices in the profession are held to the same standard of competence as more experienced members of the profession. We will discuss malpractice in greater depth in Chapter 12.

NEGLIGENCE *PER SE*

In some cases reasonable conduct is established by statute. A statute mandating that freeway drivers are limited to speeds under 65 mph establishes a safety standard. A defendant who violates this statute and who injures someone as a result of this violation will be considered "negligent *per se*" ("negligent in itself") in most courts. This doctrine, as applied by the majority of the courts, requires that (1) the violated statute be applicable to the facts of the case and that (2) a causal link between the act constituting a violation of the statute and the plaintiff's injury be established (see Table 7–1). In a few courts, however, a statutory violation is considered mere evidence of negligence and may be outweighed by other evidence of due care.

In order to prove negligence *per se* the plaintiff must first show that he or she is a member of the class of persons whom the statute was intended to protect. The plaintiff must also show that the statute was designed to protect against the kind of harm that was sustained.

The following case illustrates these two requirements. Plaintiffs were driving along a country dirt road when they approached an intersection. At the intersection they looked for cars and when they saw none they proceeded through the intersection; there they were hit by an oncoming car. The plaintiffs claimed that their view was obstructed by weeds growing in a ditch along

TABLE 7.1 Questions Relating to Negligence *Per Se*

NEGLIGENCE *PER SE*
• Is violated statute applicable to facts of case? • Is plaintiff member of class protected by statute? • Is act causing injury a violation of the statute? • Is harm that occurred intended to be prevented by statute?

the roadway. Pointing to a statute criminalizing the "shipping, selling or permitting [of] growing of noxious weeks," they sued the county for negligence *per se*.

They argued that the county had violated the statute by permitting weeds to grow in the ditch. The court, however, held that the defendants were not negligent *per se* because the plaintiffs did not belong to the class of persons whom the statute was designed to protect. The statute, the court reasoned, was designed to protect farmers and ranchers from an infestation of weeds and was not designed to protect travelers on the highway (*Hidalgo v. Cochise County*, 13 Ariz. App. 27 (1970)). Note also that the harm the statute was intended to protect against was the spread of weeds and not the prevention of accidents on the highways.

The determination as to whether the type of harm that occurred was that anticipated by statute has been particularly problematic in those cases involving keys left in cars. In such cases someone usually uses the keys to steal the car and ultimately becomes involved in an accident. The question then becomes whether the driver who left the keys in the car should be liable for the injuries caused by the person who stole the car. Plaintiffs in those states having statutes that prohibit the leaving of keys in a car have argued negligence *per se* in these cases. If the purpose of the statute is to prevent reckless driving by thieves, plaintiffs making this argument should prevail but if there is some other purpose for the statute, the elements of negligence *per se* are not satisfied. Even if negligence *per se* cannot be proved, however, plaintiffs can cite statutory violations as evidence of negligence.

In some cases the statute in question is a criminal one. Some penal statutes specifically provide that their violation will result in civil liability but ambiguity exists where no reference to civil liability is made. Under the majority rule and out of deference to the legislature, the courts will apply the criminal statutory standard to civil cases as a matter of law.

DEFENSES TO NEGLIGENCE *PER SE*

In rare instances courts have found an absolute duty to comply with a statute and have refused to accept even reasonable excuses for failure to comply. A defendant violating a statute prohibiting the sale of firearms to minors would likely be found negligent despite his good faith argument that he believed the minor to be an adult.

For the most part, however, statutes are not deemed to impose an absolute duty of compliance. In some jurisdictions the violation of a statute is construed as setting forth a presumption of negligence, which the defendant can rebut by introducing evidence of reasonable care. Other courts treat a statutory violation as negligence *per se* but accept excuses for noncompliance. Under the Restatement (Second) of Torts "excuse" approach, violation of a statute is excused for the following reasons:

a. "the violation is reasonable because of the actor's incapacity;
b. "he neither knows nor should know of the occasion for compliance;
c. "he is unable after reasonable diligence or care to comply;
d. "he is confronted by an emergency not due to his own misconduct;
e. "compliance would involve a greater risk of harm to the actor or to others." (Restatement (Second) of Torts Sec. 288A(2)).

Even if negligence *per se* is established, the defendant can still assert the defenses of contributory negligence and assumption of risk so long as the statute does not impose an absolute duty on the defendant.

One might conclude from the foregoing discussion that compliance with a statute establishes that a defendant was not negligent. But that is not true. The trier of fact is always free to conclude that a reasonable person would have taken precautions beyond that mandated by statute.

AUTOMOBILE GUEST STATUTES

Whereas some statutes have been used to establish a minimal standard of care, other statutes, specifically the automobile guest statutes, have been used to limit the duty of care. Such statutes hold a driver of a vehicle liable to a guest in his or her car only under circumstances of extreme misconduct. Typically such statutes require that the driver's misconduct must be willful and wanton, grossly negligent, or reckless before he or she will be held liable.

In an effort to evade these statutes plaintiffs have spent considerable effort in litigating the question of who is a "guest" as well as what specific acts by the driver constitute the conduct defined by statute. Beginning in the 1970s a number of automobile guest statutes were either repealed or found to be unconstitutional. Today only a few states still have such statutes in effect.

RES IPSA LOQUITUR

Suppose the plaintiff in a medical malpractice case is injured while on the operating table. If several doctors and nurses are present during the operation and could contribute to the plaintiff's injuries, the plaintiff, because she was unconscious, will have difficulty proving who did and who did not act negligently. A court-developed doctrine that makes the plaintiff's task easier is the doctrine of *res ipsa loquitur*, which means, literally, "the thing speaks for itself." This doctrine allows the plaintiff to create an inference that the defendant was negligent without actually providing direct evidence of that negligence (see Table 7–2).

Before a plaintiff can rely on the doctrine of *res ipsa loquitur*, he or she must prove the following:

- The instrument that caused the plaintiff's injury was under the exclusive

TABLE 7.2

ELEMENTS OF *RES IPSA LOQUITUR*
•Event that resulted in plaintiff's injuries does not usually happen except as a result of negligence. •Instrument that caused plaintiff's injury was under the defendant's exclusive control. •Plaintiff did not cause his own injuries. •Defendant is in better position to explain events causing plaintiff's injuries than is plaintiff.* *Not all courts require proof of this element.

control of the defendant or, stated another way, the negligence was probably due to the defendant.

- The experience suffered by the plaintiff was of a type that does not ordinarily occur except as a result of someone's negligence.
- The plaintiff did not voluntarily contribute to his or her own injuries.
- Some courts also require that the plaintiff show that the defendant is better able to explain the events that transpired than the plaintiff.

Let us examine each of these factors in some detail.

DEFENDANT IN CONTROL OR CAUSE OF INJURIES

Older cases required the plaintiff to show that the instrumentality that caused the harm was under the exclusive control of the defendant. Modern courts have required instead that the plaintiff show that the negligence was due to the defendant and not to someone else. To do this the plaintiff must often produce evidence demonstrating that it is more probable that the defendant caused the plaintiff's injuries than that someone else did. If it is just as likely that someone other than the defendant caused the injury, *res ipsa loquitur* will not apply.

Proving responsibility becomes particularly problematic in cases involving multiple defendants. In such cases the plaintiff may be able to demonstrate that the injury was caused by the negligence of at least one of the defendants but may not be able to show which defendant. The medical malpractice scenario at the beginning of this section is an illustration of just such a situation. How does the plaintiff know which of the doctors and nurses contributed to her injuries? Some courts in such cases have allowed the application of *res ipsa loquitur,* relying on the rationale that since the defendants had control over the plaintiff they should bear the responsibility of explaining what happened. The courts seem less willing, however, to apply *res ipsa loquitur* if the defendants were strangers to one another and acted independently of one another.

INJURY IS CONSEQUENCE OF NEGLIGENCE

The plaintiff must demonstrate that the accident would have been unlikely to occur in the absence of negligence. He or she is not required to show that only negligence is the cause of such events but must prove that such events are generally a consequence of negligence. In some cases that awareness will lie within the experience of the jury and will not have to be proved explicitly by the plaintiff. It could probably be presumed by a modern-day jury, for example, that an airplane that crashed for no apparent reason probably did so because of negligence. That inference might not have been justified in the early days of flight, but it can be readily drawn today in light of modern safety records. The plaintiff need not prove, however, that there was no other possible cause of the accident, only that it was more likely than not that negligence was the cause of the accident.

LACK OF CONTRIBUTORY NEGLIGENCE

The plaintiff must also provide evidence showing that he or she acted properly. If the plaintiff was contributorily negligent, the doctrine is probably not applicable. On the other hand, if the plaintiff's contributory negligence does not reduce the likelihood that the defendant was also negligent, the doctrine may still be applied.

EVIDENCE MORE AVAILABLE TO DEFENDANT

Some courts also require the plaintiff to show that evidence of negligence was more available to the defendant(s) than to the plaintiff. Most courts, however, apply the doctrine of *res ipsa loquitur* even where evidence is no more available to the defendant than to the plaintiff. This element seems to be more of a rationale for applying the doctrine than it does to be an evidentiary requirement.

PROCEDURAL CONSEQUENCES

The procedural consequence in most courts of the plaintiff's use of *res ipsa loquitur* is that the jury is allowed to infer negligence. In some courts, meeting the requirements of the doctrine creates a presumption of negligence, which the defendant must rebut to avoid a directed verdict. In a few courts once *res ipsa loquitur* applies, the defendant must prove by a preponderance of the evidence that he or she did not act negligently.

APPLICATION

Breach of duty is the key question in the case against the Baxters. Teddy and Mr. Dooright will have to prove that the Baxters acted unreasonably by failing to lock the gate to their backyard. If statutes or ordinances within their jurisdiction mandate that dogs be confined in an area that is inaccessible to children, the Baxters could be found negligent *per se*. At the very least, statutes and ordinances could be used to establish the reasonable standard of care expected of dog owners. Compliance with these statutory requirements would not necessarily absolve the Baxters, however, since their conduct could still be deemed unreasonable. Even if found negligent *per se*, they could assert that the defendants were contributorily negligent or assumed the risk.

The plaintiffs could integrate the Learned Hand formula into any arguments before the court by showing that the probability of harm occurring if Gertrude was not locked in the yard and the gravity of injuries that would occur if she attacked someone greatly outweighed the minimal inconvenience of ensuring that the gate was locked. They would have to assign numerical figures to these factors to make this formula meaningful. Since this formula is somewhat esoteric and designed to provide a guideline to the courts in assessing defendants' conduct, the attorneys would present the formula in arguments to the court and not to the jury.

The Baxters would argue that Teddy fell short of the conduct expected of a child of his age, intelligence, and experience. They would especially want to emphasize that Teddy was aware of Gertrude's propensity to defend her domain and that, having been forewarned to stay out of the Baxters' yard, he was aware of the danger inherent in entering that yard without the Baxters being present. If the Baxters tried to argue that Mr. Dooright behaved negligently by interjecting himself in the altercation between Teddy and Gertrude, they would probably fail. As long as Mr. Dooright acted reasonably considering the frightening circumstances in which he became involved he would not be found negligent. Reasonableness does not preclude acts of heroism.

SUMMARY

Breach of duty raises the question of whether the defendant engaged in unreasonable conduct. We presume that a reasonable person will avoid creating an unreasonable risk of harm for others. Under the Learned Hand formula, a defendant has breached his or her duty if the probability of the harm his or her act presents multiplied by the gravity of such harm exceeds the defendant's burden of taking precautions to avoid the harm. An objective standard is used in assessing the defendant's conduct.

Generally, special allowances are not made for defendants who are emotionally unstable, of substandard intelligence, or insane. The physical characteristics of a defendant are, however, taken into consideration. Children are held to the standard of care of a child of similar age, intelligence, and experience. The fact that a defendant acted in an emergency situation is taken into consideration in determining the reasonableness of the conduct. The custom of a particular industry or community is looked at in reviewing the reasonableness of a defendant's conduct. Professionals are held to the standard of care commonly exercised by members in good standing of their profession while specialists are held to a specialist's standard of care.

If a defendant violates a statute that is applicable to the facts of the case and if someone is injured as a result of that violation, the defendant will be considered negligent *per se*. The plaintiff must show that he or she is a member of the class of persons whom the statute is intended to protect and that the statute was designed to protect against the type of harm sustained. Criminal as well as civil statutes may be used to prove negligence *per se*. Generally, however, statutes do not impose an absolute duty of compliance and their violation may be excused for a number of reasons.

In contrast to the doctrine of negligence *per se*, automobile guest statutes absolve defendants of liability unless their conduct is willful and wanton, grossly negligent, or reckless. Few states continue to have such statutes in operation.

In some cases the plaintiff is unable to prove negligence because he or she lacks any direct evidence. The doctrine of *res ipsa loquitur* allows the plaintiff to create an inference of negligence. Under this doctrine the plaintiff must prove: (1) the negligence was due to the defendant and not to someone else, (2) the experience suffered by the plaintiff was of a sort that does not ordinarily occur except as a result of negligence, (3) the plaintiff did not voluntarily contribute to his or her own injuries, and, in some courts, (4) the defendant is better able to explain the event that occurred than is the plaintiff.

PRACTICE POINTERS

One of the easiest ways in the litigation process to gain information from the opposing side is through the use of interrogatories. In comparison to depositions, interrogatories are relatively inexpensive to prepare. They do not, however, provide the same type of information that depositions do.

Depositions give attorneys an opportunity to see how an individual reacts to pressure and allows them, in general, to assess the individual's probable performance on the witness stand. Additionally, depositions allow attorneys to follow up immediately on questions and to pursue a line of questioning aggressively without giving the individual an opportunity to collect his or her thoughts. Although depositions are typically a more helpful discovery device, their expense precludes extensive use. Therefore, law firms spend considerable time preparing and answering interrogatories.

Interrogatories give more insight into the attorney's thoughts than to the client's. This is because attorneys assist clients in responding to interrogatories and, in some cases, actually prepare the answers for the client's signature. Generally, attorneys strive to avoid answering any questions they do not absolutely have to and they try to reveal no more information than is ethically required.

Since attorneys often delegate the task of drafting interrogatories to their legal assistants, you should become familiar with this process. Interrogatories should be as specific and narrow as possible. General questions promote general answers. If you want to know how the plaintiff was injured, do not ask broad questions such as "How did the accident occur?" Design questions that call for specific information. Divide the accident into relatively short time sequences and ask questions pertaining to each sequence. Ask, for example, what the defendant was doing immediately preceding the accident, which direction he was headed in, what time of day it was, what the lighting conditions were, what intersection the accident occurred at, when the defendant first observed the plaintiff, and so on.

Avoid asking questions that can be truthfully answered with "yes" or "no" unless you intend to follow up with detail-seeking questions. Include specific requests for names, addresses, and titles of witnesses.

Continued on next page

PRACTICE POINTERS—Continued

Ask whom the other side intends to call as witnesses and what their anticipated testimony will be. Also ask about the documentation and exhibits opposing counsel intends to use at trial.

Phrase questions carefully to prevent opposing counsel from having an excuse for evading any question. Questions that violate any privileges (such as the privilege against self-incrimination, the attorney-client privilege, or the attorney work-product rule) should be avoided as should questions that are irrelevant or overly burdensome for opposing counsel to respond to.

In formulating questions it is often helpful to mentally walk through the chain of events that led up to the plaintiff's injury and that ultimately culminated in the plaintiff seeking legal assistance. The sequence of your questions should follow that same chronological order. Imagine that you are photographing the scene as it unfolds and that now, as you ask your questions, you have slowed down the camera speed so that you can see one frame at a time. Try to ask at least one question for each frame of action. Even where this proves impractical, this frame-by-frame approach will encourage you to ask extremely narrow questions.

When you review your questions, check to see that they are straightforward and concise. Confusing or convoluted questions often beget confusing, convoluted answers. Simplicity and precision are the key to effective interrogatories.

TORT TEASERS

1. How would you go about determining whether the Baxters breached their duty to Teddy and Mr. Dooright? Suppose in your research you found a statute in your state that read as follows: "Owners of dogs known to have dangerous propensities must adequately restrain such dogs so as to prevent injury to others." The Restatement (Second) of Torts Sec. 509 provides that:

> A possessor of a domestic animal that he knows or has reason to know has dangerous propensities abnormal to its class, is subject to liability for harm done by the animal to another, although he has used the utmost care to prevent it from doing the harm.

What arguments would you make on behalf of the Baxters? On behalf of Teddy and Mr. Dooright?

2. If you were to interview Teddy and his parents, what questions would you ask them to help establish that the Baxters violated their duty of care?

3. Review the sample interrogatories in Figure 7–3. What additional ques-

FIGURE 7.3 Sample Interrogatories

1. How long have you owned your German sheperd, Gertrude? ____________

2. Describe in detail all of the obedience classes and other forms of training that Gertrude has received since you have owned her. ____________

3. Has Gertrude ever threatened or attempted to attack anyone? If yes, describe in detail, each such incident. Include the date and approximate time of the event, who was present and what allegedly instigated the attack or attempted attack. ____________

4. (A) Give detailed descriptions of any injuries sustained as a result of the attacks described above, the type of treatment administered and the outcome of that treatment. ____________

(B) Give the name and address of all victims of the attacks described above and describe the nature of your relationship to each victim. ____________

5. Have you in any way encouraged or trained Gertrude to protect your property? If yes, explain specifically what training or encouragement you have provided. ____________

6. Have you ever been sued as a result of damages inflicted by Gertrude? If yes, specify the date each such suit was filed, the nature of the claim against you and the outcome of the suit. ____________

7. On the date of the incident involving Gertrude and Teddy, what did you observe when you pulled up to your house? ____________

Continued on next page

8. Give the name, address and telephone number of any insurance carrier that does or may provide coverage for the incident alleged in Plaintiff's complaint.

____

9. With respect to each of the above listed insurance carriers, provide the following:

A. Limits of liability (both aggregate and per person). ______________________________

B. Medical payments coverage (both aggregate and per person). ______________________________

10. Describe in detail each and every precaution you have taken to keep others from entering your backyard and the date that each such precaution was taken.

____

tions would you consider asking the Baxters and for what reason would you ask them?

4. Suppose the Baxters alleged that Teddy and Mr. Dooright were both contributorily negligent. If you were representing the Baxters what arguments would you raise to show that Teddy's conduct was unreasonable? What arguments would you make to show that Mr. Dooright's actions were unreasonable?

5. Plaintiff and Defendant are both driving down the road when Defendant attempts to pass Plaintiff's vehicle. In doing so his left rear tire blows out, causing him to swerve into Plaintiff's vehicle. Testimony is presented showing that the tire was very worn but defendant claims that he was unaware of the dangerous condition of the tire. Was Defendant's failure to examine his tire unreasonable conduct? *Delair v. McAdoo,* 188 A.181 (Pa. 1936).

6. Defending attorney represents a wife in a divorce proceeding. Under California community property law she is entitled to a claim to her husband's retirement benefits. Defendant fails to make this claim for his client because he erroneously believes that the wife is not entitled to the benefits. The law, in fact, is relatively clear on this issue and provides that retirement rights are community property. Defendant does not research the issue. Was Defendant negligent? How would you assess the reasonableness of his actions? *Smith v. Lewis,* 530 P.2d 589 (Cal. 1975).

7. A statute provides that the seller of a "deadly weapon" receive positive identification "of the purchaser from two residents of the state" and that he keep a record of the name, age, address, and other details pertaining to the purchaser. Defendant sells a gun and fails to comply with the statute. The purchaser uses it on Plaintiff in the course of committing an armed robbery. Was defendant negligent *per se? Hetherton v. Sears, Robuck & Co.,* 593 F.2d 526 (3rd Cir. 1979).

8. Plaintiff drinks from a bottle of coca-cola he purchased from the drugstore and spits up a fly. Defendant introduces evidence that the bottling plant was operated under sanitary conditions and that coca-cola bottles can be opened and their caps replaced without any obvious indication of tampering. Is the doctrine of *res ipsa loquitur* applicable? *Crystal Coca-Cola Bottling Co. v. Cathey,* 317 P.2d 1094 (Ariz. 1957).

NEGLIGENCE: CAUSATION

CHAPTER OBJECTIVES

In this chapter you will learn to:

- Distinguish between actual cause and proximate cause.
- Prove the element of actual cause.
- Distinguish between the Cardozo and Andrews approach to proximate cause.
- Identify the exceptions to the Cardozo rule of foreseeability.
- Distinguish between an intervening and a superseding cause.

If Teddy and Mr. Dooright are able to hurdle the "duty" and "breach of duty" obstacles, they must then set their sights on the element of causation. Causation entails two separate considerations: actual cause (sometimes referred to as causation in fact) and proximate cause (or legal cause). **Actual cause** means, quite literally, that the defendant's actions were the actual and factual cause of the plaintiff's injuries. **Proximate cause**, on the other hand, means that the defendant's conduct was so closely connected to the plaintiff's injuries that the defendant should be held liable. If the plaintiff is injured by a bizarre and extraordinary chain of events that is only remotely connected to the defendant's negligence, proximate cause is lacking.

ACTUAL CAUSE

"BUT FOR" TEST

The question of whether the defendant was the actual cause of the plaintiff's injuries is usually a factual one (see Table 8–1). The "but for" or "sine qua non" test is usually used to determine actual cause. Under this test if the plaintiff's injuries would not have occurred *but for* the defendant's negligence, the defendant will be deemed the actual cause of the plaintiff's injuries (Restatement (Second) of Torts Sec. 432).

Let us apply this test to an actual situation. The mate of the defendant's steam trawler falls overboard and disappears immediately. The defendant's lifeboat is equipped with only one oar which is lashed to the deck instead of being suspended from the davits. As a result the lashings have to be cut before the boat can be launched. Is the defendant's negligence the actual cause of the plaintiff's death (*Ford v. Trident Fisheries Company,* 122 N.E. 389 (1919))? Since the plaintiff disappeared immediately after falling overboard and no evidence shows that the defendant's negligence in any way contributed to the plaintiff's death, the defendant would not be considered the actual cause of the plaintiff's death.

Notice that the "but for" test makes for an extremely broad net into which many a defendant can be snared. If this test were to be taken to its logical extreme the parents of every defendant could be found liable for the acts of their child since "but for" their procreation the defendant would never have been born and, hence, the plaintiff would never have been injured. This facetious example illustrates the ridiculous extremes to which the test can be taken.

SUBSTANTIAL FACTOR TEST

As sweeping as the "but for" test is, it does not encompass situations involving concurrent causes of harm to the plaintiff. Concurrent causes are those events that combine (concur) to cause the plaintiff's harm, although either one of them alone could cause the harm without any contribution from the other. Under the substantial factor test, an alternative to the "but for" test, the question is whether the defendant was a substantial factor in producing the plaintiff's injury. If the concurrent causes produce a single, indivisible harm in which the damage from one event cannot be separated from that caused by the other, the courts have generally found both events to be a substantial factor in producing the plaintiff's injuries.

TABLE 8.1 Actual Cause

BUT-FOR TEST	SUBSTANTIAL FACTOR TEST	BURDEN OF PROOF
"But-for" defendant's negligence plaintiff would not have been injured.	Two or more concurrent or successive events combine to cause the plaintiff's injury and each of them is a "substantial factor" in producing the injury.	Plaintiff bears burden of proof **Except:** 1. Alternate Liability (Summers vs. Tice) 2. Market Share Liability (Sindell vs. Abbott Labs) 3. Concerted Action

To illustrate the application of this test, suppose the plaintiff is riding down a narrow road in his horse-drawn wagon when two motorcycles roar around him, one on each side. The frightened horse bolts and the plaintiff is injured. Although either motorcycle by itself would have been sufficient to frighten the horse the harm created by both of the motorcycles produces a single, indivisible harm. Consequently, both motorcyclists are the actual cause of the plaintiff's injuries (*Corey v. Havener,* 65 N.E. 69 (Mass. 1902)).

PROOF OF ACTUAL CAUSE

The plaintiff bears the burden of proving actual causation by a preponderance of the evidence. In other words, she must prove that it is probable that the injury would not have occurred but for the defendant's acts. Suppose, however, the defendant argues that the plaintiff would have been injured even if the defendant had not been negligent. The plaintiff must then show that the defendant's negligence greatly enhanced the chances of harm occurring in order to sustain the burden of proof.

If two defendants are negligent but only one could have caused the plaintiff's injury, the burden of proof will be thrust back on the defendants to show who actually caused the harm (Restatement (Second) of Torts Sec. 433B(3)). Under the theory of alternate liability, as developed in *Summers v. Tice,* 199 P.2d 1 (Cal. 1948), each negligent tortfeasor must prove that his or her actions did not cause the plaintiff's injuries. In the result of failure to make such proof both defendants will be found liable. In *Summers v. Tice* the plaintiff and the two defendants went hunting together. The defendants simultaneously shot at a quail and the plaintiff was struck by one of the shots. Since it could not be determined from which gun the bullet was fired, the court held that each of the defendants had the burden to show that it was the other's shot that wounded the plaintiff.

This theory has been expanded to encompass three or more defendants in the area of product liability. The so-called "market share liability" theory was developed in *Sindell v. Abbott Laboratories,* 607 P.2d 924 (Cal. 1980), to allow recovery to the plaintiff who can show only that the defendants were negligent but cannot prove which of the defendants caused the injury. In *Sindell* at least 200 manufacturers used an identical formula to produce diethylstilbestrol (DES). The plaintiff, whose mother took the drug during pregnancy, alleged that her cancer was a direct result of her mother's consumption of DES. The plaintiff sued five drug companies, which she maintained manufactured 90 percent of the DES ever marketed, but was unable to show which of the manufacturers produced the drug that her mother actually took.

The court concluded that it was impossible for the plaintiff to provide such proof, in part because the ill effects caused by the drug did not become apparent for many years after consumption. The court reasoned that when it came down to a conflict between an innocent plaintiff and negligent defendants, the latter should bear the cost of any injuries. The court also opined that the defendants were better able to bear the cost of injury since they could discover and guard against any defects and could also warn consumers of potential harmful effects. Any defendant unable to prove that it did not produce the particular dosages consumed by the plaintiff's mother would be liable for the portion of the judgment that represented the defendant's share of the overall DES market at the time of the mother's consumption.

Notice that market share liability differs from *res ipsa loquitur* in that the latter is used when a plaintiff has no way of proving the nature of the defendant's conduct. If the plaintiff can meet the proof requirements of *res ipsa loquitur* the defendant's negligence will be inferred. With market share liability the plaintiff can show that all of the defendants were negligent (or produced a dangerous product) but is unable to pin the injuries on one specific defendant.

Other courts, when confronted with multiple defendants, have imposed liability using a concerted action theory set forth in the Restatement (Second) of Torts Sec. 876. Under this theory plaintiffs must show that a tacit agreement existed among the defendants to perform a tortious act. To do this the plaintiff must show the existence of a common plan or that the defendants assisted or encouraged each other in accomplishing a tortious result. Regardless of which theory the court relies on, clearly a defendant may be considered the actual cause of the plaintiff's injury even if another defendant's negligence also contributed to that harm.

PROXIMATE CAUSE

If the plaintiff is successful in showing that the defendant's negligence was the actual cause of the injury, he or she must then show that the defendant proximately caused the injury. Some writers feel that the term *legal cause* is more descriptive since it reflects a judicial concern that limits should be put on a defendant's liability. This judicial constraint arises from a sense that a defendant should not be liable for a highly improbable or extraordinary consequence stemming from his or her negligence. In reading cases you will discover that some courts blur the concepts of actual causation and proximate cause. For example, if a court finds that a defendant's conduct was not the actual cause of the plaintiff's harm, it may label this a failure of proximate cause. Throughout this text, however, we will treat these two concepts separately.

FORESEEABILITY

The question of proximate cause basically boils down to a question of foreseeability. Was the plaintiff's injury a reasonably foreseeable consequence of the defendant's conduct? The difficulty that the courts grapple with is where to draw the line in holding defendants liable.

Suppose a defendant knifes the plaintiff, causing relatively mild injuries. In which of the following circumstances do you think the defendant should be held liable for the plaintiff's death?

a. The plaintiff, attempting to escape the defendant, runs in front of a car and is killed.
b. The plaintiff contracts gangrene and dies as a result of negligence on the part of the doctor who treats him.
c. The ambulance transporting the plaintiff to a hospital is involved in an accident and the plaintiff dies.
d. The plaintiff refuses medical care, contracts an infection that can be traced to the injuries he received from the defendant, and dies as a result of that infection.

We will deal with these situations later on in this chapter. But be aware only limited consensus exists in the area of proximate cause. The courts have struggled, and continue to struggle, with their determination of what is fair to a defendant.

PALSGRAF

The most famous case dealing with the issue of foreseeability is *Palsgraf v. Long Island R. R. Company,* 162 N.E. 99 (N.Y. 1928). In *Palsgraf* one of the defendant railroad's employees, attempting to assist a man running to board the defendant's train, accidentally dislodged a package from the passenger's arm. Unbeknownst to anyone, the package contained fireworks, which exploded when they fell. As a result of the shock of the explosion some scales at the other end of the platform fell and hit the plaintiff. Arguably, the defendant's employee was negligent in pushing the passenger in his effort to assist him. The real question, however, was whether the defendant's negligence toward the passenger should give rise to liability to the plaintiff, who was injured by a series of fluke events.

Palsgraf v. Long Island R. Co.
Court of Appeals of New York. May 29, 1928.
162 N.E. 99 (N.Y. 1928)

CARDOZO, C.J. Plaintiff was standing on a platform of defendant's railroad after buying a ticket to go to Rockaway Beach. A train stopped at the station, bound for another place. Two men ran forward to catch it. One of the men reached the platform of the car without mishap, though the train was already moving. The other man, carrying a package, jumped aboard the car, but seemed unsteady as if about to fall. A guard on the car, who had held the door open, reached forward to help him in, and another guard on the platform pushed him from behind. In this act, the package was dislodged, and fell upon the rails. It was a package of small size, about fifteen inches long, and was covered by a newspaper. In fact it contained fireworks, but there was nothing in its appearance to give notice of its contents. The fireworks when they fell exploded. The shock of the explosion threw down some scales at the other end of the platform many feet away. The scales struck the plaintiff, causing injuries for which she sues.

[1–3] The conduct of the defendant's guard, if a wrong in its relation to the holder of the package, was not a wrong in its relation to the plaintiff, standing far away. Relatively to her it was not negligence at all. Nothing in the situation gave notice that the falling package had in it the potency of peril to persons thus removed. Negligence is not actionable unless it involves the invasion of a legally protected interest, the violation of a right. "Proof of negligence in the air, so to speak, will not do." . . . "Negligence is the absence of care, according to the circumstances." . . . The plaintiff, as she stood upon the platform of the station, might claim to be protected against intentional invasion of her bodily security. Such invasion is not charged. She might claim to be protected against unintentional invasion by conduct involving in the thought of reasonable men an unreasonable hazard that such invasion would ensue. These, from the point of view of the law, were the bounds of her immunity, with perhaps some rare exceptions, survivals for the most part of ancient forms of liability, where conduct is held to be at the peril of the actor. . . . If no hazard was apparent to the eye of ordinary vigilance, an act innocent and harmless, at least to outward seeming, with reference to her, did not take to itself the quality of a tort because it happened to be a wrong, though apparently not one involving the risk of bodily insecurity, with reference to some one else. "In every instance, before negligence can be predicated of a given act, back of the act must be sought and found a duty to the individual complaining, the observance of which would have averted or avoided the injury." . . . "The ideas of negligence and duty are strictly correlative." . . . The plaintiff sues in her own right for a wrong personal to her, and not as the vicarious beneficiary of a breach of duty to another.

A different conclusion will involve us, and swiftly too, in a maze of contradictions. A guard stumbles over a package which has been left upon the platform. It seems to be a bundle of newspapers. It turns out to be a can of dynamite. To the eye of ordinary vigilance, the bundle is abandoned waste, which may be kicked or trod on with impunity. Is a passenger at the other end of the platform protected by the law against the unsuspected hazard concealed beneath the waste? If not, is the result to be any different, so far as the distant passenger is concerned, when the guard stumbles over a valise which a truckman or a porter has left upon the walk? The passenger far away, if the victim of a wrong at all, has a cause of action, not derivative, but original and primary. His claim to be protected against invasion of his bodily security is neither greater nor less because the act resulting in the invasion is a wrong to another far removed. In this case, the rights that are said to have been violated, the interests said to have been invaded, are not even of the same order. The man was not injured in his person nor even put in danger. The purpose of the act, as well as its effect, was to make his person safe. If there was a wrong to him at all, which may very well be doubted, it was a wrong to a property interest only, the safety of his package. Out of this wrong to property, which threatened injury to nothing else, there has passed, we are told, to the plaintiff by derivation or succession a right of action for the invasion of an interest of another order, the right to bodily security. The diversity of interests emphasizes the futility of the effort to build the plaintiff's right upon the basis of a wrong to some one else. The gain is one of emphasis, for a like result would follow if the interests were the same. Even then, the orbit of the danger as disclosed to the eye of reasonable vigilance would be the orbit of the duty. One who jostles one's neighbor in a crowd does not invade the rights of others standing at the outer fringe when the unintended contact casts a bomb upon the ground. The wrongdoer as to them is the man who carries the bomb, not the one who explodes it without suspicion of the danger. Life will have to be made over, and human nature transformed, before prevision so extravagant can be accepted as the norm of conduct, the customary standard to which behavior must conform.

The argument for the plaintiff is built upon the shifting meanings of such words as "wrong" and "wrongful," and shares their instability. What the plaintiff must show is "a wrong" to herself; i.e., a violation of her own right, and not merely a wrong to some one else, nor conduct "wrongful" because unsocial, but not "a wrong" to any one. We are told that one who drives at reckless speed through a crowded city street is guilty of a negligent act and therefore of a wrongful one, irrespective of the consequences. Negligent the act is, and wrongful in the sense that it is unsocial, but wrongful and unsocial in relation to other travelers, only because the eye of vigilance perceives the risk of damage. If the same act were to be committed on a speedway or a race course, it would lose its wrongful quality. The risk seasonably to be perceived defines the duty to be obeyed, and risk imports relation; it is risk to another or to others within the range of apprehension. . . . This does not mean, of course, that one who launches a destructive force is always relieved of liability, if the force, though known to be destructive, pursues an unexpected path. "It was not necessary that the defendant should have had notice of the particular method in which an accident would occur, if the possibility of an accident was clear to the ordinarily prudent eye." . . . Some acts, such as shooting are so imminently dangerous to any one who may come within reach of the missile however unexpectedly, as to impose a duty of prevision not far from that of an insurer. Even to-day, and much oftener in earlier stages of the law, one acts sometimes at one's peril. . . . Under this head, it may be, fall certain cases of what is known as transferred intent, an act willfully dangerous to A resulting by misadventure in injury to B. . . . These cases aside, wrong is defined in terms of the natural or probable, at least when unintentional. . . . The range of reasonable apprehension is at times a question for the court, and at times, if varying inferences are possible, a question for the jury. Here, by concession, there was nothing in the situation to suggest to the most cautious mind that the parcel wrapped in newpaper would spread wreckage through the station. If the guard had thrown it down knowingly and willfully, he would not have threatened the plaintiff's safety, so far as appearances could warn him. His conduct would not have involved, even then, an unreasonable probability of invasion of her bodily security. Liability can be no greater where the act is inadvertent.

[4] Negligence, like risk, is thus a term of relation. Negligence in the abstract, apart from things related, is surely not a tort, if indeed it is understandable at all. . . . Negligence is not a tort unless it results in the commission of a wrong, and the commission of a wrong imports the violation of a right, in this case, we are told, the right to be protected against interference with one's bodily security. But bodily security is protected, not against all forms of interference or aggression, but only against some. One who seeks redress at law does not make out a cause of action by showing without more that there has been damage to his person. If the harm was not willful, he must show that the act as to him had possibilities of danger so many and apparent as to entitle him to be protected against the doing of it though the harm was unintended. Affront to personality is still the keynote of the wrong. . . .

The law of causation, remote or proximate, is thus foreign to the case before us. The question of liability is always anterior to the question of the measure of the consequences that go with liability. If there is no tort to be redressed, their is no occasion to consider what damage might be recovered if there were a finding of a tort. We may assume, without deciding, that negligence, not at large or in the abstract, but in relation to the plaintiff, would entail liability for any and all consequences, however novel or extraordinary. . . . There is room for argument that a distinction is to be drawn according to the diversity of interests invaded by the act, as where conduct negligent in that it threatens an insignificant invasion of an interest in property results in an unforeseeable invasion of an interest of another order, as, e. g., one of bodily security. Perhaps other distinctions may be necessary. We do not go into the question now. The consequences to be followed must first be rooted in a wrong.

The Judgment of the Appellate Division and that of the Trial Term should be reversed, and the complaint dismissed, with costs in all courts.

ANDREWS, J. (dissenting). Assisting a passenger to board a train, the defendant's servant negligently knocked a package from his arms. It fell between the platform and the cars. Of its contents the servant knew and could know nothing. A violent explosion followed. The concussion broke some scales standing a considerable distance away. In falling, they injured the plaintiff, an intending passenger.

Upon these facts, may she recover the damages she has suffered in an action brought against the master? The result we shall reach depends upon our theory as to the nature of negligence. Is it a relative concept—the breach of some duty owing to a particular person or to particular persons? Or, where there is an act which unreasonably threatens the safety of others, is the doer liable for all its proximate consequences, even where they result in injury to one who would generally be thought to be outside the radius of danger? This is not a mere dispute as to words. We might not believe that to the average mind the dropping of the bundle would seem to involve the probability of harm to the plaintiff standing many feet away whatever might be the case as to the owner or to one so near as to be likely to be struck by its fall. If, however, we adopt the second hypothesis, we have to inquire only as to the relation between cause and effect. We deal in terms of proximate cause, not of negligence.

Negligence may be defined roughly as an act or omission which unreasonably does or may affect the rights of others, or which unreasonably fails to protect one's self from the dangers resulting from such acts. Here I confine myself to the first branch of the definition. Nor do I comment on the word "unreasonable." For present purposes it sufficiently describes that average of conduct that society requires of its members.

There must be both the act or the omission, and the right. It is the act itself, not the intent of the actor, that is important. . . . In criminal law both the intent and the result are to be considered. Intent again is material in tort actions, where punitive damages are sought, dependent on actual malice—not on merely reckless conduct. But here neither insanity nor infancy lessens responsibility. . . .

As has been said, except in cases of contributory negligence, there must be rights which are or may be affected. Often though injury has occurred, no rights of him who suffers have been touched. A licensee or trespasser upon my land has no claim to affirmative care on my part that the land be made safe. . . . Where a railroad is required to fence its tracks against cattle, no man's rights are injured should he wander upon the road because such fence is absent. . . . An unborn child may not demand immunity from personal harm. . . .

But we are told that "there is no negligence unless there is in the particular case a legal duty to take care, and this duty must be one which is owed to the plaintiff himself and not merely to others." . . . This I think too narrow a conception. Where there is the unreasonable act, and some right that may be affected there is negligence whether damage does or does not result. That is immaterial. Should we drive down Broadway at a reckless speed, we are negligent whether we strike an approaching car or miss it by an inch. The act itself is wrongful. It is a wrong not only to those who happen to be within the radius of danger, but to all who might have been there—a wrong to the public at large. Such is the language of the street. Such is the language of the courts when speaking of contributory negligence. Such again and again their language in speaking of the duty of some defendant and discussing proximate cause in cases where such a discussion is wholly irrelevant on any other theory.

Due care is a duty imposed on each one of us to protect society from unnecessary danger, not to protect A, B, or C alone.

It may well be that there is no such thing as negligence in the abstract. "Proof of negligence in the air, so to speak, will not do." In an empty world negligence would not exist. It does involve a relationship between man and his fellows, but not merely a relationship between man and those whom he might reasonably expect his act would injure; rather, a relationship between him and those whom he does in fact injure. If his act has a tendency to harm some one, it harms him a mile away as surely as it does those on the scene. We now permit children to recover for the negligent killing of the father. It was never prevented on the theory that no duty was owing to them. A husband may be compensated for the loss of his wife's services. To say the wrongdoer was negligent as to the husband as well as to the wife is merely an attempt to fit facts to theory. An insurance company paying a fire loss recovers its payment of the negligent incendiary. We speak of subrogation—of suing in the right of the insured. Behind the cloud of words in the fact they hide, that the act, wrongful as to the insured, has also injured the company. Even if it be true that the fault of father, wife, or insured will prevent recovery, it is because we consider the original negligence, not the proximate cause of the injury. . . .

In the well-known Polhemis Case, . . . Scrutton, L. J., said that the dropping of a plank was negligent, for it might injure "workman or cargo or ship." Because of either possibility, the owner of the vessel was to be made good for his loss. The act being wrongful, the doer was liable for its proximate results. Criticized and explained as this statement may have been, I think it states the law as it should be and as it is. . . .

The proposition is this: Every one owes to the world at large the duty of refraining from those acts that may unreasonably threaten the safety of others. Such an act occurs. Not only is he wronged to whom harm might reasonably be expected to result, but he also who is in fact injured, even if he be outside what would generally be thought the danger zone. There needs be duty due the one complaining, but this is not a duty to a particular individual because as to him harm might be expected. Harm to some one being the natural result of the act, not only that one alone, but all those in fact injured may complain. We have never, I think, held otherwise. . . .

If this be so, we do not have a plaintiff suing by "derivation or succession." Her action is original and primary. Her claim is for a breach of duty to herself—not that she is subrogated to any right of action of the owner of the parcel or of a passenger standing at the scene of the explosion.

The right to recover damages rests on additional considerations. The plaintiff's rights must be injured, and this injury must be caused by the negligence. We build a dam, but are negligent as to its foundations. Breaking, it injures property down stream. We are not liable if all this happened because of some reason other than the insecure foundation. But, when injuries do result from our unlawful act, we are liable for the consequences. It does not matter that they are unusual, unexpected, unforeseen, and unforeseeable. But there is one limitation. The damages must be so connected with the negligence that the latter may be said to be the proximate cause of the former.

These two words have never been given an inclusive definition. What is a cause in a legal sense, still more what is a proximate cause, depend in each case upon many considerations, as does the existence of negligence itself. Any philosophical doctrine of causation does not help us. A boy throws a stone into a pond. The ripples spread. The water level rises. The history of that pond is altered to all eternity. It will be altered by other causes also. Yet it will be forever the resultant of all causes combined. Each one will have an influence. How great only omniscience can say. You may speak of a chain, or, if you please, a net. An analogy is of little aid. Each cause brings about future events. Without each the future would not be the same. Each is proximate in the sense it is essential. But that is not what we mean by the word. Nor on the other hand do we mean sole cause. There is no such thing.

Should analogy be thought helpful, however, I prefer that of a stream. The spring, starting on its journey, is joined by tributary after tributary. The river, reaching the ocean, comes from a hundred sources. No man may say whence any drop of water is derived. Yet for a time distinction may be possible. Into the clear creek, brown swamp water flows from the left. Later, from the right comes water stained by its clay bed. The three may remain for a space, sharply divided. But at least inevitable no trace of separation remains. They are so commingled that all distinction is lost.

As we have said, we cannot trace the effect of an act to the end, if end there is. Again however, we may trace it part of the way. A murder at Serajevo may be the necessary antecedent to an assassination in London twenty years hence. An overturned lantern may burn all Chicago. We may follow the fire from the shed to the last building. We rightly say the fire started by the lantern caused its destruction.

A cause, but not the proximate cause. What we do mean by the word "proximate" is that, because of convenience, of public policy, of a rough sense of justice, the law arbitrarily declines to trace a series of events beyond a certain point. This is not logic. It is practical politics. Take our rule as to fires. Sparks from my burning haystack set on fire my house and my neighbor's. I may recover from a negligent railroad. He may not. Yet the wrongful act as directly harmed the one as the other. We may regret that the line was drawn just where it was, but drawn somewhere it had to be. We said the act of the railroad was not the proximate cause of our neighbor's fire. Cause it surely was. The words we used were simply indicative of our notions of public policy. Other courts think differently. But somewhere they reach the point where they cannot say the stream comes from any one source.

Take an illustration given in an unpublished manuscript by a distinguished and helpful writer on the law of torts. A chauffeur negligently collides with another car which is filled with dynamite, although he could not know it. An explosion follows. A, walking on the sidewalk nearby, is killed. B, sitting in a window of a building opposite, is cut by flying glass. C, likewise sitting in a window a block away, is similarly injured. And a further illustration: A nursemaid, ten blocks away, startled by the noise, involuntarily drops a baby from her arms to the walk. We are told that C may not recover while A may. As to B it is a question for court or jury. We will all agree that the baby might not. Because, we are again told, the chauffeur had no reason to believe his conduct involved any risk of injuring either C or the baby. As tho then he was not negligent.

But the chauffeur, being negligent in risking the collision, his belief that the scope of the harm he might do would be limited is immaterial. His act unreasonably jeopardized the safety of any one who might be affected by it. C's injury and that of the baby were directly traceable to the collision. Without that, the injury would not have happened. C had the right to sit in his office, secure from such dangers. The baby was entitled to use the sidewalk with reasonable safety.

The true theory is, it seems to me, that the injury to C, if in truth he is to be denied recovery, and the injury to the baby, is that their several injuries were not the proximate reason of the negligence. And here not what the chauffeur had reason to believe would be the result of his conduct, but what the prudent would foresee, may have a bearing—may have some bearing, for the problem of proximate cause is not to be solved by any one consideration. It is all a question of expediency. There are no fixed rules to govern our judgment. There are simply matters of which we may take account. We have in a somewhat different connection spoken of "the stream of events." We have asked whether that stream was deflected—whether it was forced into new and unexpected channels. . . . This is rather rhetoric than law. There is in truth little to guide us other than common sense.

There are some hints that may help us. The proximate cause, involved as it may be with many other causes, must be, at the least, something without which the event would not happen. The court must ask itself whether there was a natural and continuous sequence between cause and effect. Was the one a substantial factor in producing the other? Was there a direct connection between them, without too many intervening causes? Is the effect of cause on result not too attenuated? Is the cause likely, in the usual judgment of mankind, to produce the result? Or by the exercise of prudent foresight, could the result be foreseen? Is the result too remote from the cause, and here we consider remoteness in time and space. . . . Clearly we must so consider, for the greater the distance either in time or space, the more surely do other causes intervene to affect the result. When a lantern is overturned, the firing of a shed is a fairly direct consequence. Many things contribute to the spread of the conflagration—the force of the wind, the direction and width of streets, the character of intervening structures, other factors. We draw an uncertain and wavering line, but draw it we must as best we can.

Once again, it is all a question of fair judgment, always keeping in mind the fact that we endeavor to make a rule in each case that will be practical and in keeping with the general understanding of mankind.

Here another question must be answered. In the case supposed, it is said, and said correctly, that the chauffeur is liable for the direct effect of the explosion, although he had no reason to suppose it would follow a collision. "The fact that the injury occurred in a different manner than that which might have been expected does not prevent the chauffeur's negligence from being in law the cause of the injury." But the natural results of a negligent act—the results which a prudent man would or should foresee—do have a bearing upon the decision as to proximate cause. We have said so repeatedly. What should be foreseen? No human foresight would suggest that a collision itself might injure one a block away. On the contrary, given an explosion, such a possibility might be reasonably expected. I think the direct connection, the foresight of which the courts speak, assumes prevision of the explosion, for the immediate results of which, at least, the chauffeur is responsible.

It may be said this is unjust. Why? In fairness he should make good every injury flowing from his negligence. Not because of tenderness toward him we say he need not answer for all that follows his wrong. We look back to the catastrophe, the fire kindled by the spark, or the explosion. We trace the consequences, not indefinitely, but to a certain point. And to aid us in fixing that point we ask what might ordinarily be expected to follow the fire or the explosion.

This last suggestion is the factor which must determine the case before us. The act upon which defendant's liability rests is knocking an apparently harmless package onto the platform. The act was negligent. For its proximate consequences the defendant is liable. If its contents were broken, to the owner; if it fell upon and crushed a passenger's foot, then to him; if it exploded and injured one in the immediate vicinity, to him also as to A in the illustration. Mrs. Palsgraf was standing some distance away. How far cannot be told from the record—apparently 25 or 30 feet, perhaps less. Except for the explosion, she would not have been injured. We are told by the appellant in his brief, "It cannot be denied that the explosion was the direct cause of the plaintiff's injuries." So it was a substantial factor in producing the result—there was here a natural and continuous sequence—direct connection. The only intervening cause was that, instead of blowing her to the ground, the concussion smashed the weighing machine which in turn fell upon her. There was no remoteness in time, little in space. And surely, given such an explosion as here, it needed no great foresight to predict that the natural result would be to injure one on the platform at no greater distance from its scene than was the plaintiff. Just how no one might be able to predict. Whether by flying fragments, by broken glass, by wreckage of machines or structures no one could say. But injury in some form was most probable.

Under these circumstances I cannot say as a matter of law that the plaintiff's injuries were not the proximate result of the negligence. That is all we have before us. The court refused to so charge. No request was made to submit the matter to the jury as a question of fact, even would that have been proper upon the record before us.

The judgment appealed from should be affirmed, with costs.

POUND, LEHMAN, and KELLOGG, JJ., concur with CARDOZO, C. J.

ANDREWS, J., dissents in opinion in which CRANE and O'BRIEN, JJ., concur.

Judgment reversed, etc.

The court, in an oft-quoted decision authored by Judge Cardozo, held that the defendant was not liable (see Table 8–2). The court reasoned that the defendant's conduct did not create an unreasonable risk of harm to the plaintiff and that the injury she sustained was not a foreseeable one. "Proof of negligence in the air," the court said, "will not do." The wrong in relationship

TABLE 8.2

PROXIMATE CAUSE	
MAJORITY RULE	**MINORITY RULE**
CARDOZO •Defendant is liable for all reasonably foreseeable consequences of his negligence. He owes a duty of care to the reasonably foreseeable plaintiff.	ANDREWS •Defendant owes a duty to world at large and not just to those in "danger zone." • Similar to "direct causation" : defendant is liable for all consequences flowing directly from his actions no matter how unforeseeable.
EXCEPTIONS TO CARDOZO RULE	
•"Eggshell skull" rule - defendant must take plaintiff as he finds him. •Defendant is liable for harm occurring in an unforeseen manner if harm is of the same general type that made defendant's conduct negligent. •Defendant is liable if plaintiff is member of class to which there is general foreseeability of harm even if plaintiff was not particularly foreseeble. •Defendant is liable even if there is an unforeseeable intervening cause leading to same type of harm threatened by defendant's negligence.	

to the passenger holding the package did not extend to the plaintiff. According to the Cardozo rule, which is generally followed today, ". . . [a] wrong is defined in terms of the natural and probable, at least when unintentional."

Judge Andrews, in his famous dissent, argued that the defendant had a duty to "protect society from unnecessary danger, not to protect A, B or C alone." According to Andrews, "every one owes to the world at large the duty of refraining from those acts that may unreasonably threaten the safety of others. . . . Not only is he wronged to whom harm might reasonably be expected to result, but he also who is in fact injured, even if he be outside what would generally be thought the danger zone." (Cardozo's formulation of foreseeability is often referred to as the "zone of danger" test.) Judge Andrews did realize that liability must be cut off at some point. Although he fell short of defining the cutoff point, he did suggest that if the result were "too remote from the cause" in terms of time and space or if there were too many "intervening causes," the defendant's negligence should not be considered the proximate cause of the plaintiff's injuries.

DIRECT CAUSATION

Andrews' position parallels that of a view commonly known as direct causation. Under this view a defendant is liable for all consequences of his or her negligent acts, no matter how unforeseeable those consequences may be, so long as they flow directly from his or her actions. A famous case that illustrates the direct causation view is *In Re Polemis,* 3 K. B. 560 (Eng. 1921). In *Polemis,* while the defendants were unloading a ship, which they had chartered from the plaintiffs, they negligently dropped a plank into the hold. Somehow the plank struck a spark, which ignited petroleum the ship was carrying, and the resulting fire destroyed the ship. Although plainly no one could reasonably have foreseen that dropping a plank would strike a spark and destroy the entire ship, the defendants were held liable because the fire was the direct result of their negligent act.

Although the direct causation rule is commonly criticized because a logical extension of the rule would result in limitless liability, proponents of the view argue that a loss should be borne by the guilty rather than by the innocent. The courts that follow the direct causation rule will not take into account the extent of the harm, the foreseeability of the result, the manner in which the injury occurred, or the timing of the cause and effect.

DUTY VS. PROXIMATE CAUSE

You will probably notice in the course of reading opinions that courts frequently blur the issues of duty and proximate cause together. In fact, the *Palsgraf* opinion itself was centered around a discussion of duty. The question, as posed by Cardozo, was whether the defendant had a duty of care to the plaintiff. Whether phrased in terms of duty or proximate cause, the question is essentially the same. A defendant is liable only if his or her conduct poses a foreseeable risk to the plaintiff. Similarly, a defendant owes a duty of care only if there is a foreseeable risk to the plaintiff. Keep in mind, however, that proximate cause is basically a policy question. It allows the courts to cut off liability in those cases where it would be inherently unfair to hold a defendant liable.

EXCEPTIONS TO THE CARDOZO RULE

Although the Cardozo position has generally been followed by American courts, there are a few notable exceptions. Under these exceptions recovery is allowed even though the consequences are arguably unforeseeable.

"EGGSHELL SKULL" RULE

The first exception requires that a defendant must "take his plaintiff as he finds him" (*Watson v. Rinderknecht*, 84 N.W. 798 (Minn. 1901)). Under the so-called "eggshell skull" rule, if the plaintiff suffers any foreseeable injury, the defendant is also liable for any additional unforeseen physical consequences. In other words, if a defendant inflicts a relatively minor impact on a plaintiff who dies because he has a skull of eggshell thinness, the defendant will be liable for his death. Suppose a defendant assaults a plaintiff who, unbeknownst to him, has AIDS. If the plaintiff dies from these injuries because of his weakened condition, the defendant will be liable for his death even though such injuries would have been considered minor to any healthy individual.

SAME GENERAL TYPE OF HARM BUT UNUSUAL MANNER

In the second exception to the *Palsgraf* general rule a defendant is liable if the harm suffered by the plaintiff is of the general type that made the defendant's conduct negligent even if the harm occurs in an unusual manner. Suppose a defendant hands a loaded pistol to a small child, who carries it over to the plaintiff. In the process of handing the pistol to the plaintiff, if the child drops it and the gun goes off and wounds the plaintiff, the defendant is liable. The rationale is that the risk of accidental discharge is the same kind of general risk that made the defendant's conduct negligent initially. The fact that the discharge occurs by an unforeseeable means (dropping the gun) is irrelevant.

If, however, the child drops the gun on someone's foot, causing injuries, the defendant is not liable. The risk of injuring someone by dropping a gun on his foot is not one of the risks that makes the defendant's conduct negligent. (Restatement (Second) of Torts Sec. 281, illustration 3).

PLAINTIFF MEMBER OF FORESEEABLE CLASS

The same rationale is applicable when injury occurs to a plaintiff that is not a particularly foreseeable plaintiff. As long as the plaintiff is a member of a class to which there is a general foreseeability of harm, the defendant is liable. To illustrate, suppose a defendant's car carelessly collides with a car containing dynamite and the plaintiff, a pedestrian on a sidewalk near the collision point, is injured by the ensuing explosion. Even though there is no way she could have known the car contained dynamite, the defendant is liable because a reasonable driver should realize that careless driving can injure pedestrians. Therefore, the plaintiff is a member of a class (pedestrians) to whom harm is a foreseeable consequence of reckless driving. The fact that the harm occurs in a different manner than might be anticipated does not absolve the defendant of liability (Restatement (Second) of Torts Sec. 281, illustration 2).

INTERVENING CAUSES

An **intervening cause** is anything that occurs after the defendant's negligent act and that contributes to the plaintiff's injury (Restatement (Second) of Torts Sec. 441(1)). If the intervening cause rises to such a level of importance that it precludes the defendant's negligence from being the proximate cause of the plaintiff's injury, it becomes a superseding cause (Restatement (Second) of Torts Sec. 440). A **superseding cause** supersedes or cancels out the defendant's liability. If the defendant should have foreseen the possibility that an intervening cause or one like it might occur, he or she remains liable (see Table 8–3).

Examples of intervening forces can be seen in the hypothetical cases listed above in the section on Foreseeability. In the scenario in which the wounded plaintiff died as a result of the doctor's malpractice, the doctor would be considered an intervening cause. Similarly, the person who caused the accident in which the plaintiff's ambulance was involved would also be an intervening cause. The question in these cases is whether the negligence of others was sufficiently foreseeable that the defendant was negligent in not anticipating and guarding against such negligence. If the negligence of third persons is not surprising, then any acts of the defendant that precipitate the third person's conduct will be considered a proximate cause of the plaintiff's injuries.

Is it surprising that an ambulance might be involved in an accident as a result of someone's negligence? Probably not, and if not, the defendant will

TABLE 8.3

LIABILITY	
DEFENDANT IS LIABLE	DEFENDANT IS NOT LIABLE
Intervening acts	Superseding acts
Accidents	"Act of God"
Medical malpractice of doctor occurring after defendant's negligence	Gross medical malpractice of doctor occurring after defendant's negligence
Escape attempts	Bizarre escape response to defendant's negligence
Rescue	Grossly careless acts of rescuer
Foreseeable negligence of others	Unforeseeable negligence
Foreseeable criminal or intentionally tortious conduct	Unforeseeable criminal or intentionally tortious conduct

remain the proximate cause of the plaintiff's injuries. Is it surprising that someone admitted to a hospital might be further injured as a result of the negligence of his caretaker? Most courts have found medical malpractice to be sufficiently foreseeable, as long as it is not gross malpractice, and therefore not a superseding cause. Similarly, if the defendant causes the plaintiff to be in a weakened state, making him susceptible to disease or accidents, he will be held liable for any subsequent disease or accidents the plaintiff suffers. In the scenario in which the plaintiff is killed in an attempt to flee from the defendant, the plaintiff's attempted escape will not be a superseding cause as long as the plaintiff's response was not totally extraordinary or bizarre. If someone attempts to rescue the plaintiff and causes part or all of the plaintiff's injuries, the defendant will be liable to the plaintiff and to the rescuer as well for any injuries sustained by either. If the rescuer, on the other hand, is grossly negligent, his conduct will be considered a superseding cause.

The rationale that the foreseeable negligence of others will not be considered a superseding cause has been used to hold tavern owners liable for the negligence of their intoxicated patrons. Although courts are less likely to impose such liability on social hosts, some courts have done so when the guest served was known to the host to be one who would be driving.

A third person's criminal conduct or intentional tortious act may also, in some cases, be sufficiently foreseeable that such conduct will not be considered a superseding cause. As a practical matter, however, proving that the risk of such criminal or tortious conduct was actually foreseeable is often difficult. Suppose a defendant negligently causes a traffic accident. As a result of the accident gasoline leaks onto the road. A passerby throws down a match, igniting the gasoline, causing an adjoining forest to burn down. The question is whether the passerby's act was intentional or negligent and if intentional whether it was sufficiently foreseeable that the defendant should be held liable for the damage sustained to the forest.

SUPERSEDING CAUSES

An "act of God," such as being struck by lightning, is considered a superseding cause since it is an act of nature that is extraordinary and not foreseeable. If our plaintiff in the hypothetical cases given above were killed by a bolt of lightning while in the process of running from the defendant, the lightning would be considered a superseding cause that would relieve the defendant of liability.

Another example of a superseding cause is a common carrier's negligent delay in the transporting of goods, resulting in the destruction of the goods by a natural catastrophe, such as a flood or fire. Even though the delay might clearly be the cause of the damage, since the goods would not have been destroyed had there been no delay, most courts would consider the act of nature a superseding cause. To avoid this holding a plaintiff must show that an increase in the risk of such a catastrophe as a result of the delay was foreseeable.

UNFORESEEABLE INTERVENTION

Thus far we have looked at cases where the intervening cause was foreseeable. If the intervention was not foreseeable but, in fact, led to the same type of harm as that threatened by the defendant's negligence, the courts typically find the intervention not to be a superseding cause (Restatement (Second) of Torts Sec. 442B). The reasoning is that the defendant exposed the plaintiff to an unreasonable risk of harm of the same type as that which occurred. Allowing the defendant to escape liability simply because the harm was produced by an unforeseeable intervention would be unfair.

Let us consider the case of *Derdiarian v. Felix Contracting Corp.*, 414 N.E.2d 666 (N.Y.Ct.App. 1981) as an illustration of this principle. In this case the plaintiff, an employee of a subcontractor, was sealing a gas main at a work site in the street when he was struck by a driver who had just suffered an epileptic seizure and lost control of his vehicle. When struck, the plaintiff was catapulted into the air and landed in 400°F liquid enamel, causing him to be ignited into a fireball, from which he miraculously survived. The plaintiff alleged that the defendant contracting company had failed to take adequate measures to ensure the safety of workers on the excavation site. The defendant argued that the plaintiff was injured as a result of the driver's negligence and that there was no causal link between the defendant's breach of duty and the plaintiff's injuries. The court refused to find the driver's negligence a superseding cause, noting that an intervening act does not serve as a superseding cause "where the risk of the intervening act occurring is the very same risk which renders the actor negligent."

JURY QUESTION

The issue of proximate cause is a jury question as long as there is a possibility that reasonable persons could differ on this issue. The judge must first formulate the appropriate legal rule in the form of a jury instruction. But once that standard has been formulated, the final decision is a factual one left to the jury.

APPLICATION

In the case of Gertrude's attack on Teddy and Mr. Dooright, Gertrude was unquestionably the actual cause of Teddy's and Mr. Dooright's injuries. Of course, the Baxters might argue that Mr. Dooright's injuries were due to Teddy's negligence in entering their backyard. Under the "but for" test, however, the rebuttal would be that but for the Baxters' negligence in leaving their gate unlocked Teddy would not have been able to enter the yard. Even under the substantial factor test the Baxters' failure to lock their gate would be a significant factor in the cause of Mr. Dooright's injuries. Assuming that Teddy would not have been able to enter the Baxters' backyard except for the presence of the unlocked gate, both he and the Baxters would be considered causes of Mr. Dooright's injuries. As such they would both be liable for his injuries.

The Baxters would also be considered the proximate cause of Teddy's and Mr. Dooright's injuries. It is reasonably foreseeable that if a person fails to lock a gate to a yard housing a watchdog, someone, especially a child, will enter the yard and be attacked.

The Baxters might argue that Mr. Dooright's volunteering to rescue Teddy, which was of his own volition and not a duty imposed upon him, was a superseding cause that should absolve them of liability. Remember, however, that rescue is not considered an intervening cause unless it is performed in a grossly negligent manner. Based on the famous Cardozo rationale that "danger invites rescue," a rescue is foreseeable where the defendant's negligence has created a danger that could result in injury to somebody. An argument on the part of the Baxters that Teddy's negligence was a superseding cause would also fail. Such negligence was reasonably foreseeable if children were able to gain access to the Baxters' backyard via the unlocked gate.

SUMMARY

The issue of causation consists of two separate considerations—actual cause (causation of fact) and proximate cause (legal cause). If the plaintiff can prove that the defendant's actions were the actual and factual cause of her injuries, she has proven actual cause. If the plaintiff can further prove that her injuries were a reasonably foreseeable result of the defendant's conduct, she can show proximate cause.

The "but for" and "substantial factor" tests are used in proving actual cause. The plaintiff bears the burden of proving actual cause and must do so by a preponderance of the evidence. If the plaintiff cannot prove which defendant actually caused his injuries, he can shift the burden back on the defendants to show who actually caused the harm using the theory of alternate liability or market share liability. If the tortfeasors are unable to prove they did not cause the plaintiff's injuries, they will all be found liable. If a plaintiff can prove the existence of a common plan or that the defendants assisted or encouraged each other in accomplishing a tortious result, he has proved actual causation using the concerted action theory.

The purpose of proximate or legal cause is to restrict a defendant's liability by absolving him or her of liability where the plaintiff's injury occurred as a result of a series of highly improbable or extraordinary events stemming from the defendant's negligence. The question of proximate cause is a policy question; the question of actual cause is a factual one. The issue of foreseeability was addressed most notably in *Palsgraf* in which Judge Cardozo denied recovery to the plaintiff because she was not a foreseeable one. Justice Andrews, on the other hand, argued that one owes a duty to the "world at large" and not just to those in the "danger zone." Andrews' position parallels the view of those courts who espouse the theory of direct causation.

The Cardozo position is generally followed by most American courts. There are, however, a few notable exceptions. First, under the so-called "eggshell skull" rule, if a plaintiff suffers any foreseeable injury, the defendant is liable for any additional unforeseeable physical consequences. Second, a defendant is liable if the harm suffered by the plaintiff is of the general type that made the defendant's conduct negligent even if the harm occurs in an unanticipated manner. Third, a defendant is liable as long as the plaintiff is a member of a class to which there is a reasonable foreseeability of harm even if the plaintiff herself is not a particularly foreseeable plaintiff.

PRACTICE POINTERS

Answering interrogatories is often a task delegated to paralegals because, quite frankly, most attorneys do not enjoy it. Nevertheless, it is an important job and requires careful consideration since those answers can be used in court against the client.

Attorneys vary in their philosophy as to how much information should be disclosed in responding to interrogatories. Remember that the spirit of discovery is to promote the open exchange of information so that settlement of the case can be facilitated. One does not, however, unnecessarily divulge information that weakens one's case. One should answer questions as candidly as possible without revealing information that is not specifically requested. Attorneys who take a somewhat obstructionist view of discovery read questions extremely narrowly and respond by giving only that information that is absolutely required under the ethical rules of conduct. When confronted with such attorneys your firm may be forced to go to court to secure an order mandating disclosure.

You should be aware that under certain circumstances you are not required to answer interrogatories. For example, if the questions are protected by any type of privilege or fall under the attorney work-product rule, you should object and refuse to answer them. Similarly, interrogatories that are burdensome and require excessive expense or work to answer might also be objectionable. Discovery can be used as a tool of intimidation, as when one side burdens the other with reams of interrogatories that require unreasonable amounts of time and investigatory work to complete and that provide little useful information. Some courts have taken steps to curtail this kind of abuse and have limited the number of interrogatories each side can ask.

Assuming the questions before you are not privileged and are reasonable, you will need to read the entire case file before drafting any answers. Some firms ask that clients provide a first draft of their answers, while other firms request that the client answer interrogatories in conjunction with an attorney or legal assistant. Tangible evidence must be available to support every answer. You must have witness statements, documents, expert testimony, or other comparable evidence to justify your answer. Reasonable efforts must be made to answer all questions. Nonresponsive or evasive answers can lead to sanctions under the rules of discovery.

Sample Answers To Interrogatories

1. Give a concise statement as to how Plaintiff contends the incident complained of in his complaint occurred.

I entered the Baxters' yard through their back gate so that I could get my ball. The gate was not latched so all I had to do was pull up on the latch and the gate opened. I walked across the lawn to pick up my ball

Continued on next page

PRACTICE POINTERS—Continued

and was halfway back when Gertrude came running toward me. Her teeth were bared as she lunged at me and knocked me down. I tried to get back up but she grabbed my right leg and wouldn't let go. I was in horrible pain during this whole time and hurt so bad I felt like throwing up. The more I screamed and cried the more she bit into my leg and hurt me.

Finally a man (Mr. Dooright) came running into the yard and began kicking and yelling at Gertrude. When she went after him she let loose of me and I was able to limp away. I was still in horrible pain but I was so afraid that I was able to drag myself, with the help of my friend, Jonathan Turner, over to the gate.

2. List each and every witness to the incident complained of in Plaintiff's complaint.

See Plaintiff's response to Interrogatory No. 1.

3. State the substance and content of every report of which Plaintiff is aware that concerns the incident complained of in Plaintiff's complaint.

See attached Police Report dated June , 19 , prepared by officer Smart of the Paradise Police Department and bearing the number DR#91-7763.

4. State the substance of each and every conversation between Plaintiff and any third party relating to any actions complained of in Plaintiff's complaint.

Objection to this question as it relates to conversations between Plaintiff and Plaintiff's attorney in violation of the attorney-client privilege.

With respect to all other conversations, summaries are as follows:

Plaintiff told his mother that Gertrude hurt him badly and that he had been terrified during the attack. . . .

A defendant is expected to foresee the possibility of an intervening cause. Even if the intervening cause is not foreseeable but the kind of harm suffered by the plaintiff is, the defendant will remain liable. If an intervening cause rises to such a level that it becomes a superseding cause, the defendant is absolved of liability. The foreseeable negligence of others is not considered a superseding cause. Neither is a person's criminal or intentionally tortious conduct considered a superseding cause if it is sufficiently foreseeable.

TORT TEASERS

1. Assume you are working for the firm representing the Baxters. Draft answers to the interrogatories found at the end of Chapter 7. Give truthful, responsive answers but phrase them in such a manner that you answer only that which is requested. Provide no more information than what is necessary to answer the question as it is written. Do you have any basis for arguing that any of the questions are objectionable?

2. Plaintiff tries to put a can of freon in his automobile air conditioner. Defendant company, which produced the refrigerant, failed to put a warning on the can about the danger of attaching the can to the wrong side of the compressor. The evidence shows Plaintiff failed to read any instructions that were on the can. Is Defendant's failure to warn an actual cause of Plaintiff's injury? *Technical Chemical Co. v. Jacobs*, 480 S.W.2d 602 (Tex. 1972).

3. Just before Defendant's industrial "dinky" engine collides with a train on a crossing, the engineer of the "dinky" reverses the engine, shuts off the steam, and jumps. The collision causes the throttle to jar loose and the "dinky" engine backs up, gathers momentum, and travels around a loop to a second crossing where it collides with a train. Plaintiff, who is a passenger on the train, is injured in the second collision. Even though the second collision occurred in an unforeseeable manner, should Defendant be held liable? *Bunting v. Hogsett*, 21 A.31 (Pa. 1890).

4. Suppose Defendant drives a truck at excessive speed. Which of the following consequences do you think are foreseeable?

a. The truck narrowly misses a pregnant woman, who is frightened into a miscarriage. *Mitnick v. Whelan Bros.*, 163 A. 414 (Conn. 1932).

b. Defendant injures a man who suffers a second accident six months later while he is walking on crutches as a result of the first accident. *Squires v. Reynolds*, 5 A.2d 877 (Conn. 1939).

c. A truck knocks a taxi cab up against a stone wall, the wall is weakened, and as a result a stone falls off the top of the wall as the taxi is being disengaged from the wall. A pedestrian is injured when the stone falls on her. *In Re Guardian Casualty Co.*, 2 N.Y.S.2d 232 (1938).

5. A waitress employed at Defendant's restaurant spills hot coffee on Plaintiff's lap, resulting in first-degree burns. When Plaintiff jumps up she strikes her knee on an adjoining stool, requiring her leg to be put in a cast. Because of her obesity and neurotic anxiety, Plaintiff is disabled for eight months. If the normal recovery time is one to two weeks, should Defendant be held liable for the full extent of damages? *Thompson v. Lupone*, 62 A.2d 861 (Conn. 1948).

6. Defendant railroad company carries a young girl past her station and puts her off the train near a "hobo jungle," the favorite haunt of many unsavory criminal characters. On the way back to town she is raped by two unidentified persons. Is the defendant the proximate cause of the plaintiff's injuries? *Hines v. Garrett,* 108 S.E. 690 (Va. 1921).

7. A rock radio station with an extensive teenage audience sponsors a contest that rewards the first contestant to locate a particular disc jockey. Two minors, driving in separate automobiles in pursuit of the illustrious disc jockey, reach speeds of up to 80 mph. One of the minors negligently forces another car off the highway, killing the driver. A wrongful death action is filed against the radio station. Should the rock station be held liable or is the negligence of the minor a superseding cause? *Weirum v. RKO General Inc.,* 539 P.2d 36 (Cal. 1975).

KEY TERMS

■ **Intervening cause**
Act that contributes to the plaintiff's injuries but does not relieve the defendant of liability.

■ **Superseding cause**
Act that contributes to the plaintiff's injuries to the extent that the defendant is relieved of liability.

NEGLIGENCE: DAMAGES

CHAPTER OBJECTIVES

In this chapter you will learn to:

- Categorize damages.
- Recognize the various components of damages.
- Appreciate the practical problems inherent in calculating damages.
- Recognize the limitations on what a plaintiff can recover.
- Appreciate the controversy surrounding punitive damages.
- Distinguish between wrongful death and survival actions.

Liability without damages is like a car with no wheels. If the defendant is clearly liable but the plaintiff suffers minimal injuries, recovery will also be minimal. Clearly, if the attorney's fees exceed the anticipated recovery, the client cannot afford to have an attorney take the case. Therefore, the attorneys representing Teddy and Mr. Dooright will want to determine early if the anticipated damages warrant the expenditure of time and resources necessary to litigate the case.

CATEGORIES OF DAMAGES

Damages are generally divided into three categories: compensatory damages, punitive damages, and nominal damages (see Table 9–1). **Compensatory damages** are designed to compensate the victim for her losses and restore her to

TABLE 9.1 Categories of Damages

COMPENSATORY	PUNITIVE	NOMINAL
•To compensate and restore. 1. Special damages are damages that are special to plaintiff. 2. General damages are damages that are generally anticipated.	•Designed to punish.	•No actual damages.

the position she was in before she sustained her injuries. **Punitive damages** are intended to punish the defendant. **Nominal damages** are awarded when no actual damages are proved but a tort is shown to have been committed.

Compensatory damages are further divided into two categories: general damages and special damages. **General damages** are those that generally result from the kind of conduct engaged in by the defendant; **special damages** are special or unique to the plaintiff. A good example of general damages is compensation for pain and suffering. Anyone injured in a motor vehicle accident, for example, will be expected to endure a certain amount of pain and suffering as a result of the injuries. Examples of special damages are medical expenses, lost wages, and future impairment of earnings. In most cases, special damages must be specifically pleaded in a complaint while general damages do not have to be.

The purpose of punitive damages is to deter future misconduct by the defendant and similarly situated defendants. Punitive damages are not intended to make the plaintiff whole but instead are used to punish defendants who have acted with ill-will or in conscious disregard for the welfare of others. Such damages are reserved for those defendants who act in a particularly egregious manner.

Nominal damages are awarded in intentional and strict liability cases where liability is established but where no actual harm occurred. A jury could find the defendant liable for assaulting the plaintiff. But it could conclude that the plaintiff, although wronged, suffered no actual harm and could award nominal damages of $10. Nominal damages cannot be awarded in a negligence case since negligence requires proof of an actual injury. Nominal damages allow a plaintiff to be vindicated but do nothing in the way of compensating either the plaintiff or the attorneys involved. If nominal damages are anticipated, an hourly or set fee will usually be the basis for reimbursement rather than a contingency fee arrangement.

Table 9–2 lists some questions plaintiffs and defendants may have about damages. The remainder of the chapter will be structured around these questions.

TABLE 9.2

QUESTIONS PLAINTIFFS ASK ABOUT DAMAGES
•Can they prove pain and suffering? •Can they prove impaired present and future earning capacity? •Are they entitled to recover for shortened life expectancy? •Can they recover for expenses for which they have already been reimbursed? •Can they recover attorney's fees? •Are they entitled to punitive damages? •What can they recover for property damage? •Can spouses, parents or children of victims recover for "loss of consortium?" •Can spouses, parents or children recover if the victim dies?

QUESTIONS DEFENDANTS ASK ABOUT DAMAGES
•Should plaintiffs be compensated for pain and suffering? •Can an award be discounted to present value? •Can an award be paid using a structured settlement? •Did the plaintiff mitigate her damages? •Did the plaintiff suffer actual physical harm?

ILLUSTRATION OF DAMAGES

Let us consider the facts of a real case to illustrate the various components of damages. In *Anderson v. Sears, Roebuck & Co.*, 377 F.Supp. 136 (E.D.La. 1974), the plaintiff was a young child who was severely burned when the house in which she was living was consumed by a fire that was started by a heater negligently manufactured by the defendant. The child was burned over 40 percent of her body, with third-degree burns covering 80 percent of her scalp. She was hospitalized for twenty-eight days, during which time she developed infections and related problems and underwent repeated skin grafts. Furthermore, she had to undergo extensive subsequent operations and treatment.

The plaintiff's compensatory damages were divided into five categories: past and future medical expenses, past physical and mental pain, future physical and mental pain, permanent disability and disfigurement, and impaired earning capacity. Future medical expenses included the anticipated cost for plastic surgeons, psychiatrists, sociologists, and private tutors. The $250,000 allocated for these damages was also intended to cover the cost of future operations.

PAIN AND SUFFERING

The jury awarded the plaintiff $600,000 for past physical and mental pain. The pain included the pain she endured during her initial and subsequent hospitalizations as well as the mental and emotional trauma she underwent, manifesting in bed wetting, having nightmares, withdrawing, and developing speech impediments. She was further awarded $750,000 for future physical and mental pain. The pain anticipated here was that of an estimated twenty-seven future operations along with the pain and crippling caused by the extensive scarring she had sustained. These damages were also intended to compensate her for the likely deprivation of social life that she would surely suffer.

The jury awarded $1,000,000 for permanent disability and disfigurement. Examples of the types of permanent losses she was expected to suffer included permanent loss and use of her legs, permanent injury to the left elbow and left arm, permanent destruction of 40 percent of her skin, permanent impairment of speech, and permanent impairment of a normal social, recreational, and educational life. The obvious problem in awarding damages in this area is that no accurate monetary value can be affixed. How does one assign a monetary value to a person's suffering? Could one million dollars, two million dollars, or any amount of money compensate the plaintiff in this case for the excruciating pain she suffered and the social rejection she would experience in the future?

Some attorneys have attempted to concretize this process by assigning a numerical value to the amount of suffering experienced on a daily, hourly, or even a minute-by-minute basis. That number is then multiplied by the total number of days, hours, or minutes the pain is expected to last. This so-called "per diem" technique has been disallowed by some courts because it can lead to deceptively high figures. The majority of courts have, however, allowed the use of this argument and leave it up to defendants to dissuade juries as to its reasonableness.

Melvin Belli, who first advocated the per diem argument, gave the following closing argument to illustrate how one might use this approach. The case involved a man with an irreparably injured back and a thirty-year life expectancy.

> You are asked to evaluate in dollars and cents what pain and suffering is. This honorable court will instruct you that a man of this age has a life expectancy of thirty years. Let's put it to you bluntly, what's pain and suffering worth? You've got to answer this question. You've got to award for this as well as the special damages and loss of wages. Let's take Pat, my client, down to the waterfront. He sees Mike, an old friend. He goes up to him and says, "Mike, I've got a job for you. It's a perfect job. You're not going to have to work any more for the rest of your life. . . . you don't have to work even one second. All you have to do is to trade me your good back for my bad one and I'll give you $5.00 a day for the rest of your life. Do you know what $5.00 a day for the rest of your life is? Why that's $60,000.00! Of course, I realize that you not going to be able to do any walking, or any swimming, or driving an automobile, or be able to sit in a movie picture show; you're going to have excruciating pain and suffering with this job, 31,000,000 seconds a year, and once you take it on, you'll never be able to relieve yourself of this, but you get $60,000,00!" Do you think Mike would take on that job for $60,000.00? M. Belli, *The Use of Demonstrative Evidence in Achieving "The More Adequate Award,"* 33–34 (1952).

Criticism of Pain and Suffering Awards. The problem of subjectivity in reference to the awarding of damages for pain and suffering has been the subject of much debate. Quantification of such damages is often difficult. Nevertheless, some argue that if the law is able to redress a businessperson who sustains commercial damage, it can do no less for those who have suffered "a more poignant infliction" (*Gray v. Washington Power Company*, 71 P. 206 (Wash. 1930)). Even though no gauge is available for measuring such damages, which are to some degree sentimental, sentiment, it has been observed, is an element in all damages. Furthermore, the reasoning goes, the lack of precision in assessing damages should not preclude their approximate measurement and they should be submitted to the best judgment of the jury.

The concept of compensating plaintiffs for their pain has been criticized, however. Some maintain that such damages should be allowed only where there is a physiological basis for the pain. Cornelius Peck, at the University of Washington Law School, argues that pain is a social and psychological as well as a physiological phenomenon (Peck, *Compensation for Pain: A Reappraisal in Light of New Medical Evidence*, 72 Mich.L.Rev. 1355 (1974)). One study he uses to illustrate his point involves a comparison between soldiers wounded in battle and civilians who had undergone surgery. Although the battle wounds probably provided a greater physiological basis for pain than did the incisions required by surgery, only a little more than 25 percent of the soldiers required relief for pain while 87 percent of the civilians requested treatment for pain (Beecher, *Relationship of Significance of Wound to Pain Experienced*, 161 J.A.M.A. 1609 (1956)). This study seems to indicate that the cause of the injury creating the pain has some bearing on the individual's perception of that pain. Therefore, pain sustained as a result of some noble endeavor may be more easily borne than pain stemming from some capricious or inexplicable cause.

The usual argument given to justify compensation for pain is that compensation brings consolation to one who has suffered. Peck argues, however, that this consolation may actually provide a reinforcement for pain behavior and may serve to increase the pain of those who are to be consoled.

One of the objectives of tort law is to allocate risks to those who cause injury rather than to innocent victims. But Peck points to a study conducted by the U.S. Department of Transportation that indicates that compensation for pain and suffering fails to achieve this objective in any kind of equitable fashion. For example, the study shows that those persons suffering losses of less than $500 recovered 4.5 times more than the economic losses they suffered whereas those victims who suffered economic losses of $25,000 or more recovered only 30 percent of their losses (1 U.S. Dept. of Transportation, *Economic Consequences of Automobile Accident Injuries*, 17 (1970)).

Equitable compensation of victims remains an illusory albeit noble goal of tort law. The struggle continues in the allocation of damages to balance the needs of plaintiffs, defendants, and the rest of society.

IMPAIRED EARNING CAPACITY

The last item addressed in *Anderson* is that of impaired earning capacity. The court concluded that the plaintiff's injuries would preclude her from earning a living for the rest of her life and that, therefore, the jury's award of $330,000 for impaired earning capacity was appropriate.

Two types of recovery fall under the category of impaired earnings: recovery for past earnings and recovery for prospective future losses. In dealing with past earnings, recovery is relatively simple to calculate if the plaintiff was employed at fixed wages. If he or she was unemployed or if the wages cannot be computed exactly, the plaintiff will have to use circumstantial evidence to show impairment of earning capacity.

Future loss of earning capacity is more difficult to compute. Jurors must first determine how long a plaintiff might be expected to live. Mortality tables published by insurance actuaries are used in this process. Jurors are also allowed to take into consideration the plaintiff's personal habits, prior health, and individual characteristics in determining the plaintiff's projected life span. Some creative attorneys use economists as experts to testify to a diminution of the plaintiff's earning capacity. Loss of future earnings is, of course, applicable only when the plaintiff can show that the injuries are permanent.

SHORTENED LIFE EXPECTANCY

Although damages for loss of prospective earnings have been allowed, damages for the shortening of the plaintiff's life expectancy traditionally have been denied. Under the common law damages for loss of life were precluded unless provided for by statute. The courts have reasoned that the same rule must be applicable to damages for a shortened life. Furthermore, there has been a desire to avoid an issue so fraught with incalculable variables as well as a fear that such compensation would result in a duplication of damages. A few courts have, however, considered shortening of life expectancy as a distinct compensable harm.

COLLATERAL SOURCE RULE

A plaintiff is often reimbursed for her out-of-pocket expenses, including lost wages and payments for medical care, by her insurance company. Nevertheless, under the **collateral source rule** she is entitled to recover for these damages again from the defendant. Similarly, a plaintiff can recover for lost wages even if she has been reimbursed through sick pay provided by her employer or by disability benefits through worker's compensation. Social Security disability benefits and welfare payments also do not count against a plaintiff's recovery under this rule. Even if a plaintiff receives free services from friends or family members, she may recover the reasonable value of those services. In some cases, such as worker's compensation, statutory requirements mandate that the plaintiff pay back the benefits she receives.

The rationale underlying the collateral source rule is that the tortfeasor ought not to gain from benefits received by the plaintiff. Furthermore, in many cases the benefits received by the plaintiff are ones for which he has indirectly paid. If a plaintiff has paid premiums on an insurance policy, denying him double recovery would deprive him of the benefits of his investment. Furthermore, allowing the defendant to benefit from the plaintiff's investment would be unfair. In many cases the company making the plaintiff's payment has a right of reimbursement out of any judgment the plaintiff receives (known as the right of subrogation). A medical insurance plan typically requires that the plaintiff reimburse the company out of any judgment he receives, thereby precluding double recovery. Most courts have held that evidence of collateral benefits is inadmissible.

EXPENSES OF LITIGATION

Although in England the winning party is entitled to recover her expenses of litigation, including attorney's fees, such is not the case in the United States. Most personal injury cases are handled on a contingency fee basis, in which the attorney agrees to provide services for a fee based on a percentage of the client's recovery. If there is no recovery, the attorney receives nothing. Typically, the percentage of the fee depends on whether the case is settled or litigated. A common contingency fee arrangement provides for payment of 33 ⅓ percent of the settlement and 40 percent of a final judgment. Some have suggested that, as a practical matter, punitive damages and awards for pain and suffering in effect allow a plaintiff to pay attorney's fees and still retain compensation for his or her own losses.

The contingency fee arrangement has been the subject of frequent criticism. Some maintain that it creates a conflict of interest between the attorney and the client in reference to settlement offers. In some cases attorneys receive much more than would be considered a reasonable fee for the efforts they expended. On the other hand, such a fee arrangement allows those persons who would ordinarily be financially incapable of pursuing their claims to do so. Also, remember that attorneys do not win all their cases and so those cases in which they receive nothing may balance those for which they may be overcompensated.

DAMAGES FOR PHYSICAL HARM TO PROPERTY

Damages for physical harm to property are tied to the value of the property. If the property is completely destroyed, damages are measured according to the value of the property at the time and place the tort occurred. If the property is damaged but not destroyed, the damages are measured by the difference in value before and after the tort, although the amount cannot exceed the replacement cost. If the plaintiff is merely deprived of use of the property, damages consist of the value of the use of which the plaintiff was deprived.

When we refer to value of property we are alluding to its **fair market value.** Fair market value is defined as the amount that the property could have been sold for on the open market. The assumption in this definition is that it involves a voluntary sale by a leisurely seller to a willing buyer. Note that market value is usually determined on the basis of the market at the place and time that the wrong occurred. Furthermore, market value constitutes the highest price one seeking to sell the property could have realized and not the lowest price at which it could have been sold.

Market value does not always provide adequate compensation, particularly in those cases where the property has personal value to the plaintiff and no one else. In such cases the court considers the original cost of the property, the use made of the property, and its condition at the time of the tort. The mental distress that the plaintiff suffers as a result of being deprived of the property is, however, not usually compensable.

DAMAGES IN PRODUCT LIABILITY CASES

Damages in the context of product liability cases require special consideration and will be treated separately in Chapter 14.

PUNITIVE DAMAGES

Punitive damages, which are sometimes referred to as exemplary damages, are designed to punish the tortfeasor and to deter similarly situated wrongdoers. In negligence cases they can be awarded only when the defendant's conduct is "reckless," "willful or wanton," or "with an evil mind." Punitive damages are also permitted when the defendant commits an intentional tort, such as assault or intentional infliction of emotional harm. Punitive damages are considered a windfall to the plaintiff and a jury can use its discretion to refrain from awarding them.

Punitive damages have been criticized as constituting undue compensation to the plaintiff. Some maintain that these damages are in essence criminal fines that should be paid to the state and not to the plaintiff. The counterargument is that such damages act as a deterrent to those with evil motivations. They also compensate plaintiffs for the expenses of litigation, such as attorney's fees, which they would normally have to bear themselves.

Punitive damages are more and more commonly being awarded in product liability cases. A defendant who knows of a defect and makes the product anyway is liable for punitive damages. A problem in this area that has concerned some commentators and judges is that a defendant could be bankrupted if every jury that awarded compensatory damages were also to award significant punitive damages. Hundreds of potential victims might exist to whom the defendant might be liable for millions of dollars in punitive damages. As a result the defendant could become bankrupt and future plaintiffs could be precluded from recovering even compensatory damages.

One question that arises in the area of punitive damages is whether employers, who are generally liable for the torts of their employees, should be made to pay punitive damages. The courts are split in this area but many follow the Restatement (Second) of Torts Sec. 909, which requires the payment of punitive damages only in cases where the employer had personal culpability or where the employee was working in a managerial capacity.

FORD PINTO CASE

In the infamous Ford Pinto case defendant Ford Motor Company argued that it should not be liable for punitive damages because no evidence of corporate ratification of the alleged misconduct was presented (*Grimshaw v. Ford Motor Company*, 119 Cal.App. 3d 757, 174 Cal. Rptr. 348 (1981)). In this case one plaintiff was killed and another severely injured when the Pinto in which they were riding burst into flames after being struck from the rear. The fire occurred because of a design defect in the Pinto fuel system. Ford executive management was aware of this defect but failed to alter it because of what management perceived as the prohibitive cost involved in making such a change. The appellate court concluded that substantial evidence was presented from which the jury could reasonably have inferred that Ford's management went ahead with the production of the Pinto with full knowledge of the design defect. The defect rendered the fuel tank extremely vulnerable on rear impact at low speeds and endangered the safety and lives of its occupants. The court categorized Ford's executive decision-making process as corporate malice and the jury awarded $125,000,000 in punitive damages, which was later reduced by the trial judge to $3,500,000.

One of the issues raised in this case was the propriety of the punitive damage award. Ford contended that the $3.5 million award exceeded many times over the highest award ever upheld in California as well as the maximum civil penalties that could be enforced under federal and state statutes against a manufacturer. The court was unpersuaded by this argument and pointed out that amounts awarded in other cases were irrelevant. In deciding whether an award was, as a matter of law, excessive the court considered the following factors: the degree of reprehensibility of the defendant's conduct, the amount of compensatory damages, the wealth of the defendant, and the amount that would serve as a deterrent to the defendant and others who might be inclined to engage in similar conduct.

In applying these criteria the court noted that the conduct of Ford's management was reprehensible, "endanger[ing] the lives of thousands of people" and exhibiting a "conscious and callous disregard of public safety in order to maximize corporate profits." The court also noted that even a punitive damage award of $125,000,000 amounted only to approximately .005 percent of Ford's net worth and approximately .03 percent of its 1973 net income. The court concluded that the award was far from excessive in light of its purpose as a deterrent.

RECOVERY FOR LOSS OF CONSORTIUM

Under the common law, a husband and wife were considered one. Therefore, if the wife were injured the husband could recover for **loss of consortium,** which encompasses recovery for lost services, such as companionship, sex, earnings outside the home, and so on. But since the wife had no right to services from her husband, she could recover nothing if he were injured. Under modern law, husbands and wives are both entitled to recover for loss of services.

A loss of consortium claim is a **derivative claim** in that it is derived from the spouse's underlying claim. If a husband, for example, is injured in a motor vehicle accident and successfully sues the negligent driver, the wife can then sue for loss of her husband's consortium.

Since both spouses can recover this leads to the possibility of double recovery. If the spouses were to sue in two separate actions, the wife might recover for medical expenses in one action and the husband might later recover for the same expenses by arguing that he was the one who in fact paid the expenses. To preclude double recovery, many states require that such actions be brought together.

In most jurisdictions parents can recover for medical expenses incurred as a result of injury to a child. They are also entitled to recovery for the lost services and earnings of a minor child. In cases where the child has died, more and more courts are allowing recovery for loss of the child's companionship.

Typically, children have not been allowed to recover for loss of companionship of a parent who has been injured. More recently, however, a few courts have allowed such recovery where the child is a minor and is dependent on the parent for its nurturing and development. Courts have been reluctant to get involved in this area because of the difficulty in quantifying the damages. Furthermore, the potential for duplicative claims exists when the injured parent has several minor children.

WRONGFUL DEATH AND SURVIVAL ACTIONS

Under the common law when a plaintiff died as a consequence of injuries inflicted on him by the defendant his tort action died along with him. At that point his spouse and children also lost any right to recovery. The reasoning behind this rule was that it was immoral to put a monetary value on a human life. Unfortunately, this rule increased the likelihood that defendants would kill their plaintiffs since it was cheaper for the defendant if the plaintiff died.

Lord Campbell's Act, passed in England in 1846 and after which most modern statutes are patterned, allowed recovery to families of individuals killed by tortious conduct. In accord with this act all states have passed some kind of **survival** statute, which allows the injured party's claim to survive his or her death (see Table 9–3). In most states the cause of death is irrelevant but in a few states if the death resulted from the defendant's tort, a wrongful death action and not a survival claim must be filed. All survival statutes provide that a cause of action for injury to tangible property survives the death to the plaintiff. The majority allow personal injury actions to survive

TABLE 9.3

SURVIVAL STATUTES	WRONGFUL DEATH STATUTES
•Injured party's claim survives his death. •Damages awarded to deceased's estate.	•Third parties can recover for losses they sustain as a result of victim's death. •Proceeds go to spouses, parents, or children of deceased.

as well. A few states permit claims pertaining to intangible interests, such as infliction of emotional distress and defamation, to survive. Most allow a tort action to be maintained or even initiated after the defendant's death as well. Similarly, **wrongful death** statutes have also been passed, which allow third persons, usually the decedent's spouse and children, to recover for losses they sustained as a result of the decedent's death.

The issue of wrongful death is unique in the field of tort law because it centers around the interpretation of statutes. Litigants in this area are forced to engage in statutory construction and determination of legislative intent. This is often onerous since most of the statutes were written over 100 years ago.

TYPES OF RECOVERY ALLOWED

In situations where a survival action is filed separately from a wrongful death action, the possibility of double recovery exists. To preclude this from happening, many states limit survivor actions to those losses occurring prior to the decedent's death. Damages are restricted, therefore, to the decedent's medical expenses, lost earnings prior to death, and pain and suffering. Consequently, in such states if the death is instantaneous no survival action exists at all since no damages occurred prior to death (see Restatement (Second) of Torts Sec. 926, comment a).

Under Lord Campbell's Act and the wrongful death legislation patterned after that act, damages were to be limited to pecuniary or economic losses caused by the decedent's death. Typically, the loss is measured in terms of the monetary contributions that the decedent would have made during his or her lifetime to the plaintiff beneficiary. In more recent years a pecuniary value has been attached to the companionship, sexual relationship, and moral guidance provided by the decedent. Furthermore, several states allow recovery for grief and other mental suffering of the survivors. Some of those states have imposed a cap on those damages, however, to protect against runaway awards.

Recovery in this area becomes particularly problematic when parents bring a wrongful death action due to a child that has been killed. Usually the expense of raising a child far surpasses any earnings the child can be expected to bring home. Many courts allow recovery of a substantial reward for loss of companionship of the child. Other courts have allowed consideration of what the decedent child might have brought to his or her parents in terms of support in their old age. In one case, for example, $100,000 was allowed for loss of a very intelligent seven-year-old who exhibited talent as a cartoonist (*Haumerson v. Ford Motor Co.*, 257 N.W.2d 7 (Iowa 1977)).

DISCLOSURE OF REMARRIAGE

Another issue that arises in wrongful death and survival actions is whether a surviving spouse who remarries is entitled to keep this information from the trier of the fact. The concern is that a jury in particular may be inclined to give a lower verdict if it learns of the remarriage. Of course, defendants are eager to disclose this information during *voir dire* and argue that they need to do so in case prospective jurors are acquainted with the new spouse. Most courts, however, refuse to allow evidence of remarriage even if used for this limited purpose.

WHO RECOVERS?

Survival actions are usually brought by the executor or administrator of an estate. Recovery becomes an asset of that estate and may be reached by creditors. It is often distributed in accordance with state testacy and intestacy laws. Some argue that survival actions may result in a windfall to distant relatives who had little or no contact with the decedent. On the other hand, relatives who were not named beneficiaries in a wrongful death action may be able to recover in a survival action. Recovery for pain and suffering in survival actions is allowed only if the decedent was conscious of pain. Courtroom battles often revolve, therefore, around the issue of the decedent's consciousness, particularly if he or she survived only a few seconds or minutes after being injured (such as in a mid-air collision of an aircraft).

DEFENSES

Although any defenses that could have been raised against the decedent are still available to the defendant in a survival action, considerable disagreement exists as to which defenses should be allowed in a wrongful death action. Most states resolve this by allowing the defendant to assert any defenses he or she would have been able to use against the decedent if the decedent were still alive. In such cases, for example, the defendant may argue that the decedent was contributorily negligent or that he or she assumed the risk.

Statutes of limitations are another concern in wrongful death and survival actions. Suppose, for example, the decedent failed to file an action until after the statute of limitations had run. Would a wrongful death or survival action be barred? Most courts have answered "no" and indicate that the death action begins to run from the date of death.

Remember that survival actions and wrongful death actions are statutory creatures and are therefore subject to statutory construction. Be sure to examine the statutory scheme in your state dealing with these types of claims.

DISCOUNTING FUTURE DAMAGES

A plaintiff, in a sense, receives a windfall by collecting in the present for future losses. The rationale is that a lump sum paid now for future loss is worth more to the recipient than future payments because a lump sum has the potential of creating more money through investment. In practical terms, having $10,000 in the bank now, invested at a modest rate of return, is more advantageous than having $10,000 ten years from now. To illustrate, the present value of a dollar payable at 5 percent compound interest in one year is $.95 while the present value of $1.00 in ten years is $.61 and the present value of $1.00 payable in twenty years is $.38. Recognition of the earning power of money has resulted in many courts requiring juries to reduce or **discount** awards to the **present value** of lost future earnings. Discounting an award prevents the plaintiff from realizing an unwarranted windfall and reduces losses to the defendant.

Life expectancy tables, annuity tables, and work expectancy tables are used for determining earning expectancy. The present value of anticipated earnings can be computed by calculating the present value of a dollar at a particular rate of interest and multiplying that by the average monthly earnings for the designated period of time. The present value, for example, of twenty-five annual payments of $10,000 per year ($250,000 total) would be $127,833 if an interest rate of 6 percent were assumed. As you can see, the defendant receives a type of "interest" on the advance payment when the plaintiff is awarded the present value of the losses (Restatement (Second) of Torts Sec. 913A). See "Practice Pointers" at the end of this chapter for more details on the calculation of present values.

Some attorneys have argued that inflation offsets the discounting of present value awards. The argument is that claiming future damage for present value does not fully compensate the victim since the upward movement of prices can generally be anticipated. In one case, for example, the court concluded that inflation and present value canceled each other out. (*Pierce v. N. Y. Central R. Co.*, 304 F.Supp 44 (W.D. Mich. 1969)). The court noted that a dollar invested that would earn 5 percent per year now would increase in value to $2.30 after twenty-six years. However, if the purchasing power of that same dollar were reduced 5 percent per year, then in twenty-six years it would take $2.30 to purchase what it presently cost a dollar to buy. Other courts have rejected this argument as being too speculative.

STRUCTURED SETTLEMENTS

Traditionally under the common law past and future damages were paid in a single lump sum. More recently, large future damages have been paid using a periodic-payment settlement, often referred to as a **structured settlement.** Two reasons are generally given for the use of a structured settlement. First, the plaintiff does not have the responsibility of making arrangements to invest the money if he or she receives periodic payments over a long period of time. Second, the income tax that the plaintiff has to pay is usually minimized using a structured settlement. While tax does not have to be paid on a lump sum amount, it does have to be paid on any income resulting from an investment of a lump sum damage award.

We will not explore any of the intricacies involved in structuring such a settlement. Suffice it to say that federal tax law is crucial in shaping the form of a settlement. Some attorneys, however, feel that the advantages of structured settlements are illusory and that such arrangements better serve the interests of the insurance company than they do that of the plaintiff. (See A. Fuchsberg, "Pitfalls in Structured Settlements," *Trial* 42 (Sept., 1989).) Structured settlements are required by statute under certain circumstances in some states and are generally supported by the defense bar.

MITIGATION OF DAMAGES

The *duty to mitigate damages* required under contract law is also required under tort law. Under this rule, also referred to as the **avoidable consequences** rule, a plaintiff cannot recover for any damages he or she could reasonably have avoided. Recovery will not be allowed, for example, for the additional medical expenses necessary to treat an infection incurred by the plaintiff's failure to seek prompt medical care for a wound caused by the defendant's negligence. The burden would be on the defendant, however, to prove that the plaintiff could have avoided the harm.

Although this rule is usually applied to the plaintiff's conduct after the accident, in some states it has been used to argue that the plaintiff should have taken certain safety precautions before the accident. In states mandating the wearing of seat belts or motorcycle helmets the argument has been made that the plaintiff suffered injuries that he would not have sustained had he or she taken the precautions required by statute. The defendant's argument in such cases is that passage of such statutes represents legislative recognition of the capacity to avoid injuries by the wearing of seat belts or motorcycle helmets. In other states, failure to take such safety precautions is considered contributory negligence.

MENTAL SUFFERING

In a typical negligence case the plaintiff must show that he suffered some kind of physical harm. If he sustained only mental harm with no physical symptoms, he will usually be precluded from recovering. Where there is physical injury, damages from mental suffering are often called **parasitic** because they attach to the physical injury.

When the plaintiff sustains no physical injury, the courts are reluctant to permit recovery for emotional suffering because of a fear that the suffering may be feigned. Suppose a woman eats cottage cheese containing broken glass. She is not cut nor in any way physically injured but she is frightened at the prospect of possibly having swallowed some glass. She is slightly nauseated and unable to sleep that evening. The vast majority of courts will deny her recovery if she is unable to point to any nontransitory (ongoing) physical symptoms of her emotional distress. The theory is that the lack of objective physical symptoms greatly increases the risk of fraudulent claims and therefore recovery is denied. (Restatement (Second) of Torts Sec. 436A, comments b and c, illustration 1).

Many courts have allowed an exception to this general rule in cases involving the negligent mishandling of corpses (such as the misplacement or dismemberment of a corpse) or in cases involving the negligent transmission of a message by telegraph (such as an erroneous message regarding the death of a family member). Such cases are thought by their very nature to cause actual suffering and therefore minimize the risk of fake claims.

A small minority of courts follow the "impact rule," predicating recovery for mental suffering on the plaintiff experiencing some type of physical "impact." An impact could be an electric shock, a slight jarring, inhalation of smoke, dust in the eye, or any contact even of a trivial nature. Impact was achieved in a particularly novel way in one case in which a circus horse defecated in the plaintiff's lap. (*Christy Brothers Circus v. Turnage,* 144 S.E. 680 (1928)). The vast majority of courts have abandoned the impact rule in favor of requiring the plaintiff to exhibit some physical manifestation if he or she is to recover for mental disturbances.

ATTEMPTS TO CIRCUMVENT THE PHYSICAL HARM REQUIREMENT
If the defendant's conduct was intentional or willful, the courts have been much more willing to allow recovery for pure emotional distress. If the plaintiff suffers emotional distress that subsequently manifests in the form of physical consequences, the vast majority of courts also allow recovery even if the manifestation of physical consequences is not immediate.

Some states have abandoned the rule altogether where the facts are such that one could readily believe there could have been actual mental distress. In one notable case a plaintiff was allowed to recover against the defendant doctors and hospital who had mistakenly told his wife that she had syphilis (*Molien v. Kaiser Foundation Hospitals,* 616 P.2d 813 (Cal. 1980)). As a result of this disclosure the plaintiff's wife became suspicious that the plaintiff was having an extramarital affair and their marriage broke up. The court rejected the artificial physical harm requirement and concluded that the jurors were in the best position to determine whether the defendants' conduct could have caused emotional distress.

Some courts presented with the physical harm problem in the context of a plaintiff who has seen injury occur to others have taken the *Palsgraf* "zone of danger" approach. They have held that a plaintiff who is not within the "zone of danger" and who is therefore not endangered by the defendant's conduct is owed no duty. Such a plaintiff cannot recover for emotional distress as a result of another's injury even if this distress leads to physical harm.

A growing number of states have, however, begun to abandon the physical harm requirement if the plaintiff was near the scene of the accident, personally observed it, and was closely related to the victim. In one such case a young girl was run down by the defendant's automobile in front of her mother and her sister (*Dillon v. Legg,* 441 P2d 912 (Cal. 1968)). The sister, who was standing a few feet away, was in the "zone of danger" while the mother, who was standing on the sidewalk, was still in view of the accident but was not in any direct danger and was therefore outside the "zone of danger." The court, in allowing the mother to recover, pointed out the inconsistency that would arise if the sister were allowed to recover and the mother were denied recovery when both had experienced the same kind of distress.

APPLICATION

Although neither Teddy nor Mr. Dooright would be entitled to recover for punitive damages since the Baxters' negligence did not rise to the level of recklessness, they would both be entitled to compensatory damages if the Baxters were found liable. Both could certainly recover for their medical expenses and for their pain and suffering, both past and future. Proof of their past medical expenses would probably be relatively straightforward, but future medical expenses might be more difficult to quantify. Teddy, for example, might require ongoing psychiatric care as a result of his phobic disorder. Since estimating the length and cost of such treatment would be difficult, a concrete dollar figure would also be difficult to calculate. If Mr. Dooright might have to endure future operations, the expenses of those operations, along with all other future medical expenses, would have to be estimated. Remember, too, that Mr. Dooright's spouse and Teddy's parents could also file a claim for loss of consortium.

The pain and suffering endured by this duo, while less tangible than their physical injuries, would be a crucial element in their recoveries. Teddy's attorney would want to point to the physical trauma that Teddy experienced as well as the ongoing psychological pain he could be expected to suffer for the remainder of his life in relationship to his fear of dogs. His attorney would want to paint a vivid picture of the limitations stemming from this emotional trauma. If Teddy were unable to secure a job as a paper carrier as a result of his phobia or if he became so chronically anxious that his social life were disrupted, his attorney would point to this as evidence of the long-term effects of Gertrude's attack. Mr. Dooright's attorney, on the other hand, would focus more on the life-changing consequences of Gertrude's actions in bringing Mr. Dooright's concert pianist career to an abrupt end. Again, the challenge in this case would be in converting the intangible but real suffering of a human being into a dollar figure. Both parties would also be able to recover for any permanent disfigurement, such as scarring, that they sustained.

At a more tangible level, Mr. Dooright's attorney would have to project Mr. Dooright's loss of income resulting from the termination of his career. Obviously, one could anticipate conflict between counsel in reference to the relative values of a concert pianist's career and a piano teacher's career. Both counsel would have to dig out as many facts as possible to substantiate their positions. This is what makes litigation so challenging! Any other limitations that Mr. Dooright suffered as a result of his disabled hand would also have to be quantified. Specific, concrete evidence illustrating such disability would be necessary.

The Baxters might argue that the plaintiffs in this case failed to mitigate their damages if, for example, they failed to seek immediate medical treatment. They would also want to minimize the pain and suffering experienced by the plaintiffs and would want to do everything in their power to present evidence that the plaintiffs magnified their damages. They would argue that any recoveries by the plaintiffs should be discounted to present values and would likely push for some form of structured settlement.

SUMMARY

Damages can be divided into three categories: compensatory, punitive, and nominal damages. Compensatory damages are further divided into two categories: general and special.

The difficulty in assigning a monetary award for pain and suffering is in the assigning of a numerical value. Some attorneys, in an effort to quantify suffering, have used a per diem technique. Attempts to compensate plaintiffs for pain and suffering have been subject to criticism.

Plaintiffs can be compensated for loss of future earning capacity. In calculating these damages jurors are expected to project the anticipated life span of the plaintiff. Generally plaintiffs may not be directly compensated for their shortened life expectancy. Under the collateral source rule, plaintiffs are entitled to recover for those damages for which they have been reimbursed by a collateral source, such as an insurance company. Plaintiffs are not entitled to compensation for the expenses of litigation although some have suggested that, as a practical matter, punitive damages and awards for pain and suffering in effect provide for such compensation.

Damages for physical harm to property are tied to the fair market value of the property. Fair market value is considered the highest price one seeking to sell the property could have realized and not the lowest price at which a sale could have been made.

Punitive damages are reserved for those defendants who act in a particularly egregious manner. These damages have been criticized as constituting undue compensation to the plaintiff and as having the potential of bankrupting defendants, especially in product liability cases.

Spouses can recover for loss of consortium, which is considered a derivative claim. Parents are also entitled to recover for the lost services and earnings of their minor children. Some courts have allowed minor children to recover for loss of consortium when a parent on whom they were dependent dies or is seriously injured.

Survival statutes allow an injured party's claim to be sustained after his or her death. Wrongful death statutes allow third persons, usually a decedent's spouse and children, to recover for losses they sustained as a result of the decedent's death. Survival actions are typically brought by the executor or administrator of an estate and recovery becomes an asset of the estate, which may be reached by creditors. Although at one time wrongful death actions were limited to economic losses caused by the decedent's death, in more recent times they have been extended to the loss of companionship of the decedent. Most states have ruled that wrongful death and survival actions begin to run from the date of the decedent's death. Both survival and wrongful death actions are subject to statutory construction.

To prevent plaintiffs who recover for future losses from receiving a windfall many courts require juries to "discount" awards to a "present value." Some have argued that the discounting of awards is unfair to plaintiffs because inflation offsets the discounting of present value awards. Large future damages are frequently paid using a periodic-payment settlement, called a structured settlement. Arguably, this type of settlement relieves the plaintiff of the responsibility of making arrangements to invest the money and minimizes the amount of income tax required.

Under the avoidable consequences rule, a plaintiff has a duty to mitigate his or her damages by avoiding any harm that reasonably could have been avoided. This rule has been used as a defense in seat belt and motorcycle helmet cases.

A plaintiff in a negligence claim must typically show that he or she suffered some kind of physical harm or, in a few states, some kind of impact. Some courts have abandoned this rule in circumstances where one could readily believe the plaintiff actually suffered mental distress. Some courts have denied compensation for emotional distress to any plaintiff not within the "zone of danger" while others have allowed recovery where the plaintiff was near the scene of the accident, personally observed it, and was closely related to the victim.

PRACTICE POINTERS

As a paralegal you may be called on to provide the evidence necessary to prove or disprove a claim for damages (see Table 9–4). Here we will consider the practical implications of proving past and future medical expenses, loss of earning capacity, and pain and suffering.

Past Medical Expenses
In terms of proving past medical expenses, the plaintiff has the burden of proving the amount of the expenses and that the expenses were necessary and reasonable. The best way to prove past expenses is, of course, through the use of bills that reflect the charges made. Alternatively, the plaintiff can testify to the amount of the bill or have a doctor or the person who prepared the bill testify as to the amount of the charge made. It is important to keep a running account of all bills. These bills should be tabulated on a monthly basis and may be submitted to the

TABLE 9.4 Proving Damages

TYPES OF DAMAGES	EVIDENCE USED TO PROVE
PAST MEDICAL EXPENSES	•Bills from doctors, hospitals, radiology, etc. •Testimony from expert showing necessity of treatment.
FUTURE MEDICAL EXPENSES	•Expert testimony. •Award is discounted to present value.
LOSS OF EARNING CAPACITY	•Plaintiff's work record showing hours lost due to injuries. •Wage stubs, W-4 forms or IRS records (showing value of lost earnings). •Evidence of lost profits and loss of fringe benefits. •Extent of plaintiff's education and training (showing earning potential).
PAIN AND SUFFERING	•Plaintiff's testimony. •Testimony of those who have observed plaintiff's suffering "Day-in-the-life" video.

Continued on next page

PRACTICE POINTERS—Continued

insurance company and to defense counsel on an ongoing basis. Some plaintiffs' counsel feel that the continual amassing of medical expenses into an ever-burgeoning file has a psychological impact on the defendant. Defense counsel, for obvious reasons, deny this.

In most jurisdictions proof of medical bills plus proof of payment raises the presumption that the bill was necessary and reasonable. In some states, however, testimony from a doctor, druggist, or other expert is required. The reasonableness and necessity of treatment become particularly problematic when dealing with preexisting conditions. If the plaintiff was not suffering from the preexisting condition at the time of the injury, the expenses will probably be recoverable. If, however, the plaintiff was under treatment for that condition at the time of the injury, he or she will have difficulty proving which expenses were necessitated by the aggravation caused by the defendant's negligence and which expenses stemmed from the preexisting condition. The plaintiff may therefore by unable to recover any of the medical expenses.

Future Medical Expenses

Future medical expenses are much less subject to quantification. No doctor can state with absolute certainty how long future treatment will be needed nor what exact amount of future medical expenses will be incurred. Courts are aware of this ambiguity and do not require the same degree of mathematical proof that they do for past expenses. In some jurisdictions future medical expenses are left for the jury to determine based on the amount of past medical expenses, the nature of the plaintiff's injuries, and the condition of the plaintiff at the time of trial. Other jurisdictions require medical testimony regarding a dollar amount and do not allow a jury to award more than the amount supported by testimony.

As was noted in the text of this chapter future awards are often discounted to present value. Discounting is based on the idea that a dollar today is worth more than a dollar ten years from now because of the investment potential of that dollar. Present value tables, an example of which is shown on page 159, allow one to calculate the present value of future awards.

Let us use a hypothetical scenario to illustrate the use of these tables. Suppose $1,000 is to be awarded the plaintiff in year 1, $2,000 in year 2, and $3,000 in year 3. Using an interest rate of 10 percent, what would be the present value of that award? Locate 10 percent on the table. Notice that next to year 1 in the third column is the number 0.90909, which indicates that the value of a dollar received a year from now is worth $.90909 now. Therefore, $1,000 a year from now would be worth $909.09 today. By the same token $2,000 in year 2 would be worth $2,000 × .82645 or $1,652.90; $3,000 in year 3 would be worth $3,000 × .75132 or $2,253.96. Therefore, the total present value would be $4,815.95:

Continued on next page

PRACTICE POINTERS—Continued

PRESENT VALUE OF $1

Paid at End of Year	8%	9%	10%	11%	12%
1	0.92593	0.91743	0.90909	0.90090	0.89286
2	0.85734	0.84168	0.82645	0.81162	0.79719
3	0.79383	0.77219	0.75132	0.73119	0.71178
4	0.73503	0.70843	0.68302	0.65873	0.63552
5	0.68058	0.64993	0.62092	0.59345	0.56743
6	0.63027	0.59627	0.56448	0.53464	0.50663
7	0.58349	0.54704	0.51316	0.48166	0.45235
8	0.54027	0.50187	0.46651	0.43393	0.40388
9	0.50025	0.46043	0.42410	0.39093	0.36061
10	0.46319	0.42241	0.38555	0.35219	0.32197
15	0.31524	0.27454	0.23939	0.20901	0.18270
20	0.21455	0.17843	0.14865	0.12404	0.10367
25	0.14602	0.11597	0.09230	0.07361	0.05882
30	0.09938	0.07537	0.05731	0.04368	0.03338
35	0.06764	0.04899	0.03559	0.02592	0.01894
40	0.04603	0.03184	0.02210	0.01539	0.01075

$1,000 × .90909 = $ 909.09
$2,000 × .82645 = $1,652.90
$3,000 × .75132 = $2,253.96
Total Present Value = $4,815.95

Loss of Earning Capacity

To prove loss of earning capacity, you must first prove that the injuries creating the plaintiff's physical disability impaired his or her ability to work and earn money. Second, you must prove the value of that incapacity. To prove the latter you must obtain copies of the plaintiff's wage stubs, W-4 forms, and/or IRS records (not admissible in some states). The defense will want to show that the plaintiff's work record was sporadic, that the earnings for the years at issue were unusually high, or that for some reason the plaintiff would not be able to earn comparable wages in the years ahead for reasons other than the disability sustained.

Proof of earning capacity becomes more problematic if the plaintiff was temporarily disabled prior to the injuries or was for some reason not able to work before sustaining the injuries. In such cases the jury will be left to determine the value of the lost earning capacity based on their own common sense and sense of fair play.

Proof of lost earning capacity can also be difficult when the plaintiff was self-employed. In such cases a difference in profits prior to and after the plaintiff's injuries is not considered a measure of damages because factors other than the plaintiff's incapacity, such as changes in the market, could account for the decrease in profits. The plaintiff is obligated to prove that it was inability to work rather than other economic

Continued on next page

PRACTICE POINTERS—Continued

factors that caused the loss of business income.

Other types of evidence you might want to consider using to show a plaintiff's earning potential would be evidence of education and on-the-job training, as well as evidence of fringe benefits, such as bonuses, insurance programs, tips, and pensions. Prospective earnings from reasonably anticipated promotions or advancements may also be submitted as well as evidence that the plaintiff was studying or in other ways taking steps to advance into better paying work.

Evidence of income that the plaintiff receives that is unrelated to work is inadmissible. The fact that the plaintiff receives Social Security benefits, worker's compensation benefits, welfare benefits, dividends from stocks, or monies from other investments is irrelevant and therefore inadmissible unless used to impeach the plaintiff.

Pain and Suffering

Damages for pain and suffering are by their very nature not amenable to quantification. Therefore, all a plaintiff can do is prove that the physical pain and mental anguish were in fact experienced. The most direct evidence of pain and suffering is testimony by the plaintiff as to objective symptoms, such as the actual injuries received, and subjective symptoms, such as headaches. Mental anguish may take the form of fear, worry, depression, or humiliation.

Elicit detailed descriptions from the plaintiff, complete with specific incidents that illustrate the nature and depth of the pain and anguish and the limitations such suffering imposed on his or her lifestyle. In major personal injury lawsuits plaintiffs' attorneys frequently use "day in the life of" videotapes to illustrate graphically to the jury the full extent of the plaintiff's injuries. Such videos chronicle in a simple but poignant way the everyday suffering of the plaintiff and those who care for him or her. If your firm is without such resources the attorney must create vivid word pictures in the jurors' minds through the process of direct examination. In preparing the plaintiff for such testimony you must draw his or her attention to all those events in the course of a day that are rendered more difficult as a result of the injuries.

Doctors as well as others who are familiar with the plaintiff can testify regarding their observations that are indicative of pain and suffering. In working with these potential witnesses it is important to strive for detailed information that can be used to create a visual picture for the jury. Generalizations and vague statements are not helpful and will not create the kind of jury empathy plaintiff's counsel desires.

The defendant will want to rebut the plaintiff's claim of physical and mental anguish by presenting evidence that the plaintiff is pain-free and relatively happy or, alternatively, that the plaintiff's suffering is caused by factors other than the injuries. The courts are reluctant, however, to

Continued on next page

PRACTICE POINTERS—Continued

admit evidence of collateral events causing the plaintiff's suffering because such evidence may be highly prejudicial to the plaintiff. Therefore, a defendant who wants to introduce such evidence must show that the connection between the collateral event and the plaintiff's suffering is not purely conjectural.

TORT TEASERS

1. Suppose your firm represents Mr. Dooright and you have been asked to interview him to ascertain the full extent of his damages. Write down a list of the questions that you would want to ask him in reference to his medical expenses, lost income, lost future income, and pain and suffering.

2. If your firm were representing Teddy, what information would you want to elicit from the medical doctors and psychologists who treated Teddy?

3. Your client is injured in an automobile accident and as a result suffers a fractured dislocation of his right ankle. He is determined to have a remaining work life of twenty-nine years. Medical testimony indicates that he will be unable to work from one to five years at anything other than a sedentary type of job that would require no prolonged walking, running, or heavy lifting. Your client receives a medical discharge from the Air Force after the accident, receiving a 60 percent disability compensation, 40 percent of which is attributed to his ankle and the remaining 20 percent to other medical problems not related to the accident. *Beaulieu v. Elliott,* 434 P.2d 665 (Alas. 1967).

a. What types of damages would you attempt to recover in this case?

b. How would you go about determining a monetary value for each of these damages?

c. What arguments do you anticipate your opponents will make in reference to the payment of damages?

4. A twenty-one-year-old college student dies allegedly as a result of improper diagnosis and care as well as the administration of unsafe drugs. Her parents bring a claim under the wrongful death statute on their behalf and under the survival statute on behalf of their daughter's estate. *Warner v. McCaughan,* 460 P.2d 272 (Wash. 1969).

a. What problems would you anticipate with the parents filing a wrongful death action?

b. What damages would you attempt to recover under the survival statute?

c. What arguments would you want to make if you were the defense in this case as to why the parents should not be able to recover for their daughter's pain and suffering?

KEY TERMS

■ **Avoidable consequences rule**
Obligation of a plaintiff to minimize (mitigate) her damages.

■ **Collateral source rule**
Right of a plaintiff to recover twice for damages.

■ **Derivative claim**
Claim derived from underlying claim, e.g., loss of consortium is a derivative claim.

■ **Discounting an award**
Reducing an award to its present value.

■ **Fair market value**
Amount property could be sold for on the open market.

■ **General damages**
Damages that generally result from conduct engaged in by defendant.

■ **Loss of consortium**
Loss of services, including companionship, sex, and earnings outside of the home.

■ **Parasitic damages**
Damages attached to physical injury, e.g., mental suffering.

■ **Present value**
Current value of money that is to be paid in the future, based on the assumption that money received today is worth more than money received in the future because of the investment potential of money.

■ **Special damages**
Damages that are unique to the plaintiff.

■ **Structured settlement**
Agreement to pay damages in installments rather than a lump sum.

■ **Survival action**
Action that survives the decedent's death.

■ **Wrongful death action**
Action brought by third parties to recover for losses they suffered as a result of the decedent's death.

NEGLIGENCE: DEFENSES

CHAPTER OBJECTIVES

In this chapter you will learn to:

- Identify the elements of contributory negligence, comparative negligence, and assumption of risk.
- Recognize the exceptions to the contributory negligence rule.
- Recognize the problems that arise in the administration of a comparative negligence system.
- Differentiate between contributory negligence and assumption of risk.
- Identify situations in which immunity can be raised as a defense.
- Recognize the purpose behind the problems inherent in a statute of limitations defense.

If Teddy and Mr. Dooright are able to prove their claims of negligence against the Baxters, the Baxters will certainly want to raise some form of defense (see Table 10–1). The three defenses they will consider are contributory negligence, comparative negligence, and assumption of risk. If Teddy and Mr. Dooright were **contributorily negligent**—if they contributed in some way to their own injuries—they would be totally barred from recovery. On the other hand, if the state in which the suit is filed has adopted a **comparative negligence** rather than a contributory negligence system, their recovery will be reduced in direct proportion to their own degree of negligence. For example, suppose Teddy suffered damages of $10,000 and was shown to be 20 percent negligent. His recovery would be reduced to $8,000, i.e., $10,000 −

TABLE 10.1

DEFENSES TO NEGLIGENCE	
CONTRIBUTORY NEGLIGENCE	Plaintiff barred from recovery.
COMPARATIVE NEGLIGENCE	Plaintiff's recovery reduced.
ASSUMPTION OF RISK	Plaintiff either barred from recovery or recovery is reduced.
IMMUNITY	Plaintiff barred from recovery.
STATUTE OF LIMITATIONS AND STATUTE OF REPOSE	Plaintiff barred from recovery.

$2,000 (20 percent of $10,000). Under the doctrine of **assumption of risk,** if it can be shown that Teddy and Mr. Dooright voluntarily consented to take the chance that harm would occur, they might, at the worst, be precluded from recovery and, at best, have their recovery reduced.

CONTRIBUTORY NEGLIGENCE

The defense of contributory negligence in essence shifts the loss from the defendant to the plaintiff by totally barring the negligent plaintiff from recovery. The plaintiff is barred even though the defendant was negligent and, in most cases, was more negligent than the plaintiff.

The rationale for this judge-created rule stems from the notion that negligent plaintiffs should be punished for failing to protect their own safety. Additionally, some argue that the plaintiff's negligence becomes the proximate cause of his or her injuries, thus removing the defendant as the proximate cause. This argument does not hold water, however, in light of the principles of proximate cause discussed in Chapter 8. Remember that if several events contribute to the plaintiff's injuries, each of them will be considered a distinct proximate cause. A more practical explanation of the creation of contributory negligence lies in judges' historical distrust of juries and their fear that, given free rein, juries would hamper the growth of industry by awarding huge awards to injured plaintiffs.

EXCEPTIONS TO THE CONTRIBUTORY NEGLIGENCE RULE

The results rendered by the rule of contributory negligence are often harsh and unjust. Worthy plaintiffs are often denied recovery and blameworthy defendants go unscathed. As a result the courts have developed various escape mechanisms by which plaintiffs can avoid this rule. One way, which has been adopted in every jurisdiction that adheres to the contributory negligence system, is the requirement that contributory negligence be proved and specifically pleaded by the defendant. Additionally, in most jurisdictions the question of contributory negligence is left to the jury. Arguably juries have an opportunity to apply a comparative negligence standard in those cases in which application of such a standard would lead to unfair results.

Most states require that the plaintiff's negligence meet the standards of the "but for" or substantial factor test of actual causation in order to be barred from recovering. A few courts, however, bar the plaintiff's recovery if his or her negligence contributed in any way to the result, no matter how slight that contribution might have been.

In most cases, the same rules that apply in determining proximate cause in terms of the defendant's conduct also apply to the plaintiff. In one instance, however, proximate cause is construed more narrowly in the case of contributory negligence that it is in the case of the defendant's negligence. If the harm that is likely to occur as a result of the plaintiff's negligence occurs in some unforeseen manner, the plaintiff's conduct is usually held not to be the proximate cause of the harm. Suppose a pedestrian crosses a street without looking and is injured, not by an oncoming vehicle, but by an explosion that occurs when a truck carrying dynamite strikes an automobile. In such a case the plaintiff's negligence would not be considered the proximate cause of the injuries because the injury came about as a result of an unforeseen risk (an explosion) and not the foreseeable risk of being run over. Since the harm that occurred came about in a different way than the harm that was threatened, the plaintiff would not be barred from recovery (Restatement (Second) of Torts Sec. 468).

Last Clear Chance Doctrine. The most significant way in which the contributory negligence defense has been limited has been through the use of the **"last clear chance"** doctrine. Under this doctrine, if the defendant has an opportunity that is unavailable to the plaintiff to prevent the harm that occurs and does not take advantage of it, the defendant will remain liable despite the plaintiff's contributory negligence. In essence the defendant's failure to take advantage of an opportunity to prevent the harm negates or wipes out the plaintiff's contributory negligence. Although the courts have used various explanations to rationalize this doctrine, it most likely stems from an attempt to mitigate the harshness of the contributory negligence defense.

The last clear chance doctrine was first utilized in the case of *Davies v. Mann*, 152 Eng. Rep. 588 (1842), in which the plaintiff had chained up his ass and left it blocking the roadway and the defendant ran his wagon into the animal. Since the defendant could have taken measure to avoid the collision and the plaintiff was at a loss to do anything at the time of the accident, the defendant was held liable.

The courts have struggled with the variations to this last clear chance doctrine (see Table 10–2.). The courts are unanimous in holding the defendant liable if the plaintiff is unable to avoid the predicament and the defendant is aware of but negligently failed to circumvent the harm. Less consensus exists, however, if the plaintiff is helpless and the defendant negligently fails to discover the plaintiff's situation because the defendant is inattentive. Suppose the plaintiff negligently turns her vehicle in front of the defendant and the

TABLE 10.2

LAST CLEAR CHANCE DOCTRINE "VARIATIONS ON A THEME"	
PLAINTIFF IS HELPLESS AND:	
1. Defendant discovers danger but negligently fails to avoid it.	Plaintiff can recover in all courts.
2. Defendant fails to discover danger because he is inattentive.	Plaintiff can recover in most courts.
PLAINTIFF IS INATTENTIVE BUT NOT HELPLESS AND:	
1. Defendant discovers danger but negligently fails to avoid it.	Plaintiff can recover in most courts.
2. Defendant fails to discover danger because he is inattentive.	Plaintiff cannot recover.
DEFENDANT IS UNABLE TO AVOID HARMING PLAINTIFF (even though he is aware of danger) because of defendant's earlier negligence ("First Clear Chance Doctrine").	Plaintiff cannot recover in most courts.

defendant, who could have avoided the accident had he been paying attention instead of talking with his passenger, is unable to avoid the plaintiff by the time he sees her. Most, but not all, courts would apply the last clear chance doctrine, thereby holding the defendant liable.

Suppose the plaintiff is inattentive rather than helpless and negligently fails to extricate himself from the danger. If the defendant discovers the plaintiff's predicament but negligently fails to respond to it, most courts will adhere to the last clear chance doctrine. A train engineer, for example, may be liable if she fails to blow the train's whistle a second time or slow the train down once she becomes aware that a person standing on the track has not heard or has disregarded the first blow of the whistle (Restatement (Second) of Torts Sec. 480, comment b).

When the Last Clear Chance Doctrine Is Not Applicable. When is the last clear chance doctrine not applicable? If both the defendant and the plaintiff are inattentive so that neither discovers the danger, the last clear chance doctrine is not applicable. Also, if the defendant discovers the plaintiff's peril but cannot avoid it because of the defendant's earlier negligence, the majority of courts will not allow the last clear chance doctrine. Suppose the defendant is driving a car with defective brakes and as a result, although he sees the plaintiff turning in front of him, he cannot stop in time. Should the last clear chance doctrine be applied? Most courts have refused to apply the doctrine in this so-called "first clear chance" case. The general rule is that the last clear chance doctrine is inapplicable when the defendant's original act of negligence precludes her from avoiding the accident after she discovers the plaintiff's peril (Restatement (Second) of Torts Sec. 479, illustration 3).

WHEN CONTRIBUTORY NEGLIGENCE IS NOT A DEFENSE

Contributory negligence is not a defense to an intentional tort (see Table 10–3). A defendant in a battery case cannot, for example, argue that the plaintiff was negligent in failing to duck. Similarly, contributory negligence is not allowed as a defense if the defendant's conduct was "willful and wanton" or "reckless" unless the plaintiff's conduct was also "willful and wanton" or "reckless." The rationale for these rules is that defendants who intentionally or recklessly harm others should not be able to escape liability simply because those whom they harmed are negligent.

A defendant who is "negligent *per se*" might not be able to raise the defense of contributory negligence. If the statute upon which the defendant's negligence is based was enacted for the sole purpose of protecting a class of persons of which the plaintiff was a member and the statute's intent was to place sole responsibility upon the defendant, contributory negligence is not a viable defense. Such a statute is one prohibiting the sale of liquor to minors.

Finally, some kinds of contributory negligence are not considered defenses in strict liability actions. A consumer, for example, who fails to inspect a defective product before using it and is injured as a result will not be prevented from recovery damages even though he or she was contributorily negligent. (See Chapter 14, "Product Liability," for further discussion of this topic.) Some statutes explicitly abolish the defense of contributory negligence and others do so implicitly by imposing a strict liability standard.

TABLE 10.3

EXCEPTIONS TO CONTRIBUTORY NEGLIGENCE RULE
•Plaintiff's negligence does not meet standards of "but for" or "substantial factor" tests.
•Harm likely to occur as a result of plaintiff's negligence occurs in unforeseen manner.
•Last Clear Chance Doctrine - defendant did not take advantage of opportunity to avoid accident and plaintiff had no such opportunity. (Not applicable if neither plaintiff nor defendant discovers danger due to inattentiveness or if defendant's original act of negligence made it impossible for him to avoid accident.)
•Defendant committed an intentional tort.
•Defendant was "willful and wanton" or "reckless."
•Defendant was negligent *per se*. (Unless statute's intent was to place sole responsibility on defendant and was enacted to protect class of people to which plaintiff belongs.)

COMPARATIVE NEGLIGENCE

Comparative negligence was created as an alternative to the all or nothing approach of the contributory negligence system (see Table 10–4). Under comparative negligence the plaintiff's recovery is reduced in direct proportion to her degree of negligent contribution to her own injuries. Therefore, if a plaintiff is found to be responsible for 20 percent of her injuries and suffers damages of $1,000,000, her recovery will be reduced by 20 percent of the $1,000,000 or $200,000. Today all but a handful of states have adopted a comparative negligence system by statute or through a state court decision.

The states that have adopted comparative negligence have, for the most part, adopted either a pure comparative negligence standard or a 50 percent approach. Under the pure system the plaintiff can recover no matter how extensive his negligence. For example, if the plaintiff is found to be 80 percent negligent by the jury, under a pure comparative negligence system he can still recover 20 percent of his damages. Contrast this with the 50 percent approach in which such a plaintiff would be precluded from recovering because he was more than 50 percent responsible for his own injuries.

Two subsystems of the 50 percent approach have been developed: the "not as great as" and the "not greater than" approaches. Although subtle in terms of language, the differences in these two systems can have a profound impact on the plaintiff. Under the "not as great as" approach the plaintiff's claim is barred as soon as her negligence is as great as the defendant's negligence; under the "not greater than" approach the plaintiff is barred only when her negligence is greater than the defendant's. The reason this subtle distinction can give rise to tremendous differences in outcome results from juries' tendency to assign a 50–50 apportionment in terms of blame. In a 50–50 apportionment the plaintiff would be barred under the "not as great as" approach (because her negligence would be as great as the defendant's) but would not be barred under the "not greater than" approach (because her negligence would not be greater than the defendant's).

TABLE 10.4 Comparative Negligence

TYPES OF COMPARATIVE NEGLIGENCE	PROBLEMS RELATED TO COMPARATIVE NEGLIGENCE
•Pure •50% Approach 1. Not as great as 2. Not greater than	•How is fault assigned, especially where there are multiple defendants? •Is the Last Clear Chance doctrine applicable? •Should a negligent plaintiff's recovery be reduced if the defendant was negligent *per se*?

ADMINISTRATIVE PROBLEMS

The administration of the comparative fault system creates some practical problems. For example, how should the percentage of fault be assigned to the plaintiff and defendant? Should fault be based on the extent that the party's conduct contributed to the resulting harm, as suggested by the Uniform Comparative Fault Act? Or should fault be based on the extent to which the plaintiff's conduct deviated from a reasonable standard of care? Both methods are used and can lead to different outcomes.

What if some persons are not parties to an action? Should fault be assigned to their actions? How is negligence assigned if there are more parties than just the plaintiff and defendant? Under a pure comparative negligence system the answer is simple since the negligence of all parties will be considered and the plaintiff will be allowed to recover in direct proportion to the negligence of those parties. A problem arises, however, in jurisdictions where the plaintiff may recover only if her negligence is less than that of the defendants. Should such a plaintiff be allowed to recover if her negligence is less than that of all the defendants combined but greater than that of a particular defendant? Suppose, for example, the plaintiff is responsible for 40 percent of her injuries, Defendant A is 30 percent responsible, Defendant B is 20 percent responsible, and Defendant C is 10 percent responsible. Should the plaintiff be able to recover since her negligence exceeds that of each individual defendant even though she is less negligent than all of the defendants combined? Most state statutes have failed to answer this question.

OTHER ISSUES AFFECTING COMPARATIVE NEGLIGENCE

Is the last clear chance doctrine applicable in a comparative negligence system? Although some jurisdictions have continued to apply the last clear chance doctrine, the Uniform Comparative Fault Act expressly rejects its use. Comparative negligence generally is not used in reference to intentional torts to reduce the plaintiff's damages so that a defendant who commits an intentional tort may not use the argument that the plaintiff contributed to his own injuries. The defendant whose conduct is "willful and wanton" or "reckless," however, may still rely on the defense of comparative negligence to reduce the plaintiff's recovery.

Most states adopting the comparative negligence approach have allowed for the reduction of the negligent plaintiff's recovery in cases where the defendant violated a safety statute and was therefore negligent *per se*. Unlike contributory negligence, the same stance is taken even where the statute is designed to protect members of the plaintiff's class and to place all responsibility on the defendant. Some states, however, have denied apportionment, arguing that it would defeat the purpose of the statute in question.

ASSUMPTION OF RISK

A plaintiff who volunteers to take the chance that harm will occur is said to have **assumed the risk**. Under the common law such a plaintiff was completely barred from recovery. Most courts today have discontinued that practice but do take into account the plaintiff's assumption of risk when determining how to apportion damages.

COMPARISON TO CONTRIBUTORY NEGLIGENCE

Some states have in effect abolished the doctrine and consider assumption of risk to be a form of contributory negligence. The justification behind this merger is that often a plaintiff who has assumed the risk has also been contributorily negligent. A plaintiff who voluntarily but unreasonably decides to take a risk can also be said to have behaved in a negligent manner.

In some situations, however, a plaintiff is not negligent simply because he has assumed the risk. If the plaintiff's decision to entertain a risk is reasonable in light of the circumstances, he will not be considered negligent, particularly if few options are available to him other than engaging in risky behavior. Suppose a father uses a car with defective brakes because it is the only car available to him and he must use it to get his seriously injured child to the hospital. He has assumed the risk even though he has not acted negligently. In situations such as this the defense of assumption of risk can be raised even though the defense of contributory negligence cannot.

DIFFERENCES BETWEEN CONTRIBUTORY NEGLIGENCE AND ASSUMPTION OF RISK

Some states have extended assumption of risk to any situation in which the plaintiff voluntarily exposes herself to a known risk. The definition of voluntary exposure goes beyond the concept of consenting to a risk and further blurs the distinction between assumption of risk and contributory negligence (see Table 10–5). To get around this ambiguity some courts have characterized contributory negligence as "carelessness" and assumption of risk as "adventurousness." A plaintiff who deliberately walks down defective steps when

TABLE 10.5 Differences Between Assumption of Risk and Contributory Negligence

CONTRIBUTORY NEGLIGENCE	ASSUMPTION OF RISK
Characterized as "recklessness."	Characterized as "adventurousness."
Plaintiff compared to reasonable person (objective standard).	Did plaintiff understand risk? (subjective standard)
Not a defense to reckless conduct.	Is a defense to reckless conduct.
Not generally a defense in strict liability cases.	Is a defense in strict liability cases.

others, only slightly more inconvenient, are available may voluntarily assume the risk of confronting a known hazard, even though she exercises due care on the stairs. Such a plaintiff is said to assume the risk but not to be contributorily negligent if assumption of risk is defined as adventurousness. (*Hunn v. Windsor Hotel Company*, 193 S.E.57 (1937)).

If the plaintiff's conduct constitutes both assumption of risk and contributory negligence, the defendant can choose to assert either defense or, in some jurisdictions, both. In deciding which of the defenses to raise, the defendant should consider the standards used to assess the plaintiff's conduct. An objective standard is used to assess the reasonableness of the plaintiff's conduct in the case of contributory negligence. A subjective standard is used in cases involving assumption of risk. It requires that the plaintiff actually understood the risk that he undertook and not merely that a reasonable person would have understood.

Contributory negligence cannot be raised as a defense if the defendant is reckless and cannot generally be used as a defense in strict liability cases. Conversely, assumption of risk can be used as a defense of reckless conduct and in strict liability cases.

COMPARATIVE NEGLIGENCE AND ASSUMPTION OF RISK

Those states that have adopted comparative negligence statutes have, for all intents and purposes, removed assumption of risk as a separate defense and have merged it, in part at least, into the defense of comparative negligence. Therefore, a plaintiff who unreasonably places himself in danger is considered negligent and his recovery is reduced although not barred completely. If his conduct in exposing himself to the danger is reasonable, he is not considered negligent at all.

EXPRESS ASSUMPTION OF RISK

A plaintiff can either expressly or impliedly assume the risk. A plaintiff who signs a release in which she agrees to assume all risk of injury to herself and her property has expressly assumed the risk. Even an express agreement, however, may not be enforced by the courts if the defendant has unusual bargaining power, if she is the sole or unique provider of a service, and if she uses her power to compel the plaintiff to waive liability.

By the same token, agreements involving common carriers, public utilities, or other regulated industries are unlikely to be enforced. The courts usually feel that such entities are obligated to provide reasonable service and will not allow them to escape their responsibility through the use of waivers.

A plaintiff must actually be aware of any risk he is said to have assumed. If a limitation on liability is buried in fine print where the plaintiff is unlikely to see it, it will not be binding on him. Additionally, waivers of liability are valid only in reference to the defendant's negligence and not for his intentional tortious acts nor for his "gross" or "willful and wanton" negligence. One area in which the courts are unwilling to uphold a waiver, no matter how well informed that waiver is, is in the field of medical care. Agreements, for example, in which patients waive potential malpractice claims in exchange for reduced fees are unenforceable.

IMPLIED ASSUMPTION OF RISK

A plaintiff is said to have impliedly assumed the risk when her conduct shows that she was aware of the risk in question and voluntarily agreed to bear that risk herself. Suppose a plaintiff watches as her friend mounts the defendant's horse and is subsequently bucked off. If the plaintiff then climbs aboard the same horse she will have impliedly assumed the risk for any injuries she sustains.

For this principle to be applicable the plaintiff must actually be aware of the particular risk in question. It is not enough that the plaintiff merely should have known of the risk involved. The plaintiff must also voluntarily consent to the risk. Consent is not voluntary if the plaintiff had no reasonable choice but to confront a danger.

The consent principle is colorfully illustrated in a case in which the plaintiff, who was a tenant of the defendant, fell through a hole in the outhouse floor when she submitted to a "call of nature." The court held that the plaintiff did not voluntarily assume the risk even though she was aware of the defective floor since she had no choice but to use the facilities at her disposal. The court concluded that she was under no legal obligation to seek other facilities (*Rush v. Commercial Realty Company*, 145 A. 476 (N.J. 1929)). If the plaintiff in this case had been faced with a reasonable alternative, such as another intact outhouse on the same property, she might have been held to have assumed the risk.

What if a plaintiff protests against being asked to assume a risk but ultimately agrees to do so? In most cases the courts will hold that he waived his objection and assumed the risk. Even if the risk the plaintiff is exposed to is not created by the defendant, he is still considered to have voluntarily accepted the risk. A plaintiff who is badly injured in an accident and who requests that the defendant drive him to the hospital despite his knowledge that the defendant's car has bad brakes assumes the risk of injury caused by the defective brakes. Although the risk involved is not due to the defendant's wrongdoing, the plaintiff is still deemed to have assumed the risk (Restatement (Second) of Torts Sec. 496E, illustration 1).

IMMUNITIES

Immunity is a complete defense to tort liability in that it completely absolves the defendant of all liability. It is granted to those entities that bear a particular relationship to the plaintiff, such as a spouse, or who occupy a status, such as that of a governmental or charitable entity (see Table 10–6).

GOVERNMENTAL IMMUNITY

Federal Government. Under the common law the immunity of the king was based on the precept that "the king can do no wrong." American courts applied this adage early by adopting the principle that the United States government could not be sued without its consent. To get around this principle Congress passed private bills authorizing particular plaintiffs to sue on certain claims. Obviously this process created considerable inconvenience for

TABLE 10.6 Immunities

GOVERNMENTAL IMMUNITIES	PARENT-CHILD IMMUNITY
•Federal government immunity (limited by Federal Tort Claims Act) •State government immunity •Local government immunity (for governmental but not proprietary functions) •Public official immunity	•(abolished in majority of states and limited in others today)
INTER-SPOUSAL IMMUNITY	**CHARITABLE IMMUNITY**
•(abolished by majority of states today)	•(abolished in some states and limited in others today)

Congress. The fear of being inundated by thousands of private bills upon the return of servicemen after World War II prompted Congress in 1946 to pass the Federal Tort Claims Act (FTCA).

In general the FTCA provides that money damages can be recovered against the United States "for injury or loss of property or personal injury or death caused by the negligent or wrongful act or omission of any employee of the government while acting within the scope of his office or employment, under circumstances where the United States, if a private person, would be liable to the claimant" (28 USCA Sec. 1346 (B)). Thousands of claims are filed against the federal government each year, more than half of which arise out of automobile accidents.

Several exceptions limit the scope of the FTCA. The United States is not liable, for example, for intentional torts, such as assault, battery, false imprisonment, false arrest, abuse of process, or malicious prosecution except when they are committed by federal law enforcement officials. Questions regarding interpretation often arise when construing what types of claims should and should not be permitted under the FTCA. In one case, for example, a surgeon in a veterans hospital operated on the wrong hip and leg of the plaintiff and the court found no liability under the FTCA because, technically, under the law of Minnesota, the surgeon had committed a battery, which is excluded under the FTCA (*Moos v. U.S.*, 118 F.Supp. 275 (D. Minn. 1954)).

One of the most troubling exclusions to the FTCA pertains to a federal agency's or federal employee's exercise or failure to exercise a **discretionary function** or duty. No liability exists when a discretionary function is involved even if that discretion is abused (28 U.S.C.A. Sec. 2680 (A)). Deciding what constitutes a discretionary function has caused the courts considerable grief.

The U.S. Supreme Court has provided some guidance by indicating that discretion is involved "where there is room for policy judgment and decision" (*Dalehite v. U.S.*, 346 U.S. 15, 34–36 (1953)).

State Government. Traditionally, state governments enjoyed sovereign immunity as well but today most of them have abolished it to some extent. Many courts that have abolished governmental immunity have done so because of the availability of public liability insurance. Some have viewed taking responsibility for the torts of public employees as being part of the cost of administering a government. Regardless of the state's stance towards immunity, judges and legislators are almost never liable for their acts. Similarly, the making of "basic policy decisions" rarely results in liability (Restatement (Second) of Torts Sec. 895B(3)).

Local Government. Local governmental entities, such as police and fire departments, school systems, and public hospitals, have traditionally enjoyed at least partial immunity. The key legal argument that arises in the context of local government is whether the function being performed is a **governmental** or a **proprietary function**. A proprietary function is one that could be performed as well by a private corporation as by the government. A proprietary function is usually being performed in activities that produce revenue for the government, such as those carried out by gas and water utilities and city airports. Police and fire departments and school systems, on the other hand, are almost exclusively involved in governmental functions.

Governmental functions are subject to immunity while proprietary functions are not. To date, many courts have abolished local government immunity or have allowed suit where liability insurance is available. Administrative policy decisions as well as judicial and legislative actions still enjoy immunity.

For an interesting discussion of the duty owed by a municipality to its citizens when immunity is abolished read *Riss v. City of New York*. Notice the difference in how the majority and dissent characterize the nature of the city's duty to protect its citizens. You may find it interesting to know that Burton Pugach, the attorney who hired the man who maimed Linda Riss, served a fourteen-year sentence. After his release he proposed to Ms. Riss and they were ultimately married.

Public Officials. Legislators and judges, as well as some other public officials, receive complete immunity so long as the act complained of is within the scope of their duties. The rationale for this immunity is that a public official must be given free rein to carry out the difficult tasks of his or her office, unfettered by fear of being sued. Furthermore, by granting immunity competent people are not deterred from seeking public office out of fear of being sued. This protection extends even to those officials who are obviously operating out of a sense of greed or malice toward the plaintiff. Exception is made only where the official's act is outside the jurisdiction of the office.

To illustrate the extremes to which this doctrine can be taken, consider the Supreme Court decision involving a judge who ordered a fifteen-year-old plaintiff to be sterilized. The order was given as a result of a petition by the plaintiff's mother. No notice was given to the plaintiff nor did any statutory authorization exist for such a judicial order. Nevertheless, the court held that the judge did not act wholly beyond his jurisdiction and he was therefore immune from suit (*Stump v. Sparkman*, 435 U.S. 349 (1978)).

22 N.Y.2d 579
Linda RISS, Appellant,
v.
CITY OF NEW YORK, Respondent.
Courts of Appeals of New York.
Argued Feb. 27, 1968.
Decided July 2, 1968.

BREITEL, Judge.

This appeal presents, in a very sympathetic framework, the issue of the liability of a municipality for failure to provide special protection to a member of the public who was repeatedly threatened with personal harm and eventually suffered dire personal injuries for lack of such protection. The facts are amply described in the dissenting opinion and no useful purpose would be served by repetition. The issue arises upon the affirmance by a divided Appellate Division of a dismissal of the complaint, after both sides had rested but before submission to the jury.

It is necessary immediately to distinguish those liabilities attendant upon governmental activities which have displaced or supplemented traditionally private enterprises, such as are involved in the operation of rapid transit systems, hospitals, and place of public assembly. Once sovereign immunity was abolished by statute the extension of liability on ordinary principles or tort law logically followed. To be equally distinguished are certain activities of government which provide services and facilities for the use of the public, such as highways, public buildings and the like, in the performance of which the municipality or the State may be liable under ordinary principles of tort law. The ground for liability is the provision of the services or facilities for the direct use by members of the public.

In contrast this case involves the provision of a governmental service to protect the public generally from external hazards and particularly to control the activities of criminal wrongdoers. . . . The amount of protection that may be provided is limited by the resources of the community and by a considered legislative/executive decision as to how those resources may be deployed. For the courts to proclaim a new and general duty of protection in the law of tort, even to those who may be the particular seekers of protection based on specific hazards, could and would inevitably determine how the limited police resources of the community should be allocated and without predictable limits. This is quite different from the predictable allocation of resources and liabilities when public hospitals, rapid transit systems, or even highways are provided.

Before such extension of responsibilities should be dictated by the indirect imposition of tort liabilities, there should be a legislative determination that that should be the scope of public responsibility. . . .

It is notable that the removal of sovereign immunity for tort liability was accomplished after legislative enactment and not by any judicial arrogation of power. . . . It is equally notable that for many years, since as far back as 1909, in this State, there was by statute municipal liability for losses sustained as a result of riot. . . . Yet even this class of liability has for some years been suspended by legislative action . . ., a factor of considerable significance.

When one considers the greatly increased amount of crime committed throughout the cities, but especially in certain portions of them, with a repetitive and predictable pattern, it is easy to see the consequences of fixing municipal liability upon a showing of probable need for and request for protection. To be sure these are grave problems at the present time, exciting high priority activity on the part of the national, State and local governments, to which the answers are neither simple, known, or presently within reasonable controls. To foist a presumed cure for these problems by judicial innovation of a new kind of liability in tort would be foolhardy indeed and an assumption of judicial wisdom and power not possessed by the courts.

Nor is the analysis progressed by the analogy to compensation for losses sustained. It is instructive that the Crime Victims Compensation and "Good Samaritan" statutes, compensating limited classes of victims of crime, were enacted only after the most careful study of conditions and the impact of such a scheme upon governmental operations and the public fisc. . . . And then the limitations were particular and narrow.

For all of these reasons, there is no warrant in judicial tradition or in the proper allocation of the powers of government for the courts, in the absence of legislation, to carve out an area of tort liability for police protection to members of the public. Quite distinguishable, of course, is the situation where the police authorities undertake responsibilities to particular members of the public and expose them, without adequate protection, to the risks which then materialize into actual losses. . . .

Accordingly, the order of the Appellate Division affirming the judgment of dismissal should be affirmed.

KEATING, Judge (dissenting).

Certainly, the record in this case, sound legal analysis, relevant policy considerations and even precedent cannot account for or sustain the result which the majority have here reached. For the result is premised upon a legal rule which long ago should have been abandoned, having lost any justification it might once have had. Despite almost universal condemnation by legal scholars, the rule survives, finding its continuing strength, not in its power to persuade, but in its ability to arouse unwarranted judicial fears of the consequences of overturning it.

Linda Riss, an attractive young woman, was for more than six months terrorized by a rejected suitor well known to the courts of this State, one Burton Pugach. This miscreant, masquerading as a respectable attorney, repeatedly threatened to have Linda killed or maimed if she did not yield to him: "If I can't have you, no one else will have you, and when I get through with you, no one else will want you". In fear for her life, she went to those charged by law with the duty of preserving and safeguarding the lives of the citizens and residents of this State. Linda's repeated and almost pathetic pleas for aid were received with little more than indifference. Whatever help she was given was not commensurate with the identifiable danger. On June 14, 1959 Linda became engaged to another man. At a party held to celebrate the event, she received a phone call warning her that it was her "last chance". Completely distraught, she called the police, begging for help, but was refused. The next day Pugach carried out his dire threats in the very manner he had foretold by having a hired thug throw lye in Linda's face. Linda was blinded in one eye, lost a good portion of her vision in the other, and her face was permanently scarred. After the assault the authorities concluded that there was some basis for Linda's fears, and for the next three and one-half years, she was given around-the-clock protection.

No one questions the proposition that the first duty of government is to assure its citizens the opportunity to live in personal security. And no one who reads the record of Linda's ordeal can reach a conclusion other than that the City of New York, acting through its agents, completely and negligently failed to fulfill this obligation to Linda.

Linda has turned to the courts of this State for redress, asking that the city be held liable in damages for its negligent failure to protect her from harm. With compelling logic, she can point out that, if a stranger, who had absolutely no obligation to aid her, had offered her assistance, and thereafter Burton Pugach was able to injure here as a result of the negligence of the volunteer, the courts would certainly require him to pay damages. (Restatement, 2d, Torts, § 323.) Why then should the city, whose duties are imposed by law and include the prevention of crime . . . and, consequently, extend far beyond that of the Good Samaritan, not be responsible? If a private detective acts carelessly, no one would deny that a jury could find such conduct unacceptable. Why then is the city not required to live up to at least the same minimal standards of professional competence which would be demanded of a private detective?

Linda's reasoning seems so eminently sensible that surely it must come as a shock to her and to every citizen to hear the city argue and to learn that this court decides that the city has no duty to provide police protection to any given individual. What makes the city's position particularly difficult to understand is that, in conformity to the dictates of the law, Linda did not carry any weapon for self-defense. . . . Thus, by a rather bitter irony she was required to rely for protection on the City of New York which now denies all responsibility to her.

It is not a distortion to summarize the essence of the city's case here in the following language: "Because we owe a duty to everybody, we owe it to nobody." Were it not for the fact that this position has been hallowed by much ancient and revered precedent, we would surely dismiss it as preposterous. To say that there is no duty is, of course, to start with the conclusion. The question is whether or not there should be liability for the negligent failure to provide adequate police protection.

The foremost justification repeatedly urged for the existing rule is the claim that the State and the municipalities will be exposed to limitless liability. The city invokes the specter of a "crushing burden" . . . if we should depart from the existing rule and enunciate even the limited proposition that the State and its municipalities can be held liable for the negligent acts of their police employees in executing whatever police services they do in fact provide. . . .

The fear of financial disaster is a myth. The same argument was made a generation ago in opposition to proposals that the State waive its defense of "sovereign immunity". The prophecy proved false then, and it would now. The supposed astronomical financial burden does not and would not exist. No municipality has gone bankrupt because it has had to respond in damages when a policeman causes injury through carelessly driving a police car or in the thousands of other situations where, by judicial fiat or legislative enactment, the State and its subdivisions have been held liable for the tortious conduct of their employees. Thus, in the past four or five years, New York City has been presented with an average of some 10,000 claims each year. The figure would sound ominous except for the fact the city has been paying out less than $8,000,000 on tort claims each year and this amount includes all those sidewalk defect and snow and ice cases about which the courts fret so often. . . . Court delay has reduced the figure paid somewhat, but not substantially. Certainly this is a slight burden in a budget of more than six billion dollars (less than two tenths of

Availability of Insurance

1 percent) and of no importance as compared to the injustice of permitting unredressed wrongs to continue to go unrepaired. That Linda Riss should be asked to bear the loss, which should properly fall on the city if we assume, as we must, in the present posture of the case, that her injuries resulted from the city's failure to provide sufficient police to protect Linda is contrary to the most elementary notions of justice.

The statement in the majority opinion that there are no predictable limits to the potential liability for failure to provide adequate police protection as compared to other areas of municipal liability is, of course, untenable. When immunity in other areas of governmental activity was removed, the same lack of predictable limits existed. Yet, disaster did not ensue.

Another variation of the "crushing burden" argument is the contention that, every time a crime is committed, the city will be sued and the claim will be made that it resulted from inadequate police protection. Here, again, is an attempt to arouse the "anxiety of the courts about new theories of liability which may have a far-reaching effect". . . . And here too the underlying assumption of the argument is fallacious because it assumes that a strict liability standard is to be imposed and that the courts would prove completely unable to apply general principles of tort liability in a reasonable fashion in the context of actions arising from the negligent acts of police and fire personnel. The argument is also made as if there were no such legal principles as fault, proximate cause or foreseeability, all of which operate to keep liability within reasonable bounds. No one is contending that the police must be at the scene of every potential crime or must provide a personal bodyguard to every person who walks into a police station and claims to have been threatened. They need only act as a reasonable man would under the circumstances. At first there would be a duty to inquire. If the inquiry indicates nothing to substantiate the alleged threat, the matter may be put aside and other matters attended to. If, however, the claims prove to have some basis, appropriate steps would be necessary.

The instant case provides an excellent illustration of the limits which the courts can draw. No one would claim that, under the facts here, the police were negligent when they did not give Linda protection after her first calls or visits to the police station in February of 1959. The preliminary investigation was sufficient. If Linda had been attacked at this point, clearly there would be no liability here. When, however, as time went on and it was established that Linda was a reputable person, that other verifiable attempts to injure her or intimidate her had taken place, that other witnesses were available to support her claim that her life was being threatened, something more was required—either by way of further investigation or protection—than the statement that was made by one detective to Linda that she would have to be hurt before the police could do anything for her.

In dismissing the complaint, the trial court noted that there are many crimes being committed daily and the police force is inadequate to deal with its "tremendous responsibilities". The point is not addressed to the facts of this case. Even if it were, however, a distinction must be made. It may be quite reasonable to say that the City of New York is not required to hire sufficient police to protect every piece of property threatened during mass riots. The possibility of riots may even be foreseeable, but the occurrence is sufficiently uncommon that the city should not be required to bear the cost of having a redundancy of men for normal operations. But it is going beyond the bounds of required judicial moderation if the city is permitted to escape liability in a situation such as the one at bar. If the police force of the City of New York is so understaffed that it is unable to cope with the everyday problem posed by the relatively few cases where single, known individuals threaten the lives of other persons, then indeed we have reached the danger line and the lives of all of us are in peril. If the police department is in such a deplorable state that the city, because of insufficient manpower, is truly unable to protect persons in Linda Riss' position, then liability not only should, but must be imposed. It will act as an effective inducement for public officials to provide at least a minimally adequate number of police. If local officials are not willing to meet even such a low standard, I see no reason for the courts to abet such irresponsibility.

It is also contended that liability for inadequate police protection will make the courts the arbiters of decisions taken by the Police Commissioner in allocating his manpower and his resources. We are not dealing here with a situation where the injury or loss occurred as a result of a conscious choice of policy made by those exercising high administrative responsibility after a complete and thorough deliberation of various alternatives. There was no major policy decision taken by the Police Commissioner to disregard Linda Riss' appeal for help because there was absolutely no manpower available to deal with Pugach. This "garden variety" negligence case arose in the course of "day-by-day operations of government". . . . Linda Riss' tragedy resulted not from high policy or inadequate manpower, but plain negligence on the part of persons with whom Linda dealt. . . .

More significant, however, is the fundamental flaw in the reasoning behind the argument alleging judicial interference. It is a complete oversimplification of the problem of municipal tort liability. What it ignores is the fact that indirectly courts are reviewing administrative practices in almost every tort case against the State or a municipality, including even decisions of the Police Commissioner. Every time a municipal hospital is held liable for malpractice resulting from inadequate record-keeping, the courts are in effect making a determination that the municipality should have hired or assigned more clerical help or more competent help to medical records or should have done something to improve its record-keeping procedures so that the particular injury would not have occurred. Every time a municipality is held liable for a defective sidewalk, it is as if the courts are saying that more money and resources should have been allocated to sidewalk repair, instead of to other public services.

The situation is nowise different in the case of police protection. Whatever effects there may be on police administration will be one of degree, not kind. . . .

The truth of the matter, however, is that the courts are not making policy decisions for public officials. In all these municipal negligence cases, the courts are doing two things. First, they apply the principles of vicarious liability to the operations of government. Courts would not insulate the city from liability for the ordinary negligence of members of the highway department. There is no basis for treating the members of the police department differently.

Second, and most important, to the extent that the injury results from the failure to allocate sufficient funds and resources to meet a minimum standard of public administration, public officials are presented with two alternatives: either improve public administration or accept the cost of compensating injured persons. Thus, if we were to hold the city liable here for the negligence of the police, courts would no more be interfering with the operations of the police department than they "meddle" in the affairs of the highway department when they hold the municipality liable for personal injuries resulting from defective sidewalks, or a private employer for the negligence of his employees. In other words, all the courts do in these municipal negligence cases is require officials to weigh the consequences of their decisions. If Linda Riss' injury resulted from the failure of the city to pay sufficient salaries to attract qualified and sufficient personnel, the full cost of that choice should become acknowledged in the same way as it has in other areas of municipal tort liability. Perhaps officials will find it less costly to choose the alternative of paying damages than changing their existing practices. That may be well and good, but the price for the refusal to provide for an adequate police force should not be borne by Linda Riss and all the other innocent victims of such decisions.

What has existed until now is that the City of New York and other municipalities have been able to engage in a sort of false bookkeeping in which the real costs of inadequate or incompetent police protection have been hidden by charging the expenditures to the individuals who have sustained often catastrophic losses rather than to the community where it belongs, because the latter had the power to prevent the losses.

Although in modern times the compensatory nature of tort law has generally been the one most emphasized, one of its most important functions has been and is its normative aspect. It sets forth standards of conduct which ought to be followed. The penalty for failing to do so is to pay pecuniary damages. At one time the government was completely immunized from this salutary control. This is much less so now, and the imposition of liability has had healthy side effects. In many areas, it has resulted in the adoption of better and more considered procedures just as workmen's compensation resulted in improved industrial safety practices. To visit liability upon the city here will no doubt have similar constructive effects. No "presumed cure" for the problem of crime is being "foisted" upon the city as the majority opinion charges. The methods of dealing with the problem of crime are left completely to the city's discretion. All that the courts can do is make sure that the costs of the city's and its employees' mistakes are placed where they properly belong. Thus, every reason used to sustain the rule that there is no duty to offer police protection to any individual turns out on close analysis to be of little substance. . . .

By statute, the judicially created doctrine of "sovereign immunity" was destroyed. It was an unrighteous doctrine, carrying as it did the connotation that the government is above the law. Likewise, the law should be purged of all new evasions, which seek to avoid the full implications of the repeal of sovereign immunity.

No doubt in the future we shall have to draw limitations just as we have done in the area of private litigation, and no doubt some of these limitations will be unique to municipal liability because the problems will not have any counterpart in private tort law. But if the lines are to be drawn, let them be delineated on candid considerations of policy and fairness and not on the fictions of relics of the doctrine of "sovereign immunity". Before reaching such questions, however, we must resolve the fundamental issue raised here and recognize that, having undertaken to provide professional police and fire protection, municipalities cannot escape liability from damages caused by their failure to do even a minimally adequate job of it.

The Appellate Division did not adopt the "no duty" theory, but said there was no negligence here because the danger was not imminent. Despite the fact that the majority of the Appellate Division "agree[d] that certain rulings, and particularly the manner in which they were made, did not add to the appearance of a fair trial", and which, in fact, resulted in a wholly inadequate hearing, the majority found that the "facts brought out on this trial do not show the presence of such imminent danger that extraordinary police activity was so indicated that the failure to take it can be deemed unreasonable conduct." This finding does not stand examination and to its credit the city does not argue that this record would not support a finding of negligence. The danger to Linda was indeed imminent, and this fact could easily have been confirmed had there been competent police work.

Moreover, since this is an appeal from a dismissal of the complaint, we must give the plaintiff the benefit of every favorable inference. The Appellate Division's conclusion could only have been reached by ignoring the thrust of the plaintiff's claim and the evidence in the record. A few examples of the actions of the police should suffice to show the true state of the record. Linda Riss received a telephone call from a person who warned Linda that Pugach was arranging to have her beaten up. A detective learned the identity of the caller. He offered to arrest the caller, but plaintiff rejected that suggestion for the obvious reason that the informant was trying to help Linda. When Linda requested that Pugach be arrested, the detective said he could not do that because she had not yet been hurt. The statement was not so. It was and is a crime to conspire to injure someone. True there was no basis to arrest Pugach then, but that was only because the necessary leg work had not been done. No one went to speak to the informant, who might have furnished additional leads. Linda claimed to be receiving telephone calls almost every day. These calls could have been monitored for a few days to obtain evidence against Pugach. Any number of reasonable alternatives presented themselves. A case against Pugach could have been developed which would have at least put him away for a while or altered the situation entirely. But, if necessary, some police protection should have been afforded.

Perhaps, on a fuller record after a true trial on the merits, the city's position will not appear so damaging as it does now. But with actual notice of danger and ample opportunity to confirm and take reasonable remedial steps, a jury could find that the persons involved acted unreasonably and negligently. Linda Riss is entitled to have a jury determine the issue of the city's liability. This right should not be terminated by the adoption of a question-begging conclusion that there is no duty owed to her. The order of the Appellate Division should be reversed and a new trial granted.

FULD, C. J., and BURKE, SCILEPPI, BERGAN and JASEN, J. J., concur with BREITEL, J.

KEATING, J., dissents and votes to reverse in a separate opinion.

Order affirmed, without costs.

In some states high-ranking administrative officials receive the same complete immunity that legislators and judges do. In others they have limited immunity, which protects them only if they do not act in bad faith.

A public official's immunity is separate from governmental immunity. Therefore, if governmental immunity is abolished, the public official may still be protected by his or her own immunity. On the other hand, even if the government is immune, the public official may still be liable.

The subject of immunity is a crucial one when deciding whom to sue. It is imperative before instigating suit that you review applicable state or federal statutes as well as any case decisions pertaining to immunity. A case involving the state as a defendant that looks particularly appealing under the "deep pocket" theory (the theory that one should go after the defendant with the most money) can take on a different light when the issue of immunity is considered.

INTERSPOUSAL IMMUNITY

Under the common law spouses were immune from suit by their spouses and parents were immune from suit by their children. Spousal immunity arose out of the precept that a husband and wife were one entity and could not therefore sue each other. Consequently, a wife, for example, could not sue her husband if she was injured while a passenger in a car that he negligently drove.

The majority of states have now abolished interspousal immunity, rejecting the common law notion of the unity of the husband and wife as well as the arguments that allowing such suits would create family discord and encourage fraud. The claim that the abolition of this immunity would result in a flood of litigation has not materialized. Some fraudulent cases have arisen in which the defendant spouse has failed to fully litigate a claim against him so that the other spouse could collect the insurance. But most courts have chosen to weed out those claims from the meritorious claims rather than bar all interspousal cases.

Even those states that have not completely abolished interspousal immunity have applied certain limitations. Some, for example, have abolished immunity in reference to automobile accidents or where the tort committed was an intentional one.

PARENT-CHILD IMMUNITY

Some of the same reasons given to justify interspousal immunity were also given under the common law to bar suits by children against their parents and vice versa. Briefly, the fear was that such suits would breed disharmony in the family, encourage collusion and fraud among family members, and create a flood of litigation.

Some states have chosen to abolish this immunity, particularly in cases involving motor vehicle accidents. The reason commonly given is that most suits are between a family and its insurance company and not between individual members of a family. Even in those states that have not abolished such immunity, many have allowed suit where the tort was intentional, where it involved loss of property or other pecuniary loss, where the injury occurred in the course of a business activity, where the child was legally emancipated or was a stepchild of the defendant, or where the parent-child relationship was terminated by the death of one of the parties prior to the suit. No immunity exists between siblings nor in other family relationships.

One of the problems that can arise in the context of parent-child suits is the matter of negligent supervision. Consider the case of a child left unsupervised by her mother and who, as a result of this lack of supervision, is run over by the defendant. Should the defendant be allowed to bring a third-party claim against the plaintiff's mother for negligent failure to supervise the child? Some courts have said no, arguing that permitting such claims would in effect reduce the child's compensation by allowing the defendant to obtain contribution from the parent. Others have allowed such claims and have created a "reasonable parent" standard in determining the duty of supervision owed to a child.

CHARITABLE IMMUNITY

Charitable organizations, including educational and religious organizations, received immunity under the common law. The purpose of such immunity was to protect charitable institutions from tort claims and thereby promote their existence. Some courts have argued that the beneficiaries of charitable organizations impliedly waive their right to sue as a result of accepting the benefits offered by that organization. Other courts have characterized this so-called *implied waiver theory* as a legal fiction that has no relevance in emergency situations, such as the receipt of emergency aid from a charitable hospital.

The other rationale used to justify charitable immunity is sometimes referred to as the *"trust fund" theory*. This theory is based on the premise that those funds given for charitable purposes should not be used to pay judgments resulting from tort claims. The refutation of this argument is that the trust fund theory refers to how a judgment should be satisfied and not to the root question as to whether an individual has a right to bring an action. In short, the argument goes, the question of liability should not be based on the charity's ability to satisfy a judgment.

The majority of states have abolished charitable immunity altogether while others have abolished it only in reference to charitable hospitals. Some, in deference to the trust fund theory, have allowed liability when liability insurance is available but have denied it when a judgment would have to be paid out of trust funds. Still others, relying on the rationale of the implied waiver theory, have allowed those who are not beneficiaries of the charity, such as employees or visitors, to sue.

STATUTES OF LIMITATIONS AND STATUTES OF REPOSE

A **statute of limitations,** as the name indicates, is a statute limiting the time in which an action can be brought. Any action not commenced within that time period is barred. The purpose of such statutes is to protect individuals from having to defend stale claims. They also allow people to have some measure of stability and predictability in their lives by limiting the time frame in which they can anticipate being sued.

Since most statutes of limitations begin to run when a cause of action **"accrues,"** the question is when does accrual take place. Most courts have held that accrual occurs when there has been an actual injury to the plaintiff's person or property. Problems arise, however, when the plaintiff could not reasonably have discovered her injury until after the statute had run. Suppose, for example, the statute of limitations on medical malpractice claims is five years but that the plaintiff did not begin to suffer complications from the medical procedures she underwent until six years later. By the time she discovered she had a cause of action she would be barred from pursuing it.

To mitigate the harshness of a statute that precludes recovery in a case such as this, many courts have created the so-called *discovery doctrine,* which provides that the statute does not begin to run until the injury is, or should have been, discovered. Many states apply this rule to all surgical cases, but some have limited it to those claims in which an object was left in the patient's body. Still others have held that the statute begins to run when the doctor-patient relationship terminates, regardless of whether the plaintiff has discovered her injury at that time.

Some have argued that the discovery doctrine has contributed to the rising cost of medical malpractice insurance. Many policies cover a physician's conduct during a particular year even though a claim based on that conduct may not arise for several years. As a result of the actuarial projections necessitated by this type of policy, premiums are very high. Arguably, premiums could be reduced if policies were issued on a "claims made" basis so that only those claims filed against the physician that year, regardless of when the act of malpractice occurred, would be covered. Alternatively, some argue that a maximum time limit should be set for discovery under the discovery doctrine.

A similar issue arises in the case of malpractice by lawyers and other professionals. When should the statute of limitations begin to run when a lawyer negligently prepares a will? What if a latent construction defect does not show up until many years after the completion of construction? In some states the discovery doctrine has been applied.

It is important to consult the statutes in your state to determine the applicable statute of limitations and to ascertain when a cause of action accrues. This is one of the first questions that an attorney must answer when deciding whether to take a case. Failure to determine the appropriate statute of limitations could be grounds for malpractice.

Whereas the statute of limitations begins to run at the time of injury, a **statute of repose** begins to run at the date of sale of a product. Such statutes are designed to limit a manufacturer's liability, to lower insurance costs for manufacturers, and to introduce a sense of certainty in the area of product liability litigation. Most statutes of repose are five to twelve years and in some cases may bar suit even before injury occurs. As a practical matter, however, few suits are actually prevented since few plaintiffs are injured by old, defective products. The effects are devastating, however, to certain victims, such as those who were injured by DES or asbestos or by some kinds of long-lasting machinery. Some courts have found statutes of repose to be constitutionally impermissible.

APPLICATION

The Baxters will likely claim that Teddy and Mr. Dooright were contributorily negligent. If they prevail in this claim and they live in a contributory negligence state both Teddy and Mr. Dooright will be precluded from recovering. If, however, they live in a comparative negligence state their recoveries will be reduced in direct proportion to their percentage of negligence. Whereas Teddy would likely be found negligent, Mr. Dooright would probably not be found negligent as long as he acted reasonably in rescuing Teddy. The last clear chance doctrine is inapplicable since the Baxters were not present during the time of Teddy's attack and Mr. Baxter did everything he could to rescue Mr. Dooright when he became aware of Gertrude's attack.

Arguably Teddy impliedly assumed the risk by going into the Baxter's backyard since he was aware of Gertrude's presence and of her propensity to attack. The defendants will have to prove, however, that Teddy actually knew that there was a risk and not merely that he ought to have known. Again, because of his classification as a rescuer, Mr. Dooright will probably be successful in rebutting any claim that he assumed the risk.

As a result of the consideration of the defenses that can be raised in this case, it is likely that Teddy's attorney will opt for a strict liability claim if at all possible. Remember that contributory negligence is generally not a defense to strict liability although assumption of risk will usually be a complete defense. Nevertheless, assumption of risk requires subjective proof, putting the burden on the Baxters to show that Teddy knew the risk that he was confronting. The Baxters' task in proving assumption of risk would be more difficult than proving contributory negligence, in which an objective standard would be used to evaluate Teddy's conduct.

Although no immunities could be raised as defenses, consideration of the applicable statute of limitations would be important. If Teddy and Mr. Dooright "sat" on their cases for a considerable period of time, their attorneys would be required to conduct their initial investigations expeditiously and file immediately before the statute of limitations was to run. If the attorneys failed to file in a timely manner and their clients were precluded from filing due to the statute of limitations, the attorneys would be subject to malpractice claims.

SUMMARY

The three defenses most commonly raised in negligence cases are contributory negligence, comparative negligence, and assumption of risk. Because the contributory negligence rule is sometimes viewed as harsh and unjust courts have developed various escape mechanisms by which plaintiffs can avoid this rule. The most significant exception to the contributory negligence defense is the last clear chance doctrine. This doctrine does not apply if neither the defendant nor the plaintiff discovers the danger as a result of their inattentiveness. The doctrine is also inapplicable if the defendant's act of negligence precedes the plaintiff's predicament and precludes him or her from avoiding the accident after discovering the plaintiff's peril.

Contributory negligence cannot be used as a defense against an intentional tort. Nor is it allowed if the defendant's conduct was "willful and wanton" or "reckless" unless the plaintiff's conduct was also "willful and wanton" or "reckless." Contributory negligence can be raised in the case of negligence *per se* unless the statute on which the defendant's negligence is based was enacted solely to protect a class of persons of which the plaintiff is a member and the statute's intent was to place sole responsibility on the defendant.

All but a few states have adopted a comparative negligence system. Under a pure comparative negligence system the plaintiff recovers regardless of the extent of his or her negligence. Under the 50 percent approach, a plaintiff's claim is barred if his or her negligence is either "as great as" or "not greater than" the defendant's negligence. Difficulty is often encountered in assigning fault to the parties, particularly when there are more parties involved than just the plaintiff and defendant.

As with contributory negligence, comparative negligence cannot be raised as a defense to an intentional tort. It can be raised if the defendant's conduct

PRACTICE POINTERS

Physical Evidence
Physical evidence or statements (written or oral) are often needed in order to support or rebut the plaintiff's claim. Therefore, attorneys frequently turn to their legal assistants to conduct certain kinds of rudimentary investigation.

Witness Statements
The process of interviewing was discussed in Chapter 4 and will be alluded to here only briefly. Having interviewed a witness you may decide that you want to take his statement. Several means can be used to do that. As mentioned in chapter 4, you may wish, with the permission of the witness, to tape record his statement. Alternatively, you may ask him to write out his statement, although it is rare that individuals do an adequate job. Frequently, investigators write out the person's statement and have the witness sign it. The obvious drawback to this procedure is that the witness can later deny having made the statement or can say he signed it even though he was never given an opportunity to read it. In such cases the statement may be inadmissible and the investigator may be forced to take the stand to testify as to the witness' statement. Although expensive, another alternative is the use of a court reporter. This method virtually precludes the witness from denying he made the statement but if he does a court reporter, who is a disinterested third party, rather than an investigator, will be called to testify.

Statements should be as specific as possible. Detailed, specific information rather than abstract generalizations are the goal. Be sure to get the witness' actual observations and not his opinions since opinions of lay witnesses are generally not admissible.

Photographing Physical Evidence
The existence of physical evidence can be recorded through notes, sketches, photographs, or by the actual preservation of such evidence. Photographs are extremely helpful in relating a story to a jury. They should be accompanied by notes and sketches, which will allow the investigator at the time of trial to testify as to the relative location of each piece of evidence. The inclusion of units of measurements, such as a ruler, may be necessary with certain types of physical evidence. Shoe prints, for example, must be photographed using a ruler so that the actual size of the shoes can later be determined. Any sketches should also show the location of witnesses and the parties. All of this information will assist the jury in piecing together what actually happened.

Careful attention must be given to the photographic process. Keep in mind that the purpose of photographing evidence is for evidentiary and not aesthetic purposes. Therefore, black and white film rather than color

Continued on next page

PRACTICE POINTERS—Continued

film will be used in certain instances because black and white produces sharper details. Always try to fill the frame as much as possible, blocking out any distracting background. Lighting is especially crucial. When photographing shoe prints or tire impressions oblique (low angle) lighting is essential in order to bring out the unique characteristics of the evidence.

Also be careful to make sure that the photographs accurately reflect the scene as it occurred. Since distortions are so easily created through the use of photography the attorneys who cross-examine you will be interested in finding out the precise manner in which you took each photograph. To help jog your memory you should record details, such as camera speed, lighting conditions, and camera location for each photograph. Never alter any evidence in photographing it since such alterations will render the photograph inadmissible.

Sometimes a series of photographs will be necessary. For example, if the plaintiff has been bruised the discoloration will not appear for awhile and the bruises will have to be photographed over time. Accident scenes should also be photographed in a series of shots, recreating the scene from the viewpoint of the drivers. Begin shooting from the direction of your client's vehicle about 500 feet from the point of impact and move progressively closer to the point of impact. Repeat this sequence from the viewpoint of the other driver. Take these photographs at the eye level of the driver so that they represent the scene from the driver's vantage point.

Remember that a photograph is indeed "worth a thousand words." Never skimp on film to save a little money. Photograph every square inch of an accident scene from every conceivable angle. Take several photographs of damaged areas of vehicles, including less visible damages such as scratches or paint scrapings. A piece of evidence that may at the time seem trivial to you may be the very evidence upon which the whole case hinges at trial. Taking photographs in the investigative process is an exacting science. If possible, you should consider taking courses or at least reading extensively in this area to enhance your expertise.

Preservation of Evidence

In some cases it may be necessary to preserve evidence. When at all possible, submit tangible evidence to a jury rather than photographs or verbal descriptions. Additionally, inspection of such evidence by experts may lead to new insights as to how the plaintiff's injury occurred.

The general rule of thumb to keep in mind in preserving evidence is to do nothing that would in any way alter the evidence. Do not, for example, package two pieces of evidence together. Packaging in this

Continued on next page

PRACTICE POINTERS—Continued

manner creates the possibility that the two pieces of evidence will alter one another if they come in contact.

Be aware that some evidence, particularly biological evidence, will change over time if not properly preserved. Blood, semen, perspiration, urine, and saliva will decompose unless refrigerated as soon as possible. Furthermore, plastic bags lead to the decomposition of almost all biological evidence and, because they absorb moisture, can cause rusting and deterioration of nonbiological materials.

As a general rule avoid the use of plastic bags for preserving evidence; instead, use paper bags whenever possible. Anything suspected of containing a volatile compound, such as gasoline, should be preserved in paint cans or sealed glass jars so that the gases cannot escape. Again, avoid plastic bags when packaging volatile materials.

Keep in mind that trace evidence such as paint particles or fibers may be present and could accidentally be removed with careless handling. Treat every piece of evidence with care and protect it from contamination by outside sources. Avoid the unnecessary handling of documents and never fold or cut any document since such alteration may ruin its evidentiary value.

Evidence preservation is another area in which you can improve your effectiveness as an investigator if you will simply familiarize yourself with the basic rules. You can easily do this by consulting any reference book in the area of criminalistics or criminal investigations.

was "willful and wanton," "reckless," or negligent *per se*. Some jurisdictions continue to apply the last clear chance doctrine although the Uniform Comparative Fault Act expressly rejects its use in a comparative negligence system.

The distinction between contributory negligence and assumption of risk is often a blurred one. Contributory negligence is something characterized as "carelessness" while assumption of risk is sometimes perceived as "adventurousness." In the defense of contributory negligence, an objective standard is used while in assumption of risk a subjective standard is relied on. Assumption of risk, unlike contributory negligence, can be used as a defense to reckless conduct and in a case of strict liability.

A plaintiff can either expressly or impliedly assume the risk. An express waiver will not be enforced if the defendant has unusual bargaining power or if the plaintiff is unaware of the risk. In terms of implied consent the plaintiff will not be considered to have acted voluntarily if she had no reasonable choice but to confront the danger. Those states that have adopted comparative negligence have, to some degree, removed assumption of risk as a separate defense.

Immunity is a complete defense to tort liability. Immunity of federal government officials has been curtailed by the Federal Tort Claims Act. Federal officials performing discretionary functions are immune from suit. State governments traditionally enjoyed sovereign immunity although most states have abolished it to some extent. Local governmental entities have enjoyed at least partial immunity. Immunity is typically granted for governmental functions but not allowed for proprietary functions. Legislators, judges, and some other public officials receive complete immunity as long as they are acting within the scope of their duties.

The majority of states have now abolished interspousal immunity or at the least have imposed various limitations on such immunity. Similarly, some states have chosen to abolish parent-child immunity. Charitable immunity has been abolished altogether in the majority of states. Some courts have adhered to the trust fund theory and have denied liability if the judgment would have to be paid out of trust funds. Still other courts have adhered to the implied waiver theory and have allowed recovery only to those who are not beneficiaries of the charity.

Statutes of limitations and statutes of repose prevent the bringing of stale claims and allow some measure of stability and predictability in people's lives. The key question that arises in reference to these statutes is the question of accrual. Under the discovery doctrine a statute does not begin to run until the injury is or should have been discovered. A statute of repose begins to run at the date of sale of a product.

TORT TEASERS

1. The so-called "seat belt defense" is used by defense counsel to argue that the plaintiff was contributorily negligent or negligent *per se* in his failure to wear a seat belt. Assume you are representing a defendant in a motor vehicle accident case and argue: (a) the plaintiff was contributorily negligent; (b) the plaintiff was comparatively negligent; (c) the plaintiff assumed the risk; (d) the plaintiff failed to mitigate his damages; and (e) the plaintiff was negligent *per se*. Be as specific as possible in terms of the type of legal argument you would want to make and the type of evidence that you would want to introduce. Would you rather argue that the plaintiff contributed to his own injuries or that he assumed the risk? Why?

Then assume you are representing the plaintiff and argue that the seat belt defense is inappropriate. In your arguments consider whether the plaintiff has a duty to use a seat belt and whether his failure to do so constitutes the proximate cause of the accident. Furthermore, you might want to consider when the plaintiff's duty to mitigate his damages arises.

2. A State Board of Pardons and Paroles grants parole to an individual despite information that he is an extremely dangerous person and has a definite potential for violence. The parolee subsequently kills one person and seriously injures another. The injured man and the parents of the deceased file a personal injury and wrongful death suit against the Board of Pardon and Paroles. The board argues that it and its individual members enjoy absolute immunity from civil suit for decisions granting parole. In the alternative the board argues for qualified immunity. Discuss whether or not the same type of immunity that is given to judges should be granted to a Board of Pardons and Paroles. If granted qualified immunity, should such immunity extend to the grossly negligent release of a highly dangerous prisoner? *Grimm v. Arizona Bd. of Pardons and Paroles*, 564 P.2d 1227 (1977).

3. The plaintiff, a participant, in a "National Lap Sitting Contest" promoting wrinkle-free slacks, is injured when the chair in which he is sitting collapses because he was holding fourteen girls on his lap. What defenses do you think should be raised in this case and why? *Wyly v. Burlington Industries*, 452 F.2d 807 (5th Cir. 1971).

KEY TERMS

■ **Accrual**
Time at which a statute of limitations begins to run, usually at the time the plaintiff is injured.

■ **Assumption of risk**
Defense that the plaintiff voluntarily consented to take the chance that harm would occur if he or she engaged in certain conduct.

■ **Comparative negligence**
Defense that the plaintiff's recovery should be reduced in direct proportion to the plaintiff's percentage of contribution to his or her own injuries.

■ **Contributory negligence**
Defense that the plaintiff contributed to his or her own injuries and should therefore be barred from recovery.

■ **Discretionary function**
Act of a government employee requiring the use of judgment.

■ **Governmental function**
Task typically performed by a governmental entity.

■ **Immunity**
Absolute defense derived from the defendant's status (e.g., a government official) or relationship to the plaintiff (e.g., spouse of the plaintiff).

■ **Last clear chance doctrine**
Doctrine that allows the plaintiff to recover in a contributory negligence system despite the plaintiff's negligence.

■ **Proprietary function**
Function performed by the government that could just as easily be performed by a private entity.

■ **Statute of limitations**
Statute that limits the time period in which a claim can be filed.

■ **Statute of repose**
Statute of limitations in product liability cases that limits the time period during which suit can be filed.

DEFAMATION

CHAPTER OBJECTIVES

In this chapter you will learn to:

- Distinguish between libel and slander.
- Identify the elements of defamation and the damages that can be recovered.
- Recognize the importance of distinguishing between private and public figures.
- Distinguish between absolute and qualified privileges of defendants.

The headlines of the *National Snoop* proclaim that the current "heartthrob" of a daytime soap opera has impregnated his co-star. In reality, the young lady with whom he is romantically linked on the show is in fact pregnant. Further adding fuel to this story is the fact that in real life the couple has been seen together on several occasions. The actor, however, vehemently denies that he is the father of the child. What would he have to show if he wants to claim libel? Suppose that stories of his purported fatherhood circulate around the studio but are never published. Will he have any more difficulty proving slander than he will proving libel? Let us consider the elements of defamation and the distinction between libel and slander as we attempt to answer these questions.

LIBEL VS. SLANDER

Defamation is considered to be one of the most complex torts. Its complexity is due in part to First Amendment concerns that have to be reconciled with an individual's right to privacy. Defamation encompasses the two related torts of libel and slander (see Table 11–1). **Libel** refers to written defamatory statements; **slander** refers to oral statements. Libel encompasses communications occurring in "physical form" (according to many modern courts and the Restatement (Second)). Under this definition defamatory statements on records and computer tapes are considered libel rather than slander. Spoken words that are intended to be written down, such as words dictated to a stenographer, are also categorized as libel. A radio or television program that originates from a written script is considered libel although the courts are not in agreement about how to classify a program that is "ad-libbed."

SPECIAL HARM

The distinction between libel and slander is sometimes blurred but it is a significant one. To prove slander a plaintiff must establish that he or she suffered some kind of **special harm.** Special harm need not necessarily be proved in the case of libel. The special harm that must be established generally involves harm of a **pecuniary** (monetary) nature. Loss of friendship and emotional upset are not generally considered to have a pecuniary value. However, if a plaintiff is able to prove pecuniary loss she can attach any emotional damages to her pecuniary loss.

Four exceptions to the special harm requirement for slander exist. In these four cases of **slander *per se*** pecuniary harm can be assumed. The four categories encompass statements alleging (1) that the plaintiff engaged in criminal behavior, (2) that the plaintiff suffers from some type of venereal or otherwise loathsome and communicable disease, (3) that the plaintiff is unfit to conduct his or her business, trade, or profession, and (4) that the plaintiff has engaged in sexual misconduct.

Under the common law special harm did not have to be proved and damages were presumed in cases of libel in which the defamatory nature of the statement was obvious. **Presumed damages** are those damages that ordinarily flow from defamation, thereby precluding the necessity of the plaintiff proving actual harm. If damages are presumed, a plaintiff can recover an amount that approximates the damages that normally result from a defamatory statement

TABLE 11.1 Libel vs. Slander

LIBEL	SLANDER
•Written statements (including records, computer tapes, dictation by stenographer). •No need to prove special harm. •Presumed damages awarded if: (a) actual malice is shown and matter involved is of public concern or (b) matter involved is a private concern and no actual malice is shown.	•Oral statements. •Must prove special harm unless slander *per se*. •Presumed damages not awarded.

like the one made by the defendant. Recovery is allowed even though the plaintiff produces no evidence of any actual harm, such as loss of business or friends.

Recent Supreme Court decisions, however, have substantially limited the courts in their right to award presumed damages. In cases involving matters of public concern, a plaintiff cannot be awarded presumed damages if he or she is unable to prove "actual malice" (*Gertz v. Robert Welch, Inc.*, 418 U.S. 323 (1974)). A defendant who acts with **actual malice** knows either of the falsity of his statement or acts with reckless disregard in reference to the truth or falsity of his statement. If the plaintiff is able to prove actual malice, then presumed damages may be awarded. In matters involving purely private concerns, the plaintiff can recover presumed damages even without a showing of actual malice.

WHAT IS A DEFAMATORY STATEMENT?

The Restatement (Second) of Torts defines a statement as being defamatory if it tends to harm one's reputation, thereby lowering him or her in the estimation of the community or deterring others from associating with him or her (see Table 11–2). **Defamation** requires proof that the defendant's statement was defamatory and that it was published, that is, communicated to someone other than the plaintiff. Furthermore, the defendant must, at the very least, act negligently (although a greater degree of fault is required under certain circumstances).

HARM OF REPUTATION

To be considered defamatory, a statement must have a tendency to harm the reputation of the plaintiff (Restatement (Second) of Torts Sec. 559). The plaintiff's reputation need not actually be injured. A statement is sufficiently harmful if the plaintiff's reputation would have been injured if those who heard the statement had believed it. Therefore, even if everyone who hears a defamatory statement believes it to be false, this statement can still be considered defamatory.

TABLE 11.2

ELEMENTS OF DEFAMATION
•Plaintiff's reputation is harmed or tended to be harmed. •Statement is reasonably interpreted by at least one person as referring to plaintiff. •At least one interpretation of statement could reasonably be considered defamatory. •Statement is false. •Statement is seen or heard by someone other than plaintiff (publication). •Defendant acts with actual malice (if plaintiff is a public official or public figure).

A plaintiff may recover even if his or her reputation is tarnished in the eyes of only a certain segment of a community as long as the segment consists of a significant and "respectable" minority of people. In one case, for example, the defendant mistakenly published the plaintiff's picture next to a testimonial signed by a nurse praising the medicinal merits of Duffy's pure malt whiskey. As Judge Holmes noted, "if the advertisement obviously would hurt the plaintiff in the estimation of an important and respectable part of the community, liability is not a question of majority vote" (*Peck v. Tribune Co.*, 214 U.S. 185, 190 (1909)). Nonetheless, the statement must contain some element of "disgrace." Although referring to a Democrat as a Libertarian, for example, might engender some feelings of hostility, such a statement could not be construed as defamatory.

REASONABLE INTERPRETATION

The plaintiff must also prove that the statement was reasonably understood by at least one person as referring to the plaintiff. The defendant need not refer to the plaintiff but someone must interpret the statement as pertaining to the plaintiff. Furthermore, the defendant need not refer to the plaintiff by name as long as it is reasonably understood to whom the defendant is referring. A plaintiff will often have a difficult time recovering if the defendant's statement is made in reference to a group to which the plaintiff belongs. The statement probably will not be considered defamatory unless the group is a relatively small one.

BURDEN OF PROVING TRUTH

Statements can often be interpreted in several different ways. The plaintiff must show that the statement is defamatory in accordance with at least one interpretation that a reasonable person might make, and must also prove that at least one person interpreted it in a defamatory way. Before the jury can declare a statement defamatory, a judge must first determine that the statement is subject to at least one reasonable interpretation that is defamatory.

To illustrate this point, consider the case involving the famous attorney Melvin Belli, in which a newspaper alleged that, while on an expense-paid appearance before the Florida bar, Belli "took" the bar by charging hundreds of dollars worth of clothing to his hotel bill. The trial judge ruled that the statement was not defamatory and refused to submit the case to the jury. The appellate court, however, held that the statement had a clear defamatory meaning (indicating Belli was dishonest) as well as a nondefamatory meaning (indicating Belli was clever) and that the case should have been submitted to the jury (*Belli v. Orlando Daily Newspapers, Inc.*, 389 F.2d 579 (5th Cir. 1967)).

Sometimes the defamatory content of a statement may not be recognizable unless certain extrinsic facts are known. A birth announcement, for example, may not be defamatory on its face but if the recipient of that announcement is made aware that the plaintiff has been married for only six months then the defamatory implications become clearer. The plaintiff must specifically show in his or her pleadings the **innuendo,** which refers to the way in which the extrinsic facts convey a defamatory meaning. The plaintiff in the case pertaining to the birth announcement would be required to allege that because of the fact that the plaintiff had been married for only six months, the birth announcement created a false impression that the plaintiff had been unchaste prior to marriage.

A statement must be obviously false to be considered defamatory. A statement that is substantially true even though it may not be literally true in all respects is considered a true statement. Under the common law the defendant had the burden of proving the truth of his or her statement. Recent Supreme Court decisions, however, have limited a state's ability to require the defendant to bear such a burden. Today the plaintiff bears the burden of proving that a statement was false if the statement involves a matter of "public interest" and the defendant is a media defendant. (*Philadelphia Newspapers v. Hepps'*, 106 U.S. 1558 (1986)). Even plaintiffs who are private figures must bear this burden of proof. Whether a defendant may be required to bear the burden of proving the truth of his or her statements if the statements are not of public interest and the plaintiff is a private figure is not clear.

WHO CAN BE DEFAMED?

Only living persons can be defamed. Therefore, survivors of the deceased may not sue for defamation because of statements made against the deceased. If the words defame a living person by implication, however, recovery is allowed. For example, a statement that the deceased was unwed when she gave birth to her child tends to defame that child. A corporation, partnership, or association may be defamed only if the statement "tends to prejudge it in the course of its business or to deter others from dealing with it" (Restatement (Second) of Torts Sec. 561 and 562).

OPINION

Under the common law an opinion could be defamatory unless it fell under the privilege of "fair comment" or matter of public concern. Recent Supreme Court decisions point to the conclusion that a pure expression of opinion cannot be defamatory (Restatement (Second) of Torts Sec. 566 comment c). A statement that implies factual matters, however, can be considered defamatory.

The difference between fact and opinion is not always clear, but the courts look at a number of factors in making that distinction. The more precise a statement is, the more likely a court will consider it a fact. A statement that is almost impossible to verify is likely to be considered an opinion. The literary context in which the statement is made is also considered. Readers are generally assumed to understand, for example, that statements made by reviewers constitute opinion rather than objectively verifiable facts. Statements implying undisclosed facts may be actionable even though they are opinions. A statement such as "I think George is an alcoholic" may be defamatory even though the declarant is apparently expressing an opinion. The implication from the statement is that the declarant knows or has factual information about George's alcohol consumption that would justify rendering an opinion as to George's alcoholic condition (Restatement (Second) of Torts Sec. 566, illustration 3).

PUBLICATION

The term **publication,** when used in the context of defamation, is a term of art requiring that the statement be seen or heard by someone other than the plaintiff. The publication may be intentional or negligent. Merely overhearing a statement made by the defendant to the plaintiff does not constitute publication. The publication must also be understood by the person who hears it. A defamatory statement made in a language not understood to the person hearing it does not meet the requirement of publication.

Repetition of a defamatory statement is considered publication. One who repeats a statement is just as liable as if he or she were the first person to make the statement, even if the one repeating the statement does not believe it to be true (Restatement (Second) of Torts Sec. 578 comment e). Those who distribute or sell defamatory matter, such as news dealers and libraries, are not liable if they can show they had no reason to believe that the materials were defamatory. Under the *single publication rule* most courts hold that an entire edition of a book or periodical should be treated as one publication. Therefore, even if several copies of a book are sold, only one defamation can be alleged.

INTENT

Under the common law, defamation was essentially a strict liability tort since defendants could be liable even if they had every reason to believe that a statement they made was true. That has changed, however, with recent U.S. Supreme Court decisions. Under the court's first landmark decision in this area, *New York Times Co. v. Sullivan*, 376 U.S. 254 (1964), the court held that if a plaintiff is a public official, he or she can recover only by showing that the defendant acted with actual malice. Actual malice is defined as having the knowledge that a statement is false or acting with "reckless disregard" with reference to the truth or falsity of the statement. Actual malice differs from the lay definition of the term, which normally implies some type of ill will. Reckless disregard has been defined as evidence indicating that the defendant in fact "entertained serious doubts" as to the truth of his or her statements (*St. Amant v. Thompson*, 390 U.S. 727 (1969)).

The actual malice requirement was extended to public figures in a later case. The Supreme Court defined a **public figure** as "one who has achieved pervasive fame or notoriety" or who "voluntarily injects himself or is drawn into a particular public controversy" (*Gertz v. Robert Welch, Inc.*, 418 U.S. 323 (1974)). In *Gertz* the plaintiff was a locally well-known lawyer who represented the family of a young man killed by a policeman. The defendant, publisher of a John Birch Society magazine, falsely accused the plaintiff of being a criminal and a Communist. The court held that a person does not become a public figure merely because he becomes involved in a controversy of public interest. Therefore, the plaintiff in *Gertz* was not a public figure merely because the newspapers took an interest in the lawsuit. The *Gertz* court's reasoning for giving less protection to public figures was that those in the public eye "usually enjoy significantly greater access to the channels of effective communication and hence have a more realistic opportunity to counteract false statements than private individuals normally enjoy." Whether *New York Times* and *Gertz* apply to nonmedia defendants is not clear.

The public figure issue is discussed at length in *Street v. National Broadcasting Co.*, a historically interesting case that emanates from the famous "Scottsboro

Boys" case involving the alleged rape of two white women by nine black youths. Once the *Street* court concludes that the plaintiff is a public figure it is faced with the question of how long she retains that status. Pay particular attention to the court's public policy arguments and note its application of the actual malice standard.

If a plaintiff is neither a public official nor a public figure, the constitution does not require that he or she prove actual malice. Strict liability, however, is not sufficient. The plaintiff must, at the very least, prove that the defendant acted negligently.

CASE

Victoria Price STREET,
Plaintiff-Appellant,
v.
NATIONAL BROADCASTING CO.,
Defendant-Appellee.
No. 77-1682.
United States Court of Appeals,
Sixth Circuit.
Argued Nov. 28, 1979.
Decided March 13, 1981.
645 F.2d 1227 (1981).

MERRITT, Circuit Judge.

This is a Tennessee diversity case against the National Broadcasting Company for libel and invasion of privacy. The plaintiff-appellant, Victoria Price Street, was the prosecutrix and main witness in the famous rape trials of the Scottsboro boys, which occurred in Alabama more than forty years ago. NBC televised a play or historical drama entitled "Judge Horton and the Scottsboro Boys," dramatizing the role of the local presiding judge in one of those trials.

The movie portrays Judge Horton as a courageous and tragic figure struggling to bring justice in a tense community gripped by racial prejudice and intent on vengeance against nine blacks accused of raping two white women. In the movie Judge Horton sets aside a jury verdict of guilty because he believes that the evidence shows that the prosecutrix—plaintiff in this action—falsely accused the Scottsboro defendants. The play portrays the plaintiff in the derogatory light that Judge Horton apparently viewed her: as a woman attempting to send nine innocent blacks to the electric chair for a rape they did not commit.

This case presents the question of what tort and First Amendment principles apply to an historical drama that allegedly defames a living person who participated in the historical events portrayed. The plaintiff's case is based on principles of libel law and "false light" invasion of privacy[1] arising from the derogatory portrayal. . . .

1. False light invasion of privacy is one of four generally recognized forms of the tort of invasion of privacy. It differs from the other three forms in that falsity is one of its essential elements.

At the end of all the proof, District Judge Neese directed a verdict for defendant on the ground that even though plaintiff was not a public figure at the time of publication the defamatory matter was not negligently published. We affirm for the reason that the historical events and persons portrayed are "public" and distinguished from "private." A malice standard applies to public figures under the First Amendment, and there is no evidence that the play was published with malice.

I. STATEMENT OF FACTS

A. Historical Context

In April 1931, nine black youths were accused of raping two young white women while riding a freight train between Chattanooga, Tennessee, and Huntsville, Alabama. The case was widely discussed in the local, national, and foreign press. The youths were quickly tried in Scottsboro, Alabama, and all were found guilty and sentenced to death. The Alabama Supreme Court affirmed the convictions. . . . The United States Supreme Court reversed all convictions on the ground that the defendants were denied the right to counsel guaranteed by the Sixth Amendment. *Powell v. Alabama,* 287 U.S. 45, 53 S.Ct. 55, 77 L.Ed. 158 (1932). The defendants were retried separately after a change of venue from Scottsboro to Decatur, Alabama. Patterson was the first defendant retried, and this trial was the subject of the NBC production. In a jury trial before Judge Horton, he was tried, convicted, and sentenced to death. Judge Horton set the verdict aside on the ground that the evidence was insufficient. Patterson and one other defendant, Norris, were then tried before another judge on essentially the same evidence, convicted, and sentenced to death. The judge let the verdicts stand, and the convictions were affirmed by the Alabama Supreme Court. . . . The United States Supreme Court again reversed, this time because blacks were systematically excluded from grand and petit juries. . . . At his fourth retrial, Patterson was convicted and sentenced to seventy-five years in prison. . . . Defendants Weems and Andrew Wright were also convicted on retrial and sentenced to a term of years. Defendant Norris was convicted and his death sentence was commuted to life imprisonment by the Alabama governor. Defendants Montgomery, Roberson, Williams, and Leroy Wright were released without retrial. Powell pled guilty to assault allegedly committed during an attempted escape. The last Scottsboro defendant was paroled in 1950.

The Scottsboro case aroused strong passions and conflicting opinions in the 1930s throughout the nation. Several all white juries convicted the Scottsboro defendants of rape. Two trial judges and the Alabama Supreme Court, at times by divided vote, let these verdicts stand. Judge Horton was the sole trial judge to find the facts in favor of the defendants. Liberal opinion supported Judge Horton's conclusions that the Scottsboro defendants had been falsely accused.

During the lengthy course of the Scottsboro trials, newspapers frequently wrote about Victoria Price. She gave some interviews to the press. Thereafter, she disappeared from public view. The Scottsboro trials and her role in them continued to be the subject of public discussion, but there is no evidence that Mrs. Street sought publicity. NBC incorrectly stated in the movie that she was no longer living. After the first showing of "Judge Horton and the Scottsboro Boys," plaintiff notified NBC that she was living, and shortly thereafter she filed suit. Soon after plaintiff filed suit, NBC rebroadcast the dramatization omitting the statement that plaintiff was no longer living.

B. The Dramatization

The script for "Judge Horton and the Scottsboro Boys" was based on one chapter of a book by Dr. Daniel Carter, an historian, entitled *Scottsboro: A Tragedy of the American South* (Louisiana State University Press, 1969). The movie is based almost entirely on the information in Dr. Carter's book, which, in turn, was based on Judge Horton's findings at the 1933 trial, the transcript of the trial, contemporaneous newspaper reports of the trial, and interviews with Judge Horton and others. NBC purchased the movie from an independent producer.

Plaintiff's major libel and invasion of privacy claims are based on nine scenes in the movie in which she is portrayed in a derogatory light. The essential facts concerning these claims are as follows:

1. After an opening prologue, black and white youths are shown fighting on a train. The train is halted, and the blacks are arrested. The next scene shows plaintiff standing next to Ruby Bates at the tracks. Plaintiff claims that this scene, in effect, makes her a prejurer because she testified at the 1933 trial and in this case that she fainted while alighting from the train and did not regain consciousness until she was taken to a local grocery store. Judge Horton, in his opinion sustaining the motion for a new trial, found that the observations of other witnesses and the testimony of the examining doctor contradicted her testimony in this respect. Horton concluded that it was unlikely that Victoria Price had fainted.

2. As plaintiff and Ruby Bates are led away from the tracks by the sheriff and his men, the sheriff in the play calls the two women a "couple of bums." There is no indication in Judge Horton's opinion, in the 1933 trial transcript, or in Dr. Carter's book that this comment was actually made.

3. In a pretrial conversation between two lawyers representing the defendant, the play portrays one of them as advising restraint in the cross-examination of plaintiff Price. He says to the other defense lawyer: "The Scottsboro transcripts are really clear. . . . The defense at the last trial made one thing very clear, Victoria was a *whore*, and they got it in the neck for it. . . ." (Emphasis added.) There is no evidence that this specific conversation between the two defense lawyers actually occurred. Dr. Carter does state in his book that one of the purposes of the defense in cross-examining plaintiff was to discredit her testimony by introducing evidence that she was a common prostitute. . . .

4. Plaintiff in this action contends that the movie falsely portrays her as defensive and evasive during her direct and cross-examination. Judge Horton found in his 1933 opinion granting a new trial that plaintiff was not a cooperative witness: "Her manner of testifying and her demeanor on the stand militate against her. Her testimony was contradictory, often evasive, and time and again she refused to answer pertinent questions."

5. Plaintiff claims that the last question put to her on cross-examination in the play is inaccurate. In the movie the defense attorney asks: "One more question: have you ever heard of a white woman being arrested for perjury when she was the complaining witness against Negroes in the entire history of the state of Alabama?" According to the 1933 trial transcript, the actual question was, "I want to ask you if you have ever heard of any single white woman ever being locked up in jail when she is the complaining witness against Negroes in the history of the state of Alabama?" Plaintiff objects to the insertion of the word "perjury" in the play.

6. In the play, Dr. Marvin Lynch, one of the doctors who examined plaintiff after she alighted from the train, approaches Judge Horton outside the courtroom and confides that he does not believe that the two women were raped by the Scottsboro boys. Dr. Lynch refuses to go on the witness stand and so testify, however. Plaintiff argues that this scene is improper because it is not supported in the 1933 trial record. This is true. Neither the 1933 trial transcript nor Judge

Horton's opinion make reference to this incident. The Carter book does state, however, that Judge Horton told the author in a later interview that this incident occurred. . . .

7. The play portrays events leading up to plaintiff's trip to Chattanooga with her friend, Ruby Bates. It was on the return trip to Alabama that the rape alleged occurred. Lester Carter, a defense witness in the play, testifies that he had intercourse with Ruby Bates on the night before the trip to Chattanooga and the plaintiff had intercourse with Jack Tiller. During the testimony there is a flashback that shows an exchange in a boxcar in which Ruby Bates suggests that they all go to Chattanooga and plaintiff says, "[m]aybe Ruby and me could hustle there while you two [Carter and Tiller] got some kind of fill-in work. What do you say?" This is an accurate abridgement of the substance of the actual testimony of Lester Carter at the 1933 trial, although Price denied, both at the 1933 trial and in the defamation trial below, that she had had intercourse with Tiller. Judge Horton specifically found that she did not tell the truth. The dramatization quoted or closely paraphrased substantial portions of Judge Horton's 1933 opinion. Judge Horton concluded that the testimony of Victoria Price "is not only uncorroborated, but is contradicted by other evidence," evidence that "greatly preponderates in favor of the defendant":

When we consider, as the facts hereafter detailed will show, that this woman had slept side by side with a man the night before [the alleged rape] in Chattanooga, and had intercourse at Huntsville with Tiller on the night before she went to Chattanooga . . . the conclusion becomes clearer and clearer that this woman was not forced into intercourse with all of these Negroes upon the train, but that her condition [the presence of dead sperm in her vagina] was clearly due to the intercourse that she had on the nights previous in this time.

8. Lester Carter also testifies in the play that plaintiff urged him to say that he had seen her raped. The 1933 trial transcript reveals that Carter actually testified that he overheard plaintiff tell another white youth that "if you don't testify according to what I testify I will see that you are took off the witness stand. . . ." Judge Horton in his opinion observed that there was evidence presented at the trial showing that Price encouraged others to support her version of what had happened.

9. Another witness in the play, Dallas Ramsey, testifies that he saw plaintiff and Ruby Bates in a "hobo jungle" near the train tracks in Chattanooga the night before the train trip back to Alabama. Ramsey testifies that plaintiff states that she and her husband were looking for work and that "her old man" was uptown scrounging for food. The play dramatizes Ramsey's testimony while he is on the stand by a flashback to the scene at the "hobo jungle." The flashback gives the impression that plaintiff is perhaps inviting sexual advances from Ramsey, although the words used do not state this specifically. The substance of Ramsey's testimony, as portrayed in the play, is found in the 1933 trial transcript. The record provides no basis for the suggestive flashback.

The facts recited above illustrate that the play does cast plaintiff in an extremely derogatory light. She is portrayed as a perjurer, a woman of bad character, a woman who falsely accused the Scottsboro boys of rape knowing that the result would likely be the electric chair. The play is a gripping and effective portrayal of its point of view about her, the Scottsboro boys, and Judge Horton. As an effective dramatic production, the play has won many awards, including the George Foster Peabody Award for playwriting and awards from the Screenwriters' Guild and the American Bar Association. . . .

III. THE FIRST AMENDMENT DEFENSES

A. Plaintiff was a Public Figure During the Scottsboro Trials

Since common law defenses do not support the directed verdict for NBC, we must reach the constitutional issues, particularly the question whether plaintiff should be characterized as a "public figure." In *Gertz*, the Supreme Court held that one characterized as a "public figure," as distinguished from a private individual, "may recover for injury to reputation *only on clear and convincing proof* that the defamatory falsehood was made *with knowledge of its falsity or with reckless disregard for the truth.*" . . . (emphasis added). In balancing the need to protect "private personality" and reputation against the need "to assure to the freedoms of speech and press that 'breathing space' essential to their free exercise," the Supreme Court has developed a general test to determine public figure status.

Gertz establishes a two-step analysis to determine if an individual is a public figure. First, does a "public controversy" exist? Second, what is "the nature and extent of [the] individual's participation" in that public controversy? . . . Three factors determine the "nature and extent" of an individual's involvement: the extent to which participation in the controversy is voluntary, the extent to which there is access to channels of effective communication in order to counteract false statements, and the prominence of the role played in the public controversy. . . .

The Supreme Court has not clearly defined the elements of a "public controversy." It is evident that it is not simply any controversy of general or public interest. Not all judicial proceedings are public controversies. For example, "dissolution of a marriage through judicial proceedings is not the sort of 'public controversy' referred to in *Gertz.*" *Time, Inc. v. Firestone*, . . . (1976). Several factors, however, lead to the conclusion that the Scottsboro case is the kind of public controversy referred to in *Gertz*. The Scottsboro trials were the focus of major public debate over the ability of our courts to render even-handed justice. It generated widespread press and attracted public attention for several years. It was also a contributing factor in changing public attitudes about the right of black citizens to equal treatment under law and in changing constitutional principles governing the right to counsel and the exclusion of blacks from the jury.

The first factor in determining the nature and extent of plaintiff's participation is the prominence of her role in the public controversy. She was the only alleged victim, and she was the major witness for the State in the prosecution of the nine black youths. Ruby Bates, the other young woman who earlier had testified against the defendants, later recanted her incriminating testimony. Plaintiff was left as the sole prosecutrix. Therefore, she played a prominent role in the public controversy.

The second part of the test of public figure status is also met. Plaintiff had "access to the channels of effective communication and hence . . . a . . . realistic opportunity to counteract false statements." . . . The evidence indicates that plaintiff recognized her importance to the criminal trials and the interest of the public in her as a personality. The press clamored to interview her. She clearly had access to the media and was able to broadcast her view of the events.

The most troublesome issue is whether plaintiff "voluntarily" "thrust" herself to the forefront of this public controversy. It cannot be said that a rape victim "voluntarily" injects herself into a criminal prosecution for rape. . . . In such an instance, voluntariness in the legal sense is closely bound to the issue of truth. If she was raped, her participation in the initial legal proceedings was involuntary for the purpose of determining her public figure status; if she falsely accused the defendants, her participation in this controversy was "voluntary." But legal standards in libel cases should not be drawn so that either the courts or the press must first determine the issue of truth before they can determine whether an individual should be treated as a public or a private figure. The principle of libel law should not be drawn in such a way that it forces the press, in an uncertain public controversy, to guess correctly about a woman's chastity.

When the issue of truth and the issue of voluntariness are the same, it is necessary to determine the public figure status of the individual without regard to whether she "voluntarily" thrust herself in the forefront of the public controversy. If there were no evidence of voluntariness other than that turning on the issue of truth, we would not consider the fact of voluntariness. In such a case, the other factors—prominence and access to media—alone would determine public figure status. But in this case, there is evidence of voluntariness not bound up with the issue of truth. Plaintiff gave press interviews and aggressively promoted her version of the case outside of her actual courtroom testimony. In the context of a widely-reported, intense public controversy concerning the fairness of our criminal justice system, plaintiff was a public figure under *Gertz* because she played a major role, had effective access to the media and encouraged public interest in herself.

B. Plaintiff Remains a Public Figure for Purposes of Later Discussion of the Scottsboro Case

The Supreme Court has explicitly reserved the question of "whether or when an individual who was once a public figure may lose that status by the passage of time." *Wolston v. Reader's Digest Ass'n, Inc.*, 443 U.S. 157 . . . (1979). In *Wolston* the District of Columbia Circuit found that plaintiff was a public figure and retained that status for the purpose of later discussion of the espionage case in which he was called as a witness. The Supreme Court found that the plaintiff's role in the original public controversy was so minor that he was not a public figure. It therefore reserved the question of whether a person retains his public figure status.

Plaintiff argues that even if she was a public figure at the time of the 1930s trial, she lost her public figure status over the intervening forty years. We reject this argument and hold that once a person becomes a public figure in connection with a particular controversy, that person remains a public figure thereafter for purposes of later commentary or treatment of *that controversy*. This rule finds support in both case law and analysis of the constitutional malice standard.

On this issue the Fifth Circuit has reached the same conclusion as the District of Columbia Circuit in *Wolston*. In *Brewer v. Memphis Publishing Co., Inc.*, 626 F.2d 1238 (5th Cir. 1980), plaintiff sued when a newspaper implied that she was reviving a long-dormant romantic relationship with Elvis Presley. The Fifth Circuit concluded that although the passage of time might narrow the range of topics protected by a malice standard, plaintiff remained a public figure when the defendant commented on her romantic relationship. The court noted that plaintiff's name continued to be connected with Presley even after her retirement from show business. . . .

Our analytical view of the matter is based on the fact that the Supreme Court developed the public figure doctrine in order that the press might have sufficient breathing room to compose the first rough draft of history. It is no less important to allow the historian the same leeway when he writes the second or the third draft.

Our nation depends on "robust debate" to determine the best answer to public controversies of this sort. The public figure doctrine makes it possible for publishers to provide information on such issues to the debating public, undeterred by the threat of liability except in cases of actual malice. Developed in the context of contemporaneous reporting, the doctrine promotes a forceful exchange of views.

Considerations that underlie the public figure doctrine in the context of contemporaneous reporting also apply to later historical or dramatic treatment of the same events. Past public figures who now live in obscurity do not lose their access to channels of communication if they choose to comment on their role in the past public controversy. And although the publisher of history does not operate under journalistic deadlines it generally makes little difference in terms of accuracy and verifiability that the events on which a publisher is reporting occurred decades ago. Although information may come to light over the course of time, the distance of years does not necessarily make more data available to a reporter: memories fade; witnesses forget; sources disappear.

There is no reason for the debate to be any less vigorous when events that are the subject of current discussion occurred several years earlier. The mere passage of time does not automatically diminish the significance of events or the public's need for information. A nation that prizes its heritage need have no illusions about its past. It is no more fitting for the Court to constrain the analysis of past events than to stem the tide of current news. From Alfred Dreyfus to Alger Hiss, famous cases have been debated and reinterpreted by commentators and historians. A contrary rule would tend to restrain efforts to shed new light on historical events and reconsideration of past errors.

The plaintiff was the pivotal character in the most famous rape case of the twentieth century. It became a political controversy as well as a legal dispute. As the white prosecutrix of nine black youths during an era of racial prejudice in the South, she aroused the attention of the nation. The prosecutions were among the first to focus on the conscience of the nation on the question of the ability of our system of justice to provide fair trials to blacks in the South. The question persists today. As long as the question remains, the Scottsboro boys case will not be relegated to the dusty pages of the scholarly treatise. It will remain a living controversy.

C. Evidence Insufficient to Support Malice[6]

A plaintiff may not recover under the malice standard unless there is "clear and convincing proof" that the defamation was published "with knowledge of its falsity or with reckless disregard for the truth." *Gertz*. . . . There is no evidence that NBC had knowledge that its portrayal of Victoria Price was false or that NBC recklessly disregarded the truth. The derogatory portrayal of Price in the movie is based in all material respects on the detailed findings of Judge Horton at the trial and Dr. Carter in his book. When the truth is uncertain and seems undiscoverable through further investigation, reliance on these two sources is not unreasonable.

We gain perspective on this question when we put to ourselves another case. Dr. Carter, in his book, persuasively argues, based on the evidence, that the Communist Party financed and controlled the defense of the Scottsboro boys. A different playwright might choose to portray Judge Horton as some Southern newspapers portrayed him at the time—

6. The District Court found that even if plaintiff was a public figure forty years ago, she no longer was a public figure at the time of publication. The court then directed a verdict for NBC on grounds that there was no evidence of negligence. The evidence indicates, however, that there is arguably some proof of negligence by NBC. NBC was notified between the first and second showings of the film that not only was plaintiff alive but that she objected to her characterization in the movie. NBC made no attempt to verify the factual presentation in the movie thereafter. This arguably presents a jury-submissible case of negligence, as Judge Peck's dissent points out.

as an evil judge who associated himself with a Communist cause and gave his approval to interracial rape in order to curry favor with the eastern press. The problem would be similar had Judge Horton—for many years before his death an obscure private citizen—sued the publisher for libel.

Some controversial historical events like the Scottsboro trials become symbolic and take on an overlay of political meaning. Speech about such events becomes in part political speech. The hypothetical case and the actual case before us illustrate that an individual's social philosophy and political leanings color his historical perspective. His political opinions cause him to draw different lessons from history and to see historical events and facts in a different light. He believes the historical evidence he wants to believe and casts aside other evidence to the contrary. So long as there is no evidence of bad faith or conscious or extreme disregard of the truth, the speaker in such a situation does not violate the malice standard. His version of history may be wrong, but the law does not punish him for being a bad historian.

The malice standard is flexible and encourages diverse political opinions and robust debate about social issues. It tolerates silly arguments and strange ways of yoking facts together in unusual patterns. But it is not infinitely expandable. It does not abolish all the common law of libel even in the political context. It still protects us against the "big political lie," the conscious or reckless falsehood. We do not have that in this case.

Accordingly, the judgment of the District Court is affirmed.

DAMAGES

A plaintiff who successfully proves defamation can recover for pecuniary as well as nonpecuniary losses, such as lost friendship, illness, and humiliation. As a constitutional matter, punitive damages may not be awarded to private figures in suits involving matters of public interest unless the plaintiff is able to prove that the defendant acted with actual malice (*Dun & Bradstreet, Inc. v. Greenmoss Builders, Inc.*, 472 U.S. 749 (1985)). Punitive damages may still be awarded, however, in matters pertaining to issues of merely private concern where only negligence is shown.

Recall that under the common law presumed damages were allowed in most cases of libel and in cases involving slander *per se*. Thus, the plaintiff could recover even if she could not prove that she suffered any actual harm because she could recover for the harm that "ordinarily" stems from a defamatory statement. Recent U.S. Supreme Court decisions, however, cut back on this allowance by requiring the plaintiff to prove that the defendant acted at least with reckless disregard of the truth if she is to recover presumed damages. Therefore, in those states requiring plaintiffs to prove mere negligence, plaintiffs are constitutionally precluded from recovering presumed damages. If a matter is not one of public interest, however, presumed damages may be awarded even if the plaintiff proves only mere negligence.

Even though a plaintiff suffers no quantifiable loss he may still be motivated to go to court in an effort to "clear his name." Such a plaintiff is often willing to accept only nominal damages just to be given the opportunity to "have his day in court."

The majority of states, in an effort to discourage defamation suits, have enacted *retraction statutes*. These statutes essentially bar a plaintiff from recovery if a defendant retracts a defamatory statement within a certain time period. Other statutes merely require the defendant to provide the plaintiff with response time and do not bar the plaintiff's recovery.

PRIVILEGES

A plaintiff may lose even if she proves defamation if the defendant can establish that he was privileged. Privileges can either be **absolute,** in which the privilege applies regardless of the defendant's motives, or **qualified,** in which case they apply only when the defendant acts on the basis of certain well-defined purposes (see Table 11–3).

ABSOLUTE PRIVILEGES

Absolute privileges emanate largely from the nature of the defendant's job or function. Judges, lawyers, parties and witnesses enjoy an absolute privilege for the statements they make during judicial proceedings, regardless of the motives for their statements. Such statements must, however, bear some relation to the matter at issue (Restatement (Second) of Torts Sec. 585-589). Similarly, legislators acting in furtherance of their legislative function during a legislative hearing enjoy an absolute privilege. Witnesses testifying before the legislature are also absolutely privileged. All federal officials, governors, and high ranking state officials have absolute immunity while acting in their official capacity. The states are in disagreement, however, as to whether absolute immunity extends to lower ranking officials, such as police officers.

TABLE 11.3 Privileges

ABSOLUTE PRIVILEGES
•Judges, lawyers, parties and witnesses during judicial proceedings. •Legislators acting in furtherance of legislative function. •Witnesses testifying before legislature. •Federal officials, governors and high-ranking state officials acting in official capacity. •Husband-wife communications.

QUALIFIED PRIVILEGES
•Reports of public proceedings (e.g., judicial and legislative hearings). •Statement made to someone with capacity to act in the public interest. •Statement made to protect one's own interests as long as not for the purpose of obtaining a competitive advantage.

Note that no privilege applies to statements issued outside the course and furtherance of the defendant's job.

Absolute immunity can also evolve out of a relationship. Husband-wife communications, for example, are absolutely privileged. If, however, the defamation originates with a third person and is relayed from one spouse to another, the repetition will still be considered a publication and the third person will be liable for the privileged repetition of his or her defamatory statement. Any publication to which a plaintiff consents is considered absolutely privileged.

QUALIFIED PRIVILEGES

Reports pertaining to public proceedings, such as court cases and legislative hearings, enjoy a qualified privilege of immunity. Because of *Sullivan* and *Gerst* the privilege is no longer necessary in those cases involving public officials or public figures unless the plaintiff can prove the defendant acted with actual malice. If the report involves a private figure, the actual malice requirement is not applicable and the press is limited to a right to comment accurately on a public proceeding.

A statement made to one who has the capacity to act in the public interest, such as a public official, is subject to a qualified privilege. An accusation to a prosecutor about purported criminal activity, for example, is privileged unless the person making the accusation makes it recklessly. A defendant is also privileged in protecting his or her own interests as long as those interests are sufficiently important and the defamation is directly related to those interests. A defendant who protects his property, for example, by telling the police about his suspicions that the plaintiff stole his property is privileged.

Making a defamatory statement for the purpose of gaining a competitive advantage is not privileged, such as telling potential customers about the poor workmanship of the competition. A defendant may be qualifiedly privileged to act for the protection of the recipient of his or her statement if the recipient is someone to whom making such a statement would be considered "within the generally accepted standards of decent conduct" (Restatement (Second) of Torts Sec. 595 (1)(b)). Statements made within the parameters of "decent conduct" must be made in response to a request and within the context of a close personal or business relationship. Credit-reporting agencies, for example, enjoy a qualified privilege in many states in giving their subscribers credit-worthiness reports on potential customers (Restatement (Second) of Torts Sec. 595, comment h).

A qualified privilege can be lost if it is abused. For example, a defendant who makes a statement knowing it to be false or who acts in reckless disregard as to the truth or falsity of the statement will lose the privilege. If the primary purpose behind the defendant's statement is something other than protecting the interest for which the privilege was originally granted, the privilege will be lost. Suppose an employee's former employer informs his new employer about the employee's alleged dishonesty. These allegations will not be privileged if the primary motivation is preventing the employee from leaving his employment rather than warning the new employer. A privilege is also considered abused if a statement is made to more people than is reasonably necessary to protect the interest in question. In the same vein, the privilege is abused if more damaging information is added than is reasonably necessary. A defendant who reports her suspicions to the police that the plaintiff has stolen her property will probably lose the privilege if she adds her belief that the plaintiff is promiscuous (Restatement (Second) of Torts Sec. 605).

SUMMARY

Defamation consists of the related torts of libel and slander. A statement is defamatory if it tends to harm the reputation of another so as to lower him in the estimation of the community or deter others from associating with him. In addition to proving that a statement is defamatory a plaintiff must also prove publication and, at the very least, negligence.

Slander requires proof of suffering of some kind of special harm except in cases of slander *per se*. Under the common law special harm did not have to be proved because damages were presumed. Under recent Supreme Court decisions in cases involving matters of public concern, however, a plaintiff cannot be awarded presumed damages unless she can prove actual malice.

A defamatory statement must have a tendency to harm the reputation of the plaintiff even though the plaintiff's reputation is not in fact injured. If the statement involves a matter of public interest and the defendant is a media defendant, the plaintiff must prove that the statement was false. At least one person must reasonably interpret the statement as being defamatory even if the statement could be interpreted in several different ways. If the defamatory content of the statement is not recognizable unless certain extrinsic facts are known, the plaintiff must specifically show the innuendo in his or her pleadings. Expressions of opinion generally are not considered defamatory.

Defamation requires publication. Mere repetition of a defamatory statement is considered publication even if the person repeating the statement does not believe it. An entire edition of a book or periodical is treated as one publication under the single publication rule.

Under *New York Times Co. v. Sullivan* public officials and public figures are required to prove actual malice. A public figure is one who has achieved "pervasive fame or notoriety" or who "voluntarily injects himself or is drawn into a particular public controversy."

A successful plaintiff can recover for compensatory damages, including such nonpecuniary losses as loss of friendship, illness, and humiliation. Punitive damages can be recovered in matters of public interest if the plaintiff is able to prove the defendant acted with actual malice and in matters of private concern where only negligence is shown.

In certain circumstances defendants may be able to claim an absolute or qualified privilege of immunity. Judges, lawyers, parties and witnesses, for example, have absolute immunity for the statements they make during judicial proceedings. Reports pertaining to public proceedings as well as statements made to those having the capacity to act in the public interest are subject to a qualified privilege. Qualified privileges can be lost if they are abused.

PRACTICE POINTERS

Attorney-Client and Work-Product Privileges

Since legal assistants are frequently involved in the discovery process, you must fully understand the implications of the attorney-client and work-product privileges. Be aware, however, that the rules governing these privileges vary from state to state, so you should consult your local rules. In accordance with the attorney-client privilege, any confidential information between an individual and his or her attorney cannot be disclosed unless the individual consents to disclosure. This privilege may be claimed by the individual, his or her attorney, or anyone authorized to claim the privilege on behalf of the individual, such as a representative of the client's estate. All employees of an attorney or law firm are also subject to any prohibitions regarding disclosure.

Any information exchanged between a client and his or her attorney that is not disclosed to a third person is considered confidential. Disclosure to a third person does not waive the privilege if the person to whom the information is disclosed receives it for the purpose of furthering the client's interest or the disclosure is necessary for the communication of information. If, for example, an attorney writes a letter to a private investigator outlining the case so that the investigator has sufficient information to begin work, the letter is considered privileged because the information is intended to further the client's interest. Suppose a client asks her neighbor to translate correspondence from her attorney because the client cannot read English. The communication is still privileged because the disclosure is necessary for a translation to be made. If the client shares this correspondence with her neighbor simply to get her neighbor's reaction to the content, the privilege is lost. Most importantly, once the privilege is lost it cannot be regained. Therefore, never do anything that might jeopardize an attorney-client privilege.

The work-product privilege protects the disclosure of any attorney work product, which is defined as any material that reflects an attorney's impressions or conclusions. The results of any research done in anticipation of litigation or when acting in a legal capacity are also considered part of the work product. Analysis of written data and testimony of nonparty witnesses are both examples of attorney work products. Also, any communications between an attorney and an expert witness who has not been designated as a trial witness are protected under the work-product rule.

A court may circumvent a work-product privilege if the party requesting the information can demonstrate a substantial need for a particular item as well as an inability to obtain the substantial equivalent of that item without undue hardship. To prevail the party must be able to demonstrate his need using specific facts. Under no circumstances, however, will a court order the production of an attorney's notes on a case.

Continued on next page

PRACTICE POINTERS—Continued

Since the client and not the attorney holds the privilege, the client must grant specific approval for any waiver. Remember, however, that a waiver is not selective. Therefore, if opposing counsel is granted access to one or two pieces of privileged information, the waiver of the privilege will not end there. Once a waiver is given opposing counsel will be permitted access to all documents covered by the privilege, to issue interrogatories delving into those areas, and to conduct depositions of those persons whose testimony would otherwise be considered privileged. Avoid inadvertent waiver of a privilege when responding to an interrogatory, a request for production of documents, or a request for admission. Once access is allowed to a privileged document or once deposition testimony is permitted in a privileged area, the privilege will be considered waived and further discovery will be possible.

TORT TEASERS

1. Review the hypothetical scenario at the beginning of this chapter. What will the "heartthrob" have to prove if he sues for defamation? Are there any elements you anticipate he will have difficulty proving? Do you think he would be considered a public figure? Would it be easier for him to prove libel or slander? Why?

What must the plaintiff prove in cases 2–4?

2. *Time Magazine* publishes a report that Plaintiff and her husband, both of whom are wealthy socialites, were granted a divorce based on adultery when in fact the divorce was granted on other grounds. The court's final judgment reads (in part):

> According to certain testimony in behalf of the defendant, extramarital escapades of the plaintiff were bizarre and of an amatory nature which would have made Dr. Freud's hair curl. Other testimony, in plaintiff's behalf, would indicate that defendant was guilty of bounding from one bedpartner to another with the erotic zest of a satyr. The court is inclined to discount much of this testimony as unreliable. Nevertheless, it is the conclusion and finding of the court that neither party is domesticated, within the meaning of that term as used the Supreme Court of Florida. . . . In the present case, it is abundantly clear from the evidence of marital discord that neither of the parties has shown the least susceptibility to domestication, and that the marriage should be dissolved.

Time's article reads as follows:

> Divorced. By Russell A. Firestone Jr., 41, heir to the tire fortune: Mary Alice Sullivan Firestone, 32, his third wife; a onetime Palm Beach schoolteacher, on grounds of extreme cruelty and adultery; after six years of marriage, one son; in West Palm Beach, Fla. The 17-month intermittent trial produced enough testimony of extramarital adventures on both sides, said the judge, "to make Dr. Freud's hair curl." *Time, Inc. v. Firestone,* 424 U.S. 448 (1976).

3. The manager of Defendant's motel sends a certified letter to Plaintiff, who had been a guest at the motel. In the letter he alleges that Plaintiff had left without making payment and had "accidentally packed" several items of motel property. The letter is received by Plaintiff's maid and read by Plaintiff's wife. Defendant is unaware that the Plaintiff is married. *Barnes v. Clayton House Motel,* 435 S.W.2d 616 (Tex. 1968).

4. Defendants author a book in which they claim that the models at Neiman-Marcus are "call girls" and that most of the salesmen are "fairies." Fifteen of the total of twenty-five salesmen sue on their own behalf and on behalf of the others and all nine models sue for defamation. *Neiman-Marcus v. Lait,* 13 F.R.D.311 (S.D.N.Y. 1952).

5. What might the defendants want to argue in the following case? Defendants file a letter with the grievance committee of the Association of the Bar of the City of New York alleging that Plaintiff has been fraudulent and dishonest in his practice as an attorney. Plaintiff claims that such allegations are defamatory. *Wiener v. Weintraub,* 239 N.E.2d 540 (N.Y. 1968).

KEY TERMS

■ **Absolute privilege**
Absolute defense to defamation, regardless of defendant's motives.

■ **Actual malice**
Acting with knowledge of the falsity of one's statement or with reckless disregard to the truth or falsity of one's statement.

■ **Defamation**
Statement that tends to harm the reputation of another, encompassing both libel and slander.

■ **Innuendo**
Use of extrinsic facts to convey the defamatory meaning of a statement.

■ **Libel**
Written defamatory statements.

■ **Pecuniary**
Monetary; that which can be valued in terms of money.

■ **Publication**
Hearing or seeing a defamatory statement by someone other than the plaintiff.

■ **Public figure**
One who has achieved persuasive fame or notoriety or who becomes involved in a public controversy.

■ **Presumed damages**
Damages that ordinarily stem from a defamatory statement and that do not require the showing of actual harm.

■ **Qualified privilege**
Privilege that applies only when a defendant acts on the basis of certain well-defined purposes.

■ **Slander**
Oral defamatory statements.

■ **Slander *per se***
Slander in which pecuniary harm can be assumed.

■ **Special harm**
Harm of a pecuniary nature.

12 MALPRACTICE

CHAPTER OBJECTIVES

In this chapter you will learn to:

- Explain the standard of care to which a professional is held.
- Identify ways in which professional negligence is committed.
- Explain the informed consent doctrine.
- Recognize defenses that can be raised in response to a professional negligence claim.
- Appreciate the reasons for the increase in professional negligence claims.

The attorney by whom you have just been hired is a recent law school graduate. Early in his career, he discovers, through personal experience, many of the legal land mines on which an attorney can step. First, he advises a woman who was injured in an automobile accident that she has no viable cause of action. Two days after the statute of limitations runs out she consults with another attorney on a separate matter. This attorney advises her that she did indeed have a good cause of action for which she probably could have netted a considerable recovery.

Next, unaware of the malpractice noose now dangling over his head, your attorney blithely decides not to relay a settlement offer to another client because in his opinion the client should not accept the offer. When the case goes to trial the client is awarded less than he would have received under the terms of the offer. The client is most displeased when he discovers that the terms of the settlement offer were never relayed to him.

Finally, you forget to file a list of exhibits and witnesses on the date it is due. As a result, the judge refuses to allow your key witness to testify and the case is lost when it goes to trial. What will clients in each of these cases have to prove if they allege professional negligence? What might the attorney argue in his defense?

WHAT IS REASONABLE CARE?

As we discussed in Chapter 6, the duty of care required of professionals is one of reasonableness. A professional is required to have the skill and learning commonly possessed by members in good standing within that profession. The question that frequently arises is whether professionals should be required to meet national or local standards. For example, should a physician who practices in a rural area be held to the same standard of care as one who practices in an urban, high-tech office? In the medical area many states have opted for a local standard, apparently with an implicit acknowledgment that expectations of reasonableness are dependent on locale. Some courts, however, influenced by the elevated expectations of professionals resulting from enhanced communications, have discarded the "locality rule" in favor of a national standard.

Negligence is not necessarily equated with unfavorable outcome. Simply because a course of action ultimately yields undesirable results does not make it negligent. Hindsight, as we all know, is perfect but reasonable foresight is all that is required of a professional. A veterinarian, for instance, may recommend surgery for an ailing dog but if the dog dies from complications, the veterinarian is not necessarily negligent even though the outcome proves the prognosis incorrect. The veterinarian's recommendation need only be reasonable, not accurate.

PROCANIK BY PROCANIK v. CILLO
543 A.2d 985 (N.J. Super. A.D. 1988).

Pressler, P.J.A.D.

This case sounds in legal malpractice. Defendants Lee Goldsmith, an attorney at law of this state having special expertise in medical malpractice litigation, and Greenstone, Greenstone and Naishuler, the New Jersey firm with which he was associated at the time the operative events occurred, appeal from a jury verdict finding them liable to plaintiffs Rosemarie and Michael Procanik and their son Peter because of Goldsmith's alleged professional dereliction in failing to provide them with an adequate expression of his reasons for declining to represent them in their claims against Mrs. Procanik's obstetricians. We reverse. We conclude that this record does not raise a *prima facie* case of professional negligence against defendants and hence that the complaint should have been dismissed prior to its submission to the jury.

This case, as it is presently postured, comes to us by way of a tortuously complex route. The salient facts are, however, largely undisputed, and the following factual recitation is based on uncontested facts appearing in pretrial documents and adduced at trial.

The litigation arises out of the tragic circumstances of the birth on December 26, 1977 of a rubella-syndrome child, Peter Procanik, who by reason of his mother's German measles infection early in her pregnancy has grave vision and auditory disabilities, serious mental deficiencies, and a variety of other physical and mental problems. His parents believed that Mrs. Procanik's obstetrician, defendant Joseph Cillo, who was in practice with defendants Herbert Langer and Ernest Greenberg, had negligently failed to realize that she had had German measles in her first month of pregnancy and had in fact advised her that the rash-producing illness which she had then suffered was not German measles. By so doing, she claimed, defendant Cillo deprived her of the opportunity for which she would have opted of terminating the pregnancy by voluntary abortion. Her prospective cause of action and that of the child were, consequently, those which have come to be known as wrongful birth and wrongful life.

Several months after Peter's birth, the Procaniks consulted Harold Sherman, a New Jersey attorney, with respect to their potential claims against the obstetricians. Although generally experienced in personal injury litigation, Sherman was not experienced in complex medical malpractice matters. He knew, however, of Goldsmith's expertise as the result of his attendance at a lecture on the subject given by Goldsmith, whose credentials include a medical degree earned prior to his law degree. In the fall of 1978 Sherman asked Goldsmith if he would be willing to represent the Procaniks in litigation against the obstetricians. Goldsmith expressed preliminary interest, making it clear, however, that he would have to make both a medical and legal evaluation before he could commit to the undertaking. Working with Sherman, the Procaniks' attorney, rather than with the Procaniks themselves, Goldsmith obtained the pertinent medical records and a statement from Mrs. Procanik asserting that she would have chosen to terminate the pregnancy had she known that she had had German measles. Goldsmith also submitted the medical information and his own precis of the case for evaluation and report to a medical expert, Dr. Leslie Iffy, a noted perinatologist and experienced forensic witness. In addition, he did legal research and discussed the case from time to time with the senior partners of the Greenstone firm.

During the entire period in which this evaluation process was being conducted, the controlling law in this state was *Gleitman v. Cosgrove*, 49 *N.J.* 22, 227 *A.*2d 689 (1967), which had held that no cause of action on behalf of either parent or child lies based on the failure of a physician to advise the mother of a risk of a defective fetus provided the physician has neither caused nor contributed to the defect and provided he is without the capacity to remedy it. Goldsmith was, of course, aware of *Gleitman.* He also learned that on December 27, 1978 the New York Court of Appeals in *Becker v. Schwartz, . . .* overruled prior decisional law in that state by recognizing the parents' cause of action for wrongful birth but limiting their damages to those expenses incurred and to be incurred for the care and treatment of the child attributable to the child's congenital disabilities. The New York Court, however, refused to recognize either the parents' right to damages for emotional or psychic harm or the child's right to a cause of action for her "wrongful" life. Goldsmith was also aware, of course, that the United States Supreme Court's decision in *Roe v. Wade, . . .* permitting voluntary abortion during the first trimester of pregnancy at the mother's option, might have affected some of the underpinnings of the *Gleitman* ruling.[1] He

1. Goldsmith was, however, unaware that on September 5, 1978 the New Jersey Supreme Court granted plaintiffs' petition for certification in *Berman v. Allan, . . .* A notice of the grant of certification appeared in the *New Jersey Law Journal* on December

apparently hoped, therefore, that he could engage the interest of the Greenstone firm in accepting the case and, on January 29, 1979, wrote the following memorandum to the senior partners, Herbert E. Greenstone and Allen Naishuler, both now deceased:

> We have, in the office, a Procanik file. This is a case in which a woman had a last menstrual period in May, measles at the end of May, then went to a gynecologist at the beginning of June; rubella test done, showed that she did have antibodies to it and apparently never informed of this so as to get an abortion. Gave birth to a deformed child in the following year.
>
> This case would fall into the area of *Gleitman v. Cosgrove* . . . The decision in this case was in 1967, at a time when abortions were still illegal. The decision was 4 to 3, and was, in part, based on the fact that abortions were illegal.
>
> Recently, in New York, (and a copy of this decision is enclosed) there were two cases decided, *Becker v. Schwartz* and *Park v. Jessen* . . . which in effect reverses *Gleitman v. Cosgrove*, and the New York case, *Stuart v. Long Island Hospital*. I think that now, at this time, it is an appropriate time to determine clearly whether or not we wish to take on *Gleitman v. Cosgrove*, going up to the Supreme Court. I think the time is right, and I think we have a good shot at reversal. The reason for the memo, then, is please read *Becker v. Schwartz* which is enclosed as well as *Gleitman*, so that we can discuss it and discuss our options. The damages are heavy.

About a month after he wrote that memorandum, Goldsmith received Dr. Iffy's report, about which we will have more to say hereafter. At the time Dr. Iffy's report arrived, Goldsmith and Greenstone were trying a case in a distant county, and it was not until sometime in mid-March 1979 that Goldsmith and Greenstone, who had occasionally discussed the Procanik case with each other, finally met with Naishuler to decide whether or not to undertake the representation. According to Goldsmith's answers to interrogatories and his trial testimony, both entirely undisputed, Herbert Greenstone, in addition to his trial expertise, was also the firm's primary appellate practitioner, Goldsmith being then relatively uninitiated in that area of practice. Greenstone, based upon his consideration of all of the accumulated materials, factual, medical and legal, was disinclined to accept the representation, understanding that because of *Gleitman* it would, at best, involve a dismissal of the complaint at the trial level at some stage or other; a losing appeal to the Appellate Division, which would also be bound by *Gleitman*; an effort to solicit the interest of the Supreme Court sufficiently to induce its grant of a petition for certification; the prosecution of the appeal in the Supreme Court if certification were granted; and then finally, years down the road and after, presumably, substantial financing by the firm, the opportunity to prepare the case for trial by way of the extensive discovery typical of the "heavy" medical malpractice case and the ensuing opportunity to try it before a jury with all the risks and difficulties characteristic of serious malpractice litigation. It was clearly a project

28, 1978 on an inside page continuation of the "Appeals Pending in the Supreme Court" column. . . . The statement of the issue encompassed by the certification read as follows: "Are infant afflicted with Down's Syndrome and her parents entitled to damages as a matter of law for a 'wrongful birth'?"

The trial court, in its published opinion denying these defendants' motion for summary judgment, held that their failure to have noticed or otherwise become aware of the *Law Journal* report of the *Berman* certification did not constitute actionable negligence or a breach of professional duty on their part. . . . Although plaintiffs' notice of cross-appeal includes among the challenged rulings that of the trial judge "barring evidence of an attorney's duty to read the *New Jersey Law Journal*," that issue was not briefed or otherwise addressed on this appeal, and we consequently deem it waived. . . . We, therefore, do not consider it and consequently deal with the issues presented to us as if that *Law Journal* report had never appeared.

fraught with obstacles and uncertainties at every stage, and Greenstone was not interested in pursuing it.

It was Goldsmith's trial testimony that while the final decision not to take the case was Greenstone's, he, Goldsmith, concurred with it. In any event, it is not disputed that he acceded to it and communicated that decision to Sherman by letter dated April 26, 1979, which read in full as follows:

Dear Harold:

We have finally come to a decision as to what to do with the Procanik case, after a great deal of discussion here in the office because of the problems presented by the case. Let me outline those problems to you as this forms the basis of our turning down this case.

The Procanik case basically falls into the area of a woman who had measles which was not definitively diagnosed, and, at approximately the same time was diagnosed as being pregnant. No steps were taken at that time. We are aware that Mrs. Procanik indicated that had she known of the potential problem, she would have undergone an abortion. We sent out the questions in the form of a possible malpractice case to an obstetrician/gynecologist, who felt that it was an extremely difficult position to put an obstetrician/gynecologist in. We did, however, decide not to leave it there and went ahead and reviewed the following:

1) *Gleitman v. Cosgrove*, . . . As you are probably aware, this case prohibits the kind of action that would have to be brought herein. In other words, that type of action would be either a wrongful birth or an action for the purpose of trying to obtain damages for children who were born, and who would otherwise not have been born.

2) In January, 1979 two cases came down, reported as Nos. 559 and 560 of the Court of Appeals, New York entitled, *Becker v. Schwartz* and *Park v. Chessin*. These actions both are similar to *Gleitman v. Cosgrove*, and in effect, in New York, render a different opinion. It is possible that *Gleitman* could be reversed and it is further possible that the New Jersey courts could follow *Becker v. Schwartz* and *Park v. Chessin*. These cases do allow a person to sue under the circumstances of Procanik, and would allow the possibility of damages for life. It would mean, however, in Procanik, that the case would have to be started, face a dismissal at this level, and then obviously be appealed to the Supreme Court in the hopes of obtaining a reversal of *Gleitman v. Cosgrove*.

Considering the fact that the expert is somewhat weak on the case and considering the fact that it would have to be taken to the Supreme Court in order to obtain a reversal before a valid case could be brought, we have decided not to proceed. *The law is dead against us in the State and the reversal would be necessary.*

I am returning herewith all the hospital records that you were kind enough to send us. I will, if you like, send you a copy of the report of the expert. We have checked out every avenue and I think in all probability Mrs. Procanik did have measles, did become pregnant while she had the measles, and was not so informed. But because of the many and sundry other problems, we would not proceed.

Will you please be good enough to inform the Procaniks.

Cordially,
/s/ Lee
LEE S. GOLDSMITH

Sherman thereafter met with his clients, the Procaniks, and explained to them his understanding of Goldsmith's letter, advising them that their chance of success was "50/50." He also told them that while he could not represent them on a contingent fee basis, he would consider undertaking the action on an hourly rate, a proposal they declined. And finally, in order to avoid any misunderstanding he wrote them this "sign-off" letter:

Dear Mr. & Mrs. Procanik:

This will confirm that we have had a personal meeting to discuss the letter which I received from Mr. Lee Goldsmith, to whom I had referred the possible mal-practice claims, along with the materials and records collected up to this point.

The sad truth is that while the probabilities are that the facts you relate are true, that under the law of New Jersey as it presently stands, the case would not survive a dismissal at the trial level. For your information, Mr. Goldsmith is not interested in handling the matter, and his judgment is one on which I would certainly rely.

Accordingly, I have returned the materials to you with the caution that you are free to consult another attorney, who after all, might feel differently about the case. You are also advised that, while the infant's claim survives until two years from attaining his 18th birthday, it is advisable to bring these cases within two years after the parents know or should have known that there was a possible mal-practice claim, because the parents' claims for loss of services and medical expenses may be barred within two years, even though the infant's claim for injury might survive, as previously stated. It is also true that witnesses become less available, including doctors, and the same applies to records and other necessary documents.

I would, therefore, suggest that if you want to pursue this further, you contact another attorney immediately. I will provide any such attorney with a copy of Mr. Goldsmith's letter, should that request be made.

You will recall that you advanced us $200.00 towards costs, which were as follows:

Rahway Hospital Records:	$ 54.00
Presbyterian Hospital Records:	48.00
Children's Hospital Records:	18.00
Total:	$120.00

Accordingly, enclosed find our check for $80.00.

Very truly yours,
HAROLD A. SHERMAN

That was the last communication of any of the attorneys with plaintiffs, and plaintiffs did not then seek to retain other counsel.

On June 26, 1979 the Supreme Court filed its opinion in *Berman v. Allan* . . . *Berman* adhered to that portion of the *Gleitman* decision which had rejected the viability of a child's cause of action for wrongful life. It overruled, however, the *Gleitman* rejection of the parents' cause of action for wrongful birth. In recognizing such a cause of action, however, it limited damages to the parents' emotional suffering, declining to permit recovery of the "medical and other expenses that will be incurred in order to properly raise, educate and supervise the child." . . .

About eighteen months following the declination of their case by Sherman, the Procaniks, on the advice of a friend, consulted with their present counsel, who filed a complaint on their behalf in April 1981. The complaint alleged a wrongful life complaint against the obstetricians on behalf of the child, a wrongful birth complaint against the obstetricians on behalf of the parents, and a legal malpractice complaint on behalf of the parents against Goldsmith, the Greenstone firm, and Sherman. The gravamen of the legal malpractice count, as it evolved, was that defendant attorneys, by improperly discouraging the Procaniks from commencing a timely action against the obstetricians, caused them to miss the statute of limitations on their wrongful birth claim against them.

More than six years elapsed between the filing of that complaint and the ultimate trial of this cause. The relevant procedural events which took place during that period began with a motion by the defendant obstetricians for dismissal of the infant's claim against them on the ground that it was precluded by *Berman* and for dismissal of the parents' claim against them on the ground that it was precluded by the statute of limitations.

The motion was granted by an order certifying it as final pursuant to *R.* 4:42–2. Plaintiffs, having virtually conceded on the argument of the motion that the action had been commenced more than two years after their discovery of the physicians' negligence, appealed to this court only from that portion of the order dismissing the infant's wrongful birth claim. We affirmed in an unreported opinion in which we deemed ourselves bound by *Berman,* and the Supreme Court granted certification. In its decision, *Procanik by Procanik v. Cillo,* . . . rendered on August 1, 1984, the Court noted that in *Schroeder v. Perkel,* . . . decided two years after *Berman,* it had extended the scope of damages recoverable in the parents' wrongful birth claim to include expenses for the care of the child directly attributable to his disabled condition. Further noting that these damages were not obtainable by the Procaniks in this case by reason of the loss of their cause of action on account of the running of the statute of limitations, . . . the Court then addressed the question of whether those damages were recoverable by the child himself. The Court concluded that it would recognize a wrongful life cause of action for the sole purpose of permitting the child to seek those damages, provided, however, that they were recoverable only once, either in the child's wrongful life action, or the parents' wrongful birth action. . . . The matter was then remanded for trial of the child's wrongful life cause of action against the obstetricians, limited to recovery of the expenses of care and treatment required by the rubella syndrome, and for trial of the parents' malpractice action against the defendant attorneys for the emotional distress damages they could have sought against the obstetricians but for the bar of the statute of limitations.

Following the remand, the defendant attorneys moved for summary judgment dismissing the malpractice count. The trial judge granted Sherman's motion but denied the motion of Goldsmith and Greenstone. . . . Thereafter, discovery was finally conducted and the matter was tried in 1986 before the same judge who decided the summary judgment motions. Trial was bifurcated, the infant's wrongful life claim against the obstetricians proceeding first and resulting in a substantial verdict for "special expense" damages in his favor. The legal malpractice count against Goldsmith and Greenstone was tried immediately thereafter but by a different jury. The trial judge, over plaintiff's objection, instructed the jury on the issue of whether their negligence contributed to the missing of the statute of limitations, and the jury returned a liability verdict finding them to have been 15 percent at fault and the attorney-defendants 85 percent at fault. It also returned a substantial verdict in their favor to compensate them for the loss of their medical malpractice action, a verdict then reduced by the judge to reflect their degree of negligence.

There is no appeal from the order dismissing the complaint as to Sherman. Defendants Goldsmith and Greenstone appeal from the denial of their summary judgment motion as well as from the judgment entered after trial on the jury verdict. Plaintiffs cross-appeal, complaining of the trial court's submission to the jury of the issue of plaintiffs' negligence, its denial of their motion to assess against defendant attorneys prejudgment interest on a portion of the judgment recovered against the physicians, and its ruling barring evidence of an attorney's duty to read the *New Jersey Law Journal* in full. As noted in note 1, *supra,* we deem the last of these issues as waived, and we do not address the remaining two issues because of our disposition of defendants' appeal in their favor.

In addressing the issues which are properly before us, it is first necessary for us to make clear what this appeal is *not* about. On the summary judgment motion the trial judge had held, among his other rulings, that neither Goldsmith nor Sherman had a duty subsequent to Sherman's "sign-off" letter to the Procaniks to advise them that the law had in fact changed. He also ruled that Goldsmith was barred from raising the contention that the complaint against the obstetricians had been timely filed. Addressing these matters in reverse order, we need not consider the law of the case ruling since we conclude that these defendants were not negligent. We do, however, note our reservations respecting the trial judge's ruling. . . . We also do not consider the post-termination issue because it has not been raised on appeal.

With respect to the trial judge's conclusion on the summary judgment motion that an attorney-client relationship existed between Goldsmith and plaintiffs, we point out first that that ruling was, insofar as we are able to determine, based on a fact which later turned out to be incorrect. The trial court's factual recitation noted that Sherman had engaged Goldsmith to give his opinion and advice as to the Procaniks' prospective cause. By the time of trial it appeared that the characterization was not accurate. Sherman had not submitted the matter to Goldsmith for a specialist's opinion but rather asked Goldsmith if he would be interested in accepting the representation. The relational posture was therefore not of an undertaking to render advice by a "specialist" attorney but merely his declination to accept a proferred representation. It is clear that an attorney must affirmatively accept a professional undertaking before the attorney-client relationship can attach, whether his acceptance be by speech, writing, or inferred from conduct. . . . This case is about an affirmative refusal of a professional undertaking, not its acceptance. There was thus no attorney-client relationship between Goldsmith and plaintiffs.

We nevertheless do not intend to suggest that threshold communications between attorney and prospective client do not impose certain obligations upon the attorney. But it is only the nature of the attorney's obligation in that threshold context, an obligation we address hereafter, which we must consider, not the whole panoply of fiduciary responsibilities and duties which come into play when an attorney-client relationship is formed. Thus, the sole dispositive issue as we perceive it is whether, based on the undisputed facts and plaintiffs' proofs at trial, plaintiffs established a *prima facie* case of attorney negligence against Goldsmith in that context.

That issue is narrowly focused. First, plaintiff concedes that the Greenstone firm committed no act of independent or separate attorney negligence. Its liability is predicated exclusively on principles of agency and *respondeat superior*. Second, plaintiffs concede that Goldsmith was not guilty of any intentional conduct against them but only of negligent conduct. Third, plaintiffs concede that in declining to take the case, Goldsmith had no obligation to state any reason at all for his decision. What this case is consequently about is plaintiffs' theory, accepted by the trial judge both on the summary judgment motion and at trial, that if an attorney, and particularly a specialist, undertakes to give any reason at all for declining the case, he must give his full, complete and informed judgment. Plaintiffs assert that Goldsmith failed to do so.

The entire factual predicate on which plaintiffs construct their theory of Goldsmith's professional negligence is based on two alleged flaws in his letter of April 26, 1979 to Sherman which we have quoted in full. The first flaw was Goldsmith's failure to iterate in his letter to Sherman the statement he made in his January 29, 1979 memorandum to Greenstone respecting *Gleitman*, namely, that "I think the time is right, and I think we have a good shot at reversal." Their point is that Goldsmith thereby misled them respecting the strength of their case on appeal. The second is that Goldsmith mischaracterized Dr. Iffy, the proposed forensic expert, as "somewhat weak on the case," whereas, they claim, his report was strong. We reject both of these theses.

While we agree with the proposition that an attorney, in declining a representation, need give no reason at all, we disagree with the notion that if he gives any reason, it must fully explain his entire mental processes. In our view, if an attorney, including a specialist, voluntarily undertakes to give any reason for declining a case, whatever he does say must be professionally reasonable in the circumstances. We are also persuaded that there is not a scintilla of proof in this case that Goldsmith failed to comply with that standard.

We consider first the reason given by Goldsmith to Sherman respecting the state of the law on wrongful birth and wrongful life. Plaintiffs concede that Goldsmith's letter to Sherman was entirely accurate. They acknowledge, moreover, that the letter not only correctly stated the then settled law in New Jersey, but also explained that the law was evolving elsewhere and hence that "it is possible that *Gleitman* could be reversed and it is further possible that the New Jersey courts could follow" the recent New York decision. And, they acknowledge, the letter correctly outlined the appellate procedure which would have to be prosecuted "in the hopes of obtaining a reversal of *Gleitman v. Cosgrove*." They complain only that Goldsmith did not say to Sherman, as he had to Greenstone, that the chances for reversal were good and the time was right for a change.

We regard the letter in this respect to be entirely reasonable and adequate as a matter of law. We wholly disagree with the trial judge's conclusion that Goldsmith was obliged to convey any private thoughts he might have had about the prospect of the success of an appeal seeking an overruling of the clearly stated decisional law. It was certainly enough that he communicated the information respecting the recent change in New York and the possibility of an overruling of *Gleitman* engendered thereby. Obviously, predicting the future course of the evolution of legal principle is at best a risky business. Predicting that the state's highest court will, in a particular case, overrule a legal doctrine theretofore expressly embraced by it is even riskier, and this is particularly true where, as here, the issues involved are inordinately complex, involving broad and profound moral, ethical and public policy issues as well as jurisprudential ones and as to which there is a wide disparity of view among the jurisdictions. . . . Consequently, a lawyer who correctly explains the existing decisional law of the jurisdiction, the recent disparate view of a sister jurisdiction, the consequent fact of potential change of decisional law on appeal, and the procedures for obtaining change has fulfilled any obligation he may have to explain his state-of-the-law reasons for declining the case. It is not a professional dereliction for him to withhold his gratuitous prediction of the prospect of success of an appeal which would be taken to obtain a change in the law.

Our conclusion is based on what we believe to be established principle governing an attorney's communication respecting the state of the law whether to a client or a prospective client. First, where, as here, there is no attorney-client relationship, an attorney is free to decline the representation without stating any reason at all. He is not, however, without obligation with respect to a reason he does undertake to give. . . . We have no doubt that when an attorney, and particularly one specializing in a specific area of the law, declines a representation because of the state of the law which he undertakes to express, he knows or should know that the prospective client will depend on the reliability of that expression. Nor is there any doubt here that Goldsmith knew that plaintiffs would so rely on his letter to Sherman. Indeed he asked Sherman to "please be good enough to inform the Procaniks."

We also regard as well settled the scope and nature of the duty of a lawyer who does undertake to state the law to a client or a prospective client. If the law is settled, he is expected to know what it is and to state it accurately. . . . If the law is unsettled, debatable or doubtful, he is not required to be correct, usually determinable only by hindsight, but only to exercise an informed judgment based on a reasoned professional evaluation. . . . As explained by Mallen and Levit, . . .

> Implicit in the immunity afforded attorneys for their exercise of judgment on debatable or unsettled points of law is the recognition that an attorney is not required to anticipate correctly the view the courts may ultimately embrace. An attorney is not negligent because he advocates a different view of the law than that ultimately adopted.

Nor is an attorney obliged to anticipate a change in settled law. . . . And if, as here, the attorney has a degree of expertise in a complex and volatile area of the law which leads him to believe, because of developments elsewhere, that change in settled law is possible, it is surely enough for him to point out that that is so and why—just as Goldsmith did here. That explanation need not and perhaps ought not be accompanied by a prediction of the likelihood that he can effect that change in the decisional law in that very case. Surely any experienced practitioner must understand the uncertainty of that prospect even if he believes that the time for seeking change is right and the chances reasonably good. And it is that very uncertainty which ultimately precludes imposition of liability based on his withholding of such a prediction. We concur with the observation of Mallen and Levit that

> The status of a legal proposition varies with time. That which seems indisputably correct today may be deemed clearly erroneous tomorrow. Conversely, that which now appears erroneous may in the future be revealed as correct. Lawyers should not be penalized for either following an erroneous view which the ordinary lawyer perceives to be correct or for urging the correct view which the ordinary lawyer considers to be erroneous. . . .

Nor *a fortiori* can a lawyer be penalized when he not only accurately states the existing rule of law but also points out a reasoned basis supporting the possibility of its change. There was, in sum, nothing actionable in Goldsmith's legal explanation to Sherman.

The second factual predicate of plaintiffs' action was Goldsmith's characterization of Dr. Iffy's expert opinion respecting the obstetrician's medical malpractice as "somewhat weak." Plaintiffs contend that it was not weak at all but highly supportive of their medical malpractice claim. In the light of plaintiffs' stipulation that Goldsmith did not intentionally misrepresent his evaluation of Dr. Iffy's report, the legal issue, as we view it, is simply whether the "somewhat weak" characterization was a reasonable one to have been made by a lawyer skilled in medical malpractice litigation. We note that this is, in effect, the same standard which would apply in the case of an attorney-client relationship, wherein the attorney, although not a guarantor against errors in judgment, is nevertheless required to exercise "the knowledge, skill and ability ordinarily possessed and employed by members of the legal profession similarly situated." . . .

The first question, of course, is what "somewhat weak" means. That question raises the conundrum of the glass that is half full and therefore also half empty. Thus "somewhat weak," in our view, may also connote "somewhat strong." We are, however, persuaded that at the very most all that that phrase could be reasonably understood to have meant was that the report of Dr. Iffy was not unequivocal respecting the strength of plaintiffs' claim of medical malpractice liability. In short, he saw some problems. So viewed, we are also persuaded that the characterization was, on the face of the report itself, not unreasonable. Dr. Iffy, the forensic expert and versed in medical-legal matters, did not expressly state that the obstetrician's conduct was contrary to the accepted community standard of medical practice. He noted the failure of the obstetrician's records to include critical conversations between patient and physician which Mrs. Procanik had related to Sherman, thereby leaving the door open to a significant credibility issue at a potential trial. He pointed out, with respect to Mrs. Procanik's blood test ordered by defendant Dr. Cillo, that "the titer of rubella antibodies was not very high and it was compatible, therefore, with a rubella infection before, rather than during, gestation." And he further expressed the view that even after further investigation of the nature of the illness plaintiff had had early in her pregnancy, it was possible that it "could not have been resolved conclusively." Despite these problems, Dr. Iffy did conclude that in that eventuality

> the decision with regard to the fate of the gestation would have rested upon the detailed analysis of all relevant facts and would have incorporated the opinion of experts, including a specialist of infectious diseases. In that case the patient herself would have been involved in the decision making with full awareness of the options and their respective implications. I regret to conclude that the obstetrician's failure of exploring the background of the relevant data deprived this patient of this opportunity.

Based on the foregoing, we are satisfied that a medical malpractice expert aware of the context and difficulties of proving a plaintiff's medical malpractice case could, beyond any factual dispute, reasonably have characterized the report as Goldsmith did.

Even if we were to assume that Goldsmith's characterization of the Iffy report raised a potential factual question triable by a jury, we are satisfied that plaintiff failed to adduce proof that it was unreasonable. Plaintiffs' legal expert, not a medical malpractice expert, did not testify that the characterization, as he understood its meaning, was unreasonable but only that in his opinion Dr. Iffy's report was strong. Obviously, the fact that his opinion was different from Goldsmith's does not constitute proof that Goldsmith's opinion, even if erroneous, was unreasonable. We also regard as irrelevant the testimony of plaintiffs' medical expert, also a perinatologist, who testified as to his understanding and evaluation of the Iffy report. The issue was not what the report meant to another physician but how it could be reasonably interpreted by a lawyer, and that was not an issue as to which a physician was competent to express an opinion.

In conclusion, we have substantial doubt as to the propriety of the denial of these defendants' motion for summary judgment. Beyond that, we are persuaded that the trial proofs did not raise a jury question as to Goldsmith's breach of any duty he owed the Procaniks. We recognize that this is a tragic case and that the Procanik family has suffered anguish and will continue to suffer in the future. But we nevertheless fail to perceive any professional error in Goldsmith's conduct which could make him or his employers answerable to the Procaniks in damages. We do not, of course, intend to relieve any attorney from the consequences of his breach of duty or professional conduct which deviates from the required standards of reasonable skill and judgment. By the same token, we cannot hold attorneys to a standard of clairvoyance or make them guarantors of success in every case.

Reversed and remanded for entry of judgment dismissing the complaint as to defendants Goldsmith and Greenstone, Greenstone and Naishuler.

The standard of care expected of professionals is well illustrated in *Procanik v. Cillo,* 543 A.2d 985 (N.J.Super. A.D.1988). In *Procanik* an attorney was sued for professional negligence because his declination of representation allegedly discouraged the parents of a rubella-syndrome child from filing a timely negligence action against their obstetrician. The facts are particularly important in this case, so read them carefully. The court carefully describes what is expected of an attorney in relating the status of the law to clients and notes that an attorney is "not a guarantor against errors in judgment" but that he or she is expected to exercise "the knowledge, skill and ability ordinarily possessed and employed by members of the legal profession similarly situated."

In many instances several possible options are available to the professional. The rule of reasonable care does not require that all other professionals would have chosen the same course of action as that decided upon by the defendant professional. The fact that other dentists, for example, might testify that they personally would have opted for a different procedure than that used by the defendant does not necessarily make the defendant's conduct negligent. If, however, only one recognized method of treatment is used by dentists in good standing in the profession and the defendant dentist chooses another course of action, the choice will likely be considered negligent.

HOW NEGLIGENCE CAN OCCUR

Negligence can occur in a number of ways (see Table 12–1). A professional may lack the requisite training to perform a given task. He or she may fail to ask for the information necessary to make an informed recommendation to the plaintiff, or may fail to refer his or her client to a specialist when the situation dictates such a referral. An attorney in general practice with no training or experience in securities fraud, for example, could be negligent if she represented a client in a securities fraud case to the detriment of that client.

Even if a professional chooses an appropriate course of conduct, he may be negligent if he fails to use due diligence and care. Professionals who resort to unorthodox procedures are more likely to be found negligent if the client ultimately suffers some kind of damage than professionals who rely on more conventional techniques. The degree of innovation that will be considered

TABLE 12.1

WHAT CONSTITUTES PROFESSIONAL NEGLIGENCE

- Failure to have skills and learning commonly possessed by members in good standing within a profession.
- Failure to use good judgment in choosing course of action to the extent that the action chosen constitutes a deviation from the standard of care reasonably expected of professionals in the field.
- Failure to ask for essential information from client.
- Failure to make referrals when appropriate.
- Failure to keep abreast of changes in profession.
- Failure to follow up on client's progress, condition, or status.
- Failure to adhere to specialist's standard of care when appropriate.
- Failure to provide informed consent.

legally acceptable will be determined largely by the seriousness of the situation. If a physician uses a method unknown or disapproved of by her peers when dealing with a critically ill patient, she is more likely to be found negligent than if she is dealing with someone suffering a minor illness. In extremely difficult cases the professional may be expected to consult with someone else in the field. A general physician, for example, who identifies a condition that he is ill equipped to handle has an obligation to consult with a specialist.

A professional is obligated to keep abreast of new developments in the field. Accountants are expected to be aware of recent changes in tax law. Physicians are expected to be aware of innovations in medications and procedures.

Professionals are obligated to pay attention to their clients' complaints and feedback. A physician who fails to remain apprised of her patient's change in condition may be negligent. In one case a patient with a history of attacking women was involuntarily committed to a mental hospital where, several years later, a committee of three psychiatrists decided to discharge him. After this decision was made but before he was released he had to be put in restraints because he went beserk. The psychiatrists failed to reevaluate him and when he was released on schedule he attacked two women within twenty minutes of his release. The court held that the psychiatrists' failure to reexamine him constituted negligence. (*Homere v. New York,* 361 N.Y.S.2d 820 (1974)).

SPECIALISTS

Specialists are held to a higher standard of care than generalists. They must adhere to the standard of the "reasonably careful and prudent specialist" in that field. Therefore, a neurosurgeon is held to the standard of care of the average neurosurgeon rather than the average physician. As a result a specialist may be found negligent in a situation in which a general practitioner doing the same thing might not.

Specialists are typically required to adhere to a national standard of care in their field rather than a local one. The reasoning is that clients particularly seek out a specialist because they want someone who is aware of advances in the field. A pediatrician, for example, who failed to make a standard PKU test on a newborn was found negligent even though the hospitals in his community did not use such a test. Since these tests were in general use by pediatricians throughout the rest of the country, the defendant's conduct was held against the national standard of care and he was found negligent (*Naccarato v. Grob,* 180 N.W.2d 788 (Mich.1970)).

Attorneys are held to a general standard of care unless they present themselves as certified specialists. Those who set themselves out through their advertising as certified specialists are held to the standard of care of a specialist.

INFORMED CONSENT

Professionals have a **fiduciary relationship** with their clients in that their relationship is one of trust and confidence. Therefore, they have an obligation to disclose all relevant facts to their clients so that the clients can make informed decisions. The principle of autonomy underlying the **informed consent** doctrine requires clients to be given ultimate dominion over their bodies and those events that affect their lives.

Particularly in the area of medical treatment the issue of consent is very important. Certainly every human being has a right to determine what is to be done with his or her body and no physician may force unwanted treatment on anyone. Under the doctrine of informed consent a physician has a duty to warn patients of possible hazards, complications, and expected and unexpected results of treatment, as well as risks of any alternative treatments. Particularly if a therapy is new or experimental, the physician has a duty to warn the patient that all side effects of the treatment are not completely known. The duty to warn increases as the probability or severity of risk to the patient increases. Any patient who is unaware of the inherent risk of a proposed procedure cannot voluntarily consent to that procedure.

If alternative treatments exist, a physician is obligated to advise a patient about those alternatives. Failure to explain an alternative may in itself constitute negligence. If a physician does not think that an alternative would work in a particular patient's case, however, he or she has no obligation to suggest that alternative. In emergency situations when a patient is unconscious or so ill that he or she is unable to comprehend what is being said, the physician has a right to render treatment without informing the patient of the risks involved.

In determining what should and should not be disclosed to a patient, some courts look at the practice of a reasonably careful practitioner in the same or similar community under the same or similar circumstances. Others consider this a paternalistic standard that leaves the choice to the medical community. They look to the expectations of a reasonable lay person and ask what a patient in that position would reasonably need to know to make an informed decision. The question boils down to whether a reasonable patient in that situation would have submitted to the procedure had he or she been advised of the risks involved.

NATURE OF RISK INVOLVED

A physician must, however, balance the need to provide information versus the effect such information will have on the patient's morale. Recent studies show a close connection between a patient's mental state and his or her response to treatment, so physicians naturally want to avoid doing anything to jeopardize the healing process. If a risk is highly improbable and advising the patient of this risk would in the physician's opinion induce the patient to forego necessary treatment or would severely reduce the efficacy of any treatment, the physician may not be compelled to disclose this information. If the probability of the risk is statistically high, however, the patient should be informed regardless of the effect it might have on his or her morale. Even if the probability of the risk is statistically low but the consequence is extremely severe, the patient should be informed. If the probability of harm is statistically low and its severity is relatively minor, the physician can tailor the warning to avoid unnecessarily exciting the patient.

BATTERY V. NEGLIGENCE

Plaintiffs alleging lack of consent may sue on a theory of either battery or negligence (based on lack of informed consent). If a patient is in total ignorance of what is to be done or if the physician obtains consent for one procedure and then performs another, an action for battery will lie. In the more typical case, however, the patient is aware of the procedure and in fact signs a consent form but does not clearly understand some of the risks inherent in the procedure. In this case a more appropriate cause of action is negligence. Today negligence has for the most part displaced battery as a basis for liability. The practical difference between the two theories is that if battery is alleged, lay witness testimony is sufficient. In cases of negligence, however, expert witnesses are required to testify to the standard of care and the fact that it was breached. Also, the statute of limitations for battery is typically longer than the statute for negligence.

If the cause of action is one of negligence, the primary issue is whether the risks that were not disclosed were material risks. In determining what is and is not material, the courts consider the severity of the consequences and the probability of their occurrence as well as the feasibility of any alternatives. The plaintiff is also required to prove that the outcome was a foreseeable risk and not an unpredictable consequence. If the risk pertaining to that outcome is remote, recovery will not be allowed.

DEFENSES TO PROFESSIONAL NEGLIGENCE

A plaintiff attempting to prove professional negligence must prove both the standard of care expected within the profession and the defendant's deviation from that standard. To do this requires expert testimony, which is usually provided by a professional in that same area of practice. If the defendant is a specialist, the expert is typically a specialist in the same area. The expert witness must be familiar with the procedures or techniques used in the case although he or she need not follow the same practices. In those courts that follow the locality rule the expert must be familiar with the standard of care in the relevant community or similar communities. The plaintiff also has the burden of proving that his or her injuries more probably than not resulted from the negligence of the professional.

The professional can then choose either to refute the plaintiff's factual allegations of negligence or to raise the affirmative defenses of contributory negligence, comparative negligence; or assumption of risk. In order to allege contributory negligence, the defendant must show that the plaintiff's negligence was concurrent with his or her own. If the plaintiff's negligence merely added to the effects of the defendant's negligence, the defendant will not be relieved of liability. The damages awarded to the plaintiff, however, may be reduced. Table 12–2 lists defenses to the charge of professional negligence.

CONTRIBUTORY NEGLIGENCE

Typically, when the defense of contributory negligence is raised, the defendant argues that the client refused to comply with his or her instructions or

TABLE 12.2

DEFENSES TO PROFESSIONAL NEGLIGENCE
•Rebut plaintiff's factual allegations. •Prove plaintiff was negligent and that plaintiff's negligence was concurrent with professional's. •Prove plaintiff assumed the risk by knowingly and voluntarily consenting to risks involved in treatment. •Prove state of emergency (in medical situations).

was otherwise uncooperative. If a client lies to his attorney about the facts of the case, he cannot later claim the attorney was negligent since the attorney relied on the client's veracity in making strategic decisions. If, however, the client's negligence merely compounded the attorney's negligence, the attorney will remain liable and the plaintiff's damages will simply be reduced. In the medical arena, a physician may argue that the patient contributed to her injuries by delaying so long in seeking medical attention that the condition became untreatable. The physician would then have to prove that the untoward affects suffered by the patient were the sole result of the patient's procrastination and that the physician was not in any way negligent himself.

ASSUMPTION OF RISK

Related to the issue of informed consent is the doctrine of assumption of risk. A patient who understands the risk involved in treatment and knowingly consents to that treatment can be said to have assumed the risk. Of course, if those risks are not carefully explained or the plaintiff does not clearly understand them, this defense is inapplicable. No client can assume the risk of negligent care. For example, a physician who advises a patient regarding the risk involved if given improper care and then provides improper care cannot claim that the patient assumed the risk.

EMERGENCY SITUATIONS

In medical situations the defense of emergency can also be used. Treatment that is given during a life and death emergency is not required to be of the same level of care as that provided under less stressful circumstances. If death is imminent and treatment is absolutely necessary for the patient's protection, the defense of emergency may be a viable defense to a claim of negligent treatment. A patient who suffers brain damage subsequent to being treated for a cardiac arrest, for example, may file a negligence claim for her damages but will most likely meet with the defense of emergency. However, if the emergency is caused by the physician's negligence, he cannot use it as a defense. The physician in such cases bears the burden of proving that an emergency in fact existed and that it was not due to any fault of his.

What constitutes adequate care in an emergency depends on the circumstances in which the emergency occurs. A doctor intent on treating a severe head injury who fails to notice a fractured arm may or may not be considered negligent for her failure to diagnose the fracture. Such a question would be submitted to the jury for its determination of whether the doctor's conduct conformed with the expectations of a reasonable doctor working under those conditions.

MAINTAINING ADEQUATE RECORDS

Maintenance of adequate records on a client's case may be of critical importance in proving that no negligence occurred. Professionals should therefore allocate time for the completion of such records even though it may seem a frivolous expenditure of valuable time when being done. The passage of time weakens our memories. Therefore, a professional confronted with a lawsuit one, two, or more years after he has last seen the client may not remember anything about the case. He will be grateful in that circumstance if he can locate records that will disclose facts that can be used to refresh his recollection and that he can use to establish his defense. Of course, such records can also be used to build the plaintiff's case.

Acquiring medical records may present a problem since the physical record itself is considered the property of the health care provider. The content of the record, however, is usually considered to be the patient's property and if the patient will waive the physician-patient privilege most state laws require that the record be released to him or her. Trial courts have uniformly ordered the release of such records. In a personal injury case in which the plaintiff has made his or her medical problems the subject of litigation, all relevant medical records are subject to subpoena by the defendant. If the defendant professional, for example, claims that the plaintiff's injuries preceded the damages the plaintiff alleges were caused by the defendant, the defendant has a right to subpoena the records of physicians who previously treated the plaintiff for related complaints.

UNDERLYING CAUSES OF PROFESSIONAL NEGLIGENCE SUITS

Professional negligence claims appear to be on the rise, particularly those involving physicians and attorneys. Mandatory continuing legal education programs in almost every state and the increasing cost of malpractice insurance premiums attest to the increased incidence of professional negligence suits against attorneys.

Although the public has become more sophisticated in terms of its legal rights, the primary culprit behind many malpractice claims is a breakdown in communication. Poor client relations is probably the single most important contributing factor to these claims. The most common complaint levied against attorneys, according to most state bar organizations, is lack of communication. Many attorneys are notoriously bad about returning telephone calls to clients or advising clients about the status of their case. Professionals can maintain a good rapport with their clients by talking openly with clients about their problems, listening to their complaints, and behaving in a manner that indicates they respect their clients. Those who do so are far less likely to be sued for negligence even when they make mistakes than are those who treat clients in a paternalistic, disdainful manner.

Another possible explanation for the increase in malpractice claims is the unreasonable expectations that many plaintiffs have as a result of what they hear from friends and what they learn from the media. The media tend to over glamorize any personal injury cases, for example, by heavily publicizing large jury awards and then only casually mentioning when those awards are reduced or the verdicts are overturned. People compare these multimillion-dollar awards to their own claims and unrealistically extrapolate what their damages should be. Those watching television shows about life in the medical and legal fields may expect professionals they deal with to have the same charismatic personas and demonstrate the same infallibility they see depicted on television. When reality does not conform to their expectations, some seek recourse by filing suit.

HOW TO PREVENT PROFESSIONAL NEGLIGENCE SUITS

Although professionals can do little to counteract this glorified publicity, they can take several steps to improve client relations. First, they can ensure that their workload does not exceed their capacity to perform. Many professionals, fearful of experiencing a dearth of clients in the future, take on more clients than they can possibly handle at one time. Juggling an unrealistic workload forces them to cut corners and the corner usually cut is client communication. Therefore, professionals should accept no more clients than they can reasonably handle.

Second, professionals need to learn how to manage their businesses. Most have dedicated many years of their lives to honing their technical skills, but few have allocated much time or attention to consideration of the management of their practice. Simple, inexpensive management devices that would make them more efficient and less likely to commit silly errors of omission are often overlooked.

Third, professionals must be willing to dedicate the amount of time necessary to handle a client's problem competently. Consequently, if research should be done or if other practitioners should be consulted, the professional must be willing to expend the time and money necessary to do this. Professionals who constantly take shortcuts in this area are flirting with the specter of malpractice claims.

ROLE OF LEGAL ASSISTANTS

Legal assistants can do their part to prevent professional negligence claims by improving client relations. They can maintain close contact with clients, informing them of the progress of their cases, listening to their concerns, and answering their questions. By doing these things they can shield their attorneys from some of the time-consuming interpersonal tasks that make for good rapport with clients but are often avoided by attorneys because of their limited time.

Legal assistants can also assume responsibility for meeting filing dates. By using management tools, such as "tickler" systems, to alert them to upcoming deadlines, they can minimize the chances of missing important filing and court dates. Because legal assistants must be intimately familiar with the procedural rules and customs of the courts in their jurisdiction, you should pay special attention to procedural law courses in your program of study.

MEDICAL MALPRACTICE CRISIS

Because of the perceived current "medical malpractice crisis," most legislatures have passed statutes that affect medical malpractice litigation in some way. This "crisis" has arisen because of the increase in the amount of litigation since the 1960s, the size of the judgments sometimes awarded, and the concomitant increase in the cost of medical malpractice insurance. Legislators attempting to slay the "malpractice dragon" have enacted legislation resulting in modification of the informed consent doctrine, the burden of proof, evidentiary rules, statutes of limitation, the awarding of punitive damages, and the setting of the standard of care. You would be prudent, therefore, to consult the statutes in your state when getting involved in a medical malpractice case.

SUMMARY

Professionals are held to a reasonable standard of care in that they are required to have the skill and learning commonly possessed by members in good standing within their profession. Choosing a course of action that other professionals might not have chosen or that results in an undesirable outcome does not necessarily make a professional negligent. Lack of proper training, failure to refer to a specialist when necessary, failure to stay abreast of new discoveries, and failure to follow up on a client's progress may all constitute negligence. Specialists are held to the standard of care of a "reasonably careful and prudent specialist." Unlike generalists, specialists must adhere to a national standard of care rather than a local one.

The doctrine of informed consent requires that a physician warn patients of possible hazards, complications, and expected and unexpected results of treatment as well as possible risks of alternative treatments. This duty increases as the probability or severity of risk to the patient increases. How much information must be disclosed to the patient depends on the situation, but sufficient information must be given so that the patient can make an informed decision. If no information is disclosed or if the physician obtains consent for one procedure and then opts to perform another, the patient may sue for battery. If, however, the patient is simply uninformed as to the nature of the risks involved, he or she may sue for negligence. With the latter cause of action, the key question is whether the risks that were not disclosed were material risks. Adequate records should always be maintained so that the professional's memory can be refreshed in the event of a lawsuit.

PRACTICE POINTERS

The defendant may request that the plaintiff submit to an independent physical or mental examination to verify injuries claimed and to justify expenses and suffering alleged. In most jurisdictions, however, the plaintiff is required to submit to only one examination. The examination cannot take place at a location unduly far from the plaintiff's residence and must not include any procedure that is particularly painful or intrusive. Physical examinations must be conducted by a licensed physician or health care professional and mental examinations must be conducted by a licensed physician or clinical psychiatrist.

Typically, the defendant submits a written demand for physical examination to the plaintiff. Such a demand must include the time and location that the examination is to take place, the identity and specialty of the examining physician, and a description of the conditions, scope, and nature of the examination. This demand is served on all other parties to the action but is not filed with the court. The plaintiff must then file a response to the demand indicating whether he or she will comply with the terms of the demand. Alternatively, the plaintiff can insist that certain modifications be made, such as a change in the time or location of the examination. If the defendant then concludes that the plaintiff's request for changes or refusal to appear is unwarranted, he or she may move the court for an order compelling compliance with the demand.

If a physical examination of someone other than the plaintiff is requested or if a mental examination of any person is demanded, a court order must be obtained unless all other parties stipulate to allowing an examination. A motion for medical examination must include the same elements as a demand for physical examination. Additionally, it must contain a declaration showing that the parties have attempted to resolve the issue by stipulation. If an examination is a long distance from the plaintiff's residence (more than seventy-five miles according to federal rules), a court will order attendance only if the requesting party can show good cause for requesting an examination at this distance and if the moving party agrees to advance travel expenses. If a party seeking recovery for personal injuries stipulates that no claim is being made for mental or emotional distress (other than that normally anticipated to arise from a physical injury) and that no expert testimony will be used to show unusual mental and emotional distress, a court may not order a psychological examination.

Most states prohibit the presence of anyone other than the examinee at a psychological examination. In many cases, however, the examiner or the examinee may tape record a mental examination. An attorney for the examinee does, however, have a right to attend a physical examination as well as to tape record that examination. The attorney has a right to suspend the examination if, in his or her opinion, the physician

Continued on next page

PRACTICE POINTERS—Continued

uses tests or procedures that were not included in the order for physical examination. Either the physician or the attorney may suspend an examination if they believe it necessary to secure a protective order.

After submitting to a medical examination, the party may, by written demand, obtain a written report setting forth the findings of the examiner. This report should include the examiner's conclusion, the results of all tests, and copies of any previous reports prepared by the examiner in reference to the examinee. If the demanding party fails to receive these reports in a timely manner, it may move the court for an order compelling delivery. If a party fails to comply with this court order, the court must exclude the testimony of the examiner whose report was not delivered. By the same token, the party who conducts the examination, at the time it serves the demanded report, is entitled to any reports prepared as a result of an examination of the same condition. Additionally, that party is entitled to the identity of any physician who conducts an examination but does not prepare a report as well as the identification of any physician who later examines the patient.

Demand for Physical Examination

Carbuncle and Boyle
1620 Blissful Lane
Suite 6200
Carefree, Arizona 85254
(602) 897-1334
Alma Carbuncle
Steven Boyle
Attorneys for the Defendants

Superior Court for the State of ____________
For the County of ____________

CASE NUMBER C 6096-ABC

THEODORE JONES, et al.,
Plaintiffs
v.
STEVEN AND MILDRED BAXTER,
husband and wife
Defendants

DEMAND FOR PHYSICAL EXAMINATION

TO ALL PARTIES AND TO THEIR ATTORNEYS OF RECORD HEREIN:

A demand is hereby made upon Plaintiff THEODORE JONES to submit to a physical examination.

Continued on next page

PRACTICE POINTERS—Continued

The examination will take place on April 4, 19 __ at 10:30 am at the office of Dr. Bryon Happytimes, Do It Now Medical Center, 4700 Harmony Lane, Suite 200, Scottsdale, Arizona.

The examination will be conducted by Dr. Happytimes, a board certified dermatologist.

February 22, 19 __

Carbuncle and Boyle

Alma Carbuncle
Attorney for Defendants

TORT TEASERS

1. Review the hypothetical scenario at the beginning of this chapter. Has professional negligence been committed? What defenses can be raised?

2. An attorney in general practice tries but fails to create a trust that would have given his client a tax advantage. While conceding his inexperience, the attorney argues that he did a fair job of working on the matter and that he did not have a duty to refer the client to a tax specialist. Do you think the attorney should be found negligent for his failure to seek assistance? *Horne v. Peckham,* 158 Cal.Rptr. 714 (Ct.App.1979).

3. The father of a small child takes the child to an emergency room and tells the attendants that the child has ingested a large quantity of aspirin. The attendants specifically tell the father to advise the physician of this fact but the father fails to make mention of it. The physician diagnoses the child as having the flu. The child dies shortly thereafter and the parents sue the physician for negligence. Should the parents be able to recover? What defense might the physician raise? *Hudson v. St. Paul Mercury Ins. Co.,* 219 So.2d 524 (La.1969).

4. A physician tells his patient he is going to perform a biopsy on her breast and in fact performs a mastectomy. Before performing surgery he specifically indicates that he is not going to perform a mastectomy. On what theory should the patient base her cause of action and why? *Corn v. French,* 289 P.2d 173 (Nev.1955).

5. A troubled, twenty-four-old man consults the head pastor of a church and several of its pastoral counsel. Severely depressed, he tells them he has contemplated suicide. Defendants advise him that suicide is an acceptable alternative in some cases. Defendants visit him in the hospital after he unsuccessfully attempts suicide and he tells them he will reattempt suicide when he is released. Defendants do not advise the doctors or the young man's family about this conversation. Two weeks after he is released from the hospital the young man commits suicide. Plaintiffs, the parents of the young man, sue for wrongful death, alleging, among other things, "clergyman malpractice." How would you go about determining whether Defendants were negligent? *Nally v. Grace Community Church of the Valley*, 763 P.2d 948 *cert. denied*, 109 S.Ct.1644 (Cal.1989).

KEY TERMS

■ **Fiduciary relationship**
Relationship based on trust and confidence that imposes an obligation to act in good faith; an example is the attorney-client relationship.

■ **Informed consent**
Knowledgeable consent based on disclosure of all relevant facts, allowing one to make an informed decision.

13 STRICT LIABILITY

CHAPTER OBJECTIVES

In this chapter you will learn to:

- Identify those circumstances in which animal owners are strictly liable for damages caused by their animals.
- Describe abnormally dangerous activities.
- Describe the defenses that can be raised in response to a strict liability claim.

In this high-tech era of powerful but potentially dangerous sources of energy we are now faced with the problem of waste disposal. We are just beginning to awaken to the horrendous potential posed by chemicals and are taking our first faltering steps toward safeguarding future generations. But some in our society have already begun to experience the repercussions of our ignorance. Suppose a woman comes to your supervising attorney and claims she has contracted cancer as a result of the leakage of toxic chemicals into her home. She wants to sue the city for approving the construction of the housing development in which she lives. She tells you that fifteen years before the land was developed into a residential area, it was used as a disposal site for chemical wastes. Is the city liable for the residents' injuries even if those who allowed the dumping of wastes were, at the time, completely unaware of the potential medical dangers posed by such wastes?

OVERVIEW OF STRICT LIABILITY

In such a case your attorney might choose a theory of strict liability as an alternative to a negligence theory. **Strict liability** is applicable even when a defendant is neither negligent nor has any intent of wrongdoing (see Table 13–1). It is a particularly useful theory in those situations involving **"abnormally dangerous"** activities. Injuries involving defective products and dangerous animals are two other areas in which strict liability is imposed. An in-depth discussion of product liability is presented in Chapter 14.

In cases involving strict liability, defendants who engage in particularly dangerous kinds of activities must pay for any damage that results even if they carry out those activities in the most careful manner possible. Liability is imposed even though a defendant is not at fault. This lack of fault is what distinguishes strict liability from negligence.

Some courts refer to strict liability as "absolute liability." The latter description, however, is somewhat misleading because defenses to strict liability actions can be raised; therefore, liability is not "absolute." Others refer to strict liability as "liability without fault." This term is also a misnomer since liability without fault exists under an intentional tort basis of liability. Therefore, we will use the term *strict liability* throughout the text.

Remember that the key distinction between negligence and strict liability lies in the area of fault. In a strict liability cause of action a defendant may be liable even if he or she did not intentionally injure the plaintiff and adhered to an objective standard of reasonable care.

TABLE 13.1

STRICT LIABILITY	
ANIMALS	•Trespassing •Wild
PRODUCT LIABILITY	
ABNORMALLY DANGEROUS ACTIVITIES*	**Abnormally Dangerous Acts** •Crop dusting •Storage of flammable liquids (urban areas) •Toxic waste disposal •Use of poisonous gas exterminators •Testing of rocket fuel **Not Abnormally Dangerous Acts** •Airplane flight (except ground damage) •Defective electrical wiring •Water damage from burst dam •Defective plumbing •Household use of gas, water or electricity

*The courts are not in agreement as to what does and does not constitute an "abnormally dangerous" activity. The examples given are representative of the majority position but should not be considered definitive.

STRICT LIABILITY FOR HARM CAUSED BY ANIMALS

TRESPASSING ANIMALS

Under the English common law, owners of animals were liable for property damage caused when animals trespassed on another's land. Owners could not escape liability even if they used the utmost care to prevent their animals from escaping. Luckily for animal owners, the rule applied only to animals likely to roam, such as cattle, horses, sheep, and goats and not to household animals, such as dogs and cats.

Most American jurisdictions follow the English rule of strict liability in reference to trespassing animals. Historically, the Western states, whose economic base relied on cattle that were customarily allowed to graze at large on open range, rejected the common law rule. Many of these states have, however, adopted "fencing in" statutes, which provide that an owner is not strictly liable if he or she attempts to fence in the animals but is strictly liable if he or she does not. On the other hand, under the "fencing out" statutes, property owners who properly fence their land have a strict liability claim against those whose animals trespass onto their land.

NONTRESPASSING ANIMALS

One who keeps *dangerous animals* is strictly liable for the harm done by those animals. The definition of dangerous depends on whether the animal is considered wild or domesticated. A domesticated animal, according to the Restatement (Second) of Torts Sec. 506(2), "is by custom devoted to the service of mankind." Under this definition, the courts have generally held that bulls and stallions, while often very dangerous, are domesticated. The apparent reasoning is that ownership of animals serving a valid social purpose should not be discouraged.

According to the Restatement (Second) of Torts, people who keep wild animals are strictly liable for all damage caused by such animals if the damage results from a "dangerous propensity" typical of that particular species (Restatement (Second) of Torts Sec. 507). Javelinas and foxes are examples of animals that are considered wild. Liability also exists where the damage stems from a dangerous tendency of the particular animal in question of which the owner is or should be aware. Some courts have moved away from a strict liability standard to a negligence standard when dealing with those who display wild animals to the public (as in a zoo, for example).

Strict liability is imposed in the case of domestic animals where the owner knows or has reason to know that the animal has vicious propensities. If an animal has unsuccessfully attempted to bite someone in the past or in general has a vicious temperament, the owner will be deemed to have reason to know of the pet's dangerous tendencies and will be held liable for any damage caused. The oft-repeated phrase "Every dog is entitled to one free bite" is an illusion and should not be relied on to evade liability. Note, too, that the common law regarding liability for dog bites has been changed by statute in many states. Furthermore, statutory provisions, such as those requiring dogs to be leashed or muzzled, may also affect liability. Failure to comply with such statutes may render an owner negligent *per se*.

ABNORMALLY DANGEROUS ACTIVITIES

DOCTRINE OF *RYLANDS v. FLETCHER*

The path to strict liability for abnormally dangerous activities was paved in the English case of *Rylands v. Fletcher*, L.R. 3 H.L. 330 (1868). In *Rylands* the defendants hired an engineer and contractors to plan and construct a reservoir in order to supply their mill with water. When the defendants filled the reservoir, the water broke through into some abandoned mine shafts and then flooded into adjacent mine shafts owned by the plaintiffs. An arbitrator found that while the defendants themselves were not guilty of any negligence, the engineer and contractors were negligent in their failure to use proper care. The case reached the House of Lords, the final appellate tribunal in England. The court, in finding for the plaintiff, established the rule that ". . . the person who for his own purposes brings on his lands and collects and keeps there any thing likely to do mischief if it escapes, must keep it in at his peril, and if he does not do so, is prima facie answerable for all the damage which is the natural consequence of its escape."

The majority of American courts, along with the Second Restatement, have adopted the rationale of *Rylands* and imposed strict liability in cases involving abnormally dangerous activities. The Restatement (Second) of Torts Sec. 520 suggests consideration of six factors in determining whether an activity is abnormally dangerous:

- High degree of risk: "High degree of risk of some harm to the person, land or chattel of others."
- Risk of serious harm: "Likelihood that the harm that results from it will be great."
- Cannot be eliminated even by due care: "Inability to eliminate the risk by the exercise of reasonable care."
- Not a matter of common usage: "Extent to which the activity is not a matter of common usage."
- Inappropriateness: "Inappropriateness of the activity to the place where it is carried on."
- Value: "Extent to which its value to the community is outweighed by its dangerous attributes."

In determining whether strict liability should be imposed, the courts consider all of the factors listed above (see Table 13–2). Read *Yukon Equipment, Inc. v. Firemen's Fund Insurance Company* to see an application of the six-factor test (although observe that the court ultimately rejects this test). Any one factor alone is generally not sufficient to warrant strict liability; on the other hand, all of the factors need not be present to find strict liability. The essential question is whether the risk created is so unusual (either because of its magnitude or because of the circumstances surrounding it) to justify strict liability even though the activity was carried out with all reasonable care. An example of such an activity is the transportation of nuclear materials. This activity necessarily involves a major risk of harm to others no matter how carefully it is carried out. (Note: Federal statutes impose a ceiling on liability for any nuclear mishaps.)

Be aware that the following examples of activities the courts have or have not considered abnormally dangerous are highly fact-specific. In other words,

TABLE 13.2

IS AN ACTIVITY ABNORMALLY DANGEROUS? SIX-FACTOR TEST (RESTATEMENT (SECOND) OF TORTS)
• Is there a high degree of risk of harm to person or property?
• Is any harm that results from the activity likely to be serious?
• Can the risk of harm be eliminated by exercising reasonable care?
• Is the activity a matter of common usage?
• Is the activity inappropriate in reference to the place where it is carried on?
• Is the value of the activity to the community out-weighed by its dangerousness?

if the fact pattern had varied slightly in any of these cases, the court could have arrived at a different conclusion. Therefore, do not categorize certain activities as being either abnormally dangerous or not. Rather, look at these cases as being illustrative of the courts' reasoning in the context of specific fact patterns.

YUKON EQUIPMENT, INC., an Alaska Corporation, and E. I. du Pont de Nemours Company, a Delaware Corporation, Petitioners,
v.
FIREMAN'S FUND INSURANCE COMPANY et al., Respondents.
No. 3308
Supreme Court of Alaska.
Nov. 3, 1978.
585 P.2d 1206 (Alas. 1978)

MATTHEWS, Justice.

A large explosion occurred at 2:47 A.M. on December 7, 1973, in the suburbs north of the city of Anchorage. The explosion originated at a storage magazine for explosives under lease from the federal government to petitioner E. I. du Pont de Nemours and Company, which was operated by petitioner Yukon Equipment, Inc. The storage magazine is located on a 1,870 acre tract of federal land which had been withdrawn by the Department of the Interior for the use of the Alaska Railroad for explosive storage purposes by separate orders in 1950 and 1961. The magazine which exploded was located 3,820 feet from the nearest building not used to store explosives and 4,330 feet from the nearest public highway. At the time of the explosion it contained approximately 80,000 pounds of explosives. The blast damaged dwellings and other buildings within a two-mile radius of the magazine and, in some instances, beyond a two mile radius. The ground concussion it caused registered 1.8 on the Richter scale at the earthquake observation station in Palmer, some 30 miles away.

The explosion was caused by thieves. Four young men had driven onto the tract where the magazine was located, broken into the storage magazine, set a prepared charge, and fled. They apparently did so in an effort to conceal the fact that they had stolen explosives from the site a day or two earlier.

This consolidated lawsuit was brought to recover for property damage caused by the explosion. Cross-motions for partial summary judgment were filed, and summary judgment on the issue of liability was granted in favor of the respondents. Respondents presented alternative theories of liability based on negligence, nuisance, absolute liability, and trespass. The court's order granting partial summary judgment did not specify the theory on which the liability was based.

Petitioners contend that none of the theories may be utilized to fix liability on them by summary judgment and further that the intentional detonation of the magazine is a superseding cause relieving them of liability under any theory. Respondents argue that the summary judgment is sustainable under the theory of absolute liability and that the intentional nature of the explosion is not a defense. We agree with respondents and affirm.

I

The leading case on liability for the storage of explosives is *Exner v. Sherman Power Constr. Co.*, 54 F.2d 510 (2d Cir. 1931). There dynamite stored by the defendant exploded causing personal injury and property damage to the plaintiffs who resided some 935 feet away from the storage site. A distinguished panel of the Circuit Court of Appeals for the Second Circuit held the defendant liable regardless of fault:

> Dynamite is of the class of elements which one who stores or uses in such a locality, or under such circumstances as to cause likelihood of risk to others, stores or uses at his peril. He is an insurer, and is absolutely liable if damage results to third persons, either from the direct impact of rocks thrown out by the explosion (which would be a common law trespass) or from concussion.

Id. at 512–13. The court pointed out that while the general principle of absolute liability expressed in the English case of *Rylands v. Fletcher* had been accorded a mixed reception at best in United States courts, there had been no such reluctance to impose absolute liability in blasting cases. The court then noted that some authorities had made a distinction between damage done by rocks or debris hurled by an explosion, as to which there would be absolute liability, and damage caused by a concussion, as to which a negligence standard applied. The court concluded that such a distinction was without a logical basis and rejected it. *Id.* at 514. The court also determined that there was no reason for attaching different legal consequences to the results of an explosion "whether the dynamite explodes when stored or when employed in blasting." The court expressed the policy behind the rule of absolute liability as follows:

> The extent to which one man in the lawful conduct of his business is liable for injuries to another involves an adjustment of conflicting interests. . . . When, as here, the defendant, though without fault, has engaged in the perilous activity of storing large quantities of a dangerous explosive for use in his business, we think there is no justification for relieving it of liability, and that the owner of the business, rather than a third party who has no relation to the explosion, other than that of injury, should bear the loss.

Id. at 514. *Exner* has been widely followed, and was based on many earlier authorities imposing absolute liability for explosions. . . .

> The storage and transportation of explosive substances are ultra-hazardous activities because no precautions and care can make it reasonably certain that they will not explode and because the harm resulting from their explosion is almost certain to be serious.

Comment (e) addresses the question of common usage, stating:

> While blasting is recognized as a proper means of clearing woodlands for cultivating and of excavating for building purposes, the conditions which require its use are usually of brief duration. It is generally required because of the peculiar character of the land and it is not a part of the customary processes of farming or of building operations. Likewise, the manufacture, storage, transportation and use of high explosives, although necessary to the construction of many public and private works, are carried on by a comparatively small number of persons and, therefore, are not matters of common usage.

Thus the particular rule of *Exner*, absolute liability for damage caused by the storage of explosives, was preserved by the Restatement and a general rule, inferred from *Exner* and the authorities on which it was based, and from *Rylands v. Fletcher* and its antecedents, was stated which imposed absolute liability on any other activity which met the definition of ultra-hazardous.

The Restatement (Second) of Torts (1977), adopted by the ALI after the explosion in this case, does not reflect a *per se* rule of liability for the storage of explosives. Instead it lists six factors to be considered in determining whether an activity is "abnormally dangerous" and therefore subject to the rule of absolute liability. The factors are:

> (a) existence of a high degree of risk of some harm to the person, land or chattels of others;
>
> (b) likelihood that the harm that results from it will be great;
>
> (c) inability to eliminate the risk by the exercise of reasonable care;
>
> (d) extent to which the activity is not a matter of common usage;
>
> (e) inappropriateness of the activity to the place where it is carried on; and
>
> (f) extent to which its value to the community is outweighted by its dangerous attributes.

Id. § 520.

Based in large part on the Restatement (Second), petitioners argue that their use was not abnormally dangerous. Specifically they contend that their use of the magazine for the storage of explosives was a normal and appropriate use of the area in question since the storage magazine was situated on lands set aside by the United States for such purposes and was apparently located in compliance with applicable federal regulations. They point out that the storage served a legitimate community need for an accessible source of explosives for various purposes. They contend that before absolute liability can be imposed in any circumstance a preliminary finding must be made as to whether or not the defendant's activity is abnormally dangerous, that such a determination involves the weighing of the six factors set out in section 520 of the Restatement (Second) of Torts, and that an evaluation of those factors in this case could not appropriately be done on motion for summary judgment.

If we were to apply the Restatement (Second)'s six factor test to the storage of explosives in this case we would be inclined to conclude that the use involved here was an abnormally dangerous one. Comment (f) to section 520 makes it clear that all of the factors need not be present for an activity to be considered abnormally dangerous:

> In determining whether the danger is abnormal, the factors listed in clauses (a) to (f) of this Section are all to be considered, and are all of importance. Any one of them is not necessarily sufficient to itself in a particular case, and

> ordinarily several of them will be required for strict liability. On the other hand it is not necessary that each of them be present, especially if others weigh heavily.

The first three factors, involving the degree of risk, harm, and difficulty of eliminating the risk, are obviously present in the storage of 80,000 pounds of explosives in a suburban area. The fourth factor, that the activity not be a matter of common usage, is also met. Comment (i) states:

> Likewise the manufacture, storage, transportation and use of high explosives, although necessary to the construction of many public and private works, are carried on by only a comparatively small number of persons and therefore are not matters of common usage.

The fifth factor, inappropriateness of the activity, is arguably not present, for the storage did take place on land designated by the United States government for that purpose. However, the designation took place at a time when the area was less densely populated than it was at the time of the explosion. Likewise, the storage reserve was not entirely appropriate to the quantity of explosives stored because the explosion caused damage well beyond the boundaries of the reserve. The sixth factor, value to the community relates primarily to situations where the dangerous activity is the primary economic activity of the community in question. Thus comment (k) states that such factor applies

> particularly when the community is largely devoted to the dangerous enterprise and its prosperity largely depends upon it. Thus the interests of a particular town whose livelihood depends upon such an activity as manufacturing cement may be such that cement plants will be regarded as a normal activity for that community notwithstanding the risk of serious harm from the emission of cement dust.

The comment further states that

> in Texas and Oklahoma, a properly conducted oil or gas well, at least in a rural area, is not regarded as abnormally dangerous, while a different conclusion has been reached in Kansas and Indiana. California, whose oil industry is far from insignificant, has concluded that an oil well drilled in a thickly settled residential area in the City of Los Angeles is a matter of strict liability.

Since five of the six factors required by section 520 of the Restatement (Second) are met and the sixth is debatable, we would impose absolute liability here if we were to use that approach.[8]

[2, 3] However, we do not believe that the Restatement (Second) approach should be used in cases involving the use or storage of explosives. Instead, we adhere to the rule of *Exner v. Sherman Power Constr. Co.* and its progeny imposing absolute liability in such cases. The Restatement (Second) approach requires an analysis of degrees of risk and harm, difficulty of eliminating risk, and appropriateness of place, before absolute liability may be imposed. Such factors suggest a negligence standard.[10] The six factor

8. *Cf. Siegler v. Kuhlman,* 81 Wash.2d 448, 502 P.2d 1181 (1972), *cert. denied* 411 U.S. 983, 93 S.Ct. 2275, 36 L.Ed.2d 959 (1973), holding that hauling gasoline on public highways is abnormally dangerous as a matter of law, utilizing the six factors identified in a tentative draft of the Restatement (Second).

10. In the analogous area of strict liability for defective products we have rejected the approach of § 402(a) of the Restatement (Second) of Torts which requires proof that a product is "unreasonably dangerous." "It represents a step backwards in the development of products liability cases. The purpose of strict liability is to overcome the difficulty of proof inherent in negligent and warranty theories, thereby insuring that the costs of physical injuries are borne by those who market defective products." *Butaud v. Suburban Marine & Sporting Goods, Inc.,* 543 P.2d 209, 214 (Alaska 1975).

analysis may well be necessary where damage is caused by unique hazards and the question is whether the general rule of absolute liability applies, but in cases involving the storage and use of explosives we take that question to have been resolved by more than a century of judicial decisions.

The reasons for imposing absolute liability on those who have created a grave risk of harm to others by storing or using explosives are largely independent of considerations of locational appropriateness. We see no reason for making a distinction between the right of a homesteader to recover when his property has been damaged by a blast set off in a remote corner of the state, and the right to compensation of an urban resident whose home is destroyed by an explosion originating in a settled area. In each case, the loss is properly to be regarded as a cost of the business of storing or using explosives. Every incentive remains to conduct such activities in locations which are as safe as possible, because there the damages resulting from an accident will be kept to a minimum.

II

[4] The next question is whether the intentional detonation of the storage magazine was a superseding cause relieving petitioners from liability. In *Sharp v. Fairbanks North Star Borough*, 569 P.2d 178 (Alaska 1977), a negligence case, we stated that a superseding cause exists where "after the event and looking back from the harm to the actor's negligent conduct, it appears to the court highly extraordinary that it should have brought about the harm." 569 P.2d at 182, quoting from Restatement (Second) of Torts § 435 (1965). We further explained in *Sharp*,

> [w]here the defendant's conduct threatens a particular kind of result which will injure the plaintiff and an intervening cause which could not have been anticipated changes the situation but produces the same result as originally threatened, such a result is within the scope of the defendant's negligence.

Id. at 183 n. 9. The considerations which impel cutting off liability where there is a superseding cause in negligence cases also apply to cases of absolute liability.

Prior to the explosion in question the petitioners' magazines had been illegally broken into at least six times. Most of these entries involved the theft of explosives. Petitioners had knowledge of all of this.

[5] Applying the standards set forth in *Sharp, supra,* to these facts we find there to have been no superseding cause. The incendiary destruction of premises by thieves to cover evidence of theft is not so uncommon an occurrence that it can be regarded as highly extraordinary. Moreover, the particular kind of result threatened by the defendant's conduct, the storage of explosives, was an explosion at the storage site. Since the threatened result occurred it would not be consistent with the principles stated in *Sharp, supra,* to hold there to have been a superseding cause. Absolute liability is imposed on those who store or use explosives because they have created an unusual risk to others. As between those who have created the risk for the benefit of their own enterprise and those whose only connection with the enterprise is to have suffered damage because of it, the law places the risk of loss on the former. When the risk created causes damage in fact, insistence that the precise details of the intervening cause be foreseeable would subvert the purpose of that rule of law.

The partial summary judgment is AFFIRMED.

RABINOWITZ, Justice, concurring.

Although I concur in the result reached by the court, I disagree with its adoption of the approach of *Exner v. Sherman Power*

Construction Co., 54 F.2d 510 (2d Cir. 1931), which imposes absolute or strict liability in all cases involving the use or storage of explosives. I am persuaded that sections 519 and 520 of the Restatement (Second) of Torts (1977) embody a sounder rule of law. On balance, I think it is preferable that the court, in making the determination whether an activity is "abnormally dangerous" and therefore subject to absolute liability, employ the criteria articulated in section 520 to analyze the particular acts and circumstances of the case. In my view, consideration of these criteria offers a rational solution to the problem of determining whether a particular activity is abnormally dangerous.

Despite the foregoing, I can agree with the court's overall disposition of this appeal since application of section 520 to the facts of the case leads to the conclusion that the activity in question was abnormally dangerous. Thus absolute liability was properly imposed.

EXAMPLES OF ACTIVITIES SOME COURTS HAVE CONSIDERED ABNORMALLY DANGEROUS

Crop Dusting. The plaintiffs were organic farmers who used no nonorganic fertilizers, insecticides, or herbicides in their farming; they sold their produce to organic food buyers. The defendant, a crop duster, while spraying land adjoining plaintiffs' land, during one spraying pass began spraying while over plaintiffs' property. The residue rendered plaintiffs' produce unfit to sell to buyers of organic food. The court, considering each of the six factors set forth in the Second Restatement, held that the defendant was strictly liable for the damage caused by his aerial spraying. The court emphasized that the risk of harm was accentuated by the fact that the drift of chemicals in aerial spraying is particularly unpredictable. The court also noted that the likelihood that harm would result was dependent upon what adjoining property owners did with their land. In balancing the risk of harm versus the utility of the activity, the court concluded that an equitable balancing of social interests could be attained only if the defendants were made to pay for the consequences of their acts (*Langan v. Valicopters, Inc.*, 567 P.2d 218 (Wash.1977)).

Poisonous Gases. In an effort to kill cockroaches, the defendant, an exterminator, put hydrocyanic acid gas in the basement of a commercial building one evening while the building was unoccupied. The next morning the plaintiff was almost fatally poisoned because he was unable to smell the fumes due to having a cold and because he was unaware of the defendant's nocturnal activities. The court found that the defendant had engaged in an ultrahazardous activity that was likely to cause injury even though the utmost care was used. The court also concluded that the defendant knew or should have known injury might result and that the use of gas in this case was not "common usage" since even though the gas was commonly used by fumigators, it was not used generally by the public (*Luthringer v. Moore*, 190 P.2d 1 (Cal.1948)).

Other activities the courts have held subject to strict liability include the following:

- Storage of flammable liquids in urban areas.
- Disposal of hazardous waste.
- Testing of rocket fuel.

EXAMPLES OF ACTIVITIES SOME COURTS HAVE CONSIDERED NOT ABNORMALLY DANGEROUS

Airline Crash. An airline crash resulted in fire damage to a nearby apartment building. The court held for the defendant after concluding that flying is not an abnormally dangerous activity and that there was no intent to crash and no control over the plane after the mid-air collision preceding the crash (*Wood v. United Air Lines, Inc.*, 223 N.Y.S.2d 692, affirmed 226 N.Y.S.2d 1022, appeal dismissed, 230 N.Y.S. 207 (1961)).

In the early days of commercial aviation, airlines were held to a strict liability standard. Modern safety records no longer warrant classifying flying as an abnormally dangerous activity and most courts have retreated to a negligence standard in this area. In many states strict liability continues to apply to ground damage caused by an airline crash, although an increasing number of states appear to be abandoning that position.

Irrigation Dam. A saboteur ruptured the defendant's irrigation dam causing damage to the plaintiff's property. The appellate court held that reservoir owners are not absolutely liable for damage to the property of others caused by escaping waters if due to an "act of God," due to a public enemy, or due to the malicious act of a third person. The court noted that in a semiarid climate an irrigation reservoir does not qualify as an uncommon usage or an ultrahazardous activity (*Wheatland Irrig. Dist. v. McGuire*, 537 P.2d 1128, rehearing granted in part, 552 P.2d 1115, rehearing, 562 P.2d 287 (Wyo.1975)).

Falling Tree. The plaintiff, a motorist, was injured when his automobile was struck by a falling tree. The plaintiff alleged that the defendant's construction of an irrigation canal was abnormally dangerous conduct that caused the roots of the tree to weaken. The court held that the defendant's acts were not abnormally dangerous since building an irrigation canal was not an uncommon activity in a rural area and did not involve an abnormally high degree of risk (*Stroda v. State By and Through State Highway Commission*, 539 P.2d 1147 (Ore.App.1975)).

Other activities the courts have concluded are not abnormally dangerous include the following:

- A defective lawn sprinkler that resulted in an automobile crash.
- Defective plumbing that caused damage to plaintiff's lower floor apartment.
- Defective electric wiring that resulted in property damage.

The courts are not in agreement as to what does and does not constitute an abnormally dangerous activity. Public policy appears to influence that determination since an overview of the cases in several jurisdictions indicates that courts are more likely to classify an activity as abnormally dangerous if the activity occurs in a highly populated area and less likely to do so if the activity occurs in an isolated area. Courts are more likely, for example, to hold strictly liable those who store flammable liquids or explosives in densely populated areas than they are those who store these materials in rural areas. By the same token, courts appear reluctant to classify the household use of gas, water, or electricity as an abnormally dangerous activity.

PRODUCT LIABILITY

The rationale underlying strict liability in the area of product liability is that it is easier for the defendant to bear the risk of loss than for the plaintiff. Advocates of strict liability reason that merchants and manufacturers have the ability to internalize the costs of accidental losses and can distribute such losses among the consumers who purchase their products.

Another reason given for imposing strict liability is that product safety is better promoted by a strict liability theory than by traditional negligence theory. Once courts render decisions imposing strict liability on defendants even though they were not negligent, defendants arguably have a strong incentive to prevent the occurrence of future harm. Preventing future harm is a primary goal for those who advocate strict liability. This theory of liability will be discussed at length in Chapter 14.

LIMITATIONS ON STRICT LIABILITY

A defendant can raise either of two defenses in a strict liability case. First, a defendant can argue lack of proximate cause, i.e., that the damage that occurred was not the result of the kind of risk that made the activity abnormally dangerous. Second, a defendant can argue that a plaintiff who has "assumed the risk" should be barred from recovery.

PROXIMATE CAUSE

A defendant is strictly liable only for those damages that result from the kind of risk that made the activity abnormally dangerous. The Restatement (Second) of Torts illustrates this point using an example of a pedestrian run over by a truck transporting dynamite. Although transporting dynamite is an abnormally dangerous activity, the plaintiff will not be able to sue on the basis of strict liability because the risk of hitting pedestrians is not one of the things that makes such transportation abnormally dangerous.

A related rule is that a defendant will not be strictly liable if the harm occurred only because the plaintiff was conducting an "abnormally sensitive" activity. The case commonly used to illustrate this point is one in which plaintiff's female minks killed their young as a result of the mothers' frightened reactions to the defendant's blasting operation being conducted more than two miles from the plaintiff's mink ranch (*Foster v. Preston Mills Co.*, 268 P.2d 645 (Wash.1954)) The court reasoned that blasting operations are unusually dangerous because of "the risk that property or persons may be damaged or injured by coming into direct contact with flying debris, or by being directly affected by vibrations of the earth or concussions of the air." Here, since the minks were harmed only because of their "exceedingly nervous disposition," the court held that the defendant was not strictly liable. Strict liability does not protect against "harms incident to the plaintiff's extraordinary and unusual use of land."

Some courts will also relieve defendants of liability if the harm occurred in an unforeseeable manner. An "act of God," for example, is often enough to relieve a defendant of strict liability. Although the Restatement (Second) of

Torts rejects the "act of God" exception, many courts have been reluctant to impose liability where the harm that occurred was clearly out of the control of the defendant. Courts have refused to impose strict liability where, for example, extraordinary rainfall washed out a dam or where a hurricane caused water to overflow from a hydroelectric plant, resulting in flood damage.

Although the courts are not uniform in where they draw the line on strict liability, most courts impose liability for a narrower range of harm in cases involving strict liability than in those cases involving negligence. That is, a court is more likely to find proximate cause in a negligence case than in a strict liability case. Likewise, a court is more likely to deny liability if there is an unforeseen, intervening cause in a strict liability case than in a negligence case. This willingness to curtail liability in strict liability cases is most likely due to the fact that the defendant is without fault.

ASSUMPTION OF RISK

A plaintiff who knowingly, voluntarily, and either reasonably or unreasonably subjects himself or herself to danger is barred from recovering on the basis of strict liability. For example, a plaintiff who insists on driving through an area where blasting is being done after seeing warning signs and being detained by a flagman assumes the risk if he is injured by the blasting (Restatement (Second) of Torts Sec. 523, illustration 2). Note, however, that contributory negligence usually will not bar a plaintiff from recovery. In the example above, if the driver had been merely inattentive and had missed the warning signs, this contributory negligence would not have barred him from recovery. Even though the driver in that situation did not discover a risk he should have discovered, full responsibility would lie with the party who created the abnormal risk (Restatement (Second) of Torts Sec. 524, comment a).

SUMMARY

Strict liability is a cause of action that can be used in cases involving abnormally dangerous activities, dangerous animals, and product liability. A plaintiff can recover damages even if the defendant acted without fault. The rationale underlying strict liability is that those people who engage in unusually dangerous activities must be responsible for any damages resulting from those activities.

Animal owners who are or should be aware of the vicious propensities of their domesticated pets are strictly liable for damages caused by those pets. Under the common law owners were liable for property damage created by trespassing animals if those animals were likely to roam. This rule was modified by the "fencing in" and "fencing out" statutes adopted by the Western states.

Abnormally dangerous activities are those activities involving a high degree of risk of serious harm that cannot be eliminated with due care. Furthermore, the activity must not be a matter of common usage, must be inappropriate to the place where it is carried out, and its value to the community must be outweighed by its dangerous attributes. Crop dusting and the storage of flammable liquids are both examples of abnormally dangerous activities. Pub-

PRACTICE POINTERS

Part of the discovery process is the submission of Requests for Production of Documents and Things to the opposing party. This is a request to view and copy any tangible evidence of the opposition, including written statements, photographs, records, drawings, graphs, and charts. Requests can also be made to test or sample tangible items in the custody of the opposition, which is frequently done in product liability cases.

Requests for Production can be served at any time after the complaint is filed but many attorneys opt to serve them when they send out interrogatories to the opposition. The request must be in writing and must set forth the time and place for production. A request should generally be drafted broadly rather than calling for specific documents so that the party complying with the request is obligated to produce documents that the requesting party may be unaware of. The requested material can be viewed in the requesting attorney's office if it is relatively small

FIGURE 13.1 Sample Request for Production of Documents and Things

SUPERIOR COURT OF THE STATE OF ARIZONA
COUNTY OF MARICOPA

------------------------) Suzy Smith,) Plaintiff) vs.) Jake Garcia,) Defendant)	Civil Action No. 90-1495

Pursuant to Rule 34 of the Arizona Rules of Civil Procedure, Plaintiff SUZY SMITH (hereinafter "Plaintiff") hereby requests that Defendant JAKE GARCIA (hereinafter "Defendant") produce for inspection and photocopying the documents described in Exhibit A at the Offices of Edwards & Edwards, Seven Shea Boulevard, Suite 800, Phoenix, Arizona 85031 at 10:00 am on April 22, 19___.

Dated: February 22, 19__.

____

Stan Edwards
Attorney for the Plaintiff

Continued on next page

PRACTICE POINTERS—Continued

and easily transportable. If such a viewing is impracticable, the material can be viewed in the opposing counsel's office or the location where the material is permanently stored.

A responding party may object to a Request for Production, including such grounds as privilege or work product. Alternatively, a party may indicate it is unable to comply with the request by stating that a diligent and reasonable effort was made to comply but that compliance was impossible because the requested item was never in the party's possession, was stolen, lost or destroyed, or never existed.

Deciding which documents are relevant to a Request for Production is a sometimes prodigious task that is frequently assigned to legal assistants. Disclosure can involve production of hundreds or, in some complex cases, millions of pages of documents. A production summary, as shown on page 250, can be used to assist in organizing the assimilation of materials. This summary correlates the general material being requested with the sources and descriptions of the specific materials that will be used to comply with each request. The summary should be reviewed with the supervising attorney before a meeting is scheduled with the client. The client should be consulted to determine the types of responsive documents that are available as well as their location. All materials must be reviewed to see if they are relevant and producible. All produced documents should be numbered systematically. Relevant materials can either be supplied to the requesting party or can be made available for inspection at a mutually agreeable time.

FIGURE 13.2

Exhibit "A"

1. Copies of all reports prepared by police officials investigating the accident involving Plaintiff and Defendant on October 19, 19__.

2. Copies of Defendant's automobile insurance policies that may provide satisfaction of all or part of any judgment entered against Defendant in this proceeding, including declaration pages and pages setting forth policy limits.

3. Copies of any written communications between Defendant and Plaintiff or any agent or representative of Plaintiff, including, but not limited to, attorneys, insurance company representatives, family members, friends, etc.

4. Photographs, diagrams or other depictions of the accident scene that are in the Defendant's possession.

5. Copies of any and all written reports prepared by experts for Defendant.

TABLE 13.3 Sample Production Summary

Production Summary
Smith vs. Garcia
Request Date: Feb. 22, 19__
Response Date: April 22, 19__

REQUEST NUMBER	MATERIAL REQUESTED	TYPES OF DOCUMENTS	SOURCE	WRITTEN RESPONSE
1	Investigative reports	Police reports	Phoenix Police	Will produce
2	Insurance policies	State Farm policy	Client	Will produce
3	Written communications	Letter from State Farm; Letter from plaintiff's mother	Client	Will produce
4	Depictions of accident scene	Photos & diagrams	Phoenix Police	Will produce
5	Expert reports			None prepared at this time

lic policy concerns appear to affect the courts' classification of activities as being abnormally dangerous.

A defendant can be absolved of liability if the plaintiff assumes the risk by voluntarily and knowingly exposing himself or herself to the danger created by the defendant. If proximate cause is lacking in that the damage that occurred did not result from the kind of risk making the activity abnormally dangerous, the defendant is not liable.

TORT TEASERS

1. Remembering the hypothetical scenario presented at the beginning of the chapter, what arguments would you make if you wanted to allege that those who dispose of hazardous wastes, such as toxic chemicals, are strictly liable for the consequences of their dumping? Analogize to the cases in this chapter, arguing that your case is most like those cases used to illustrate abnormally dangerous activities and unlike those cases used to illustrate activities that are not abnormally dangerous.

2. Plaintiff, while employed by defendants to look after their children, is startled by defendants' pet bird when it lights on her face. In trying to avoid the bird she steps back, falls, and fractures her hip. Defendants often let the bird out of its cage and do not lock the cage even though they are aware that they could do so. Should Defendants be held strictly liable? *Neagle v. Morgan*, 277 N.E. 483 (Mass.1971).

3. Plaintiff boards his mare in a pasture with other horses. One day while trying to feed his mare Plaintiff leads the mare away from the other horses in the pasture. Defendant's colt approaches him in a menacing manner and Plaintiff, who is aware of the colt's vicious propensities, drives the colt away and returns to feeding his mare. The colt waits and then stealthily comes up behind Plaintiff and kicks him in the behind. Do you think this is a case of strict liability? What defenses might be raised and why? *Sandy v. Bushey*, 128 A. 513 (Me.1925).

4. The court's synopsis of the facts in this particular case certainly bears repeating. "On September 14, 1907, the plaintiff was the owner of a thoroughbred Holstein-Friesian heifer, which was born on January 9, 1906, and had been thereafter duly christened 'Martha Pietertje Pauline.' The name is neither euphonious nor musical, but there is not much in a name anyway. Notwithstanding any handicap she may have had in the way of a cognomen, Martha Pietertje Pauline was a genuine 'highbrow,' having a pedigree as long and at least as well authenticated as that of the ordinary scion of effete European nobility who breaks into this land of democracy and equality, and offers his title to the highest bidder at the matrimonial bargaining counter. The defendant was the owner of a bull about one year old, lowly born and nameless as far as the record discloses. This plebeian, having aspirations beyond his humble station in life, wandered beyond the confines of his own pastures, and sought the society of the adolescent and unsophisticated Martha, contrary to the provisions of Sec. 1482, . . . As a result of this somewhat morganatic mesalliance, a calf was born July 5, 1908." What would a court consider in deciding whether Defendant should be held strictly liable for Plaintiff's damages? *Kopplin v. Quade*, 130 N.W. 511 (Wis.1911).

5. Plaintiff, a fireman, suffers severe chemical bronchitis as the result of inhaling antimony pentachloride gas when he responds to a call to give assistance to two men trapped in a tank. When Plaintiff arrives at the scene, he is told that the men have been extricated and that he should return to the station. While at the scene he encounters gas in the form of a haze or fog coming from an unknown source. Plaintiff never puts on a face mask to protect himself. While Plaintiff experiences some irritation resulting from his contact with the gas, he is unaware of the potential danger created by exposure to the gas. Should Plaintiff be able to recover on the basis of strict liability? *Langlois v. Allied Chemical Corporation*, 249 So.2d 133 (La.1971).

6. Defendants' gasoline trailer breaks away from the truck towing it, leaves the highway, and falls onto a road below. Thousands of gallons of gasoline spill onto the road and a motorist driving across the road is killed when the gas explodes and his car is engulfed in flames. Plaintiff brings a wrongful

death action against defendants, one of whom is the owner of the truck and the other of whom is the driver. Do you think strict liability should be imposed? *Siegler v. Kuhlman*, 502 P.2d 1181 (Wash.1973).

KEY TERMS

■ **Abnormally dangerous activity**
Activity for which a defendant is strictly liable if someone is injured; characterized as an activity having a high degree of risk of serious harm that cannot be eliminated with due care and whose value is outweighed by its dangerous attributes.

■ **Strict liability**
Liability imposed without a showing of intent or negligence.

14 PRODUCT LIABILITY

CHAPTER OBJECTIVES

In this chapter you will learn to:

- Differentiate between negligence, warranty, and strict liability causes of action.
- Appreciate the importance of classifying losses as personal injury losses, property damage, or economic losses.
- Identify characteristics and examples of manufacturing defects, design defects, and defective warnings.
- Recognize when it is appropriate to sue on the basis of negligence, strict liability, and breach of warranty.
- Identify the characteristics of express and implied warranties.
- Explain the rationale behind strict liability.
- Outline the elements of a strict liability claim.
- Identify the defenses that can be raised in negligence, strict liability, and warranty causes of action.

Having spent several years desperately trying to have children, Husband and Wife go to Doctor to determine the reason for Wife's inability to conceive. After running several tests Doctor concludes that Husband's sperm count is so low that he probably will never be able to impregnate Wife. Doctor suggests that they might be able to impregnate Wife using semen from a sperm bank. After studying in depth the procedures used in artificial insemination, Husband and Wife opt for this technique. Based on a list that Husband and Wife prepare as to the traits they wish their child to have, Doctor selects a specific anonymous donor. Wife becomes pregnant as a result of the artificial insemination and conceives a boy. Unfortunately, when the child is quite young, it is discovered that he has a serious congenital birth defect. Husband and Wife sue Doctor for the harm caused to their child.

Are the doctor and sperm bank negligent in supplying a defective product, i.e., sperm that contains faulty genetic coding? Did they breach any implied warranties? Should they be held strictly liable for the injuries sustained by the child? Can the child as well as the parents sue for his damages? What defenses can the doctor and the sperm bank raise?

OVERVIEW OF PRODUCT LIABILITY

"Product liability" refers to the liability of a manufacturer, seller, or other supplier of a chattel which, because of a defect, causes injury to a consumer, a user, or in some cases a bystander. Liability can be based on any of three theories of recovery: (1) negligence; (2) warranty; or (3) strict liability.

TYPES OF LOSSES

Defective products can cause three types of losses: personal injury, property damage, and economic loss. Injury to a person resulting from a defective product is, logically enough, referred to as *personal injury,* whereas physical injury to property is referred to as *property damage.* **Economic loss** is defined as a diminution in the value of the product and includes such items as the cost of repairs, the cost of replacement, and the loss of profits.

For example, if a computer in a car malfunctions, resulting in an explosion and ensuing fire, any damage to the car is classified as property damage, while any injuries to the driver of the car are considered personal injuries. If the computer malfunction results in the driver of the car being late for work and thereby losing his job, such loss is deemed an economic loss.

Most courts do not allow recovery under a strict liability theory for purely economic loss in the absence of personal injury or property damage. However, the method for categorizing a loss as either economic loss or property damage varies tremendously among the states. Some courts consider damage to the product itself as property damage; others consider such damage economic loss. If the computer malfunction mentioned above results in damage only to the computer and not to any other part of the car, the question is whether that constitutes property damage or economic loss. A claim classified as an economic loss in one state (and therefore not recoverable) may be classified as property damage (and therefore recoverable) in another state. Because the classification of economic loss is an unsettled area of the law, you should consult the case law in your state when dealing with damages of an economic nature.

TYPES OF DEFECTS

Most product liability causes of action involve products that are defective in some way. The three major defects plaintiffs typically allege are: (1) manufacturing defects; (2) design defects; and (3) defective warnings (see Table 14–1). A **manufacturing defect** results from a deviation in the manufacturing process, which causes the item that injures the plaintiff to be different from others manufactured by the defendant. In a **design defect** case all products manufactured by the defendant are the same but possess a feature whose design is unreasonably dangerous. **Defective warning** cases involve a failure to give adequate warnings or directions for use.

Since the definition of defective lies at the core of all product liability cases, we will examine the three categories of defects in some detail. We will then consider the three theories of recovery, which are negligence, warranty, and strict liability (see Table 14–2).

MANUFACTURING DEFECTS

A classic example of a manufacturing defect is found in the landmark case of *MacPherson v. Buick Motor Company*, 111 N. E. 1050 (N.Y. 1916). Buick Motor Company made a car that it sold to a retail dealer, who in turn sold it to the plaintiff. One of the wheels was made of defective wood and its spokes crumbled into fragments, causing injury to the plaintiff when the car suddenly collapsed. The defendant manufacturer was found liable even though it had not manufactured the wheel. The court reasoned that the manufacturer could have discovered this defect by reasonable inspection and that its failure to do so constituted a breach of its duty of care. Notice that what was at issue here was the faulty construction of one of the wheels and not the design of the wheel.

TABLE 14.1

WHAT IS A DEFECT?	
MANUFACTURING DEFECT	Results from deviation in manufacturing process.
DESIGN DEFECT	Feature in design of product is unreasonably dangerous. Structural. Safety feature. Misuse of product.
DEFECTIVE WARNING	Failure to give adequate warnings or directions.

TABLE 14.2

	WHO CAN SUE?
NEGLIGENCE	Direct purchaser Remote purchaser User (if reasonably foreseeable)
EXPRESS WARRANTY	Direct purchaser Remote purchaser User (if member of general class expected to be reached by warranty.
IMPLIED WARRANTY	Direct purchaser Remote purchaser User (some courts)
STRICT LIABILITY	Direct purchaser Remote purchaser User Bystanders (some courts)

	WHO CAN BE SUED?
NEGLIGENCE	Manufacturer User or manufacturer of component part Retailer (difficult to prove) Lessor Seller of real estate Supplier of service
EXPRESS WARRANTY	Manufacturer User or manufacturer of component part Retailer Lessor Seller of real estate Supplier of service
IMPLIED WARRANTY	Manufacturer User or manufacturer of component part Retailer (except for sealed containers [in some courts]) Lessor Seller of real state (in some courts) Seller of service (in some courts)
STRICT LIABILITY	Manufacturer User or manufacturer of component part Retailer Lessor Seller of real estate Supplier of service

TABLE 14.2 Continued

	WHAT CAN YOU RECOVER?
NEGLIGENCE	Personal injuries Property damage Economic loss (although pure economic loss is difficult to recover)
EXPRESS WARRANTY	Personal injuries Property damage Pure economic loss Incidental and consequential damages
IMPLIED WARRANTY	Personal injuries Property damage Pure economic loss Incidental and consequential damages (direct purchaser only)
STRICT LIABILITY	Personal injuries Property damage Economic loss if accompanied by personal injury or property damage

Whereas *MacPherson* was based on a theory of negligence, the famous case of *Henningsen v. Bloomfield Motors, Inc.*, 161 A.2d 69 (N.J. 1960), was based on a breach of warranty. In *Henningsen* defendant Chrysler Corporation produced a car with a defective steering mechanism. One of its dealers, defendant Bloomfield Motors, sold the car to Mr. Henningsen, who gave it to his wife. While Mrs. Henningsen was driving the car the steering mechanism failed, causing the car to veer sharply to the right and into a wall, resulting in her injury. The court held that Mrs. Henningsen could recover from Chrysler for breach of implied warranty of merchantability. As in *MacPherson*, the defect was peculiar to this particular car and was not inherent in the design of the car.

Manufacturing defects are not restricted to man-made products. They can also be found in food that is improperly produced, processed, or stored. A manufacturer or retailer, for example, can be found liable for a manufacturing defect if a consumer contracts botulism as a result of purchasing a can of improperly stored food.

DESIGN DEFECTS

The key issue in a design defect case is whether the defendant chose a design that posed an unreasonable danger to the plaintiff in light of the availability of some other design. For instance, a sanding machine that contains no guards or shields to protect the operator of the machine might be found defective if the manufacturer, with little cost or inconvenience, could have created a design that had a shield or guard.

Design defect claims, even though cast in strict liability terms, have attributes of negligence claims. Negligence analysis typically revolves around the reasonableness of the manufacturer in placing the product on the market. Is the product an essential item? Is it likely to cause injury and is any such injury likely to be serious? These questions are representative of the types of questions a court will contemplate in determining whether a manufacturer acted in a reasonable manner.

Strict liability analysis focuses instead on the consumer's expectations, i.e., whether the product performed as safely as an ordinary consumer would expect. A court will consider how much the consumer paid for the product in determining what the reasonable expectations should be. Use by the consumer extends to any reasonably foreseeable use even if it is not the use intended by the manufacturer. Whether phrased in negligence or strict liability terms, the key element in a design defect case is whether the defendant chose a design that posed an unreasonable danger to the plaintiff in light of the availability of affordable, safer alternative designs.

Defendants will often raise the *"state-of-the-art"* defense, in which they argue that the level of technology existing at the time they made the product precluded them from utilizing a safer design. Although courts generally allow such a defense, defendants relying on this argument will not necessarily be absolved of liability. A jury could conclude, for example, that even though no reasonable alternative design existed at the time, the risk created by producing such an item outweighed its utility.

In defective design cases the plaintiff will frequently try to bring out the fact that the defendant redesigned the product to make it safer after the plaintiff received injuries. Such evidence is generally inadmissible to prove defectiveness. The rationale underlying this rule is that the admission of this evidence would inhibit manufacturers from redesigning products to make them safer.

If the plaintiff does recommend an alternative design, the burden rests on him or her to show that the alternative is practicable. Plaintiffs must, in other words, conduct a type of cost-benefit analysis in which they produce evidence that their alternative design is an economically viable one.

Any design defect alleged by a plaintiff must fall into one of three categories: (1) structural defect; (2) absence of safety features; and (3) misuse of product.

Structural Defects. A *structural defect* exists when the defendant's choice of materials results in a structural weakness, causing the product to be dangerous. A stepladder that collapses when anyone of more than average weight steps on it might, for example, be structurally defective. Defendants are not, however, obliged to provide the most durable design. Nor are they expected to make products that last forever. Their only obligation is to make products that are reasonably safe.

Safety Features. In determining whether a *safety feature* must be installed, one must consider the expense of installation of the feature in comparison with the cost of the product and the magnitude of the danger that exists without such a safety feature. If the expense is relatively minimal, any design not incorporating the safety feature is likely to be considered defective.

Defendants often claim that their product is as safe as that of the competition. Although often successful, such a defense is unpersuasive in situations in which the entire industry has been negligent in the installation of safety devices.

A defendant may also argue that the danger was so obvious that the plaintiff could have protected himself or herself even in the absence of any safety device. Even though the obviousness of the danger is considered when determining the degree of dangerousness, most courts will not automatically dismiss the need for protective devices even though the defect is obvious. A manufacturer could, for example, be found liable for failing to provide protective guard rails for a machine even though the potential danger inherent in getting too close to the machine might be patently obvious.

Foreseeable Misuse. One of the most common design defect arguments is that the product, while not dangerous when used in the manner intended by the manufacturer, becomes dangerous when put to some other use. If such misuse is reasonably foreseeable by the manufacturer, most courts will require the manufacturer to employ reasonable design precautions to protect the plaintiff from the danger resulting from that misuse.

The most common foreseeable misuse cases center around the production of "crashworthy" vehicles. Plaintiffs reason that manufacturers should protect vehicle occupants involved in "second collisions," the collisions that occur inside the vehicle following the initial accident. Most modern courts have found that secondary collisions are clearly foreseeable and that manufacturers have an obligation to take reasonable precautions to make their cars reasonably safe in the event of an accident.

TURNER v. GENERAL MOTORS CORPORATION
514 S.W.2d 497 (Tex. Civ. App. 1974).

COULSON, Justice.

This is an appeal from an order sustaining a plea of privilege in a products liability case. Appellant Robert Turner sued General Motors Corporation, appellee, and Raymond Kliesing d/b/a Kliesing Motor Company in strict liability in tort for personal injuries received when his car rolled over in an accident. Suit was brought in Brazoria County, where Turner purchased the automobile from Kliesing Motors. General Motors filed a plea of privilege to be sued in the county of its residence in Texas, Harris County. Turner filed a controverting affidavit asserting that venue for General Motors was proper in Brazoria County. . . . Turner sued General Motors and Kliesing in strict liability in tort for a defectively designed roof on his automobile which enhanced his injuries, but did not cause the accident. The trial judge, in his findings of fact, found all the facts necessary for this alleged cause of action, if such a cause of action does exist; the sustaining of a plea of privilege was, in effect, a holding that no such cause of action exists in Texas.

The question here is whether a manufacturer and retailer may be held strictly liable in tort for a defectively designed automobile which enhances the injuries of plaintiff, but does not cause the accident.

At the plea of privilege hearing, Turner testified that in April of 1971 he was driving on a two-lane farm-to-market road in his 1969 four-door, Chevrolet Impala, hardtop sedan with a center post. He was following a truck, which started to pull onto the right shoulder. Turner accelerated to fifty or sixty miles per hour to pass the truck, but the truck attempted to make a left-hand turn when Turner came up to it. Turner pulled to the right to avoid a collision and left the road. When he attempted to return to the road, he overturned and the car landed on its top. Turner estimated his speed immediately before the roll-over at twenty to thirty miles per hour. Turner's seat belt was buckled, but the right-front portion of the roof collapsed and came into contact with his head. This contact paralyzed Turner's hands and legs.

Mr. James Barron, called as an expert witness by Turner, stated that he had worked as a design engineer for the Chevrolet Division of General Motors from 1963 to 1965, and had then worked in the same capacity for American Motors for over five years. Barron testified that General Motors designed for future production five years in advance and that he was involved in the design of the 1969 Impala. Barron informed his superiors at General Motors of the desirability of putting a roll bar in the roof of their cars, and Barron worked on a roll bar program. He testified that a roll bar would be expensive as an option, but relatively inexpensive if put on all cars at their birth on the assembly line. The roll bar program was discontinued, and Barron was told this was due "primarily [to] cost reasons and cost in conjunction with the fact that the consumer could not see what he was paying for." His supervisor told him that "it is difficult to pass on something to the consumer and charge him money for it if he cannot see it."

Barron testified that it would be impossible to design a crash proof car. He defined the term "crashworthiness" as the ability of a car "to withstand normal hazard conditions." Crashworthiness was broken down into the following categories: the structural integrity of the car's shell; the elimination of sharp or protruding objects in the interior; passenger restraint devices; and the elimination of post-crash fire. Barron estimated that, in the context of all possible types of accidents, roll-overs occur in twenty percent of all accidents involving "principal" injuries.

Barron drew a diagram of the Impala's roof structure and termed the roof "cosmetic," in that it provided protection from sun and rain, but it would not provide adequate protection in an overturn regardless of the speed. He categorized the roof as definitely defective, "uncommonly dangerous," and "unreasonably dangerous." The design of the Impala's roof was called perhaps the weakest way to design a roof, and Barron said that all of the roof structure in this Impala had collapsed. There was nothing in the roof of the car which would support the car in an overturn.

Barron suggested that there were many alternative ways to design a roof more safely and specifically proposed the roll bar or roll cage (the latter is, in effect, a connected double roll bar forming a rectangle with a bar at each corner attaching the frame to the body of the car). Roll bars and roll cages had been known to Barron since 1952, and he stated that General Motors put them on test cars and racing cars. In Mr. Barron's opinion, roll bars would greatly minimize roll-over injuries. Barron admitted that no mass-produced automobile in the United States had ever come equipped with a roll bar or roll cage and conceded that the Impala's roof was no more dangerous than the roof in any other car produced at that time. He frankly stated that he considered the roofs on all American cars defectively designed, including those currently manufactured (West Germany's Porsche Targa was the only production car cited by Barron as being equipped with a roll bar).

Raymond Kliesing, the defendant dealer, testified that, based upon his forty-five years of sales experience, the average consumer believes that a sedan vehicle will be a reasonably safe product in a roll-over.

The trial judge sustained General Motors' plea of privilege and filed findings of fact and conclusions of law. The trial judge found that Kliesing was an authorized General Motors dealer, that Turner's roof collapsed and injured him in the accident, and that the auto immediately before the accident was in substantially the same condition it was in when sold. The court's crucial finding is that the car was

> defectively designed in that the roof was not a sufficient structural support to prevent the roof from collapsing and thereby injuriously encroaching into the passenger compartment in the event of an overturn of the automobile and this defective design rendered the automobile unreasonably dangerous to the user or consumer, i.e., dangerous to an extent beyond that which would be contemplated by the ordinary user or consumer with the knowledge available to him as to the characteristics of a 1969 Chevrolet four-door sedan with a center post.

The defect was found by the trial judge to be a proximate and producing cause of the injuries, and the possibility of overturn accidents was held to be clearly foreseeable by General Motors.

The trial judge's sustaining of General Motor's plea of privilege was a ruling, in effect, that Turner had failed to prove a bona fide claim against Kliesing. In light of the trial judge's findings of fact, it is clear that his implicit conclusion of law was that strict tort liability in Texas does not encompass the liability of a manufacturer or retailer of a defective product when the defect enhances the injuries of a plaintiff, but plays no role in causing the accident. The question thus presented is one of first impression in Texas.

The genesis of this issue can be found in Evans v. General Motors Corporation. . . . There the plaintiff sued under general negligence, strict liability, and implied warranty principles with the argument that the manufacturer of his automobile should be liable for his enhanced injuries due to the "X" frame without side rails on his car, despite the fact that this defect had not caused the collision. The Seventh Circuit held that the manufacturer owed no duty to design or make an accident-proof or fool-proof car. The court also said that the intended purpose of a car does not include its participation in collisions. In Larsen v. General Motors Corporation, . . . the plaintiff claimed under negligence principles that his car was defectively designed in that the steering shaft protruded in front of the axle so that his injuries were enhanced when his car was struck in the left front. The Eighth Circuit said that an auto manufacturer has a duty to design and construct its product to be reasonably fit for its intended use and free of hidden defects which would render it unsafe for that use. The court found that the real issue was one of intended use and said that the intended use of an automobile necessarily entails the risk of injury-producing accidents; such injuries are foreseeable as an incident to the normal and expected use of a car. Since Evans and Larsen, more than twenty jurisdictions have addressed the issue of crashworthiness and have split evenly. . . . We are persuaded by the logic of Larsen. . . .

Before addressing the merits of the Evans-Larsen controversy, it is necessary to discuss several Texas cases which General Motors feels have implicitly rejected the doctrine of crashworthiness. In Muncy v. General Motors Corp., . . . an automobile was alleged to be negligently designed because the key could be removed from the ignition while the car was in gear and the engine was running. The court held that the appellant "was not using the car in the manner and for the purpose for which it was intended—at least appellants have failed to prove that the car was being so used." Kahn v. Chrysler Corporation, . . . involved an allegation of negligent design in regard to sharp, protruding tailfins on a car. The plaintiff was a boy who had ridden his bicycle into a fin. The court, relying heavily on Muncy, held that the "duty of the automobile manufacturer extends to the ordinary use of the vehicle. . . . But the manufacturer has no obligation to so design his automobile that it will be safe for a child to ride his bicycle into it while the car is parked." . . . Because of the Supreme Court's decision in Otis Elevator Company v. Wood, . . . which will be discussed *infra,* we believe that both these decisions have taken an overly narrow and restrictive view of the standard of "intended use." General Motors also cites Kerby v. Abilene Christian College, . . . which involved a finding of contributory negligence on the part of the plaintiff in failing to close the sliding door of his van; this act had substantially increased the plaintiff's injuries but had played no part in causing the accident. The court held . . . :

> We draw a sharp distinction between negligence contributing to the accident and negligence contributing to the damages sustained. Contributory negligence must have the causal connection with the accident that but for the conduct the accident would not have happened. Negligence that merely increases or adds to the extent of the loss or injury occasioned by another's negligence is not such contributory negligence as will defeat recovery.

This holding explicitly restricts the basic scope of contributory negligence, does not deal with actionable primary negligence, and we think, simply expresses the Court's rejection of the harsh doctrine of denying a plaintiff any recovery because of an omission playing no part in causing the accident from which his injuries flow. General Motors would construe Kerby to stand for the general proposition that pre-existing negligence which causes injury is not actionable if another's intervening negligence specifically sparks the accident. This is not the law of Texas. . . .

General Motors cites one case applying Texas law which does deal with the issue of defective design and crashworthiness. In Willis v. Chrysler Corporation, . . . plaintiff was traveling at seventy miles per hour and was struck head-on by another car moving at an undetermined but extremely high rate of speed. The plaintiff's auto broke completely in two, directly behind the front seat, and suit was brought for breach of the manufacturer's warranty. The court held that a manufacturer has "no duty to design an automobile that could withstand a high speed collision and maintain its structural integrity." The court then agreed with Evans that the intended purpose of a car does not include its participation in collisions. While we simply disagree with the court's acceptance of Evans as the law of Texas, we do not believe that Larsen imposes a duty to design an automobile which will withstand the type of high-speed, head-on collision described in Willis.

We find pertinent and agree with South Austin Drive-In Theatre v. Thomison. . . . In that case, the driver of a riding lawn mower backed the vehicle into a child and knocked him down. The driver attempted to pull the boy away, but found him pinned by the machine. The boy lost a leg. The court rejected the manufacturer's arguments of foreseeability, misuse, and industry custom. The manufacturer was held to have negligently designed the mower in failing to have a guard over the drive chain and gear sprocket, despite the fact that this design had not caused the accident. The court said, . . .

> We believe it is a correct statement of the law to say that [the manufacturer] owed a duty to use reasonable care in the design and manufacture of its power mower to prevent injury to the user and to persons [the manufacturer] should reasonably expect to be in the vicinity of the mower's probable use.

Preliminary to a discussion of the question of crashworthiness, it must be noted that the issues and arguments pertinent to the question are essentially the same whether suit is brought under general negligence or under strict tort liability. Most of the decisions from other jurisdictions involving crashworthiness were brought under negligence, but they are nevertheless applicable here. The issue of a manufacturer's exercise of due care under negligence becomes the issue of whether he has put an unreasonably dangerous product into the stream of commerce under strict liability, and the issues of foreseeability and intended use under negligence are transformed into the issue of normal use under strict liability.

General Motors concedes that it could foresee that its products would be involved in accidents of an infinite variety, including roll-overs. Its argument is that foreseeability cannot be equated with duty. General Motors characterizes the Larsen argument as being that, since car accidents can be foreseen, there is a duty to design cars to reduce the injuries from these accidents. If duty were commensurate with foreseeability, then an automobile manufacturer would be an insurer. . . . However, duty has never properly been defined solely by foreseeability. . . . This argument was expressed by the Seventh Circuit in Evans as follows . . . :

> The intended purpose of an automobile does not include its participation in collisions with other objects, despite the manufacturer's ability to foresee the possibility that such collisions may occur. As defendant argues, the defendant also knows that its automobiles may be driven into bodies of water, but it is not suggested that defendant has a duty to equip them with pontoons.

We agree that foreseeability alone cannot define an automobile manufacturer's duty; this would create the duty to design a crash-proof car. However, Larsen seeks merely to hold the manufacturer to the duty of designing a crashworthy vehicle. While all agree that there is no duty to design a crash-proof car, one court has termed it a "non sequitur" to use this truism as a basis for thus saying there is no duty to design a crashworthy car. . . . The rule of Larsen is not grounded upon foreseeability, but upon the *unreasonable* risk of injury in the event of a collision. Under strict liability the question of liability in each case turns upon whether the product is in a defective condition which is "unreasonably dangerous."

The controlling issue in the crashworthiness inquiry is not foreseeability, but intended use. General Motors argues that the normal and proper use of an automobile does not include its participation in collisions. The Evans court said that collisions are not an intended purpose of the automobile even though the manufacturer may foresee the "possibility" of collisions. The Larsen court terms collisions a "probability;" the court stated that between one-fourth and two-thirds of all automobiles are involved during their life in a collision producing injury or death. . . . It is irrelevant whether the occurrence of an accident involving a particular car is a possibility or a probability. What is germane is the fact that collisions are so frequent and common that they must be considered an unavoidable incidence of the normal and proper use of automobiles. Misuse of an automobile may occur, such as the intentional use of a car as a bulldozer. However, the normal use of an automobile is to transport people *safely* over the public roads. It cannot be argued that a manufacturer should not be liable for a defect which causes an accident, and no logical distinction can be drawn between that situation and one in which a defect causes injury in a foreseeable accident. We hold that an automobile manufacturer may be held strictly liable for a defective design which produces injuries, but not the accident. . . .

The doctrine of crashworthiness does not make insurers of automobile manufacturers. The Fourth Circuit, in adopting Larsen, noted that the question of whether a manufacturer had created an unreasonable risk of injury involves a traditional balancing of the gravity and likelihood of harm against the burden of precautions to avoid the harm. Dreisonstock v. Volkswagenwerk. . . . The court stated that the burden of taking precautions included a consideration of the particular purpose of the vehicle, the style or aesthetic appeal of the model, and the cost of the change and of the vehicle. So viewed, it is obvious that manufacturers are not required to produce the safest possible car, but only a reasonably safe one. For instance, if a change in design would add little to safety, render the vehicle ugly or inappropriate for its particular purpose, and add a small fortune to the purchase price, then a court should rule as a matter of law that the manufacturer had not created an unreasonable risk of harm.

The same type of balancing of factors takes place under strict liability. Section 402A states that a manufacturer is strictly liable for a product in a defective condition "unreasonably dangerous" to the user or consumer. Comment i to § 402A defines "unreasonably dangerous" as "dangerous to an extent beyond that which would be contemplated by the ordinary consumer who purchases it, with the ordinary knowledge common to the community as to its characteristics." . . .

When Comment i is applied to crashworthiness, Dreisonstok's balancing test for negligence governs characteristics of a product which lie within the ordinary knowledge of the community. . . . This approach would reply to the Evans' pontoon argument that, while the average consumer as a matter of law does not expect his car to float, he may well expect the roof of that car to maintain its structural integrity in a roll-over accident.

The moderate approach of Dreisonstok to the issue of crashworthiness should dispel General Motors' fears of absolute liability. This approach may be contrasted with that of Cronin v. J. B. E. Olson Corporation. . . . There, a clasp holding bread trays on a delivery truck failed to hold the trays in a collision, sending the driver through the windshield. The plaintiff recovered under his allegation of defective design in strict liability. The court adopted Larsen and then stated that it was not necessary for a plaintiff to establish that the product was unreasonably dangerous after he had shown a defect and causation, because such a requirement would place too onerous a burden upon plaintiffs. Such an approach to crashworthiness does indeed make insurers of manufacturers.

The courts adopting Evans often say that safety standards must be left to Congress, because courts lack the expertise for dealing with such complex matters, because sporadic and ad hoc court decisions will result in wrong and even contradictory standards, and because Congress had already proceeded to set safety standards. In 1966 (eighteen months before Larsen), Congress enacted the National Traffic and Motor Vehicle Safety Act, 15 U.S.C.A. §§ 1381–1431. Section 1392 instructs the Secretary of Transportation to establish motor vehicle safety standards.[1] Section 1397(a) prohibits the manufacture of vehicles not in compliance with these standards. However, § 1397(c) provides: "Compliance with any

1. The Secretary's Standard No. 216 ("roof crush resistance—passenger cars") provides that a force equal to one and one-half the weight of the vehicle or 5,000 pounds, whichever is less, applied to the corner of the roof must not move the roof more than five inches. 49 C.F.R. § 571.216 (1973).

Federal motor vehicle safety standard issued under this subchapter does not exempt any person from any liability under common law." It is obvious from this language that the federal standards were meant to supplement rather than obviate the law of negligence and products liability. It has been suggested that, while the federal regulations propounded by the Secretary do not preempt the common law, they may serve as strong evidence of negligence, if not negligence per se, in regard to vehicles before the effective date of each regulation. . . . The question of whether safety standards *should* be left to federal regulation presents a separate question from that of congressional intent. However, we are not aware that the argument of the necessity of federal regulation has been made in regard to design defects which cause accidents, and we cannot see any reason why design defects which cause injuries are any more in need of federal control. The danger that juries will arrive at conflicting conclusions is a hazard every manufacturer who distributes nationally runs. The complex, technical questions facing juries, aided by expert testimony, cannot be more difficult than the questions in such fields as medical malpractice. Finally, the argument that a single jury verdict may have profound consequences disrupting an essential industry has been characterized as contending that the desirability of immunity from liability is directly proportional to the magnitude of the risk created. . . .

Assuming the existence of liability for a design defect causing injuries, but not the accident, General Motors argues that the trial judge's finding of defective design is supported by no evidence, insufficient evidence, or is contrary to the great weight and preponderance of the evidence. The expert witness below admitted that no mass-produced automobile had ever been manufactured in the United States with a roll bar or roll cage, and he agreed that the roof of Turner's vehicle was no more unsafe than the roof on other vehicles of the same manufacturing era.

General Motors relies principally upon two cases for these evidence point. Dyson v. General Motors Corporation, . . . involved roof deformation in the roll-over accident of a hardtop. General Motors argued that to require roofs which would be perfectly safe in a roll-over would be to declare convertibles unreasonably dangerous per se. The court adopted Larsen and said . . . ,

> [T]he manufacturer was not necessarily under an obligation to provide a hardtop model which would be as resistant to roll-over damage as a four-door sedan; but the defendant was required, in my view, to provide a hardtop automobile which was a reasonably safe version of such model, and which was not substantially less safe than other hardtop models.

In Dreisonstok, *supra*, a 1968 Volkswagen van was involved in a front-end collision. Such a vehicle does not have the engine in front, but plaintiff's experts declared the van to be defectively designed by comparing it to a 1966 mid-sized Ford passenger car. The Fourth Circuit, amplifying upon Dyson, held that this was impermissible; vehicles of the same type must be compared in order to determine defective design. These two cases do not stand for the proposition that defective design *must* be shown by comparing plaintiff's vehicle to similar vehicles. The expert below indicted the entire industry, a possibility which Dreisonstok does not foreclose. This is in accord with the law of Texas that, while conformance to industry custom is admissible on the question of negligence, the custom itself may be shown to be negligent. . . . (Tex.Sup.1961). We think the expert's condemnation of the industry for its failure to install roll bars constitutes a sufficient showing that the custom itself was unreasonably dangerous. General Motors' evidence points are overruled.

The judgment of the trial court is reversed, and judgment here rendered that General Motors' plea of privilege is overruled.

Turner v. General Motors Corp., 514 S.W.2d 497 (Tex.Civ.App. 1974) contains an interesting analysis of the doctrine of crashworthiness. Note the court's conclusion that automobile manufacturers have an obligation to make cars reasonably safe in a collision. In arriving at this conclusion the court advocates the use of a balancing test in which the gravity and likelihood of harm resulting from a particular design are weighed against the burden of precautions necessary to avoid the harm. It is noteworthy that the *Turner* court found the General Motors car to be unreasonably unsafe even though no American car had ever been manufactured with the roll bar recommended by the design engineer. Clearly, industry custom itself may be found to be negligent.

The issue of crashworthiness has also arisen in the relatively new area of litigation surrounding air bags. Since automobile manufacturers have a duty to build reasonably safe cars based on state-of-the-art technology and feasibility considerations, the question exists as to whether manufacturers who have failed to install air bags have fully complied with that duty. The controversy centers around the question of whether air bags are necessary to make a car reasonably safe in case of an accident. Air bag proponents argue that air bag systems are within the realm of state-of-the-art protection, while automobile manufacturers assert that air bags have not been proven to be reliable and might be potentially hazardous to car occupants. Consumer advocates and representatives of the automobile industry also clash over the potential cost of air bag systems as well as the public's desire to have such systems.

Defective Warnings. The absence of a warning regarding the possible dangers of a product may also lay the groundwork for a defective product claim. A seller may be required to give directions or warnings on a container to keep the product from being deemed unreasonably dangerous. In determining what warnings or instructions will suffice, a court looks at the likely number and severity of accidents that could be avoided by having a warning or instruction. The court then weighs these factors against the difficulty of providing such warnings or instructions.

In cases involving the manufacture of drugs, courts look at whether the warnings clearly convey the nature, gravity, and likelihood of the known or knowable risks of the drugs. An advertising or publicity campaign for a drug, however, may dilute the warning to the point that it becomes inadequate. For example, a warning that blood disorders are a possible side effect of using a drug may in effect be canceled by the manufacturer's "detail men" who, when speaking with physicians, downplay the dangers of using the drug (*Incollingo v. Ewing*, 282 A.2d 206 (Pa. 1971)).

Some plaintiffs have used the defective warning theory to attack the warnings on cigarette packages. The argument that these warnings are inadequate has thus far been unsuccessful for sales made after 1966. Warnings on packages manufactured after that date contain the text specified by Congress and have been deemed reasonable by law by those courts that have considered the question. Federal statutes imposing certain labeling requirements preempt state common-law causes of action, in essence negating the argument that a warning is insufficient. One jury did find a tobacco company liable for sales made before 1966, however, because the packages failed to warn the plaintiff of the dangers of cigarettes. The Third Circuit overturned the judgment and remanded the case back to the trial court (*Cipollone v. Liggett Group*, 693 F.Supp. 208 (D.N.J. 1988), rev'd ___ F.2d ___ (3rd Cir. 1990)). Interestingly, the Circuit Court concluded that the jury should be allowed to decide whether the risks of smoking were commonly known to ordinary consumers before 1966, and if they were not, whether the risks of smoking outweigh the benefits of smoking.

If the defendant can show that it neither knew nor should have known of the danger at the time of the sale of the product, most courts have held that the defendant has no duty to warn. Manufacturers are not to be the insurers of their products. So if a drug manufacturer can show that it had subjected a drug to reasonable testing procedures and did not discover any adverse side effects, it would escape liability for injuries to consumers resulting from long-term side effects not known to either the manufacturer or researchers at the time the drug was produced. In some rare cases, however, such as those involving asbestos, the defense of ignorance has failed. The courts have held asbestos manufacturers liable even if they were unaware of the danger, essentially holding them to a strict liability standard.

Obviousness of danger is a factor that is considered in determining the defendant's obligation to warn. But obviousness of danger alone does not preclude a duty to warn. Indeed, a product may be so dangerous that it should not be marketed at all. A light fixture with exposed (noninsulated) wiring, for example, is dangerous with or without a warning attached advising consumers of the danger. In such a case giving a warning would not protect the defendant from liability.

THEORIES OF RECOVERY

NEGLIGENCE

Anyone who negligently manufactures a product is liable for any personal injuries proximately caused by his or her negligence. A manufacturer, as we discussed earlier, may be negligent in the way it designs or manufactures its product. It may be negligent in its failure to conduct a reasonable inspection or test of its finished products. Furthermore, a manufacturer may be negligent in its failure to package and ship its products in a reasonably safe manner.

Users and Makers of Components Parts. Similarly, the manufacturer of a component part may be liable for failure to use reasonable care. Additionally, a manufacturer who uses components prepared by others may be liable if it does not take reasonable care to obtain them from a reliable source or does not make a reasonable inspection of the components before incorporating them. Thus an automobile manufacturer who assembles a chassis using components prepared by other manufacturers is liable for any malfunctions that result from a defect in the component parts if the manufacturer does not make a reasonable inspection of those components before incorporating them.

Retailers. A manufacturer is liable if a retailer fails to make an inspection that it is under an obligation to make. If, however, the retailer learns of the defect either by inspection or through some other means and fails to warn the customer, many courts have found the chain of causation to be broken and have absolved the manufacturer of any liability.

Retailers as well as manufacturers may be found negligent, but suits against retailers on the basis of negligence are often unsuccessful. The sale of a negligently manufactured or designed product is not enough by itself to show negligence. Generally, a retailer has no duty to inspect goods unless it has reason to believe they may be dangerous because even if it did inspect it would have no chance of finding the defect. A retailer selling microwave ovens, for example, has no duty to break open the boxes in which the ovens are packaged to inspect the ovens. A majority of courts have, however, imposed a duty to make at least a superficial examination, especially where the retailer is a car dealer. The consequences of a defect in a car are likely to be severe and the retailer is much more likely than the buyer to discover any defects. If a retailer knows or should know that a product is unreasonably dangerous, it is negligent if it does not at least warn customers. Generally, plaintiffs suing retailers opt for warranty or strict liability theories for reasons we will discuss later in this chapter.

Lessors, Real Estate Agents, and Sellers of Services. Lessors of goods may also be liable in negligence for failing to discover defects. Rental car companies that lease defective cars, for example, may be found negligent. The sellers of real estate as well as suppliers of services (e.g., the providers of blood transfusions) may also be found negligent.

Privity. Before *MacPherson v. Buick Motor Company* a plaintiff in a negligence action was required to contract directly with the defendant. This so-called **privity** requirement was abolished in *MacPherson,* allowing a plaintiff who buys a product from a retailer and not directly from the defendant manufacturer to still recover. Therefore, a plaintiff can sue the manufacturer, the retailer, or the lessor of a product. Users of products who do not purchase the products can also recover under a negligence theory if they are "reasonably foreseeable" plaintiffs. (See *Palsgraf* in Chapter 8 for a discussion of foreseeability.)

Damages In Negligence Cases. Although plaintiffs generally seek to recover damages resulting from personal injuries, they can also recover for property damage. Suppose a defendant fails to use due care in manufacturing a television set and the defect in the electrical wiring in the television causes it to catch fire and burn down the plaintiff's house. The plaintiff can recover for the resulting property damage.

Plaintiffs in negligence actions generally have a hard time recovering for pure economic loss. Breach of warranty, rather than negligence, is the preferred theory to be utilized in recovering for economic damages. As mentioned previously, the distinction between property damage and economic loss is not always clear. Is the destruction of the plaintiff's property or of the product itself considered property damage or economic loss? Similarly, does the fact that the product no longer works or is now worthless because of the defect constitute property damage or economic loss? Consult the case law in your state to see how the courts in your jurisdiction have resolved these issues.

WARRANTY

Combination Of Tort and Contract Law. A cause of action based on breach of warranty is a hybrid one, containing characteristics of both tort and contract law. Originally the action was deemed a form of misrepresentation and was therefore considered a tort. But since most warranties arose under the common law in situations involving a contract of sale, contract law was also applicable. Today this amalgamated form of law is made even more confusing by the Uniform Commercial Code's efforts to deal with warranties on a statutory basis.

Pay particular attention to the fact that the public policy justifications underlying tort law and contract law are quite different. Tort remedies are designed to protect the public from dangerous products. The purpose of strict liability is to protect consumers and allocate the risk to manufacturers, who are better able than consumers to bear the risk of loss. Contract remedies, on the other hand, are designed to compensate parties for the loss of the benefit of their bargain. Under the Uniform Commercial Code the free flow of commerce is encouraged (see U.C.C. Sec. 1–102, Official Comment 2) and commercial parties of equal bargaining power are allowed to allocate the risk of loss between themselves. A party to a commercial contract may, for example, choose to forego a remedy in exchange for a lower purchase price. Presumably merchants are better able to protect themselves from economic loss than are consumers.

In deciding whether to apply contract law or tort law, a court must consider the nature of the defect in the product and the type of loss for which the plaintiff seeks compensation. In a tort claim the plaintiff is alleging that he or she has been exposed by means of a hazardous product to an unreasonable risk of injury. In a contract case, on the other hand, the plaintiff is alleging that the product failed to perform in accordance with the expectations one would have for a product of a particular quality and fit for ordinary use. Tort law, then, is reserved for those defects that result in an unreasonably dangerous product. Contract remedies are more appropriate when the defect involves only the quality of the product and presents no unreasonable danger to persons or property.

The type of loss, i.e., personal injury, property damage, or economic loss, also determines whether the plaintiff will select a contract or tort claim. Although a majority of jurisdictions restrict contract liability to recovery for commercial or economic loss and restrict tort liability to recovery for damage to persons or property, this distinction has been challenged by several modern courts. Some, such as the Arizona courts, have reasoned that if the plaintiff's only loss is an economic one, the parties are best left to their commercial remedies. If the plaintiff's economic loss is accompanied by some physical damage to a person or other property, the party's interests are best protected via tort liability. Consult the case law in your state to determine how the courts in your jurisdiction have analyzed this issue.

EXPRESS WARRANTY

There are two types of warranties—express and implied. With an **express warranty** a seller expressly represents that the goods possess certain qualities.

A description of a windshield by a manufacturer as being "shatter proof" is an example of an express warranty. If the purchaser can later show that the product does not possess such qualities (if, for example, the windshield shatters after being hit by a stone), he or she may sue for breach of warranty. An express warranty may be made in one of three ways:

- An "affirmation of fact or promise" regarding the goods.
- A description of the goods.
- Use of a sample or model of the goods. (U.C.C. Sec. 2–313)

A seller might describe goods as being water resistant, for example, or might use a model to demonstrate how the product works, thus suggesting to consumers that the product they buy is similar in nature.

Who May Recover? In a sense, breach of express warranty is a type of strict liability claim. The plaintiff need not show that he or she believed the seller's representations to be true nor, in most cases, that he or she was even aware of the express warranty. All the plaintiff need show is that the representation was in fact false. A drug company that produced a drug it believed to be nonaddictive and that it advertised as such was found liable when a consumer became addicted to the drug and ultimately died from his addiction. (*Crocker v. Winthrop Laboratories,* 514 S.W.2d. 249 (Tex. 1974)). The court discounted the reasonableness of the company's belief in the nonaddictiveness of the drug. It focused on the falsity of the company's representations and the disastrous results of the physician's misplaced reliance on such representations.

Plaintiffs may recover for breach of express warranty even when they are not in privity with the seller in that they did not purchase directly from the seller. According to some courts, a plaintiff who is a user and not a purchaser of a product must show that he or she is a member of the general class of the public that the manufacturer expected or should have expected to be reached by the warranty. In many cases express warranties, such as the warranty of shatter-proofness, would be considered to be addressed to the public at large. Therefore, a remote buyer, user, or even bystander would probably be held to be part of the general class to which the warranty was addressed.

What May Be Recovered? A plaintiff whose damages are solely economic, such as lost profits, can recover the difference between what the product would have been worth had it been as it was warranted and what it was in fact worth with its defect (U.C.C. Sec. 2–714 (2)). The buyer can also recover for incidental and consequential damages (U.C.C. Sec. 2–715). As in the case of negligence, plaintiffs can certainly recover for property damage and personal injuries resulting from the defective product.

Implied Warranty. A seller also makes certain **implied warranties** by virtue of offering a product for sale. The two most common types of implied warranties are warranty of merchantability and warranty of fitness for a particular purpose.

A **warranty of merchantability** is implied in a contract for the sale of goods if the seller is a merchant in the regular business of selling the kind of goods in question. According to the U.C.C., Sec. 2–314, for goods to be merchantable they must (among other things):

- Be "fit for the ordinary purposes for which such goods are used."
- Be "within the variations permitted by the agreement, of even kind, quality and quantity within each unit and among all units involved."
- Be "adequately contained, packaged, and labeled as the agreement may require."
- "Conform to the promises or affirmations of fact made on the container or label, if any."

The courts have consistently held that retailers impliedly warrant the merchantability of their products. A few courts, however have created what is known as the "sealed container" doctrine, which absolves retailers who sell sealed containers of any liability. Under the U.C.C., the merchantability warranty is applicable to the sale of food or drink. The code does not apply, however, to services and to real estate transactions, although some courts have creatively applied warranty theory to such transactions. Some courts, for example, have utilized an "implied warranty of habitability" in finding liability on the part of builders of homes where purchasers of such homes have suffered injuries. The courts are in disagreement as to whether an implied warranty of merchantability exists for sellers dealing in used goods.

An **implied warranty of fitness for a particular purpose** is created when a seller who knows that a buyer wants goods for a particular (noncustomary) purpose makes a recommendation on which the buyer relies (U.C.C. Sec. 2–315). Suppose, for example, a consumer asks advice from a salesman at the hardware store regarding what type of lumber he should purchase for a particular construction project. If the type of lumber he purchases turns out to be unsuitable for such use, the consumer can sue the hardware store on the basis of breach of implied warranty.

What Can Be Recovered? A direct purchaser, i.e., one who buys directly from the defendant, can certainly recover on the basis of breach of implied warranty for personal injury and property damage resulting from the product, and also for solely economic damages, such as lost profits. As with express warranties, a direct purchaser can recover the difference between what the product would have been worth had it been as warranted and what it is worth with its defect. The direct buyer can also recover for incidental and consequential damages.

A purchaser can recover for personal injury on the basis of implied warranty even though he or she bought the product from a dealer and not the defendant manufacturer. Some states allow such remote purchasers to recover for property damage alone on the basis of breach implied warranty. A remote purchaser, however, probably would not be able to recover for purely economic damages, such as lost profits. According to the majority position a nonprivity plaintiff should instead sue the immediate seller for economic damages resulting from a breach of an implied warranty. Many states permit a nonpurchaser (user), such as an employee of a purchaser, whose use of the product was foreseeable, to recover for personal injuries from the manufacturer or others in the distributive chain. There is a great deal of variation among states regarding privity requirements in reference to implied warranties. The U.C.C. itself suggests three alternatives for dealing with privity requirements. Therefore, it is important that you check the case law and statutes in your state pertaining to recovery by remote purchasers and nonpurchasers.

Who Can Be Held Liable? Breach of warranty actions can be brought against manufacturers, retail dealers, and component manufacturers (those who manufacture components that are incorporated into a larger product). Considerable controversy exists as to whether warranty liability can be imposed on the sellers of used goods. But by analogizing to the U.C.C., the courts do allow recovery on the basis of implied warranty in cases involving lessors of goods, sellers of real estate, and sellers of services. A mass producer of homes, for example, can be held liable for breach of an implied warranty of habitability for having installed faulty plumbing.

Comparison With Strict Liability Claims. Many plaintiffs opt for strict liability over warranty claims because strict liability is easier to prove than breach of warranty and in many respects is virtually identical to warranty claims. In a few instances, however, the plaintiff may have an advantage in suing on a warranty theory. A plaintiff who is the direct purchaser and whose damages are solely economic will likely sue for breach of warranty rather than for strict liability or negligence because of the generosity of the U.C.C. in providing for damages. Remember that under the U.C.C., whether a warranty is expressed or implied, a direct purchaser can recover the difference between what the product would have been worth had it been as it was warranted and what it is worth with its defect. The buyer can also recover for incidental and consequential damages. Under the U.C.C. a remote purchaser who has suffered only economic harm may recover on the basis of breach of express warranty whereas he or she would be precluded from doing so on the basis of strict liability or negligence. Furthermore, in many states the statute of limitations used in warranty actions is the contract statute of limitations, which is typically longer than the tort statute of limitations used in strict liability claims.

STRICT LIABILITY

Rationale Justifying Strict Liability. Strict liability theories now constitute the primary basis for liability for manufacturers of products. Three basic reasons are given to support the premise that manufacturers should be held strictly liable for defects in their products. Foremost is the idea that sellers of defective products, rather than consumers, should bear the cost of compensating tort victims for the injuries they sustain from defective products. Proponents argue that manufacturers are in a better economic position than consumers to bear such costs.

Second, some feel that sellers should be made to internalize the cost of any injuries their products inflict, forcing them to incorporate the cost of liability into the product itself and thereby raising the market price of the product. The reasoning is that consumers, when faced with the higher costs of such products, will purchase cheaper and presumably safer products.

The third argument is that the sophistication of modern products precludes the average consumer from pinpointing the act of negligence responsible for his or her injuries. When some of the evidentiary obstacles to recovery found under negligence analysis are removed, more consumers are able to recover under a strict liability theory and manufacturers are deterred from producing unsafe products.

Many courts and commentators refute these arguments, however. Some have pointed out that empirical evidence of strict liability's effect on product safety is lacking. Some feel that the pendulum has swung too far in favor of consumer protection and needs to reach a more moderate position so that manufacturers are not unduly hampered in their efforts to meet consumer demands.

Section 402A of the Restatement. One of the first decisions dealing with strict liability was rendered by Justice Traynor, who was disenchanted with the warranty theory. In *Greenman v. Yuba Power Products, Inc.*, 377 P.2d 897 (Cal. 1963), Justice Traynor held that the plaintiff's failure to give timely notice of breach of warranty to the defendant, as required by California law, did not bar his recovery because the defendant was strictly liable. Traynor noted that "a manufacturer is strictly liable in tort when an article he places on the market, knowing that it is to be used without inspection for defects, proves to have a defect which causes injury to a human being." Traynor reasoned that manufacturers who put defective products on the market should bear the cost of injuries resulting from such defective products rather than the injured parties who, he believed, were powerless to protect themselves. Consumers, he concluded, were better protected under a strict liability theory than under a warranty theory.

Traynor's opinion laid the foundation for Section 402A of the Restatement (Second) of Torts, which has been adopted by the majority of American jurisdictions. Section 402A reads as follows:

> Section 402A. Special liability of seller of product for physical harm to user or consumer.
>
> (1) One who sells any product in a defective condition unreasonably dangerous to the user or consumer or to his property is subject to liability for physical harm thereby caused to the ultimate user or consumer, or to his property, if
>
> (a) the seller is engaged in the business of selling such a product, and
>
> (b) it is expected to and does reach the user or consumer without substantial change in the condition in which it is sold.
>
> (2) The rule stated is subsection (1) applies although
>
> (a) the seller has exercised all possible care in the preparation and sale of his product, and
>
> (b) the user or consumer has not brought the product from or entered into any contractual relation with the seller.

Under Section 402A, as interpreted by most courts, the plaintiff must prove five elements:

- A product was sold.
- The product was defective.
- The defective product was the cause in fact and proximate cause of the plaintiff's injuries.
- The defect existed at the time the product left the defendant's hands.
- The item was manufactured or sold by the defendant.

Unlike the plaintiff proving negligence, the plaintiff who has opted for a strict liability claim need not prove that the manufacturer or seller failed to use due care. In other words, the defendant in a strict liability case is liable even if he or she was not at fault (see Table 14–3).

Sale of A Product. Section 402A applies only to the sale of products and not to the provision of services. This sales-service dichotomy is a point of contention, for example, in the so-called "bad blood" cases in which the plaintiffs contract a disease after receiving contaminated blood in the form of transfusions. The question is whether a transfusion involves the sale of a product (blood) or is part of the package of services provided by a hospital and is therefore not a sale but a service. (The same issue arises in the context of warranty cases since the U.C.C. applies only to goods sold and not to services rendered.)

Defective Conditions. We have discussed the three categories of defects (manufacturing defects, design defects, and defective warnings) but now we need to consider what constitutes a defective condition for purposes of strict liability. In most strict liability cases the courts focus on whether the product is in "a defective condition unreasonably dangerous." According to the Restatement (Second) of Torts Section 402A, comment i, a product is in a *"defective condition unreasonably dangerous"* if it is "dangerous to an extent beyond that which would be contemplated by the ordinary consumer who purchases it, with the ordinary knowledge common to the community as to its characteristics." Good whiskey, therefore, is not considered unreasonably dangerous merely because some people will become drunk and injure themselves. Bad whiskey containing a dangerous amount of isopropyl alcohol, however, is considered in a "defective condition unreasonably dangerous." The phrase "defective condition unreasonably dangerous" is a term of art and so the words "defective condition" should not be separated from the words "unreasonably dangerous."

Some courts look at the acts of a reasonable consumer, using the "consumer expectation" test, to determine whether a product is in a "defective condition unreasonably dangerous." Others look at the acts of a reasonable defendant, using what is commonly referred to as the "risk-utility" test. Under this test,

TABLE 14.3

ELEMENTS OF STRICT LIABILITY CLAIM

- Was a product sold (as opposed to a service)?
- Was the product defective (in a "defective condition unreasonably dangerous")?
- Was the defective product the proximate cause and cause in fact of the plaintiff's injuries?
- Did the defect exist at the time the product left the defendant's hands?
- Was the product manufactured or sold by the defendant?

the court imputes knowledge of a defective condition of the product to the defendant. The core inquiry is whether a reasonable person would conclude that the perceived risks created by the design and marketing of the product outweigh the benefits. Would the defendant, as a reasonable person, have put the product into the stream of commerce if he or she had knowledge of its defective condition? This test was used in *Turner v. General Motors Corp.*, referred to above, to determine whether General Motors' design of the Impala's roof was defective.

A "defective condition unreasonably dangerous" can arise not only from the characteristics of the product itself but also from foreign objects contained in the product, from decay or deterioration before sale, or from the way in which the product was prepared or packaged. A carbonated beverage that is bottled under excessive pressure and explodes upon being opened or a beverage that contains bits of glass is in a "defective condition unreasonably dangerous."

Unavoidably Unsafe Products. **"Unavoidably unsafe products"** are those products that are incapable of being made safe for their intended and ordinary use. If the benefits of such products outweigh their risks, the courts will not hold their manufacturers strictly liable for harm coming to the consumers. Experimental drugs exemplify "unavoidably unsafe products." Their absolute safety cannot be assured because of insufficient research data and lack of medical experience. Those who sell these drugs are not held strictly liable for any untoward consequences resulting from their use as long as they prepare and market the drugs properly and give adequate warnings to consumers (Section 402A, comment k). Note, however, that if a manufacturer were negligent in failing to make adequate tests before selling the drugs, a plaintiff could recover for negligence.

Many courts have classified blood as an "unavoidably unsafe product." Additionally, many states have precluded by statute strict liability suits by those receiving "bad" blood. In one case in which the plaintiff contracted serum hepatitis as a result of receiving a blood transfusion, the court held that neither the hospital nor the blood bank was strictly liable (*Hines v. St. Josephs Hospital*, 527 P.2d 1075 (N.M. 1974)). No technology existed at the time to determine whether a particular specimen was infected with hepatitis even though blood banks were aware that a percentage of all specimens would be infected with hepatitis. The court concluded that the blood was "incapable of being made safe for its intended and ordinary use." The defendants fulfilled their duty to warn of the defect by warning the doctor and the hospital (through labeling) even though they never warned the plaintiff herself.

Remember that plaintiffs generally cannot introduce evidence that the defendant redesigned the product to make it safer. Such evidence is, however, admissible for the limited purpose of rebutting the defendant's argument that the product is "unavoidably unsafe" because of the extreme cost involved in removing the defect.

Causation. The plaintiff must also show that the product was the cause in fact and proximate cause of his or her injuries. Suppose, for example, the plaintiff eats a food product manufactured by the defendant and becomes ill several hours later. He must establish that it was the defendant's product and not some other factor that caused his illness.

Frequently, defendants will argue that intervening events were the proximate cause of the plaintiff's injuries or that other factors were the sole cause in fact of the accident. Remember from our discussion on strict liability (Chapter 13) that the courts are more likely to find a superseding cause in a strict liability cause of action than in a negligence case. Generally, if the act was reasonably foreseeable, it will not be considered a superseding act. If the act was unforeseeable but caused the same type of harm that made the product dangerous, then once again the act will not be considered superseding.

Unique causation problems have been raised in the diethylstilbestrol (DES) litigation. In one of the first DES cases, *Sindell vs. Abbott Laboratories*, 26 Cal.3d 588, 607 P.2d 924, *cert. denied*, 101 S.Ct. 285 (1980), the plaintiff was unable to identify the manufacturer responsible for making the DES taken by her mother while the plaintiff was in utero. Sympathizing with the plaintiff's plight, the court determined that since the plaintiff had sued five of the manufacturers of DES, whom she asserted produced 90 percent of the DES marketed, the burden of proof shifted to the defendants to demonstrate that they could not have supplied the DES that caused the plaintiff's injuries. Furthermore, the court reasoned that each defendant that failed to make such a showing would be held liable for the proportion of the judgment represented by its share of the DES market.

The theory of alternate liability (see Chapter 8 for further discussion), adopted by the Restatement (Second) of Torts Section 433B(3), preceded the "market share liability" theory of *Sindell.* It has been used by at least one AIDS victim (a hemophiliac), who could not identify the manufacturer that made the blood product from which he contracted AIDS (*Poole vs. Alpha Therapueutic Corp.*, 696 F.Supp. 351 (N.D.Ill. 1988)). Under this theory, if two or more persons have committed a tortious act and it can be proven that the harm done to the plaintiff was done by only one of them, but there is uncertainty as to which one did the harm, the burden is on each defendant to prove that he or she did not cause the harm. Any defendant that cannot prove his or her actions did not cause the plaintiff's injuries will be found liable. In *Poole* once the plaintiff was able to identify all of the defendants that could possibly have caused him to contract AIDS, the burden of proof shifted to the defendants to prove that they were not responsible for the plaintiff's injuries.

When Defect Existed. Finally, the plaintiff must show that the defect existed at the time the product left the hands of the defendant manufacturer. If it is just as likely that the defect developed in the hands of an intermediate dealer, the plaintiff cannot sustain his or her burden of proof against the manufacturer. Proof of this is exacerbated in cases where the product passed through several middlemen before it was used by the plaintiff. Most courts, however arc fairly liberal in allowing the plaintiff to at least get to the jury on this issue.

Strictly speaking, *res ipsa loquitur* is not applicable in a strict liability case but some of the inferences made under that doctrine are applicable. The fact that a product malfunctioned and no one else tampered with it may give rise to a permissible inference that the product was defective and that the defect existed when it left the hands of the defendant. The principles of *res ipsa loquitur* were successfully used in one strict liability case where shortening exploded when the user drained it from a fryer into a can. In light of the fact that the plaintiff had properly handled and used the shortening, there was no possible explanation for the explosion other than a defect in the shortening since shortening does not normally explode (*Franks v. National Dairy Products Corp.*, 414 F.2d 682 (5th Cir. 1969)).

Who May Be A Defendant? Strict liability applies to anyone in the business of selling goods, whether or not he or she is the manufacturer. A retail dealer in the business of selling goods is therefore strictly liable for the sale of any defective goods even if the sale is not a predominant part of the business. An owner of a movie theater, for example, is strictly liable for any defective popcorn or candies he sells even though such sales are presumably a by-product of his main business. A private individual, on the other hand, who sells her furniture is not strictly liable since she is not in the business of furniture selling. Component manufacturers are usually held to a standard of strict liability if the plaintiff can show that the defect existed at the time the component left the manufacturer's shop. Many courts have been willing to impose strict liability on lessors of defective goods (where the lessor is in the business of leasing) as well as sellers of real estate and sellers of services. Those who sell used goods, however, generally are not held to a standard of strict liability unless the plaintiff can show that the defects were created by the seller.

Who May Be A Plaintiff? Strict liability allows recovery for anyone who is the "ultimate user or consumer." Consumers include those who prepare a product for consumption (such as the husband who opens a bottle of beer for his wife to drink), those who passively enjoy the benefit of a product (such as passengers in an airplane), as well as those who use the product for the purpose of doing work on it (such as a serviceman making repairs on an automobile). (Restatement (Second) of Torts Section 402A, comment l.)

Many courts have been willing to extend strict liability protection to bystanders whose presence was reasonably foreseeable. One court reasoned that bystanders are entitled to greater protection than consumers or users because they do not have the same opportunity to inspect products for defects that consumers and users do (*Elmore v. American Motors Corp.*, 451 P.2d 84 (Cal. 1969)).

The courts have struggled with where to draw the line in reference to the protection of bystanders. Should a father, for example, be able to sue a manufacturer of birth control pills on behalf of his twin Down's syndrome daughters, one of whom is living and one of whom is deceased, on the theory that the pills altered the mother's chromosome structure, causing the resultant birth defects (*Jorgensen v. Meade Johnson Laboratories, Inc.*, 483 F.2d 237 (10th Cir. 1973))? The *Jorgensen* court held that the plaintiffs' claim for pain and suffering, mental retardation, and deformity, all of which were prenatal injuries, could be maintained since the children were born alive. While recognizing the father's right to bring this cause of action, the circuit court saw the key problem as being one of causation, i.e., presenting sufficient medical evidence to prove that the contraceptives did in fact cause the Down's syndrome.

Damages. Plaintiffs suing under a strict liability cause of action may recover for property damage as well as damages resulting from personal injuries. Lost profits and other intangible economic harm are generally not recoverable under a strict liability theory unless the plaintiff can show he or she also suffered injury or property damage.

A prime example of a case in which the court classified the plaintiff's losses as economic and therefore unrecoverable involved the purchase by the plaintiff cattle-breeding company of semen for its cattle (*Two Rivers Co. v. Curtiss Breeding Serv.*, 624 F.2d 1242 (5th Cir. 1980)). The semen had a recessive genetic defect that resulted in some of the calves being stillborn and that lowered the market value of those calves who survived. The court reasoned that the policy reasons underlying strict liability were not compelling in a case in which the plaintiff's commercial expectations were not realized and concluded that contract law (the U.C.C.'s warranty provisions) rather than tort law should be applied.

DEFENSES

NEGLIGENCE

The plaintiff's contributory negligence, comparative negligence, or assumption of risk are defenses to product liability claims based on a theory of negligence (see Table 14–4). For a complete discussion of those defenses see Chapter 9.

TABLE 14.4 Defenses to Product Liability Claims

NEGLIGENCE	WARRANTY	STRICT LIABILITY
•Contributory negligence •Comparative negligence •Assumption of risk •Statute of limitations/ Statute of repose	•Contributory negligence •Comparative negligence •Assumption of risk •Disclaimer of warranty •Limitation of remedies •Failure to discover breach in reasonable time •Statute of limitations/ Statute of repose	•Contributory negligence (only if plaintiff misused product or used it in abnormal fashion) •Comparative negligence (subject to much controversy) •Assumption of risk •Statute of Limitations/Statute of repose

WARRANTY

The rules pertaining to contributory negligence are generally applicable to cases involving warranty claims. If a buyer discovers that a good is defective and uses it anyway, his or her action rather than the breach of warranty may be considered the proximate cause of the injuries. The buyer's unreasonable failure to examine goods before using them may also constitute a defense to a breach of warranty claim. The courts tend to be more lenient, however, with consumers than with merchants in terms of their obligation to examine goods.

If the plaintiff's negligence is due to his or her misuse or abnormal use of the product, many courts will analyze the warranty action as involving a proximate cause or duty problem rather than as involving an affirmative defense. If a plaintiff, for example, misuses a bottle in attempting to remove its cap, a court might hold that the defendant had no duty to produce a bottle that could withstand unreasonable handling or, alternatively, that the makeup of the bottle was not the proximate cause of the plaintiff's injuries. The only real significance in this difference in analysis lies in the burden of proof. If the court uses a duty or proximate cause analysis, then the burden of proof lies with the plaintiff. If, however, the court treats the misuse as an affirmative defense, then the burden of proving that misuse lies with the defendant.

In addition to contributory negligence, assumption of risk is also generally a valid defense in warranty actions.

Disclaimers. Under the U.C.C. a seller can *disclaim* both implied and express warranties. To disclaim a warranty of merchantability the U.C.C. requires that the seller use language that is conspicuous and that specifically mentions merchantability (U.C.C. Section 2–316). Alternatively, an implied warranty of merchantability is disclaimed if the product is sold "as is" or if the buyer has an opportunity to examine the goods but refuses to do so. Federal law (under the Magnuson-Moss Federal Trade Commission Improvement Act, 15 U.S.C. Sec. 2301, *et. seq.)* precludes any manufacturer that provides a consumer with a written warranty from disclaiming any implied warranty. Any written warranty provided by a manufacturer must therefore include the implied warranty of merchantability.

Limitations of Remedies. Sellers sometimes try to limit the remedies available to plaintiffs for breach of implied warranties by providing that they (sellers) will not be liable for consequential damages. "[L]imitation of consequential damages for injury to the person in the case of consumer goods is prima facie unconscionable . . ." (U.C.C. Sec. 2–719(3)). Therefore, provisions limiting the seller's liability to repair or replacement of goods will not be enforced in cases involving personal injuries resulting from defects in products designed for personal use. Limitation of damages is not unconscionable, however, where the loss is commercial, i.e., involving intangible economic loss (U.C.C. Sec. 2–719(3)).

Time Limits. A seller can also argue that a buyer must "within a reasonable time after he discovers or should have discovered any breach" notify the seller of the breach (U.C.C. Sec. 2–607(3)). Courts frequently refuse to enforce this requirement when the plaintiff is not in privity with the defendant.

STRICT LIABILITY

A plaintiff's contributory negligence is not a defense to a strict liability claim if the plaintiff fails to discover the defect or to guard against the possibility of its existence. A valid defense may exist, however, if the plaintiff misuses the product or uses it in an abnormal fashion. Examples of the misuse or abnormal use of a product include knocking a bottled beverage against a radiator to remove the cap and overeating a product to the point of becoming ill (Restatement (Second) of Torts Section 402A, comment h). On the other hand, if the abuse or misuse is reasonably foreseeable, the manufacturer has a duty to anticipate such misuse and to make the product safe against it. Drivers inadvertently trying to start their vehicles from the "drive" position might, for example, be foreseeable. In that case manufacturers would have a duty to protect consumers from the consequences of their negligence. As we discussed in the section on defenses to warranty actions, cases of misuse or abnormal use can be phrased in terms of a duty or proximate cause analysis rather than as an affirmative defense.

Suppose the manufacturing defect is not the sole proximate cause of the plaintiff's injuries, but, in fact, the plaintiff's own negligence is an additional proximate cause. The plaintiff can still recover if he or she can show that the acts were not so unforeseeable that they should be considered superseding acts.

In comparative negligence jurisdictions considerable controversy exists as to whether a plaintiff suing on the basis of strict liability should have recovery reduced in proportion to his or her own negligence. Some courts have construed their comparative negligence statutes so as to find them applicable to strict liability situations, in effect reducing the plaintiff's recovery. The Uniform Comparative Fault Act suggests that the plaintiff's strict liability recovery should be reduced in proportion to the degree of fault.

Assumption of risk is basically treated in the same fashion in strict liability cases as it is in negligence cases. A plaintiff who discovers a defect and voluntarily and unreasonably proceeds to use the product is barred from recovery.

STATUTE OF LIMITATIONS

A defendant must look at the plaintiff's pleadings to determine the appropriate statute of limitations. The general tort statutes, which are usually relatively short, are applicable to negligence claims. The U.C.C.'s statute of limitations (Section 2–725) usually applies to breach of warranty actions and gives the plaintiff four years from the time of the sale of the product in which to sue. In strict liability cases the courts are in disagreement as to whether the U.C.C. or the general tort statutes are applicable.

Some states have adopted **statutes of repose,** which provide a fixed period of time from the date of the original sale during which a product liability suit can be brought. Unlike a statute of limitations, which begins to run at the time of injury, a statute of repose begins to run at the date of sale. Consequently, some product liability suits may be barred by a statute of repose before the injury even occurs. Victims of DES or AIDS, whose injuries become apparent years after the initial exposure, will often be precluded from filing suit if a statute of repose exists. Since the majority of bodily injuries occur within five years of purchase, however, statutes of repose have little effect on most claims.

SUMMARY

Product liability cases can be based on theories of negligence, breach of warranty, or strict liability. All three types of actions involve products in a defective condition, which can involve manufacturing defects, design defects, or defective warnings. Design defects include structural defects, absence of safety features, and misuse of a product if the misuse is reasonably foreseeable.

Plaintiffs recovering on the basis of negligence can sue the manufacturer, retailer, or lessor of a product whose defect was the proximate cause of their injuries. They can recover for personal injuries and property damage but will have difficulty recovering for pure economic loss.

Warranty actions, which are a hybrid of contract and tort law, can be based on breach of an express or implied warranty. The most common implied warranties are warranties of merchantability and warranties of fitness for a particular purpose. A plaintiff who is a direct purchaser will, because of the generosity of the U.C.C., likely opt for a warranty theory over a negligence or strict liability theory if the damages are solely economic. Privity requirements, which vary from state to state, dictate who may and may not be sued.

Strict liability is the most commonly used cause of action in product liability cases. Plaintiffs must prove that the product was in a "defective condition unreasonably dangerous," that the defect was the cause in fact and proximate cause of the plaintiff's injuries, that the defect existed at the time the product left the defendant's hands, and that the product was manufactured or sold by the defendant. Strict liability extends to the ultimate user or consumer of a product, including, for many courts, bystanders whose presence was reasonably foreseeable. Anyone in the business of selling goods, including manufacturers, retailers, and lessors can be held strictly liable for the defective products they pass on to others.

Contributory and comparative negligence and assumption of risk are defenses to negligence and warranty claims. With certain restrictions warranties can be disclaimed under the U.C.C. and sellers can limit the remedies available in the event of a breach. Contributory negligence is not a defense in a strict liability case unless the plaintiff abused the product in an unforeseeable way. Assumption of risk is generally a defense to strict liability. Plaintiffs must determine the appropriate statute of limitations and must consider any statute of repose when filing claims.

PRACTICE POINTERS

Meeting with and preparing witnesses for trial is a task that sometimes falls to legal assistants. Bear in mind that the purpose of this preparation is not to coach witnesses as to what they should say but rather to remind them of facts they have previously attested to. Transcripts of previous testimony as well as prior statements should be brought in for their review. If time permits they should be put through a mock cross-examination so that they will know the types of questions they can anticipate fielding on the witness stand. At the very least they should be asked to give a narrative of the events and facts about which they are being called to testify.

Several general suggestions can also be offered that will enhance their credibility and overall effectiveness as witnesses. Most importantly, remind them that the trier of fact is the one they are relating to and, therefore, the one to whom they should direct their attention. Direct communication with jurors is particularly important since jurors will quickly become apathetic and inattentive if a witness fails to establish eye contact with them and talks only to the attorneys. Caution witnesses against volunteering any information that is not specifically solicited since doing so can open the floodgates to an outpouring of additional questions. Advise them to listen carefully to the question being asked, answering that question as directly as possible and asking for clarification if they do not understand the question. Urge them to be as truthful and candid as possible and to avoid speculation. Finally, warn them never to lose their tempers and to refrain from engaging in verbal battles with counsel. Patience and an engaging smile will gain them greater rapport with a jury than a quick wit and acid tongue.

You may also wish to forewarn witnesses about a few "tricks of the trade" that attorneys sometimes employ as part of their cross-examination techniques. Anything attorneys can do to fluster or anger a witness often works to their advantage so witnesses should be alert to any attempts to bait or confuse them. Attorneys who repeat the same question over and over or a variation thereof are looking for inconsistency in answers. An attorney who continues to stare at a witness who has completed his answer is using body language to pressure the witness into volunteering more information. Constant interruptions are both a way to establish dominance over a witness as well as a way to disrupt the flow of communication between the witness and the trier of fact. A favorite tactic of many attorneys is to box a witness into a "yes" or "no" answer. If a question cannot in all candor be answered "yes" or "no," a witness should be aware that she can advise the judge of the inadequacy of either answer and request that she be given an opportunity to give a more complete and more honest answer.

TORT TEASERS

What type of defect would you argue exists in each of the following cases?

1. Plaintiff, a twenty-six-year-old woman, is given a prescription for oral contraceptives by her physician. The pill dispenser she receives is labeled with the warning "Oral contraceptives are powerful and effective drugs which can cause side effects in some users and should not be used at all by some women," and that "[t]he most serious known side effect is abnormal blood clotting which can be fatal." The warning also refers Plaintiff to a booklet that contains detailed information about the medication, including the increased risk to vital organs. The booklet specifically notes the possibility of the brain being damaged by abnormal blood clotting. The word "stroke" does not appear on the dispenser warning or in the booklet. Three years after commencing use of the pills, Plaintiff suffers a stroke rendering her disabled. *MacDonald v. Ortho Pharmaceutical Corp.*, 475 N.E.2d 65 (Mass. 1985).

2. The petcock in the undercarriage of a bus is unprotected from debris on the road. One night while Plaintiff is driving his heavily overloaded bus down the highway, the petcock becomes disengaged by the debris, allowing the brakes to drain. The resultant brake failure causes an accident. *Carpini v. Pittsburgh and Weirton Bus Company*, 216 F.2d 404 (3rd Cir. 1954).

3. Plaintiff decides he wants to buy a Shopsmith, a combination power tool that can be used as a saw, drill, and wood lathe. He sees a Shopsmith demonstrated by a retailer and then studies a brochure prepared by the manufacturer. He buys the Shopsmith along with necessary attachments and uses the Shopsmith as a lathe. While making a chalice, Plaintiff is struck on the forehead by a piece of wood when it flies out of the machine and he is seriously injured. Plaintiff had used the Shopsmith as a lathe on several previous occasions with no difficulties. *Greenman v. Yuba Power Products, Inc.*, 377 P.2d 897 (Cal. 1963).

In each of the following cases which of the three theories of recovery (negligence, breach of warranty, or strict liability) would you use as a basis for recovery and why?

4. After being injured by an armed robber, Plaintiff brings suit against the manufacturer of "Saturday night specials." Such guns are characterized by "short barrels, light weight, easy concealability, low cost, use of cheap quality materials, poor manufacture, inaccuracy, and unreliability." These weapons are basically useless for legitimate purposes and are used mainly by criminals. *Kelley v. R. G. Industries*, 497 A.2d 1143 (Md. 1985).

5. After selling a plastic molding press to Company A, a manufacturer learns that the press has a dangerous tendency to crush the hands of people using it and that it violates state safety laws. When Company A sells the machine to Company B the manufacturer learns of this transaction through repair records and offers Company B a safety device for the machine for $500. Company B declines this offer and Plaintiff, one of its employees, gets her hand crushed. *Balido v. Improved Machinery, Inc.*, 105 Cal. Rptr. 890 (Cal. Ct. App. 1973).

6. Defendant manufacturer advertises its rifle as being suitable for "big game hunting." When Plainttiff uses this gun on a foreign safari and it fails he sues the manufacturer for the cost of that safari. *Thomas v. Olin Mathieson Chemical Corp.*, 63 Cal. Rptr. 454 (1967).

What would you argue as the defendant in the following cases? How would you, as the plaintiff, respond to the defendant's arguments?

7. Plaintiff buys a car with a defective seat belt from Defendant. When Plaintiff brings the car back for a new belt Defendant tells him that nothing can be done until a new one is received from the factory. While waiting for the new belt, Plaintiff drives without a belt and is involved in an accident. *DeVaney v. Sarno*, 311 A.2d 208 (N.J. 1973).

8. A strict liability claim is brought against the manufacturer of the Opel automobile on behalf of the driver who is killed as a result of an alleged defect in the door latch. The evidence shows that the driver was not using a shoulder harness, did not lock the door, and was intoxicated at the time of the accident. *Daly v. General Motors Corp.*, 575 P.2d 1172 (Cal. 1978).

9. Salt River Project (SRP), an electric utility company, purchases a gas turbine generator from Westinghouse. After a year of using the generator, SRP complains to Westinghouse about frequent computer malfunctions in the generator. In response to this complaint Westinghouse develops a Local Maintenance Controller (LMC) that permits manual operation of the turbine. SRP orders the LMC; Westinghouse responds with a standardized acceptance form containing the following warranty:

> This warranty . . . is exclusive and in lieu of any warranty of merchantability, fitness for purpose, or other warranty of quality, whether express or implied.
> Limitation of Liability—Neither party shall be liable for special, indirect, incidental or consequential damages. The remedies of the purchaser set forth herein are exclusive, and the liability of Westinghouse with respect to any contract or sale or anything done in connection therewith, whether in contract, in tort, under any warranty or otherwise, shall not, except as expressly provided herein, exceed the price of the product or part on which such liability is based.

Two years after the LMC was installed, an explosion and fire occurred, which SRP alleges resulted from a malfunction in the LMC. *Salt River Project Agri-*

cultural Improvement and Power District v. Westinghouse Electric Corp., 694 P.2d 198 (Ariz. 1985).

10. Recall the hypothetical problem posed at the beginning of this chapter.
a. Which of the three theories of recovery would you use if you decided to sue the doctor and the sperm bank? What would be the reasoning underlying your choice?
b. Outline the elements you would have to prove if you decided to sue on the basis of negligence. Then do the same for warranty and strict liability.
c. Develop a list of questions you would want to ask your potential clients, Husband and Wife, at the initial interview.
d. Draft some interrogatories that you would want to submit to the sperm bank.
e. Compile a list of questions you would want to submit to a doctor you are thinking about using as an expert witness.
f. Prepare a list of the documents and correspondence you would want to request during discovery from the doctor and the sperm bank.

KEY TERMS

■ **Defective warning**
Defect arising out of a manufacturer's failure to give adequate warnings or directions for use.

■ **Design defect**
Defect arising out of a manufacturer's use of an unreasonably dangerous design.

■ **Economic loss**
Diminution in the value of a product.

■ **Express warranty**
Express representation by a seller that a product possesses certain qualities.

■ **Implied warranty**
Representations as to a product's qualities that are implied by virtue of the product being offered for sale.

■ **Manufacturing defect**
Defect arising out of a deviation in the manufacturing process.

■ **Privity**
Requirement that the plaintiff must contract directly with the defendant in order to recover for losses.

■ **Unavoidably unsafe products**
Products incapable of being made safe for their ordinary and intended use.

■ **Warranty of fitness for a particular purpose**
Implied warranty that goods are suitable to be used for a particular (noncustomary) purpose.

■ **Warranty of merchantability**
Implied warranty that goods are fit for the ordinary purpose for which they are used.

15 INTENTIONAL TORTS

CHAPTER OBJECTIVES

In this chapter you will learn to:

- Identify the elements of assault, battery, false imprisonment, and infliction of mental distress.
- Identify the elements of trespass to land, trespass to chattels, and conversion.
- Recognize those circumstances in which it is appropriate to raise the defenses of consent or necessity.
- Recognize when force can be used to defend self, others, property, to regain possession of chattels, or to reenter land.

Suppose you come home one evening to discover that your teenage son "borrowed" your car and went on the following spree. First, he dropped by his girlfriend's house to pick her up but once there met with considerable resistance from her parents. Not to be intimidated by her father, who stood menacingly in front of the car as he started the engine, your son yelled out the window that he would run over her father if he did not get out of the way. The father, who doggedly stood his ground until the last possible moment, barely escaped injury when he finally jumped aside.

Unbeknownst to either your son or his girlfriend, her younger brother had crawled into the back of the car during the fracas with the father. Once under way, the little boy screamed to be released from the car. Your son, who harbored some latent hostility toward the little brother, took great delight in holding him captive for several miles before letting him out of the car to walk home.

Next the twosome headed to a remote place in the country to enjoy a little privacy. Deeply involved in professing their love for each other, neither noticed the approach of a man brandishing a gun. The man punctuated each demand to get off his land by firing a shot in the air. Thoroughly frightened, the two lovers beat a hasty retreat but, with one last act of bravado, your son took aim at a sign on the man's property and obliterated it with the car. Later your son, as an afterthought, casually mentioned to you that before leaving the property he took the opportunity to fire a few shots in the man's direction with a gun that he had "borrowed" from you.

Ultimately, he arrived safely at home with a car that was only slightly scratched from its close encounter with a sign. In the course of his escapade what intentional torts did your son commit and what defenses might he raise to justify his conduct? To answer these questions let us first consider the nature of an intentional tort.

WHAT IS AN INTENTIONAL TORT?

The state of the tortfeasor's mind separates an intentional tort from a negligent one. Although negligent torts can be committed unintentionally, **intentional torts,** as the name implies, require that the tortfeasor intend or have a desire to bring about a particular consequence. The tortfeasor need not desire to harm a person, but he or she must be aware that certain consequences are substantially certain to result from his or her acts. If, for example, the defendant intends to do nothing more than play a practical joke on the plaintiff and has absolutely no desire to injure him, he may still be liable if he harms the plaintiff. The intent to bring about a particular result is what is important. The fact that he wishes no harm to the plaintiff has no bearing on his intent.

If a defendant knows with substantial certainty that a result will occur, he or she will be liable for the consequences. An individual who throws a firecracker into the middle of a dense crowd, for example, may not actually want to hit anyone but if she knows with substantial certainty that someone will get hit, she has acted intentionally. If the consequences are merely highly likely but not substantially certain, the defendant will be considered negligent but will not be deemed to have acted intentionally. Note that intent can be distinguished from motive. Intent is the desire to bring about a consequence; motive is connected to the reason for desiring such a consequence.

You will recall that intentional torts can also be crimes. An assault is both a tort and a crime as is trespass and false imprisonment. A police officer who deliberately and unlawfully detains an individual can be sued for the damages sustained by the detainee (false imprisonment) and can be punished criminally as well (although the crime is often referred to as unlawful imprisonment). Be cautious, however, in drawing too many analogies between tort law and criminal law. Since the purposes and historical derivations of criminal and tort law are different, the terms and concepts used in the criminal area do not necessarily correspond to those used in tort law.

TRANSFERRED INTENT DOCTRINE

If a tortfeasor intends to punch A but A ducks and the tortfeasor inadvertently strikes B, the intent to strike A will be transferred from A to B. Under the

transferred intent doctrine, the intent with respect to one person is transferred to the person who is actually injured. Therefore, in such cases the tortfeasor is deemed to have committed an intentional tort. This same rule is applicable if the tortfeasor intends to commit one kind of tort and in fact commits another. If the tortfeasor uses his dog to terrorize A (an assault) and the dog escapes and bites B (a battery), the tortfeasor will be liable for the battery even though he intended an assault.

CATEGORIZATION OF INTENTIONAL TORTS

Intentional torts are generally divided into two categories: intentional torts against persons and intentional torts against property. The torts against persons that will be discussed in this chapter are battery, assault, false imprisonment, and infliction of mental distress (see Table 15–1). The torts against property that will be discussed are trespass to land, trespass to chattels, and conversion.

INTENTIONAL TORTS AGAINST PERSONS

BATTERY

If two people become engaged in a heated argument and one pushes the other to the ground, the person who does the shoving commits a battery. **Battery** is defined as the intentional infliction of a harmful or offensive contact upon a person. If the tortfeasor intends only to frighten the victim and accidentally makes "harmful or offensive contact," he or she has still committed a battery. As indicated above, whether the tortfeasor intends to actually injure the plaintiff is irrelevant. To satisfy the elements of battery the tortfeasor must only intend to make contact and that contact must actually be made.

What Is Considered Contact? The function of battery is to protect individuals from undesired and unpermitted contacts. This tort extends to contact with any part of a person's body or anything attached to or identified with the body. Contact with a purse, with an object in the plaintiff's hand, or with

TABLE 15.1 Intentional Torts Against Persons

BATTERY	ASSAULT
Intentional infliction of harmful or offensive contact.	Intentional causing of apprehension of harmful or offensive contact.
FALSE IMPRISONMENT	**INFLICTION OF MENTAL DISTRESS**
Intentional confinement of another.	Intentional infliction of severe emotional or mental distress as a result of extreme and outrageous conduct (can also be committed recklessly).

the car in which the plaintiff is riding all constitute contact for the purposes of battery. In one case the plaintiff, a black man, was attending a luncheon at the defendant's hotel. One of the defendant's employees grabbed the plate from the plaintiff's hand while he was waiting to be served and shouted that the plaintiff could not be served in the club because he was black. Although the plaintiff was never actually touched or frightened by defendant's employee, he did suffer a battery because the intentional snatching of the plate from his hand constituted an offensive invasion of his person (*Fisher v. Carrousel Motor Hotel, Inc.*, 424 S.W.2d 627 (Tex. 1967)).

The defendant need not actually touch the plaintiff with his body. A person who orders his dog to attack or who throws water on someone has committed a battery (Restatement (Second) of Torts Sec. 18, comment c).

Neither must the plaintiff suffer pain or bodily damage to recover for battery. The contact need only be "offensive." In determining whether a contact is offensive, the question is whether a person with a reasonable sense of dignity would be offended. If a woman gently taps her boyfriend on the shoulder to get his attention, she has not committed a battery. Touching by a friend is not offensive to an ordinary person and is not therefore actionable.

Awareness Of Contact. The plaintiff is not required to have any awareness of the contact at the time it occurs. If the plaintiff gives consent for a biopsy to be done and the doctor decides while the patient is under anesthetic to go ahead and perform surgery, the doctor has committed battery. Even though she obtained consent for the biopsy, she lacks the plaintiff's consent to perform the surgery. The fact that the plaintiff is unaware of the doctor's actions at the time of the surgery is irrelevant.

Extent of Liability. The defendant who commits battery is held liable for any consequences regardless of how unforeseen they may be. Suppose the defendant grabs the plaintiff around the waist and playfully squeezes her in a manner that would normally cause no bodily harm. Because the plaintiff is suffering from osteoporosis, however, she sustains extensive damage to her ribs, resulting in long suffering. The defendant is liable for the full extent of the plaintiff's bodily harm even though he could not have reasonably anticipated that harm.

Assault

Assault is defined as the intentional causing of an apprehension of harmful or offensive contact. Apprehension does not mean fear but does require the plaintiff to be aware of the impending contact. A woman who shakes her broom at someone to frighten or chase him away has committed assault if the object of her threats believes she is trying to strike him. A defendant can commit assault by either intending to commit a battery or merely intending to frighten the plaintiff with no intent of actual contact. A defendant, for example, who attempts to strike the plaintiff but misses commits an assault but so does the defendant who makes a fist at the plaintiff with no intent of actually hitting him.

The doctrine of transferred intent is as applicable to assault as it is to battery. Therefore, if a defendant throws a stone at A and B fears being hit, the defendant will be liable to B for assault even though he never intended to hit or frighten B.

Plaintiff's Attitude. Unlike battery, a plaintiff alleging assault must be aware of the threatened contact. So if A intends to frighten B by discharging a pistol behind him but B, who is stone deaf, does not hear the pistol, A will not be liable to B for assault (Restatement (Second) of Torts Sec. 22, illustration 1).

An individual will not be able to recover for assault if his apprehension is that someone else will be touched and not himself. If a husband for example disarms a robber just before he shoots the husband's wife, the husband cannot recover for assault since the attack was directed at his wife and not himself (Restatement (Second) of Torts Sec. 26).

A plaintiff need not be fearful that he will be harmed. A plaintiff confident in his ability to protect himself can still be the victim of assault. His awareness that he could be harmed if he failed to take defensive action is sufficient.

Defendant's Ability To Carry Out Threat. A defendant must appear to the plaintiff to have the present ability to carry out the threatened contact. In one case the plaintiff entered a telegraph office that was managed by the defendant and reminded him that he had contracted to fix her clock. The defendant, who was standing behind the counter, said "If you will come back here and let me love you and pet you, I will fix your clock." He then leaned forward across the counter and attempted to touch the plaintiff. If the counter was so wide that the defendant could not have touched the plaintiff, no assault could have been committed (*Western Union Telegraph Co. v. Hill,* 150 So. 709 (Ala. 1933)). If a plaintiff believes the defendant has the ability to carry out his threatened contact even though he actually does not, the elements of assault are met.

What Constitutes A Threat? Any threats of harm must be imminent to constitute an assault. Threats of future harm are not sufficient although they may satisfy the criteria for the tort of intentional infliction of mental distress. If A threatens to shoot B, for example, but must go to her car to get her revolver, A has not committed assault (Restatement (Second) of Torts Sec. 29, illustration 4).

The courts are in some disagreement as to whether words alone constitute an assault. Some courts require that words be accompanied by some overt act that tends to enhance the threatening character of the words; other courts, in accordance with the Restatement (Second), require no accompanying overt act. If a member of a juvenile gang, holding a knife in his hand, approaches a member of another gang and, without movement, says, "You die," many courts would conclude that an assault had been committed.

Note that the tort of assault is complete as soon as the plaintiff apprehends the contact. If, after the plaintiff's apprehension, the defendant suddenly abandons his plan, he will still be liable for assault.

FALSE IMPRISONMENT

The tort of **false imprisonment** is committed when a person intentionally confines another. Originally confinement was restricted to actual incarceration but today confinement includes restraint in an open street or in a moving vehicle. The restraint must be more than a mere obstruction of the plaintiff's right to go wherever she pleases. Blocking the plaintiff's path in one direction only does not constitute confinement as long as alternative routes are available. The doctrine of transferred intent is applicable to this tort. If the defendant, in his intent to confine one person, inadvertently confines another as well, he will be liable to both for false imprisonment.

What Constitutes Confinement? The plaintiff is not required to subject herself or her property to any risk of harm in an effort to extricate herself from her confinement. Suppose a defendant closes off every exit except one. If the plaintiff can escape only by exposing herself to the possibility of substantial bodily harm, the defendant has confined her. Similarly, if the defendant blocks all doors except one and steals the plaintiff's clothing, leaving the plaintiff naked, and the plaintiff can leave only by walking through a room filled with persons of both sexes, the defendant has confined the plaintiff (Restatement (Second) of Torts Sec. 36, illustrations 3 and 5).

Confinement can be achieved by something less than physical force. If a defendant threatens by his body language alone to harm the plaintiff if the plaintiff tries to escape, he has still confined the plaintiff. Threats need not be aimed directly at the plaintiff, either. If the defendant threatens to harm another if the plaintiff leaves the confined area, the defendant has committed false imprisonment. Any threats, however, must be of imminent harm. Threats of future harm are not sufficient. Finally, the plaintiff must be aware of her confinement at the time it occurs. If a person does not discover until after her release that she was confined she cannot claim she was falsely imprisoned.

False Imprisonment In Law Enforcement. False imprisonment most often occurs in the context of law enforcement. A valid defense to the allegation of false imprisonment is the police officer's assertion of the legal right to make an arrest. An officer can claim such a defense even if the arrest or detention later turns out to be unlawful. He or she is required only to act reasonably and in good faith in carrying out the arrest. An officer who serves the plaintiff with an invalid arrest warrant but who reasonably believes the warrant to be valid has not committed false imprisonment.

Shoplifting. In most states today a merchant who reasonably believes that a customer has stolen property has a right to detain the suspected individual for a short period of time for the purposes of investigation. The right to detain is very restricted, however, and will be lost if the detention is unreasonably long, if the plaintiff is bullied or insulted, if the plaintiff is publicly accused of shoplifting, or if the detention is used to coerce payment or the signing of a confession. In most states the right to detain is limited to detention on the defendant's premises and is lost when the plaintiff leaves the premises. The pivotal question is whether the merchant had reasonable grounds for the detention. Consult the statutes and common law in your state to ascertain more specifically the rights of merchants in your jurisdiction.

INFLICTION OF MENTAL DISTRESS

A relative newcomer to tort law is the claim of infliction of mental distress. This tort can be committed either intentionally or recklessly. If committed intentionally, the tortfeasor must want to bring about a particular consequence or must know with substantial certainty that a certain result is likely to occur. If the tort is committed recklessly, the defendant must act in deliberate disregard of the emotional distress that he knows he is very likely to cause the plaintiff. Such recklessness rises above negligence. All of the elements of this tort are presented and discussed in full in *Harris v. Jones.*

William R. HARRIS v. H. Robert JONES et al.
No. 58. Courts of Appeals of Maryland. Dec. 9, 1977.
380 A.2d 611 (1977).

MURPHY, Chief Judge.

In *Jones v. Harris,* 35 Md.App. 556, 371 A.2d 1104 (1977), a case of first impression in Maryland, the Court of Special Appeals, in a scholarly opinion by Judge W. Albert Menchine, recognized intentional infliction of emotional distress as a new and independent tort in this jurisdiction. It found that a majority of the states now recognize intentional infliction of emotional distress as a separate and distinct basis of tort liability, apart from any other tort, thus repudiating earlier holdings that claims for emotional distress could not be sustained except as a parasitic element of damage accompanying a recognized tort. We granted certiorari to review the decision of the Court of Special Appeals and to decide whether, if intentional infliction of emotional distress is a viable tort in Maryland, the court erred in reversing judgments entered on jury verdicts for the plaintiff on that cause of action.

The plaintiff, William R. Harris, a 26-year-old, 8-year employee of General Motors Corporation (GM), sued GM and one of its supervisory employees, H. Robert Jones, in the Superior Court of Baltimore City. The declaration alleged that Jones, aware that Harris suffered from a speech impediment which caused him to stutter, and also aware of Harris' sensitivity to his disability, and his insecurity because of it, nevertheless "maliciously and cruelly ridiculed . . . [him] thus causing tremendous nervousness, increasing the physical defect itself and further injuring the mental attitude fostered by the Plaintiff toward his problem and otherwise intentionally inflicting emotional distress." It was also alleged in the declaration that Jones' actions occurred within the course of his employment with GM and that GM ratified Jones' conduct.

The evidence at trial showed that Harris stuttered throughout his entire life. While he had little trouble with one syllable words, he had great difficulty with longer words or sentences, causing him at times to shake his head up and down when attempting to speak.

During part of 1975, Harris worked under Jones' supervision at a GM automobile assembly plant. Over a five-month period, between March and August of 1975, Jones approached Harris over 30 times at work and verbally and physically mimicked his stuttering disability. In addition, two or three times a week during this period, Jones approached Harris and told him, in a "smart manner," not to get nervous. As a result of Jones' conduct, Harris was "shaken up" and felt "like going into a hole and hide."

On June 2, 1975, Harris asked Jones for a transfer to another department; Jones refused, called Harris a "troublemaker" and chastised him for repeatedly seeking the assistance of his committeeman, and representative who handles employee grievances. On this occasion, Jones, "shaking his head up and down" to imitate Harris, mimicked his pronunciation of the word "committeeman," which Harris pronounced "mmitteeman." As a result of this incident, Harris filed an employee grievance against Jones, requesting that GM instruct Jones to properly conduct himself in the future; the grievance was marked as satisfactorily settled after GM so instructed Jones. On another occasion during the five-month period, Harris filed a similar grievance against Jones; it too was marked as satisfactorily settled after GM again instructed Jones to properly conduct himself.

Harris had been under the care of a physician for a nervous condition for six years prior to the commencement of Jones' harassment. He admitted that many things made him nervous, including "bosses." Harris testified that Jones' conduct heightened his nervousness and his speech impediment worsened. He saw his physician on one occasion during the five-month period that Jones was mistreating him; the physician prescribed pills for his nerves.

Harris admitted that other employees at work mimicked his stuttering. Approximately 3,000 persons were employed on each of two shifts, and Harris acknowledged the presence at the plant of a lot of "tough guys," as well as profanity, name-calling and roughhousing among the employees. He said that a bad day at work caused him to become more nervous than usual. He admitted that he had problems with supervisors other than Jones, that he had been suspended or relieved from work 10 or 12 times, and that after one such dispute, he followed a supervisor home on his motorcycle, for which he was later disciplined.

Harris' wife testified that her husband was "in a shell" at the time they were married approximately seven years prior to the trial. She said that it took her about a year to get him to associate with family and friends and that while he still had a difficult time talking, he thereafter became "calmer." Mrs. Harris testified that beginning in November of 1974, her husband became ill-tempered at home and said that he had problems at work. She said that he was drinking too much at that time, that on one occasion he threw a meat platter at her, that she was afraid of him, and that they separated for a two-week period in November of 1974. Mrs. Harris indicated that her husband's nervous condition got worse in June of 1975. She said that at a christening party held during that month Harris "got to drinking" and they argued.

On this evidence, the case was submitted to the jury after the trial court denied the defendants' motions for directed verdicts; the jury awarded Harris $3,500 compensatory damages and $15,000 punitive damages against both Jones and GM. . . .

Illustrative of the cases which hold that a cause of action will lie for intentional infliction of emotional distress, unaccompanied by physical injury, is *Womack v. Eldridge,* 214 Va. 338, 210 S.E.2d 145 (1974). There, the defendant was engaged in the business of investigating cases for attorneys. She deceitfully obtained the plaintiff's photograph for the purpose of permitting a criminal defense lawyer to show it to the victims in several child molesting cases in an effort to have them identify the plaintiff as the perpetrator of the offenses, even though he was in no way involved in the crimes. While the victims did not identify the plaintiff, he was nevertheless questioned by the police, called repeatedly as a witness and required to explain the circumstances under which the defendant had obtained his photograph. As a result, plaintiff suffered shock, mental depression, nervousness and great anxiety as to what people would think of him and he feared that he would be accused of molesting the boys. The court, in concluding that a cause of action had been made out, said:

> "[M]ost of the courts which have been presented with the question in recent years have held that there may be a recovery against one who by his extreme and outrageous conduct intentionally or recklessly causes another severe emotional distress. . . .

* * * * * *

> "A great majority of cases allowing recovery for such a cause of action do so when the act was intentional and the wrongdoer desired [to inflict] the emotional distress or knew or should have known that it would likely result. [citations omitted]

The court in *Womack* identified four elements which must coalesce to impose liability for intentional infliction of emotional distress:

(1) The conduct must be intentional or reckless;

(2) The conduct must be extreme and outrageous;

(3) There must be a causal connection between the wrongful conduct and the emotional distress;

(4) The emotional distress must be severe.

Essentially, these are the elements of the tort set forth in § 446 of the Restatement, *supra*. . . .

As to the first element of the tort, § 46 of the Restatement, *supra*, comment i, states, and the cases generally recognize, that the defendant's conduct is intentional or reckless where he desires to inflict severe emotional distress, and also where he knows that such distress is certain, or substantially certain, to result from his conduct; or where the defendant acts recklessly in deliberate disregard of a high degree of probability that the emotional distress will follow.

Whether the conduct of a defendant has been "extreme and outrageous," so as to satisfy that element of the tort, has been a particularly troublesome question. Section 46 of the Restatement, comment d, states that "Liability has been found only where the conduct has been so outrageous in character, and so extreme in degree, as to go beyond all possible bounds of decency, and to be regarded as atrocious, and utterly intolerable in a civilized community." The comment goes on to state that liability does not extend, however:

> "to mere insults, indignities, threats, annoyances, petty oppressions, or other trivialities. The rough edges of our society are still in need of a good deal of filing down, and in the meantime plaintiffs must necessarily be expected and required to be hardened to a certain amount of rough language, and to occasional acts that are definitely inconsiderate and unkind. . . ."

Comment f states that the extreme and outrageous character of the conduct "may arise from the actor's knowledge that the other is peculiarly susceptible to emotional distress, by reason of some physical or mental condition or peculiarity." The comment continues:

> "The conduct may become heartless, flagrant, and outrageous when the actor proceeds in the face of such knowledge, where it would not be so if he did not know. It must be emphasized . . . that major outrage is essential to the tort. . . ."

In his now classic article, *Mental and Emotional Disturbance in the Law of Torts,* 49 Harv.L.Rev. 1033 (1936), Professor Calvert Magruder warned against imposing liability for conduct which is not outrageous and extreme; he observed at 1035 that "Against a large part of the frictions and irritations and clashing of temperaments incident to participation in a community life, a certain toughening of the mental hide is a better protection than the law could ever be," and at 1053, he said:

> "there is danger of getting into the realm of the trivial in this matter of insulting language. No pressing social need requires that every abusive outburst be converted into a tort; upon the contrary, it would be unfortunate if the law closed all the safety valves through which irascible tempers might legally blow off steam."

In determining whether conduct is extreme and outrageous, it should not be considered in a sterile setting, detached from the surroundings in which it occurred. . . . The personality of the individual to whom the misconduct is directed is also a factor. "There is a difference between violent and vile profanity addressed to a lady, and the same language to a Butte miner and a United States marine." . . .

Without indicating our approval or rejection, cases decided by other courts reflect an application of these principles. For example, in *Pakos v. Clark, supra,* the court held that the conduct of a police officer who told the plaintiff that he was crazy as a bedbug and would be put back in an asylum and his children taken from him, and the conduct of another official who puffed up his cheeks and bulged his eyes 7 or 8 times at the plaintiff, was not extreme and outrageous conduct. In *Paris v. Division of State Compensation Ins. Funds,* . . . a supervisor delivered a letter of reprimand to the plaintiff, a paraplegic, which contained the statement: "You must realize that your job was created for you because of your handicap." The court there affirmed the trial court's ruling that this conduct was not so outrageous as to support an action for the intentional infliction of emotional distress. . . .

It is for the court to determine, in the first instance, whether the defendant's conduct may reasonably be regarded as extreme and outrageous; where reasonable men may differ, it is for the jury to determine whether, in the particular case, the conduct has been sufficiently extreme and outrageous to result in liability. Restatement, *supra,* § 46, comment h . . .

In cases where the defendant is in a peculiar position to harass the plaintiff, and cause emotional distress, his conduct will be carefully scrutinized by the courts. . . . Thus, in *Alcorn, supra,* the court referred to comment e of the Restatement, *supra,* § 46, *i.e.,* that the extreme and outrageous character of the defendant's conduct may arise from his abuse of a position, or relation with another person, which gives him actual or apparent authority over him, or power to affect his interests. In that case, the Supreme Court of California said that a plaintiff's status as an employee should entitle him to a greater degree of protection from insult and outrage than if he were a mere stranger. It there found an employer's conduct toward a black employee to be extreme and outrageous, and to support an action for intentional infliction of emotional distress where the employer, "standing in a position or relation of authority over plaintiff, aware of his particular susceptibility to emotional distress, and for the purpose of causing plaintiff to suffer such distress, intentionally humiliated plaintiff, insulted his race [by calling him a 'nigger'], ignored his union status, and terminated his employment, all without just cause or provocation."

The Court of Special Appeals found that Jones' conduct was intended to inflict emotional distress and was extreme and outrageous. As to the other elements of the tort, it concluded that the evidence was legally insufficient to establish either that a causal connection existed between Jones' conduct and Harris' emotional distress, or that Harris' emotional distress was severe.

While it is crystal clear that Jones' conduct was intentional, we need not decide whether it was extreme or outrageous, or causally related to the emotional distress which Harris allegedly suffered. The fourth element of the tort—that the emotional distress must be severe—was not established by legally sufficient evidence justifying submission of the case to the jury. That element of the tort requires the plaintiff to show that he suffered a *severely* disabling emotional response to the defendant's conduct. The severity of the emotional distress is not only relevant to the amount of recovery, but is a necessary element to any recovery. . . . Comment j of § 46 of the Restatement, *supra*, elaborates on this requirement:

> "Emotional distress passes under various names, such as mental suffering, mental anguish, mental or nervous shock, or the like. It includes all highly unpleasant mental reactions, such as fright, horror, grief, shame, humiliation, embarrassment, anger, chagrin, disappointment, worry, and nausea. It is only where it is extreme that the liability arises. Complete emotional tranquility is seldom attainable in this world, and some degree of transient and trivial emotional distress is part of the price of living among people. The law intervenes only where the distress inflicted is so severe that no reasonable man could be expected to endure it. The intensity and the duration of the distress are factors to be considered in determining its severity. Severe distress must be proved; but in many cases the extreme and outrageous character of the defendant's conduct is in itself important evidence that the distress has existed. . . .
>
> "The distress must be reasonable and justified under the circumstances, and there is no liability where the plaintiff has suffered exaggerated and unreasonable emotional distress, unless it results from a peculiar susceptibility of such distress of which the actor has knowledge. . .
>
> "It is for the court to determine whether on the evidence severe emotional distress can be found; it is for the jury to determine whether, on the evidence, it has in fact existed."

The "severe emotional distress" required to support a cause of action for intentional infliction of emotional distress was discussed by the Supreme Court of Illinois in *Knierim v. Izzo*, . . .

> ". . . not . . . every emotional upset should constitute the basis of an action. Indiscriminate allowance of actions for mental anguish would encourage neurotic overreactions to trivial hurts, and the law should aim to toughen the psyche of the citizen rather than pamper it. But a line can be drawn between the slight hurts which are the price of a complex society and the severe mental disturbances inflicted by intentional actions wholly lacking in social utility." 174 N.E.2d at 164. . . .

Thus, in *Johnson v. Woman's Hospital*, . . . the Court of Appeals of Tennessee found that severe emotional distress was established by evidence showing nervous shock sustained by a mother whose newly born deceased infant was displayed to her in a jar of formaldehyde. . . . In *Swanson v. Swanson*, . . . the court held that severe emotional distress was not shown by evidence of plaintiff's nervous shock resulting from the deliberate refusal of his brother to inform him of their mother's death, or to publish her obituary.

Assuming that a causal relationship was shown between Jones' wrongful conduct and Harris' emotional distress, we find no evidence, legally sufficient for submission to the jury, that the distress was "severe" within the contemplation of the rule requiring establishment of that element of the tort. The evidence that Jones' reprehensible conduct humiliated Harris and caused him emotional distress, which was manifested by an aggravation of Harris' pre-existing nervous condition and a worsening of his speech impediment, was vague and weak at best. It was unaccompanied by any evidentiary particulars other than that Harris, during the period of Jones' harassment, saw his physician on one occasion for his nerves, for which pills were prescribed—the same treatment which Harris had been receiving from his physician for six years prior to Jones' mistreatment. The intensity and duration of Harris' emotional distress is nowhere reflected in the evidence. All that was shown was that Harris was "shaken up" by Jones' misconduct and was so humiliated that he felt "like going into a hole and hide." While Harris' nervous condition may have been exacerbated somewhat by Jones' conduct, his family problems antedated his encounter with Jones and were not shown to be attributable to Jones' actions. Just how, or to what degree, Harris' speech impediment worsened is not revealed by the evidence. Granting the cruel and insensitive nature of Jones' conduct toward Harris, and considering the position of authority which Jones held over Harris, we conclude that the humiliation suffered was not, as a matter of law, so intense as to constitute the "severe" emotional distress required to recover for the tort of intentional infliction of emotional distress.

JUDGMENT AFFIRMED; COSTS TO BE PAID BY APPELLANT.

What Is "Extreme and Outrageous" Conduct? It is not enough for this tort that the defendant act unreasonably; the conduct must be "extreme and outrageous." Outrageous conduct is any conduct considered intolerable in any civilized society and characterized as exceeding all possible bounds of decency. For example, if the defendant tells the plaintiff that her husband has been critically injured in an accident, when in fact no such accident has occurred, the defendant is liable for any emotional distress the plaintiff suffers (Restatement (Second) of Torts Sec. 46, illustration 1).

Mere insults and petty manipulation of others are not sufficient for this tort. However, a defendant who uses his or her position abusively may be liable for any emotional distress this causes. A high school principal, for example, who browbeats a student, threatening her with public disgrace and even prison unless she confesses to immoral conduct with certain men, will probably be liable for any emotional distress suffered by the student (Restatement (Second) of Torts Sec. 46, illustration 6).

The peculiar characteristics of the plaintiff may be taken into consideration in evaluating the defendant's conduct. A defendant who takes advantage of a plaintiff of below-average intelligence may be liable for any distress she causes the plaintiff even though that same conduct would not be deemed outrageous if the plaintiff were an adult of average intelligence. An extensive discussion of the consideration of individual personalities is discussed at some length in *Harris v. Jones*.

Transferred Intent Doctrine. The doctrine of transferred intent is generally not applicable in cases of intentional infliction of mental distress. To apply this doctrine would be to open the courthouse doors to all those who suffered emotional distress as a result of viewing tortious acts being intentionally committed against others. An exception to this general prohibition occurs when the defendant directs his or her conduct against a member of the plaintiff's immediate family and is aware that the plaintiff is present at the time. For example, if a man severely beats a child's father and is aware at the time of the beating that the child is watching, he will be liable for the emotional distress suffered by that child.

The transferred intent doctrine also is not applicable if the defendant fails to commit the tort he intended to commit and succeeds only in causing the plaintiff emotional distress. A defendant who is weary of the incessant barking of his neighbor's dog and who shoots at the dog with the intent to kill it but misses will not be liable for the emotional distress suffered by the dog's owner. His intent to commit conversion, in other words, is not transferred to the emotional distress he actually causes (Restatement (Second) of Torts Sec. 47, illustration 2).

Type of Harm Suffered. A plaintiff must prove that he or she actually suffered severe emotional distress and must, at the very least, have sought medical attention. Some courts require that the plaintiff suffer some kind of physical harm although most modern courts have no such requirement. A plaintiff who suffers harm only because of a peculiar vulnerability or sensitivity will not be allowed to recover if the defendant is not aware of these vulnerabilities or sensitivities.

Higher Standard for Those in Public Service. Common carriers and public utilities are held to a higher standard of conduct than the rest of the populace and can be held liable, for example, for highly insulting language. While an insult to an ordinary person would almost never be considered actionable, an insult to a customer by an employee of a utility or carrier would be considered cause for an infliction of mental distress claim. This rule apparently stems from a concern that those who provide such services not be rude to their customers.

INTENTIONAL TORTS AGAINST PROPERTY

TRESPASS TO LAND

A person who enters or wrongfully remains on another's land has committed the tort of **trespass** (see Table 15–2). By the same token, trespass occurs if an individual fails to remove an object from another's land if she is under a duty to remove it. Historically, trespass was a strict liability tort, allowing liability even if the defendant's contact with the land was unintentional. Today, almost all courts have rejected strict liability except when the defendant is engaging in an abnormally dangerous activity, such as blasting.

Defendant's Intent. The defendant's only intent must be to make physical contact with the plaintiff's land. He or she need not intend any harm to the plaintiff's property nor be aware that any harm might even occur. A defendant is still liable for trespass even if his or her contact with the plaintiff's land is the result of a reasonable mistake. An intentional trespass is committed, for

TABLE 15.2 Intentional Torts Against Property

TRESPASS TO LAND	TRESPASS TO CHATTELS	CONVERSION
Intentionally entering or wrongfully remaining on another's land.	Intentional interference to another's use or possession of chattel (personal property).	Intentional interference with another's use or possession of chattel to the extent fairness requires that the defendant pay the full value of the chattel.

example, if a defendant walks on another's land thinking it to be his own or believing he is entitled to enter the land.

Type of Contact Required. The defendant need not enter or make contact with the land himself; an indirect invasion is sufficient. If a child fires his BB gun at the plaintiff's barn, for example, he is liable for trespass even if he never sets foot on the plaintiff's property. Furthermore, a defendant who does not intend to enter the plaintiff's land but who knows that such an entry is reasonably certain to happen is liable for trespass. If a person builds up an embankment next to his adjoining neighbor's land and during an ordinary rain the dirt washes from his land to the other's land, he is liable for trespass. Even a defendant who allows gases or particles to enter the plaintiff's property will, according to most modern courts, be liable for trespass. Similarly, most courts today hold that a trespass is committed when the defendant sets off a blast that causes concussions or vibrations on the plaintiff's property.

Since landowners, under the common law, are considered to own the airspace above their property and the surface below their property, those who violate such space can be sued for trespass. Someone who fires a gun over the plaintiff's property may be liable for trespass even though no bullet lands on the property. In this day of general aviation, however, landowners cannot be allowed to sue for any invasion of their airspace. The airspace above certain minimum flight altitudes, as established by federal statutes and administrative regulations, is considered public domain. Therefore, damages cannot be awarded for any flights occurring above these altitudes. A landowner who can show that he has suffered actual harm resulting from the flight of aircraft over his property at permissible altitudes may, however, be able to sue on the basis of a nuisance theory. This theory of recovery will be discussed in more detail in Chapter 17, "Miscellaneous Torts."

Revocation of Permission to Enter. Trespass is also committed if a defendant who has permission to enter the plaintiff's land refuses to leave when the permission is revoked. Similarly, if the defendant refuses or neglects to remove something when she is supposed to, she may be liable for trespass.

For example, a person who is given permission to park his car on the plaintiff's land for a month and who at the end of the month removes the car but forgets to remove the gas can that he put beside the car has committed a trespass.

Extent of Liability. A defendant is liable for almost all consequences of the trespass, no matter how unpredictable those consequences might be. Even if a defendant has no reason to believe that the plaintiff or others will be injured as a result of his trespass, he will be liable. In some courts he will be liable as well for any emotional distress suffered as a result of the trespass even if the plaintiff suffers no physical harm.

TRESPASS TO CHATTELS

Trespass to chattels is committed by the intentional interference of the plaintiff's use or possession of **chattel** (personal property). A defendant who damages the plaintiff's china or who deliberately hides his bicycle so as to deprive him of its use has committed trespass to chattels. The length of the deprivation is irrelevant. Recovery will be allowed even if the loss of possession is only temporary. The owner of the chattel need not be in possession of the chattel at the time the trespass occurs. Both the owner and possessor of a chattel are entitled to sue.

The only intent required for this tort is the intent to interfere in some way with the plaintiff's chattel. The defendant need not intend to cause harm to the property. Neither is the defendant's mistaken belief that the property is his own a defense.

Unlike the plaintiff who sues for trespass, however, the plaintiff who sues for trespass to chattels must prove actual harm. A child who climbs on the back of a dog and pulls on its ears has not committed trespass to chattels as long as the dog is not harmed in any way (Restatement (Second) of Torts Sec. 218 illustration 2).

CONVERSION

If the defendant's interference with the plaintiff's property is so substantial that justice demands that he or she pay the plaintiff the full value of the property, the defendant has committed the tort of **conversion.** As with trespass to land and trespass to chattels no intent to harm the plaintiff's property or possessory rights is required. An innocent mistake by the defendant is sufficient. The plaintiff must show only that the defendant intended to interfere with his or her possessory rights. As with trespass to chattels the plaintiff in a conversion action need not be the owner but can be the person in possession of the property at the time of the conversion.

Distinction Between Conversion and Trespass to Chattels. From the defendant's standpoint the distinction between trespass to chattels and conversion is an important one. A defendant who is in possession of the chattel at the time suit is brought has the right to return the goods in the case of trespass to chattels. Returning the goods is an effort to mitigate the plaintiff's damages. In the case of conversion, however, title is deemed to have transferred from the plaintiff to the defendant because of the defendant's interference. As a result the defendant is required to pay the full value of the property. In a sense, conversion may be looked on as a "forced sale" since the defendant pays for the full value of the property rather than just for the damage done.

Indicia of Conversion. Six factors are taken into consideration in determining whether a defendant's interference with the plaintiff's property rises to the level of conversion (Restatement (Second) of Torts Sec. 222A). These factors are:

- The extent and duration of the defendant's exercise of control over the property.
- The extent and duration of the resulting interference with the plaintiff's right to control.
- The defendant's intent to assert a right inconsistent with the plaintiff's right of control.
- The defendant's good faith.
- The harm done to the chattel.
- The inconvenience and expense caused to the plaintiff.

To illustrate how these factors are weighed, consider a defendant who, upon leaving a restaurant, mistakenly picks up the plaintiff's hat, believing it to be his own. When he reaches the sidewalk he discovers his mistake and promptly reenters the restaurant and returns the hat. Since no harm was done, the defendant acted in good faith, and his interference with the plaintiff's right of control was limited, no conversion would be committed (Restatement (Second) of Torts Sec. 222A, illustration 1).

Suppose that the defendant keeps that hat for three months before discovering his mistake and returning the hat. Such a lengthy confiscation of the hat would be considered a conversion because of the defendant's substantial interference with the plaintiff's use of his property. The defendant's acting in good faith would not make it any less a conversion (Restatement (Second) of Torts Sec. 222A, illustration 2).

When the defendant gets to the sidewalk, if a sudden gust of wind blows the hat into an open manhole, he will be liable for conversion since the plaintiff's property interest is completely destroyed. Again, the defendant's good faith would not change the outcome (Restatement (Second) of Torts Sec. 222A, illustration 3).

Suppose the defendant knowingly takes the plaintiff's hat but returns it to the restaurant because he sees a police officer coming toward him. He has committed a conversion because of his bad faith even though the duration of his control of the hat is relatively short (Restatement (Second) of Torts Sec. 222A, illustration 4). Although the distinction between trespass to chattels and conversion is a blurred one, these guidelines will assist you in making reasonable distinctions.

Removal and Transfer of Goods. Conversion can be committed by ways other than taking possession of the plaintiff's property. A defendant may also be liable for conversion by the removal of goods. The removal must create a relatively serious interference with the plaintiff's right to possession and control of his or her property. Suppose, for example, the defendant takes possession of a house of which the plaintiff and defendant are co-owners. If the defendant removes the plaintiff's furniture when they become engaged in a dispute about ownership, he will be liable for conversion if he refuses to make the furniture available when the plaintiff demands it back. On the other hand, if the defendant complies with the plaintiff's request, the defendant's interference will constitute trespass to chattels but not conversion. In the latter case the defendant's interference is not so severe as to constitute conversion but is considered intermeddling with the plaintiff's goods, which is the essence of trespass to chattels.

Conversion also occurs when the defendant transfers chattel to someone who is not entitled to it. A parking lot attendant, for example, who gives a car to the wrong person commits conversion if he creates an interference with the car owner's rights that are sufficiently severe. By the same token, a parking lot attendant who intentionally refuses to return the plaintiff's car to him is liable for conversion if his refusal is done in bad faith and the resultant interference with the plaintiff's right to possession is substantial.

Conversion of Intangibles. In recent years a number of courts have allowed conversion suits for intangibles, such as stock certificates, promissory notes, insurance policies, and savings bank books. Generally, however, these intangible rights must be linked to some kind of document to support a conversion action. A defendant who steals a plaintiff's customer, for example, is not liable for conversion although he or she may be liable for some other tort, such as interference with contractual relations (discussed in Chapter 17).

DEFENSES

MISTAKE

Mistake in and of itself is not a defense to an intentional tort. A defendant who intentionally enters the land of another, acting in the honest and reasonable belief that the land is her own, is still liable for the tort of trespass. Mistake is, however, an element of consideration in some of the other defenses discussed in this chapter. A defendant who reasonably but mistakenly believes he must defend himself or another can still claim self-defense even though his acts are premised on an erroneous belief. The effect of mistake will be considered throughout the remaining sections of this chapter.

CONSENT

In general, a defendant is not liable for an intentional tort if the plaintiff consents to the defendant's intentional interference (see Table 15–3). In most cases the plaintiff does not explicitly consent but the consent may be implied from the plaintiff's conduct or from any customs surrounding such conduct. Since defendants are not expected to be mind readers, the issue of whether a plaintiff has consented is determined by objective manifestations and not by the plaintiff's subjective mental state. Simply put, the question is whether a reasonable person in the defendant's shoes would have believed that the plaintiff consented to an invasion of his interest. Suppose a man announces to his date while they are standing at her front door that he is going to kiss her goodnight. If she says or does nothing to indicate her displeasure, it can be inferred from her conduct that she has given consent.

Consent or lack of consent can also be inferred from custom. One court, for example, allowed a professional football player to bring a tort action against another football player who intentionally struck him on the back of his head and neck. The court concluded that the customs of football do not encompass intentional punching or striking of others from the rear (*Hackbart v. Cincinnati Bengals, Inc.*, 601 F.2d 516 (10th Cir. 1979)).

Capacity to Consent. Consent is not a defense if the plaintiff is incapable of or incompetent to give consent. Someone who is unconscious or obviously intoxicated, for example, is incapable of giving consent. Consent will be implied, however, if emergency action is immediately necessary to save an incapacitated person's life, if no indication exists that he would have refused to give consent, and if a reasonable person would have consented under like circumstances. A patient's consent is implied, for example, when a doctor performs emergency surgery that is immediately necessary to save the patient.

Generally, if a plaintiff consents only because she is mistaken about some material fact, her consent will still be considered effective. If, however, the defendant either knows of or induces the plaintiff's mistake, the plaintiff's consent will be deemed ineffective. If the defendant, for example, induces the plaintiff to engage in sexual intercourse with him by staging what he knows to be a fake wedding ceremony, he will be liable for battery since her consent will be considered ineffective.

The question of mistaken consent most often arises in the context of medical cases in which the plaintiff alleges that the doctor did not adequately inform her about the risks involved in the proposed treatment. Generally, the courts consider consent to be ineffective if the doctor fails to disclose the consequences of a procedure that he or she knows will definitely follow from the treatment. If, however, the doctor simply fails to mention a minor risk that may or may not be a consequence of the treatment, most courts will consider the plaintiff's consent to be effective.

The courts are split in reference to the effectiveness of a plaintiff's consent to a criminal act. The majority of courts find such consent ineffective. A minority of courts and the Restatement (Second) consider the consent effective unless the crime is intended to protect a class of persons against their own poor judgment and the plaintiff is a member of that protected class. A defendant who commits statutory rape, for example, is liable regardless of the plaintiff's consent. Because the plaintiff is a member of the class the statute is intended to protect, she cannot give her consent.

Voluntariness of Consent. If a plaintiff consents only because she is under duress and that duress creates an immediate and serious threat to herself or another, her consent will be deemed involuntary. Threats of future harm and threats involving economic duress are generally not sufficient to render a plaintiff's consent involuntary. A plaintiff who agrees to have sex with the defendant because of his threat to blackmail her in the future cannot claim duress because the threat pertains to future action.

Scope of Consent. A defendant must not exceed the scope of the plaintiff's consent. A defendant who invades a plaintiff's interest in a way that sub-

TABLE 15.3

DEFENSES TO INTENTIONAL TORTS	
CONSENT	If a plaintiff who has the capacity to consent to interference with his person or property voluntarily does so, either explicitly or implictly, the defendant will not be liable for such interference.
SELF DEFENSE	A defendant is entitled (priviledged) to use reasonable force to protect himself or another against imminent harm if he reasonably believes it is necessary to do so (most courts require that any person being aided must be privileged to act in self-defense).
DEFENSE OF PROPERTY	A defendant is entitled to use reasonable (not deadly) force to protect his property against imminent harm if he reasonably believes it is necessary to do so and he verbally demands that the intruder stop first (if circumstances permit).
REGAINING POSSESSION OF CHATTELS	A property owner is entitled to use reasonable force to regain possession of chattel if the chattel was wrongfully taken and the owner is in fresh pursuit.
REENTRY ON LAND	In some states a land owner may use resonable force to reenter his land although the majority of courts deny that right to landlords attempting to evict tenants.
NECESSITY	
PUBLIC NECESSITY	A defendant may harm the property interest of another when necessary to prevent a disaster to the community or a substantial number of people. No reimbursement of the plaintiff is required.
PRIVATE NECESSITY	A defendant may harm the property interest of another if necessary to protect his own interests or those of a few private citizens because no less damaging way to prevent the harm exists. Reimbursement of the plaintiff is required if there is substantial harm to the plaintiff's property.

stantially deviates from that consented to will be liable for his or her act. Suppose a plaintiff consents to gallbladder surgery but the surgeon decides to remove her appendix as well. Since the plaintiff's consent did not extend to her appendix, the doctor will be liable for battery. However, if the condition of the patient's appendix justified an emergency removal, the patient will be deemed to have implicitly consented to that operation. The issue of consent in the area of medical practice is largely academic today since most hospitals require patients to fill out extremely general consent forms, which, unless unduly vague, protect hospitals from liability.

SELF-DEFENSE

In the area of self-defense two questions are generally raised. Was the defendant privileged to use force to defend herself and was the degree of force that she used reasonable? A person may defend herself against any threatened harmful or offensive bodily contact as well as any threatened confinement. Whether the threat posed is intentional or negligent does not matter. The defendant need not even actually be harmed to invoke this defense.

Defendant's Belief. The defendant must reasonably believe that a threat exists, even if he or she is wrong. This result is probably based on the idea that "self-preservation is the first law of nature." Suppose a police officer apprehends a suspect known to her to be armed and dangerous. If the suspect reaches into his pocket for what the officer mistakenly believes to be a gun and the officer shoots him, the officer will be deemed to have acted in self-defense so long as her mistaken belief is a reasonable one. If the officer were exceptionally timid or paranoid, unreasonably believed that the suspect was about to shoot her, and no objective facts supported her perception, she could not claim self-defense.

What Constitutes Reasonable Force? A defendant may use only that force that is reasonably necessary to protect herself against a threatened harm. She cannot use force to defend herself against words alone unless those words are accompanied by some type of hostile act. Nor can she use force to protect herself against future harm. Any threat of harm must appear to the defendant to be imminent. Furthermore, she must reasonably believe that she has no reasonable alternative to the use of force to protect herself from the impending danger.

For obvious reasons a defendant may not claim self-defense if he uses force against someone who is helpless. If A takes a swing at B and in the process slips and falls flat on his back, rendering him incapacitated, B cannot take that opportunity to avenge himself. Nor can self-defense be used to justify any retaliation for a previously committed tort. If a small child throws a snowball at the defendant, hitting her in the eye, the defendant is not justified in using force to punish the child (Restatement (Second) of Torts Sec. 63, illustration 4). In summary, the use of force is not considered reasonable if it is used against someone who is helpless, in response to a threat of future harm, in retaliation for a previously committed tort, or in response to words unaccompanied by a hostile act.

How much force a defendant may use depends on the degree of force necessary to prevent the impending harm. Suppose A threatens B with clenched fists. B cannot claim self-defense if she responds using a knife because her response exceeds the amount of force necessary to protect herself. Furthermore, a defendant may not use deadly force (defined as that force likely to cause death or serious bodily injury) unless she is in danger of death or serious bodily harm herself (Restatement (Second) of Torts Sec. 65–66). Consequently, someone threatened with rape or some other type of serious bodily harm may defend herself using deadly force whereas someone threatened with trespass to chattels may not. This rule is based on an objective standard in that the conduct of the defendant is compared to that of a reasonable person under similar circumstances.

Defense of Home. A common question that arises in the area of self-defense pertains to the use of force when someone invades another's home. The oft-quoted advice that if someone shoots a person who is outside her house, she must drag the body inside in order to claim self-defense, is erroneous. All one need show is that she reasonably believed she was in imminent danger of death or serious bodily harm and that no lesser degree of force was sufficient to prevent the harm.

The courts are split, however, on whether a defendant has a duty to retreat. Some courts, giving homage to individual honor and dignity, allow a defendant to use deadly force even if she can safely retreat. Other courts, attaching more importance to the sanctity of human life, require a defendant to retreat if she can do so safely. Even the latter courts, however, do not require someone who is attacked in her own home to retreat. This result is apparently based on the precept that "one's home is one's castle."

Prevention of Felonies. According to the Restatement, deadly force may also be used to prevent certain types of felonies, such as robbery, kidnapping, and rape. The defendant must believe that the felony cannot otherwise be prevented and the type of harm threatened must involve death or serious bodily injury (Restatement (Second) of Torts Sec. 143). Notice that the defendant in this case is entitled to use force even though he or she is not personally endangered.

Defense of Others. Reasonable force may be used to protect others, including complete strangers. To claim the privilege of defense of another, the defendant must reasonably believe that the circumstances would support a claim of self-defense and that his or her intervention is immediately necessary for the protection of the other person.

Problems arise when the defendant intervenes on behalf of another, mistakenly believing assistance is necessary. Suppose A sees B being tackled and injured by C and he intervenes on B's behalf. If it turns out that C is an undercover police officer attempting to arrest B, should A be able to claim the privilege of defense of another as long as he reasonably believes that B is in imminent danger? Most courts reason that the intervenor (A) "steps into the shoes of the person he has sought to champion (B)." If it turns out that the person being rescued is not privileged to act in self-defense, the intervenor is precluded from claiming such a privilege. A minority of courts, including the Restatement (Second), however, allow the intervenor to claim the privilege as long as he reasonably believes the person he is aiding would have been privileged to use self-defense.

DEFENSE OF PROPERTY

The same rationale used in defense of persons applies to defense of property. A property owner may use only that degree of force that is reasonably necessary to protect the property. Furthermore, the owner must verbally insist that an intruder stop before he or she is justified in using force. An exception to this general rule is allowed if the defendant reasonably perceives that the request to stop will be useless or that the harm will occur immediately (Restatement (Second) of Torts Sec. 77 (c)). Beyond this an owner may not use deadly force to protect property unless she believes such force is immediately necessary to prevent death or serious bodily harm to herself or another or to prevent certain types of felonies.

Mechanical Devices. Property owners frustrated by frequent burglaries that the local police appear impotent to prevent sometimes turn to mechanical devices for protection. These devices can range from strings of barbed wire to spring guns, which are mechanically rigged guns designed to go off automatically when someone enters the premises. As a general rule, a property owner is entitled to use such a device only if she could use a similar degree of force if she herself were present when the intruder entered. Since such devices are usually considered deadly force, they may be used only to prevent death or serious bodily harm or the commission of certain felonies. A homeowner will be liable, therefore, if a trespasser is seriously injured by an electric fence erected by the homeowner. Since the owner would not be justified in using deadly force against the trespasser if she confronted the trespasser in person, she would not be justified in using a mechanical device that constituted deadly force.

The classic case of *Katko v. Briney*, 183 N.W.2d 657 (Iowa 1971), aptly illustrates the principle regarding the use of mechanical devices. In *Katko* the defendants owned an unoccupied, boarded-up farmhouse that had been broken into many times. To prevent further burglaries the defendants constructed a spring gun that was designed to discharge if a person entered the bedroom. The plaintiff, who broke into the house in an effort to steal bottles and jars that he believed to be antique, was severely injured when the gun went off. The court held that a property owner may not use deadly force against a trespasser unless that trespasser is endangering human life or committing some violent felony.

Media reports of this case reflected that the entry was into the Brineys' home rather than into an abandoned farmhouse. As a result, public outcry regarding the decision resulted in the introduction of "Briney Bills" in several state legislatures. These bills legalized the use of any means necessary to protect one's person, family, or property from intrusion.

If an owner intends to use some nondeadly mechanical device, such as barbed wire, he must post some type of warning that will put others on notice that the device is present. Even a warning will not suffice, however, in the case of a mechanical device that constitutes the use of deadly force. No warning of the spring gun, for example, would have relieved the defendants in *Katko* of liability.

[You may find it interesting to know that the Brineys were forced to sell eighty acres of their 120-acre farm in order to satisfy the judgment in this case. Since no bids above the minimum price of $10,000.00 were made, three neighbors purchased the land for a dollar more, expecting to hold it for the Brineys until they won their appeal. After the Brineys lost their appeal, the neighbors leased the land back to them for enough money to pay their taxes and the interest on the money they had borrowed. Years later the neighbors decided to sell the property and one of them bought it for $16,000.00 and sold it to his son for $16,500.00. Briney and Katko then joined together and jointly sued the neighbors. Just before the case came to trial it was settled for a large enough sum that the Brineys were able to pay the remainder of their judgment to Katko.]

REGAINING POSSESSION OF CHATTELS

Under limited circumstances a property owner may use force to regain possession of chattels taken from her by someone else. Since the owner becomes an aggressor by her use of force, she is not given the same latitude by the courts as one who is taking a less aggressive stance in defending her possession of chattels.

Reasonable Force. To claim this defense, the owner must first show she used reasonable force in securing the chattels. Deadly force is never allowable unless justified under the doctrine of self-defense.

Property Wrongfully Taken. Second, the property must have been wrongfully taken. If the owner willingly gives up possession and is later entitled to repossession of the property, she cannot use force to regain it. A seller who attempts to repossess a stereo unit sold to a consumer who has missed several payments cannot break into the consumer's house to regain possession. If, however, the consumer uses fraud to gain possession and the seller promptly discovers the fraud, she may use reasonable force to recover possession (Restatement (Second) of Torts Sec. 101(1)(a) and 106). No greater force than that required can be used and deadly force is impermissible unless necessary for the defendant to protect herself against ensuing violence.

Fresh Pursuit. Third, the property owner must be in "fresh pursuit." Therefore, if the owner delays for a substantial period of time before attempting to get her property back, she may no longer use reasonable force to secure possession. Instead she must turn to the courts for redress. Although the courts have never clearly defined the meaning of "fresh pursuit," it appears that prompt and persistent efforts must be made to reclaim the property. Owners are privileged to use force to recapture property only because of the concern for the delay created by the cumbersome, time-consuming legal process. If, however, they fail to make timely efforts to regain possession, they will be relegated to the legal process.

Mistake. Any mistakes on the part of the owner will cause her to lose the privilege. If, for example, she mistakenly (albeit reasonably) believes that someone is in possession of her goods, she will not be justified in using force to retake the goods. Similarly, if she reasonably but mistakenly believes that force is necessary to reclaim the goods, she will lose the privilege. The owner is expected to bear the consequences of any mistakes.

Detention of Shoplifters. The issue of recapture of goods most frequently occurs in the context of merchants detaining suspected shoplifters. As discussed earlier in this chapter, many courts have granted merchants the privilege of temporarily detaining any person they reasonably suspect of shoplifting. As you will recall, the detention must be relatively short in duration and the merchant or its agent must not attempt to coerce a payment or a confession from the suspect, nor may the merchant or its agent purport to arrest the suspect.

REENTRY ON LAND

The issue of reentry on land typically occurs in the case of a landlord who attempts to forcibly evict a tenant who overstays his lease (referred to as a holdover tenant). The majority of American courts do not permit the use of force by landlords. Landlords, it is felt, should be restricted to the legal process to resolve these disputes since the law typically provides procedures allowing for expeditious resolutions. In short, landlords are discouraged from taking the law into their own hands. A landlord may, however, enter the land if she does so without force. Furthermore, if a provision in the lease allows for reentry through the use of force, some courts will uphold a forcible entry as long as only reasonable force is used.

NECESSITY

In the privileges discussed thus far, the defendant has prevailed in her cause of action because of some wrongdoing on the plaintiff's part. In some circumstances, however, the defendant is privileged not because the plaintiff has done anything wrong but because of unusual circumstances that justify the defendant's actions. The privilege of **necessity** justifies the defendant's harming of the plaintiff's property in emergencies. For example, a person who trespasses on another's land in an attempt to avoid a criminal attack can claim the privilege of necessity.

Distinction Between Public and Private Necessity. Cases involving necessity fall into two categories: public necessity and private necessity. The conduct of a defendant protecting only her own interests or those of a few private citizens falls into the realm of *private necessity.* On the other hand, if the class of persons being protected is the public as a whole or a substantial number of persons, the privilege is referred to as *public necessity.* The only reason for distinguishing between these two kinds of necessities is that the defendant does not have to pay for damages caused in cases of public necessity but is required to do so in cases involving private necessity.

Public Necessity. The privilege of public necessity arises when interference with the land or chattels of another is required to avert a disaster to the community. In one case, for example, the defendant sprayed fire-retardant chemicals on the plaintiff's land while fighting a forest fire that threatened the entire county. When the plaintiff sued for the damage incurred by his trees, the court permitted the defendant to raise the privilege of necessity (*Stocking v. Johnson Flying Service,* 387 P.2d 312 (1963)). The defendant who successfully claims the privilege of public necessity will not be required to reimburse the plaintiff for the damages he suffers. Although the common law does not require the community as a whole to compensate the victim, several states have enacted statutes that provide for such compensation.

Private Necessity. A person may claim the privilege for private necessity when she damages the property of another to prevent injury to herself or her property. The privilege also extends to the protection of a third person or the property of that person. Furthermore, the privilege requires that no less damaging way of preventing the harm exist. In contrast to cases of public necessity, private necessity applies even when the danger is not severe. A driver, for example, can claim the privilege of private necessity if she is forced to trespass on private land because the public roadway on which she is traveling is obstructed and the only conceivable path of avoidance is through the adjoining land of a private owner.

Damages. In determining whether a privilege exists, the harm to the plaintiff's property must be weighed against the severity and likelihood of the danger the defendant is seeking to avoid (Restatement (Second) of Torts Sec. 263, comment d). If the defendant causes no substantial harm to the plaintiff's property, the privilege of private necessity is a complete defense. If, however, the defendant causes actual damage to the plaintiff's property, the privilege will be limited and the defendant will be required to pay for the damages caused. Suppose a man is lost in the forest and comes upon someone's cabin. If he enters the cabin and takes food because he is starving, he will not be liable for the trespass. He will, however, be required to compensate the owner of the cabin for the food he takes.

One of the benefits of invoking the privilege of private necessity is that the person whose property has been harmed has no right to use reasonable force to prevent the exercise of the privilege. Furthermore, one who resorts to such retaliatory force will be liable for any damages she causes (Restatement (Second) of Torts Sec. 263, comment b).

SUMMARY

An intentional tort requires that the tortfeasor intend or have a desire to bring about a particular consequence. The fact that the defendant wishes no harm to the plaintiff has no bearing on whether he acted intentionally. If he knows with substantial certainty that a result will occur, he will be liable for an intentional tort. Under the transferred intent doctrine, a tortfeasor's intent with respect to one person may be transferred to the person who is actually injured.

The intentional infliction of a harmful or offensive contact upon a person's body or anything attached to or identified with the body is referred to as battery. The plaintiff need not suffer actual pain or bodily injury nor even be aware of the contact at the time it occurs.

If a tortfeasor intentionally causes an apprehension of a harmful or offensive contact, he commits assault. Assault requires an intent either to commit a battery or to frighten the plaintiff. The victim of assault, unlike the victim of battery, must be aware of the threatened contact. The plaintiff need not actually fear that he will be harmed but he must believe that the defendant has the present ability to carry out the threatened contact.

The tortfeasor who intentionally confines another commits the tort of false imprisonment. The plaintiff must be aware of his confinement at the time it occurs but is not required to subject himself to any risk of harm in order to extricate himself from his confinement. As with assault and battery, the doctrine of transferred intent is applicable and threats of harm must be imminent.

The tort of infliction of mental distress can be committed either intentionally or recklessly, but in either case the defendant's conduct must be "extreme and outrageous." The peculiar characteristics of the plaintiff may be taken into consideration in evaluating the defendant's conduct. Generally, the doctrine of transferred intent is not applicable although some exceptions exist. A plaintiff must prove she actually suffered severe emotional distress and in some courts must prove she experienced some kind of actual physical harm.

A person who enters or wrongfully remains on another's land commits the tort of trespass. The defendant's only intent must be to make physical contact with the plaintiff's land. He need not intend any harm to the plaintiff's property nor be aware that any harm might occur. An indirect invasion of the land is sufficient as is an invasion of the airspace above or the surface below the plaintiff's property. A defendant who refuses to leave the plaintiff's land when his permission has been terminated also commits trespass.

Intentional interference with the plaintiff's use or possession of chattels constitutes trespass to chattels. As with trespass, the only intent required is the intent to interfere. The defendant need not intend to cause harm to the property. As with trespass, the mistaken belief that the property is his own is not a defense. In contrast with trespass, the plaintiff is required to prove actual harm.

If the defendant's interference with the plaintiff's property is so substantial that the defendant must compensate the plaintiff for the full value of the property, the defendant has committed the tort of conversion. The defendant need not desire to harm the plaintiff's property. With trespass to chattels, the defendant has a right to return the goods to mitigate the plaintiff's damages, but the defendant in a conversion action is required to pay the full value of the property.

One of the defenses that can be raised in response to an intentional tort is consent. If a plaintiff implicitly or explicitly consents to the defendant's intentional interference, the defendant is not liable for his conduct. Consent is determined by objective manifestations of the plaintiff but can be inferred from custom. The plaintiff must be capable of giving consent and must do so voluntarily. If a defendant exceeds the scope of the plaintiff's consent, he will be liable for his conduct.

A defendant may use reasonable force to protect himself against threatened harmful or offensive bodily contact or threatened confinement. He cannot raise the defense in response to threats of future harm or when he is threat-

PRACTICE POINTERS

A trial notebook contains the documents and information essential for a trial attorney to litigate a case. If organized properly it allows for the prompt retrieval of information and the orderly presentation of evidence at trial. A well-prepared trial notebook helps an attorney impress the trier of fact with his or her organizational skills.

A trial notebook can be prepared using one or more three-ring binders, which can be subdivided into clearly identifiable sections using colored tab dividers. The content of a trial notebook is subject to some variation but the following sections are representative of the types of materials generally found:

1. Pleadings
2. Statement of facts
3. *Voir dire*
4. Opening statements
5. Closing arguments
6. Witnesses
7. Exhibits
8. Jury instructions
9. Medical and other expenses
10. Motions

Let us consider each of these components individually. Pleadings, although rarely needed during a trial, should be included so they are available for reference if necessary. A statement of facts should also be available and should include such information as the date and time of injury, a diagram of the accident (if applicable), the type of injuries sustained, the names of the defendants and so on. With all of the pertinent facts condensed to a single sheet of paper, the attorney can then refer to one source during the trial to refresh her memory. The *voir dire* section should contain key questions that the attorney wishes to ask along with authority that supports the asking of such questions.

The section for opening statements should contain an outline of the key points the attorney anticipates covering in her opening statements. Similarly, the closing arguments section should sketch out the main ideas the attorney plans to cover during her closing arguments. Notes of opposing counsel's opening statements should also be included in this section to ensure that proper rebuttal is made.

Information pertaining to all possible witnesses should be included in the notebook. A list of witnesses should be compiled, indicating, among other things, whether a witness is to testify for the plaintiff or the defendant, whether his deposition is to be read into evidence, if the witness lives out of town, and if so, what the name, address, and telephone number of his hotel are. Next to each witness' name an identifying statement that quickly clues the attorney in as to the nature of

Continued on next page

PRACTICE POINTERS—Continued

the witness' testimony should be added. A brief summary of the anticipated testimony of each witness can also be included along with key questions that the attorney intends to ask. You may want to put each witness' testimony in a separate section or, if necessary, a separate binder. In this section you may also include such things as deposition digests, interview statements, police reports, answers to interrogatories, or anything else relating to the testimony of witnesses.

A list of all exhibits expected to be offered as evidence should be prepared, including the number assigned each exhibit, along with a brief description of the exhibit. Provision should be made to insert notations when the exhibit is received into evidence. When permitted by the court, exhibits should be marked prior to trial. When that is done, copies of the list of exhibits should be provided prior to trial to opposing counsel, the judge, and the court reporter. If necessary, an exhibit envelope should be included in this section of the trial notebook so that smaller exhibits, such as money, can be readily produced.

The section on jury instructions should include the requested instructions as well as those that are actually given. In this way the attorney will have a complete record to use to prepare any appeal.

A list of all expenses, including doctors' bills, drug expenses, hospital expenses, property damages, loss of earnings, and other financial losses should be included in the exhibit section. Copies of each bill should also be available.

Access to all motions, including motions for summary judgment, motions for a new trial, motions *in limine* and so on, should be provided in a good trial notebook. Space to make notations indicating the court's ruling on each of these motions should also be included. Deposition digests or outlines should ideally be available for ready reference. The material should be indexed so that it can be easily accessed for impeachment purposes.

The content, style of organization, and time of preparation of a trial notebook will vary from firm to firm. The common denominator of any good trial notebook, however, is its ability to allow the attorney to access information quickly and comfortably while under the stress of trial.

ened with words alone, unless those words are accompanied by some kind of hostile act. Deadly force may be used only in response to a threat of death or serious bodily injury. A defendant who uses force to protect against the invasion of his home must show that he was in threat of death or serious bodily harm and that no lesser degree of force was sufficient. The courts are split on whether a defendant has a duty to retreat before resorting to force.

If the circumstances would support a claim of self-defense and the defendant's intervention is immediately necessary for the protection of a third person, a defendant may use reasonable force to protect another. If the person being rescued would not be privileged to act in self-defense, the defendant, according to most courts, will be precluded from claiming the privilege. A minority of courts, however, allow the privilege as long as the defendant reasonably believes that the person he is aiding would have been privileged to use self-defense.

A property owner may use only that degree of force that is reasonably necessary to protect his property. He must first verbally insist that an intruder stop unless it reasonably appears that the request to stop will be useless or that the harm will occur immediately. Mechanical devices that are used to protect property are generally considered deadly force and may be used only to prevent death, serious bodily harm, or the commission of certain felonies.

In some circumstances a property owner may use force to regain possession of chattels. Reasonable force is required and deadly force is never allowed unless justified under the doctrine of self-defense. Furthermore, the property must have been wrongfully taken and the property owner must be in "fresh pursuit." If the property owner is mistaken in any way, he will lose the privilege even if his mistake is a reasonable one.

The use of force to gain reentry on land is usually not allowed by the courts. Landlords, who most frequently argue that force is necessary to evict a tenant, are generally restricted to the legal process to resolve their disputes.

A defendant who is justified in harming the plaintiff's property because of an emergency may claim the privilege of either public necessity or private necessity. Interference required to avert a disaster to the community is classified as a public necessity; interference necessary to prevent injury to a few private citizens is classified as a private necessity. In a case of public necessity the defendant is not required to reimburse the plaintiff for the damages he suffers.

TORT TEASERS

1. What intentional torts were committed in the hypothetical scenario given at the beginning of this chapter? What defenses could have been raised by each of the actors who committed a tort?

2. In December, 1941, the United States Army destroyed vital parts of the plant of an oil company in Manila to prevent it from falling into the hands of the advancing Japanese Army. Was this conduct privileged? *U.S. v. Caltex, Inc.*, 344 U.S. 149 (1952).

3. An eighty-six-year-old member of a Catholic order experiences cardiac arrest subsequent to a hernia operation. Previously he had expressed a desire not to have his life artificially prolonged by use of a respirator if he were ever to become permanently unconscious. Should his request be granted? *Matter of Storar*, 420 N.E.2d 64 (1981).

4. Defendant sees Plaintiff break into a vending machine. He yells at Plaintiff to stop, drop his weapon, and wait for the police but Plaintiff and his companions continue to run. The thieves are carrying a money box, a tire tool, and a lug wrench. When they are seventy to seventy-five yards away defendant fires three shots, one of which strikes Plaintiff in the back. Should Defendant be held liable? *Bray v. Isbell,* 458 So.2d 594 (La. App. 1984), *cert. denied,* 462 So.2d 210 (La. 1985).

5. Plaintiff is injured by Defendant's vicious dog when he trespasses on Defendant's land. Defendant has posted a sign warning outsiders of the presence of the dog. Should Defendant be held liable? *Hood v. Waldrum,* 434 S.W.2d 94 (1968).

6. Plaintiff takes a can of hair spray to the checkout counter but after she stands in line for several minutes decides to leave and puts the hair spray on a counter inside the store. After she leaves the store she is accosted by a security guard, who identifies herself by displaying a badge. When asked by the guard where the hair spray is, Plaintiff asks, "What hair spray?" At this point the security guard flips open Plaintiff's jacket and says, "The hair spray you took out of the store." At the security guard's request, Plaintiff returns to the store and shows the guard where she put the can of hair spray. The security guard then just walks away. Is Defendant store entitled to detain Plaintiff to investigate the alleged shoplifting? Would Defendant store have been justified in using force had Plaintiff actually taken the can of hair spray out of the store? *Moore v. Pay'N Save Corp.,* 581 P.2d 159 (Wash. App. 1973).

7. What should the defendants in each of the following cases be found liable for?

a. Auctioneer sells stolen goods. *Judkins v. Sadler-MacNeil,* 376 P.2d 837 (Wash. 1962).

b. Plaintiff and Defendant are involved in an action to quiet title. Before any judgment is rendered Defendant forcibly breaks into the premises, which are occupied by Plaintiff, posts "No Trespassing" signs, and changes the locks. Defendant then removes Plaintiff's personal property and puts it in storage. Defendant informs Plaintiff that he can secure possession of his personal property by contacting his attorney but Plaintiff makes no response. Defendant never uses the goods during the four months they are kept in storage. *Zaslow V. Kroenert,* 176 P.2d 1 (Cal. 1946).

c. Plaintiff owns a tract of land on a hill. Defendant discovers the entrance to a cave on the land adjoining his own. The cave extends a considerable distance under Plaintiff's land. Defendant develops the cave, advertises it, and conducts tours through it. *Edwards v. Sims,* 24 S.W.2d 619 (1929).

d. A man touches a woman in an indecent manner. *Skousen v. Nidy,* 367 P.2d 248 (Ariz. 1961).

e. Defendant threatens plaintiff with an unloaded gun. *Allen v. Hannaford,* 244 P.700 (Wash. 1926).

f. Plaintiff is an eccentric old woman who believes that a pot of gold is buried in her back yard and is constantly digging for it. Defendants deliberately bury a pot filled with rocks and dirt in a place where they know

she will dig it up. When she does so they escort her in a mock triumphal procession to City Hall where she opens the pot under circumstances causing her extreme public humiliation. *Nickerson v. Hodges*, 84 So.37 (La. 1920).
g. Defendant, a police officer, observes Plaintiff's dog running loose in violation of the city's "dog leash" ordinance. When Defendant demands that Plaintiff produce her driver's license or go to jail, she refuses to do so although she does volunteer her name and address. Defendant arrests her, charging her with a violation of the dog leash ordinance. *Enright v. Groves*, 567 P.2d 851 (Colo. App. 1977).

KEY TERMS

■ **Assault**
Intentional causing of an apprehension of harmful or offensive contact.

■ **Battery**
Intentional infliction of a harmful or offensive contact upon a person.

■ **Chattels**
Personal property.

■ **Conversion**
Substantial interference with another's property to the extent that justice demands payment for the full value of the property.

■ **False imprisonment**
Intentional confinement of another.

■ **Intentional tort**
Tort in which the tortfeasor intends to bring about a particular consequence or knows with substantial certainty that a result will occur.

■ **Necessity**
Privilege that justifies the defendant's harming of the plaintiff's property in an effort to prevent great harm to the defendant or others.

■ **Transferred intent**
Intent with respect to one person (or tort) is transferred to another person (or tort).

■ **Trespass to chattels**
Intentional interference with another's use or possession of chattels.

■ **Trespass to land**
Intentionally entering or wrongfully remaining on another's land.

16 MISREPRESENTATION

CHAPTER OBJECTIVES

In this chapter you will learn to:

- Distinguish among intentional, negligent, and innocent misrepresentation and identify the elements of each.
- Identify those situations in which one is entitled to rely on the representations of another.
- Identify the two ways in which a plaintiff's damages can be measured.

A few months after you buy a home in which you have invested your life savings, you start experiencing strange phenomena—dishes that suddenly go hurtling across the room, pictures that for no explicable reason fall down, and so on. After doing some research you discover that the son of the previous owner was violently murdered in the house a year before your purchase and that events similar to those you are now experiencing also plagued the sellers. The sellers told you they were moving only because of job opportunities in another state and that, given a choice, they would have remained in the home indefinitely. In fact, they were terrified and would have gone to any lengths to get out of the house.

Can you hold them liable for misrepresentation? What if these statements had been made by their real estate agent and not the sellers personally? Would the outcome be any different if they had never experienced these paranormal events themselves but had heard stories of "weird" things happening from their renters and had forgotten to tell you about what they had heard? Did the sellers have an obligation to disclose their son's murder in the house even if no related question was ever posed to them? With these questions in mind, let us consider the tort of misrepresentation.

DEVELOPMENT OF MISREPRESENTATION AND ITS RELATIONSHIP TO OTHER TORTS

Misrepresentation (which is basically the making of false representations) can be found interwoven among other types of tortious behavior. A conversion, for example, can be committed by making false representations. A battery can be committed by a person who uses deceit to induce the plaintiff to consent to physical contact. A claim for intentional infliction of emotional distress may arise out of a maliciously spread lie.

Misrepresentation as a distinct cause of action arose out of the common law action of **deceit.** Typically, in a case of deceit the plaintiff lost money or property as a result of reliance on the defendant's representations. Today, however, the law of misrepresentation is broader than an action for deceit. Although deceit was usually based on an intent to deceive, misrepresentation can be based on intentional deception, negligent deception, or innocent deception (strict liability).

INTENTIONAL MISREPRESENTATION

Intentional misrepresentation corresponds to what was known as "deceit" or "fraud" under the common law. The elements of intentional misrepresentation are as follows (see Table 16–1):

■ The defendant misrepresents something with the intent of inducing the plaintiff's reliance on that misrepresentation.

■ The defendant knows that the representation is false or acts with reckless indifference to the truth.

■ The plaintiff justifiably relies on the defendant's misrepresentation.

■ The plaintiff suffers damages stemming from this reliance.

WHAT CONSTITUTES A MISREPRESENTATION?

A defendant commits misrepresentation by affirmatively making a false statement. Alternatively, he or she can intentionally conceal a fact from the plaintiff. A seller of a house, for example, who deliberately paints the ceiling to conceal from the plaintiff-buyer the fact that the roof is leaking commits misrepresentation. Actions alone may constitute misrepresentation. The seller of a car

TABLE 16.1

ELEMENTS OF INTENTIONAL MISREPRESENTATION
•Defendant makes a misrepresentation with intent of inducing plaintiff's reliance. •Defendant knows the misrepresentation is false or acts with reckless indifference to truth or falsity of representation. •Plaintiff justifiably relies on misrepresentation. •Plaintiff suffers damages as a result of reliance.

who turns back the odometer misrepresents the mileage on that car even though he says nothing (Restatement (Second) of Torts Sec. 525, illustration 1).

Under the common law mere failure to disclose a material fact (as opposed to deliberate concealment) was not considered a misrepresentation. In the modern view, however, nondisclosure may be considered concealment under certain circumstances, especially when the defect is **latent** (not visible to the buyer). A duty to disclose, for example, is frequently set forth in the so-called "termite" cases, in which the homeowner fails to tell the purchaser that the house has been infested with termites. In *Universal Investment Co. v. Sahara Motor Inn, Inc.*, the court discusses an obligation to disclose when dealing with latent rather than **patent** defects. The court uses the term "fraud" rather than "intentional misrepresentation" but this difference in terms does not affect the analysis.

UNIVERSAL INVESTMENT COMPANY, a corporation, as trustee, Plaintiff/Appellant, v. SAHARA MOTOR INN, INC., a corporation, Defendant/Appellee. No. 2 CA-CIV 3516. Court of Appeals of Arizona, Division 2. Sept. 17, 1980. Rehearing Denied Oct. 22, 1980. Review Denied Nov. 13, 1980. 619 P.2d 485 (1980)

OPINION

RICHMOND, Judge.

This is a suit on a promissory note received by appellant Universal Investment Co. as part payment in the sale of a Tucson motel. Sahara Motor Inn, Inc., the buyer, in its answer raised the affirmative defense of fraud and filed a counterclaim for rescission and damages based on fraudulent concealment. The trial court entered judgment that neither party take anything. Only the seller has appealed.

The determinative question is whether the seller had a duty to disclose the fact that a defect in the electrical system violated city code provisions, even though the buyer knew or should have known of the defect and the sales contract contained an "as it" clause. We reverse.

On March 25, 1978, the buyer agreed to purchase the Thunderbird Motel in Tucson for $250,000. The contract states that the property "will be accepted in an 'as is' condition, except the pool will be cleaned and painted." In part payment the buyer executed a promissory note for $57,289.03 with interest at eight percent per annum from March 29, 1978, which was secured by deed of trust. Buyer assumed seller's obligations under a pre-existing contract of sale, which also was secured by deed of trust.

Buyer inspected and approved the premises. After closing, the buyer was notified by the City of Tucson that the motel's electrical system was in violation of the city code. Electrical service was discontinued and the motel closed on July 10, 1978, because the buyer failed to repair the system.

Buyer made none of the agreed payments on the promissory note or the assumed contract. Under the acceleration clause the seller sued for the entire amount.

In its judgment the trial court found and concluded:

1. The Plaintiff [seller] knew or should have known of the electrical code violations;
2. That these electrical code violations were material;
3. That the Plaintiff failed to convey the information respecting the electrical violations to Defendant;
4. That Defendant was justified in not making the payments on the note;
5. That Defendant knew, or should have known, of the defects on the said premises;
6. That Defendant was anxious for a quick deal.

Other than failure to mitigate damages, the only defense asserted against the seller's claim was fraudulent concealment. The court's findings do not support that defense, nor is there evidence in the record to support it.

Fraud will not be presumed and must be proved by clear and convincing evidence. . . . Concealing a material fact when there is a duty to disclose may be actionable fraud. . . . The evidence supports findings that the seller failed to disclose violations of the city code in the electrical system which were known to it prior to closing and that violations were material under the circumstances, but the questions remain whether the seller had a legal duty to disclose the violations to the buyer or the buyer had a right to rely on the seller's silence.

Though generally no duty to disclose exists between a buyer and seller, certain circumstances may give rise to such a duty. If there is a confidential relationship between the parties and one reasonably relies on the trustworthiness of the other, the duty arises. . . . This was an arm's length transaction. Consequently, no special relationship existed that would give rise to a duty to disclose. . . .

Inquiry by the buyer about the condition of the electrical system would have imposed a duty on the seller to disclose all it knew. Here, however, the buyer made no inquiry and made its own inspection of the system. The evidence supports the court's finding that the buyer knew or should have known of the defects. The "as is" clause in the contract itself implies that the property was in some way defective and the buyer could not justifiably rely on the seller's silence as a representation that the electrical system met code specifications.

Buyer cites California cases as authority requiring disclosure of code violations to a buyer in a land sale. . . . In each of those cases, however, the courts found a duty to disclose only when the defect or code violation was latent and not discoverable through diligent investigation by the buyer. In this case the defects were patent and the court found the buyer knew or should have known of them. There was no evidence to establish the buyer could not have discovered the extent of the defects with reasonable investigation, and there was evidence that it could have discovered the code violations through such investigation once it learned of the defects. Under those circumstances it had no right to rely on the seller's silence.

The judgment is reversed and the case remanded with instructions to enter judgment for Universal Investment Co. . . .

Similarly, liability may be imposed if a defendant makes a "half-truth," a statement that although literally true tends to be misleading. A statement such as "We have no termites in this house" is a half-truth if the termites have been long-term residents up until a month before the statement was made. If a **fiduciary relationship** exists between the parties, such as that between parent and child or attorney and client, the law imposes a more demanding obligation to disclose than if a transaction occurs at *"arm's length"* (i.e., no special relationship exists between the parties). For example, a businessman selling property to his business partner (assuming they have a fiduciary relationship for purposes of the transaction involved) has an obligation to disclose information that he would not be required to disclose if he were conducting an arm's length transaction with a stranger.

The courts are more likely to find misrepresentation if a nondisclosed fact is essential to the transaction. If a seller of land fails to disclose to a buyer that nothing can be grown on the land even though she is aware that the buyer intends to use the land to grow crops, she is likely to be found liable for misrepresentation. Even if a plaintiff is unable to recover damages for nondisclosure, he can get rescission (which results in the canceling of the contract) if the nondisclosed fact is a material one.

TO WHOM MUST THE MISREPRESENTATION BE MADE?

Under the traditional common law, a defendant was liable only to those persons whom he or she intended to influence by the misrepresentation. A debtor, for example, who misrepresented his credit record to a creditor and then failed to make payments was not liable to a party who bought the debtor's note from the creditor. The requirement has been relaxed in recent times. Presently a plaintiff can recover if he or she is a member of a class whom the defendant could reasonably expect to learn of and rely on the misrepresentation.

Additionally, the plaintiff's reliance must occur in the "type of transaction" the defendant could reasonably expect the plaintiff to engage in as a result of the reliance (Restatement (Second) of Torts Secs. 531 and 533). Suppose an architect supplies erroneous specifications to a builder, who in turn subcontracts the electrical work. If the subcontractor suffers pecuniary (monetary) damages because of the faulty specifications, the subcontractor will be allowed to recover from the architect. Recovery will be allowed even if the architect is unaware of the identity of the subcontractor when he gives the specifications to the builder (Restatement (Second) of Torts Sec. 531, illustration 5).

Another exception to the rule requiring intent to induce reliance occurs in the context of commercial documents. Those who incorporate misstatements into commercial documents are liable to persons who suffer as a result of their justifiable reliance on the truth of those statements. A company that markets clover seed intentionally mislabeled as alfalfa seed is liable to those who plant the seeds in reliance on the label and consequently suffer a loss. Again it does not matter whether the seed company intended to make contact with those buyers (Restatement (Second) of Torts Sec. 532, illustration 2).

REQUIRED STATE OF MIND

Proof of intentional misrepresentation also requires showing that the defendant knew of the falsity of the statement or acted with reckless disregard to the truth. A defendant who lacks grounds for his representation or confidence in its accuracy possesses the state of mind required for intentional misrepresentation. State of mind is what distinguishes intentional misrepresentation from negligent misrepresentation.

A defendant is also culpable if he makes a statement that is merely a belief but represents it as being actual knowledge. In one case the officers of a corporation told one of the company's creditors that the company was making money. They also sent him some erroneous financial statements. In reliance on the officers' statements, the plaintiff refrained from collecting his debt. In fact, the company was losing money and when the plaintiff finally sought reimbursement he was unable to collect the monies owed him. The defendant officers were found liable in this case, not because their statements were false but because they made statements regarding the solvency of the company without knowing whether the company was making money or not. Their culpability lay in their representation of belief as knowledge (*Sovereign Pocohontas Co. v. Bond,* 120 F.2d 39 (D.C. Cir. 1941)).

RELIANCE ON THE MISREPRESENTATION

A plaintiff must also show that she relied on the defendant's misrepresentation. The question that commonly arises is whether the plaintiff made any independent investigation of her own and whether her reliance was on the misrepresentation, her investigation, or both. Suppose the seller of a horse fraudulently misrepresents the breeding potential of the horse and the plaintiff, wishing to confirm these representations, checks with other experienced horse breeders. If the plaintiff relies totally or almost totally on her own investigation, she will be deemed not to have relied on the seller's misrepresentation. If, however, the seller's misrepresentation is a substantial factor in inducing the plaintiff's reliance, the reliance requirement will be fulfilled and the seller will be found liable.

WAS THE RELIANCE JUSTIFIABLE?

A related question is whether the plaintiff's reliance was justifiable. Is a plaintiff entitled to rely on an opinion offered by the defendant? Traditionally, courts have been reluctant to allow plaintiffs to recover on the basis of any of the defendant's statements that could be characterized as opinion.

In some circumstances, however, such reliance may be justified. If a defendant and plaintiff have a fiduciary relationship or if the defendant has worked to secure the confidence of the plaintiff, the plaintiff may be justified in relying on the defendant's opinion. Also, if the defendant purports to have special knowledge that the plaintiff does not have, the plaintiff may be justified in relying on the defendant. Similarly, if the defendant is aware that the plaintiff is particularly gullible or unintelligent and will be easily misled by any kind of opinion, a justifiable reliance will more likely be found. A horse trader, for example, who tells an ignorant investor that a particular horse is worth $500,000 may be found liable for misrepresentation if, in fact, any knowledgeable investor would recognize that figure as being wholly unrealistic (Restatement (Second) of Torts Sec. 542).

"Puffing." Mere "puffing" is not actionable. A used car dealer who tells a customer that this car is "the best deal you will ever make" is not liable for the statement even though the dealer does not actually believe that the car is a particularly good deal (Restatement (Second) of Torts Sec. 542, comment e).

Opinion of Disinterested Party. The result may be different if the plaintiff reasonably perceives that the opinion is being expressed by a "disinterested" party. In that case the plaintiff's reliance is more likely to be considered reasonable. If a consumer advocacy group indicates that a particular brand of off-road vehicle is safe and the plaintiff is injured in that vehicle, the consumer group's argument that its endorsement was merely an opinion is likely to fail. By holding itself out as a disinterested party that examined and ultimately endorsed the product, the group likely will be deemed as possessing special information upon which the public was reasonably justified in relying.

Opinion Implying Facts. If a defendant renders an opinion implying that no facts incompatible with that opinion exist, the plaintiff may be able to recover if he or she can show that the defendant was aware of such incompatible facts. For example, a corporation president who, in an effort to sell stock, represents his company as being a "gold mine" when in fact he knows the company to be losing money may be found liable for misrepresentation (*Ragsdale v. Kennedy*, 209 S.E.2d 494 (N.C. 1974)).

Remember that the line between fact and opinion is a tenuous one at best but if the defendant crosses over that line by making a statement of fact that she knows to be false, she can be found liable. A statement of value that would normally be considered opinion may become a factual statement because of the context in which it is expressed. A defendant who says "The land across the street sold for $10,000 an acre last year" has made a statement of fact for which he will be liable if he is aware that the land actually sold for much less.

Predictions. A prediction that a certain event is bound to happen will almost always be regarded as an opinion. If, however, the defendant knows of facts inconsistent with that prediction, he or she may still be found liable for misrepresentation. A landowner who predicts that the value of her land will increase 10 percent a year for the next five years could be held liable if the plaintiff could show that the landowner was aware that the property was about to be condemned.

Statement of Intentions. If a defendant makes a statement as to her own intentions, a plaintiff's reliance on that statement will frequently be considered justifiable. If a party to a contract is unable to sue for breach of contract because the opposing party can raise a contract defense, such as the Statute of Frauds, the party wanting to sue may be able to claim misrepresentation if she relied on the defendant's statements. Suppose a defendant promises to buy the plaintiff's house for $50,000 but at the time she makes this promise she actually has no intention of buying the house. When the plaintiff sues for breach of contract, if the defendant raises a Statute of Frauds defense (because the contract was not in writing), the plaintiff can sue on the basis of misrepresentation, arguing that the defendant never intended to keep her contract. If the plaintiff can prove this was the defendant's intent, most courts will not allow the defendant to raise the Statute of Frauds, the parol evidence rule, lack of consideration, or any other contract defense in order to bar liability.

PROXIMATE CAUSE

The plaintiff in a suit for misrepresentation must prove that he or she sustained actual damages that were proximately caused by the defendant's misrepresentation. In other words, the loss must be a "reasonably foreseeable" result of the misrepresentation. Suppose, for example, the plaintiff purchases stock in reliance on the defendant's misrepresentation. If the market value of the stock declines due to causes unrelated to those misrepresentations, the defendant will not be considered the proximate cause of the plaintiff's losses (Restatement (Second) of Torts Sec. 548A, illustration 1).

DAMAGES

Damages for misrepresentation may be measured in two ways. First, the plaintiff may be asked to be put in the position he or she was in before the misrepresentation (referred to as the *reliance measure*). Alternatively, the plaintiff may be asked to be put in the position he or she would have been had the misrepresented facts been true (referred to as the *benefits of the bargain measure*). The majority of courts use the latter measure of damages.

To exemplify these approaches, suppose that a plaintiff pays $20,000 for a horse that is actually worth $10,000. If the horse would have been worth $50,000 if the misrepresentation about the horse had actually been true, under the benefit of the bargain approach the plaintiff will receive $40,000 (the difference between the actual value of the horse, $10,000, and what it would have been worth if it had been as it was represented, $50,000). Under the reliance method of measurement the plaintiff will recover $10,000 (the difference between the actual value of the horse, $10,000, and what the plaintiff paid, $20,000). Note that in assessing damages the fact that the plaintiff would have made a bad bargain even if the defendant had made no misrepresentations is irrelevant.

Table 16–2 lists the aspects of misrepresentation we have been discussing.

NEGLIGENT MISREPRESENTATION

Although historically recovery for negligent misrepresentation was not permitted, today most American courts allow such a claim. Other than intent, the requirements for an action of negligent misrepresentation are essentially the same as those for intentional misrepresentation.

The courts are most inclined to allow recovery for negligent misrepresentation when the defendant makes false statements during the course of his or her business or profession or has a pecuniary interest in the transaction at hand. In one case the defendant sold stove blacking to the plaintiff and negligently told him that is was safe to use on a hot stove. "The warmer the stove the better it works," he told the plaintiff. But the blacking exploded when the plaintiff used it on a hot stove and the defendant was held liable for the harm caused by his erroneous directions (*Cunningham v. C. R. Pease House Furnishing Co.*, 68 A. 120 (1908)).

The defendant is not required to receive compensation directly. If a prospective client comes to an attorney's office and the attorney negligently gives him incorrect advice as part of a "free first consultation," the defendant is still liable for his misrepresentation (Restatement (Second) of Torts Sec. 552, comment d).

One who negligently misrepresents something, however, is liable to a narrower class of third persons than is one who intentionally misrepresents something. One who makes an intentional misrepresentation is liable to any-

TABLE 16.2

WHAT IS A MISREPRESENTATION?

- False statement.
- Concealment by actions.
- Failure to disclose material fact that is essential to transaction.
- Telling of half-truth.

TO WHOM MUST MISREPRESENTATION BE MADE?

- Plaintiff belongs to class of persons that defendant could reasonably expect to learn of and rely on misrepresentation.
- Plaintiff is involved in the type of transaction defendant could reasonably expect plaintiff to engage in as a result of reliance.
- Defendant incorporates misstatements into commercial documents.

DEFENDANT'S STATE OF MIND?

- Is aware of falsity of representation.
- Acts with reckless disregard for truth or falsity of representation.
- Has mere belief but acts as if he or she has actual knowledge.

WHAT IS JUSTIFIABLE RELIANCE?

Defendant offers an opinion and:

- Defendant and plaintiff have fiduciary relationship.
- Defendant has worked to gain plaintiff's confidence.
- Defendant is aware plaintiff is gullible or unintelligent.
- Plaintiff is likely to perceive that opinion is offered by "disinterested" party.
- Defendant suggests no facts incompatible with opinion exist when he or she is aware such facts exist.
- Defendant makes prediction and is aware of facts inconsistent with prediction.
- Defendant states what his or her intentions are, knowing the actual intentions are different.

HOW ARE DAMAGES PROVED?

Reliance: Putting plaintiff in position he or she was in prior to misrepresentation
Benefit of the bargain: Putting plaintiff in position he or she would have been in had the misrepresented facts been true.

one whom he or she reasonably expects to learn about the statement (under the modern view). One who makes a negligent misrepresentation, on the other hand, is liable only to those whom he or she intends to reach with the information or knows the recipient of the information intends to reach.

Nevertheless, as long as the defendant is aware that a negligent misrepresentation will be passed on to a limited number of people, he or she will be liable even if unaware of their precise identity. Suppose a surveyor negligently provides a landowner with an erroneous description of her land. If the surveyor is aware that the owner is planning to sell her land, he will be liable to the purchaser for his errors even though he does not know the name of the purchaser. By the same token, a lawyer who negligently drafts a will may be liable to the beneficiaries even though he may be unaware of the identity of those beneficiaries.

The courts deny recovery, however, when the class of people intended to be reached by the negligent misrepresentation is not limited. Suppose a stock ticker service negligently reports information to its customer brokers. The plaintiff, a stock owner, reads the news at his broker's office and immediately sells his stock because he expects stock prices to fall. The stock ticker service is not liable because the plaintiff did not subscribe directly to its service; therefore, the "limited number of persons" requirement is not met (*Jaillet v. Cashman*, 139 N.E. 714 (N.Y. 1923)).

INNOCENT MISREPRESENTATION

Until relatively recently, the courts have been unwilling to impose liability for innocent misrepresentations, which are, in effect, representations for which a defendant is strictly liable. At least two circumstances exist, however, in which many courts are now willing to allow recovery. If a party involved in a sale, rental, or exchange transaction makes a material misrepresentation to the other in an effort to close a deal, he or she will be liable even if the misrepresentation is innocent (Restatement (Second) of Torts Sec. 552C (1)). If a seller of land, for example, represents in good faith that he is selling property that he in fact does not own, he will be liable to the purchaser for his misrepresentation even though it is perfectly innocent. The sale, rental, or exchange must be directly between the plaintiff and the defendant. Suppose a manufacturer makes a representation to a retailer, who in turn passes it on to the plaintiff in order to induce her to buy the product. In that case strict liability does not apply (Restatement (Second) of Torts Sec. 552C).

Cases involving innocent misrepresentations can also be brought on the basis of an implied or express warranty theory. The plaintiff may opt for the strict liability theory because certain contract defenses that can be raised in a warranty suit are inapplicable in a strict liability suit. The parol evidence rule, for example, which precludes the admission of oral and written evidence external to a contract, is inapplicable in a strict liability suit but is certainly appropriate in a warranty suit.

Innocent misrepresentation also arises in the context of product liability. Similar to the "express warranty" provisions of the U.C.C., a seller of goods

TABLE 16.3

WHEN IS RECOVERY ALLOWED FOR NEGLIGENT MISREPRESENTATION?	WHEN IS RECOVERY ALLOWED FOR INNOCENT MISREPRESENTATION?
•Misrepresentation is made during course of defendant's business or profession. •Misrepresentation is made during transaction in which defendant has a pecuniary interest. •Plaintiff is someone defendant intends to reach with representation or knows recipient of representation intends to reach. •Defendant is aware misrepresentation will be passed on to limited number of persons although he does not know their identities.	•Defendant makes mispresentation during course of sale, rental, or exchange in effort to close the deal. •Defendant makes misstatement on product label or in course of public advertising.

that makes misrepresentations on a label or through public advertising is strictly liable for any physical injury that results from such misinformation. Even if the plaintiff does not buy the product from the defendant, the defendant remains liable.

SUMMARY

Misrepresentation arose out of the common law action of deceit. Intentional misrepresentation, corresponding to fraud under the common law, requires (1) that the defendant makes a misrepresentation with the intent of inducing the plaintiff's reliance on that misrepresentation, (2) that the defendant knows the representation is false or acts with reckless indifference to the truth, (3) that the plaintiff justifiably relies on the defendant's misrepresentation and (4) that the plaintiff suffers damages stemming from his or her reliance.

A misrepresentation may consist of a false statement or an intentional concealment of a fact or an action by itself. Under modern law, mere failure to disclose a material fact may be considered concealment under certain circumstances.

A plaintiff can recover if he or she is a member of the class whom the defendant can reasonably expect to learn of and rely on the misrepresentation. The plaintiff must also show that his or her reliance occurred in the type of transaction the defendant could reasonably expect the plaintiff to engage in as a result of the reliance. A defendant must know that his or her statement is false or act with reckless disregard to the truth or falsity of the statement. In reference to the issue of reliance, the question is whether the plaintiff made

PRACTICE POINTERS

Summarizing Depositions

Legal assistants are often asked to summarize depositions. A well-composed deposition summary can provide an attorney with easy access to testimony in the form of a compact document. Not only are deposition summaries usually included in trial notebooks, they are used to prepare for subsequent depositions and pretrial motions such as motions for summary judgment. They also are helpful when compiling discovery documents such as interrogatories and requests for admissions, and when preparing witnesses for trial. These summaries analyze testimony by breaking it down into its relevant components and restructuring it in a form that highlights the significant issues. The writing style must be concise and clear.

Before attempting to summarize a deposition, you should be familiar with the case file. If you must summarize a deposition for an unfamiliar case, you should read the pleadings and motions in the case file and be able to develop a sense of the chronology of the pertinent events. You should also write out the legal issues you believe are at stake and then verify these with your supervising attorney.

Several different methods can be used to summarize depositions; your choice should be dictated by your attorney's preference. One straightforward method requires a *page-by-page summary* of the witness' testimony. This is really nothing more than a condensed version of the original transcript but it allows the attorney who took the deposition to follow the summary easily. Reference to the page and line number where the testimony can be found in the transcript is provided in the left-hand column. A brief summary of the testimony is recorded at the right.

Page:Line	*Summary*
6:02	*Work History:* Worked as teaching assistant from 9/83 to 5/87. Private piano lessons from 6/85 to 9/88. Music consultant for theatre from 4/88 to present. Went on concert tour 1986.
8:22	*Work History:* Part of string ensemble that went on tour in 1982.
10:01	Explanation of activities involved in teaching piano.
12:22	*Damages to career as result of injury:* Unable to perform as concert pianist. Unable to participate in upcoming competition for which he had spent a year preparing. Restricted now to consultant work and giving piano lessons. No possibility of recording contract.

A *topical index* of the main subjects covered during the witness' testimony is another organizational method used in deposition summaries.

Continued on next page

PRACTICE POINTERS—Continued

Less detailed than the previous method, it provides a list of the main subjects designated by page and line number. This method is especially helpful when it is necessary to cross-reference numerous deposition summaries. For example, if an attorney wants to review all the testimony pertaining to a particular exhibit, he or she can use this type of summary to locate the relevant testimony quickly.

Topic	*Transcript Page:Line*
Work history	6:02
Damages due to injury	12:22
Medical expenses	32:07
Pain and suffering	36:15

Issues can be used as a means of structuring a deposition summary. In this method all testimony relating to a particular subject matter is grouped together. This method is useful for impeaching witnesses if complete quotations of significant testimony are included. Since this method sometimes requires reorganization of the material, a word processor is useful. If a word processor is not available, you might consider photocopying the deposition and using a "cut and paste" technique to group related statements together.

Subject	*Page:Line*
Work History	
Worked as teaching assistant, gave piano lessons, and served as music consultant to a theater. Went on concert tour in 1986.	6:02
Was part of a string ensemble that went on tour in 1982.	8:22
Worked as assistant in recording studio.	20:19

The writing style used in deposition summaries is also a matter of choice. Some attorneys prefer a terse writing style in which all nonessential words, such as "a," "and," and "the" are eliminated; others prefer complete sentences. Regardless of the summarizing method you use, your summary should include the following information:

- Name of the deponent.
- Time, date, and location of deposition.
- Names of those in attendance at deposition.
- Case name and number.

any independent investigation of his or her own and whether reliance was on the misrepresentation, the investigation, or both.

The plaintiff is not usually entitled to rely on an opinion offered by the defendant. If, however, the defendant and plaintiff have a fiduciary relationship or if the defendant has worked to secure the plaintiff's confidence or purports to have special knowledge the plaintiff may be justified. Mere "puffing" is not actionable unless the plaintiff reasonably perceives that the opinion being offered is being made by a disinterested party. Predictions are almost always considered opinion unless the defendant is aware of facts inconsistent with that opinion.

To recover for misrepresentation, the plaintiff must show that the losses suffered were the "reasonably foreseeable results" of the misrepresentation. A plaintiff may ask either to be put into the position he or she was in before the misrepresentation (reliance measure) or to be put in the position he or she would have been in had the misrepresented facts been true (benefit of the bargain measure).

Most courts today allow a claim for negligent misrepresentation. Recovery is most likely to be allowed when a defendant makes false statements during the course of his or her business or profession or has a pecuniary interest in the transaction in which he or she is involved. One who makes a negligent misrepresentation is liable only to those he intends to reach with his information or whom he knows the recipient of his information intends to reach.

Recovery for innocent misrepresentation is allowed if a party makes an innocent but material misrepresentation in the course of a sale, rental, or exchange transaction. The seller of goods who makes misrepresentations on a label or through public advertisement is also liable for any innocent misrepresentations resulting in physical injury.

TORT TEASERS

1. Answer the questions posed in the hypothetical scenario given at the beginning of this chapter.

2. A law firm writes an opinion letter for its client in which it indicates that the client is a general partnership. In fact, some of the members claim to be limited partners and are therefore not subject to full liability. Does the law firm have a duty to disclose this information to Plaintiff, who is contemplating making loans to the partnership? *Roberts v. Ball, Hunt, Hart and Barerwitz*, 57 Cal.App.3d 104, 128 Cal.Rptr. 901 (1976).

3. An attorney negligently give erroneous "curbstone advice" to his client. Can he be held liable for misrepresentation? *Buttersworth v. Swint*, 186 S.E.77 (1936).

4. Plaintiff, who is interested in buying a boiler, requests that Defendant inspect the boiler. Defendant negligently provides Plaintiff with a report that the boiler is in good condition when in fact it is not. Defendant is aware that his report is to be passed on to the seller, who can be expected to rely on the report in giving warranties. When the seller does sell the boiler it proves to be defective and the seller suffers pecuniary loss when he incurs liability for breach of warranty. Is Defendant liable for misrepresentation? *Du Rite Laundry v. Washington Elec. Co.*, 263 App.Div. 396, 33 N.Y.S.2d 925 (1942).

5. Plaintiff is a strong believer in spiritualism. She receives a "Spanish prisoner" letter from Mexico, which states that the writer is unjustly imprisoned and that he has a draft for $20,000 that he has been unable to cash, located in a New York bank. He promises Plaintiff that this draft will be turned over to her if she will deliver $8,500 to a designated agent of the writer. Plaintiff consults Defendant, a spiritualist medium, who tells Plaintiff that the letter is legitimate. Relying on this assurance, Plaintiff mortgages her house, pays the $8,500, and loses it. Should Plaintiff be allowed to recover from Defendant? *Hyma v. Lee*, 60 N.W.2d 920 (1953).

6. A violin expert tries to sell an instrument purported to be a genuine Stradivarius to a purchaser who is also a violin expert. Should the seller be liable for his misrepresentation? *Banner v. Lyon and Healy Co.*, 249 App. Div. 569, 293 N.Y.S. 236 (1937).

KEY TERMS

■ **Deceit**
Common law cause of action equated with intentional misrepresentation; also referred to as fraud.

■ **Fiduciary relationship**
Relationship based on trust and confidence imposing an obligation to act in good faith.

■ **Latent defect**
Defect that is invisible or not readily discoverable.

■ **Patent defect**
Defect that is visible or readily discoverable.

MISCELLANEOUS TORTS

CHAPTER OBJECTIVES

In this chapter you will learn to:

- Distinguish between public and private nuisance and identify the elements of both.
- Distinguish among the four torts that are considered an invasion of privacy and identify the elements of each.
- Recognize the torts involving interference with family relations.
- Distinguish among the torts involving interference with business relations and identify the elements of each.
- Distinguish among the torts involving misuse of the legal process and identify the elements of each.

After meeting your sister's fiancé, you suspect that he is not all that he pretends to be. You ask a friend of yours, who is a private investigator, to conduct a background check on him. You discover, among other things, that your prospective brother-in-law had an affair with a woman who was married to a prominent businessman. When the husband discovered their relationship and terminated their affair, your sister's boyfriend sought revenge. First he went to the attorney general's office and tried to convince an attorney to prosecute the husband for price fixing even though he was aware that such claims were utterly false. In a further act of petulance he sent letters to several of the husband's customers giving intimate details of the husband's sex life, including the fact that the husband was impotent. Not being one to forgive and forget, your brother-in-law-to-be is currently trying to purchase property next to the husband's business. He plans to open a bookstore that features the sale of pornographic materials. Since the husband operates a religious bookstore, he is confident that this will, at the very least, have a detrimental effect on the husband's business and, more likely, he hopes, contribute to its demise.

What torts has this potential bane of your existence committed? Has he committed nuisance, invasion of privacy, interference with family relations, interference with business relations, injurious falsehood, or misuse of legal process? Let us see.

NUISANCE

A precise definition of the term **"nuisance"** has eluded the courts for centuries. The most than can be said is that a defendant's interference with a plaintiff's interest constitutes nuisance. A nuisance can be either a public nuisance or a private nuisance. The essence of a *public nuisance* is an interference with "a right common to the general public" (Restatement (Second) of Torts Sec. 821B(1)). A *private nuisance*, on the other hand, is an unreasonable interference with the plaintiff's use and enjoyment of his or her land (Restatement (Second) of Torts Sec. 822). The key to private nuisance is the need for the plaintiff to have an interest in the land that has been affected by the defendant's activities. The maintenance of a feedlot or a house of prostitution in close proximity to a residential area are examples of public nuisance; the playing of extremely loud music at 2:00 A.M. in a residential area exemplifies a private nuisance. Table 17–1 defines the aspects of public and private nuisances.

PUBLIC NUISANCE

To sustain a claim for public nuisance, the plaintiff must show that the public at large was actually injured or was exposed to the possibility of injury. Only the plaintiff being injured, even if he or she is injured in a public place, is not sufficient. Furthermore, the harm must be a substantial one. Under the

TABLE 17.1

PUBLIC NUISANCE	PRIVATE NUISANCE
•Substantial interference. •Affects right common to general public. •Public must be injured or exposed to injury. •Plaintiff need not have interest in land. •Plaintiff must suffer damages peculiar to him.	•Substantial interference. •Affects plaintiff's use and enjoyment of land. •Plaintiff must suffer substantial interference with use or enjoyment of land. •Plaintiff must have interest in land.

common law only conduct that constituted a crime met the requirement of a public nuisance. Most modern courts no longer require conduct to be criminal although such conduct is still more likely to be deemed a public nuisance than conduct that is not.

The plaintiff must also show that he suffered damage peculiar to him that was not shared by the rest of the public. Suffering the same inconvenience or being exposed to the same threat as everyone else in the community is not sufficient. The rationale for this rule is that wrongs to the community as a whole should be redressed by the community's representatives to avoid duplication of legal actions.

The courts, however, have struggled with this notion of "particular damage." Some have allowed recovery if the plaintiff suffered greater economic loss than others in the community while others have denied recovery in similar cases. If the plaintiff's pecuniary loss precludes him from performing on a contract or causes him additional expense in his performance, many courts have allowed the plaintiff to recover. Similarly, if the defendant has interfered with the plaintiff's commercial use of his land, many courts allow recovery for public nuisance. Commercial fisheries, for example, have been allowed to recover for losses due to pollution even though ordinary citizens who used the polluted waters could not recover.

PRIVATE NUISANCE

The key to suing on the basis of private nuisance, as mentioned earlier, is the plaintiff's ability to show she has an interest in the affected land. Tenants, as well as family members of an owner or tenant, are considered to have such an interest. The plaintiff must prove the use and enjoyment of her land was substantially interfered with and that the defendant's conduct was either negligent, intentional, or abnormally dangerous.

Nuisance vs. Trespass. The difference between a private nuisance and trespass is subtle. A trespass consists of an interference with the plaintiff's right to *possession* of his or her property; nuisance consists of an interference with the plaintiff's right to *enjoy* and *use* his or her property. Nuisance can occur, therefore, even if nothing physically enters the plaintiff's property. Furthermore, the fact that the interference must be substantial also differentiates nuisance from trespass. Recall that a plaintiff may recover for trespass even though suffering no substantial harm since the tort requires only an intentional invasion of the plaintiff's property. Most conduct that constitutes a trespass typically meets the criteria for a nuisance as well. Blasting activities in the vicinity of the plaintiff's land, for example, obviously create a nuisance in light of the noise and vibrations that are produced. But if rocks and other debris are cast on the plaintiff's land, a trespass is also committed.

What Constitutes Substantial Interference. Substantial interference no doubt occurs when the plaintiff is injured or her property is damaged. The interference may also be substantial if the plaintiff is inconvenienced or subjected to unpleasant sensory awarenesses, such as obnoxious odors or blaring sounds. The plaintiff must show that a person of normal sensitivity would be seriously bothered by the defendant's conduct. An abnormally sensitive plaintiff, therefore, will be precluded from recovery. What comprises substantial interference will, of necessity, hinge on the type of neighborhood in which the activity occurs. Activities that constitute a nuisance in a quiet suburban area might not qualify as a nuisance in a densely populated urban area.

Intentional and Unreasonable Interference. Although a defendant's conduct can be either negligent, intentional, or abnormally dangerous, most private nuisance claims arise out of intentional conduct. A defendant must, in other words, know with substantial certainty that interference will occur even if he has no desire to interfere with the plaintiff's use and enjoyment of his land.

If the defendant's interference is intentional, the plaintiff must also prove that such interference is unreasonable. To determine whether interference is unreasonable some courts have balanced the utility of the defendant's conduct against the plaintiff's harm. In accordance with this test a plaintiff may be barred from recovery even though she suffered substantial harm if the utility of the defendant's conduct exceeds the harm the plaintiff suffered.

The Restatement (Second) has rejected this balancing test for reasonableness and deemed that interference is unreasonable if one of two things is true. Either the plaintiff's harm must outweigh the utility of the defendant's conduct, or alternatively, the harm caused by the conduct must be substantial and greater than anything any individual should be required to bear without compensation (Restatement (Second) of Torts Sec. 829A). Under this criterion even if the defendant's activity is socially useful, he will be required to compensate the plaintiff unless so many people are affected by the defendant's conduct that requiring the defendant to pay damages would make it impossible for him to continue the activity.

In one case a coal-burning electric generating plant emitted 90 tons of sulphur-dioxide gas into the atmosphere each day, causing extensive crop damage and other harm. The defendant claimed it had used due care in constructing and operating the plant. Nevertheless, the emissions from the plant were determined to be a nuisance. Even though the economic and social utility of the plant outweighed the harm to the farmers, the court required the plant to compensate the farmers for their damages (*Jost v. Dairy Cooperative,* 172 N.W.2d 647 (Wis. 1970)).

Remedies. A plaintiff alleging private nuisance may seek either compensatory damages or an injunction. If the nuisance is likely to be permanent, she can recover for both past and prospective damages in the same action. However, if it is unclear whether the harm will be an ongoing one, she can recover only for those damages sustained at the time of suit and must bring future actions for subsequent harm.

If damages would be an insufficient remedy, the plaintiff may be entitled to an injunction. If she seeks an injunction, she must prove that the harm to her outweighs the utility of the defendant's conduct. Compare this to the Restatement approach discussed above in which a plaintiff can recover damages even if the harm to her does not outweigh the utility of the defendant's conduct as long as it would be unfair to deprive her of payment.

Defenses. Both contributory negligence and assumption of risk can be raised as defenses in private nuisance claims. One way a plaintiff can assume the risk is if he "comes to the nuisance" by purchasing property having advance notice that the nuisance exists. A plaintiff who purchases a home adjacent to an industrial plant that is in full operation and spewing gases and waste into the environment is said to have "come to the nuisance." Although at one time the courts treated "coming to the nuisance" as an absolute defense, modern courts look at that fact as merely one of many factors to be considered in deciding whether the plaintiff should be allowed to recover. To bar recovery to all plaintiffs who "come to the nuisance" would allow defendants, in essence, to condemn the land in their vicinity so that the land would become valueless to others. The courts expect defendants to contemplate the possibility that others will eventually want to settle in the area and to anticipate that nuisance claims may arise in the future.

This point is illustrated in one interesting case involving a defendant cattle feedlot that produced "over a million pounds of wet manure per day" in a rural area outside of Phoenix. The plaintiff developer constructed a retirement development, "Sun City," one portion of which adjoined the feedlot. The plaintiff alleged that the flies and odor from the feedlot rendered this portion of the development unhealthy and virtually uninhabitable. The court concluded that the plaintiff had indeed "come to the nuisance" in its building of a subdivision in the vicinity of an already existing feedlot. Nevertheless, the court enjoined the defendant from operating the feedlot because the rights of innocent third parties, the residents of "Sun City," were also involved. Because the plaintiff had "come to the nuisance," however, the court required the plaintiff to indemnify the defendant for its moving costs (*Spur Industries, Inc. v. Del E. Webb Development Co.*, 494 P.2d 700 (Ariz. 1972)).

INVASION OF PRIVACY

The right to privacy, sometimes referred to as "the right to be let alone," has a unique origin. Prior to 1890 such a tort had never been recognized by the English or American courts. But in that year Samuel Warren and Lewis Brandeis, fueled by their perception that individuals needed protection from what they viewed as an increasingly invasive press, authored a *Harvard Law Review* article proposing the creation of a new tort. Their proposal was the subject of extensive academic debate and was accepted as a basis of recovery in some lower courts. The New York Court of Appeals generated a storm of public disapproval when it denied recovery to a plaintiff whose picture had been used to advertise flour without her consent. The New York legislature went on to pass a statute allowing recovery in such cases. Today every state except Rhode Island has recognized the right to privacy in some form or another.

Invasion of privacy is actually comprised of four distinct torts, dissimilar in every respect except that they all protect the plaintiff from unreasonable interference with his or her privacy. These four torts are appropriation, unreasonable intrusion, public disclosure of private facts, and false light (see Table 17–2).

TABLE 17.2 Invasion of Privacy

APPROPRIATION	UNREASONABLE INTRUSION
Value of plaintiff's name or picture is used by defendant for financial gain.	Defendant intentionally intrudes upon seclusion of plaintiff and the intrusion is highly offensive to a reasonable person.
PUBLIC DISCLOSURE OF PRIVATE FACTS	**FALSE LIGHT**
Defendant publicizes details of plaintiff's private life and matter publicized is highly offensive to a reasonable person.	Defendant puts plaintiff before public in false light that would be highly offensive to a reasonable person.

APPROPRIATION

If the value of a plaintiff's name or picture is used by a defendant for his or her own financial gain, the plaintiff can sue for this **appropriation**. Note that the value of the plaintiff's name must be appropriated and not the name itself. In other words, the mere use of a name the same as that of the plaintiff's does not impose liability. The purpose for the appropriation, however, typically may be for either commercial or noncommercial purposes, although some state statutes limit recovery to commercial appropriations. The unauthorized use of an actress' photograph for the purposes of advertising could give rise to a cause of action for appropriation. Notice that appropriation was one of the allegations made by Robyn Douglas in *Douglas v. Hustler Magazine, Inc.*

Robyn DOUGLASS, Plaintiff-Appellee-Cross-Appellant. v. HUSTLER MAGAZINE, INC., Defendant-Appellant-Cross-Appellee, and Augustin Gregory, Defendant. Nos. 84-2919, 84-2985. United States Court of Appeals, Seventh Circuit. Argued April 24, 1985. Decided June 17, 1985. Rehearing and Rehearing En Banc Denied Aug. 22, 1985.

Reversed and remanded.

769 F.2d 1128 (7th Cir. 1985).

POSNER, Circuit Judge.

Robyn Douglass, the actress and model, obtained $600,000 in damages in this diversity suit against the corporation that publishes *Hustler* magazine, for invasion of her right of privacy. . . . *Hustler* (as we shall call the magazine and its publisher interchangeably) has appealed, raising questions of tort law, freedom of the press, and trial procedure; Douglass has cross-appealed, complaining about the judge's action in reducing the punitive damages awarded by the jury.

Robyn Douglass moved to Chicago in 1974 and began a career as an actress and model. That year she posed nude together with another woman for the freelance photographer Augustin Gregory, a codefendant with *Hustler* in the district court. The photographs were intended for a forthcoming feature in *Playboy* magazine, the "Ripped-Off" pictorial. Gregory testified that he required all his photographic models to sign releases allowing him to do with the photographs whatever he wanted. Robyn Douglass testified (and the jury was entitled to believe) that all she signed was a release authorizing *Playboy* to publish or otherwise use the photographs "for any lawful purpose whatsoever, without restrictions." The release does not refer to sale as such; but in granting rights not only to *Playboy* but to its "assigns and licensees," Douglass in effect gave *Playboy* carte blanche to dispose of the photos in any lawful way it wanted. Some of the photographs were published in *Playboy* in March 1975 as planned. Gregory had in 1974 also taken nude photographs of Douglass for a "Water and Sex" pictorial, also intended for *Playboy;* and there is a similar conflict over the release.

Douglass's career throve in the following years. She appeared eight times nude in *Playboy* but also made television commercials for Chicago advertising agencies and appeared in television dramas and in movies—notably "Breaking Away," where she had a starring role. Meanwhile in 1980 Gregory had become the photography editor of *Hustler*. This move was not unconnected with his earlier photographing of Douglass. The magazine wanted to publish nude photos of celebrities and in negotiations over becoming *Hustler's* photography editor Gregory had shown management some of his photographs of Douglass. After he was hired, management asked Gregory for releases authorizing publication of these photographs. He testified that he couldn't find the releases at first but that eventually he submitted to *Hustler* two releases signed by Douglass, one for the photo session for the "Ripped-Off" pictorial, the other for the "Water and Sex" pictorial. At trial *Hustler* was able to produce only photostats of the releases allegedly signed by Douglass. The parties stipulated that, if called as a witness, a handwriting expert would testify that Douglass's signature had been forged on one of the releases and that the photostat of the other was too poor to allow the authenticity of the signature on it to be determined.

Douglass heard that there was to be a photo feature on her in the January 1981 issue of *Hustler* (an acquaintance had seen an announcement of it in a previous issue). She complained to the magazine that it had no authority to publish any photos of her. It responded with photostatic copies of the alleged releases, which within two or three days she denounced to *Hustler* as forgeries. The issue containing the feature had already been printed and distributed to retailers; and though it had not yet appeared on newsstands or been mailed to subscribers, *Hustler* made no effort to recall the issue, and it was widely sold. The feature, entitled "Robynn Douglass Nude," contained nude photographs from the two photo sessions for *Playboy* and stills (not nude) from two of her movies. The magazine paid Gregory a fee, over and above his regular salary, for the photographs he had supplied.

This suit charges that Gregory and *Hustler* invaded Douglass's right to privacy under the common law of Illinois by publishing "Robynn Douglass Nude." The feature, she charged, invaded her right of privacy in two ways: it cast her in a "false light," and it appropriated valuable commercial rights that belong to her. At trial she presented evidence that the publication of the feature had caused her emotional distress, and had killed her career of making commercials in Chicago because advertisers thought she had voluntarily appeared in what they considered an extremely vulgar magazine. An economist testified that the present value of her lost earnings was $716,565 at the time of trial (1983).

The judge gave the jury a verdict form with a blank beside each defendant's name for the amount of compensatory damages if the jury found either defendant liable, and a separate blank beside each name for punitive damages. The jury found both defendants liable and awarded the plaintiff $500,000 in compensatory damages against each defendant and $1,500,000 in punitive damages against *Hustler*. The judge remitted all but $100,000 of the punitive damages and Douglass accepted the remittitur. The award of compensatory damages against Gregory was not executed because on the eve of trial he had made an agreement with Douglass that if he testified truthfully, and consistently with his deposition, she would not execute any judgment against him. Hence the real judgment was only $600,000. Gregory has not filed an appearance in this court.

Hustler argues that the facts, even when viewed favorably to the plaintiff, do not make out a cause of action under the Illinois common law of privacy, so that the judgment should be reversed with directions to dismiss the complaint; or that if they do, still the complaint must be dismissed because the plaintiff failed to prove "actual malice" by clear and convincing evidence, as required by the Constitution. Alternatively it argues that a new trial should be ordered because of errors in the instructions to the jury, and other trial errors.

First of all, *Hustler* denies that Illinois even recognizes the "false light" tort. Illinois' substantive law governs this suit, apart from the defendants' First Amendment defense; and no Illinois court has ever found liability for such a tort, . . . In cases in which that tort has been charged, albeit unsuccessfully, the Illinois courts have proceeded as if it existed in Illinois. In *Leopold v. Levin*, . . . the only false-light case decided by the Illinois Supreme Court, Leopold, the surviving defendant in the Leopold and Loeb murder case, brought suit against the author of a book about the case, charging that the book *(Compulsion)* placed Leopold in a false light. The Illinois Supreme Court held that Leopold had no cause of action. He had forfeited any right of privacy by the notoriety of his crime; the book was represented to the public as a fictionalized rather than literal account; Leopold was a public figure; and to award tort damages would have unduly limited freedom of expression. These points would have been unnecessary to make if the court had thought that the false-light tort was not part of the common law of Illinois. . . . Incidentally, we do not read *Leopold v. Levin* to deny the protection of the tort to any and all public figures (Robyn Douglass, as we shall see, is a public figure). Leopold's status as a public figure was relevant to but not, as we read the opinion, conclusive on whether his rights had been violated.

Like every other division of the tort law of privacy, the "false light" tort . . . can be criticized, especially for overlapping with the tort of defamation. . . . Why should a plaintiff be able to circumvent the technical limitations with which the tort of defamation is hedged about by calling his suit one for placing him in a false light? Several answers are possible, however:

1. Some of those limitations seem not to reflect considered policy, but instead to be fossil remnants of the tort's prehistory in the discredited practices of Star Chamber and the discredited concept of seditious libel. . . . If they are gotten around by allowing a plaintiff to plead invasion of privacy, there is no great loss.

2. The principal limitations concern the requirement of proving special damages in some cases. . . . Since Robyn Douglass proved special damages (i.e., a pecuniary loss), these limitations would not have impeded her even if she had brought this

suit as one for defamation. As for the other limitations in the law of defamation, *Hustler* has not shown how any of them, either, would have posed an embarrassment for Douglass on the facts of this case. And if she had sued for defamation she would not have had to prove (though it was not difficult to prove) that the offending materials had been widely publicized, an element of invasion of privacy that has no counterpart in the law of defamation.

3. Part of Douglass's claim is that *Hustler* insinuated that she is a lesbian; and such a claim could of course be the basis for an action for defamation. But the rest of her claim fits more comfortably into the category of offensive rather than defamatory publicity. The difference is illustrated by *Time, Inc. v. Hill*, 385 U.S. 374, 87 S.Ct. 534, 17 L.E.2d 456 (1967). *Life* magazine had presented as true a fictionalized account of the ordeal of a family held hostage by escaped convicts. The members of the family were shown being subjected to various indignities that had not actually occurred. The article did not defame the family members in the sense of accusing them of immoral, improper, or other bad conduct, and yet many people would be upset to think that the whole world thought them victims of such mistreatment. The false-light tort, to the extent distinct from the tort of defamation (but there is indeed considerable overlap), rests on an awareness that people who are made to seem pathetic or ridiculous may be shunned, and not just people who are thought to be dishonest or incompetent or immoral. We grant, though, that the distinction is blurred by the fact that a false statement that a woman was raped is actionable as defamation, . . . though in such a case the plaintiff is represented to be a victim of wrongdoing rather than a wrongdoer herself.

At all events, the criticisms of the false-light tort have to our knowledge persuaded the courts of only one state that recognizes a tort of invasion of privacy to withhold recognition of this subtype of the tort—North Carolina, . . . Almost all signs point to Illinois' recognizing it when a suitable case arises. A more difficult question is whether the facts of this case make out a false-light tort. We must decide in what light *Hustler* may be said to have cast Robyn Douglass, and (by comparison with her activities as a *Playboy* model) in what if any sense the light could have been found to be a false one. To answer these questions we shall have to enter imaginatively into a world that is not the natural habitat of judges—the world of nude modeling and (as they are called in the trade) "provocative" magazines.

The feature "Robyn Douglass Nude" in the January 1981 issue of *Hustler* occupies three full pages about a third of the way from the end of the magazine. The first page is dominated by a picture of Douglass, shown from the front, rain-splattered, wearing only an open raincoat. This is one of the photos that had been taken for the "Water and Sex" pictorial. Her mouth is open and her eyes closed. The text on the page reads:

> She played Katherine, the Midwestern coed in the film *Breaking Away*, and Jamie, the shapely newspaper reporter in the TV series *Galactica 1980* (below). But in HUSTLER seductive young actress Robyn Douglass plays herself. In these never-before-published photos this hot new star strips away her screen image to reveal the flesh of a real woman. An accomplished stage performer and TV-commercial model (Orbit gum, Gatorade and United Airlines), Robyn has been trained to use her body as a tool of her trade. These photos show just how well she's learned to use that tool.

The "below" reference is to an innocuous still photo from the television series.

The second page of the feature is given over to four more photographs of Douglass, two from "Water and Sex" and two from the "Ripped-Off" pictorial. (To be precise, these and the other nude photos in "Robyn Douglass Nude" were photos that had been taken for the two *Playboy* pictorials but, apparently, had not actually been published.) The photographs from "Water and Sex" again show Douglass from the front with the raincoat playing out behind her. In one picture her mouth is open while in the other she seems to be looking abstractedly at herself. In the two photos from "Ripped-Off," Douglass, now wearing a slip rather than a raincoat, appears to be engaged in erotic play with the other woman in the pictorial.

The last page of the feature has the following text beneath a picture of Douglass, fully clothed, on a motorcycle:

> When asked to audition for the role of Katherine in *Breaking Away* (above), Robyn sought out the character's most emotional scene to read for director Peter Yates. "You only have a short time to prepare; so I went through the script to try to find the climactic moments for Katherine." From the looks of Robyn (who's blond in the photos of her and a female friend), she's never had difficulty finding climactic moments.

The rest of the page is given over to two photographs from the "Ripped-Off" pictorial. The underwear visible in the other two photographs from this session has indeed been ripped off; the two women are naked. Douglass is straddling the other woman and the two appear to be engaged in sexual activity.

Douglass argues that the *Hustler* feature casts her in a false light in two respects. First, it insinuates that she is a lesbian, which (all agree) she is not. Second, it insinuates that she is the kind of person willing to be shown naked in *Hustler*. Nothing in the feature itself suggests that the nude photographs of her are appearing without her permission and against her will, and readers might well assume that she had cooperated in the preparation of the feature in order to stimulate interest in her films. Moreover, she had been described in a previous issue of *Hustler* as a forthcoming "Hustler celebrity-exclusive," and in another issue *Hustler's* chairman, Larry Flynt, had announced in an editorial column that he does not publish photographs of women without their consent. It is (or so a jury could find) as if *Hustler* had said, "Robyn Douglass is proud to pose nude for *Hustler* magazine." To complete this part of her argument Douglass asserts that voluntary association with *Hustler* as a nude model is degrading.

We would not ourselves think that *Hustler* was seriously insinuating—or that its readership would think—that Robyn Douglass is a lesbian. *Hustler* is a magazine for men. Few men are interested in lesbians. The purpose of showing two women in apparent sexual embrace is to display the charms of two women. Moreover, the photos obviously are posed rather than candid shots; they show what the photographer wanted the women to do, not necessarily what the women wanted to do. Nevertheless we cannot say that a reasonable jury seeing the pictures and reading the accompanying text with its references to "climactic moments" and "female friend" could not infer that Douglass was being represented to be a lesbian.

The question whether she was also being depicted in a degrading association with *Hustler* invites attention to the difference between libel and false light. It would have been difficult for Douglass to state this claim as one for libel. For what exactly is the imputation of saying (or here, implying) of a person that she agreed to have pictures of herself appear in a vulgar and offensive magazine? That she is immoral? This would be too strong a characterization in today's moral climate. That she lacks good taste? This would not be defamatory. . . . The point is, rather, that to be shown nude in such a setting before millions of people—the readers of the magazine—is degrading in much the same way that to be shown beaten up by criminals is degrading (although not libelous, despite the analogy to being reported to have been raped), though of course if Douglass consented to appear nude in this setting she is responsible for her own debasement and can get no judicial redress.

That the setting is indeed a degrading one requires only a glance through the issue of *Hustler* in which "Robyn Douglass Nude" was published to confirm. The cover shows a naked woman straddling and embracing a giant peppermint stick. The titles of several articles in the issue are printed on the cover, next to the picture, including along with some titles that are not related to sex "New Discovery: How to Give Women Vaginal Orgasms." This is directly below "Nude Celebrity: Robyn Douglass, Star of Galactica and Breaking Away." The inside cover is a full page of advertisements for pornographic video cassettes. On page 5 there is the "publisher's [Larry Flynt's] statement"—a call to tax the churches. This sounds another theme of Hustler: "irreverence," which has the practical meaning in *Hustler* of hostility to or contempt for racial, ethnic, and religious minorities. Then there is a "World News Roundup"—the news is all concerned with sex—and a page of coarse advice to readers who have sexual problems. Between these two features is a full-page advertisement entitled "Get Any Girl *Within 5 Minutes* or YOU PAY NOTHING!" with subtitles such as "Turn Women Into Putty." The issue contains many similar sexual advertisements, some with obscene pictures and text. . . .

We shall leave off here, . . . having sufficiently indicated the character of the magazine. To be depicted as *voluntarily* associated with such a sheet . . . is unquestionably degrading to a normal person, especially if the depiction is erotic . . . for although the magazine is offensive on several planes, the sexual is the one most emphasized. These features of the case help to distinguish *Ann-Margret v. High Society Magazine, Inc.*, 498 F.Supp. 401, 404–06 (S.D.N.Y. 1980), where a seminude still of an actress was published without her authorization in a magazine *(High Society Celebrity Skin)* described by the judge merely as "tacky," *McCabe v. Village Voice, Inc.*, 550 F.Supp. 525, 529 (E.D.Pa. 1982), a case like *Ann-Margret* except that the magazine was completely inoffensive; and [*Brewer v. Hustler Magazine, Inc.*, 749 F.2d 527, 530 (9th Cir.1984),] where a previously published photograph was republished in a "sexually explicit" magazine—none other than *Hustler* itself—but apparently the plaintiff did not argue that the magazine was degrading, as distinct from merely explicit. And the photograph was of Brewer pretending to shoot himself in the head (for unexplained reasons, he had had this photograph printed on his business cards); he was not associated with the magazine's view of sex. More important, in none of these cases was it argued that the subject was being represented as appearing voluntarily in the magazine, and (except in *McCabe*) the photographs had previously been published elsewhere. These points are related. If a photograph has been published previously the implied representation that its present publication is with the consent of the subject is weakened; the first publication may have put the photograph in the public domain. But the nude photographs of Robyn Douglass that *Hustler* published had not been published before.

Hustler argues that publication of "Robyn Douglass Nude" could not be degrading to one who had posed nude for *Playboy*. This fact distinguishes the case from the two cases that give the most support to Douglass's false-light claim: [*Wood v. Hustler Magazine, Inc.*, 736 F.2d 1084 (5th Cir.1984),] where the plaintiff was not a model or actress and her nude photo (taken by her husband) had not been published previously and had not been intended to be published; and [*Braun v. Flynt*, 726 F.2d 245 (5th Cir.1984),] where the photo of the plaintiff that was published on the same page with offensive matter in another "provocative" magazine published by Flynt *(Chic)* was not a nude photo; the plaintiff was wearing a bathing suit. . . [(It should be apparent by now that this little niche of the law of privacy is dominated by Larry Flynt's publications.)

To evaluate *Hustler's* contention required the jury to compare the two magazines. We shall use for comparison the issue of *Playboy* in which the "Ripped-Off" pictorial appeared, though the jury had other issues of *Playboy* to peruse as well. The cover shows a young woman with partially naked buttocks and thighs but otherwise clothed. The only (other) suggestion of sex on the cover is the words "Ripped Off! A Torrid Nine-Page Pictorial," which by its position on the cover appears to be a reference to the cover girl. The inside cover is a conventional advertisement for Scotch whisky. Besides advertisements (none sexual), the issue contains fiction, a column of sexual advice (more refined than its *Hustler* counterpart), book reviews (only one of a book on sex), and articles. None of the stories or articles is obscene, though one story is erotic (a "Ribald Classic") and there are many bawdy cartoons and jokes (but not vicious ones, like many of those in *Hustler*) and four nude pictorials. In one of the pictorials a woman is doing exercises and being massaged; some of the frames contain an erotic suggestion of a mild sort. Two of the other pictorials show nude women in various poses but there is no suggestion that they are engaged in erotic activity. The last nude pictorial is "Ripped-Off," which turns out to consist of photographs of nude women (some in erotic poses) by different photographers. Two of the photographs are by Gregory, and one of them is of Robyn Douglass, though she is not identified by name. Although she is shown removing the slip of the other woman, as in the *Hustler* pictures, the text beneath the picture weakens any inference of lesbianism: "How long since you've seen a girl—let alone two—in lingerie like this? 'I pick very feminine, almost outdated slips for the girls to wear in this scene,' says photographer Gregory. 'To me, that made it more of a fantasy, more of a turn-on.' " Among other pictures in "Ripped-Off," one could be taken to be an (obviously simulated) photograph of sexual intercourse.

Although many people find *Playboy*, with its emphasis on sex and nudity, offensive, the differences between it and *Hustler* are palpable. *Playboy*, like *Hustler*, contains nude pictorials, but the erotic theme is generally muted, though there are occasional photographs that an earlier generation would have considered definitely obscene. And unlike *Hustler*, *Playboy* does not carry sexual advertisements, does not ridicule racial or religious groups, and avoids repulsive photographs—though most of the jokes and cartoons have sex as their theme, and not all are in good taste. We cannot say that it would be irrational for a jury to find that in the highly permissive moral and cultural climate prevailing in late twentieth-century America, posing nude for *Playboy* is consistent with respectability for a model and actress but that posing nude in *Hustler* is not (not yet, anyway), so that to portray Robyn Douglass as voluntarily posing nude for *Hustler* could be thought to place her in a false light even though she had voluntarily posed nude for *Playboy*. Apart from the evidence of the magazines themselves, Douglass presented evidence that advertising agencies in Chicago were afraid of their clients' reactions if she appeared in commercials after her appearance in *Hustler*, but cared nothing about her appearing nude in *Playboy*. And of course the issue for us is not whether the jury was right but whether a reasonable jury could have found a false-light tort on the facts of this case.

However, since Douglass gave a general release to *Playboy*, it can be argued that she consented to have her photographs appear in any lawful setting; and there is no contention that "Robyn Douglass Nude," or the issue of *Hustler* in which it appeared, could lawfully have been suppressed on obscenity or other grounds. The jury could find, however, that only Douglass or *Playboy* could give consent to the publication of the photographs and that neither had done so. True, by giving *Playboy* a general release Douglass took a risk that her nude photographs would end up in an offensive setting that would damage her career as a model for television commercials, and it might seem that someone who takes such a risk cannot have a high regard for her privacy. But the risk she took and the risk that materialized were not the same. She took what may have seemed a trivial risk that *Playboy* would resell her photographs to a competitor, not the risk that the competitor would steal them. *Playboy* has an interest, on which Douglass could reasonably rely in executing a release to *Playboy,* in not degrading its models and in maintaining exclusive rights to its photos of them. The woman in the *Wood* case assumed the risk that her husband would sell *Hustler* the nude photograph that he took of her, but this did not deprive her of the right to sue for invasion of privacy when *Hustler* published the photograph having gotten it from someone who had broken into her house and stolen it.

We conclude that Robyn Douglass has a cause of action against *Hustler* for portraying her in a false light. Further, we think the jury did not exceed the bounds of reason in finding that *Hustler* also violated her rights under the commercial-appropriation branch of the right of privacy—what is sometimes called the "right of publicity," which *Hustler* concedes is a part of the common law of Illinois. This is the right to prevent others from using one's name or picture for commercial purposes without consent. Although originally the forbidden use was putting one's name or picture into an advertisement, it is apparent from *Zacchini v. Scripps-Howard Broadcasting Co.,* 433 U.S. 562, . . . (1977), that the right can extend to publication in the nonadvertising portions of a magazine or broadcast. This extension is closely related to copyright. . . . Zacchini had perfected a "human cannonball" act that lasted about 15 seconds. A television station broadcast the whole act as part of a news program. The station argued that the act was newsworthy; in copyright terms this would make the broadcasting of it a "fair use." *Hustler* makes a similar argument here—Robyn Douglass is newsworthy and "Robyn Douglass Nude" was fair comment on her career. But the station could have done a story on Zacchini without showing his entire act; and showing the whole act was likely to shrink the paying audience for it—people could see it on television for nothing. Thus there was an invasion of Zacchini's rights, analogous to copyright, under state tort law. Similarly, Robyn Douglass or her agents must have control over the dissemination of her nude photographs if their values is to be maximized. *Hustler* can run a story on her and use any photographs that are in the public domain or that it can buy but it cannot use photographs made by others for commercial purposes and (temporarily) withheld from public distribution. . . .

The unauthorized publication did impair the commercial exploitation of Douglass's talents, though probably not as much as she asserts and mainly because of where they were published. But an important aspect of the "right of publicity" is being able to control the places as well as time and number of one's public appearances; for example, no celebrity sells his name or likeness for advertising purposes to all comers. In any event, Douglass was not paid by *Hustler* for the right to publish nude photos of her.

Of course the issue in *Zacchini* was not whether the common law created a right of action against the television station—let alone the common law of Illinois (the case came from Ohio)—but whether the Constitution barred such a right of action if it existed in state law. There are no Illinois cases like *Zacchini.* But forced to guess, we guess that Illinois would recognize a "right of publicity" on the facts of *Zacchini* and the analogous facts of the present case. Indeed, this may be an easier case than *Zacchini,* where the performance had been in public, though in a different medium. This case approaches very closely to a violation of common law copyright, as in the theft and unauthorized publication of an author's manuscript. Of course Douglass would have no claim if Gregory had gotten a general release from her. But by executing only a limited release, she retained a right in the photos he took of her that, if not quite a property right, is nevertheless given legal protection under the (misleading) rubric of privacy.

But it was error to allow the jury to find an invasion of Douglass's right of publicity in the fact that *Hustler* published stills from her movies and television shows—whether reversible error we need not decide (for reasons to appear). Apparently these stills were in the public domain, for they had been published and *Hustler* is not accused of copyright infringement in republishing them. Republishing previously published, uncopyrighted photographs of a celebrity is a fair use justified by the newsworthiness of celebrities, and it therefore does not violate the right of publicity. . . . To forbid *Hustler* to publish any photographs of people without their consent, merely because it is an offensive, though apparently a lawful, magazine, would pretty much put *Hustler* out of the new business, would probably violate the First Amendment, and would in any event cross outside the accepted boundaries of the right of publicity. But as noted earlier the nude photographs of Douglass that *Hustler* published had not been published before. They were, in a sense that tort law recognizes, part of her portfolio. She had a legally protected interest in deciding at least their first place of publication, provided *Playboy* did not exercise its right to publish them or to license their publication to others, a right for which Douglass had been compensated in executing the release to *Playboy*.

Although we reject *Hustler's* argument that Douglass failed to prove an invasion of her right of privacy, we must also consider among other issues whether a reasonable jury could have found "actual malice" by *Hustler*. For failure to show actual malice would (possibly subject to qualification, as we shall see) be a defense, based on the First Amendment, to her tort suit. As the term is used in relation to the limitations that the First Amendment has been held to place on suits for defamation and "false light" invasion of privacy, it means knowledge of falsity or reckless disregard for truth. . . .

As *Hustler* does not so much as argue that it ever believed that Douglass was a lesbian, it was at the very least reckless in representing her as one, which we said a reasonable jury could have found it had done in "Robynn Douglass Nude." With regard to "actual malice" in representing her as voluntarily associating with the magazine, the only question is whether *Hustler* knew that it was acting without authorization—knew, in other words, that Douglass was not voluntarily associating herself with the magazine—or didn't care. *Hustler* argues that it relied on Gregory to supply authentic releases and cannot be found to have acted with actual malice if he submitted forged ones. The absence of any release from the other woman in the "Ripped-Off" pictorial undermines this claim; but a more important point is that Gregory was *Hustler's* photography editor, acting within the scope of his employment, so that his knowledge of the falsity of the releases was the corporation's knowledge. It makes no difference whether in submitting the photographs he was acting as an independent contractor, as *Hustler* argues, or as an employee. As photography editor, which is to say in his capacity as an employee, he had some—it does not matter precisely how much—responsibility for the provenance of the photographs that were published. If someone had submitted nude photographs of Robyn Douglass to him without a release and he had told his superiors there was a release, he would have been acting within the scope of his employment. It makes no difference that in fact he was the seller as well as the buying agent. The doctrine of respondeat superior is fully applicable to suits for defamation and invasion of privacy, notwithstanding the limitations that the First Amendment has been held to place on these torts. . . .

Although there is no basis for ordering the complaint dismissed, there were a number of trial errors which together persuade us that there must be a new trial. The first relates to the judge's failure to instruct the jury that it must find actual malice by "clear and convincing" evidence. This is one of the requirements that the Supreme Court has imposed in the name of freedom of the press on suits for defamation . . . and we can think of no reason why it might be inapplicable to suits against the press for invasions of privacy, at least when the invasion takes the form of casting the plaintiff in a false light—a form of invasion of privacy that, as we have seen, overlaps the tort of defamation. Courts have assumed as a matter of course that the requirement of proving actual malice by clear and convincing evidence indeed applies to the false-light tort. . . .

The judge here said that his error did not matter because the evidence of actual malice *was* clear and convincing. It may have been, but that did not make the error harmless. Douglass was not entitled to a directed verdict. Therefore the error in the instruction on burden of proof was not harmless. . . .

All of this assumes of course that actual malice must be proved regarding even so mundane a question as whether consent was obtained to publish some photographs, which is the only question on which *Hustler's* knowledge is a matter of fair debate. As an original matter we would have our doubts. The purpose of requiring proof of knowledge of falsity, or reckless disregard for the truth, is to lighten the investigative burdens on the press of determining the truth of what it writes. It is no great burden to determine whether a release has been executed; it is not like ascertaining the truth about allegations that a government official took a bribe or engaged in insider trading or fudged casualty statistics. A requirement that the plaintiff prove that the defendant was negligent in mistaking the existence of the release might be quite enough to protect the press from having to make costly investigations. The contrary argument is that the law under the First Amendment is complicated enough without attempting to make distinctions among the types of fact as to which actual malice is required in torts so closely related as defamation and false light. The qualification, however, and the analogy to copyright which supports Douglass's right-of-publicity claim, suggest that knowledge or even care is irrelevant at least to that claim; for it is no defense to copyright infringement that the infringer reasonably but mistakenly thought he had a license. . . .

Fortunately we need not try to unravel this tangled skein. The plaintiff does not argue that she was excused from having to prove actual malice because of the nature of her claim or the nature of *Hustler's* falsity in regard to her. She does argue that she was excused from having to prove actual malice because she is not a public figure. But a successful actress and model who has appeared nude many times in *Playboy* magazine cannot be called a "private person"; she is a public figure in a literal sense. The lifting of the burden of proving actual malice in defamation cases from the shoulders of plaintiffs who are not public figures reflects two things: the fact that people who do not thrust themselves into the public eye have on average a greater sense of privacy than those who do; and the difficulty that obscure people have, compared to celebrities, in commanding the media's attention to efforts to rebut innuendoes about them (whether defamatory, or merely offensive in a false-light sense). . . . But not only is Robyn Douglass no shrinking violet; she is a budding celebrity eager to be seen in the nude by millions of people—she *had* been seen in the nude by millions of people, the readers of *Playboy*, before *Hustler* got hold of her photographs. She is not like the plaintiff in *Braun v. Flynt, supra,* who did not become a public figure merely because her job in a local amusement park included feeding "Ralph, the Diving Pig" from a bottle of milk while treading water.

As an original matter one might want to confine the class of public figures to government officials and other politicians; freedom of political speech, and in particular freedom to criticize government officials and aspirants to public office, was the original concern of the First Amendment. But it is too late in the day to make such a distinction, at least at this judicial level. Art, even of the questionable sort represented by erotic photographs in "provocative" magazines—even of the artless sort represented by "topless" dancing—today enjoys extensive protection in the name of the First Amendment. . . . And so with news about art and entertainment. Entertainers can therefore be public figures for purposes of a publisher's or a broadcaster's First Amendment defense to a charge of false-light invasion of privacy. . . . Robyn Douglass clearly is one.

There is, incidentally, some question whether a plaintiff in a false-light case, merely because he (or she) is not a public figure, is relieved from having to prove actual malice, as would be true in a defamation case. The question was left open in *Cantrell v. Forest City Publishing Co., supra,* 419 U.S. at 250–51, 95 S.Ct. at 469. An argument can be made that the injury that being cast in a false light creates is less serious than that created by being defamed, and therefore the plaintiff should have a tougher row to hoe. We need not resolve the question here, but mention it lest our discussion of whether Robyn Douglass is a public figure be taken to have resolved it implicitly. . . .

The judgment is reversed and the case remanded for a new trial. No costs in this court.

REVERSED AND REMANDED.

UNREASONABLE INTRUSION

A defendant who intentionally intrudes upon the seclusion of another is liable for invasion of privacy if his intrusion would be considered "highly offensive to a reasonable person" (Restatement (Second) of Torts Sec. 652B). Physical intrusion includes the use of mechanical devices, such as binoculars or wiretaps. A private detective, for example, who in the process of seeking evidence for a lawsuit rents a room in a house adjoining the plaintiff's residence and monitors the plaintiff's activities for a period of time using a telescope will be considered to have invaded the plaintiff's privacy. Unreasonable intrusion may also be committed by opening the plaintiff's private mail, searching her purse, or examining her private bank account.

When consumer advocate Ralph Nader planned to publish a book attacking the safety of automobiles manufactured by General Motors, the company attempted to harass Nader by making threatening telephone calls, interviewing his acquaintances, tapping his phone, eavesdropping on him using electronic equipment, using women to make illicit proposals to him, and conducting surveillance on him in public places. The court held that Nader had a cause of action for invasion of privacy because of the wiretapping and electronic eavesdropping. The other activities, however, did not constitute invasion of privacy because the court did not consider them unreasonably intrusive (*Nader v. General Motors Corp,* 255 N.E.2d 765 (N.Y. 1970)).

PUBLIC DISCLOSURE OF PRIVATE FACTS

By the same token, publicizing the details of the plaintiff's private life may also constitute invasion of privacy. The matter publicized must be of the type that would be "highly offensive to a reasonable person" and must "not be of legitimate concern to the public" (Restatement (Second) of Torts Sec. 652D).

For example, a disgruntled creditor who posts a notice in the window of his store saying that the plaintiff owes him money invades the plaintiff's privacy (Restatement (Second) of Torts Sec. 652D, illustration 2).

No invasion of privacy exists if the details publicized are contained in a public record. If the name of a deceased rape victim is broadcast on television, the victim's parents have no claim for invasion of privacy because the victim's name would be available in an indictment, which would be available for public inspection at the suspect's trial (*Cox Broadcasting Corp. v. Cohn*, 420 U.S. 469 (1975)). Similarly, a murder suspect whose past history and daily life are recorded in the newspaper cannot claim invasion of privacy because his activities would be considered matters of legitimate concern to the public (Restatement (Second) of Torts Sec. 652D, illustration 13).

FALSE LIGHT

A plaintiff put before the public eye in a **false light** that would be highly offensive to a reasonable person can also sue for invasion of privacy (Restatement (Second) of Torts Sec. 652E). Suppose that a newspaper publishes an article about local taxi drivers cheating on their fares and uses the plaintiff's photograph to illustrate the article. If the photograph clearly implies that the plaintiff resorts to such practices (and in fact he does not), the plaintiff may recover for invasion of privacy. Such "false light" actions can be brought only if the plaintiff can show that the defendant deliberately portrayed the plaintiff in a false light or acted in reckless disregard of the issue (*Time, Inc. v. Hill*, 385 U.S. 374 (1967)).

A "false light" case may or may not be considered grounds for defamation. The *Douglass* court (on page 338) considers the similarities and dissimilarities between false light and defamation and discusses why a plaintiff may opt for a false light claim rather than a defamation claim. In addition to being easier to prove in some respects than defamation, the court points out, the tort of false light allows recovery for offensive publicity (depicting a plaintiff as pathetic or ridiculous) and not just defamatory publicity (depicting the plaintiff as immoral or dishonest).

Suppose a movie is made about a war hero's life and the movie contains details regarding the fictitious private life of the war hero, including a nonexistent romance. Even if the moviemaker were aware of the falsity of some of the portrayal, the plaintiff could not sue for defamation as long as the movie did not tend to harm the plaintiff's reputation. He could, however, sue for invasion of privacy if the presentation would be considered "highly offensive to a reasonable person" (Restatement (Second) of Torts Sec. 652E, illustration 5).

INTERFERENCE WITH FAMILY RELATIONS

Under the common law a jilted spouse could recover for "alienation of affections" or "criminal conversation." Recovery for **alienation of affections** was allowed against anyone who caused the plaintiff's spouse to lose affection for the plaintiff. The defendant did not necessarily have to be a romantic rival but could be a friend or relative who convinced the spouse to leave the plaintiff

(Restatement (Second) of Torts Sec. 683). A claim for **criminal conversation** could be alleged against anyone who had sexual intercourse with another's spouse. The fact that the spouse rather than the defendant initiated the act or that the spouse falsely represented that he or she was unmarried was not considered a defense (Restatement (Second) of Torts Sec. 685). Many states have eliminated both causes of action by statute.

Although a parent will not usually have a tort claim against anyone who alienates his or her child's affections, a few exceptions exist. If the defendant causes a minor child to leave home, the parent may have a claim for alienation of affections. Many tort claims filed against Reverend Sung Yung Moon and his followers were based on this tort. Such claims were particularly appropriate since defendants are not relieved of liability even though they act out of kindness or affection for the child. Similarly, a parent who has been awarded sole custody of a child may sue the noncustodial parent for abducting the child or inducing him or her to leave the custodial parent's home. A parent can also maintain a tort claim against anyone who has sexual intercourse with his or her minor daughter even though the daughter gave consent and was above the statutory age of consent (Restatement (Second) of Torts Sec. 701). Interestingly, such a claim will not lie for a minor son.

INTERFERENCE WITH BUSINESS RELATIONS

Three tort actions specifically protect business interests. They are interference with existing contractual relations, interference with prospective contractual relations, and injurious falsehood (see Table 17–3).

TABLE 17.3 Interference with Business Relations

INTERFERENCE WITH EXISTING CONTRACTUAL RELATIONS	INTERFERENCE WITH PROSPECTIVE CONTRACTUAL RELATIONS
Defendant intentionally and actively induces another to breach a contract with plaintiff.	Defendant unlawfully and maliciously induces another to stop doing business with plaintiff.

INJURIOUS FALSEHOOD
•TRADE LIBEL: Defendant falsely disparages plaintiff's goods or business. •SLANDER OF TITLE: Defendant disparages plaintiff's property rights.

INTERFERENCE WITH EXISTING CONTRACTUAL RELATIONS

One commits interference with existing contractual relations by inducing another to breach a contract with the plaintiff. The defendant's interference must be intentional (negligence is not sufficient) and improper. Several factors are taken into consideration when deciding if a tort has been committed. They include the purpose and motive of the defendant, the means used to create the interference, the type of interest with which the defendant interferes, as well as the social interest involved in protecting both the defendant's freedom of action and the contractual interest of the plaintiff (Restatement (Second) of Torts Sec. 766 and 767).

One of the first and certainly most famous decisions imposing liability for intentional inducement of a breach of contract was *Lumley v. Gye*, 118 Eng.Rep. 749 (Q.B. 1853). In *Lumley* the plaintiff's theater entered into a contract with an opera singer in which she agreed she would not perform for anyone else during a period of time. The defendant deliberately enticed the singer to refuse to perform and was held liable for improper interference with a contractual relationship.

In more modern times, liability for contractual interference was found in a case in which an attorney, after terminating his employment with a law firm, actively engaged in an attempt to procure business for his new law firm. He contacted some of the firm's clients with whom he had been working and advised them that he was leaving the firm and that they could choose to be represented by him, the firm, or any other firm or attorney. Additionally, he mailed these clients form letters that could be used to discharge the firm as counsel and create a contingency fee agreement between him and the client. The court reasoned that the attorney used his position of trust and responsibility to unfairly prejudice the firm. The court also concluded that no public interest was served in allowing such use of confidential information (*Adler, Barish, Daniels, Levin and Creskoff v. Epstein*, 393 A.2d 1175 (Pa. 1978)).

Active Interference. The defendant must actively interfere with the contract. Merely offering a better price to a third person, knowing that this might cause the third person to breach his contract with the plaintiff, is not sufficient. On the other hand, suppose the defendant says "I'll give you a better price than the plaintiff is offering and if you accept my offer you'll save enough money to afford to break your contract with the plaintiff and still come out ahead." By this statement the defendant actively induces a breach of contract (Restatement (Second) of Torts Sec. 766, illustration 3).

Kind of Contract Involved. Some kinds of contracts cannot serve as a basis for this tort. The plaintiff cannot recover if a contract that is illegal or "contrary to public policy" is breached. Similarly, most courts will not hold the defendant liable if he or she induces the breach of a contract that is terminable at will. An **at will employee** is one who, because of the employment agreement into which he entered with his employer, can be discharged at any time for any reason. The Restatement (Second) and a growing number of courts, however, do consider the inducing of a breach of an at-will contract to be contractual interference. The reasoning behind this approach is that a plaintiff has a right to expect that the contract will not be tampered with until it is in fact terminated. Contracts that are unenforceable for other reasons, such as lack of consideration or because they are not in conformance with the Statute of Frauds, can serve as a basis for contractual interference.

Remedies. The plaintiff may certainly recover for pecuniary losses he or she sustains as a result of the interference and also, according to some courts, may be allowed to recover for emotional harm. The plaintiff can recover for breach of contract against the person the defendant induced to breach the contract.

In one case, the plaintiffs, a black family that contracted to buy a house in a white neighborhood, were allowed to recover for mental suffering from the defendants, their would-be neighbors, who induced the owner not to go through with the sale. They were also allowed to seek specific performance from the seller as well as incidental expenses they incurred as a result of the breach. The plaintiffs were not, however, entitled to recover twice for the same damages. They could not, for example, recover from the seller the interest they had to pay while waiting for their suit and then recover that sum again from the defendants who induced the breach (*Duff v. Engelberg*, 47 Cal.Rptr. 114 (Cal.Dist. Ct.App. 1965)).

Privileges. If a defendant merely tries to protect his own existing contractual rights, he will be privileged to induce a breach as long as his motive is not trying to gain business for himself. If a buyer is aware, for example, that a manufacturer of goods has promised to deliver goods to both himself and another buyer, he can ask that the manufacturer fulfill his contract even if he is aware that the manufacturer will be unable to fulfill both contracts.

If an individual induces a breach for the purpose of promoting social interests, he or she will also be privileged. One unusual case illustrating this point involved a burlesque troupe known as the Wu Tut Tut Revue, whose manager so underpaid the performers that they were forced to eke out an existence by resorting to prostitution. The defendant persuaded the theater owners with whom the troupe had contracted to perform to cancel the contract unless higher wages were paid to the performers. The defendant's action was considered justified and therefore not tortious (*Brimelow v. Casson*, 1 Ch. 302 (1924)).

INTERFERENCE WITH PROSPECTIVE CONTRACTUAL RELATIONS

Essentially the same rules apply to interference with prospective contractual relations as to interference with existing contractual relations except for one major difference. Since no contract actually exists, the defendant is given greater leeway as to what he can do to interfere. Although a defendant cannot interfere with an existing contract for the purpose of obtaining business for himself, he is privileged to do so where only a potential contract is involved. He is even privileged to drive a plaintiff out of business as long as he does not use unlawful means, such as price fixing or monopolization. But if he acts out of sheer malice his conduct will not be privileged.

Interference with a plaintiff's nonbusiness expectations of financial gain can be the basis for this tort. If the defendant induces a testator to leave the plaintiff out of his will, he can be held liable. Interference with a plaintiff's potential legal claim can also be tortious. A defendant may be liable if he tampers with medical records or conceals facts from the plaintiff that if known would reveal a cause of action.

INJURIOUS FALSEHOOD

Injurious falsehood protects plaintiffs against false statements made against their business, product, or property rights. If the plaintiff's goods or business are falsely disparaged, the tort committed is typically referred to as **trade libel** but if the disparagement refers to property rights of the plaintiff, the tort is usually referred to as **slander of title.**

Trade Libel. To recover for trade libel the plaintiff must show that the defendant made a false statement clearly referring to the plaintiff's goods or business that disparaged those goods or business. A defendant who falsely claims during an interview on national television that his company is the only one of its kind may be liable for disparaging a plaintiff's business that is identical to his.

Note that trade libel differs from defamation in that the false statement need not ridicule or disgrace the plaintiff. As with defamation, however, the plaintiff must show the statement was published and that he suffered some kind of pecuniary harm. The defendant must also either know his statement was false, act with reckless disregard for the truth or falsity of his statement, or (according to some courts) act out of spite toward the plaintiff.

The same defenses that are applicable to defamation are applicable to trade libel. A defendant is also privileged to fairly compete with a plaintiff by making general comparisons between his product and the plaintiff's. A competitor is in fact permitted to "puff" even if he is aware that his statements are false and are made for the purpose of taking business away from the plaintiff. The defendant is not privileged, however, if he makes specific false allegations about the plaintiff's product.

Slander of Title. If a defendant falsely disparages the property right of another he commits slander of title. For example, if he interferes with the plaintiff's right to hold or dispose of property by filing a false document, such as a mortgage or levy of execution, he commits slander of title. Leases, mineral rights, trademarks, copyrights, and patents may all be subjected to slander of title. The same intent, defenses, and privileges applicable to trade libel apply to slander of title. Additionally, a defendant has a qualified privilege to protect his own interest by asserting a bona fide claim to property. An assertion of infringement on a patent right is privileged as long as the assertion is made in good faith and in the absence of any motive of a desire to do harm.

MISUSE OF LEGAL PROCESS

A plaintiff who has been subjected to unwarranted judicial proceedings may sue on the basis of malicious prosecution, wrongful institution of civil proceedings, or abuse of process (see Table 17–4). Notice that the plaintiff in

TABLE 17.4 Misuse of Legal Process

MALICIOUS PROSECUTION	WRONGFUL INSTITUTION OF CIVIL PROCEEDINGS
Defendant institutes criminal proceedings against plaintiff but has no probable cause and acts out of motives other than a sense of bringing plaintiff to justice.	Defendant institutes civil proceedings against plaintiff but has no probable cause and acts out of motives other than seeking compensation for wrong suffered.

ABUSE OF PROCESS
Defendant uses litigation devices for improper purposes.

these cases was originally the defendant in the cause of action leading to the suit involving the misuse of legal process. Suppose an individual became the target of a criminal investigation resulting in his becoming the defendant in a criminal trial. If the individual believed the prosecutor's chief witness fabricated the story involving the defendant and actively sought to bring criminal proceedings against the defendant out of vengeance because of a squabble the two had had years earlier, the defendant in the criminal action could sue the prosecutor's witness, who would become the defendant in the malicious prosecution suit.

MALICIOUS PROSECUTION

A defendant whose motives are for some purpose other than bringing the plaintiff to justice and who, without probable cause, institutes criminal proceedings against another commits *malicious prosecution* (Restatement (Second) of Torts Sec. 653). For the plaintiff to recover, the proceedings must conclude in the plaintiff's favor and the defendant must actively participate in instigating the prosecution. A defendant who leaves the decision in the hands of the prosecutor is not considered to have actively participated in the prosecution. Rather, the defendant must have lied to the prosecutor or attempted in some way to influence his decision to prosecute. The proceedings are deemed to have concluded in favor of the plaintiff if the prosecutor decides not to prosecute, the grand jury refuses to indict, or the case is dismissed because of the weakness of the case. A plaintiff's plea of guilty in acceptance of a plea bargain is not considered a favorable conclusion for the plaintiff.

The most difficult hurdle for plaintiffs to overcome in malicious prosecution cases is the probable cause requirement. If a defendant reasonably believes that the plaintiff committed certain acts, he will be deemed to have probable cause. If it turns out that the defendant's belief is mistaken, his mistake will not constitute lack of probable cause as long as the mistake is a reasonable one. An acquittal does not necessarily indicate a lack of probable cause since an acquittal may occur because of reasonable doubt rather than lack of probable cause. Therefore, even if the plaintiff is acquitted, the defendant has a right to, in essence, retry the plaintiff. If he can show by a preponderance of the evidence that the plaintiff was guilty, he can establish the existence of probable cause.

In showing improper purpose, the plaintiff must show that the defendant acted out of malice or for some reason other than seeing that justice was done. A creditor, for example, who uses the criminal process to compel a debtor to pay her debt has an improper purpose (Restatement (Second) of Torts Sec. 668, comment g).

Prosecutors are almost always immune from malicious prosecution suits. Immunity is also generally given to police officers as long as they are acting within the general scope of their duties.

WRONGFUL INSTITUTION OF CIVIL PROCEEDINGS

Although the tort of malicious prosecution normally applies to criminal proceedings, most states allow similar actions for *wrongful institution of civil proceedings*. The elements are essentially the same as for malicious prosecution although civil proceedings may encompass administrative proceedings, bankruptcy proceedings, and insanity proceedings as well as ordinary civil lawsuits. Proving lack of probable cause in a civil case is more difficult than in a criminal case since one can initiate civil proceedings with far less certainty of the facts than in a criminal proceeding. A suit brought merely to harass an opponent or to extort a settlement when the defendant is aware there is no real chance of succeeding exemplify wrongful institution of civil proceedings. A counterclaim brought solely for the purpose of delaying proceedings is another example.

ABUSE OF PROCESS

If an individual initiates a criminal or civil proceeding based on probable cause and on the basis of permissible motives, he may still be liable for **abuse of process** if he uses certain litigation devices for improper purposes. Using a subpoena, for example, to harass someone or to induce her to settle rather than for its practical purpose of obtaining testimony could be considered abuse of process (Restatement (Second) of Torts Sec. 682, illustration 3). As long as the primary purpose for the proceeding is justified the fact that the defendant has an ulterior motive or that the proceedings may be of some incidental benefit to her is irrelevant. If the instigation of bankruptcy proceedings is justified, it does not become abuse of process merely because the instigator of those proceedings hopes she will gain some benefit from the closing down of her competitor's business. Typically, abuse of process involves those situations in which a party puts undue pressure on another to induce her to engage in or refrain from a particular action.

SUMMARY

A public nuisance requires an interference with a right common to the general public; a private nuisance is an unreasonable interference with the plaintiff's use and enjoyment of his or her own land. To prove public nuisance a plaintiff must show that the public at large was injured or exposed to the possibility of injury and the harm must be a substantial one. The harm suffered by the plaintiff must be peculiar to him or her and not shared by the rest of the public. Some courts allow recovery, however, if the plaintiff suffers greater economic loss than others in the community.

Private nuisance, on the other hand, requires only that the plaintiff's use and enjoyment of his or her land is substantially interfered with and that the defendant's conduct is negligent, intentional, or abnormally dangerous. Interference is considered substantial if the plaintiff is inconvenienced or subjected to unpleasant sensory awarenesses. A plaintiff may seek either compensatory damages or an injunction. If he seeks an injunction, however, he must prove that his harm outweighs the utility of the defendant's conduct. Contributory negligence and assumption of risk can be raised as defenses in private nuisance claims.

The right to privacy consists of four separate torts: appropriation, unreasonable intrusion, public disclosure of private facts, and false light. Appropriation consists of the use of the value of the plaintiff's name or picture for the defendant's financial gain. Unreasonable intrusion occurs when the defendant intentionally intrudes upon the seclusion of another and his intrusion would be considered "highly offensive to a reasonable person." Publicizing details of the plaintiff's private life that would be "highly offensive to a reasonable person" and would "not be of legitimate concern to the public" constitutes public disclosure of private facts. If the details publicized are contained in a public record no tort is committed. The so-called "false light" cases occur when the plaintiff is put in the public eye in a false light that would be highly offensive to a reasonable person.

Under the common law a jilted spouse could recover for alienation of affections or criminal conversation. Many states have eliminated both causes of action. With a couple of exceptions, parents generally cannot bring tort claims against those who alienate their children's affections.

Three tort actions that specifically protect business interests are interference with existing contractual relations, interference with prospective contractual relations, and injurious falsehood. Intentionally and actively inducing another to breach a contract with the plaintiff constitutes interference with existing contractual relations. When deciding if this tort is committed the courts will consider the defendant's motive and purpose, the means he uses to create the interference, the type of interest with which he interferes, and the social interest involved in protecting both the defendant's freedom of action and the contractual interest of the plaintiff. Greater latitude is allowed defendants charged with interference with prospective contractual relations. A false statement made against a plaintiff's business, product, or property opens one to a claim of injurious falsehood. A false statement made in reference to the plaintiff's goods or business is usually referred to as trade libel but a false statement in reference to the property rights of the plaintiff is referred to as slander of title.

Anyone subjected to unwarranted judicial proceedings may recover on the basis of malicious prosecution, wrongful institution of civil proceedings, or abuse of process. Malicious prosecution occurs when a defendant actively participates in instituting criminal proceedings against another, lacks probable cause, and has motives other than bringing the plaintiff to justice. Wrongful institution of civil proceedings is comparable to malicious prosecution except that it involves the initiation of civil proceedings. Abuse of process occurs when an individual institutes criminal or civil proceedings on the basis of permissible motives and with probable cause but uses litigation devices for improper purposes.

PRACTICE POINTERS

Trial Exhibits

Exhibits are used at trial to explain, illustrate, and emphasize points that are of particular importance for a jury to understand. In a typical personal injury case exhibits include such things as police reports, medical reports, independent medical examination reports, photographs of the scene, and medical therapeutic devices. Legal assistants often assist attorneys in preparing these exhibits. They must be intimately familiar with the facts and issues involved in the case.

When initially identifying those documents and evidentiary items that will be used as trial exhibits, preparing a preliminary exhibit list is often helpful. This exhibit list should include a description of the critical items to be included along with the location of each item, the witness that will be used to offer it into evidence, and a tentative exhibit number.

Most courts require that each exhibit be premarked with an exhibit number. Appropriate exhibit numbers are determined either by local

PRELIMINARY EXHIBIT LIST FOR *JONES v. BAXTER*

Exhibit No.	Description	Witness
1	Teddy's medical records from St. Mary's hospital, 6/9/90 to 6/14/90. Location: S. T. Lewis deposition file	Dr. S. T. Lewis
2	8″ × 10″ photos of Teddy's injuries. Location: H. R. Jones deposition file	Harriett Jones, Mother
3	9/23/90 psychiatric report of Dr. Samuel Westphal regarding phobic reactions of Teddy. Location: S. L. Westphal deposition file	Dr. S. L. Westphal

Continued on next page

PRACTICE POINTERS

SAMPLE MASTER EXHIBIT LIST

Exhibit Number	Description	Witness	Marked for Id.	Received in evidence
Pl.Ex.1	Teddy's medical records from St. Mary's hospital, 6/9/90 to 6/14/90. Location: S. T. Lewis deposition file	S. T. Lewis	12/8/91	12/8/91
Pl.Ex.2	8/10 photos of Teddy's injuries. Location: H. R. Jones file	Harriet Jones, Mother	12/8/91	12/8/91
Pl.Ex.3	9/23/90 psychiatric report of Dr. Samuel Westphal regarding phobic reactions of Teddy. Location: S. L. Westphal file	Dr. S. L. Westphal	12/8/91	12/9/91
Def.Ex. 2	9/24/90 medical report of Dr. T. F. Shephard (independent medical examiner)	Dr. T. F. Shephard	12/12/91	12/12/91

rules or by agreement of the parties. Each exhibit must be assigned an individual number. If a large number of documents must be assigned a single exhibit number, they can be differentiated using decimal numbers (e.g., exhibits 5.0, 5.1, 5.2, 5.3, etc.).

Immediately before trial a master trial exhibit list should be prepared in conformance with the court's required format. Such a list should include the exhibit numbers, descriptions of the exhibits, and the names of the witnesses who will be testifying when the evidence is offered. Leave room to indicate at what point in the trial the evidence is marked for identification and when it is received into evidence. Copies of this master exhibit list should be distributed to the judge, the trial clerk, opposing counsel, and the testifying witnesses. An extra set of copies should be made for emergency purposes and, of course, one copy should be maintained at counsel's table.

While some jurisdictions allow copies to be used at trial, others require the use of original documents. If copies are used, make sure they are

Continued on next page

PRACTICE POINTERS—Continued

as legible as possible. If originals are mandated, you must locate the source of each exhibit.

Evidence must be identified in some manner as an exhibit. This is usually done by affixing a court-supplied sticker to the document. These documents are then retained in manila folders, which are correspondingly labeled with the appropriate exhibit number.

Trial exhibits can also include demonstrative visual aids such as charts, enlargements of important documents, anatomy models, and videotapes. Such evidence can frequently be used to complement the testimony of expert witnesses. Several points are important to keep in mind when preparing this type of evidence. Charts must be simple enough for a jury to understand them in a single glance. Lettering must be large and clear enough to be seen by all participants at the trial. Consistency in the charts is a must (for example, if blue is used in one chart to indicate something in particular it should be used in all other charts to indicate the same thing). Such evidence should generally be hidden from the jury until it is used because its impact will be considerably diminished if it is revealed prematurely. Finally, opposing counsel ought not be able to use your evidence to prove a contrary point. If opposing counsel identifies a distortion in one of your charts, he or she can use that to rebut your argument and thus deflate your persuasiveness.

Arrange for the storage of exhibits with the court clerk prior to trial if the transportation of these exhibits would become cumbersome. Check out all audiovisual aids prior to using them at trial. Interruptions in an attorney's delivery caused by equipment failure detract from the polished presentation the attorney wants to deliver and undercuts the impact of any point he or she is trying to make.

TORT TEASERS

Decide which tort you think would be appropriate to allege in each of the following cases.

1. Defendant purchases a home in a residential area and uses it to operate a funeral home. *Williams v. Montgomery,* 186 So. 302 (Miss. 1939).

2. A man sues his ex-wife for defamation because of her claims that he is homosexual and that Plaintiff is his lover. The ex-wife asks Defendant, a deputy sheriff, to secure a hair sample from Plaintiff while he is in the hospital.

Defendant pays an orderly who obtains combings from Plaintiff's hair brush and a discarded adhesive bandage. Plaintiff does not learn of this intrusion until after it occurs. *Froelich v. Werbin*, 548 P.2d 482 (Kan. 1976).

3. A bitter dispute arises between Plaintiff school district and Defendant teachers' association. The teachers' association subpoenas 87 teachers and refuses to stagger their appearances, thereby requiring the school district to hire substitutes in order to avoid a total shut-down of the schools. *Board of Ed. of Farmingdale Union Freeschool District v. Farmingdale Classroom Teachers' Assoc., Inc.*, 343 N.E.2d 278 (Ct.App. N.Y. 1975).

4. Pennzoil Company (Plaintiff) and Getty Oil negotiate a contract involving the sale of Getty Oil to Pennzoil. After a press release is issued by both parties, Getty Oil's investment banker continues to contact other companies, looking for a higher price than Pennzoil offered. While Pennzoil's attorneys work on a draft of a formal transaction agreement, Getty Oil accepts an offer from Texaco (Defendant). Pennzoil immediately contacts Getty and demands that Getty honor its agreement with Pennzoil. Evidence exists that Texaco had a strong motivation to acquire the oil reserves of Getty and that it deliberately formulated and implemented a strategy to acquire Getty Oil. *Texaco, Inc. v. Pennzoil, Co.*, 729 S.W.2d 768 (Tex.App.-Houston [First District] 1987).

5. Plaintiff, a manufacturer of loudspeaker systems and other audio equipment, claims that Defendant consumer product-testing organization published false statements in its review of Plaintiff's loudspeakers. What claim might Plaintiff file in addition to a defamation claim? *Bose Corp. v. Consumers U. of U.S., Inc.*, 508 F.Supp. 1249 (D.C.Mass 1981).

KEY TERMS

■ **Abuse of process**
Use of litigation devices for improper purposes.

■ **Alienation of affections**
Causing a plaintiff to lose affection for his or her spouse.

■ **Appropriation**
Use of the value of the plaintiff's name or picture for the defendant's financial gain.

■ **At-will employee**
Employee who, because of the nature of his or her employment contract, can be discharged at any time for any reason.

■ **Criminal conversation**
Having sexual intercourse with another's spouse.

■ **False light**
Representing the plaintiff to the public in a way that would be highly offensive to a reasonable person.

■ **Injurious falsehood**
False disparagement of a plaintiff's business, product, or property rights.

■ **Nuisance**
Substantial and unreasonable interference with a plaintiff's intent; includes public and private nuisance.

■ **Slander of title**
False disparagement of plaintiff's property right.

■ **Trade libel**
False disparagement of plaintiff's goods or business.

PART III WHOM TO SUE

18 VICARIOUS LIABILITY

CHAPTER OBJECTIVES

In this chapter you will learn to:

- Identify the circumstances in which an employer is vicariously liable for the acts of an employee or an independent contractor.
- Distinguish between an employer-employee relationship and an employer-independent contractor relationship.
- Identify the exceptions to the bailor nonliability rule as applied to the owners of automobiles.
- Recognize situations in which contributory negligence is imputed.
- Identify the circumstances in which parents are vicariously liable for the acts of their children.

Let us take a brief excursion into the not-too-distant future when you have completed your program of study and have assumed a position as a legal assistant. Suppose you are asked by your supervisoring attorney to draft a contract and the attorney, who is called out of town on a personal emergency, never reviews the contract. As he dashes out of the office he yells back at you to be sure that the contract is signed by the parties within the week. Before you can utter a word of protest he is gone. Can he be held liable for any provisions in the contract that eventually inure to the detriment of the client?

Suppose that your attorney asks you to do a research project in the library. While enroute to the library you happen to pass a very elite clothing store, which you are aware is having an outrageous one-day-only sale. Knowing that this is your only chance to take advantage of these bargains, you stop by the store for a few minutes. You put your briefcase on the floor so your hands are free to do some serious shopping. Another customer fails to notice your briefcase, catches her heel on its handles, and falls to the ground. The tumble she takes is a bad one and paramedics have to be called. Will this woman be able to sue your employer since you were engaged in your shopping diversion during your work time?

Now suppose that, unnerved by the incident at the clothing store, you rush off to the library. Once there you immerse yourself in the task at hand. Suddenly whose face appears among the bookstacks but your ex-spouse's? Since you have only recently escaped the chains of matrimony, within thirty seconds the two of you are engaged in a full-scale verbal war. Without warning some demonic urge possesses you and you find yourself using your briefcase (the same one that just wreaked havoc on the customer) as a weapon. Will your ex be able to recover from your employer for the injuries sustained as a result of your pugilistic activities? These and other related questions will be explored in this chapter.

OVERVIEW OF VICARIOUS LIABILITY

Under the doctrine of **vicarious liability**, an individual is held liable for the tortious acts of another. These acts are imputed to him because of the special relationship he holds to the tortfeasor. The most common relationship is the one between employer and employee, in which the employer is held vicariously liable for the tortious acts of his or her employee. Vicarious liability may also arise in relationships between employers and independent contractors and in activities involving joint enterprises. Furthermore, automobile consent statutes and the family purpose doctrine possess elements of vicarious liability (see Table 18–1).

EMPLOYER-EMPLOYEE RELATIONSHIP

An employer is vicariously liable for the acts of an employee under the doctrine of ***respondeat superior***, which translates as "let the person higher up answer." This doctrine applies to negligent torts, intentional torts, and strict liability

TABLE 18.1

EXAMPLES OF VICARIOUS LIABILITY
Employers - Employees
Employers - Independent Contractors
Members of Joint Enterprise
Automobile Consent Statutes
Family Purpose Doctrine

actions (see Table 18–2). The rationale most commonly used to justify this doctrine is that employers should consider the expense of reimbursing those injured by their employees as part of the cost of doing business. As a practical matter, keep in mind that typically the employee is judgment proof while the employer is the proverbial "deep pocket."

For the doctrine to be applicable the employee must be acting "within the scope and furtherance of his employment" (Restatement (Second) of Agency Sec. 229). An employee will be considered to be doing this as long as he is intending to further his employer's business purpose. Even if the means he chooses are indirect or foolish or if his intent is a combination of serving his employer and meeting his personal needs, he will be viewed as acting "within the scope and furtherance of his employment." Travel to and from work, however, is generally not included as falling within the scope of employment.

INTENTIONAL TORTS

What if an employee intentionally injures another? The employer will still be liable as long as the tort is reasonably connected to the employee's job. A company may be liable, for example, for false imprisonment committed by an overzealous security guard who unreasonably detains a customer she suspects of shoplifting or for assault and battery committed by an employee who resorts to Rambo-style techniques in trying to collect a debt for the company. The employer will not be liable if the employee's acts are driven by some purely personal motive, such as vengeance.

FROLICS AND DETOURS

An employer is not vicariously liable when an employee goes on a "frolic" or "detour" of his own. Suppose an employee of a pizza parlor, having completed his deliveries, drives twenty miles out of his way for a little rendezvous with his girlfriend. His twenty-mile side trip would likely be considered a "frolic" or "detour" and, under the traditional view, his employer would

TABLE 18.2 Employer-Employee Liability (*Respondeat Superior*)

EMPLOYER IS LIABLE	EMPLOYER IS NOT LIABLE
•Employee is acting within the scope and furtherance of employment. •Employee commits intentional tort reasonably connected to job. •Employee's deviation from business purpose is reasonably foreseeable. •Employee commits acts expressly forbidden by employer but within scope of employment. •Employee negligently delegates his or her rights and authority to another without the employer's authorization.	•Employee goes on "frolic" or "detour." •Employee is traveling to or from work.

not be vicariously liable for any acts of negligence he might commit. However, if the employee became involved in an accident while enroute back to the pizza parlor, the employer would once again become vicariously liable because once he got back on track, the employee would be acting within the scope of his employment.

Under the more modern view the employee would be seen as acting within the scope of his employment if his deviation from his business purpose was "reasonably foreseeable." Under this approach an employee whose deviation is slight in terms of time and distance is considered acting within the scope of his employment even when he is on a personal errand. The reasoning underlying this approach is that employers should be liable for those things that can generally be anticipated as one of the risks of doing business.

FORBIDDEN ACTS

Is the employer liable even if he or she explicitly forbids the employee to engage in certain acts and the employee does so anyway? Yes, as long as the acts are done within the scope and furtherance of employment. Suppose a store expressly forbids its employees from using physical force to detain someone suspected of shoplifting. The store will nevertheless be vicariously liable for the negligence of its employees who countermand those orders, and wrestle to the ground and hogtie an uncooperative customer whom they suspect of shoplifting.

DELEGATION OF AUTHORITY OR RIGHTS

Vicarious liability may or may not exist when an employee delegates his or her authority or rights to another without the employer's authorization. What if an employee hires someone without the employer's permission? Or what if he allows an unauthorized person to use the employer's property, such as the company car, and that person commits a tort? In both cases vicarious liability will exist if the employee acted negligently. If the employee knew or should have known that the individual lacked skills and would be unable to safely complete the job, the employer will be vicariously liable. Notice that the issue of vicarious liability hinges on the employee's negligence and not the third party's negligence because vicarious liability is based on the link existing between the employer and the employee.

EMPLOYERS–INDEPENDENT CONTRACTORS

Generally, one who hires an independent contractor will not be held vicariously liable for the tortious acts of that person. Several exceptions, however, can be found to that basic rule.

Before dealing with those exceptions we must first distinguish between an employee and an independent contractor. An employee is typically viewed as someone under the control of the person who hired him; an **independent contractor**, although hired to produce certain results, is considered his own boss. An independent contractor works at his own pace, in his own way, under his own supervision.

Under this definition would a newspaper carrier be considered an employee or an independent contractor? In *Santiago v. Phoenix Newspapers, Inc.* this question is raised. The court considers a number of factors, including the amount of control exercised by the employer over the carrier's work, the nature of the carrier's work, the length of employment, the method of payment, and so on. Notice that the language in the parties' contract does not determine the nature of their relationship. As you read through this opinion pay attention to the court's use of the IRAC method of analysis (discussed in Chapter 3).

CASE

Cite as
64 Ariz. Adv. Rep. 20
IN THE SUPREME COURT
OF THE STATE OF ARIZONA
En Banc
William SANTIAGO, a single man, Plaintiff/Appellant,
v.
PHOENIX NEWSPAPERS, INC., an Arizona corporation,
Defendant/Appellee.
No. CV-89-0042-PR FILED: July 3, 1990

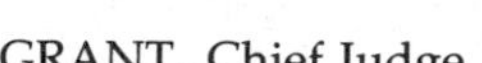

GRANT, Chief Judge.

The appellant, William Santiago (Santiago), asks this court to review the court of appeals' decision affirming the trial court's entry of summary judgment in favor of Phoenix Newspapers, Inc. (PNI). We granted review to consider whether the trial court correctly found as a matter of law that PNI was not vicariously liable for the injuries Santiago sustained in a collision with a PNI delivery agent. . . .

PROCEDURAL HISTORY

On April 20, 1986, a car driven by Frank Frausto (Frausto) collided with a motorcycle driven by Santiago. At the time Frausto was delivering the Sunday edition of the Arizona Republic on his route for PNI. Santiago filed a negligence action against Frausto and PNI, alleging that Frausto was PNI's agent. Both parties moved for summary judgment. The court, finding no genuine issues of material fact, concluded that Frausto was an independent contractor. The court of appeals agreed, stating that "[p]arties have a perfect right, in their dealings with each other, to establish the independent contractor status in order to avoid the relationship of employer-employee, and it is clear from the undisputed facts that there was no employer-employee relationship created between PNI and Frausto." . . .

FACTS

Frausto began delivering papers for PNI in August 1984 under a "Delivery Agent Agreement," prepared by PNI. The agreement provided that Frausto was an "independent contractor," retained to provide prompt delivery of its newspapers by the times specified in the contract. Although Frausto had the right to operate the business as he chose, he could engage others to deliver papers on his route for no more than 25% of the delivery days. He was free to pursue any other business activities, including delivering other publications, so long as those activities did not interfere with his performance of the PNI contract. Frausto was also required to provide PNI with satisfactory proof of liability insurance, a valid driver's license, and a favorable report from the Arizona Motor Vehicle Division.

The contract was for a period of six months, renewable at PNI's option. Either party could terminate the agreement prior to six months without cause with 28 days notice and for cause with no notice. Under the contract, cause for termination by PNI existed if complaints from home delivery subscribers exceeded an undefined "acceptable" level, or if Frausto failed to maintain "acceptable" subscriber relations or provide "satisfactory service," defined as banding and bagging newspapers to insure they were received in a dry and readable condition. PNI was also free to breach the agreement if it ceased publishing the paper, defined in the contract as "excusable non-compliance." There is no correlative definition of cause for termination by Frausto. Customers paid PNI directly and any complaints about delivery were funnelled through PNI to Frausto. Additionally, the contract required Frausto to allow a PNI employee to accompany him on his route "for the purposes of verifying distribution, subscriber service, or regular newspaper business."

Early each morning, Frausto drove to a PNI-specified distribution point to load the papers into his car. He then delivered the papers before a PNI-specified time to addresses on a delivery list provided and owned by PNI. He could deliver the papers to listed addresses only. When customers were added to and taken from this list by PNI, Frausto was required to incorporate these changes into his route. According to Frausto, the number of papers delivered fluctuated by as much as thirty papers. For these services, PNI paid Frausto a set amount each week. That amount did not vary when addresses within or beyond the contracted delivery area were added to or taken away by PNI from the delivery list. PNI provided Frausto with health and disability insurance, but did not withhold any taxes.

In ruling on the summary judgment motion, the court considered the affidavits of Frausto and David L. Miller, a delivery agent and former employee driver. Frausto stated in his affidavit that, despite the contractual nomenclature, he considered himself an employee and delivered the papers any way his supervisor directed him to. This included placing the paper in a particular spot if requested by the customer. If he did not comply with these requests, his supervisor would speak to him and he could be fired. Miller stated in his affidavit that he had been a service driver, later switched to being a delivery agent, and that, in his view, there was no significant difference between the level of supervision provided to those holding the two positions.

DISCUSSION

If the inference in this case is clear that no master-servant relationship exists, the trial court was correct in granting summary judgment; if it is not clear, the case should have been presented to the jury to decide. . . . We apply the rule in this case by asking whether the courts below correctly decided that no inferences could be drawn from the material facts suggesting Frausto was acting as PNI's employee when the accident occurred.

Section 220 of the *Restatement (Second) of Agency*, adopted by Arizona, . . . defines a servant as "a person employed to perform services in the affairs of another and who with respect to the physical conduct in the performance of the services is subject to the other's control or right to control." The *Restatement* lists several additional factors, none of which is dispositive, in determining whether one acting for another is a servant or an independent contractor. We now review those factors, along with the cases considering them, for evidence of an employer-employee relationship which could preclude the entry of summary judgment.

As a prefatory note, we reject PNI's argument that the language of the employment contract is determinative. Contract language does not determine the relationship of the parties, rather the "objective nature of the relationship, [is] determined upon an analysis of the totality of the facts and circumstances of each case." . . .

In determining whether an employer-employee relationship exists, the fact finder must evaluate a number of criteria. They include:

1. The extent of control exercised by the master over details of the work and the degree of supervision;
2. The distinct nature of the worker's business;
3. Specialization or skilled occupation;
4. Materials and place of work;
5. Duration of employment;
6. Method of payment;
7. Relationship of work done to the regular business of the employer;
8. Belief of the parties.

ANALYSIS OF RELATIONSHIP BETWEEN FRAUSTO AND PNI

1. The extent of control exercised by the master over the details of the work

Such control may be manifested in a variety of ways. A worker who must comply with another's instructions about when, where, and how to work is an employee. *See Restatement* § 220 comment h. In *Throop,* . . . the plaintiff's husband was killed in a collision with a car driven by Hennen, a salesman for the defendant company. Plaintiff sought recovery against the company on a theory of vicarious liability. At the close of evidence, the trial court granted a directed verdict in favor of the company. On appeal, we examined the record for evidence of the company's control. Hennen was required to call on accounts in person and to present all inventory items, to submit written reports on these visits and to make collections. Although Hennen had these responsibilities for a seven-year period, he could sell anywhere in the country, visit prospects whenever he chose, use his own vehicle exclusively, and select all prospects himself, visiting the office only a few times a year. Based on these facts, we agreed the trial court properly directed the verdict in the company's favor because no reasonable juror could find it had exercised sufficient control over Hennen to make him an employee.

Missing in *Throop* was the right to control the details of how Hennen made his sales. Where this right of control exists, the inference of the employer-employee relationship is strengthened. For example, an appellate court overturned the trial court's finding of no employer-employee relationship in *Gallaher v. Ricketts*. . . . The newspaper carrier in *Gallaher* provided his own transportation and was paid a commission for every dollar worth of papers delivered on his assigned route. The company conducted training programs, including tips on how to distribute the paper and stimulate sales, reimbursed him for some transportation expenses, and retained the right to terminate him at any time. The court concluded that these indices of control demonstrated that the carrier "was merely a cog in the wheel of the defendant's enterprise," and held that Ricketts was an employee. . . .

A strong indication of control is an employer's power to give specific instructions with the expectation that they will be followed. . . .

In this case, PNI designated the time for pick-up and delivery, the area covered, the manner in which the papers were delivered, *i.e.*, bagged and banded, and the persons to whom delivery was made. Although PNI did little actual supervising, it had the authority under the contract to send a supervisor with Frausto on his route. Frausto claimed he did the job as he was told, without renegotiating the contract terms, adding customers and following specific customer requests relayed by PNI.

2. The distinct nature of the worker's business

Whether the worker's tasks are efforts to promote his own independent enterprise or to further his employer's business will aid the fact finder in ascertaining the existence of an employer-employee relationship. *Tanner v. USA Today*, . . . The agent in *Tanner* contracted with USA Today to distribute papers. The agent in turn hired carriers to deliver the papers using his trucks. USA Today had no control over the choice of drivers, the trucks used, or the route taken. Under these circumstances, and despite USA Today's imposition of time parameters for delivery, the court found insufficient evidence to raise the issue of an employer-employee relationship.

A concomitant inquiry to this factor also considers whether the worker's job performance results in a profit or loss for the worker. Thus, where the worker purchases the product and then sells it at a profit or loss, the worker is more likely to be found an independent contractor. . . .

As far as the nature of the worker's business, Frausto had no delivery business distinct from that of his responsibilities to PNI. Unlike the drivers in *Tanner*, Frausto had an individual relationship and contract with the newspaper company. Furthermore, he did not purchase the papers and then sell them at a profit or loss. Payments were made directly to PNI and any complaints or requests for delivery changes went through PNI. If Frausto missed a customer, a PNI employee would deliver a paper.

3. Specialization or skilled occupation

The jury is more likely to find a master-servant relationship where the work does not require the services of one highly educated or skilled. *See Restatement* § 220 comment h. PNI argues that its agents must drive, follow directions, and be diligent in order to perform the job for which they are paid. However, these skills are required in differing degrees for virtually any job. Frausto's services were not specialized and required no particular training. In addition, an agreement that work cannot be delegated indicates a master-servant relationship. *Restatement* § 220 comment j. In this case, Frausto could delegate work but only up to twenty-five percent of the days.

4. Materials and place of work

If an employer supplies tools, and employment is over a specific area or over a fixed route, a master-servant relationship is indicated. *Restatement* § 220 comment h. In this case, PNI supplied the product but did not supply the bags, rubber bands, or transportation necessary to complete the deliveries satisfactorily. However, PNI did designate the route to be covered.

5. Duration of employment

Whether the employer seeks a worker's services as a one-time, discrete job or as part of a continuous working relationship may indicate that the employer-employee relationship exists. The shorter in time the relationship, the less likely the worker will subject himself to control over job details. *See Restatement* § 220 comment j. In addition, the employer's right to terminate may indicate control and therefore an employer-employee relationship. The "right to fire" is considered one of the most effective methods of control. . . . In this case, the contract provided for a six-month term, renewable as long as the carrier performed satisfactorily. Frausto could be terminated without cause in 28 days and with cause immediately. The definition of cause in the contract was defined only as a failure to provide "satisfactory" service. A jury could reasonably infer that an employer-employee relationship existed since PNI retained significant latitude to fire Frausto inasmuch as the "satisfactory service" provision provides no effective standards. In addition, the jury could also infer that PNI provided health insurance to encourage a long-term relationship and disability insurance to protect itself in case of injury to the carrier, both of which support the existence of an employer-employee relationship.

6. Method of payment

PNI paid Frausto each week, but argues that because Frausto was not paid by the hour, he was an independent contractor. Santiago responds that payment was not made by the "job" because Frausto's responsibilities changed without any adjustment to his pay or contract. . . .

7. Relation of work done to the employer's regular business

A court is more likely to find a worker an employee if the work is part of the employer's regular business. *Restatement* § 220 comment h. The court of appeals addressed this factor in *Anton* . . . The contractor in that case, Perkins, entered into an agreement to harvest certain trees and deliver the lumber to Southwest. Southwest gave Perkins detailed specifications for the wood which Perkins passed on verbatim to his woodcutters. Perkins hired Anton as one of these woodcutters under a written contract. That contract required Anton to fell trees, cut them into logs, stack the logs into cords, and clean up the forest afterwards, all in accordance with the Southwest specifications. Perkins reserved to himself only the task of picking up and delivering the wood to Southwest. During the process, Perkins checked Anton's work, making sure he cut the logs correctly, selected the correct quality of wood, stacked the timber as directed, cleaned the forest sufficiently, and worked quickly.

The court noted that in reality the woodcutters conducted virtually every facet of Perkins' enterprise related to the Southwest contract. In deciding whether Anton was an employee for purposes of workers' compensation, the court considered whether the work performed was an *integral* part of the employer's *regular* business. . . . It found Anton was an employee because Perkins had not limited his attempt to contract to a particularly "well-defined incidental activity . . . ancillary to the central concerns of his business . . . but rather the ongoing basic employee activity" itself. . . .

We find the *Anton* . . . [analysis] particularly apt here. Home delivery is critical to the survival of a local daily paper; it may be its essential core. As one court explained:

> The delivery of newspapers within a reasonable time after publication is essential to the success of the newspaper business. For the greater portion of its income the paper depends on advertising, and the rates for advertising are governed by the paper's circulation. Circulation is a necessity for success. The delivery boys are just as much an integral part of the newspaper industry as are the typesetters and pressmen or the editorial staff.

PNI is hard-pressed to detach the business of delivering news from that of reporting and printing it, especially when it retains an individual relationship with each carrier. . . .

8. Belief of the parties

As stated above, Frausto believed that he was an employee, despite contract language to the contrary. Even if he believed he was an independent contractor, that would not preclude a finding of vicarious liability. As the *Restatement* explains: It is not determinative that the parties believe or disbelieve that the relation of master and servant exists, except insofar as such belief indicates an assumption of control by the one and submission of control by the other." *Restatement* § 220 comment m. . . . In addition to the parties' belief, the finder of fact should look to the community's belief. "Community custom in thinking that a kind of service is rendered by servants . . . is of importance." *Restatement* § 220 comment h. The fact that the community regards those doing such work as servants indicates the relation of master and servant. The newspaper's customers did not have individual contact or contracts with Frausto. All payments, complaints, and changes were made directly to PNI. From these facts, a jury could infer that the community regarded Frausto as PNI's employee.

Again, analyzing these factors in relation to the facts of this case a jury could determine that an employer-employee relationship existed between PNI and Frausto.

CONCLUSION AND DISPOSITION

Whether an employer-employee relationship exists may not be determined as a matter of law in either side's favor, because reasonable minds may disagree on the nature of the employment relationship. A jury could infer from these facts that Frausto was an employee because PNI involved itself with the details of delivery, received directly all customer complaints and changes so as to remove much of Frausto's independence, retained broad discretion to terminate, and relied heavily on Frausto's services for the survival of its business. The jury could also infer that Frausto was an independent contractor because he used his own car, was subject to little supervision, provided some of his own supplies, and could have someone else deliver for him within limits. Therefore, the trial court erred in finding as a matter of law that Frausto was an independent contractor. Summary judgment on the vicarious liability claim was inappropriate. The opinion of the court of appeals is vacated and the case is remanded to the superior court for proceedings consistent with this opinion.

SARAH D. GRANT, Chief Judge
FRANK X. GORDON, Chief Justice
STANLEY G. FELDMAN, Vice Chief Justice
JAMES MOELLER, Justice

The mere fact that an employer refers to someone as an independent contractor is not dispositive in classifying the relationship. The nature of the relationship and not the label that is attached to the relationship determines its classification. Therefore, an employer cannot evade liability by simply casting the label of independent contractor on an employee.

EXCEPTIONS TO NONLIABILITY RULE FOR INDEPENDENT CONTRACTORS

Several exceptions to the nonliability rule for independent contractors exist. First, if the employer himself is negligent in dealing with an independent contractor, he can be found liable. For example, if the employer hires someone that he knows will not perform the work safely (such as an individual who has a poor safety record) or if he fails to inspect work after it is done, the employer can be liable even if the injuries stem from the contractor's negligence (See Table 18–3).

Nondelegable Duties. Some duties of care are so important they are nondelegable. A city that hires a private contractor to work on its streets cannot delegate to the company its duty to keep its streets in good repair. For this same reason the owner of a shopping mall can be held vicariously liable for damages resulting from an independent contractor's negligent repair of its roof. The courts have not clearly defined what is and is not a "delegable" duty but their decisions are generally motivated by a desire to prevent employers from avoiding liability by hiring independent contractors to carry out their responsibilities.

Extraordinary Risks. Employers continue to be vicariously liable if they hire independent contractors to carry out activities involving risks that require more than ordinary precautions. If an employer hires an independent contractor to relocate date palm trees, for example, special precautions obviously would have to be taken in securing the trees to ensure that transportation

TABLE 18.3

EMPLOYER-INDEPENDENT CONTRACTORS
GENERAL RULE: •Employers are not vicariously liable for torts of independent contractors. EXCEPTIONS TO NONLIABILITY RULE •Employer is negligent in dealing with independent contractor. •Employer delegates nondelegable duty to independent contractor. •Employer hires independent contractor to conduct an activity involving unusual risks that are recognizable in advance. •Employer contracts for performance of an illegal act. •Doctors are liable for negligent acts of those under their control (this doctrine has been abolished in some jurisdictions and limited in others).

along public highways was done without endangering others. In the case of an accident the employer would be vicariously liable. This special rule of liability applies only to unusual risks and not to risks arising out of ordinary forms of negligence. Suppose the contractor were asked to transport common shrubs in an enclosed truck rather than freestanding palm trees. In that case the employer would not be liable if the contractor drove negligently because the risk involved in hauling shrubs would not be an unusual one.

Employers will not be liable if the risks involved are not recognizable in advance. If a family hires a lawn care service to tend their lawn while they are on vacation and one of the caretakers decides to add water to the pool and forgets to shut it off, the family will not be vicariously liable for the flood damage to their adjoining neighbor's property. The risk of overfilling the pool would not be considered an inherent or foreseeable risk of lawn care.

Illegal Acts. Another exception to the nonliability of employers for the acts of independent contractors is in the area of illegal acts. If an employer contracts for the performance of an illegal activity, he or she will be vicariously liable for any damage caused by the contractor.

Physicians. Historically, physicians were exceptions to the nonliability rule. A physician was vicariously liable for the negligence of nurses, other physicians, paramedical personnel, and hospital administrators who, although not under her employ, were for legal purposes considered to be under her control. The courts reasoned that a physician acting in a supervisory role over other medical personnel was the "captain of the ship" and thus should be held vicariously liable for their negligent acts. The impetus behind this doctrine probably lay in the court's attempt to circumvent charitable immunity and find a solvent defendant. With the demise of charitable immunity, this doctrine has been abolished in many places and in other jurisdictions has been strictly limited to acts committed during surgery. This same rationale has been used, however, by plaintiffs to reach those hospitals that hire private franchises to carry out special functions in a hospital, such as radiology and serology.

BAILMENTS

If a party temporarily entrusts goods to the care of another, the party who hands over the goods is referred to as a **bailor** while the person who receives custody of the goods is a **bailee**. When you take your car in for repair you are the bailor and the service station is the bailee. The question in terms of vicarious liability is whether a bailor should be liable for the negligence of a bailee.

Under the common law majority rule a bailor is not vicariously liable for the acts of a bailee (see Table 18–4). So if someone rents a car from a rental agency and negligently injures a plaintiff in driving such a car, the rental agency (bailor) is not vicariously liable for the acts of the individual who rented the car (bailee). The bailor may be liable for his own negligence if he entrusts control of his property to a person that he knows or reasonably should know is likely to endanger others. Therefore, if the rental agency in the example given above were aware that the driver was intoxicated or otherwise unable to control the vehicle, it could be held vicariously liable for the driver's negligent acts.

EXCEPTIONS TO BAILOR NONLIABILITY

The courts, for the most part, have been dissatisfied with the nonliability rule regarding bailors when applied to owners of automobiles who allow others to drive. They have adopted a number of strategies by which vicarious liability can be placed on the owners of vehicles. The implicit reasoning behind the notion of owner liability is that owners are more likely to be able to pay for

TABLE 18.4

BAILMENTS
GENERAL RULE: •Bailors are not vicariously liable for the acts of a bailee. EXCEPTIONS TO NONLIABILITY RULE •Bailor negligently entrusts property to one he knows or should know will endanger others. •In some states mere presence of owner in vehicle makes owner vicarously liable for acts of driver. •Family Purpose Doctrine - driver (nonowner) is presumed to be carrying out family purpose, making owner vicariously liable. •Automobile Consent Statutes - owner is vicariously liable for negligent acts committed by anyone using the vehicle with the owner's permission. •Joint Enterprise Doctrine - owner is vicariously liable for negligent acts committed by joint venturer.

damages than those to whom they loan their vehicles and that owners, not drivers, are expected to carry insurance.

In some courts the mere presence of the owner in the car creates the presumption that the owner had control over the driving. As a result the owner is considered vicariously liable for the acts of the driver. Some courts have retreated from this position by making the presumption a rebuttable one. Others have negated the presumption altogether and treat the nondriving owner as if she were a guest in her own car. The courts will not, however, impute the driver's negligence to the owner if the owner is not present.

Family Purpose Doctrine. In their struggle to circumvent the nonliability rule for absent owners, some courts created a legal fiction called the *family purpose doctrine.* Under this doctrine the assumption is made that the driver is carrying out a "family purpose," making the family head, typically the most financially responsible person in the family, vicariously liable. This doctrine is maintained even though, typically, the driver is using the vehicle on his or her own behalf. So long as the driver is a member of the head of the family's household and has permission to use the car, the head of the family is vicariously liable for the driver's negligent acts.

The family purpose doctrine is in effect in less than half the states today and is complicated by a host of exceptions. It arises most often in those cases where a minor is relegated to driving a particular vehicle. Typically the parents provide only as much insurance on a vehicle driven by a minor as mandated by law while providing more extensive coverage on the vehicles they themselves drive. Anyone injured by the minor will find little compensation in the minor's coverage and will often be motivated to turn to the parents for relief. If the plaintiff can meet the requirements of the family purpose doctrine, she can recover from the parents instead of the minor.

Automobile Consent Statutes. Dissatisfaction with the rule of nonliability of bailors led several state legislatures to adopt *automobile consent statutes.* These statutes make the owner vicariously liable for negligent acts committed by anyone using the car with the owner's permission. If the borrower (bailee) of the car exceeds the scope of the owner's consent, the owner (bailor) is generally not vicariously liable unless the deviation is a relatively minor one. If the bailee in turn lends the car to a third person, the courts are divided in terms of the owner's liability. In one case a rental agency explicitly forbade customers from allowing anyone else to drive the car. The court found that the agency was deemed to have impliedly given consent and held the agency liable when its customer allowed a third person to drive who subsequently caused a collision (*Shuck v. Means,* 226 N.W.2d 285 (Minn. 1974)). Not all courts are in agreement with this case, however, and are less likely to find liability when the bailee is not in the vehicle at the time of the accident.

The *omnibus clause* in most automobile liability insurance policies has substantially reduced the need for automobile consent statutes. Such clauses extend insurance coverage to members of the insured's household and to any person using the automobile with the insured's permission as long as the use falls within the scope of the permission given. Consequently, plaintiffs have no incentive to find liability on the part of the owner, at least up to the policy limits.

Joint Enterprises. Another court-created doctrine designed to make the owner of an automobile vicariously liable is the joint enterprise doctrine (see Table 18–5). A **joint enterprise** consists of four elements:

1. An express or implied agreement between members of a group.
2. A common purpose or goal to be carried out by the group.
3. A common pecuniary interest in the purpose or goal.
4. An equal right of each member to control the direction of the enterprise. (Restatement (Second) of Torts Sec. 491, comment c.)

A social trip is not a joint enterprise since it involves no sharing of a pecuniary interest. The mere sharing of expenses is not enough by itself to establish a pecuniary interest. Furthermore, the courts frequently find that a passenger on a social trip has no right of control over the driver. For this doctrine to be applicable each of the joint venturers must have some say in how the car is to be driven. Each person need not have a right to arbitrarily steer the car at any time but each must have an equal say in what route will be followed, how fast the car will travel, and so on. Two partners in a law firm, for example, who car pool together would be considered members of a joint enterprise.

Once the joint enterprise requirements are met each of the joint venturers is vicariously liable for the negligence of the others. This doctrine almost always arises in the context of automobile cases. Typically the plaintiff is a passenger in another car and wishes to recover against a passenger (usually the "deep pocket") in the joint venturer's vehicle. By imputing the negligence of the driver to the passenger, the plaintiff is then allowed to recover.

TABLE 18.5

JOINT ENTERPRISE
GENERAL RULE: •All joint venturers are vicariously liable for the negligent acts of other joint venturers.
ELEMENTS OF JOINT ENTERPRISE •Express or implied agreement. •Common purpose or goal. •Common pecuniary interest. •Equal right to control direction of enterprise.

IMPUTED CONTRIBUTORY NEGLIGENCE

Suppose the driver of an automobile and a truck driver for Company X negligently collide with each other. Should the truck driver's negligence be imputed to, i.e., charged against or attributed to, Company X, making Company X contributorily negligent and thus barring it from suing the automobile driver, who was also negligent? Under traditional common law, the answer to that question was yes. The negligence of a driver was imputed to the passengers. Because of the contributory negligence imputed to him, an injured passenger could not sue the other driver. Similarly, a few courts have actually used the imputing of negligence to preclude a passenger from suing the driver of the vehicle in which he was riding when the driver and passenger are joint venturers. The driver's negligence is imputed to the passenger, who is then considered contributorily negligent and thus barred from recovering from the driver.

Under the modern rule, however, contributory negligence is imputed only if the relationship is such that the plaintiff would be vicariously liable if he or she were a defendant (Restatement (Second) of Torts Sec. 485). In the example given above of the passenger wanting to sue the driver of the vehicle with which he collided, the passenger would not be vicariously liable for the negligence of the driver of the vehicle in which he was a passenger. Therefore, no negligence would be imputed to the passenger and he could recover for his injuries (see Figure 18–1).

The rationale for not imputing a driver's negligence to a passenger is that a passenger basically has no control over the acts of the driver of the vehicle in which he or she is riding. The passenger should not, therefore, be saddled with responsibility for the driver's negligence. In other words, contributory negligence should not be imputed unless negligence can also be imputed.

In the case of the truck driver, since the employer (Company X) would be vicariously liable for the truck driver's acts, the truck driver's negligence would be imputed to the employer and the employer would be prevented from suing the other driver. Since the employer bears responsibility for the acts of his employees, imputing the negligence of employees to their employer seems neither illogical nor unfair, according to the prevailing reasoning of the courts. The negligence of the employee is not imputed to the employer, however, if the employer is suing the employee rather than a third party.

The rule regarding the imputing of negligence is in general disfavor today. In most states the negligence of one spouse is not imputed to the other (except in some community property states where recovered damages are treated as community property), nor are parents or children barred from recovery because of the negligence of the other. Under the modern rule the contributory negligence of a bailee is generally not imputed to the bailor, even where the bailor would be liable as a defendant pursuant to an automobile consent statute.

In derivative claims, such as wrongful death actions and loss of consortium claims, the contributory negligence of the injured party is imputed to the plaintiff. Because the plaintiff's claim is derived from and dependent on another person's injury, the imputed negligence doctrine is applicable. Therefore, if a driver is killed in a collision and her family sues the other driver in

FIGURE 18.1

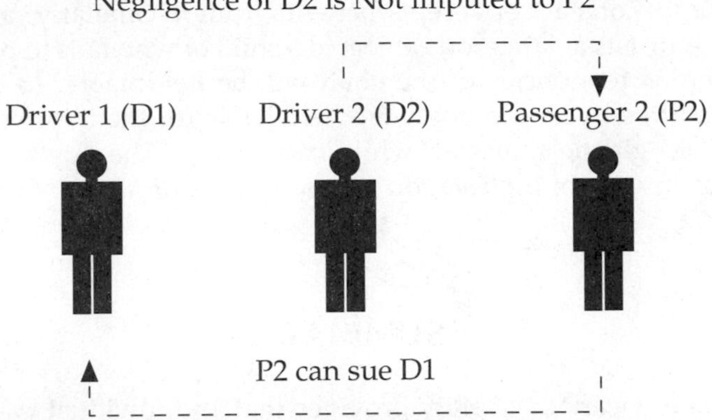
NEGLIGENCE NOT IMPUTED
Negligence of D2 is Not imputed to P2
Driver 1 (D1)
Driver 2 (D2)
Passenger 2 (P2)
P2 can sue D1

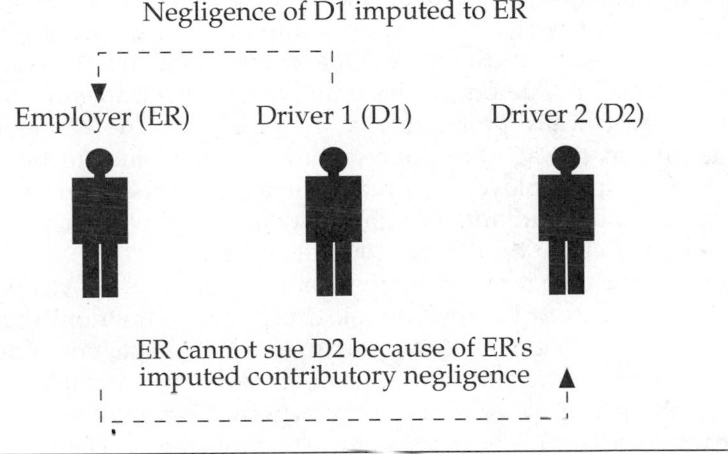
NEGLIGENCE IMPUTED
Negligence of D1 imputed to ER
Employer (ER)
Driver 1 (D1)
Driver 2 (D2)
ER cannot sue D2 because of ER's imputed contributory negligence

a wrongful death action, any negligence on the part of the decedent will be imputed to the family.

PARENTAL LIABILITY

Some states, in an effort to curb juvenile delinquency, have enacted statutes that hold parents liable for the tortious acts of their children. These torts can involve either personal injury or property damage but they must be intentional torts. Most such statutes have damage ceilings, which can be as high as several thousand dollars. A Georgia statute that provided for no such ceiling was held void under the due process clause. (*Corley v. Lewless*, 182 S.E.2d 766 (Ga.1971)).

A parent may also be vicariously liable if he or she encourages the commission of a tortious act or accepts benefits from it. Similarly, a parent who negligently entrusts a dangerous object to a child or who fails to protect others from dangerous tendencies of the child will be held liable. In one case the parents of a fifteen-year-old boy were held liable for the injuries suffered by a five-year-old girl he molested while babysitting. The boy's parents were aware of his history of molestation of young girls (*Schurk v. Christensen*, 497 P.2d 937 (Wash. 1972)).

SUMMARY

The doctrine of vicarious liability provides that an individual is liable for the tortious acts of another if he or she shares a special relationship with the tortfeasor. Examples of such special relationships are those between employers and employees, employers and independent contractors, parents and children, and parties involved in a joint enterprise. Both the family purpose doctrine and automobile consent statutes possess elements of vicarious liability.

The doctrine of *respondeat superior* is applicable if an employee is acting "within the scope and furtherance of his employment" but not if an employee goes on a "frolic" or "detour" of his or her own. Even if an employee engages in conduct specifically prohibited by the employer, the employer remains liable as long as the acts are done within the scope and furtherance of the employment. An employer also retains liability if an employee negligently delegates his or her authority or rights to a third party without the employer's authorization and the third party commits a tort.

In general one who hires an independent contractor is not vicariously liable for the tortious acts of that individual. Exceptions to the nonliability rule for independent contractors exist. An employer who is negligent in dealing with an independent contractor can be found liable as can an employer who contracts for the performance of an illegal activity. Some duties of care cannot be delegated so that, in some cases at least, employers will be prevented from evading liability by hiring an independent contractor. Employers will be vicariously liable if they hire independent contractors to carry out activities that involve risks requiring more than ordinary precautions but they will not be liable if those risks are not recognizable in advance.

Under the majority rule bailors are not vicariously liable for the acts of bailees unless they negligently entrust control of their property to a person they know or reasonably should know is likely to endanger others. Dissatisfaction with this rule as it is applied to owners of automobiles led some courts to create the presumption that an owner's mere presence in the car establishes his control over the driving, making him vicariously liable.

In accordance with the court-created family purpose doctrine a driver is assumed to be carrying out a "family purpose" as long as he or she is a member of the owner's household and has permission to use the car. Along similar lines, many state legislatures have adopted automobile consent statutes, which make an owner vicariously liable for the negligent acts committed by anyone using the car with the owner's permission unless the bailee exceeds the scope of the owner's consent. The joint enterprise doctrine, also created by the courts, renders the owner of an automobile vicariously liable for the negligence of the driver if the two are involved in a joint enterprise.

Modern courts generally impute contributory negligence only if the relationship is such that the plaintiff would be vicariously liable if he were a defendant. Under this rule an employee's negligence is imputed to the employer, which prevents the employer from suing any other third party who is negligent as well.

PRACTICE POINTERS

Legal assistants are not governed by the same ethical rules of conduct that are applicable to attorneys. Because they are not licensed to practice law, legal assistants cannot be disbarred for engaging in arguably unethical behavior. They can certainly be censored by members of their professional community and can be fired for improper conduct. Furthermore, an attorney can be disciplined for the transgressions of a legal assistant she is responsible for supervising.

One area in which legal assistants may find themselves subject to both criminal and civil sanctions is the "unauthorized practice of law." Presumably to ensure that those persons who offer legal services do so competently, the legal profession has mandated that only those individuals who have received appropriate training and who have successfully hurdled the rite of passage known as the bar exam are eligible to practice law. Legal assistants, therefore, are relegated to assisting attorneys and cannot practice law. To allow legal assistants to carry out those activities traditionally performed by lawyers, it is argued, would compromise the integrity of the profession.

Just exactly what constitutes the "unauthorized practice of law" continues to evade definition. Certainly legal assistants generally cannot represent clients in court (although some exceptions to this general prohibition exist) and they cannot offer legal advice. What constitutes the giving of legal advice is not clear. Does suggesting to a client that she might want to consider filing a particular motion constitute rendering legal advice? What about conducting research to determine the meaning of a particular statute? Case law is not generally helpful in answering these types of questions. You may find it more enlightening to consult attorney general and ethics committee opinions rendered in your state.

Most importantly, you should consult with your attorney as to what tasks you should perform. Clarify, for example, what your role should be in dealing with clients. Determine what types of questions you should

Continued on next page

PRACTICE POINTERS—Continued

answer yourself and which ones you should refer to the attorney. Most attorneys are careful about supervising the work of their legal assistants because they are aware that the ultimate responsibility for any work product lies with them. Nevertheless, some attorneys, because of their work load or outright carelessness, will be less than diligent in carrying out their supervisorial tasks. In some cases you may have to insist that an attorney review your work. If an attorney should ever gloss over his refusal to carry out his review responsibility by assuring you of his implicit trust in you, do not be appeased. For the protection of all concerned it is imperative that you work under the auspices of an attorney.

TORT TEASERS

1. Review the three hypothetical questions posed at the beginning of this chapter and determine if the attorney in each case would be liable for the acts of his employee.

2. At a Christmas office party Defendant (an employee) becomes drunk and on his way driving home negligently causes the Plaintiff injury. What would you need to know to determine if Defendant was acting within the scope of his employment? *Harris v. Trojan Fireworks Company,* 120 Cal App. 3d 157, 174 Cal. Rptr. 452 (1981).

3. Defendant collides with a car driven by Plaintiff as a result of brake failure. Defendant had her brakes overhauled by a mechanic three months prior to the accident. Defendant claims that the mechanic's negligent repair was the cause of the accident. Should Defendant be held liable? *Maloney vs. Rath,* 445 P.2d 513(Cal. 1968).

4. Employee, entrusted with a vehicle by Employer, suffers an epileptic seizure and causes an accident that results in the death of one person. Employer hired Employee six weeks before the accident. Three weeks before the accident Employee suffered dizzy spells and had minor accidents on three separate occasions, two of which were brought to the attention of Employer. Employer arranged to have Employee examined by a physician, who found nothing wrong with him. Should Employer be held vicariously liable in a wrongful death action? *Syah v. Johnson,* 55 Cal. Rptr. 741 (1966).

5. The owner of a vehicle brings his car to a car wash. It is attached to a tow line and towed without its operator through the car wash. When it emerges from the wash it rolls down an incline and strikes Plaintiff's automobile. Is the car wash liable for the damages to Plaintiff's car?

Assume that the motor vehicle code of that state provides that the negligence of one who uses or operates a vehicle with the owner's express or implied permission is imputed to the owner of the vehicle. In accordance with this statute should the vehicle owner be held liable for the property damage to Plaintiff's vehicle? *Allcity Ins. Co. v. Old Greenwich Delicatessen,* 349 N.Y.S.2d 240 (1973).

6. Defendant driver collides with a school bus while acting as a chauffeur for the owner of the vehicle he is driving. Defendant is driving with the owner's permission for the purpose of keeping the car running in good shape. If Defendant was contributorily negligent, can the owner sue the driver and owner of the school bus for the damages sustained by his vehicle? Can the two passengers in the vehicle at the time of the accident recover for their injuries? Can the driver's wife recover for her injuries (assume this is a community property state)? *Muhammad v. U.S.,* 366 F.2d 298, *cert. denied,* 386 U.S. 959 (9th Cir. 1966).

KEY TERMS

■ **Bailee**
One who is temporarily entrusted with the custody of goods.

■ **Bailor**
One who entrusts his or her goods to the temporary custody of another.

■ **Imputed negligence**
Negligence that is charged or attributed to another.

■ **Independent contractor**
Someone hired to do a job who works at his own pace, in his own way, under his own supervision.

■ **Joint enterprise**
Two or more persons who agree to a common goal or purpose, who share a common pecuniary interest, and who have an equal right to control the direction of the enterprise.

■ ***Respondeat superior***
Doctrine establishing the vicarious liability of employers for the acts of their employees.

JOINT LIABILITY

CHAPTER OBJECTIVES

In this chapter you will learn to:

- Identify those situations in which tortfeasors are jointly and severally liable for their acts.
- Apply the concepts of contribution, satisfaction, and indemnification.
- Distinguish between releases and covenants not to sue.
- Recognize the problems associated with releases in light of contribution.

You and a friend go out West for a week's vacation. While there you decide to take in the local scene by going on a trail ride through the desert. The ostentatious resort where you are staying sponsors such a ride designed for "dudes" such as yourself. It is advertised as a peaceful, scenic ride that allows you to enjoy the panoramic vistas of the desert. When you arrive at the stable, you tell the trail hands, Tex and Rex, of your ignorance about horses. Tex and Rex, engaging in a little cowboy humor, put you on Molly, a mare noted for her impulsive urges to return to her stablemates without giving any notice to her rider. Unfortunately, Molly succumbs to this urge while you are a passenger. She dumps you unceremoniously on the rocky ground, never demonstrating the least bit of remorse as she gallops back to the stable.

You suffer several broken bones and a concussion as a result of this little adventure and decide to sue Tex and Rex, the stable that employed them, and the resort that promoted the trail ride. Assuming you are able to prove liability on behalf of all the defendants, can you elect to recover your damages only from the resort even though Tex and Rex were primarily responsible for your injuries? Can the resort then turn around and seek reimbursement from the stable for its portion of the damages? If the stable is held liable only because the negligence of Tex and Rex is imputed to it, can the stable seek reimbursement from Tex and Rex? If Tex comes to you and says that the whole scheme was Rex's idea, can you agree to absolve Tex from all liability in exchange for securing his testimony against Rex? See if you can answer these questions after reading this chapter.

JOINT AND SEVERAL LIABILITY

Two or more people who act in concert to produce a negligent or intentional tort are called **joint tortfeasors.** A joint tortfeasor is *"jointly and severally" liable* in that he or she is totally liable for the entire loss suffered by the plaintiff if that loss is indivisible. A loss that cannot be apportioned among the defendants is considered indivisible. The rule of joint liability also applies to **concurrent tortfeasors,** those whose independent acts concur (combine) to cause the plaintiff's injury. Notice that joint tortfeasors act together while concurrent tortfeasors act independently, but their combined acts cause the plaintiff's injuries.

Under the rule of **joint and several liability** if a harm is indivisible and no rational apportionment is possible, each defendant can be held responsible for the entire harm or any designated portion of the harm (see Table 19–1). Although a plaintiff may recover from one or all of the joint tortfeasors, he or she may recover only once for the total damages. As a result of this rule one defendant can be held responsible for payment of all damages even

TABLE 19.1

JOINT LIABILITY	SATISFACTION	CONTRIBUTION
Each tortfeasor is liable for entire loss if loss is indivisible.	Plaintiff is entitled to only one satisfaction (payment) of judgment.	A defendant who pays more than his pro rata share of damages is entitled to contribution (partial reimbursement) from other defendants.

RELEASE	INDEMNIFICATION
A plaintiff who agrees to release a defendant absolves that defendant of all liability.	A tortfeasor who agrees to indemnify another tortfeasor accepts all financial responsibility on behalf of that tortfeasor.

though his or her contribution to the plaintiff's injuries was relatively minor. Therefore, if the plaintiff suffered damages in the amount of $10,000 and five defendants acted together to cause the injuries, the plaintiff could recover $2,000 from each defendant, $10,000 from one defendant, or $1,000 from four of the defendants and $6,000 from one of the defendants, and so on.

If the plaintiff dies as a result of the independent or concerted acts of the defendants, each defendant will be held liable for the plaintiff's death because death is not apportionable. Similarly, if the plaintiff's property is destroyed, the harm is considered indivisible and nonapportionable.

Even if one of the defendants directly causes the plaintiff's injuries, all the defendants will be held liable if a court concludes that they acted in concert. Suppose two young men are drag racing down a public street and one of them collides with the plaintiff's car. Both will be held liable even though only one of them actually came in contact with the car. The reasoning is that the tortious conduct of one encouraged the tortious behavior of the other and the combination led to the harm caused. See, e.g., *Bierczynski v. Rogers*, 234 A.2d 218 (Del. 1968).

HARM THAT CANNOT BE APPORTIONED

The rule of joint and several liability does not apply if the harm can be apportioned. In other words, if 60 percent of the harm was caused by defendant A and the remainder by defendants B and C, defendant A will be responsible for 60 percent of the damages and defendants B and C will be responsible for the other 40 percent. As discussed in Chapter 9 on damages, if the harm can be apportioned but can be done so only with great difficulty, the burden of allocating harm will shift to the defendants. If the defendants are unable to satisfactorily prove who was responsible for each percentage of the damages, all the defendants will be held jointly and severally liable.

STATUS OF JOINT AND SEVERAL LIABILITY

Joint and several liability has been abolished in some states, primarily because of the concern that the doctrine is used to go after the "deep pocket" defendant, who may actually be responsible for only a minimal portion of the harm. A corporation, for example, whose negligence contributed to only 10 percent of the plaintiff's harm may be held totally responsible for the plaintiff's damages under the rule of joint and several liability simply because the more blameworthy defendant is penniless. Other states have placed statutory limits on the doctrine by requiring that the liability of a tortfeasor whose contribution to the plaintiff's damages is below a certain percentage be limited to the tortfeasor's equitable share of the damages.

SATISFACTION

If tortfeasors A, B, and C are jointly and severally liable for a $10,000 judgment and the plaintiff recovers the full amount from A, he or she cannot collect anything from B and C. Additional recovery is not allowed because the plaintiff is entitled to only one **satisfaction** (payment) of the claim. Although she can collect from all the tortfeasors, she can collect on her judgment only once.

CONTRIBUTION

Tortfeasor A may, however, be entitled to **contribution** from B and C. In other words, A may turn to B and C for partial reimbursement since he paid more than his pro rata share of the damages. Early American courts denied contribution to intentional tortfeasors and eventually denied it to all joint tortfeasors. That common law rule was severely criticized and has today been changed by statute or judicial decision. Under the majority rule today contribution is permitted to some extent. Although typically allowed for negligent tortfeasors, contribution is often denied for intentional tortfeasors. The justification underlying contribution is that one tortfeasor should not be saddled with all the damages while allowing others to escape without any responsibility.

The courts disagree about the division of damages in the context of contribution. In some jurisdictions each defendant is required to pay an equal share of the damages. In those states that have adopted comparative negligence, the damages are generally divided in proportion to each defendant's contribution to the plaintiff's harm. A defendant to whom a jury assigns 1/4 fault but who pays the entire judgment can collect 3/4 of that amount from the other defendants in a comparative negligence state.

Contribution hinges on joint liability. If a defendant can raise a defense, such as immunity, that would bar recovery by the plaintiff, then the other defendants cannot seek contribution from him or her. Similarly, contribution cannot be sought against an employer if a worker's compensation statute prevents the plaintiff employee from suing the employer. (Under worker's compensation statutes employees can recover from insurance carried by their employers for any work-related injury, regardless of who was at fault. Employees who recover under these statutes are then barred from suing their employers in tort.)

RELEASE

Contribution becomes particularly problematic when a **release,** a document absolving a defendant of all liability, is given to one defendant. Under the common law, a plaintiff had a single, indivisible cause of action against all joint tortfeasors. Therefore, a release of one tortfeasor released all tortfeasors. To avoid the restrictive results of a release, a plaintiff who settled with one defendant would enter into a covenant not to sue, in which he or she promised not to sue that particular defendant but continued to hold all other defendants liable.

According to the Restatement (Second) of Torts Sec. 885, which reflects the majority rule, all tortfeasors are released if the release is silent regarding their continuing liability. To illustrate this point, suppose the plaintiff is injured by defendant A and seeks medical treatment from defendant B, who aggravates the injury through negligent treatment. If the plaintiff receives payment from defendant A and signs a release that does not mention defendant B, defendant B can later point to the common law rule regarding releases and escape all liability.

A plaintiff may preserve his or her rights against the other tortfeasors by specifically including a provision to that effect in the release. A desire to reserve one's right to sue may be proved by external evidence, such as verbal statements. This evidentiary rule was promulgated out of a desire to protect those who enter into such releases without legal advice but who clearly intend to reserve their rights to sue the nonsettling defendants (Restatement (Second) of Torts Sec. 885, comment d).

DIFFERENCES BETWEEN A RELEASE AND A COVENANT NOT TO SUE

Note the distinction between a release and a covenant not to sue. A plaintiff who enters into a release surrenders her claim; a plaintiff who enters into a covenant not to sue does not surrender her claim but agrees that she will not sue on it. If the plaintiff later reneges on a covenant not to sue and decides to sue, the defendant with whom she entered into the covenant will have a counterclaim for breach of contract.

Plaintiffs should be cautioned against entering into releases prematurely. If a plaintiff's injuries turn out to be more extensive than originally realized, the release may have to be set aside on the grounds of fraud or mistake. Litigation regarding the validity of releases can be avoided by simply refraining from entering into releases until the full extent of the plaintiff's injuries are known.

PROBLEMS WITH RELEASES IN LIGHT OF CONTRIBUTION

Problems arise in the context of contribution when one defendant is granted a release and the other defendants are not (see Table 19–2). Suppose the plaintiff accepts $2,000 from defendant A and releases him and then sues defendant B and obtains a judgment for $20,000. Can B obtain contribution from A? Under the traditional majority rule the answer was yes. Unfortunately, however, this rule discourages defendants from settling since they know they may be subject to contribution at a later time.

TABLE 19.2 Three approaches to the problem of releases in the context of contribution

SOLUTION A	SOLUTION B	SOLUTION C
Non-released defendant can seek contribution from released defendant. **Problem Associated with Solution A:** Discourages defendants from settling.	Non-released defendant <u>cannot</u> seek contribution but plaintiff's claim against non-released defendant is reduced. **Problem Associated with Solution B:** Discourages plaintiffs from settling.	Non-released defendant <u>cannot</u> seek contribution and plaintiff's claim is unaffected by release as long as parties negotiate in good faith. **Problem Associated with Solution C:** Leads to litigation regarding issue of good faith.

To prevent this problem some courts disallow contribution but reduce the plaintiff's claim against the nonreleased defendant on a pro rata basis. Suppose that, as in the previous example, the plaintiff releases defendant A and is later awarded damages in a jury trial against defendant B for $20,000. The plaintiff will be allowed to recover only $10,000 from defendant B since, by settling with defendant A, she liquidated half of her total right to recovery. Defendant B, however, would not be allowed to obtain contribution from defendant A. This rule is also problematic in that it discourages plaintiffs from settling as much as the previous rule discouraged defendants from settling.

To encourage settlement, therefore, some courts relieve the settling defendant from contribution liability altogether. Both the plaintiff and the settling defendant must reach settlement in "good faith." They must also show they did not act in collusion with each other. The issue of good faith often ends up being litigated under this approach.

Order and Memorandum Opinion
PANASUK v. SEATON
277 F.Supp. 979 (1968).

JAMESON, Chief Judge.

Plaintiff, Paul Panasuk, brought this action for personal injuries sustained while riding as a passenger in an automobile driven by his brother George when it collided with a truck-trailer driven by the defendant Arlynn Seaton and owned by the defendant Arden Leas. Defendants have filed an answer and also a third-party complaint against George Panasuk as third-party defendant and Leas has filed a cross-claim for damages to his truck and cargo.[2] Seaton and Leas, as third-party plaintiffs, pray, in the event a verdict is recovered against them by plaintiff, that the third-party defendant, George Panasuk, "be held primarily liable" and that they have "judgment over and against the third-party defendant, George Panasuk, for the amount recovered by plaintiff."

The third-party defendant, George Panasuk, has filed a motion to strike and dismiss the amended third-party complaint of Seaton and Leas and to dismiss the cross-claim of Leas. . . .

Third-party defendant first contends that the claim of third-party plaintiffs in effect seeks contribution between joint tortfeasors, and that this may not be done under the law of Montana. Third-party plaintiffs contend (1) that the law of Montana does not prohibit application of the doctrine of "contribution;" and (2) if the amended complaint does not state a claim for relief for "contribution," it does state a claim for relief in "indemnity."

The rule is well settled in Montana that, "if the concurrent negligence of two or

2. It is alleged in the amended third-party complaint that the third-party defendant operated his car in a grossly negligent and reckless manner, that the accident was caused solely by his negligence, and that if third-party plaintiffs were negligent, their negligence was secondary or passive, whereas the negligence of the third-party defendant was primary and active. In the Leas cross-claim it is alleged that the Panasuk vehicle was operated in a negligent and careless manner. Leas would of course be entitled to recover from third-party defendant upon proof of ordinary negligence proximately causing the accident, in the absence of contributory negligence.

more persons causes an injury to a third person, they are jointly and severally liable, and the injured person may sue them jointly or severally, and recover against one or all."[3] . . . The Montana court also recognized the general rule that "one of the several wrongdoers cannot recover against another wrongdoer although he may have been compelled to pay all the damages for the wrong done."

The "conflicting views" regarding the right of contribution as between joint tortfeasors were well-summarized in an annotation in 60 A.L.R.2d 1368, as follows:

> "A relatively large majority of jurisdictions in which the contribution rights of negligent joint tortfeasors are not controlled by statute hold that the fact that joint tortfeasors' injury-causing conduct was negligent, rather than wilful or intentional, furnishes no basis for freeing them of the burden of the general rule that there can be no contribution among joint tortfeasors." (Citing cases from Alabama, Arizona, California, Colorado, Connecticut, Florida, Illinois, Indiana, Massachusetts, Nebraska, New Hampshire, North Dakota, Ohio, Oklahoma, Oregon, Utah, Vermont, and Washington).
>
> "The minority—and, it seems, growing—view on the question presently under consideration is this: the rule which bars contribution among joint tortfeasors is not appropriately applied to joint tortfeasors guilty of nothing more than negligence; hence, there is a common-law right of contribution as between such joint tortfeasors." (Citing cases from District of Columbia, Iowa, Maine, Minnesota, Wisconsin).

Third-party plaintiffs rely upon cases from jurisdictions permitting contribution among joint tortfeasors, i.e., Iowa, Wisconsin and Minnesota, which clearly represent the minority view.

It may be, as third-party plaintiffs contend, that Montana has not expressly adopted the majority rule barring contribution among joint tortfeasors, but as noted supra, it clearly recognized the rule in Variety, Inc. v. Hustad Corporation. There is no reason for this court to assume that the Montana court will now adopt the minority view. It is my conclusion that the amended third-party complaint fails to state a claim for relief on the theory of contribution.

The question then arises as to whether the complaint states a claim for relief under applicable principles of indemnity.

In Great Northern Railway Company v. United States, . . . this court recognized the general rule that joint tortfeasors are not entitled to contribution from each other, but permitted recovery on the theory of indemnity since the act was not caused by any act of the plaintiff. The exception to the general rule was stated as follows:

> "Where the parties are not in pari delicto, and an injury results from the act of one party whose negligence is the primary, active and proximate cause of the injury, and another party, who is not negligent or whose negligence is remote, passive and secondary, is nevertheless exposed to liability by the acts of the first party, the first party may be liable to the second party for

3. It is recognized that plaintiff might recover from the defendants and not from the third-party defendant. As pointed out in brief of third-party plaintiffs, under the Montana Guest Statute (R.C.M.1947 § 32–1113), a guest passenger may not recover unless the damage is caused "directly and proximately by the grossly negligent and reckless operation" of the motor vehicle. We are not concerned here, however, with the question of whether plaintiff may recover from third-party defendant for the latter's gross negligence, but whether third-party plaintiffs may do so under the principles of "contribution" or "indemnity." This question could arise in any action by a third party (whether a guest passenger or not) where one or both of the motorists claimed the other was more culpable by reason of gross negligence and recklesness.

the full amount of damages incurred by such acts. . . .

Counsel have not cited nor have I found, any case in which indemnity, as distinguished from contribution, has been held applicable in a case involving a collision between two motor vehicles. This situation was considered in an annotation in 88 A.L.R.2d 1356. The annotation first summarizes the general situations in which indemnity may be granted:

"(1) Where the indemnitee has only an imputed or vicarious liability for damage caused by the indemnitor.

"(2) Where the indemnitee has incurred tort liability by performing at the direction of and in reliance upon the indemnitor an act not manifestly wrong.

"(3) Where the indemnitee has incurred liability by reason of his reliance, even though negligent, upon the duty of care which the indemnitor owed as a supplier of goods.

"(4) Where the indemnitee has incurred liability for failure to correct a hazardous condition which, as between indemnitor and indemnitee, it was the duty of the indemnitor to make safe.

"The ratio decidendi of cases granting indemnity has frequently been expressed in such general terms as that the indemnitee was not personally at fault (see (1) above); the parties were not in pari delicto (see (2) above); the negligence of the indemnitee was merely passive as compared to the negligence of the indemnitor which was active (see (3) above); and the liability of the indemnitee was only secondary as compared to the liability of the indemnitor, which was primary (see (4) above)."

With specific reference to whether a tortfeasor guilty of ordinary negligence may recover indemnity from a joint tortfeasor guilty of gross negligence, the annotation continues:

"* * * Hence, it would seem that such general propositions as have been adduced in support of particular results in cases allowing indemnity as an exception to the general rule will not serve as adequate standards to determine whether or not a tortfeasor guilty of ordinary negligence may recover indemnity against a tortfeasor guilty of gross negligence, wilful or wanton misconduct, or intentional wrongdoing.

"* * *

"The one case found which deals directly with the problem under consideration holds that indemnity is not available as respects the persons and situations postulated." . . .

"There are a number of cases which, without expressly referring to the distinction between ordinary negligence, on the one hand, and the wilful or wanton misconduct or gross negligence, on the other, use language indicating the court's belief that the mere fact that one of two or more persons whose misconduct contributed to the injury of a third person was guilty of more morally reprehensible conduct or of greater negligence than another is insufficient to warrant the granting of indemnity in favor of the latter." . . .

Jacobs v. General Acc. F. & L. Assur. Corp., . . . suggests several cogent reasons why the rule of indemnity should not be applied in such cases, including (1) "it seems undesirable * * * in automobile accident situations, to extend the effect of the distinction between gross and simple negligence beyond those effects already recognized;" and (2) any "rule allowing indemnity in this situation would tend to increase or prolong automobile personal injury litigation because of the advantage one defendant would hope to gain by showing that another defendant was guilty of gross negligence."

In Builders Supply Co. v. McCabe, supra, a third party obtained a judgment against Builders Supply Co. Builders sought contribution or indemnity from McCabe. In reversing a judgment in favor of Builders, the Pennsylvania Supreme Court said in part:

The right of indemnity rests upon a difference between the primary and the secondary liability of two persons each of whom is made responsible by the law to an injured party.

"It is right which enures to a person who, without active fault on his own part, has been compelled, by reason of some legal obligation, to pay damages occasioned by the initial negligence of another, and for which he himself is only secondarily liable.

"The difference between primary and secondary liability is not based on a difference in degrees of negligence or on any doctrine of comparative negligence,—a doctrine which, indeed, is not recognized by the common law.

It depends on a difference in the character or kind of the wrongs which cause the injury and in the nature of the legal obligation owed by each of the wrongdoers to the injured person. * * *"

After citing examples, the court continued:

"Without multiplying instances, it is clear that the right of a person vicariously or secondarily liable for a tort to recover from one primarily liable has been universally recognized. But the important point to be noted in all the cases is that secondary as distinguished from primary liability rests upon a fault that is imputed or constructive only, being based on some legal relation between the parties, or arising from some positive rule of common or statutory law or because of a failure to discover or correct a defect or remedy a dangerous condition caused by the act of the one primarily responsible."

Third party plaintiffs rely strongly on United Airlines, Inc. v. Wiener, . . . involving 31 cases arising out of a midair collision between a commercial airliner owned by United and an Air Force jet fighter. All of the actions were brought under the Nevada Wrongful Death Statute. Nevada has no statutes relating to contribution or indemnity. In considering whether United was entitled to indemnity, the court recognized that the "common law principles of noncontractural indemnity and contribution among persons jointly liable in tort to a third party are not susceptible of definite and precise articulation." The court analyzed the various bases of liability for indemnity, citing the annotation in 88 A.L.R.2d quoted supra. In concluding that United was entitled to indemnity in the nongovernment employee cases, the court said in pertinent part:

"United's duty to appellees' decedents was to exercise the highest degree of care; the government's duty was to exercise ordinary care. The government's negligent acts occurred literally from the start to the finish of this tragic incident. The cumulative effect of these negligent acts was to dispatch United's flight 736 and the government's high-speed jet training mission, conducted by a student pilot who was virtually blindfolded and an instructor whose cockpit preoccupations were greater than ordinarily demanded of pilots flying under VFR conditions and responsibilities, into the same area without warning to those in control of either craft. If we accept the government's assertions, the government's pilots discovered United's peril in time to effectively respond but engaged in a maneuver destined to encounter rather than to evade. Contrasted with all of this is the finding that United's pilots, to some disputed degree of probability, could have seen the jet and, in discharge of the obligation to exercise the highest degree of care for their passengers, should have seen and avoided the jet.[10] In view of the disparity of duties, the clear disparity of culpability, the likely operation of the last clear chance doctrine and all the surround-

10. In a footnote the court pointed out that it is "generally agreed * * * that the failure to discover unsafe conditions created by a joint tortfeasor constitutes 'passive' negligence and does not bar indemnity."

ing circumstances, the findings that United and the government were *in pari delicto* are clearly erroneous and we hold that there is such difference in the contrasted character of fault as to warrant indemnity in favor of United in the nongovernment employee cases."[11]

As noted supra, no case has been found where this rule has been extended to a collision between two motor vehicles. If indemnity were permitted in a case of this nature, it could arise in any action where a third person had a possible cause of action against two motorists. Each motorist could claim indemnity by alleging gross negligence of the other. This would result in the undesirable situation suggested by the Wisconsin court in Jacobs. The plaintiff in this action in order to recover from the defendants must of course prove that the defendants were negligent and that their negligence was a proximate cause of plaintiff's injury. If this is not established, there is no liability, and no question of possible indemnity could arise. It is my conclusion that this is not a case where the principles of indemnity are applicable.

In view of my conclusion that the third-party complaint should be dismissed, it is unnecessary to consider the remaining questions raised by third-party defendant.

It is ordered that the third-party complaint is dismissed for failure to state a claim, and that the cross-claim of the defendant Arden Leas is dismissed without prejudice.

11. United is distinguishable from the instant case. The United States owed a duty to warn the pilot in charge of the United craft, and its negligence in sending its training mission into the same area without warning to those in control of either craft created the unsafe condition which resulted in a midair collision.

"MARY CARTER" OR "GALLAGHER" AGREEMENTS

Plaintiffs and defendants sometimes enter into agreements known as "Mary Carter" or "Gallagher" agreements. ("Mary Carter" agreements have been so designated because of the case of *Booth v. Mary Carter Paint Company,* 202 S.2d 8 (Fla.App. 1967) in which such an agreement was first reviewed by the appellate courts.) Under these agreements the defendant (or some of the defendants) agrees to guarantee the plaintiff a certain amount of money if the plaintiff loses or recovers less than a stated amount. The plaintiff agrees to refund part of the defendant's payment in the event of a verdict against the defendants in excess of a stated amount. Numerous variations on this theme exist but the important feature is that the contracting defendant, although still a party in the case and usually a participant at the trial, benefits by the size of the judgments against the other defendants.

In effect these agreements allow parties relief from any no-contribution rule. If the no-contribution rule is in effect and a plaintiff executes a judgment against a "deep pocket" defendant, that defendant will be unable to limit his or her liability by seeking relief from the other joint tortfeasors. "Mary Carter" and "Gallagher" agreements, however, allow defendants to limit their liability, in essence circumventing rules prohibiting contribution. Some courts allow these agreements; others have found them to be a violation of public policy. Some courts require that the existence of these agreements be brought to the attention of the trier of fact. Although such innovative agreements can promote settlement, they are also potentially abusive, particularly to a nonagreeing defendant.

INDEMNIFICATION

When one tortfeasor accepts total financial responsibility for another tortfeasor he or she is said to have **indemnified** that tortfeasor. The party against whom indemnification is sought is referred to as an *indemnitor* and the party seeking to be indemnified is an *indemnitee*. Indemnification can be distinguished from contribution in that contribution involves a sharing of liability whereas indemnification involves a shift of liability from one tortfeasor to another. A discussion of the rules of both contribution and indemnity is found in *Panasuk v. Seaton* on page 387. (Carefully read the procedural history, which is found in the first two paragraphs.) The most frequent way indemnification arises is by virtue of a contractual agreement in which one party promises to indemnify another, as is often the case in contracts between general contractors and their subcontractors.

The right to indemnity also arises out of the law's attempt to avoid unjust enrichment of tortfeasors, as in cases involving vicarious liability. The "unjust enrichment" occurs when a tortfeasor is not required to reimburse a tortfeasor who pays the claim, resulting in the discharge of them both. An employer, for example, pays a judgment incurred by one of its employees only because it is vicariously liable for the torts of its employees. The courts reason that if the employer was not then indemnified by its employee so that it could recover the full amount of what it paid in damages, the employee would be unjustly enriched by being allowed to shirk his responsibility to pay for damages he caused. Since employers and employees are generally covered under a single insurance policy, however, liability of both parties is satisfied by the insurance company's payment of the claim and so indemnification is rarely sought.

In addition to situations involving vicarious liability, indemnity also applies to those defendants who are liable only because they failed to discover or to prevent another's misconduct. A retailer, for example, who innocently fails to discover a defect in goods that he sells will be indemnified by the manufacturer of the defective goods. If, on the other hand, the retailer knows of the defect, the manufacturer will not be obligated to indemnify him. Some courts also deny indemnity if the retailer acts negligently.

The issue of indemnification sometimes arises when an individual follows the directions of another and reasonably believes the directions to be lawful. Typically this occurs in the context of a principal-agent relationship in which the agent acts under the direction of the principal. But it can also take place when a sheriff is instructed to seize someone's property and no lawful basis for such seizure exists. As long as the sheriff reasonably believes that the orders are lawful and engages in no deliberate wrongdoing, he will be indemnified by the governmental agency for which he works.

Indemnity is sometimes allowed in cases where the plaintiff's injuries were aggravated by negligent treatment. If a driver, for example, pays for the total damages incurred by the plaintiff whom she injured, she can be indemnified by the doctor who aggravates the plaintiff's injuries by negligent medical care. The driver would be entitled to indemnification for that portion of the plaintiff's damages that were attributed to the negligent treatment.

Traditionally indemnity was an "all or nothing" situation, requiring that the indemnitor pay the indemnitee the full amount that the indemnitee paid the plaintiff. Under the doctrine of equitable indemnity, the amount of indemnity is dependent on the relative fault of the tortfeasors. Therefore, a tortfeasor may conceivably be indemnified for only part of the total damages he paid. Suppose a judgment is paid in full by an individual because the other defendants are penniless. In accordance with the doctrine of equitable indemnity, if that individual were to be indemnified by his principal, he would be indemnified only to the extent that he was actually responsible for the plaintiff's damages. The doctrine of equitable indemnity is inapplicable in cases in which the indemnitee's liability is purely vicarious.

SUMMARY

Joint tortfeasors are those who act together to produce a negligent or intentional tort. If the harm created is indivisible, each tortfeasor is jointly and severally liable for the harm suffered by the plaintiff. If all the defendants acted in concert all will be held liable even though only one of the defendants directly caused the plaintiff's injuries. If the harm can be apportioned (divided) the rule of joint and several liability is inapplicable. Joint and several liability has been abolished in some states and limited in others.

A plaintiff is entitled to only one satisfaction of his or her claim. A defendant who has paid more than his or her pro rata share may, however, turn to the other defendants for contribution. Although contribution was denied under the common law, it is allowed in most states for negligent torts. The courts are not in agreement as to how damages should be divided in the context of contribution.

Contribution becomes particularly problematic when a release is given to one defendant. The rules created by the courts to deal with contribution when a release has been granted have discouraged either plaintiffs or defendants from settling. Under the common law a release of one tortfeasor was a release of all tortfeasors. Under the Restatement, however, those defendants not parties to a release are absolved of liability only if the release is silent regarding their continuing liability.

Plaintiffs and defendants sometimes enter into "Mary Carter" or "Gallagher" agreements. In such agreements one (or more) of the defendants agrees to guarantee the plaintiff a certain amount of money regardless of the outcome of the case and the plaintiff agrees to reimburse the defendant if the verdict exceeds a stated amount.

Indemnification involves one tortfeasor's acceptance of total financial responsibility for another. An employer that is vicariously liable for the torts of its employee may be indemnified by that employee in that it can recover the full amount of what it paid in damages. Defendants who are liable only because they failed to discover or prevent another's misconduct may also be indemnified. The doctrine of equitable indemnity, which has been adopted by some courts, allows indemnity to be based on the relative fault of the tortfeasors.

PRACTICE POINTERS

In almost any personal injury case you will need to obtain documentation regarding your client's medical treatment as well as information demonstrating the impact of her injuries on her ability to work. Therefore, as soon as your firm agrees to represent a client, you should have her sign medical authorizations and a loss of wages authorization. Medical authorizations are used to obtain hospital records and doctors' reports on your client's behalf. Loss of wages authorizations allow you to gain access to employment information that otherwise would be considered confidential.

Your firm will have generic authorization forms, which for the sake of convenience, you should have the client sign while she is in the office. Try to anticipate approximately how many physicians and medical care facilities you expect the client to visit and have her fill out an equivalent number of forms.

The proper time to request a physician's report depends largely on the physician's practices and the amount he charges for such reports. Some doctors dictate extensive notes following each office visit; others prefer to prepare one cumulative report, based on handwritten notations. Some charge so much for reports that economy dictates reliance on hospital records and the client's recollections. In such cases only one cumulative report will be requested. Hospital records can be requested almost immediately if the client was treated in the emergency room. If her stay was lengthy, you should wait a few weeks before requesting records from the hospital medical records department. Most hospitals will forward records without any charge but it is common courtesy to offer in your cover letter to remit payment.

A loss of wages letter should not be sent until you are sure that the client has returned to a normal work schedule and that she is no longer seeing doctors or therapists. Address any such letters to the personnel department unless the client has advised you that you should communicate with a particular individual. In this letter you should request the following information:

- The client's normal work schedule and hourly wage.
- The overtime rate (which may vary depending on the time the work is done) and the anticipated overtime the client would normally be expected to have accrued if it were not for her accident.
- Whether the client's injuries resulted in an inability to perform certain overtime tasks.
- Whether the client was in line for a promotion, raise or bonus, which she is now denied because of her lost time from work or because she can no longer perform the tasks required for the new job.
- A description of any new duties your client may have been assigned, accompanied by an associated pay scale.
- Verification that the client has returned to work on a regular basis and the date she so returned.

TORT TEASERS

1. Discuss the questions raised at the beginning of this chapter. What additional information would you need to fully answer these questions?

2. A is injured as a result of the combined negligence of B and C. A settles with B for $2,000 and releases him. A then sues C and obtains a judgment for $30,000. If C pays $30,000, can he obtain contribution from B?

3. An automobile passenger injured in a one-vehicle accident enters into an agreement with his host driver to limit the amount of liability the driver will be exposed to regardless of the verdict in the passenger's action against the City. Assuming there is no evidence of unethical conduct or collusion, is such an agreement in violation of public policy? *City of Glendale v. Bradshaw,* 493 P.2d 515 (Ariz. 1972).

4. Defendant encourages an assailant to attack Plaintiff and stops others from coming to Plaintiff's aid. Is Defendant liable even though he takes no part in the attack? *Thompson v. Johnson,* 180 F.2d 431 (5th Cir. 1950).

5. Plaintiffs are injured when the car in which they are passengers collides with a taxicab. Plaintiffs sue the owner of the taxicab but not the owner of the car in which they were riding. What are the options of the taxicab owner? *Knell v. Feltman,* 174 F.2d 662 (D.D.C.1949).

KEY TERMS

Concurrent tortfeasors
Tortfeasors who independently cause the plaintiff injury.

Contribution
Partial reimbursement of tortfeasor who has paid more than his or her pro rata share of the damages.

Covenant not to sue
Promise by a plaintiff not to sue a particular defendant.

Indemnification
Total acceptance of financial responsibility by one tortfeasor for another.

Joint and several liability
Liability for an entire loss if the loss is indivisible.

Joint tortfeasors
Those who act together to cause the plaintiff's injury.

Release
Agreement to absolve a defendant of all liability.

Satisfaction
Payment of a judgment.

PART IV IS IT WORTH SUING?

OVERVIEW OF INSURANCE

CHAPTER OBJECTIVES

In this chapter you will learn to:

- Recognize the various types of insurance available.
- Distinguish between first party and third party coverage.
- Distinguish between single limits and split limits coverage.
- Differentiate among the four forms of life insurance.
- Recognize the defenses an insurer can raise.

FIRST PARTY VS. THIRD PARTY COVERAGE

In the not-too-distant past insurance was bundled into the relatively neat categories of fire, marine, inland marine, accident, and casualty insurance. These classifications do not begin to cover the vast array of insurance available today. A more appropriate differentiation of insurance in today's society is the distinction between first party and third party coverage. **First party coverage** provides reimbursement to the insured for losses directly sustained by him or her as a result of an "insured event." An insured event could be a loss caused by damage to the insured's property, losses caused by ill health or disability to work, or other losses sustained by the insured as a result of some unpredictable event.

Third party coverage indemnifies the insured for obligations she might otherwise have for damages she has caused or for which the law holds her responsible. Third party coverage includes coverage for liability caused by the insured's negligence and liability imposed by the law without regard to fault. Third party claims include claims for property damage, medical expenses, and pain and suffering caused by the insured.

The best known and most litigated insurance contract, the automobile insurance contract, has elements of both first party and third party coverage. Uninsured motorist coverage, for example, is first party coverage that reimburses the insured for losses he or she suffers that are caused by an uninsured motorist. Liability insurance, on the other hand, is third party coverage that indemnifies the insured for damages she has caused by her own negligence. Most of the entire gambit of protections provided in insurance contracts can be found in an automobile insurance contract.

Insurance taken out by an employer to provide coverage with respect to the acts of its employees is somewhat of a hybrid in that it has the characteristics of both first party and third party coverage. The protection of the employer from liability stemming from the acts of its employees is a third party characteristic. The reimbursement of the employer for damages caused to the employer itself because of its employees' wrongful acts, such as theft or embezzlement, is a first party characteristic.

TYPES OF INSURANCE COVERAGE AVAILABLE

Learning about all the different types of insurance coverage would be of little value. However, to give you some appreciation for the vast number of coverages, the table of contents of W. Freedmans, *Richards on the Law of Insurance* (6th ed., Lawyers Coop, 1991) is duplicated below (and see Table 20–1):

- accident insurance
- airplane insurance
- annuities and endowment insurance
- asbestos insurance
- automobile insurance
- boiler insurance
- burglary, robbery, theft, and larceny insurance
- burial insurance
- business interruption insurance
- casualty insurance
- condominium insurance
- confiscation insurance
- contractor's insurance
- credit insurance
- crop insurance
- directors and officer liability insurance
- disability and impairment insurance
- earthquake insurance
- elevator insurance
- employers' liability insurance
- errors and omissions insurance
- fidelity and guaranty insurance
- fire insurance
- flood insurance
- fraternal or mutual benefit insurance
- group life insurance

TABLE 20.1

OVERVIEW OF TYPES OF INSURANCE COVERAGE AVAILABLE	
FIRE INSURANCE	Covers rebuilding, repair and replacement of property damaged by fire.
ACCIDENT INSURANCE	Provides fixed benefits in event of accidental injury.
HEALTH INSURANCE	Reimbursement for expenses resulting from sickness or accidental injury.
HOMEOWNERS' INSURANCE	Reimbursement for losses related to damages to one's residence (excludes losses stemming from use of automobile).
LIABILITY INSURANCE	Reimbursement for losses for which insured is liable (usually excluding intentional and criminal acts).
LIFE INSURANCE	Payment to insured's estate or beneficiaries in event of insured's death.
MARINE INSURANCE	Reimbursement for losses incurred in shipping of goods.
MALPRACTICE INSURANCE	Reimbursement for losses stemming from professional negligence.
PRODUCT LIABILITY INSURANCE	Reimbursement for losses stemming from defective products.
PROPERTY INSURANCE	Reimbursement for losses sustained to property.
TITLE INSURANCE	Coverage for losses resulting from defective title to property.
UNEMPLOYMENT INSURANCE	Provision of compensation for losses caused an employee due to termination of employment.

- hazardous waste and environmental liability insurance
- health or sickness insurance
- homeowners' insurance
- inland marine insurance
- jewelers' block insurance
- liability insurance

- life insurance
- lightning insurance
- marine insurance
- medical and dental malpractice insurance
- plate glass insurance
- product liability insurance
- property insurance
- reciprocal or interindemnity insurance
- reinsurance
- strike insurance
- title insurance
- unemployment insurance
- use and occupancy insurance
- worker's compensation insurance

SPECIFIC TYPES OF INSURANCE

FIRE INSURANCE

As you have seen, the types of insurance available are many and varied. For the right premium an insurer can be found to insure against almost any contingency. One of the most prevalent types of insurance, however, is fire insurance. Fire insurance may be found in different types of policies but is most often encountered in the standard homeowners' policy. The 1943 New York Standard Policy provides the pattern for the standard coverage in today's homeowners' policies. This insurance prototype has been extensively reviewed by the courts and its contents are familiar to insurance regulators in all states.

One of the important provisions of the 1943 policy is the right given to the insurer to rebuild the damaged structure, repair it, or if necessary replace it. An insurer will obviously select the most economical option available. These options, which are similar to those available to the insurer under automobile collision coverage, often result in disputes between the insured and the insurer as to whether the option selected by the insurer was appropriate. Quite possibly, for example, a residence that is rebuilt because of severe fire damage may have a stigma attached to it that results in a substantial reduction of its fair market value. One vital prerequisite to recovery under any fire insurance policy is that the insured must not have intentionally caused the damage or conspired with another to intentionally cause the damage.

Irrespective of the amount of fire insurance obtained by an insured on a particular piece of property, the amount to be paid by the insurer will not be greater than the property's fair market value or replacement cost, depending on the type of insurance purchased. The mere fact that an insured purchases fire insurance for $100,000 on a building worth only $50,000 does not allow him or her to collect $100,000 in the event of the total loss of the structure.

ACCIDENT INSURANCE

Accident insurance is designed to provide the insured with specified coverage in the event of an accidental injury. A policy might provide a fixed amount for the loss of one eye, a greater amount for the loss of both eyes, a fixed sum for the loss of a leg, and so on. Often the accident insurance policy provides a fixed benefit in the case of an accidental death. Accident insurance, unlike health insurance, does not reimburse the insured for expenses incurred as the result of an accident. Rather, it provides an agreed upon payment if an accidental injury covered by the policy should occur.

HEALTH INSURANCE

Health insurance is designed to provide reimbursement for medical expenses incurred by the insured as a result of sickness or accidental injury. Most health insurance policies provide for a deductible that must be paid by the insured before benefits become payable.

In addition, most health insurance policies require the insured to be responsible for a percentage of the medical expenses incurred above the deductible, up to what is called the **co-insurance limit**. Above the co-insurance limit the insurer is totally responsible for payment of expenses. Suppose the insurer is responsible for 80 percent of the medical expenses incurred above the deductible of $1,000, to a total of $5,000 above the deductible (the co-insurance limit). If $10,000 in medical expenses were sustained, the insured would have to pay the deductible of $1,000 plus 20 percent of $5,000 ($1,000). The insurer would then be totally responsible for the remainder of the expenses ($4,000) and would have to pay 80 percent of the $5,000 above the deductible, for a total of $8,000.

Most health insurance policies have a maximum figure for which the insurer will be responsible for medical expenses as the result of any one claim. Once the policy limits are met by the insurer the insured is responsible for the payment of any shortfall. Depending on the policy, that maximum might be reinstated if the insured were to sustain medical expenses as a result of a different cause. Some policies also have lifetime maximums that will be paid irrespective of the number of claims.

The standard health insurance policy provision requires that the insured remain treatment free as a result of any preexisting conditions for a fixed period of time after the policy is issued. A **pre-existing condition** is any medical condition suffered by the insured prior to securing a policy from the insurer. The time period required varies from policy to policy but can be as short as ninety days or as long as two years. Any medical expenses incurred or treatment begun prior to the expiration of the period set forth in the policy will not be covered. The insurer may also provide specific exclusions for preexisting conditions. For example, a policy could contain an exclusion precluding payment for expenses relating to any injury to the insured's knee. Such an exclusion would be required by the insurance carrier because of prior problems with or treatment of the insured's knee.

One problem that often arises in health insurance policies is an allegation by the insurer that the insured failed to give a full and complete disclosure of a prior medical condition on the health insurance application. How the courts deal with such nondisclosure varies but most policies allow for cancelation if the insurer refunds the premiums paid. If an insured can show that the insurer would have issued a policy with only an exclusion for the type of injury that was not disclosed and that the injury that he or she sustained was not related to any misrepresentation on the application, some courts will require the insurer to pay the expenses despite the misrepresentation. Other courts look to the material misrepresentation and allow the insurer to avoid its contractual obligations, even though the misrepresentation was unrelated to the injury or sickness actually sustained by the insured.

HOMEOWNERS' INSURANCE

Homeowners' insurance policies have been designed for the owner-occupant of a single-family residence. Homeowners' insurance may provide either basic or extended coverage. *Basic coverage* provides for protection against loss due to fire, lightning, windstorm, or hail. *Extended coverage* provides personal liability protection as well as "all risk" coverage, which is coverage for all risk of physical loss to insured property except for exclusions specifically listed in the policy. Most lenders require, at the minimum, that a homeowner/insured maintain coverage for fire, windstorm, hail, vandalism, and malicious mischief. The purpose of this requirement is to ensure that any losses sustained that may affect the security of the lender will be reimbursed by the homeowner's insurance carrier.

The standard homeowners' policy specifically excludes any liability that might be imposed on the insured arising out of the operation of a motor vehicle. It may, however, provide liability coverage for the insured and the insured's family for acts that occur at locations other than the residence insured under the policy. One fertile field of litigation with respect to the standard homeowners' policy is the issue of liability for the death of minor children in a homeowner's swimming pool. Injuries caused to others by the insured or members of his or her family are also hotly litigated. If, for example, the insured's son injures his friend while engaging in unreasonably rough horseplay while on the premises or if the insured's dog bites a guest, the insured's homeowners' policy should provide coverage.

Many homeowners' insurance policies provide for medical payments insurance. They also frequently require that the insured specifically list (and pay an extra premium for) items of unusual value such as works of art, musical instruments, jewelry, excessive cash, and weapons.

LIABILITY INSURANCE

Liability insurance is one of the more comprehensive types of insurance available. Under this policy the insurer must reimburse (indemnify) the insured for any loss covered by the policy for which the insured may be responsible. Liability insurance covers damages the insured may be required to pay as a result of bodily injury or property damage caused by the insured's negligence. Illegal or intentional acts of the insured are not covered in a standard liability policy. Most policies, either by their specific language or by court interpretation, do not provide coverage for punitive damages.

Liability insurance is written either in single limit or split limits coverage. Under the **single limit** approach a set amount is all that is available to injured third parties irrespective of the total amount of the injuries they sustain. For example, a $300,000 single limit policy provides coverage for damages up to a maximum of $300,000 no matter how many claimants apply and no matter how great their actual losses are. Potentially, one claimant could recover

$300,000 and the other claimants could be left with nothing under this type of policy.

Under **split limits coverage** a fixed amount is set for each individual claim along with a different fixed amount for the total of all claims arising out of the same incident. The split limits coverage of a $100,000/$300,000 policy, for example, would allow a maximum recovery of $100,000 for each person injured and a maximum recovery of $300,000 for all persons injured. This type of coverage would prevent one claimant from usurping all of the $300,000 by putting a $100,000 cap on individual recovery.

As mentioned previously, liability insurance is a standard part of the homeowners' insurance policy. In most cases it is also a required part of the automobile insurance policy, which will be discussed in Chapter 21.

LIFE INSURANCE

Unlike the other types of insurance we have discussed, life insurance does not indemnify the insured for any losses sustained. In essence, a life insurance contract is an agreement by the insurance carrier to pay the insured's estate or the named beneficiary a fixed amount upon the insured's death. Unlike liability insurance or, for that matter, most other forms of insurance, the event insured against (death) is certain to happen.

Life insurance carriers have devised a variety of life insurance plans because of the perceived diverse needs of the American public (see Table 20–2). They have also attempted to capitalize on the tax benefits that have been granted to the life insurance industry. These tax benefits, which arguably stem from Congress' perception of life insurance as a type of savings, have provided life insurance carriers with sales pitches unavailable to other types of insurers. For example, insurers can offer policies that allow the insured to accumulate tax-free interest during the term of the policy and to pay taxes only upon actually receiving the funds. When the monies are received the insured is typically in a much lower tax bracket, according to the insurance carrier, usually as a result of retirement. Individual life insurance premiums are not tax deductible and the face amount of the policy paid to the beneficiary upon the insured's death is generally not taxable.

TABLE 20.2

ORDINARY	TERM
Insured pays fixed premium with benefits paid to estate or beneficiaries in event of insured's death.	Insured pays fixed premium with benefits paid to estate or beneficiaries in event of insured's death.
JOINT	**SURVIVORSHIP**
Benefits payable upon death of one or more insureds.	Benefits payable only to survivors of two or more insureds.

The most common types of life insurance now available are ordinary life, term life, joint life, and survivorship insurance.

Ordinary Life Insurance. An ordinary life insurance policy has a fixed monthly or yearly premium based on the age of the insured at the time the policy is taken out. This premium is paid during the life of the insured in consideration of the payment (based on the face amount of the policy) guaranteed to be paid his or her estate or beneficiary at the insured's death. Some ordinary life insurance policies are set up so that premiums are prorated through a certain age such as sixty, sixty-five, or seventy-five, at which time the policy is considered fully paid.

Typically the ordinary life insurance policy provides for the building of a cash value, which occurs after the first few years. Initially the payments provide the means for the agent to be paid a commission. As a result, the insurer pays the insured the cash value of the policy if the policy is canceled prior to his or her death. Alternatively, the insurer could loan the insured monies in an amount equal to the *loan value* of the policy, as determined by the insurance contract. The loan value of a policy varies depending on the number of years the policy has been in effect and the internal rate of return of the insured. If the insured takes a loan on the policy, the policy stays in effect as long as premiums and loan payments are paid on a timely basis.

Term Insurance. Term insurance has a fixed term, usually a year, and provides for payment only if the insured dies during that term. Unlike ordinary life insurance, the rates of term insurance vary on a periodic basis, depending on the age of the insured at the time the policy is taken out. Term insurance is more like other types of insurance in that the risk insured against (death during the term of the policy) is not certain to occur. Term insurance is often the insurance of choice for younger couples who want to provide for their dependents in the event of their own demise but who are unable to afford the higher premiums demanded by ordinary life insurance. Some term policies, while allowing the premium to vary with the age of the insured, guarantee insurability to the insured. Many waive the need for a physical examination as long as the insured renews the policy prior to the expiration of every term, so that no break in the coverage occurs.

Joint Life Insurance. With joint life insurance the benefits become payable upon the death of one of the insureds covered by the policy. Joint life insurance requires at least two insureds although a limitless number of insureds could theoretically be covered.

Joint life insurance is particularly advantageous when a small group of individuals, each of whom is vital to the group, begins a joint enterprise. Since the death of any group member could adversely affect the success of the endeavor, a joint life policy provides a fund from which the survivors can be compensated for the loss of one of their members. In contrast, term insurance, taken in the name of each individual, can result in premiums that exceed the enterprise's ability to pay. Joint life insurance, on the other hand, provides reimbursement to the enterprise at a minimal cost. Subsequent to the death of one of their group members, the survivors could obtain a second policy covering the survivors.

Survivorship Insurance. A survivorship policy is the mirror image of a joint life policy. Joint life insurance provides benefits when one of the insureds dies; survivorship insurance provides benefits when all but one of the insureds has died (i.e., it pays the last survivor). Survivorship insurance might be preferable to term insurance for a married couple in which one spouse is considerably older than the other. Although a survivorship policy would cost more than a term policy issued on the eldest spouse it would cost less than purchasing term policies for both of them. This type of policy might also be advantageous to a group in which the efforts of individual deceased members could be duplicated but a lone survivor would be unable to carry on the enterprise.

MARINE INSURANCE

Marine insurance, the oldest form of insurance, protects against losses incurred in shipping goods. It covers the loss itself as well as lost profits. Modern-day marine insurance traces its beginning to the emergence of England as a maritime power in the sixteenth century. The preeminent insurer in this area, Lloyds of London, issues the industry standard, called the "English Lloyds policy."

MALPRACTICE INSURANCE

Malpractice insurance is analogous to the *errors and omissions policy* used to protect officers and directors of major corporations. Malpractice insurance applies to professionals, who are held to the standard of care reasonably expected of similar professionals in the geographic area in which they practice. The major distinction between errors and omissions insurance and malpractice insurance lies in the standard of care. As previously noted, negligence is measured in terms of the standard of care of a "reasonable person." The standard of care for malpractice, on the other hand, is based on the expectations of a reasonable professional in a particular field and geographic area. Malpractice insurance is available for medical and dental practitioners, including pharmacists, hospitals, and nurses as well as for lawyers, psychologists, veterinarians, and other professionals.

One of the factors that differentiates malpractice insurance from errors and omissions insurance is that malpractice insurance requires state licensure while errors and omissions generally does not. Licensing is one of the first things to consider when determining what type of insurance might be available although it is not a consistent requirement. Most real estate salespeople, for example, are required to be licensed and yet their coverages are still considered errors and omissions policies rather than malpractice policies.

One recent change in malpractice policies lowers the amount of coverage available to a claimant by including the cost of his or her defense as part of the insurance coverage. Including defense costs is an illusory attempt to lower premiums while maintaining the same face value of coverage. In the past the cost of defending a lawsuit was not considered part of the policy. Under these terms, a claimant could avail herself of a sum equal to the face value of the policy minus the deductible. Under the new policy the amount available to the claimant is the face value of the policy minus the malpractice carrier's cost of defending the insured.

PRODUCT LIABILITY INSURANCE

Product liability insurance is a creation of the twentieth century. Manufacturers and producers of goods obtain product liability insurance to protect themselves against claims by the ultimate users and/or handlers of their products. Since most product liability cases are based on strict liability, the potential for loss is very high. In some industries, such as the airline industry, a single incident can result in numerous multimillion-dollar claims.

Because of this exposure, product liability insurance is very expensive but, from a practical standpoint, necessary to any entity that either manufactures or produces products. Problems arise when the cost of product liability insurance results in the production or manufacture of the product no longer being economical. At that point the maker of the goods must decide whether to go uninsured and hope no claims are made or to discontinue manufacturing the product altogether.

Testing of new products and modification of old products is often required by providers of product liability insurance. Underwriting Laboratory's "seal of approval," for example, allows manufacturers promotional advantages by being able to prominently display the "UL" symbol. But, more importantly, testing may be a prerequisite to the obtaining of product liability insurance.

In the marketplace the cost of product liability insurance unquestionably inhibits the introduction of new products. Many hope this cost will spur manufacturers to exhibit greater concern for consumers, but the cost/benefit ratio is still difficult to determine. The question remains whether the high cost of admission to the marketplace has created artificial barriers to the introduction of new and innovative concepts.

PROPERTY INSURANCE

Property insurance is an agreement by the insurer to indemnify the insured for any losses sustained to his or her property. Property insurance is included in many different types of coverage, including homeowners' coverage. Fire insurance and flood insurance are both types of property insurance. Property insurance, however, covers far more perils than fire and flood and frequently includes windstorm, lightning, rain, hail, and similar natural catastrophes.

Property insurance generally comes in two forms—**actual cash value** (the initial cost minus accrued depreciation) or **replacement cost** (the cost of replacing the article at the date of loss rather than at its depreciated value.) Therefore, most replacement cost policies require higher premiums than the premiums required for actual cash value policies.

TITLE INSURANCE

The primary purpose behind title insurance is to provide coverage to the insured for any loss that may result due to a defect in the title to property (not losses due to defects in or damage to the property itself). An insured is obligated to prove the nature and amount of the loss incurred and the insurer then indemnifies the insured against only that loss. In many instances, a problem with a title results in no or only insubstantial damages.

Suppose a title insurer issues a policy of title insurance for a parcel of land but fails to disclose an easement over the south ten feet of the property. If the title policy insured ownership of the entire parcel to the policy holder, the policy holder would be entitled to indemnification for only the loss in value due to the existence of the unknown easement. Very likely an easement for five or ten feet would be relatively insignificant with respect to the total value of the property. On the other hand, if such an undisclosed easement divided the property in half, the value of the remaining parcels might be dramatically affected.

Title insurance comes in a variety of forms, including the owner's policy, the lender's policy, and the American Land Title Association (ALTA) policy. The *owner's policy* tries to meet the needs of real estate buyers, the *lender's policy* protects the interest of the financing entity in a real estate transaction, and the *ALTA policy* provides the maximum protection to the insured. Because of its extensive coverage the ALTA policy is substantially greater in cost per dollar of coverage than other title policies.

UNEMPLOYMENT INSURANCE

Unemployment insurance is extensively regulated by state law. In most instances the benefits are fixed and mandated by statute as are the procedures for the redress of aggrieved employers and employees. Unemployment insurance matters require a very detailed examination of state statutes and the case law interpreting them.

WORKER'S COMPENSATION

Worker's compensation, like unemployment insurance, is highly regulated. All states have regulatory agencies whose purpose is to insure that employees have a source of compensation for work-related injuries. In most instances, the acceptance of worker's compensation benefits provided by statute precludes the employee from suing the employer for negligence. Worker's compensation, in general, provides benefits without regard to fault of the injured party. In other words, even though the employee was negligent in not abiding by the safety rules and regulations established by the employer, he or she is still entitled to worker's compensation benefits in the event of injury. As with unemployment insurance, the statutory framework in reference to worker's compensation claims must be extensively analyzed in light of relevant court decisions.

AUTOMOBILE INSURANCE

Perhaps nowhere in our court system is more litigation threatened or initiated than in reference to liability arising out of motor vehicle accidents. Automobile insurance, with all its variations, possesses most of the attributes of the other types of insurance. Automobile insurance will be discussed in some detail in the following chapter.

DEFENSES AN INSURANCE COMPANY CAN RAISE AGAINST ITS INSURED

The issuance of an insurance policy begins when an insured or his or her agent fills out an application. The primary purpose of the application is to answer certain relevant questions surrounding the issuance of the policy. A health insurance application, for example, deals primarily with the applicant's previous medical history. The insurer needs this information to determine whether any preexisting conditions exist that should be excluded from the policy as well as to assess the overall insurability of the applicant.

MISREPRESENTATIONS

If an applicant makes any material misrepresentations relating to any risks that are insured, the insurer may be able to void the policy should the insured make any claim relating to those risks (see Table 20–3). If the applicant attempts to conceal material facts or deliberately misrepresent material issues in the application, he or she may be denied any coverage whatsoever and may be relegated to, at most, reimbursement of the premiums paid to date. Many policies provide that after two years have elapsed from the issuance of the policy, the insurer cannot use any error or misrepresentation on the application to void the insurance contract.

FAILURE TO ABIDE BY TERMS OF POLICY

A policy can also be voided by the insured's failure to abide by the terms of the policy. Insureds are most likely to be at odds with their insurance company in one of two ways. The first involves the insured's duty to cooperate with the insurer in dealing with the claim. The second involves the policy's provisions requiring the insured to give prompt notice of any potential claim.

Failure to Cooperate. An insured potentially violates the duty to cooperate if he or she refuses to give a statement to the insurance company, refuses to make books and records available (where applicable), or refuses to allow the insurance company to enter his or her premises for inspection purposes in the case of a fire or property damage claim. The insured also violates the duty to cooperate when he or she is sued and fails to participate in the discovery process by refusing to attend depositions, answer interrogatories, respond to requests for admissions, or assist in the production of documents.

Failure to Notify. Failure to notify an insurance company of a claim is a second potential point of contention between insureds and their insurance

TABLE 20.3

DEFENSES INSURER CAN RAISE

- Insured makes material misrepresentation in application.
- Insured fails to cooperate with insurer in dealing with claim.
- Insured fails to give timely notice to insurer of potential claim.
- Insured commits intentional act.

companies. Although most policies require reasonable notice, some attempt to set an outer time limit by which any claim must be reported. Before an insured can be said to have violated the duty to give notice he or she must know or have reason to know that a claim is forthcoming. What might appear, for example, to be a minor motor vehicle collision with no property damage and no personal injury could result in a subsequent claim. If the insured reasonably believes no damage occurred and no claim will be made, failure to advise the carrier about the accident will not give the insurance company grounds for denying coverage.

In a similar vein, the insured has a duty to advise the insurance company of any suit that is actually filed against him or her. If the carrier is unable to answer the complaint because of the insured's failure to notify it in a timely manner and a default judgment is entered, the insurer can attempt to deny coverage. Alternatively, the insurer might seek reimbursement for the damages it sustained as a result of the default judgment against the insured. Suppose an insured, through his own inaction, allows a default judgment to be entered against him. The carrier may then be relieved of the responsibility of paying the judgment or may be allowed to attempt to set aside the judgment as far as it relates to its duty to indemnify the insured.

INTENTIONAL ACTS

Most insurance policies exempt coverage for intentional acts of the insured. Such acts include intentionally setting fire to insured property, suicide (although many life insurance policies cover suicide if committed after a fixed period of time following the issuance of the policy), intentionally using a motor vehicle to cause damage, or intentionally assaulting a third party.

RESERVATION OF RIGHTS

An insurer may find it difficult to immediately determine whether it has a right to deny coverage under the policy. Therefore, most insurance carriers, until they are sure they have a right to deny coverage, will defend the insured under a **reservation of rights**. Under a reservation of rights the insurer advises the insured that coverage may not be available but that it will defend the insured until that determination is made. In many cases the insurer will institute a declaratory judgment action, seeking a court determination regarding the issue of coverage. If an insurer proceeds under a reservation of rights, it may later withdraw from representation of the insured and seek reimbursement for its defense costs.

INSURER'S ACTIONS

An insurance carrier can by its own actions lose its right to assert a defense against an insured. In such cases the insurer will be deemed to have waived its rights to contest the policy and may, in some circumstances, be estopped (prevented) from asserting defenses because of its prior acts.

As with all areas of insurance, court rulings and statutory enactments affecting the policy in question must be carefully researched. In some instances the plain wording of the policy and the insurer's actions have been deemed wrongful and in violation of "public policy." Public policy attempts to reconcile legislative enactments, prior court decisions, and the public good in overriding provisions perceived as inequitable. Public policy requirements will be read into an insurance policy and terms and conditions conflicting with public policy will either be ignored or deemed unenforceable. Provisions in a policy that exclude members of an insured's family from coverage, for example, may be deemed in violation of public policy and therefore unenforceable by the insurer.

SUMMARY

Third party coverage provides an insured with funds up to the policy limit for any damages resulting from the insured's acts if those acts are covered under the insurance policy. First party coverage provides for payment directly to the insured from his or her carrier for personal losses sustained by the insured. Many insurance policies, such as automobile insurance and homeowners' policies, have both first and third party protection.

Life insurance differs from other types of insurance in that it does not reimburse insureds for losses they sustain but rather provides a fixed payment upon death. This payment depends on the amount of insurance purchased and is paid to the designated beneficiary at the death of the insured. Life insurance may be for a fixed period of time (term insurance), for a fixed premium paid during the life of the insured and based on the life expectancy of the insured (ordinary life), or paid on the death of either an individual in a group (joint life) or when only one individual in a group is left alive (survivorship insurance).

A variety of other types of insurance coverage are also available, including fire insurance, marine insurance, product liability insurance, and unemployment insurance, all of whose provisions are obvious from their names. Accident insurance provides fixed benefits for losses resulting from an accident while health insurance provides reimbursement for medical expenses incurred. Most health insurance policies deny coverage for preexisting conditions and have a co-insurance limit that limits the liability of the insurer. Homeowners' insurance policies provide either basic or extended coverage for losses due to fire, lightning, windstorm, vandalism, malicious mischief, and other risks. Liability insurance, one of the more comprehensive types of insurance, reimburses the insured for those losses for which the insured is responsible. Both single limit and split limits coverages are available. Property insurance comes in the form of either actual cash value policies or replacement cost policies. Title insurance provides coverage to the insured for losses resulting from defects in the title to property.

A policy may be voided by the insurer if the insured makes any material misrepresentations when filling out the application for a policy. Similarly, a policy can be voided if the insured fails to cooperate with the insurer in dealing with any claims or fails to give prompt notice of any potential claims. Intentional acts of insureds are exempted from coverage by most insurance policies. Most insurance carriers will defend an insured under a reservation of rights until they are able to ascertain whether they have a right to deny coverage.

PRACTICE POINTERS

Before preparing a file for any type of insurance case you must first meticulously review the insurance contract in question. Carefully analyze any applicable provisions in light of the policy's definitions and conditions to make sure that you thoroughly understand the policy language and its implications.

Once you have a good grasp of the policy provisions, you can begin organizing the file. Consider including in the file relevant cases, law review articles, and other publications relating to the issue in question. Although this information may be duplicated in other files, having it readily available will expedite answering any questions that arise.

In many jurisdictions commercial publications are available that give recent jury verdicts. Retaining copies of these reports not only helps you evaluate your client's claim but gives you some very potent "ammunition" to use in discussions with the adjustor. For a nominal fee ($100–$200) a compendium of cases that have been decided in the same general area as your claim can be obtained. This type of compendium helps you evaluate your claim, tells you how many similar types of cases your insurance carrier has litigated in your jurisdiction, and gives you some insight into jury verdict trends.

Having established a depository for the insurance policy and related information, you must then devise a mechanism for keeping track of damages. Damages include property losses, health care costs, lost wages, replacement cost of equipment, and the cost of hiring employees to replace the insured. Each type of damages should be tracked individually even though the same damages may be relevant to different claims. The cost of repairing an automobile in an accident case, for example, establishes the property damage claim for replacement of the vehicle but also demonstrates the force and extent of the collision, thus helping prove subsequent medical expenses.

Be careful when evaluating damage claims to ensure that the client receives adequate compensation. If a client's vehicle is totally demolished, for example, he should be awarded the true fair market value of his vehicle along with the sales tax on the damages and a pro rata reimbursement of his registration fees. Suppose your client's vehicle has a $20,000 price tag and a fair market value of $17,000 to $20,000. If the sales tax in your state is 7 percent and the value of the vehicle is determined to be $17,000, your client should recover an additional $1,190 along with a pro rata share of his registration fees. To determine what items he should be reimbursed for, review appropriate statutory authority and administrative rules and regulations. Even if peripheral damages are not specifically provided for under your state's laws, persuasive argument should be made that justice demands they be included in any settlement.

Medical expenses, including hospital and doctors' bills, ambulance service bills, prescription costs, radiology bills, and costs of auxiliary

Continued on next page

PRACTICE POINTERS—Continued

medical support in the form of wheelchairs, braces, and so forth should be updated regularly. A medical worksheet at the front of the file should contain a list of expenses, along with a brief description giving the dates a service was provided,by whom it was provided, and what part of the bill, if any, is already paid. Similarly, a property damage worksheet should be prepared and regularly updated. Estimates of repairs should be included and the company that ultimately makes the repairs should be indicated. Lost wages must also be documented and information regarding the client's hourly and overtime wages must be obtained as well as the number of regular and overtime hours he lost because of his injuries. Once this is known the total loss of regular and overtime wages can be calculated. A loss of wages worksheet can be helpful in keeping track of a client's work record.

TORT TEASERS

1. With respect to each of the types of insurance listed in this chapter determine whether that insurance is first party, third party, or a combination of both.

2. Review the homeowners' insurance policy in the Appendix and answer the following questions.

a. Does coverage exist for property damage resulting from fire, windstorm, hail, earthquake, volcanic eruptions, or flood and, if so, how much coverage is available?

b. How much liability insurance is provided by the policy? Is it a single limit or split limits coverage?

c. How much medical payments coverage is available?

d. When does the policy provide coverage for damage to the structure or its contents caused by water damage (i.e., from fighting the fire, burst pipes in the interior of the house or exterior to the house, after wind damage has destroyed the roof and rain water comes into the residence, when someone forgets to turn off the water in the bathtub and the overflow drain doesn't work, etc.)?

e. Is the amount of personal property coverage a percentage of the property damage limit?

f. Does the policy have any riders covering specific types of property such as art work, jewelry, coin collections, weapons, etc.?

g. Does the policy have an "intentional acts" exclusion?

h. How much, if any, coverage is provided for additional living expenses in the event of a loss?

i. Is there any limitation in the policy as to how much will be paid to clean up the debris in the event of a loss?

KEY TERMS

■ **Actual cash value**
Policy that pays the insured on the basis of the initial cost of the property minus any accrued depreciation.

■ **Co-insurance limit**
The point in a health insurance policy at which an insurer is totally responsible for payment of expenses; up to that point the insured is responsible for a percentage of the expenses (that percentage is designated in the policy).

■ **First party coverage**
Coverage providing reimbursement to the insured for losses sustained directly by the insured.

■ **Loan value**
The amount of monies that will be loaned by an insurer to an insured based on the contractually determined value of the life insurance policy.

■ **Preexisting condition**
Medical condition suffered by an insured prior to his or her application for a health insurance policy.

■ **Replacement cost policy**
Policy that pays the insured on the basis of the cost of replacing the property at the time the loss is incurred.

■ **Reservation of rights**
Decision of insurer to defend insured until it determines that it has a right to deny coverage.

■ **Single limit coverage**
Fixed amount of coverage that is available to all those injured regardless of how great their losses are.

■ **Split limits coverage**
Fixed amount of coverage that is available for each individual claim with a different fixed amount for the total of all the claims (puts a cap on individual recovery).

■ **Third party coverage**
Coverage that indemnifies the insured for damages he or she caused or for which the law holds him or her responsible.

AUTOMOBILE INSURANCE

CHAPTER OBJECTIVES

In this chapter you will learn to:

- Identify the characteristics of medical payment, collision, comprehensive, UM, UIM, and umbrella coverage.
- Recognize an insurer's subrogation and termination rights.
- Recognize when reformation of policies is appropriate.
- Describe the arbitration process used to resolve disputes.

As Pauline and Perry are leaving their local fast food restaurant, Perry prepares to make a left turn across traffic on a four-lane street immediately in front of the restaurant. Upon pulling out into traffic Pauline and Perry's 1990 Chevrolet, a one-half ton pickup, is broadsided in the second lane of traffic by Denise, who is driving a 1963 Chrysler. Her fourteen-year-old brother, David, is a passenger. Perry, who is not wearing a seat belt, is critically injured in the accident and dies ten days later. Pauline, who is wearing her seat belt, is also seriously injured. She suffers a broken shoulder, a concussion, extensive scarring to the side of her face, and severe soft tissue injuries, including cervical strain and sprain.

Neither Denise, a sixteen-year-old unlicensed driver, nor David are wearing seat belts. Denise's injuries require only minor medical treatment. David, however, is catapulted from the front seat through the windshield of the Chrysler and suffers severe facial injuries as well as nerve damage that renders him a paraplegic.

Pauline and Perry's automobile insurance policy for the pickup, set forth in the Appendix along with the applicable declarations page, provides $100,000/ $300,000 liability coverage, $10,000 medical payments coverage, $50,000 property damage coverage, and $15,000/$30,000 in both UM (uninsured motorist) coverage and UIM (underinsured motorist) coverage. They also have a $500 deductible collision coverage and a zero deductible comprehensive provision. The Chrysler that Denise is driving, which she took without her parent's permission, has no applicable insurance. Her father had purchased the car five months earlier and was in the process of restoring it.

At the time of the accident Denise is driving without her headlights on. Pauline tells the investigating officers that she was looking to the left when her husband was making his turn and did not see the Chrysler coming. Wilma, a registered nurse who was immediately behind Pauline and Perry at the restaurant exit, tells the investigating officer that she saw the Chrysler approaching even without seeing its headlights. Warren, a construction worker driving a van, tells the investigating officers that he was approximately 50 yards behind Denise at the time of the accident and that Denise was driving at the speed limit but never applied her brakes prior to impact with Perry's pickup. Warren also states that the Chrysler did not have illuminated taillights. In fact, he says, he almost ran into Denise's car earlier since the car, being dark green and unilluminated, was difficult to see at night.

Denise's father is an assembler at a local electronics plant, where he works the night shift from 4 to 12 P.M. Her mother has been hospitalized for two weeks with a serious illness, which has severely strapped the family's financial resources. Since her mother was hospitalized and her father was working Denise had the responsibility of watching out for David. For this reason she had access to the keys to the Chrysler. Prior to this joy-riding incident Denise had always been a very responsible teenager and was an honor student at her high school. We will use this scenario in the Tort Teasers section at the end of the chapter to apply the concepts presented throughout this chapter.

OVERVIEW OF AUTOMOBILE INSURANCE

As mentioned in the previous chapter more litigation arises out of the automobile insurance contract than any other type of insurance. The horrendous number of automobile accidents coupled with the mandatory insurance legislation in most states has created this proliferation of lawsuits. Failure to obtain and maintain the minimal insurance coverage required by state law can prevent an automobile owner from either registering or driving a vehicle. Additionally, in most states either civil or criminal sanctions await those who unlawfully drive without mandatory insurance coverage.

The types of automobile insurance coverage available vary, depending on whether the state is *"fault"* or *"no fault."* "No fault" insurance is based on the concept that the insured's carrier should pay for his or her damages regardless of who is at fault. Since "no fault" insurance is a relatively new concept and has been adopted by very few states, we will focus in this chapter on the traditional automobile insurance policy in effect in "fault" states.

AUTOMOBILE LIABILITY COVERAGE

The primary purpose of automobile insurance is to provide liability coverage to the insured for the bodily injury or property damage he or she causes while operating an automobile. (See Table 21–1). An example of the terms and conditions of liability and property damage coverage is set forth in coverage N (Section III) of the insurance policy in the Appendix. This coverage provides either split limits or single limit coverage. Recall that with split limits coverage each individual may recover a set amount of damages, with an aggregate amount available for damages independent of the total number of individuals injured. A single limit coverage amount for property damage resulting from the insured's negligence is usually provided.

An example of split limits coverage is the minimum limits set by many states, in which $15,000 must be available for each person injured and $30,000 must be available as an aggregate amount for all individuals injured. If a minimum of $10,000 were required to cover property damage, the liability limits of such a policy would be described as $15,000/$30,000/$10,000.

Table 21–2 lists types of automobile insurance coverage.

UMBRELLA POLICY

The total limits of liability available for bodily injury and property damage are as high as the maximum amount provided by the carrier issuing the policy. As a practical matter, however, bodily injury limits in excess of $250,000 to $500,000 and property damage in excess of $100,000 generally are not covered by the automobile policy itself but by a separate policy called an **umbrella policy**. The umbrella policy may be written by the same carrier issuing the automobile insurance policy or by a different carrier. Such a policy is usually subject to a large deductible.

The umbrella carrier is liable only after the first insurer pays the full limits of its coverage. If, for example, a primary insurer pays $500,000 to the person injured by the insured for bodily injuries but the individual actually sustains $750,000 in damages for bodily injuries, the umbrella carrier would pay the additional $250,000 (or the amount up to the limits of the insured's umbrella policy). Terms and conditions of an umbrella policy are shown in the insurance policy in the Appendix in Section V.

REFORMATION OF POLICY

If an insurance carrier attempts to issue a policy with limits less than those required by the statute, the courts will **reform the policy** by construing it to provide the minimum statutory coverage.

In some instances the insurance policy itself provides terms and conditions to conform the policy to state law in the event the cancellation or nonrenewal

TABLE 21.1

CHARACTERISTICS OF AUTOMOBILE POLICIES

- Single limit vs. split limits
- Coordination of benefits provisions
- Primary vs. secondary coverage
- Subrogation rights
- Arbitration rights

TABLE 21.2

TYPES OF COVERAGE	
LIABILITY COVERAGE	Coverage for losses caused by the insured while operating a motor vehicle.
MEDICAL PAYMENT	Reimbursement of medical expenses incurred when injured in vehicle covered by policy.
COMPREHENSIVE	Coverage for losses resulting from something other than collision.
COLLISION	Reimbursement for repair or replacement of damaged vehicle.
ACCESSORY COVERAGE	Emergency road service. Car rental. Death and disability.
UNINSURED MOTORIST COVERAGE	Coverage for losses caused by an uninsured motorist.
UNDERINSURED MOTORIST COVERAGE	Coverage for losses caused by motorist whose liability insurance is insufficient to cover the insured's losses.

provisions are contrary to the laws of the state. An example of this type of provision is shown in the policy in the Appendix in Section V, part VIII, paragraph 15.

SUBROGATION

If an insurer pays its insured, the insurer is then subrogated to the rights of the insured and can sue the responsible party. **Subrogation** allows an insurer to institute suit against the responsible person, in the name of the insured, to collect the amounts paid by the insurer to the insured. Subrogation is universally allowed with respect to uninsured motorist, collision, and comprehensive payments made by the insurer. If subrogation is allowed the insured has an obligation to cooperate with his or her insurer in the subrogation claim. Cooperation could include assisting the insurer at trial and in the discovery process.

An example of a subrogation provision is shown in the policy in the Appendix in coverage P (Section III), paragraph 6, and endorsement 303 (Section III), paragraph 6. That subrogation provision, called a trust agreement, provides that the insured will take no action that would cause the insurer to lose any of its rights of recovery against either the uninsured or underinsured motorist.

MEDICAL PAYMENT COVERAGE

Medical payment coverage provides for reimbursement of all reasonable medical expenses incurred by an insured while occupying a covered vehicle or when the insured, as a pedestrian, is struck by a different vehicle. In some states medical payment coverage is referred to as personal injury protection (PIP). If the insured is injured in a motor vehicle owned by someone other than the insured, the owner's medical payment coverage will be **primary**. In other words, the automobile owner's medical payment coverage will be primarily responsible for payment of the insured's medical expenses up to the limits of the owner's medical payment coverage.

If the insured's medical expenses exceed the owner's limits, the coverage available to the insured under his or her own medical payment coverage will kick into effect. Suppose an automobile owner's medical payment coverage is $5,000 and the individual injured has medical payment coverage of his own for $10,000. If the individual incurs reasonable medical expenses of $20,000, the first $5,000 will be paid by the owner's policy, the next $10,000 by the injured person's medical payments carrier, and the balance of $5,000 by the injured party or his own health insurance policy, assuming no third party is liable for the injuries.

Most medical payment policies provide that benefits are payable only for those medical expenses incurred within a fixed time period after the date of the accident. Typically, these time periods range from one to three years after the accident. If medical expenses are incurred after this time has elapsed, the insurer is not responsible for payment.

In most instances, an injured party may receive benefits under medical payment coverage in addition to any benefits received under any of his or her other medical policies. Some policies have a **coordination of benefits provision**, which precludes payment if other insurance is available. If neither the medical payments nor health insurance coverage has a coordination of benefits provision, the injured party can lawfully recover twice for medical expenses. Such recovery is, of course, subject to any deductible or coinsurance limit in the health insurance policy. This double recovery, allowed under the so-called collateral source rule (see Chapter 9 on damages), is premised on the fact that the insured, who is paying a separate premium for each type of coverage, may reap the benefits of his or her investment.

Many medical payment plans also provide for benefits in the event of the insured's death. Death benefits are usually fixed at a certain dollar amount and are intended, in part at least, to cover burial expenses. Medical expenses incurred by the deceased up to the date of death are also covered.

The terms and conditions of a typical medical payment provision are listed in coverage Q (Section III) of the insurance policy in the Appendix. Be aware that the exclusions are applicable to all coverages in Section III of the policy.

COMPREHENSIVE COVERAGE

Comprehensive automobile insurance provides coverage for loss to the insured vehicle and, in some cases, to a nonowned automobile for losses other than those resulting from collision. Coverage for property damage and loss caused by fire, theft, windstorm, and hail is included. Losses typically recovered under comprehensive coverage are from a shattered windshield, from the theft of valuables from a vehicle, and from the loss of a vehicle and its contents due to fire or theft. Reimbursement for a lost or damaged item is determined by its *actual cash value* (purchase price less depreciation) or its *replacement cost.* Many policies require physical signs of forced entry before the insured can be reimbursed for the stolen property. Some policies are subject to a deductible, which is the responsibility of the insured to pay.

State insurance departments do not require comprehensive coverage to be part of the standard automobile insurance contract. However, if a vehicle is being financed through some kind of financing institution, the insured may be required to maintain comprehensive as well as collision coverage. Typical provisions providing comprehensive coverage are shown in the Appendix policy under coverages R and S (Section III).

COLLISION INSURANCE

Collision insurance reimburses the insured if he or she must repair or replace a damaged vehicle. Like medical payment insurance, collision insurance provides coverage irrespective of who is to blame for the damages. In the case of a negligent motorist, the carrier is subrogated to the rights of the insured and can seek reimbursement from the motorist for any expenses it incurs in repairing the insured vehicle. If the damage is caused by the insured's own negligence, the insurer has no right to seek payment from the insured. Most collision policies are issued subject to a deductible. Typical examples of the protection provided by having collision coverage are also set forth in the policy in the Appendix under coverage T (Section III).

MISCELLANEOUS COVERAGE

The automobile insurance contract can also include coverage for emergency road service, which pays for towing and any other emergency services occurring on the road, up to a maximum amount, often $25. Its primary purpose is to provide for towing a disabled vehicle to the nearest service station. Other available coverages include death and disability insurance and car rental insurance.

Care should be taken in selecting these "accessory" coverages. Make sure the premium for the risk to be covered is in proportion to the premiums and risk covered in a regular disability or accidental death policy. The latter may provide coverage whether or not the incident triggering coverage resulted from the use of an automobile.

These types of "miscellaneous" coverage provisions are shown in the Appendix policy as endorsements 323, 334, 335, and 368 (Section III). Most provisions of this type establish the absolute maximum amount for which the insurer is liable as well as the maximum per diem expense that will be paid.

UNINSURED MOTORIST COVERAGE

Next to liability insurance the most important coverage available under the standard automobile insurance contract is uninsured motorist coverage (UM), which provides coverage only for injuries caused by an uninsured motorist. The percentage of uninsured motorists on the road is alarmingly high, especially in those states requiring automobile insurance coverage but not requiring written proof of such insurance when registering a motor vehicle. Since many uninsured motorists are financially incapable of paying any substantial award for damages they inflict, UM coverage ensures that funds are available to compensate the insured. This coverage guarantees that the insured will be compensated, up to the limits of his policy, by his own insurer to the extent that a third party (the uninsured motorist) is responsible for his injuries.

An uninsured motorist is typically defined as a motorist having no applicable automobile insurance policy for the vehicle being driven or having an applicable policy with an insolvent insurance carrier. In some policies a hit-and-run driver may be considered an uninsured motorist.

Most states require that UM coverage be provided with the issuance of a liability policy. The minimum limits of this coverage are generally set by statute and are often the same as the minimum coverage limits required for liability insurance coverage. Uninsured motorist coverage typically does not provide for any deductible to be paid by the insured. In most states the insured's carrier can reduce the amount of damages paid to its insured in proportion to the insured's own negligence.

If payment is made to the insured, the UM carrier is subrogated to the rights of its insured and can bring an action in the name of its insured against the responsible party. Subrogation relieves the insured of having to chase the uninsured motorist to either obtain or collect a judgment.

An insurance company cannot, for the most part, attempt to offset monies paid under a medical payment policy against the amount otherwise due the insured under a UM policy, especially if the policy is the minimal amount allowed by law. Suppose an insured has $10,000 in medical payment coverage and $15,000 in UM coverage (the statutory minimum). The carrier cannot credit monies paid under medical payments to the amount otherwise due the insured under his or her UM coverage. That credit might, however, be allowed if the insured has UM coverage in excess of the statutory minimum.

PRIMARY VS. SECONDARY COVERAGE

Most UM policies provide coverage regardless of whether the insured was driving the automobile specifically referred to in the policy or a different vehicle. If the insured was driving a different vehicle, the uninsured motorist coverage will be coordinated with the coverage that would otherwise be available on the vehicle being driven. Most policies designate the coverage provided with the vehicle being driven as **primary** and the policy covering the driver (the insured in this case) as **secondary**. The primary carrier is liable for all damages up to the limits of its policy. At that point the secondary carrier is liable for any damages sustained by the insured above the limits of the primary policy up to the amount of the insured's loss or the limits of the excess policy, whichever is less.

COORDINATION OF BENEFITS

If an insured has applicable insurance in addition to that provided by his or her automobile policy, the **coordination of benefits provision** of most policies will require the insurance carrier to be responsible for its pro rata share of the damages as long as the insured is driving his or her own vehicle. A carrier's pro rata share is determined by the proportion of its coverage to the total amount of available insurance. Suppose the insured has UM coverage of $50,000 per person and an additional $100,000 of coverage under a different but applicable policy. The UM insurance carrier would be responsible for no more than one-third of the damages ($50,000/$150,000), up to a total maximum liability of $50,000. Since the other carrier that provided $100,000 of coverage would probably have a comparable coordination of benefits provision, litigation between the two carriers would likely be necessary to determine their respective obligations. Coordination of benefits provisions also apply to underinsured coverage.

Typical provisions contained in a policy providing uninsured motorist coverage are set forth in coverage P (Section III) of the Appendix policy.

UNDERINSURED MOTORIST COVERAGE

Underinsured motorist (UIM) coverage protects the insured who is injured by a motorist whose liability coverage is insufficient to fully compensate the insured for his or her injuries. UIM coverage is applicable, for example, when the insured sustains $50,000 in damages but the responsible party has only $15,000 worth of liability coverage. In that case the responsible party's insurance carrier will pay $15,000 and the insured's UIM policy will compensate the insured for the remaining $35,000, assuming the UIM coverage limit is $35,000 or greater. Underinsured motorist coverage typically does not provide for any deductible to be paid by the insured.

Most states prohibit **stacking** of UM and UIM coverage. In other words UM and UIM are not available to the insured for the same accident. Therefore, an uninsured motorist who is the responsible party cannot be alleged by the insured to be both uninsured for the purposes of UM coverage and underinsured for purposes of UIM coverage. In multivehicle accidents, however, UM coverage may be applicable to one joint tortfeasor and UIM coverage may be applicable to another.

Typical provisions contained in a policy providing underinsured motorist coverage are set forth in endorsement 303 (Section III) of the Appendix policy.

ARBITRATION

Most policies require arbitration for disputes arising out of medical payment, UM, and UIM coverage with respect to the amount of damages sustained by the insured. Since most states favor the use of arbitration to resolve contractual disputes, these policy provisions are generally enforceable. Both the insured and the carrier are usually required to select and pay for an arbiter of their choosing. The two arbiters then select a third arbiter, whose compensation is split evenly by the insured and the insurer.

In a hearing before the three arbiters, where local evidentiary rules are often applied, a decision rendered by two of the arbiters is binding on both parties. Often, however, the arbitration clause provides that if an award is entered in excess of the statutory minimal limits for bodily injury, the arbitration award will not be binding. If either party contests an award, a trial "de novo," in which the issue of damages is relitigated without regard to the arbiters' findings, is held. An arbiter's findings with respect to the insured's damages are not admissible at trial.

A typical arbitration requirement is shown in the Appendix policy in paragraph 5 of coverage P (Section III). These arbitration provisions relate only to uninsured and underinsured motorist coverage claims. Most policies also require that disputes with respect to medical payments be arbitrated.

TERMINATION

An automobile insurance contract can be terminated at the request of the insured or due to the acts of the insured. If the insured chooses to terminate his or her policy, the termination is effective on the date notice is given, usually to the insured's agent. The insured is then entitled to a return, usually pro-rata, of any advance premiums paid.

Voluntary termination has been complicated in some states by mandatory insurance requirements. In certain circumstances termination can result in the insured forfeiting his or her registration rights to the vehicle unless another policy meeting state requirements is taken out. Statutes and case law should be carefully researched, therefore, to determine the implications of voluntary termination.

If the insurer initiates termination it must comply with the policy's notification requirements as well as the terms and conditions upon which termination is permitted in that state. Termination is always an option for an insurer if an insurer fails to pay his or her premiums. In most instances the insured must be given written notice. Termination for nonpayment may become effective only after a designated time period following the giving of written notice. The insurer may also terminate a policy if an insured or driver who lives with the insured has his or her license suspended or revoked. In light of current societal attitudes about intoxication, most policies allow termination if an insured is convicted of driving while intoxicated.

SUMMARY

The primary purpose of automobile insurance is to protect the insured for expenses incurred as a result of bodily injury or property damage caused while the insured is operating his or her automobile. Both single limit and split limits coverage are available. Umbrella policies are available as a sec-

PRACTICE POINTERS

Once your firm has agreed to represent an automobile accident victim, you or your attorney should immediately initiate contact with the insurance adjuster for the adverse carrier (insurer of the responsible party). If an adjuster has not yet been assigned, a letter should be written to the insurance carrier requesting that the adjuster for the accident contact your firm. The attorney, more often than the legal assistant, communicates with the adjuster, but the responsibility for keeping the files up to date often falls to the legal assistant. Therefore, you should be aware of the type of information that is conveyed and maintain relevant materials in the files.

Although a variety of means of dealing with adjusters exists, regular and timely information regarding the client's medical treatment should be provided to the adjuster. Updates of medical expenses, the names of those providing treatment, the type of treatment being utilized, and the cost of treatment should be forwarded routinely. Forcing the adjuster to review the file on a regular basis as your client's treatment progresses may result in a greater reserve for the case than when the adjuster is faced with a demand letter and copies of all medical records at the same time. The *reserve* refers to the amount of funds set aside by the insured for your claim. Although the amount of the reserve depends on the individual carrier's internal practices, theoretically it represents a fair estimate of the value of the claim. The purpose of having reserves is to allow insurers to set aside sufficient funds to pay claims as they become due as well as to provide accurate financial statements for insurers.

At the early stages of a case you need to obtain the names and records of those physicians who have previously treated the client. A review of these records allows for a determination of whether a client has been treated for similar injuries or complained of similar problems in the past. Being aware of the client's previous medical treatment allows for a more accurate evaluation of the claim and, if necessary, a rebutting of the defendant's allegations of preexisting conditions.

In many instances an adjuster may request an independent medical examination (IME) of a client. Since the client is already receiving treatment from his or her physician most attorneys do not allow an IME prior to the institution of a suit. In most jurisdictions an insurer cannot require an IME of a third party prior to suit being filed. Since an IME is for the insurer's benefit and since the IME doctor is usually very "conservative," the value of voluntarily agreeing to subject a client to an IME is questionable. If a medical payment claim is being pursued the client's duty to cooperate with the insurer requires him or her to submit to an IME. Sometimes the medical payment carrier is the same carrier that is providing liability coverage for the responsible party. In those cases the medical payment IME should not be allowed until the insurer

Continued on next page

PRACTICE POINTERS—Continued

vows that different adjusters will be handling each claim and that information provided with respect to the medical claim will not coincidentally find its way into the liability file.

Most insurers will not, as a matter of policy, disclose the limits of liability of their insured until suit is instituted, but one should never hesitate in requesting that information. Even if the responsible party's coverage is the statutory minimum, the issue of additional coverage becomes a major concern if a client's claim exceeds the statutory requirements and he or she does not have UIM coverage. If the liability coverage of a responsible party is insufficient to compensate a client, the financial resources of the responsible party must be evaluated to determine if an excess judgment could be collected against him or her. If the responsible party claims lack of financial resources, an affidavit attesting to his or her financial condition should be obtained. That affidavit should then be reviewed in accordance with state bankruptcy laws to determine what, if any, part of his or her estate might be subject to execution if a judgment were obtained. Only if diligent inquiry reveals that an excess judgment could not be satisfied from the property of the responsible party should settlement for his or her policy limits be made.

ondary source of coverage when the full limits of the primary coverage are exceeded. Courts will reform those policies whose policy limits are less than those required by statute.

The insurer is subrogated to the rights of the insured, which allows the insurer to institute suit against the responsible person in the name of the insured. Many states prohibit subrogation with respect to UIM claims. An insured has an obligation to cooperate with his or her insurer in subrogation claims.

Medical payment coverage reimburses the insured for all reasonable medical expenses incurred while occupying a covered vehicle or when, as a pedestrian, he or she is struck by a different vehicle. If an insured is injured in a motor vehicle owned by someone other than the insured, the automobile owner's medical payment coverage is primarily responsible for payment of the insured's medical expenses up to the limits of the owner's medical payment coverage. Once that limit is exceeded the insured's own medical payment coverage kicks into effect. If the medical payment coverage has a coordination of benefits provision, the injured may not be allowed to recover twice for his or her medical expenses.

Other types of available automobile insurance coverages include comprehensive, collision, and "accessory" coverages, such as towing, car rental, and death and disability insurance. Comprehensive coverage includes coverage for property damage and losses caused by fire, theft, windstorm, and hail.

Collision insurance provides coverage regardless of who is to blame for the damages.

Most states require uninsured motorist (UM) coverage. A carrier cannot credit monies paid under a medical payment policy to the amount due the insured under his or her UM coverage unless the insured has UM coverage in excess of the statutory minimum. Most UM policies provide coverage regardless of whether the insured was driving the automobile referred to in the policy or a different vehicle. Underinsured motorist (UIM) coverage protects an insured who is injured by a motorist whose liability coverage is insufficient to fully compensate the insured for the injuries sustained. Most states prohibit stacking of UM and UIM coverage.

Arbitration is usually required as a means for resolving disputes that arise with respect to coverage. An arbitration award is often not binding if it exceeds the statutory minimum limits for bodily injury.

An insured can voluntarily terminate his or her automobile insurance contract by providing notice to the agent. Likewise, an insurer can terminate the contract for nonpayment of premiums, or because the insured's license is suspended or revoked, or the insured is convicted of driving while intoxicated.

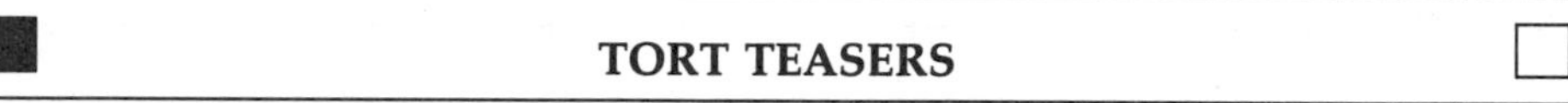

TORT TEASERS

Reread the introductory hypothetical case and, using the insurance policy in the Appendix when necessary, answer the following questions.

1. Pauline seeks legal advice to determine her rights in reference to the medical expenses incurred by her and her late husband, the damages she sustained, and Perry's wrongful death. Denise and David also see an attorney, who says that she cannot represent both Denise and David because David may have a claim against Denise. She then refers Denise to another attorney.

If the parties sustain the following damages, the questions before us are who has a claim against whom and what portions of Pauline and Perry's insurance policy are applicable.

- Perry—medical expenses of $6,000, funeral expenses of $4,000.
- Pauline—medical expenses of $15,000, personal damages of $90,000, wrongful death claim with respect to Perry of $250,000, property damage claim of $16,000.
- Denise—medical expenses of $500, personal damages of $3,500.
- David—medical expenses of $24,000, future medical expenses of $76,000, personal damages of $2,500,000.
- Denise's father—property damage claim of $840.

Use this scenario to review the concepts you have learned. To resolve issues of damages you will need to first assess the liability of the parties and determine any defenses they can raise. To assist in doing this you might want to review Chapters 6–10, 18–19.

2. How much, if any, would Perry and Pauline's insurance carrier have to pay of Pauline's medical expenses of $15,000, the $6,000 in medical expenses incurred by Perry prior to his death as well as Perry's funeral expenses of $4,000?

3. Does Pauline have a claim against Denise that should be compensated by the uninsured motorist coverage of Perry's policy?

4. If Pauline pursues a wrongful death claim who will be the appropriate party to sue? Can Pauline look to any coverage under her own policy for payment of all or a portion of the claim?

5. How much will Pauline's insurer have to pay of her property damage claim of $16,000?

6. Does Denise have a potential claim for recovery for her medical expenses and personal damages? If so, against whom should the claim be made? What defenses to her claim could be alleged?

7. Against whom does David have a claim?

8. Can Denise's negligence be imputed to David? Did David assume the risk by voluntarily going with Denise?

9. Do you think Pauline's insurance carrier will offer to settle David's claim for the policy limits of $100,000? Why or why not?

10. Does Denise's father have a claim against Perry? If so, how would you evaluate Denise's father's claim?

11. In terms of potential recovery, which of the following claims would you rather be representing? Explain why. What defenses might be raised in each case?

a. Pauline's wrongful death claim
b. Pauline's personal injury claim
c. Perry's damages claim
d. Denise's damages claim
e. David's damages claim
f. Denise's father's claim

12. Is the interspousal immunity doctrine in effect in your state? If so, does that change any of your answers to the previous question? Why or why not?

13. Is any claim by Denise barred because of her wrongful utilization of the family vehicle and lack of a driver's license?

14. Will Pauline's wrongful death claim be affected by the fact that Perry was not wearing his seat belt at the time of the accident? Assume that an accident reconstructionist will testify that while Perry would have suffered serious injuries he would not have been killed had he been wearing a seat belt.

KEY TERMS

■ **Coordination of benefits provision**
Policy provision that precludes payment to the insured if the insured has other insurance available.

■ **Primary coverage**
Insurance carrier providing initial coverage for all damages up to the limits of the policy.

■ **Reformation of a policy**
Construing a policy to provide the minimum coverage required by statute.

■ **Stacking of policies**
Using one or more policies to provide coverage for the same incident.

■ **Secondary coverage**
Insurance carrier providing coverage for damages incurred but not until the limits of the primary policy have been exhausted.

■ **Subrogation**
The right of an insurer to institute suit in the name of the insured against the responsible party to collect for monies paid by the insurer to the insured.

■ **Umbrella policy**
Policy that provides a secondary source of coverage after the deductible has been paid, usually coordinated with the limits of the underlying policy.

BAD FAITH

CHAPTER OBJECTIVES

In this chapter you will learn to:

- Identify the elements of a bad faith claim.
- Recognize the rationale behind the development of bad faith actions.
- Distinguish between first party and third party claims for purposes of bad faith and recognize the importance of that distinction.

On a Labor Day weekend Jerry and a number of his fraternity brothers and sorority sisters decide to spend their three-day holiday near a place called Rocky Point on the Gulf of Baja, California in Mexico. The entire group has to wait in line to enter the gate that allows vehicles to enter Sandy Beach. Jerry steps up on the back bumper of a jeep driven by Dick when Dick suddenly accelerates his jeep to move up in line. The sudden movement catches Jerry unaware and he is thrown backward, causing him to strike his head on the hard-packed sand. He is knocked unconscious for a few minutes and when he comes to his fraternity brothers put him in the back of a van to recuperate. After a few hours it becomes apparent that Jerry has suffered a serious injury and he is taken to a hospital. He is hospitalized for two weeks and is ultimately forced to withdraw from the first semester of his sophomore year at the university. He suffers short-term memory loss with respect to the accident and has some longer term problems with his speech, reading abilities, and retention.

Both Dick and Jerry are insured by the same automobile insurance carrier and each of their policies provides liability coverage for any accident that occurs in Mexico as long as the accident takes place within fifty miles of the United States border. Dick's policy was issued in Colorado, a no-fault state.

It does not provide medical payments coverage (called personal injury protection in Colorado) on Dick's jeep when it is outside the United States. Jerry's policy does provide medical payments coverage in Mexico if the accident occurs within 50 miles of the U.S. border.

Your attorney, who represents Jerry, submits Jerry's medical expenses to his insurance carrier but the carrier neither accepts nor rejects the claim. After eight months of inaction your attorney files suit against the carrier for bad faith. After the suit is filed the carrier hires a professor who analyzes information obtained from various witnesses (whom the carrier had not interviewed prior to the filing of the bad faith action). The professor concludes that the accident occurred somewhere between 51 and 51.5 miles outside the United States border. Your attorney hires an expert who determines that the accident occurred between 49.63 and 51 statute miles from the United States border.

The key issue is whether the accident occurred outside the 50-mile geographical limitation of Jerry's policy. The policy does not define a mile as being a statute mile (5,280 feet) or a nautical mile (6,080.1 feet). Unquestionably, if nautical miles are used the accident occurred within the 50-mile limit. The insurance carrier provides many of its insureds with maps that indicate that the area of the accident is not more than 48 statute miles from the United States border. Keep this fact pattern in mind as you read about bad faith as a cause of action.

HOW BAD FAITH IS COMMITTED

Bad faith is considered an intentional tort since mere negligence on the part of the insurance carrier is not actionable. Bad faith can occur if: (1) the insurance carrier unreasonably delays payment on a policy; (2) the carrier acts unconscionably towards its insured; or (3) the carrier engages in unfair claims practices (see Table 22–1).

HISTORICAL DEVELOPMENT OF BAD FAITH

Historically courts held that insurance carriers have an implied covenant of good faith and fair dealing in reference to their insureds. Later, courts classified some insurance contracts as adhesion contracts. **Adhesion contracts** are standardized contracts commonly used in business (an example of which is

TABLE 22.1

WHAT CONSTITUTES BAD FAITH
• Insurer unreasonably delays payment.
• Insurer acts unconscionably toward insured.
• Insurer engages in unfair claims practices.

the contract signed by consumers when financing a car). They are characterized by the courts as those contracts in which the party drafting the contract has superior bargaining power and the other party is typically unfamiliar with the terms of the contract and also has no real opportunity to negotiate what those terms will be. Focusing on the unequal bargaining power between insureds and insurers as well as the public interest in insurance contracts, the courts scrutinized insurance contracts more carefully than those contracts in which the parties were assumed to know and understand the terms of the contracts they signed. The courts also realized that insureds rely heavily on their insurance carriers to protect their interests. Therefore, the courts created various mechanisms to protect an insured's contract rights as well as his or her "reasonable expectations" regarding the policy's provisions.

In accordance with their vision of insurance contracts as adhesion contracts, courts held that certain policy provisions could not necessarily be utilized against an insured and that the insured was not presumed to understand all the terms of the insurance contract. Courts later developed a rule of law requiring contracts to be interpreted in favor of the nondrafter (the insured) so that any "ambiguities" in a contract were construed against the carrier and in favor of the insured. This rule was propagated in the hope that insureds would be protected from complex insurance contracts and that the insurance industry would be pressured into drafting contracts comprehensible to those who read them.

Interpreting contracts in favor of the nondrafter eventually evolved into the modern-day rule generally referred to as the *reasonable expectations doctrine*. This doctrine protects the insured's reasonable expectation that coverage will be provided and not defeated by provisions that would be unanticipated by the ordinary insured and that were never negotiated between the insured and the carrier. The court will reform the contract to the reasonable expectations of the insured even though a detailed review of the contract itself does not manifest those expectations.

In their efforts to curb the sometimes misused discretion of insurance carriers, courts have looked for remedies outside of those found in contract law because such remedies afford a relatively small penalty to overreaching carriers. A carrier found in breach of contract is liable only for the amount owed to the insured plus attorney's fees and court costs. Since insurance companies know that at the worst they will have to pay only a minor penalty for their indiscretions, they can afford to be rather cavalier in their actions toward their insureds. Accordingly, insurers have little incentive to be concerned about the majority of their insureds, since most insureds can ill afford the tremendous expense involved in litigating with a major company.

Some courts have found a fiduciary duty between the insurance carrier and the insured. Objectionable acts of a carrier as well as objectionable terms of an insurance contract are then found to be a breach of the fiduciary duty owed the insured. As a result, objectionable terms can be eliminated from the contract.

Some states have restricted the strict interpretation of contracts by providing the insured with standard tort remedies. For example, recovery for intentional infliction of mental distress has been allowed when an insurance company has committed especially egregious acts. In many cases, however, the physical complications required for this cause of action cannot be shown in the context of an insurer-insured relationship.

OVERVIEW OF BAD FAITH

As can be seen from this brief historical review, bad faith evolved as a means of providing relief to the insured. Bad faith is a question of fact for the jury. Only when the court determines that no reasonable person could conclude that bad faith has occurred can the court take the case from the jury.

Initially, bad faith applied only to *third party claims* (claims in which the insured paid damages to a third party). Most jurisdictions now recognize the tort of bad faith in cases of *first party claims* (claims in which an insured demands payment from his insurer in his own right).

Bad faith cases also involve a breach of contract claim as well. Some jurisdictions, however, recognize that bad faith can occur even when no contract is breached. A bad faith claim of this nature occurs when the insurer, acting unreasonably and not in good faith, denies coverage or refuses payment that a court ultimately determines the insurer had no contractual obligation to provide. An insurance carrier might, for example, deny coverage without a proper investigation of the claim and later, after being sued, discover evidence that supported its original denial of coverage. Such a discovery would not, however, diminish the carrier's initial failure to act in good faith.

SUING THE INSURED

Although theoretically possible, an insurance carrier rarely sues an insured for bad faith. The duty of good faith is an unconditional and independent contractual obligation of the insurer and most states provide relief even when the insured has not fulfilled all of his or her contractual duties. Those courts that have recognized bad faith claims against insureds have allowed the insurers to recover contractual damages only. Tort damages as well as punitive damages have been denied. Conceivably, however, comparative negligence could be used to reduce an insured's award of damages if an insured acted in bad faith.

FIRST PARTY VS. THIRD PARTY CLAIMS

In first party cases the plaintiff (insured) and defendant (insurer) are easily defined. The insured, pursuant to a contractual right emanating from his or her insurance contract, sues the insurer. As previously mentioned, most bad faith claims include a breach of contract claim and, if supported by the insurer's acts, a claim for punitive damages. Although the requisite conduct for punitive damages varies, the trend is to award punitive damages only when an "evil mind guides the evil hand."

Third party suits follow a more circuitous route to the courthouse. Most states do not allow those who have been injured by the insured and then damaged by the insurer's actions towards its insured to file suit directly against the insurance company because injured parties are not considered third party beneficiaries under the insured-insurer contract. A third party case usually reaches trial in the name of the insured only after the insured "cuts a deal" with the injured party.

RESOLUTION OF THIRD PARTY CLAIMS

A third party action often arises after the insurer fails to settle the injured party's claim against the insured for an amount less than or equal to the policy limits. After trial and the entry of an **excess judgment** (a judgment in excess of the policy limits), the insured will often assign to the injured party all of her rights under the contract, including any claims she might have for bad faith. Although many states prohibit the assignment of "pure" personal injury claims, most allow the assignment of contract rights. Since the bad faith claim arises out of a contract and is not considered a pure tort, most courts allow its assignment. Some states also allow the assignment of any right the insured might have to punitive damages.

Once the assignment is made, the injured party then pursues the insurer in the name of the insured. Because the lawsuit is filed in the insured's name, as part of the assignment, the insured must assure his or her cooperation in the action against the insurer. The lawsuit will in fact be orchestrated by the injured party.

The insured may also assign his or her rights to the injured party when the insurer denies coverage for the injured party's claim and/or agrees to defend the insured only under a "reservation of rights." As you will recall from Chapter 20, an insurance carrier that defends its insured under a reservation of rights initially tells its insured it will provide a defense to the claim. At the same time, however, the carrier reserves its rights to later deny that coverage exists, in which case it can withdraw the defense previously offered. In most cases the insurance carrier's reservation of rights letter will advise the insured to consider employing his or her own counsel.

Insured's Option When Denied Coverage. An insured's remedies upon being denied coverage are often based on whether coverage was denied outright or whether his or her position was compromised as a result of a reservation of rights. If coverage is flatly denied, the insured has no chance of indemnity for any judgment rendered against him or her, and no opportunity to mount a defense except from his or her own pocket.

Because of the vulnerability of an insured that has been denied coverage, some courts allow the insured to enter into an agreement with the injured party, stipulating to the amount of the judgment to be entered in favor of the injured party. The injured party must still present evidence to substantiate the damages claimed but with no adversary attempting to exclude evidence the injured party usually has little difficulty obtaining a large judgment. Once the judgment is entered, the insured assigns all rights under the insurance policy to the injured party. Then, once again in the name of the insured, the injured party sues the insurance carrier, seeking indemnity for the amount of the judgment entered, or garnishes the insurer.

When this procedure is allowed an insurance carrier's liability usually does not exceed the policy limits unless the carrier has denied coverage in bad faith. In that case the injured party can recover the amount of the judgment obtained (up to the policy limits) for breach of contract and can also pursue an independent bad faith claim against the insurance carrier.

Insured's Option When Insurer Defends Under a Reservation of Rights. If an insurer defends under a reservation of rights, the insured is not left completely naked. The insurer, in essence, loans him a "coat" but at the same time advises the insured that the "coat" may be recalled at any time. Under these circumstances some courts have allowed the insured to enter into an agreement with the injured party that basically protects the insured if the insurer subsequently denies coverage. Entering into such an agreement is not considered a violation of the cooperation clause found in most insurance contracts that mandates the insured's cooperation with the insurer.

In a typical reservation of rights case the insured enters into negotiations with the injured party to protect the insured from being exposed to an uninsured judgment. Any agreement normally provides for a judgment to be entered based on evidence presented to the court, usually without objection from the insured. Care must be taken to insure that no fraud is perpetrated on the court when such an agreement is entered into. After judgment is entered the insured assigns all rights under his or her insurance contract to the injured party.

In a reservation of rights case an insured must usually advise the insurer of the terms and conditions of the agreement prior to entering into any agreement. The insurer then has one last opportunity to withdraw its reservation of rights and provide an unconditional defense to the insured.

The reservation of rights case is resolved when the injured party files suit against the insurer in the name of the insured. Alternatively, the injured party can garnish the insurer. Suit is considerably different than the trial of a denial of coverage case. The injured party must prove that the insurance policy issued to the insured covers the claim and that the agreement between the insured and the injured party was not a fraud on the court. He or she must also show that the judgment entered by the court was not fraudulent and was fair and reasonable considering the issue of liability, the facts relating to actual damages, the advantages and risks of going to trial, and the risks of the insurer not being liable under the policy. Under this scenario the jury must be told the terms and conditions of the agreement and the fact that the insured was released from liability. The jury would also be advised, however, that the insurer had reserved the right to deny coverage and that is was the concern of noncoverage that motivated the insured to enter into its agreement with the injured party.

This "trial within a trial" allows the insurer to introduce all relevant evidence that counters any of the positions taken by the plaintiff (the injured party, who is acting in the name of the insured). If the jury determines no coverage exists it will enter a judgment for the defendant (insurer). If the jury determines that the judgment obtained in accordance with the agreement between the insured and the injured party was excessive, it can award damages in a lesser amount.

Failure to Settle Claim. The insurer can be subjected to bad faith even when it acknowledges coverage and provides a complete defense. This type of bad faith occurs when the insurance carrier has a reasonable opportunity to settle the injured party's claim within the policy limits. If the insurer refuses to settle, the insured can be liable for the amount of the judgment in excess of the policy limits.

Of particular concern to the insured are those areas of liability being contested where the damages are extremely large. In those instances the insurer might be tempted to "roll the dice" by going to the jury in the hope of getting a defense verdict. Since the insurer's liability does not exceed the insured's policy limits, the insurer has nothing to lose by going to trial. The insurer, after entry of an excess judgment, can pay the amount of its policy limits and leave the insured to deal with the injured party. The insured would then have a potential bad faith claim against the insurance carrier for its failure to settle the claim within the policy limits. Since the insured would probably be very happy to be relieved from having to pay the injured party, she would likely assign to that party any rights she might have against the insurer. The injured party would then proceed, in the name of the insured, in a bad faith claim against the insurer.

Some have questioned whether an insured who knows the insurer has refused to settle within the policy limits is in a position to strike a deal with the injured party prior to an excess judgment actually being entered. Most courts have held that an insured in this situation is bound to cooperate with the insurer and may not enter into an agreement with the injured party until after judgment is entered. The courts reason that the insured, having selected the limits of coverage, cannot shift her responsibility to adequately insure herself to her insurer when those limits turn out to be too low to cover the risk that actually occurred.

Damages—Third Party Claims. The amount of damages to be awarded in third party cases is based on four factors: (1) the amount of judgment entered against the insured in excess of the policy limits (i.e., the amount the insured must pay out of his or her own pocket); (2) the legal fees the insured has incurred in pursuing the claim against the insurer; (3) the emotional distress, if any, suffered by the insured; and (4) any other monetary loss or damage to the insured's credit or reputation (Table 22–2).

If the insurer's actions have been sufficiently egregious, punitive damages might also be available. Punitive damages are intended to prevent similar misconduct in the future rather than to compensate the plaintiff. Therefore,

TABLE 22.2

DAMAGE FACTORS - THIRD PARTY CLAIM
•Amount of judgment entered against insured in excess of his policy limits. •Legal fees incurred by insured. •Emotional distress suffered by insured. •Monetary loss or damaged credit reputation of insured.

the amount of punitive damages to be awarded is based on the financial condition of the insurer and the degree of its misconduct rather than the impact of its misconduct on the insured. Since the insurance business is often very lucrative, a plaintiff asking for relatively small actual damages may seek punitive damages in the millions of dollars range.

RESOLUTION OF FIRST PARTY CLAIMS

A first party bad faith case is more straightforward than a third party case because only two parties are involved. In a first party bad faith case the insured is denied the benefits of her contract with her insurer due to the insurer's failure to deal with her fairly and in good faith. An insurer acts in bad faith by either failing to investigate a claim made by the insured or by inadequately investigating a claim. If coverage is denied as a result or an unreasonably low evaluation of the damages is made, a claim for bad faith will lie.

An insurance carrier's delay tactics in investigating and evaluating a claim can also lead to bad faith. A carrier obviously benefits financially by delaying payment of a claim as long as possible. Such a delay allows the carrier to obtain the maximum benefits of its investment of the insured's premium.

Since an insurer is obligated to properly investigate its insured's claim, many courts refuse to allow information obtained after the filing of a bad faith lawsuit to be utilized by the insurer to justify its prior actions. Suppose an insurer denies coverage but never investigates the claim. The insurer usually cannot later submit evidence supporting its denial of coverage if it finds this evidence by virtue of an investigation conducted after the insured files a bad faith suit.

An additional basis for bad faith in first party cases involves fraudulent or harassing practices by the carrier. In some states violation of state statutes governing unfair claim settlement procedures can result in claims of bad faith.

Damages—First Party Claims. Determining the amount to be paid in first party cases entails consideration of elements similar to those used in third party claims (see Table 22–3). The major difference is that first party claims involve the loss of unpaid benefits while third party claims involve an excess judgment. Unpaid benefits include the insured's loss of the "benefit of the bargain," any resulting consequential damages, and lost interest on the unpaid amount due the insured.

TABLE 22.3

DAMAGE FACTORS - FIRST PARTY CLAIM

- Unpaid benefits of policy.
- Legal fees incurred by insured.
- Lost interest on unpaid amount due insured.
- Emotional distress suffered by insured.
- Any other financial losses of insured caused as a result of insurer's bad faith.

In many cases, such as those involving health or disability insurance claims, wrongful denial results in not only the insured's inability to pay bills but also in the loss of his and his family's credit rating. If such losses can be proved to stem from the wrongful acts of the insurer they can also be recovered. Care must be taken, however, in evaluating losses alleged to have occurred as a result of the insurer's bad faith. Asking a jury to stretch its concept of proximate cause may result in a backlash against the insured, who may be perceived as overreaching.

STANDARDS USED TO DETERMINE BAD FAITH

An insured is often exposed to lesser risk in first party bad faith cases than in third party matters. In first party cases the insurer does not have sole control of litigation relating to the insured's potential liability, which it has in third party cases. Additionally, in first party cases the insured makes her claim directly in her own name and does not face losses in excess of her policy limits.

Due to these differences many courts use a different standard in a first party case than in a third party case to determine whether bad faith has been committed. In first party situations the standard is based on the reasonableness of the insurer's position. Some courts consider denial of a claim reasonable (and therefore not in bad faith) if the claim is "fairly debatable." Some courts require a showing of more than mere negligent conduct before finding that an insurer acted in bad faith. For those courts an unintentional mistake, oversight, or carelessness of an insurer's employee does not constitute bad faith even though a jury, with hindsight, could objectively determine that the carrier's actions were unreasonable.

Since in third party situations the insured has almost no control over the processing of the claim against him or her, most courts have held the insurer to a higher standard of care. The courts go beyond asking whether an insurer's position was "fairly debatable." Many inquire whether the insurer gave as much consideration to its insured's interests as it did to its own (the "equal consideration" test).

General Accident Fire & Life Assurance Corporation, Ltd., Appellant, v. Irene Bernice LITTLE, Administratrix, Appellee.
No. 8466. Supreme Court of Arizona. In Banc.
July 16, 1968.
443 P.2d 690 (Ariz. 1968).

UDALL, Vice Chief Justice:

The appellee, Irene Bernice Little, brought this action as the assignee of Elza A. Allen and Claudie Beatrice Allen, who were the named insureds under an automobile public liability policy carried with the appellant, hereinafter referred to as General.

On October 11, 1959 Mrs. Allen was involved in an accident which resulted in the death of Mrs. Little's seventeen-year-old son. Appellee thereafter brought suit against the Allens, during the pendency of which General was offered an opportunity to settle for $4,000.00. This offer was rejected and a jury ultimately returned a verdict in favor of Mrs. Little, administratrix, in amount of $17,500.00. Thereafter General paid its policy limits, $5,000, and accrued costs on the judgment. With no execution being levied or any other steps being taken to collect the balance of the judgment, Mrs. Little accepted from the Allens the following assignment:

> "WE, ELZA A. ALLEN and CLAUDIE BEATRICE ALLEN, for value received, hereby assign to IRENE BERNICE LITTLE, Administratrix of the estate of JIMMY ANDREW HAVNER, deceased, her executors, administrators and assigns, all our right, title and interest in our claims, rights of action and causes of action against The General Accident Fire and Life Assurance Corporation, Ltd., and Potomac Insurance Group doing business as The General Accident Group, based on the negligence, breach of contract and bad faith of said Company in failing to settle cause No. 111201, Superior Court of Maricopa County, State of Arizona, within the policy limits of our liability policy with said company and we authorize IRENE BERNICE LITTLE, Administratrix of JIMMY ANDREW HAVNER, deceased, her executors, administrators and assigns, to commence action on, prosecute and collect thereon, and take all legal or other measures deemed proper or necessary, with the same force and effect as we could do.
>
> "This assignment is made *to secure the payment of a judgment rendered against us in cause No. 111201, Superior Court of Maricopa County, Arizona, the payment of which obligation will render this assignment void; otherwise, to be of full force and effect.*" [emphasis added]

Armed with this assignment Mrs. Little instituted the present action. The complaint herein alleged the death of Jimmy Havner, Mrs. Little's son; the prior suit and judgment, the issuance of a liability policy by General, the defense of the prior action by General, the offer and refusal of settlement within policy limits and further alleged that such refusal was based on the bad faith and negligence of General resulting in damage to the Allens in amount of $12,500 (amended complaint); and, finally, the assignment to Mrs. Little was alleged.

General defended on the basis that the complaint failed to state a claim on which relief could be granted. General admitted the accident, the issuance of the policy and the defense of the claim under the terms of the policy; but denied that the accident and death were caused by any negligence of Claudie, or that General had been negligent or had acted in bad faith in refusing to accept the offers of settlement and further denied that the Allens had sustained any damage or that any claim of the Allens had been assigned to Mrs. Little. As to the latter denial the trial court entered a pre-trial order "that the cause of action asserted by plaintiff is properly in the plaintiff by virtue of the assignment in question and the trial of said cause shall proceed on the merits."

Trial resulted in a jury verdict of $12,500. General's motions objecting to the form of judgment entered thereon (which provided for interest), for a new trial, and for judgment notwithstanding the verdict were all denied. This appeal follows.

This is only the second opportunity this court has had to review an "excess liability" case. As we noted in the earlier case the "law in this regard is of comparatively recent development and the cases are not entirely harmonious," Farmers Insurance Exchange v. Henderson . . . . *Farmers* is authority for the proposition that an insurer must give equal consideration to the interests of an insured in determining whether to settle or defend a claim, and that a failure to do so does not constitute good faith. . . .

The appellant contends that looking at all the evidence in the light most favorable to Mrs. Little, she failed to sustain her burden of proving bad faith and hence the trial court erred in overruling the motions for directed verdict and for judgment notwithstanding the verdict.

What constitutes a breach of duty to exercise good faith? In Farmers Insurance Exchange v. Henderson, supra, we said:

> "* * * It occurs to us that when the insurer is defending litigation against the insured, employs attorneys to represent the interests of both and has sole power and opportunity to make a settlement which would result in the protection of the insured against excess liability, common honesty demands that it not be moved by partiality to itself nor be required to give the interests of the insured preferential consideration. A violator of this rule of equality of consideration cannot be said to have acted in good faith. (citations omitted) The enunciation of the rule is not difficult but its application is troublesome. *It is a matter of consideration of comparative hazards.*" . . . (Emphasis added)

California also follows the "equality of consideration" doctrine and in looking to the elements of its "troublesome" application in Brown v. Guarantee Insurance Co., supra, the California court set out the following factors:

> "* * * the strength of the injured claimant's case on the issues of liability and damages; attempts by the insurer to induce the insured to contribute to a settlement; failure of the insurer to properly investigate the circumstances so as to ascertain the evidence against the insured; the insurer's rejection of advice of its own attorney or agent; failure of the insurer to inform the insured of a compromise offer; *the amount of financial risk to which each party is exposed in the event of a refusal to settle;* the fault of the insured in inducing the insurer's rejection of the compromise offer by misleading it as to the facts; and any other factors tending to establish or negate bad faith on the part of the insurer." [emphasis added] . . .

Several of the factors mentioned by the California court are not in issue in the present case. For instance there was never any discussion of contributions toward a settlement on the part of the Allens; there is nothing in the record to show General was misled by the Allens as to the facts of the original accident; it is not claimed that insured rejected the advice of its own attorney. (In fact at the time of trial the attorney for the company evaluated the settlement value of the case at $2,000 and felt the prospects of a verdict were 60–40% in favor of the defendant); there is no contention that the insurer failed to keep the insured informed as to settlement offers.

As to the adequacy of the investigation itself the record is undisputed that the company had an investigator on the job commencing with the day of the accident. On that date he obtained the statement of Claudie Allen, the statement of a witness to the accident, the police reports and photographs of the Havner motorcycle and the Allen automobile. Subsequently, and within a week of the accident a lengthy statement was taken from another eye witness, the Havner home was contacted, the accident was discussed with the Allens on numerous occasions and the results of the investigation were all submitted to the Phoenix Claims Office of the company. The file was subsequently submitted to the company attorney who, in his own further investigation, obtained knowledge about the working condition of the Havner motorcycle from a friend of the deceased Havner lad, and information from plaintiff's attorney relative to the earnings of Jimmy Havner (who had been a carry-out boy at a market, $25 to $30 a week), damages to his motorcycle, and funeral expenses. The adequacy of the investigation has not been challenged by the appellee on appeal—nor do we see how a jury could have found any bad faith in this regard.

The claim was evaluated by the company claims manager and defense counsel. No effort was made by appellee to impeach their qualifications or their competency.

Now, let us look to the strength of claimant's case on the issue of liability and damages, as it would have appeared prior to the trial. Clearly, all can now see through hindsight that it would have been better for both the insureds and the insurer to have accepted the offer of settlement, but as was said in Ferris v. Employers Mutual Casualty Company, . . .

> "* * *. Again there is the implication that we should judge the fairness of the decision not to settle by the result. We suggest that if we are to venture into the area of what counsel 'should have known' in advance of the trial of a lawsuit as shown by the final outcome, by a jury's decision, we are requiring of him the gift of foretelling the future not often given to mankind. We know of no mortal who has been vouchsafed this power since the days of the Bible prophets; and as we understand it, these ancient seers had access to some inside information not presently available to counsel in damage cases. The court placed an unfair burden on the defendant here * * *
>
> * * * * * *
>
> "* * * We may not measure the reasonableness of the offer by the ultimate result of the litigation; it must be considered in the light of the case as it fairly appeared to the insurer and its authorized agents and attorneys at the time the offer was made. Whether Mr. Mitchell was mistaken in his judgment that he could successfully defend may be argued; but a mere mistake in judgment is not enough to show bad faith * * *" . . .

This accident occurred at 8:30 in the morning. Mrs. Allen was proceeding south on 17th Avenue, came to a stop at Buckeye Road where traffic was jammed or stacked up. A Mr. Ruth, traveling west on Buckeye moved his truck a little so Mrs. Allen could traverse the intersection. She thereafter proceeded through the opening Ruth had provided. Ruth then observed the Havner boy coming east on Buckeye at a distance of some 200 to 300 feet. According to Ruth the boy was lying down on the motorcycle, bent forward from the waist; his speed was estimated at 55 to 60 miles per hour and remained constant from the first time Ruth observed the motorcycle right up to the impact. Further, according to Ruth, no attempt to apply the brakes was ever made.

The physical evidence revealed no skid marks. Both the attorney for the insured and the attorney for the claimant recognized contributory negligence as an issue in the case. In evaluating liability prospects the claims manager felt that the chances of a defense verdict were 75% and, as stated previously, the insurer's attorney felt that the odds in favor of defendant were at least 60–40.

As to the potential damage should a verdict be rendered against the insured the company saw that he was 17 years old at the time of the accident, unmarried, without dependents, and earning from 25 to 30 dollars a week. In determining what a possible verdict might be the attorney for the company felt that under our death statute the jury might well mitigate its verdict because of the fact that the boy was riding the motorcycle at the time.

With all these factors in mind the insurance attorney determined that if a jury returned a plaintiff's verdict it would range between a low of $3,000 and tops of $7,500 and the claims manager felt that it could not exceed $10,000. Within the judgment of General, then, first, that they had a fighting chance of winning the case hands down, and secondly, that if they did lose the verdict would range from $3,000 to $10,000 does it appear that they exercised equal consideration in measuring the comparative hazards of the insured and the insurer, Farmers Insurance Exchange v. Henderson, supra?

The appellee argues that the insured had only one interest and that was the financial loss they would incur if the verdict exceeded the policy limits; and that the company in refusing to accept settlement when offered within those limits gave no consideration to that interest. Mrs. Little contends that, under the well-established rule that the evidence must be viewed in the most favorable light to appellee, she established her prima facie case through the testimony of the company claims manager and the company attorney. This testimony in substance had the effect of showing that neither the claims manager nor the attorney took into consideration the policy limits in evaluating the claim, e. g.:

Q "Then you are saying that it didn't make any difference to your company that these people had only a $5,000 policy in determining what this case should be settled for, is that right?"
A [Claims Manager] "That is right."
* * *, and also

* * * * * *

A "We don't believe that limits are a factor in determining the value of a file. A broken leg is worth the same to me whether I have a $5,000 or a $100,000 policy."

* * * * * *

Q "I ask you whether or not the policy limits of the Allens played any part in your evaluation of the value of the case?

A [Attorney] "You mean the amount of the policy?"

Q "Yes."

A [Attorney] "No."

Q "Has it ever?"

A "No."

We cannot agree with appellee's argument. It is obvious that they have rested their case on a gross misconstruance of the meaning of "equal consideration." Clearly the value of an unlitigated claim is determined on its own apparent merits or lack of them, or the possibility of liability being established, and on injuries and their extent being proven, and on such other factors as the bread-winning capacities of the injured party.

Surely all would agree that an insurance company would not breach its duty of good faith to the insured if it refused to settle a claim for $4,999.99 on a $5,000 policy when the question of liability was highly debatable, the apparent injury was extremely minor, and the injured was an unemployed adolescent. We state it in the ridiculous to point up the fallacy of appellee's argument.

Thus it should be clear that the evaluation of a case should not be determined by looking to the policy limits. When an insurance company evaluates a claim without looking to the policy limits and as though it alone would be responsible for the payment of any judgment rendered on that claim its views that claim objectively, and in doing so renders "equal consideration" to the interests of itself and the insured. . . .

Where an insurance company acts honestly and in good faith upon adequate information it should not be held liable because it failed to prophecy the result. If the insurer in good faith believed that it could successfully defend, it was not bound to relieve the Allens of all possible harm that might come from their election to purchase only $5,000 coverage in the light of present day dollar values and verdicts.

The record, however, also shows and clearly that General recognized the plaintiff, Mrs. Little, would most probably be able to establish a prima facie case against Mrs. Allen and thus that the question of liability would be for jury determination.[3]

3. During cross examination of General's attorney the following was elicited:
"Q In your evaluation of this case, is it correct to say that you felt that the plaintiff would be able to establish a prima facie case of negligence on the part of your insured, Mrs. Allen?
"A That was my opinion, sir.
* * * * *
"Q So you recognized in the trial that you were facing that probably the plaintiff would sustain the burden of proof of showing that Mrs. Allen was basically negligent, and that it would be then incumbent upon the defendant to rebut this or to show that the boy who was killed was contributorily negligent, is that true?
"A That is true, sir. I thought that this would be a case for jury determination."

As has been previously pointed out the liability carrier also recognized and told their insureds that in the event a verdict were returned for plaintiff, Mrs. Little, it could "be greatly in excess of $5,000." Mr. Allen, who by virtue of the marital relationship was a co-defendant and jointly subject to such excess liability insisted or strongly urged that the lawsuit be settled.

This was a wrongful death claim and the complaint prayed for relief in amount of $100,000. A seventeen year old boy had been taken from his mother. It appears to this court that General and its attorney were being less than realistic when they estimated a potential verdict at a low of $3,000 and a high of $10,000. In Arizona there is no statutory ceiling on wrongful death verdicts and the jury "shall give such damages as it deems fair and just with reference to the injury resulting from the death to the surviving parties * * * having regard to the mitigating or aggravating circumstances attending the wrongful act, neglect or default * * *" A.R.S. § 12–613. As opposed to General's estimate it is to be noted that the attorney for the plaintiff, who testified he had handled hundreds of personal injury cases, estimated a potential plaintiff's verdict in this case of from $10,000 to $30,000.

We agree with the courts and legal writers who have noted that even with the expertise and experience afforded liability carriers and competent trial lawyers they yet are not endowed with the gift of being able to accurately prophecy a jury verdict. However, under the terms of the policy the company is contracturally given the exclusive right to determine whether a settlement offer should be accepted.

When we apply the test of *Farmers Insurance Exchange*, supra, to the facts of this case; when we note by General's own conservative and self-serving evidence that there were four chances in ten of losing this case and the possibility of suffering a verdict "greatly in excess of the policy limits"; and we note further that in accepting the settlement offer of $4,000 General would be paying only $1,500 more than its $2,500 offer of settlement, part of which would be and was spent in legal fees and court costs, we do not find it difficult to sustain the jury's finding that General did not exercise its duty of good faith. It did not give equal consideration to its own and the insured's comparative hazards.

Where policy limits should have no place in an objective evaluation of a claim, once that claim has been evaluated and there is determined, as here, at least a 40% possibility of liability being established and an obvious recognition that an adverse verdict can reasonably be expected to "greatly exceed" policy limits, equal consideration of the comparative hazards demands that the insurer give attention to the policy limits. . . .

Finally, General contends that the lower court erred in refusing to give its tendered instructions on the meaning of "bad faith" and on the proper burden of proof. We believe under the facts of this case the instructions were properly denied. It is true that actions based on fraud must be proven by "clear and convincing" evidence, . . .; and it is equally true that one obvious species of "bad faith" is fraud. But, as we have shown above, the species of "bad faith" relied upon in this case was not actual fraud but a failure on the part of General to exercise its duty of giving "equal consideration" to the comparative hazards to its own interest and the interests of the policyholder. Under the rule of Farmers Insurance Exchange v. Henderson supra, the instruction given by the trial court adequately covered the issue of good faith.

There being no contention of fraud in this case the proper burden of proof test was the usual "preponderance of the evidence."

Judgment affirmed.

Although the "equal consideration" test varies somewhat from jurisdiction to jurisdiction, the concept is illustrated in *General Accident Fire and Life Assurance Corp. v. Little,* 443 P2d 690 (1968). Eight factors deemed important to the *Little* court in determining whether the insurer had given "equal consideration" to its insured were (also see Table 22–4):

1. The relative strength of the injured party's claim in reference to the issues of liability and damages against the insured.
2. The insurer's failure to properly investigate the claim so as to determine the availability of relevant evidence.
3. The insurer's failure to advise its insured of an offer to settle within policy limits.
4. The insurer's failure to follow the advice of its own attorney or agent.
5. The extent of the financial risk to its insured if the insurer refused to settle.
6. Any attempt by the insurer to get the insured to contribute to the settlement.
7. Any action by the insured that might have influenced the insurer to reject any compromise settlement offers.
8. Any other factors that might support or disprove bad faith on the part of the insurer.

A third party bad faith claim need not have elements of each of the above considerations.

DECLARATORY JUDGMENT ACTIONS

Insurance carriers will often institute a declaratory judgment action to determine if coverage exists. In a **declaratory judgment action** the court renders an opinion with respect to a matter of law or with regard to the rights of the parties but orders no action to be taken. Such an action can serve both defensive as well as offensive purposes. Offensively, a declaratory judgment action can serve to determine that no coverage exists and that the insurer

TABLE 22.4

EQUAL CONSIDERATION FACTORS FOR THIRD PARTY CLAIMS
•Relative strength of injured party's claims in references to issues of liability and damages against insured. •Insurer's failure to properly investigate claim so as to determine availability of relevant evidence. •Insurer's failure to advise insured of offer to settle within policy limits. •Insurer's failure to follow advice of its attorney or agent. •Extent of financial risk to insured if insurer refused to settle. •Attempt by insurer to get insured to contribute to settlement. •Action by insured that might have influenced insurer to reject any compromise settlement offers. •Any other factors that might support or disprove bad faith on the part of insurer.

need not defend or compensate its insured. Defensively, such an action allows a carrier to dispute coverage as well as permit it to go before a court hoping that the potential for a bad faith claim might be minimized by its efforts to obtain a judicial determination of its position.

UNINSURED AND UNDERINSURED MOTORIST COVERAGE

Uninsured (UM) and underinsured (UIM) motorist coverage has characteristics of both first party and third party claims. One first party characteristic is that the insured is obligated to make payment directly to the insurer. A third party characteristic is that the insurer stands in the shoes of the allegedly responsible party. As such the insurer can assert any defense that the responsible party might have, including comparative or contributory negligence, assumption of risk, and denial of liability.

Most UM and UIM policies prohibit the insured from suing his or her carrier over the issue of damages. If an insurer and its insured cannot reach agreement with respect to damages, the matter is submitted to arbitration. The issue of coverage, however, is not subject to arbitration in most UM and UIM policies. Coverage is determined in a separate lawsuit.

Since many states require automobile policies to provide UM and UIM coverage, some argue that carriers should have to meet the standard appropriate for third party claims. Most courts, however, view UM and UIM claims as first party claims. As first party claims, the maximum benefit due an insured as a result of an insurer's breach of its contractual obligations is the policy limits. If a UM or UIM claim is "fairly debatable," most courts hold that the insurer is not liable to its insured on the basis of bad faith.

UM and UIM carriers have tried to convince the courts that since they stand in the shoes of the allegedly responsible party, an adversarial relationship exists between them and their insureds. This argument, for the most part, has been rejected. The courts have, however, reasoned that bad faith has not occurred if the liability of the allegedly responsible party is reasonably in question and the amount of damages that must be paid the insured is reasonably disputed.

SUMMARY

Bad faith is an intentional tort that occurs when a party to an insurance contract breaches its implied covenant of good faith and fair dealing. Most cases of bad faith involve allegations against the insurance carrier. Bad faith arises when (1) the insurer wrongly refuses to provide coverage for a client, (2) fails to adequately investigate a claim before making its decision to deny coverage or pay only a portion of the insured's claim, or (3) unreasonably refuses to settle a third party claim within the limits of the insured's policy.

In most jurisdictions the standard of care owed to an insured by the insurer depends on whether the case is a first or third party claim. In first party claims some jurisdictions use the "fairly debatable" standard. Under that standard

PRACTICE POINTERS

Once a client's medical condition has stabilized and his or her treatment has been terminated, you will need to get medical/legal narratives from the treating physicians. These narratives should detail the nature and extent of the client's injuries, the diagnoses made, the treatment given, and the prognosis for recovery as well as link the injuries to the accident in question.

Sometimes these narratives are based only on the treating physician's first-hand information. You may want to provide a physician with the notes and records of other treating physicians and, if applicable, records documenting treatment of the client prior to the accident. Without this information a narrative may, at worst, be a waste of your client's money or, at least, its impact will be greatly diminished. Providing the physician with this information allows him or her to incorporate appropriate portions of your client's medical records into the narrative and can greatly augment the value of the analysis. This information also prevents the physician from being caught unaware later of the client's prior and subsequent treatment and greatly enhances the value of the narrative for settlement purposes. Most adjusters will allege preexisting conditions and/or unnecessary treatment if your client has suffered similar symptoms in the past. You must be able to produce medical evidence showing that your own health care provider analyzed the information and concluded that previous injuries and conditions did not significantly contribute to your client's current need for treatment.

Similarly, before your client's treating physicians are deposed they must review all applicable medical information relating to your client, including independent medical exam (IME) reports by the insurer's physician and medical/legal narratives provided by other health care providers. If relevant, the physician should review X-rays taken prior to the accident to ascertain, using objective evidence, whether the injuries sustained by your client were caused by the accident in question or were carry-overs from other incidents.

if a claim submitted by an insured is fairly debatable the insurer's actions in refusing to pay the claim will not constitute bad faith. For third party claims most courts impose a higher duty on the insurer. This higher duty, sometimes referred to as an "equality of consideration" standard, requires the insurer to give the same consideration to the insured's interests as it does to its own. In most jurisdictions something more than mere negligence is required before the courts will find that the insurer has violated its implied covenant of good faith and fair dealing.

The position of an insured varies depending on whether the insurer denies coverage or defends the insured under reservation of rights. The insured is able to negotiate an agreement more freely with an injured party when coverage of the claim is denied. He or she may still be able to work out an agreement with the injured party when the insurer is defending him or her under reservation of rights. The insured does, however, have greater obligations to the insurer, including a duty to advise the insurer of the agreement so that the insurer can withdraw its reservation of rights before the agreement becomes effective.

UM and UIM coverage has aspects of both first and third party claims. Most jurisdictions treat UM and UIM claims as first party claims. UM and UIM policies generally prohibit suit over the issue of damages but the issue of coverage is often resolved in a declaratory judgment action.

TORT TEASERS

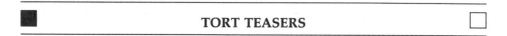

Review the hypothetical scenario at the beginning of the chapter and answer the following questions.

1. What is the significance of the insurer providing its insureds with maps showing that the Rocky Point area is within 48 statute miles of the United States border?

2. Can Jerry use these maps to prevent the insurer from alleging that the accident occurred more than 50 statute miles from the United States border?

3. Would your answer to the preceding question be different if Jerry testified that not only was he unaware of the maps that were issued by his insurer, he was also unaware at the time of the accident that he had coverage for medical payment expenses and UM in Mexico?

4. How does the insurer's actions in obtaining an expert to determine the location of the accident affect your analysis of whether bad faith has been committed?

5. If the insurer hires experts and denies coverage prior to bad faith being instituted, does that change your evaluation of Jerry's claim?

6. If the insurer institutes a declaratory judgment action prior to Jerry filing his bad faith action, does that affect your opinion as to whether the insurer acted in bad faith?

7. If the insurer argues that since it neither accepted nor denied Jerry's claim it cannot be in bad faith, how would you respond?

8. Since the insurer has determined that the accident occurred more than 50 statute miles from the United States border it has denied liability coverage to Dick and UM coverage to Jerry. Suppose Dick loses his coverage argument in the suit he institutes in the Colorado courts against his insurer. Is it possible that at the same time Jerry could win his case in the Arizona courts regarding his UM benefits?

9. What type of an agreement could Dick enter into with Jerry upon denial by Dick's insurer that he had liability coverage for the accident?

10. With respect to each of the possible claims that Jerry and Dick may have, determine what type of coverage the claim would be made under and whether it would be a first or third party claim.

KEY TERMS

■ **Adhesion contract**
Standardized contract characterized by the unequal bargaining power of the parties and the lack of negotiation regarding the terms of the contract.

■ **Declaratory judgment action**
Action in which the court renders an opinion as to a matter of law or in reference to the rights of the parties but does not order any action to be taken.

■ **Excess judgment**
Judgment in excess of the insured's policy limits.

APPENDIX I

THE COUNTRY SQUIRE

A Package of Protection for Today's Farmer and Rancher

Farm Bureau
Family of Insurance Services

Western Agricultural Insurance Company
P.O. Box 20180, 2618 South 21st Street, Phoenix, Arizona 85036-0180

A MESSAGE TO OUR POLICYHOLDERS

This is your Farm and Ranch Country Squire Insurance Policy. It is written in easy to read and understand language. We believe it provides you the best property and liability insurance coverage on the market today. Everything about this policy has been designed with today's farm and ranch family in mind.

We urge you to read this policy carefully, including the attached Declarations page. If you have any questions, your Farm Bureau agent welcomes your call.

WHERE TO LOOK–INDEX

Be sure to check your Declarations page, attached to this policy, to see which of the following apply to you.

DEFINITIONS APPLICABLE TO SEC. I, II, IV

The following definitions apply to Sections I, II and IV; they do not apply to Sections III or V:

Throughout these sections we, us and our mean the Company named in the Declarations. You and your mean the person named in the Declarations and that person's spouse if a resident of the same household. You and your also refer to a partnership, corporation, estate or trust named in the Declarations.

Bodily Injury means physical injury or death to a person caused by an **occurrence**.

Business means a trade, profession or occupation, other than **farming** or **custom farming**. **Business** includes rental of all or any part of an **insured**

location to others, or held for rental by you other than:

1. Your **residence premises** if rented occasionally;
2. Garages or stables, if not more than three (3) car spaces or stalls are rented or held for rental;
3. One-, two-, three-, or four-family **dwellings** described in the Declarations; or
4. Your farm.

Business does not include:

1. The operation of roadside stands principally for the sale of produce raised on the **insured location**; or
2. Newspaper delivery, baby-sitting, lawn care or similar activities normally performed by minors, when the activity is not the principal occupation of any **insured**.

Custom Farming means the use of any draft animal or **mobile agricultural machinery** in connection with **farming** operations for others for any charge.

Dwelling means a one-, two-, three-, or four-family **dwelling** listed in the Declarations, including its grounds and private garages.

Farm Employee means someone employed by you whose duties are in connection with the maintenance or use of the **insured location** as a farm, including the maintenance or use of your farm equipment. **Farm employee** does not include you, your spouse, or a minor child of either, but does include exchange labor.

Farm Personal Property means your personal property which is usual and incidental to the operation of a farm and is used on your farm. It includes livestock, poultry, **mobile agricultural machinery**, tools, supplies, equipment, and harvested crops used in or resulting from your **farming** operation. It includes property being purchased under an installment plan whether or not you have title to the property.

Farming means the production of fruit, nut or field crops, or the raising or keeping of livestock, poultry, fish, fur-bearing animals or bees. It includes wholesale but not retail sales, except incidental retail sales of your unprocessed farm products with the resulting gross income being less than 25 percent of your combined **farming** gross income.

Insured means you and if residents of your household:

1. Your **relatives**; and
2. Minors in the care of those named above.

Under Section II of this policy, **insured** also means a person while operating machinery, watercraft, or, in charge of your domestic or farm animals with your permission in your operations covered by this policy.

Insured Location means

1. All locations listed in the Declarations where you maintain a farm or residence, including private approaches;
2. Locations acquired by you during the policy period where you maintain a farm or residence, including private approaches;
3. Individual or family cemetery plots or burial vaults;

4. A location in which you temporarily reside but do not own; and
5. Vacant land owned by you and listed in the Declarations or acquired by you during the policy period.

Insured Location does not include property on which a **business** is conducted.

Medical Expenses means reasonable charges for medical, surgical, x-ray, dental, ambulance, hospital, professional nursing and prosthetic devices.

Mobile Agricultural Machinery means a land vehicle, including any machinery or attached apparatus, whether or not self-propelled, usual to the operation of a farm and used exclusively for agricultural purposes, not subject to registration and designed for use principally off public roads.

Mobile agricultural machinery includes implements of husbandry which are defined as a vehicle or piece of equipment or machinery designed for agricultural purposes, used primarily in the conduct of agricultural operations and used principally off the highway.

Motor Vehicle means a motorized land vehicle, trailer, or semi-trailer (including any attached machinery or apparatus) designed principally for travel on public roads. The following are not considered **motor vehicles** unless they are being towed by or carried on a **motor vehicle**:

1. A utility, boat, camping or travel trailer;
2. **Mobile agricultural machinery**;
3. **Recreational motor vehicles**;
4. Any equipment which is designed for use principally off public roads and not subject to registration or licensing.

Occurrence means an unexpected and unintended event, including continuous or repeated exposure to conditions, which results in **bodily injury** or **property damage** during the policy period. All **bodily injury** and **property damage** resulting from a common cause shall be considered the result of one **occurrence**.

Personal Property means personal property usual and incidental to the use of the **dwelling premises** as a **dwelling**.

Property Damage means injury to or destruction of tangible property caused by an **occurrence**.

Recreational Motor Vehicle or Recreational Vehicle means any motorized vehicle designed for recreation, principally used off public roads, and not subject to licensing.

Relative means a person related to you by blood, marriage, or adoption who is a resident of your household, including a ward or foster child.

Residence Employee means someone employed by you who performs duties in connection with the maintenance or use of the **residence premises**. This includes a person who performs duties for you elsewhere of a similar nature not in connection with your **business** or **farming**.

Residence Premises means a one-, two-, three-, or four-family **dwelling** which is your principal residence, including its grounds, and private garages. **Residence**

premises also means that part of any other building which is your principal residence but does not include any portion used for **business**.

GENERAL CONDITIONS APPLICABLE TO SEC. I, II, III, & IV

Unless otherwise indicated, the following conditions are applicable to Sections I, II, III, and IV:

1. **Agreement.** We will provide the insurance described in this policy and Declarations if you have paid the premium and have complied with the policy provisions and conditions. This policy is divided into four sections, some with multiple coverages. You have only the coverages for which you have paid premium. These coverages are indicated in the Declarations and are subject to the indicated limits of insurance.
   READ THE DECLARATIONS TO DETERMINE WHICH COVERAGES PERTAIN TO YOU.
2. **Abandonment of Property.** We need not pay for nor accept any property abandoned by an **insured**.
3. **Appraisal** (Not applicable to liability coverages). If you and we fail to agree on the amount of loss, either one can demand that the amount of loss be set by appraisal. If either makes a written demand for appraisal, each shall select a competent, independent appraiser and notify the other of the appraiser's identity within 20 days of receipt of the written demand. The two appraisers shall then select a competent, impartial umpire. If the two appraisers are unable to agree upon an umpire within 15 days, you or we can ask a judge of a court of record in the state where the **residence premises** is located to select an umpire. The appraisers shall then set the amount of the loss. If the appraisers submit a written report of an agreement to us, the amount agreed upon shall be the amount of the loss. If the appraisers fail to agree within a reasonable time, they shall submit their differences to the umpire. Written agreements signed by any two of these three shall set the amount of the loss. Each appraiser shall be paid by the party selecting that appraiser. Other expenses of the appraisal and the compensation of the umpire shall be shared equally.
4. **Assignment.** Assignment of this policy shall not be valid unless we give our written consent.
5. **Audit Premium.** The premium stated in the Declarations shall be computed according to our rules and rating plans. The premium is for insurance from the inception date in the Declarations (12:01 a.m.) to the expiration date in the Declarations (12:01 a.m.); date and time being at your **residence premises**. This premium, however, is an estimated premium only. We shall be permitted to examine and audit your books and records during the policy period and within three (3) years after the final termination of the policy, to obtain information about the premium basis of this insurance. The earned premium for the insurance shall be computed according to our rules and rating plans. If the earned premium exceeds the estimated premium you paid, you shall pay us the excess; if the earned premium is less, we shall return the overpayment to you.

6. **Bankruptcy of An Insured.** Bankruptcy or insolvency of an **insured** shall not relieve us of our obligations under this policy.
7. **Cancellation.** You may cancel this entire policy by mailing to us written notice stating when this cancellation shall be effective. Our cancellation rights appear on back pages of this policy labelled "Cancellation".
8. **Concealment or Fraud.** We will not provide coverage if any **insured** has intentionally concealed or misrepresented any material fact or circumstance relating to this insurance.
9. **Death.** Upon your death, we will continue through the current policy period to insure any member of your household who is an **insured** at the time of your death. We will also insure:
   a. With respect to your property, the person having proper temporary custody of the property until appointment and qualification of a legal representative; or
   b. The legal representative of the deceased, but only with respect to the premises and property of the deceased covered under the policy at the time of death.
10. **Declarations.** By acceptance of this policy, you agree that the Declarations indicate the coverages you purchased. This policy embodies the only agreements existing between you and us or any of our agents relating to this insurance.
11. **Deductible Clause.** Loss from each **occurrence** shall be adjusted separately. The deductible stated in the Declarations shall be subtracted from each adjusted loss or the limit of insurance, whichever is less. Under the special limits applicable to Coverage C, however, the deductible shall be subtracted from only the adjusted loss.
12. **Dividends or Credits.** Any obligation of ours for dividend or credit shall not in any way extend or change the policy period.
13. **Inspection and Audit.** We shall be permitted to inspect and audit your insured property and operation at any time. We are not obligated, however, to conduct inspections and any inspection or report shall not be considered a representation that the operation or property is safe.
14. **Liberalization Clause.** If we adopt any revision which would broaden the coverage under this policy without payment of additional premium within 60 days prior to or during the policy period, the broadened coverage will immediately apply to this policy.
15. **Loss Payment** (Not applicable to liability coverages). We will adjust all losses with you. Payment for loss will be made within 60 days after we receive your signed, sworn statement of loss and ascertainment of the loss is made either by agreement with you, entry of a final judgment, or the filing of an appraisal award with us. Actual cash value in this policy means replacement cost less depreciation.
16. **Mortgage Clause** (Limited to Sections I and IV). The word "mortgagee" includes a trustee of a deed of trust.

    If a mortgagee is named in this policy, any loss payable under Sections I or IV shall be paid to the mortgagee and you, as interests appear. If more than one mortgagee is named, the order of payment shall be the same as the order or precedence of the mortgages.

If we deny your claim, that denial shall not apply to a valid claim of the mortgagee, if the mortgagee:

a. Notifies us of any change in ownership, occupancy or substantial change in risk of which the mortgagee is aware;

b. Pays any premium due under this policy on demand if you have neglected to pay the premium; and

c. Submits a signed, sworn statement of loss within 60 days after receiving notice from us of your failure to do so. Policy conditions relating to Appraisal, Suit Against Us and Loss Payment apply to the mortgagee.

If the policy is cancelled by us, notice shall be mailed to the mortgagee at least 10 days before the date cancellation takes effect.

If we pay the mortgagee for any loss and deny payment to you:

a. We are subrogated to all the rights of the mortgagee granted under the mortgage on the property; or

b. At our option, we may pay to the mortgagee the whole principal on the mortgage plus any accrued interest. In this event, we shall receive a full assignment and transfer.

Subrogation shall not impair the right of the mortgagee to recover the full amount of the mortgagee's claim.

17. No Benefit to Bailee. We will not recognize any assignment or grant any coverage for the benefit of any person or organization holding, storing or transporting property for a fee regardless of any other provision of this policy.

18. Nonduplication of Insurance Benefits. No person entitled to benefits under any coverage of this policy shall recover duplicate benefits for the same elements of loss under other coverages of this policy or other policies written by us.

19. Our Option. If we give you written notice within 30 days after we receive your signed, sworn statement of loss, we may:

a. Take all or any part of the property at the agreed or appraised value; or

b. Repair or replace any part of the property damaged with equivalent property. We will not be liable for any loss resulting from delay in repair or choice of repairmen.

20. Policy Period. This policy applies only to **occurrences** which take place during the policy period.

21. Policy Renewals. Subject to our consent, you may renew this policy for successive periods by payment to us of the premium we require to renew the policy. Premium payment for any renewal period shall be due on the expiration of the preceding policy period.

22. Policy Termination. If you fail to pay the premium when due, the policy shall terminate on the expiration date of the policy without any notice or action by us.

23. Subrogation—Our Right to Recover Payment.

a. If we make payment under this policy and the person to or for whom payment was made has a right to recover damages, we will be subrogated to that right (have that right transferred to us). That person must do whatever is necessary to enable us to exercise our rights and must do nothing after the loss to prejudice our rights.

b. If we make a payment under this policy, and the person to or for whom payment was made recovers damages from another, that person must hold the proceeds of the recovery in trust for us and must reimburse us to the extent of our payment.

24. **Suit Against Us.** No action shall be brought against us unless there has been compliance with the policy provisions. No one shall have any right to join us as a party to any action against an **insured**. Further, no action with respect to liability coverages shall be brought against us until the obligation of the **insured** has been determined by final judgment or agreement signed by us.
25. **Terms of Policy to Conform to Statute.** Terms of this policy which are in conflict with the statutes of the state where the policy is issued are hereby amended to conform to such statutes.
26. **Waiver or Change of Policy Provisions.** A waiver or change of any provision of this policy must be in writing by us to be valid. Our request for an appraisal or examination shall not waive any of our rights.

SECTION I—PROPERTY INSURANCE

We cover the property insured under Section I against direct physical loss only for specified perils. The perils and our limit of liability applicable to each coverage are indicated in the Declarations.

COVERAGE A
Your Dwelling(s)

We cover the following:

1. The **dwelling** on the **residence premises** shown in the Declarations used principally as your private residence, including structures attached to the **dwelling** and outdoor equipment pertaining to the **dwelling** and materials and supplies located on or adjacent to the **residence premises** for use in the construction, alteration or repair of the **dwelling** or private garage on the **residence premises**.
2. Your **dwelling(s)** other than the **dwelling** on the **residence premises**, shown in the Declarations and used principally as a private residence, including structures attached to and outdoor equipment pertaining to them and materials and supplies on these **dwelling premises** for the construction, alteration or repair of them or their private garages.

Coverage for outdoor radio and television antennas, aerials, and satellite receivers, including their lead-in wiring, masts, and towers, is subject to a maximum payment of $250, unless such equipment is specifically insured elsewhere for a greater amount. Fences within 250 feet of the **dwelling** on the **residence premises** are covered. Field and pasture fences are excluded.

We cover detached private garages and storage sheds pertaining to the above **dwelling(s)**. Coverage for these structures shall not exceed ten percent (10%) of the amount of the insurance specified for the applicable **dwelling** as an additional amount of insurance. We do not cover these structures if used for **business**, professional or **farming** purposes. We also do not cover any garage or storage shed rented to someone other than a tenant of the **dwelling**.

COVERAGE B
Additional Living Expense
If a loss covered under Coverage A of this policy makes the **dwelling** uninhabitable, we pay the following not to exceed the applicable limit stated in the Declarations:

1. **Additional Living Expense.** Any necessary increase in living expenses incurred by you so that your family can maintain its normal standard of living. Payment shall be for the shortest time required to repair or replace the premises or, if you permanently relocate, the shortest time required for your household to settle elsewhere. This period of time is not limited by expiration of this policy.
2. **Fair Rental Value.** The fair rental value of the **dwelling premises.** Payment shall be for the shortest time required to repair or replace the part of the premises rented or held for rental. This period of time is not limited by expiration of this policy. Fair rental value shall not include any expenses that do not continue while part of the **dwelling premises** rented or held for rental is uninhabitable.
3. **Prohibited Use.** If a civil authority prohibits you from use of the **dwelling premises** as a result of direct damage to neighboring premises by a peril insured against in this policy, we cover any resulting additional living expenses or fair rental value loss incurred by you for a period not exceeding two weeks during which use is prohibited.

We do not cover loss or expense due to cancellation of a lease or agreement. No deductible applies to Coverage B.

COVERAGE C
Personal Property
We cover **personal property** owned or used by any **insured** while it is anywhere in the world. At your request, we will cover personal property owned by others while the property is in that part of the **residence premises** occupied exclusively by an **insured.** Your **personal property** in a newly acquired principal residence is covered only for thirty days immediately after you begin to move the property there. If your **personal property** is distributed between your **residence premises** and this newly acquired principal residence, the limit of liability shall apply at each location in the proportion that the value at each location bears to the total value of all property distributed between the two locations.

If you have more than one **dwelling** insured under Coverage A of this policy a different Coverage C limit of liability applies to each **dwelling.** These limits are stated in the Declarations. The limit applicable to one insured **dwelling** can not be applied to a loss at another insured **dwelling.**

Our limit of liability for your **personal property** usually situated at your **dwelling premises** insured under Coverage A, located at other than your principal **dwelling** on the **residence premises,** is five percent (5%) of the limit of liability for that **dwelling premises** insured under Coverage A, unless the

Declarations indicate you have purchased additional coverage. Any additional coverage is limited to the amount indicated for that particular location.

1. **Special Limits of Liability.** These limits do not increase the Coverage C limit of liability.

   The special limit for each following category is the total limit for each **occurrence** for all property in that category:

   a. $200 on money, bank notes, numismatic property, buillion, gold other than goldware, silver other than silverware, platinum, coins, medals, stamps, and other philatelic property;
   b. $1,000 on securities, accounts, deeds, evidences of debt, letters of credit, notes other than bank notes, manuscripts, passports and tickets;
   c. $1,000 on watercraft, including their trailers, furnishings, equipment, and outboard motors. We do not cover any loss by windstorm or hail to this property unless it is inside a fully enclosed building;
   d. $1,000 on utility trailers not otherwise insured;
   e. $1,000 on grave markers;
   f. $1,000 for loss by theft of jewelry, watches, furs, precious and semi-precious stones;
   g. $1,000 for loss by theft of firearms;
   h. $2,500 for loss by theft of silverware, silver-plated ware, goldware, gold-plated ware and pewterware.

2. **Property Not Insured.** We do not insure under Coverage C:

   a. **Farm personal property;**
   b. Animals, birds, fish or pets;
   c. Motorized land vehicles and parts, including **mobile agricultural machinery** except vehicles used to service your **dwellings** and not licensed for road use, such as power lawnmowers;
   d. Aircraft and parts;
   e. Property of roomers, tenants and boarders not related to an **insured;**
   f. **Business** personal property, including, but not limited to office equipment, supplies, furnishings, merchandise, samples, tools, and **business** papers and records;
   g. **Recreational vehicles,** trailer homes and campers;
   h. Any **personal property** located at any **dwellings** which are owned by you and not insured under Section I;
   i. Articles separately described and specifically insured by this or other insurance.

3. **Supplementary Coverages.** The following supplementary coverages do not increase the applicable limit of liability under this policy:

   a. Consequential loss. We also cover loss to property insured under Coverage C while at the **insured location** due to change in temperature as a result of physical damage to the building or equipment therein caused by a peril insured against.
   b. Credit Card, Bank Transfer Card, Counterfeit Currency and Forgery. We will pay up to $1,000 for:

   (1) The legal obligation of an **insured** to pay because of the theft or unauthorized use of credit cards or bank transfer cards issued to or registered in any **insured's** name. We do not cover credit card or bank card use if any **insured** has not complied with all terms and conditions under which the card was issued;

(2) Loss suffered by an **insured** caused by forgery or alteration of any check or negotiable instrument;

(3) Loss suffered by an **insured** through acceptance in good faith of counterfeit United States or Canadian paper currency.

We do not cover losses resulting from **business** pursuits or dishonesty of any **insured.**

COVERAGE D

Farm Personal Property

We cover your unscheduled **farm personal property** on the **insured location.** This coverage is further extended for your **farm personal property** away from the **insured location** except while:

1. Stored in or being processed in manufacturing plants, public elevators, warehouses, seed houses, or drying plants;
2. In transit by common or contract carrier; or
3. In public sales barns or sales yards.

We will cover **farm personal property** leased, rented or borrowed by you to conduct your **farming** operation. This **farm personal property** may not be available for your regular use and may not be used on a co-operative exchange basis. This coverage is excess over insurance which the owner has on the property.

1. **Livestock Coverage.** We cover your **livestock** for the specified perils only if death occurs.

   Livestock is defined as cattle, horses, mules, swine, poultry, donkeys, goats and sheep. Dogs, cats and fur-bearing animals are not covered. Our limit of liability shall in no case exceed the actual cash value of the livestock subject to the maximum per head limit stated in the Declarations. Death must result within fifteen (15) days from the date of **occurrence.**

2. **Limited Crop Coverage.** Hay, straw and fodder are covered for loss caused by peril 1 (fire) only not to exceed the amount stated in the Declarations in any one stack or building. If a stack or hay building is exposed within 125 feet by another stack or building, the applicable limit shall apply to the aggregate of all such exposed stacks or buildings. For example, if stack Y is 100 feet from stack X and stack Z is 100 feet from stack Y but 200 feet from stack X, the aggregate limit applicable to stacks X, Y and Z is the Coverage D stack limit stated in the Declarations.

3. **Coinsurance Clause.** You must maintain insurance on all your eligible unscheduled **farm personal property** to the extent of at least eighty percent (80%) of the actual cash value at the time of loss and no less than at the time of our auditing or taking inventory. For example, if at the time of loss your unscheduled **farm personal property** is worth $100,000, then the amount of insurance must be at least $80,000. If you fail to keep this agreed percentage of coverage, you will share in each loss in addition to the deductible. We will pay the proportion of each loss represented by the amount you did insure at the time of loss divided by the amount you should have insured.

If the aggregate claim for any loss under this coverage is less than two percent (2%) of the total amount of insurance under Coverage D, you will not be required to furnish an inventory of the undamaged property. This does not mean we waive any of our rights concerning the application of this coinsurance clause.

4. **Inspection and Audit.** We shall be permitted to inspect and audit your insured **farm personal property** at any reasonable time.
5. **Coverage Limitation to Records and Electronic Data Processing Property.** Our liability for loss to:
   a. Books of account, manuscripts, abstracts, drawings, card index systems and other records except electronic data processing records shall not exceed the cost of blank books, cards or other blank material, plus the cost of labor incurred by you for transcribing or copying such records;
   b. Film, tape, disc, drum, cell and other magnetic recording or storage media for electronic data processing shall not exceed the cost of such media in unexposed or blank form.
6. **Exclusions.** Coverage D does not cover:
   a. **Personal property;**
   b. Animals, other than **livestock;**
   c. Accounts, bills, currency, deeds, evidences of debt, money and securities;
   d. Vegetables (except threshed peas and beans), root crops, bulbs, fruits, cotton, tobacco and silage;
   e. Permanently installed irrigation pumps, buried water lines; and permanently installed or portable sprinkler lines and sprinkler equipment (including any sprinkler's electrical equipment);
   f. Fences, sawmill equipment, windmills, wind chargers and their towers, private power, light and telephone poles, radio and television towers and antennas, vehicles primarily designed and licensed for road use other than wagons and trailers designed for **farming** purposes and used principally on the insured premises;
   g. Trucks, automobiles, housetrailers, motorcycles, watercraft, **recreational motor vehicles,** aircraft, or their parts or accessories;
   h. Standing growing crops or stubble. However, 10% of the amount specified for Coverage D will cover standing corn, wheat, oats, barley, rye, flax, soybeans and other grains against loss by fire only;
   i. Grain, seeds, peas, beans, hay, straw, and fodder unless loss is caused by peril 1 (fire);
   j. Structures and buildings except portable buildings on skids in an amount not to exceed $300 per building;
   k. Any damage arising from wear and tear, freezing, mechanical breakdown or failure;
   l. Under collision or overturn coverage: damage to tires, unless damaged by the same cause as other loss covered under Coverage D;
   m. Bee boards or their larvae and bees;
   n. Loss to **livestock** caused by the direct or indirect result of fright, freezing, running into fences or other objects, running into streams or ditches, or smothering;
   o. Livestock losses caused by collision with any **insured's** vehicle or with the roadbed; or

p. Property which is separately described and specifically insured in whole or in part by this or any other insurance.

COVERAGE E
Additional Buildings
We cover your **dwellings,** barns, buildings, fences and structures listed on the schedule of additional buildings.

1. **Materials and Supplies.** Coverage on a building or structure is extended to cover all materials and supplies on the premises or adjacent to them intended to be used in the construction, alteration or repair of such building or structure.
2. **Coverage on Buildings.** Coverage on buildings includes permanent fixtures and sheds attached to the described buildings, but excluding fences.
3. **Utility Poles.** Coverage on private utility poles includes attached switch boxes, fuse boxes, and other electrical equipment mounted on the poles.
4. **Fences and Similar Structures.** Our liability for loss to fences, corrals, pens, chutes and feed racks shall not be for a greater proportion of any loss than the amount of insurance bears to the total value of that particular property at the time of loss.
5. **New Construction.** We will pay up to $5,000 per **occurrence** for loss to newly constructed additional dwellings, barns, or buildings when erected on the **insured location.** This includes all materials and supplies on the premises to be used in the construction. This coverage shall cease sixty (60) days from the date construction was begun or the policy expiration date, whichever occurs first. For additional coverage, you must request it and pay the required premium. This extension does not cover additions, alterations or repairs to existing dwellings, barns or buildings. Perils 1–9 apply to New Construction Coverage.

Coverage to outdoor radio and television antennas, aerials, and satellite receivers including their lead-in wiring, masts and towers, is subject to a maximum payment of $250, unless such equipment is specifically insured for a greater amount.

ADDITIONAL COVERAGES—SECTION I

No deductible applies to these additional coverages.

1. **Debris Removal.** We will pay the reasonable expense incurred by you in the removal of debris of covered property provided coverage is afforded for the peril causing the loss. Debris removal expense is included in the limit of liability applying to the damaged property. When the amount payable for the actual damage to the property plus the expense for debris removal exceeds the limit of liability for the damaged property, an additional 5% of that limit of liability will be available to cover debris removal expense.
2. **Reasonable Repairs.** We will pay the reasonable costs incurred by you for necessary repairs made solely to protect covered property from further damage provided coverage is afforded for the peril causing the loss. This

coverage does not increase the limit of liability applicable to the property being repaired.

3. **Trees, Shrubs and Other Plants** (Limited to Coverage A—Your Dwellings). We cover trees, shrubs, plants and lawns within 250 feet of the **dwelling premises** for loss caused by the following perils: fire or lightning, explosion, riot or civil commotion, aircraft, vehicles not owned or operated by a resident of the **dwelling premises,** vandalism or malicious mischief or theft. The limit of liability for this coverage shall not exceed five percent (5%) of the limit of liability specified for the Coverage A **dwelling** at the same **dwelling premises.** Our limit of liability for any one tree, shrub or plant is $500. We do not cover property grown for **business** or **farming** purposes under this paragraph. This coverage shall not increase the applicable Coverage A limit under your policy.
4. **Refrigerated Products.** If Coverage C applies to your policy, we will pay an amount not to exceed $500 for loss or damage to contents of a freezer or refrigerator at the **residence premises.** This coverage does not apply to **farm personal property.** If a different amount is stated in the Declarations, that amount applies. The loss or damage must be caused by a change in temperature resulting from:
   - **a.** Interruption of electrical service to refrigeration equipment caused by damage to the generating or transmission equipment which results in a breakdown in the system; or
   - **b.** Mechanical or electrical breakdown of the refrigeration system.

   You must exercise diligence in inspecting and maintaining refrigeration equipment in proper working condition. If interruption of electrical service, mechanical or electrical breakdown is known, you must exercise all reasonable means to protect the insured property from further damage.
5. **Fire Department Service Charge.** We will pay up to $300 for your liability assumed by contract or agreement for fire department charges incurred when the fire department is called to save or protect covered property from a peril insured against. No deductible applies to this coverage. Coverage afforded under this clause applies only if the covered property is not located within the limits of the city, municipality or protection district furnishing such fire department response. This coverage does not apply to property located in Arizona.

PERILS INSURED AGAINST—SECTION I

We cover for direct physical loss to property insured caused by the following perils:

1. **Fire** or **lightning.**
2. **Removal.**

   When property is removed because it is endangered by other insured perils, we pay for direct loss from any cause for accidental loss to that property while it is being removed and for thirty (30) days after removal to a proper place.
3. **Windstorm** or **hail.**
   - **a.** This peril does **not** include loss to the interior or contents of a building caused by rain, snow, sleet, sand or dust unless the direct force of

wind or hail damages the building causing an opening in a roof or wall through which the rain, snow, sleet, sand, or dust gets in;

b. This peril does **not** include loss caused directly or indirectly by frost, cold weather, ice (other than hail), snowstorm or sleet, all whether driven by wind or not;

c. This peril does **not** include loss to watercraft and their trailers, furnishings, equipment and outboard motors while outside a fully enclosed building.

4. Explosion.

This peril does not include:

a. Concussion unless caused by explosion;

b. Electrical arcing;

c. Water hammer;

d. Rupture or bursting of steam boilers, steam pipes, steam turbines, steam engines, or water pipes, if owned by, leased or actually operated under the control of an **insured;** or

e. Rupture or bursting due to expansion or swelling of the contents of any building or structure, caused by or resulting from water;

f. Rupture or bursting of rotating parts of machinery caused by centrifugal force; or

g. Shock waves caused by aircraft, including a sonic boom.

5. Riot or **civil commotion.**

6. Aircraft, including self-propelled missiles and spacecraft.

7. Vehicles.

This peril does **not** cover loss:

a. To a fence, driveway, walk, or structure insured under Coverage E, caused by a vehicle owned or operated by you, your employees or by a resident of the premises; or

b. To any **motor vehicle** or trailer.

NOTE: Loss by Perils 6 (Aircraft) and 7 (Vehicles) includes only direct loss by actual physical contact of an aircraft or vehicle with the covered property.

8. Smoke, meaning sudden and accidental damage from smoke.

This peril does **not** include loss caused by smoke from agricultural smudging or industrial operations.

9. Vandalism or malicious mischief, meaning only the willful and malicious damage to or destruction of the property covered.

This peril does **not** cover:

a. Loss if the **dwelling** has been vacant or unoccupied for more than thirty (30) consecutive days immediately before the loss. A **dwelling** being constructed is not considered vacant or unoccupied;

b. Wear and tear caused by tenants or members of their household.

10. Theft, including attempted theft and loss of property from a known location when it is likely that the property has been stolen.

Property of a student who is an **insured** is covered while at a residence away from home only if the student has been there at any time during the forty-five (45) days immediately before the loss.

The term "theft" shall **not** include escape, inventory shortage, wrongful conversion or embezzlement.

This peril does **not** include loss:

a. Committed by any **insured;**

b. In or to a building under construction;

c. Of materials, tools and supplies for use in the construction of a building until it is completed and occupied;

d. From any part of a **dwelling premises** rented by an **insured** to other than an **insured;**

e. Of property while in the custody of the postal service or similar government or private business;

f. Caused by tenants, their employees, or members of their households.

In the event of loss by theft, you shall give immediate notice to the nearest law enforcement officer.We will not pay any reward you offer for the return or recovery of any stolen property.

11. **Breakage of glass or safety glazing** material which is part of the covered building. This coverage extends to storm doors and storm windows in summer storage. This peril does **not** include loss if the building has been vacant more than thirty (30) consecutive days immediately before the loss. A building being constructed is not considered vacant.

12. **Weight of ice, snow,** or **sleet** which causes damage to a building or property contained in a building. This peril does **not** include loss to an awning, fence, patio, pavement, swimming pool, foundation, retaining wall, bulkhead, pier, wharf, or dock.

13. **Collapse** of a building or any part of a building.

This peril does **not** include loss to an awning, fence, patio, pavement, swimming pool, underground pipe, flue, drain, cesspool, septic tank, foundation, retaining wall, bulkhead, pier, wharf or dock unless the loss is a direct result of the collapse of a building. Collapse does **not** include: settling, cracking, shrinking, bulging or expansion.

14. **Accidental discharge or overflow** of water or steam from within a plumbing, heating or air conditioning system or from within a household appliance. We also pay for tearing out and replacing any part of the covered **dwelling** necessary to repair the system or appliance from which the water or steam escaped.

This peril does **not** include loss:

a. To a **dwelling** caused by continuous or repeated seepage or leakage for more than thirty (30) days;

b. On the **dwelling premises,** if the **dwelling** has been vacant for more than thirty (30) consecutive days immediately before the loss. A **dwelling** being constructed is not considered vacant;

c. To the system or appliance from which the water or steam escaped;

d. Caused by or resulting from freezing; or

e. On the **dwelling premises** caused by accidental discharge or overflow which occurs off the **dwelling premises.**

15. **Sudden or accidental tearing apart, cracking, burning** or **bulging** of a steam or hot water heating system, an air conditioning system, or an appliance for heating water.

We do **not** cover loss caused by or resulting from freezing under this peril.

16. **Falling objects.** This peril does **not** include loss to the interior of a building or property contained in the building unless the roof or an exterior wall of the building is first damaged by a falling object. This peril does **not** include loss to outdoor equipment, awnings, fences, and retaining walls. Damage to the falling object itself is not included.
17. **Freezing of a plumbing, heating or air conditioning** system or of a household appliance.

    This peril does **not** include loss on the **dwelling premises** while the **dwelling** is vacant, unoccupied, or being constructed unless you have:
    a. Maintained heat in the building; or
    b. Shut off the water supply and drained the system and appliances of water.
18. **Sudden and accidental damage from artificially generated electrical current.**

    This peril does **not** include loss to a tube, transistor or other electronic components.
19. **Collision with another object or overturn.** This peril does not apply to **livestock.** Impact with the ground or roadbed is not considered a collision.
20. **Electrocution.** This peril applies only to **livestock.**
21. **Attack by dogs or wild animals.** This peril applies only to **livestock.** It does **not** include attack by dogs owned by you or any person residing on the **insured location.**
22. **Accidental shooting.** This peril applies only to **livestock.** This peril does not include loss caused by any **insured,** employees of an **insured,** or persons residing on the **insured location.**
23. **Loading, unloading, collision or overturn while in transit.** This peril applies only to **livestock.** Impact with the ground or roadbed is not considered a collision.
24. **Drowning.** This peril applies only to **livestock** and excludes swine under thirty (30) days old and poultry.
25. **All risk.**

    We insure for all risks of physical loss to the property insured **except:**
    a. Those losses excluded under **"Exclusions Applicable to Section I";**
    b. Freezing of a plumbing, heating or air conditioning system or of a household appliance, or by discharge, leakage or overflow from within the system or appliance caused by freezing, while the **dwelling** is vacant, unoccupied or being constructed unless you have used reasonable care to:
    (1) Maintain heat in the building; or
    (2) Shut off the water supply and drained the system and appliances of water.
    c. Freezing, thawing, pressure or weight of water or ice, whether driven by wind or not, to a fence, pavement, patio, swimming pool, foundation, retaining wall, bulkhead, pier, wharf or dock;
    d. Theft in or to a building under construction, or of materials, tools and supplies for use in the construction until the building is completed and occupied;
    e. Vandalism and malicious mischief or breakage of glass and safety glazing materials if the building has been vacant or unoccupied for

more than thirty (30) consecutive days immediately before the loss. A building being constructed is not considered vacant or unoccupied;

f. Continuous or repeated seepage or leakage of water or steam for more than thirty (30) days within a plumbing, heating or air conditioning system or from within a household appliance;

g. Wear and tear; marring; deterioration; inherent vice; latent defect; mechanical breakdown; rust; mold; wet or dry rot; contamination; smog; smoke from agricultural smudging or industrial operations; settling, cracking, shrinking, bulging, or expansion of pavements, patios, foundations, walls, floors, roofs or ceilings; loss caused by birds, vermin, rodents, insects or domestic animals. If any of these cause water to escape from a plumbing, heating or air conditioning system or household appliance, we cover loss caused by the water. We also cover the cost of tearing out and replacing any part of a building necessary to replace the system or appliance. We do **not** cover loss to the system or appliance from which this water escaped.

If Peril 25 applies to Coverage C, the following additional exclusions also apply:

h. Breakage of eye glasses, glassware, statuary, bric-a-brac, porcelains, and similar fragile articles, other than jewelry, watches, bronzes, cameras, and photographic lenses. These items are covered, however, if breakage results from Perils 1 through 10 or 13 through 16;

i. Dampness of atmosphere or extremes of temperature unless the direct cause of loss is rain, snow, sleet or hail;

j. Loss arising from refinishing, renovating or repairing property other than watches, jewelry and furs;

k. Collision other than collision with a land vehicle; sinking, swamping or stranding of watercraft, including their trailers, furnishings, equipment and outboard motors.

Under items g and a through d above any ensuing loss not excluded is covered.

EXCLUSIONS APPLICABLE TO SECTION I

We do not cover loss under Section I resulting directly or indirectly from:

1. **Ordinance or law,** meaning enforcement of any ordinance or law regulating the construction, repair, or demolition of a building or other structure, unless specifically provided under this policy.
2. **Earth movement,** including but not limited to earthquake, landslide, mudflow, earth sinking, rising or shifting. Direct loss by fire, explosion, theft, or breakage of glass or safety glazing materials resulting from earth movement is covered.
3. **Water damage,** meaning:

   a. Flood, surface water, waves, tidal water, overflow of a body of water, or spray from any of these, whether or not driven by wind;

   b. Water which backs up through sewers or drains;

   c. Water below the surface of the ground, including water which exerts pressure on, or seeps or leaks through a building, sidewalk, driveway, foundation, swimming pool or other structure. Direct loss by fire, explosion or theft resulting from water damage is covered.

4. **Volcanic eruption.**
5. **Neglect,** meaning neglect of an **insured** to use all reasonable means to save and preserve property at and after the time of loss, or when property is endangered by a peril insured against.
6. **War,** including undeclared war, civil war, insurrection, rebellion, revolution, warlike act by military force or military personnel, destruction or seizure for use for any purpose by any governmental authority, and including any consequence of any of these. Discharge of a nuclear weapon shall be deemed a warlike act even if accidental.
7. **Power, heating or cooling failure** unless the failure results from physical damage to power, heating or cooling equipment situated on the **dwelling premises** where the loss occurs. This failure must be caused by a peril insured against.
8. **Depreciation, decay, deterioration, change in temperature or humidity, loss of market,** or from any other consequential or indirect loss of any kind.
9. **Any sound reproducing, receiving or transmitting equipment** designed for use as an eight-track player, cassette player, citizens band radio, two-way mobile radio or telephone, scanning monitor, radar detection or similar device, or any tape, wire, record, disc, or other medium for use with any such device while any of this property is in or upon any motorized vehicle, farm equipment, boat or aircraft, and capable of being operated by power supplied from these vehicles. These devices are covered if factory installed in **mobile agricultural machinery** insured under Coverage D.
10. **Nuclear hazard,** meaning any nuclear reaction, radiation, or radioactive contamination, all whether controlled or uncontrolled or however caused, or any consequence of any of these. Loss caused by the nuclear hazard shall not be considered loss caused by fire, explosion, or smoke, whether these perils are specifically named or otherwise included within the perils insured against in Section I.

    The above exclusions, 1 through 10, apply even if the following contribute to the loss: faulty, inadequate or defective planning; zoning; development; maintenance of property on or off the insured location by any person or organization.
11. **Any damage caused intentionally** by or at the direction of any **insured.**

CONDITIONS APPLICABLE TO SECTION I

1. **Insurable Interest and Limit of Liability.** Even if more than one person has an insurable interest in the property covered, we shall not be liable:
   a. To the **insured** for an amount greater than the **insured's** interest; nor
   b. For more than the applicable limit of liability.
2. **Your Duty after Loss.** In case of a loss to which this insurance may apply, you must see that the following duties are performed:
   a. Give written notice to us or our agent, as soon as practicable, and also

give notice to the police if loss is suspected to be in violation of a law. In case of loss under the credit or bank card coverage, also notify the issuing card company;

b. Protect the property from further damage, make reasonable and necessary repairs required to protect the property and keep an accurate record of repair expenditures;

c. Prepare an inventory of damaged property showing in detail, the quantity, description, actual cash value and amount of loss. Attach to the inventory all bills, receipts and related documents that substantiate the figures in the inventory;

d. As often as we may reasonably require, exhibit the damaged property and submit to examination under oath and subscribe the same;

e. Within sixty (60) days after our request, submit to us your signed, sworn statement of loss which sets forth the following information to the best of your knowledge and belief:

(1) The time and cause of loss;

(2) The interest of the **insured** and all others in the property involved and all encumbrances on the property;

(3) Other insurance which may cover the loss;

(4) Changes in title or occupancy of the property during the term of the policy;

(5) Specifications of any damaged building and detailed estimates for repair of the damage;

(6) An inventory of damaged property as described above;

(7) Receipts for additional living expenses incurred and records supporting any fair rental value loss; and

(8) Evidence or affidavit supporting a claim under the credit card or bank card coverage stating the amount and cause of loss.

3. Loss Settlement. Subject to the applicable limits stated in the Declarations, covered property losses are settled as follows:

a. Personal Property, structures that are not buildings, **farm personal property,** and buildings insured under Coverage E, at actual cash value at the time of loss but not exceeding the amount necessary to repair or replace;

b. Floor coverings, domestic appliances, awnings, outdoor antennas and outdoor equipment, whether or not attached to the buildings, at actual cash value at the time of loss but not exceeding the amount necessary to repair or replace;

c. Buildings insured under Coverage A:

(1) When the full cost of repair or replacement for loss to a building under Coverage A is less than $1500, Coverage A is extended to include the full cost of repair or replacement without deduction for depreciation.

(2) If the limit of liability on the damaged building is less than 80% of its replacement cost at the time of the loss, we pay the larger of the following:

(a) Actual cash value of the damaged part of the building; or

(b) That proportion of the replacement cost of the damaged part which our limit of liability on the building bears to 80% of the full current cost of the building.

(3) If the limit of liability on the damaged building is at least 80% of its replacement cost at the time of loss we pay the full cost of repair or replacement of the damaged part without deduction for depreciation, but not more than the smallest of the following amounts:

(a) The limit of liability applicable to the building;

(b) The cost to repair or replace the damage on the same premises using materials of equivalent kind and quality to the extent practicable; or

(c) The amount actually and necessarily spent to repair or replace the damage.

(4) When the cost to repair or replace exceeds 5% of the applicable limit of liability on the damaged building, we are not liable for more than the actual cash value of the loss until actual repair or replacement is completed. You may make a claim for the actual cash value amount of the loss before repairs are made. A claim for any additional amount payable under this provision must be made and construction started within one hundred and eighty (180) days after the loss.

4. **Increased Hazard.** We shall not be liable for any loss to property insured under this policy occurring while the hazard is increased by any means within the control or knowledge of any **insured.**
5. **Loss to a Pair or Set.** In case of a loss to a pair or set, we may elect to:
   a. Repair or replace any part or restore the pair or set to its value before the loss; or
   b. Pay the difference between the actual cash value of the property before and after the loss.
6. **Glass Replacement.** Covered loss for breakage of glass shall be settled on the basis of replacement with safety glazing materials when required by ordinance or law.
7. **Waiver of Subrogation.** You may waive in writing before a loss all right of recovery against any person. If not waived, we may require an assignment of rights for a loss to the extent that payment is made by us.
8. **Other Insurance.** If you are carrying other insurance on the property to which this policy applies, the coverage under this policy is null and void. We may permit other insurance, however, by endorsement to this policy. If other insurance is permitted, we will not be liable for a greater portion of any loss than our pro rata share in excess of any deductible.
9. **Vacancy.** When a building insured under this policy has been vacant, unoccupied or abandoned for a period of six (6) consecutive months at the initial inception date of this policy or any time after that, our liability is reduced fifty (50) percent. Outbuildings, which are in a seasonal state of vacancy or unoccupancy due to normal practices of **farming** operations, are not considered vacant or unoccupied as defined in the policy and therefore, our liability is not reduced under the provisions of this clause.

ENDORSEMENTS APPLICABLE TO SECTION I

Each of the following endorsements may be purchased by your payment of an additional premium. All policy provisions apply to these endorsements unless an endorsement specifically states otherwise. **An endorsement applies only when it is listed in the Declarations and you pay this premium.**

No. 111 Replacement Cost—Personal Property.
Losses under Coverage C shall be settled at replacement cost without deduction for depreciation.

Property Not Eligible
Property listed below is not eligible for replacement cost settlement. Any loss shall be settled at actual cash value at the time of loss but not exceeding the amount necessary to repair or replace.

1. Antiques, fine arts, paintings, statues and other articles which by their inherent nature cannot be replaced with new articles.
2. Articles whose age or history contribute substantially to their value, including but not limited to memorabilia, souvenirs, and collectors items.
3. Personal property of others.
4. Articles not maintained in good or workable condition.
5. Articles that are outdated or obsolete and are stored or not being used.

Replacement Cost

1. We will pay not more than the smallest of the following amounts:
   a. Replacement cost at time of loss without deduction for depreciation;
   b. The full cost of repair at time of loss;
   c. 400% of the actual cash value at time of loss;
   d. Any special limit of liability applicable under Coverage C; or
   e. The total limit of liability applicable to Coverage C.
2. When the replacement cost for the entire loss under this endorsement exceeds $500, we will pay no more than the actual cash value for the loss or damage until the actual repair or replacement is completed.
3. You may make a claim for loss on an actual cash value basis and then make claim within 180 days after the loss for any additional liability in accordance with this endorsement.
4. This endorsement also covers domestic appliances, floor coverings, awnings, outdoor antennas, and outdoor equipment pertaining to a **dwelling** insured under Coverage A.

No. 114 Borrowed Equipment Endorsement.
We cover under Coverage D loss to **mobile agricultural machinery** in which you have no interest, provided such machinery has been borrowed by either you or **your employees** and is actually being used in the conduct of your own farm operation, is not available for your regular use, and is not used on a cooperative exchange basis. This coverage, however, shall apply as excess over any insurance which the owner has on this borrowed property. Our limit of liability per **occurrence** under this endorsement is stated in the Declarations.

No. 120 Inflation Guard Endorsement.
It is agreed that the Limit of Liability specified in the Declarations for Section

I—Property under Coverage A (Dwelling), Coverage B (Additional Living Expense) and Coverage C (Personal Property), shall be increased at the same rate as the increase in the Company Index as developed monthly from available Governmental and Appraisal Company Indices and kept on file in the Home Office.

In no event will the limit of liability be less than the amount specified in the Declarations.

At each renewal date after this endorsement becomes effective the amount of insurance on the above coverages will be corrected to the nearest $100 in accordance with the above factor and renewal premium will be adjusted accordingly.

No. 130 Elimination of Livestock under Coverage D.

There is no coverage for **livestock** under Coverage D.

No. 171 Glass Deductible Waived.

No deductible will apply to glass breakage to the building(s) insured under Coverage A of Section I.

No. 183 Guaranteed Replacement Cost Endorsement.

We agree that our limit of liability for buildings insured under Coverage A is not limited by the amount shown on the Declarations page provided:

1. You have insured your **dwelling** and other structures to 100% of their replacement costs as we determine based on the accuracy of information you furnish, and you pay the premium we require;
2. You accept the property insurance adjustment condition in paragraph 1 above, agree to accept any annual adjustment, and pay the additional premium charged;
3. You notify us within ninety (90) days of the start of any additions or other physical changes which increase the value of your **dwelling** or other structures on the **dwelling** premises by $5,000.00 or more, and pay the additional premium charged.

   Losses under this endorsement are covered for the full cost of repair or replacement of the damaged part without deduction for depreciation, but not more than the amount actually and necessarily spent to repair or replace the damage on the same premises using materials of equivalent kind and quality to the extent practical.

   Parts c(1), (2) and (3) of the loss settlement clause of "Conditions Applicable to Section I" are deleted. This endorsement is void if you fail to comply with its provisions.

SECTION II—YOUR LIABILITY PROTECTION

COVERAGE F
Liability

If a claim is made or a suit is brought against any **insured** for damages because of **bodily injury** or **property damage** caused by an **occurrence** to which this coverage applies, we will:

1. Pay up to our limit of liability for the damages for which the **insured** is legally liable;

2. Provide a defense at our expense by counsel of our choice. We may make any investigation and settlement of any claim or suit that we decide is appropriate. Our obligation to defend any claim or suit ends when the amount we pay for damages equals our limit of liability.

COVERAGE G
Premises Medical
We will pay the necessary **medical** and funeral expenses incurred within three years from the date of an **occurrence** causing **bodily injury.** This coverage does not apply to you or regular residents of your household other than **residence employees.** As to others, this coverage applies only:

1. To a person on the **insured location** with the permission of any **insured;** or
2. To a person off the **insured location,** if the **bodily injury:**
   a. Arises out of a condition in the **insured location** or the ways immediately adjoining;
   b. Is caused by the activities of any **insured;**
   c. Is caused by the activities of a **farm** or **residence employee** in the course of employment by an **insured;**
   d. Is caused by an animal owned by or in the care of any **insured;**
   e. Is sustained by any **residence employee** and arises out of and in the course of employment.

No payment shall be made under Coverage G unless the person to or for whom such payment is made shall have signed an agreement that the amount of such payment shall be applied toward the settlement of any claim, or the satisfaction of any judgment for damages entered in the person's favor against any **insured** because of **bodily injury** to which Coverage F of this policy applies. (This paragraph is not applicable if this policy is issued in Arizona.)

COVERAGE H
Employer's Liability
If a claim is made or suit brought against you or your **relatives** because of **bodily injury** caused by an **occurrence** sustained by any **farm employee** arising out of and in the course of employment by you, we will:

1. Pay up to our limit of liability for the damages for which you are legally liable;
2. Provide a defense at our expense by counsel of our choice. We may make any investigation and settle any claim or suit that we decide is appropriate. Our obligation to defend any claim or suit ends when the amount we pay for damages resulting from the **occurrence** equals our limit of liability.

COVERAGE I
Medical Payments for Farm Employees
We will pay the necessary **medical** and funeral expenses incurred within three years from the date of **occurrence** to or for each **farm employee** who sustains **bodily injury** caused by an **occurrence** arising out of and in the course of employment by you.

No payment shall be made under Coverage I unless the person to or for whom such payment is made shall have signed an agreement that the amount of such payment shall be applied toward the settlement of any claim, or the satisfaction of any judgment for damages entered in the person's favor because of **bodily injury** to which Coverage H of this policy applies.

COVERAGE J
Medical Payments (Named Persons)
We will pay the necessary **medical** and funeral expenses incurred within three years from the date of **occurrence** to or for each person named in Coverage J of the Declarations, who sustains **bodily injury** caused by an **occurrence.**

No payment shall be made under Coverage J unless the person to or for whom such payment is made shall have signed an agreement that the amount of such payment shall be applied toward the settlement of any claim, or the satisfaction of any judgment for damages entered in the person's favor against any **insured** because of **bodily injury** to which Coverage F or H of this policy applies.

COVERAGE K
Death of Livestock by Collision
We will pay, subject to the limits of liability stated in the Declarations, for loss by death of any cattle, horse, or hybrid thereof, hog, sheep or goat owned by you and not otherwise covered, caused by collision between such animal and a **motor vehicle,** provided:

1. The **motor vehicle** is not owned or operated by an **insured** or any **insured's** employee;
2. The animal is within a public highway and is not being transported;
3. Death to the animal occurs within fifteen days after the date of the collision.

We further extend this coverage to include the death of livestock when killed by any train, provided you first present a claim in your name to the railroad company involved.

COVERAGE L
Custom Farming
Coverage F also covers your **custom farming.**

Coverage L does **not** apply to:

1. Any damage or injury to the land or crops upon which the **custom farming** is performed or is to be performed, arising from:
   a. The mixing or application of fertilizers, herbicides, pesticides, fungicides, or other chemical treatment of real property, seeds or crops;
   b. Any goods, products, or their containers manufactured, sold, handled or distributed by or on behalf of any **insured.**
2. Injury or damage resulting from:
   a. A delay in or lack of performance by or on behalf of any **insured** of any contract or agreement, written or oral; or
   b. The failure of any **insured's** products or work performed by or on behalf of any **insured** to meet the level of performance, quality, fitness or result warranted or represented by any **insured.**

COVERAGE M
Damage to Property of Others
We will pay for **property damage** to property of others caused by an **insured.** We will **not** pay for **property damage:**

1. Caused intentionally by any **insured** who is thirteen (13) years of age or older;
2. To property owned by or rented to any **insured,** a tenant of any **insured,** or a resident of any **insured's** household; or
3. Arising out of:
   a. Any **business;**
   b. The ownership, maintenance, use, loading or unloading of a **motor vehicle,** watercraft, or aircraft;
   c. Theft, mysterious disappearance, or loss of use;
   d. Mechanical or electrical breakdown, wear and tear, latent defect or inherent vice;
4. To tires.

Coverage M is subject only to the above exclusions and not to the general exclusions applicable to Section II.

Limit of Liability. Our limit of liability under Coverage M for **property damage** arising out of any **occurrence** shall not exceed the lesser of:

1. The actual cash value of the damaged property at the time of the loss; or
2. What it would then cost to repair or replace the damaged property with other of like kind and quality; or
3. The limit of liability stated in the Declarations for Coverage M.

If Section I of this policy also applies to a loss under Coverage M, Section I is primary and Coverage M is excess. You must pay any applicable Section I deductible before Coverage M applies.

We may pay for the loss in money or may repair or replace the property and may settle the claim for loss to property either with the owner or with you. Any property paid for or replaced shall, at our option, become our property.

We have no obligation under Coverage M to provide a defense against any claim or suit brought against any insured.

SECTION II—ADDITIONAL COVERAGES

Section II includes the following:

1. **Fire Legal Liability.** Coverage F is extended to cover **property damage** to a lodging place and its furnishings rented to, occupied or used by or in the care of an **insured** if such **property damage** arises out of fire, smoke or explosion. For purposes of this fire legal coverage, **insured** shall include only you and those persons listed in Paragraphs (1) and (2) of the definition of **insured.** The care, custody and control exclusion does not apply to this extension of coverage.
2. **Newly Acquired Locations.** Section II is extended to cover locations you acquire by ownership or leasehold if similar to premises or **dwellings** described in the Declarations, if you notify us of these acquisitions on or

prior to the next renewal date of this policy. The insurance afforded to these acquisitions is limited to the insurance applicable to the locations already described in the Declarations.

This extension of coverage does not apply to loss for which you have other valid and collectible insurance. You must pay any additional premium required because of the application of this insurance to such newly acquired locations.

SECTION II—ADDITIONAL PAYMENTS

Under Coverages F and H, we will pay the following expenses in addition to our limits of liability, but our obligation for these payments ceases when our obligation to defend ends:

1. Expenses for first aid to others incurred by any **insured** for **bodily injury** covered under this policy. We will not pay for first aid to you or any other **insured;**
2. Expenses incurred by us and costs taxed against any **insured** in any suit we defend;
3. Premiums on bonds required in a suit defended by us, but not for bond amounts greater than the limit of liability provided by this policy. We are not obligated to apply for or furnish any bond;
4. Reasonable expenses incurred by any **insured** at our request, including actual loss of earnings (but not loss of other income) up to $50 per day for assisting us in the investigation or defense of any claim or suit;
5. Interest on the entire judgment which accrues after entry of that part of the judgment which does not exceed the limit of liability that applies and before we pay, tender or deposit in court that part of the judgment which does not exceed the limit of liability that applies.

EXCLUSIONS APPLICABLE TO SECTION II

The following exclusions apply to all coverages under Section II except Coverage M. Section II does not cover **bodily injury** or **property damage:**

1. Arising from any **insured's business** activities or any professional service;
2. Arising from any location which an **insured** owns, rents, leases, or controls, other than an **insured location.** This exclusion does not apply to **bodily injury** of **residence employees** arising out of and in the course of employment by an **insured;**
3. Which is intentionally caused by any **insured;**
4. Arising from the maintenance, operation, use, loading or unloading of any of the following which any **insured** owns, borrows, rents, leases or operates:
   a. Any aircraft, except model aircraft of the hobby variety not used or designed for the transportation of people or cargo;
   b. Any **motor vehicle,** coverage however, applies on the **insured location** if the **motor vehicle** is not licensed for road use because it is used exclusively on the **insured location;**
   c. Any watercraft:
      (1) If powered by an inboard or inboard-outboard motor of more than fifty (50) horsepower;
      (2) If a sailing vessel twenty-six (26) feet or more in overall length.

Exclusion 4.c. does not apply while the watercraft is stored on the **insured location.**

d. Any **recreational vehicle** if the **bodily injury** or **property damage** occurs away from the **insured location.** Exclusion 4.d. does not apply to golf carts while used for golfing purposes.

Exclusions 4.c. and 4.d. do not apply to watercraft or **recreational vehicles** borrowed or rented by an **insured** for less than 10 days. Damage to the borrowed or rented **recreational vehicle** or watercraft, however, is not covered. Exclusion 4 does not apply to **bodily injury** sustained by a **residence employee** in the course of employment.

5. Arising out of the use of any aircraft, **motor vehicle, mobile agricultural machinery,** watercraft or **recreational vehicle,** while being used in or following any prearranged or organized racing, speed or stunting activity or in practice or preparation for any such contest or activity;
6. Which results from liability arising out of any contract or agreement;
7. Arising out of **custom farming** when total receipts exceed $10,000 in a calendar year. This exclusion does not apply if coverage is indicated under Coverage L in the Declarations;
8. Caused by or resulting from declared or undeclared war, civil war, insurrection, rebellion, revolution, warlike act by a military force or military personnel, destruction or seizure or use for any government purpose, and including any consequence of these. Discharge of a nuclear weapon shall be deemed a warlike act even if accidental;
9. Resulting from any act or omission of a **residence** or **farm employee** who is also an **insured** while away from the **insured location,** if the employee is under the control and direction of some person other than an **insured;**
10. Caused by a substance released or discharged from an aircraft owned or operated by an **insured** in connection with dusting or spraying operations;
11. Caused by any goods, products or containers manufactured, processed, sold, handled or distributed by an **insured,** except farm products raised on the **insured location.** Loss arising out of the failure of seed sold by an **insured** to conform to the variety, purpose or quality specified by the insured, however, is not covered. The term "seed" means seeds, bulbs, plants, roots, tubers, cuttings or other similar means of plant propagation;
12. Arising out of the discharge, dispersal, release or escape of smoke, vapors, soot, fumes, acids, alkalis, toxic chemicals, liquids or gases, waste materials or other irritants, contaminants, or pollutants into or upon land, the atmosphere or any water course or body of water. This exclusion does not apply to:
    a. Crop damage resulting from the accidental above ground contact with herbicides, pesticides, fungicides and fertilizers caused by the application of the same to an insured site which results in actual damages within one growing season of said application.
    b. Bodily injury resulting from the accidental above ground contact with herbicides, pesticides, fungicides and fertilizers caused by the application of the same to an insured site which results in medical treatment within one year (365 days) of said application.
13. Sustained by you or any **insured** as defined in paragraphs (1) and (2) of the definition of **insured;**

14. Arising out of a violation of a criminal law, except traffic violations, if committed by any **insured;** or
15. With respect to which any **insured** under this policy is also an **insured** under a nuclear energy liability policy issued by a nuclear energy liability insurance association, mutual atomic energy liability underwriters, nuclear insurance association of Canada, or any similar organization, or would be an **insured** under any such policy but for its termination upon exhaustion of its limits of liability;
16. Arising out of the entrustment by the **insured** of a **motor vehicle** to any person; coverage, however, applies on the **insured location** if the **motor vehicle** is not licensed for road use because it is used exclusively on the **insured location.**

    Exclusion 16 does not apply to bodily injury sustained by a **residence employee** in the course of employment.

Section II does not cover:

17. Property owned by, used by, rented to, or in the care, custody or control of any **insured** or his employees, or as to which any **insured** or his employees exercise physical control for any purpose (This exclusion is the care, custody and control exclusion referred to in **Section II Additional Coverages—Fire Legal Liability.**);
18. Any **property damage** to work completed by or for an **insured,** any damage arising out of such work, or out of the materials, parts, or equipment furnished in connection with such work;
19. Any **property damage** to goods or products, including containers, which an **insured** manufactures, sells, handles, raises or distributes;
20. Damages claimed for the withdrawal, inspection, repair, replacement, or loss of use of your products, or work completed by or for you or for any property of which such products or work form a part, if such products, work or property are withdrawn from the market or from use because of any known or suspected defect or deficiency;
21. Punitive or exemplary damages;
22. **Bodily injury** to any person eligible to receive any benefits required to be provided or voluntarily provided by any **insured** under any worker's compensation, non-occupational disease, disability or occupational disease law;
23. **Property damage** to an **insured location** arising out of the alienation (for example, selling, leasing, separating, etc.) of that location;
24. **Bodily injury** under Coverage G sustained by any person residing on the **insured location** except a **residence employee;**
25. Under Coverages G, I and J:
    a. **Bodily injury** involving hernia or back injury, unless it is of recent origin, it is accompanied by pain, it was immediately preceded by some accidental strain suffered in the course of employment, and it did not exist prior to the date of the alleged injury;
    b. Any person while conducting his **business** on the **insured location,** including the employees of that person;
    c. **Bodily injury** to the extent that any medical expenses are paid or payable under the provision of any:
        (1) Auto or premises insurance;

(2) Accident, disability, or hospitalization insurance;
(3) Medical or surgical reimbursement plan prepaid or otherwise;
(4) National, state or other governmental plan; or
(5) Worker's compensation or similar law.

26. Under Coverages F and G, **bodily injury** sustained by any **farm employee** arising out of employment;
27. Loss of use of property which has not been physically injured or destroyed, resulting from:
    a. A delay in or lack of performance by or on your behalf of any contract or agreement; or
    b. The failure of your products or work performed by or on your behalf to meet the level of performance, quality, fitness or durability warranted or represented by you;
28. **Bodily injury** or **property damage** which arises out of the transmission of:
    a. Acquired Immune Deficiency Syndrome (AIDs); or
    b. Genital herpes, syphilis, gonorrhea or other venereal disease caused wholly or in part by the acts of an **insured, farm employee,** or **residence employee;**
29. Any **bodily injury** sustained by any person arising out of or resulting from the molesting of minors by:
    1) any **insured,**
    2) any **farm employee** or **residence employee** of any **insured,** or
    3) any volunteer

    We shall not have any duty to defend any suit against the **insured** seeking damages on account of such **bodily injury.**

CONDITIONS APPLICABLE TO SECTION II

1. **Duties after Loss.** In case of an accident or **occurrence,** the **insured** shall perform the following duties:
   a. Give written notice to us or our agent as soon as practicable, which sets forth:
      (1) The identity of the policy and **insured;**
      (2) Reasonable available information on the time, place and circumstances of the accident or **occurrence;**
      (3) Names and addresses of any claimants and witnesses.
   b. Immediately forward to us every notice, demand, summons or other process relating to the accident or **occurrence;**
   c. At our request, assist in:
      (1) Making settlement;
      (2) The enforcement of any right of contribution or indemnity against any person or organization who may be liable to any **insured;**
      (3) The conduct of suits and attend hearings and trials;
      (4) Securing and giving evidence and obtaining the attendance of witnesses.
   d. The **insured** shall not, except at the **insured's** own cost, voluntarily make any payment, assume any obligation or incur any expense other than for first aid to others at the time of the **bodily injury;**
   e. Under Coverage M—Damage to the Property of Others—submit to us

within 60 days after the loss, a sworn statement of loss and exhibit the damaged property, if within the **insured's** control.

2. **Duties of an Injured Person**—Coverages G, I and J. The injured person or someone acting on behalf of the injured person shall:
   a. Give us a written proof of claim, under oath if required, as soon as practicable;
   b. Execute authorization to allow us to obtain copies of medical reports and records; and
   c. Submit to physical examination by a physician selected by us when and as often as we reasonably require.
3. **Cooperation of Insured**—If any **insured** fails to cooperate with us or send us legal papers as required, we have the right to refuse any further coverage for the **occurrence** or loss.
4. **Payment of Claim.** Any payment under Section II is not an admission of liability by any **insured** or us.
5. **Limits of Liability**—Coverages F and H.
   Regardless of the number of:
   (a) **insureds** under this policy,
   (b) persons or organizations sustaining **bodily injury** or **property damage,** or
   (c) claims made,
   our liability for each **occurrence** is subject to the following limitations:
   a. Our total combined single limit of liability under Coverage F for all **bodily injury** and **property damage** resulting from one **occurrence** shall not exceed the applicable limit of liability stated in the Declarations.
   b. Our total limit of liability under Coverage H for all **bodily injury** resulting from one **occurrence** shall not exceed the applicable limit stated in the Declarations.
   c. **Products Liability Limits.** The per **occurrence** combined single limit of liability for **bodily injury** and **property damage** caused by farm products produced on the **insured location** is also the total limit of our liability for all such **occurrences** during the policy period.
6. **Limits of Liability**—Coverages G, I and J. The limit of liability for Coverages G, I and J as stated in the Declarations as applicable to each person is our limit of liability for all expenses incurred by or on behalf of each person who sustains **bodily injury** resulting from an **occurrence.** Subject to the limit of liability for each person, our total limit of liability for each **occurrence** for **bodily injury** sustained by two or more persons is the per **occurrence** limit of liability stated in the Declarations.
7. **Other Insurance**—The insurance under Section II is excess over any other valid and collectible insurance except insurance written specifically to cover as excess over the limits of liability that apply in this policy.

ENDORSEMENTS APPLICABLE TO SECTION II

Each of the following endorsements may be purchased by your payment of an additional premium. All policy provisions apply to these endorsements unless an endorsement specifically states otherwise. **An endorsement applies**

only when it is listed in the Declarations and you pay this premium.

No. 204 Employer's Nonownership Liability Endorsement.

We agree that Coverage F of Section II covers the liability of you and any of your executive officers arising out of the use of any **nonowned motor vehicle** used in your farm or household **business** by any person other than you.

1. **Definitions.**

   In this endorsement only, **nonowned motor vehicle** means a land motor vehicle, trailer or semi-trailer not owned by, registered in the name of, hired or leased by, or loaned to you.

2. **Application of Insurance.**
   - **a.** This endorsement does not apply to any **motor vehicle** owned by any of your executive officers or their spouses.
   - **b.** This insurance does not apply to any **motor vehicle** owned by or registered in the name of a partner if your **business** is in the form of a partnership.

3. **Other Insurance.**

   This insurance shall be excess insurance over any other valid and collectible insurance.

SECTION III—AUTOMOBILE

DEFINITIONS

The following definitions apply to Section III:

Throughout this section, we, us, and our mean the Company named in the Declarations. You and your mean the person named in the Declarations and that person's spouse if a resident of the same household. You and your also refer to a partnership, corporation, estate, or trust named in the Declarations.

Bodily Injury means physical injury or death to a person caused by an **occurrence.**

Insured means:

1. Under Coverages N, R, S and T with respect to an **insured vehicle:**
   - **a.** You and any **relative;**
   - **b.** Anyone using an **insured vehicle** within the scope of your permission or within the scope of permission of your adult **relative;**
   - **c.** Any person or organization legally responsible for the **insured vehicle,** provided the use of the **insured vehicle** is by you or with your permission and within the scope of such permission.
2. Under Coverage N with respect to a **nonowned vehicle,** you or your **relatives** when operating a **nonowned vehicle,** or when that vehicle is operated by your agent and with your permission and within the scope of such permission.

Insured Vehicle means:

1. Any vehicle shown in the Declarations;

2. Under Coverages N, P and Q, any private passenger automobile, pickup, panel truck, farm truck, van, motorcycle or motorhome, ownership of which is acquired by you during the policy period;
3. If you have Coverages S and T, any private passenger automobile, pickup, panel truck, farm truck, **trailer,** camper, van or motorhome, ownership of which is acquired by you during the policy period provided the vehicle falls within the year model limitation indicated in the Declarations.

   The vehicles in 2 and 3 above are not **insured vehicles** unless we insure all of your vehicles and you ask us to insure the newly acquired vehicle during the policy period or within 30 days of its acquisition, whichever is shorter. A newly acquired vehicle includes a vehicle which replaces one shown in the Declarations.
4. A **temporary substitute vehicle** which is a **motor vehicle** or **trailer** you do not own while temporarily used as a substitute for a vehicle described in the Declarations when that vehicle cannot be used because of breakdown or servicing;
5. Under Coverage N only, any **trailer** while attached to a vehicle described in the Declarations. Also included is a **trailer** while being used with a **temporary substitute vehicle.**

Medical Expenses means reasonable charges for medical, surgical, x-ray, dental, ambulance, hospital, professional nursing, and prosthetic devices.

Motor Vehicle means a motorized land vehicle designed principally for travel on public roads. The term **motor vehicle** does not include a **trailer.**

Nonowned Vehicle means a **trailer** or **motor vehicle** not exceeding two-tons in capacity operated by you or your **relatives** or in the custody of you or your **relatives** provided the actual use is with the permission of the owner. This vehicle must not be owned by you or your **relatives** or be available for regular use by you or your **relatives.**

Occupying means in, on or getting in or out of.

Occurrence means an accident arising out of the ownership, maintenance or use of a **motor vehicle,** including continuous or repeated exposure to conditions, which results in unexpected **bodily injury** or **property damage** during the policy period. All **bodily injury** and **property damage** resulting from a common cause shall be considered the result of one **occurrence.**

Property Damage means injury to or destruction of tangible property caused by an **occurrence.**

Relative means a person related to you by blood, marriage or adoption who is a resident of your household, including a ward or foster child.

Trailer means a vehicle designed for towing by a private passenger automobile or farm truck. It also includes a farm wagon, farm semi-trailer or farm implement while towed by an **insured vehicle. Trailer** does not include vehicles used:

1. To haul passengers;
2. As an office, store or for display purposes;
3. As a permanent residence.

SECTION III COVERAGES

COVERAGE N

Liability

If a claim is made or a suit is brought against any **insured** for damages because of **bodily injury** or **property damage** arising out of an **occurrence** involving an **insured vehicle** or a **nonowned vehicle,** we will:

1. Pay up to our limit of liability for the damages for which the **insured** is legally liable;
2. Provide a defense at our expense by counsel of our choice. We may make any investigation and settlement of any claim or suit that we decide is appropriate. Our obligation to defend any claim or suit ends when the amount we pay for damages equals our limit of liability.

Additional Payments

We will pay the following in addition to our limits of liability, but our obligation for these payments ceases when our obligation to defend ends:

1. Expenses for first aid to others incurred by any **insured** for **bodily injury** covered under this policy. We will not pay for first aid to you or any other **insured;**
2. Expenses incurred by us and costs taxed against any **insured** in any suit we defend;
3. Premiums on bonds required in a suit defended by us, but not for bond amounts greater than the limit of liability provided by this policy. We will also pay up to $250 for the premium of any bail bond required of an **insured** because of an arrest in connection with an accident resulting from the use of an **insured vehicle.** We are not obligated to apply for or furnish any bond;
4. Reasonable expenses incurred by any **insured** at our request, including actual loss of earnings (but not loss of other income) up to $50 per day for assisting us in the investigation or defense of any claim or suit;
5. Interest on the entire judgment which accrues after entry of that part of the judgment which does not exceed the limit of liability that applies and before we pay, tender or deposit in court that part of the judgment, which does not exceed the limit of liability that applies.

COVERAGE P

Uninsured Motorist

See the back pages of this Section III entitled "Uninsured Motorist Coverage".

COVERAGE Q

Medical Payments

We will pay the necessary **medical** and funeral expenses incurred within three (3) years from the date of **occurrence** to each **insured** who sustains **bodily injury** caused by an **occurrence.**

The following are **insureds** under Coverage Q:

1. You or any person **occupying** an **insured vehicle** with your permission or the permission of an adult **relative** and sustaining **bodily injury** caused by an **occurrence** resulting from the use of this **insured vehicle;**

2. Your or your **relatives** sustaining **bodily injury** caused by an **occurrence** while **occupying** a **nonowned vehicle;**
3. Any person sustaining **bodily injury** while **occupying** a **nonowned vehicle,** if the **bodily injury** results from:
   a. Its operation by you or on your behalf by a private chauffeur or domestic servant;
   b. Its operation by a **relative.**
4. You and your **relatives** sustaining **bodily injury** while a pedestrian or a bicyclist when struck by a **motor vehicle** or **trailer.**

No payment shall be made under this coverage unless the person to or for whom such payment is made shall first execute a written agreement that the amount of the payment shall be applied toward the settlement of any claim, or the satisfaction of any judgment of damages entered in the person's favor against any **insured** because of **bodily injury** to which Coverage N or P of this policy applies. (This paragraph is not applicable if this policy is issued in Arizona.)

COVERAGE R

Fire and Theft Only

We will pay for any direct and accidental loss of, or damage to, your **insured vehicle** and its equipment caused by:

1. Fire, lightning or windstorm;
2. Smoke or smudge due to a sudden, unusual and faulty operation of any heating equipment serving the premises in which the vehicle is located;
3. The stranding, sinking, burning, collision or derailment of any conveyance in or upon which the vehicle is being transported; or
4. Theft.

If Coverage R applies to your **insured vehicle,** it will also extend to a **nonowned vehicle.**

COVERAGE S

Comprehensive

We will pay for any direct and accidental loss of, or damage to, your **insured vehicle** and its equipment not caused by collision or rollover. Loss or damage from missiles, falling objects, theft, collision with animals, or accidental glass breakage are comprehensive losses.

If Coverage S applies to your **insured vehicle,** it will also extend to a **nonowned vehicle.**

COVERAGE T

Collision and Roll Over

We will pay for direct and accidental loss to your **insured vehicle** and its equipment when it is hit by or hits another vehicle, or object, or rolls over. We will waive any applicable deductible if the collision involves **insured vehicles** of two or more of our policyholders. If Coverage T applies to your **insured vehicle,** it will also extend to a **nonowned vehicle.**

Additional Payments

1. **Loss to Luggage.**
   If as a result of other loss covered under Coverages R, S or T, damage results to clothing or personal luggage, including contents of the luggage being transported by the **insured vehicle,** we will pay up to $200 for this loss. Exclusion 13 does not apply to this coverage.
2. **Loss of Use by Theft—Reimbursement.**
   Following a theft of an **insured vehicle** covered under Coverage R or S, we will reimburse you for expenses up to $25 a day to a maximum of $500 incurred for the rental of a substitute automobile including taxi cabs. This reimbursement is limited to such expense incurred during the period commencing 48 hours after the theft has been reported to us and the police, and terminating, regardless of expiration of the policy period, on the date the automobile is returned to you and on such earlier date as we make or offer settlement for this theft.

EXCLUSIONS APPLICABLE TO SECTION III

Section III does not cover:

1. Any **insured** while using any vehicle to carry persons for a fee. This exclusion does not apply to a share-the-expense car pool;
2. Any **insured** for any vehicle rented or leased to others;
3. Any **insured** while using any vehicle in a pre-arranged race, speed contest, or other competition, or preparation for any of these activities;
4. Any damages which are intentionally caused by any **insured;**
5. Any **nonowned vehicle** while an **insured** is using it in the business of selling, repairing, servicing, storing or parking **motor vehicles,** including road testing and delivery;
6. Any damage caused by nuclear reaction, radiation, or radioactive contamination;
7. Any radar or similar detection device; any device or instrument designed for the recording, reproduction, amplification, receiving, or transmitting of sound, radio waves, microwaves, or television signals; or tapes, records, or other discs designed for use with this equipment. This exclusion does not apply to a device or instrument if it is permanently installed in the dash or console opening;
8. Damages caused by declared or undeclared war, invasion, insurrection, civil war, other assumption of power, or confiscation by a duly constituted governmental or civil authority;
9. Exemplary or punitive damages;
10. **Bodily injury** to anyone eligible to receive benefits which an **insured** either provides or is required to provide under any worker's compensation or occupational disease law;
11. Any damages arising out of the ownership, maintenance or use of any type of emergency vehicle; gas, oil, or newspaper delivery truck; logging truck; or any non-farm commercial truck;
12. Under Coverage N, **bodily injury** sustained by:

   a. You;
   b. The operator of the **insured vehicle,** or the residents of the operator's household who are related to the operator by blood, marriage or adoption, including a ward or foster child.
13. Under Coverage N, damage to property owned or transported by any **insured;**
14. Under Coverage N, damage to property rented to, used by, or in the care, custody or control of an **insured.** This exclusion does not apply to **property damage** to a residence or private garage rented to an **insured;**
15. Under Coverages N, and P, liability arising out of any contract or agreement;
16. Under Coverage Q, **bodily injury** sustained while an **insured vehicle** is used as a residence or temporary living quarters;
17. Under Coverage Q, **bodily injury** sustained by a person engaged in the maintenance or repair of an **insured vehicle;**
18. Under Coverage Q, **bodily injury** to anyone eligible to receive benefits under any:
   a. Automobile or premises insurance affording benefits for medical expenses;
   b. Worker's compensation, disability benefits or similar law;
   c. National, state or other governmental plan.
19. Under Coverages R, S and T, any loss by collapse, explosion or implosion of any tank or container;
20. Under Coverages R, S and T, any equipment or accessories contained in a motorhome, camper unit or trailer unless the equipment or accessories are built in and form a permanent part of the vehicle;
21. Under Coverages, R, S and T, loss caused by recall of an **insured vehicle;**
22. Tires, unless damaged concurrent with other loss covered under Coverages R, S, or T;
23. Damages caused by wear and tear, freezing, mechanical or electrical breakdown or failure other than burning of wiring, unless the damage results from other loss covered under Coverages R, S, or T.

CONDITIONS APPLICABLE TO SECTION III

1. **Out of State Insurance.** If you have liability insurance under this policy and if you are traveling in a state or province which has a compulsory insurance, financial responsibility, or similar law affecting nonresidents, we will automatically provide the legally required minimum amounts and types of coverages if your policy does not already provide these coverages, or the limits stated in the Declarations whichever are greater, with respect to the operation or use of the insured vehicle in that state or province. The required coverage, however, will be excess over any other collectible insurance.
2. **Two or More Vehicles.** When two or more vehicles are covered by this policy, the policy terms will apply separately to each. A vehicle, however, and an attached **trailer** will be considered one vehicle under Coverages N, P and Q and separate vehicles under Coverages R, S and T; any deductible will be applied to each vehicle.

The maximum limits of liability set forth in Paragraphs 3 and 10 of these conditions shall not be increased in any way by this paragraph.

3. **Other Vehicle Insurance in the Company.** If this policy and any other vehicle insurance policy issued to you by this company apply to the same **occurrence,** the maximum limit of our liability under all of the policies will not exceed the highest applicable limit of liability under any one policy. This is the most we will pay regardless of the number of **insureds,** claims made, **insured vehicles** or premiums.
4. **Duties after Loss.** In case of an accident or **occurrence,** the **insured** shall perform the following duties:
   a. Give written notice to us or our agent as soon as practicable, which sets forth:
      (1) The identity of the policy and **insured;**
      (2) Reasonably available information on the time, place and circumstances of the accident or **occurrence;**
      (3) Names and addresses of any claimants and witnesses;
   b. Immediately forward to us every notice, demand, summons or other process relating to the accident or **occurrence;**
   c. At our request, assist in:
      (1) Making settlement;
      (2) The enforcement of any right of contribution or indemnity against any person or organization who may be liable to any **insured;**
      (3) The conduct of suits and attend hearings and trials;
      (4) Securing and giving evidence and obtaining the attendance of witnesses.
   d. The **insured** shall not, except at the **insured's** own cost, voluntarily make any payment, assume any obligation or incur any expense other than for first aid to others at the time of the **occurrence.**
5. **Duties after Loss—Coverages R, S, and T.** In the case of the loss to which this insurance applies, you shall perform the following duties:
   a. Give written notice to us or our agent, as soon as practicable, and also give notice to the police if loss is suspected to be in violation of a law;
   b. Protect the property from further damage, make reasonable and necessary repairs required to protect the property and keep an accurate record of repair expenditures. If you fail to do these things, further damage is not insured under this policy;
   c. Prepare an inventory of damaged property showing in detail, the quantity, description, actual cash value and amount of loss. Attach to the inventory all bills, receipts, and related documents that substantiate the figures in the inventory;
   d. As often as we may reasonably require, exhibit the damaged property and submit to examination under oath and subscribe the same;
   e. Within sixty (60) days after our request, submit to us your signed, sworn statement of loss which sets forth the following information to the best of your knowledge and belief:
      (1) The time and cause of loss;
      (2) The interest of the **insured** and all others in the **insured vehicle** involved and all encumbrances on the **insured vehicle;**

(3) Other insurance which may cover the loss;
(4) Changes in title of the **insured vehicle** during the term of the policy.

6. **Duties of an Injured Person—Coverages P and Q.** The injured person or someone acting on behalf of the injured person shall:
   a. Give us a written proof of claim, under oath if required, as soon as practicable;
   b. Execute authorization to allow us to obtain copies of medical reports and records; and
   c. The injured person shall submit to physical examination by a physician selected by us when and as often as we reasonably require.
7. **Cooperation of Insured.** If any **insured** fails to cooperate or send us legal papers as required, we have the right to refuse any further protection for the **occurrence** or loss.
8. **Territory.** This policy applies only to **occurrences** within the United States of America and Canada. Section III Coverages are extended for trips into that part of the Republic of Mexico lying not more than 100 miles from the nearest boundary line of the United States of America. If applicable to your insured vehicle, our liability for Coverages R, S and T will be determined on the basis of cost at the nearest United States point.

   WARNING: Automobile accidents in the Republic of Mexico are considered a criminal offense, rather than a civil matter. The insurance provided by this policy will not meet the Mexican automobile insurance requirements. If you are in an automobile accident in Mexico and have not purchased insurance through a licensed Mexican insurance company you may be jailed and may have your automobile impounded.
9. **Payment of Claim.** Any payment under Section III is not an admission of liability by any **insured** or us.
10. **Limits of Liability.** Regardless of the number of:
    (a) **insureds** or vehicles insured under this policy,
    (b) persons or organizations sustaining **bodily injury** or **property damage,** or
    (c) claims made,

    our liability for each **occurrence** is subject to the following limitations:
    a. Our total combined single limit of liability under Coverage N for all **bodily injury** and **property damage** resulting from any one **occurrence,** shall not exceed the applicable limit of liability stated in the Declarations.
    b. Under Coverage Q the **medical** limit for each person is our limit of liability for all expenses incurred by or on behalf of each person who sustains **bodily injury** resulting from an **occurrence.**
    c. Under Coverages R, S, and T, our limit of liability will be the actual cash value of the stolen or damaged property at the time of loss. If the loss is a part of that stolen or damaged property, we will pay the actual cash value of that part at the time of loss or what it would cost to repair or replace the part with like kind and quality.
11. We will apply the combined single limit of liability to provide any separate limits required by law for **bodily injury** or **property damage.** This provision, however, will not increase our total limit of liability.

12. **Other Insurance.** The insurance under Section III is excess over any other valid and collectible insurance except insurance written specifically to cover as excess over the limits of liability that apply in this policy.
13. **Loss Payable Clause.** This clause is applicable only if a lienholder is named in the Declarations.
    a. We will pay you and the lienholder named in the policy for loss to an **insured vehicle,** as interest may appear.
    b. Section III covers the interest of the lienholder unless the loss results from fraudulent acts or omissions on your part.
    c. We may cancel the policy during the policy period. Notice of cancellation shall be mailed to the lienholder at least ten (10) days before the date the cancellation takes effect.
    d. If we make any payment to the lienholder, we will obtain his rights against any other party.

COVERAGE P

Uninsured Motorist Coverage

We will pay damages which an **insured** is legally entitled to recover from the owner or operator of an **uninsured motor vehicle** because of **bodily injury** sustained by an **insured** and caused by an **occurrence.** The owner's or operator's liability for these damages must arise from the ownership, maintenance or use of the **uninsured motor vehicle.**

The following additional definitions apply to Coverage P:

1. **Insured** means:
    a. You and any **relative;**
    b. Anyone occupying an **insured vehicle;** or
    c. Anyone **occupying** a **nonowned vehicle** while operated by you or any **relative.**
2. **Uninsured motor vehicle** means a **motor vehicle** or **trailer:**
    a. To which a **bodily injury** liability bond or policy does not apply at the time of the **occurrence;**
    b. For which an insuring or bonding company denies coverage or is or becomes insolvent; or
    c. Which is a hit-and-run vehicle and neither the driver nor the owner can be identified. The hit-and-run vehicle must hit an **insured,** and **insured vehicle** or a vehicle which an **insured** is **occupying;**
    d. Which is insured by a **bodily injury** liability bond or policy at the time of the **occurrence** but its limit of **bodily injury** liability is less than the minimum limit for **bodily injury** specified by the financial responsibility law of the state in which your **insured vehicle** is principally garaged.
3. An **uninsured motor vehicle** does not include any **motor vehicle** or **trailer:**
    a. Owned by any governmental unit or agency; (Not applicable if this policy is issued in Arizona.)
    b. Designed for use mainly off public roads while not on public roads;
    c. Used as a residence;
    d. Owned by or furnished for the regular use of you or any **relative;** or
    e. Which is an **insured vehicle.**

Exclusions

In addition to the general exclusions of Section III, the following exclusions apply to Coverage P. Coverage P does not apply to:

1. **Bodily injury** sustained by any **insured** while **occupying** a **motor vehicle** or **trailer** without the permission of the owner.
2. The direct or indirect benefit of any insurer or self-insured under any worker's compensation, disability benefits or similar law.

Conditions

In addition to the general conditions applicable to Section III, the following conditions apply to Coverage P only.

1. **Limits of Liability.**
   Our total limit of liability under Coverage P for all **bodily injury** resulting from one **occurrence** shall not exceed the applicable limit of liability stated in the Declarations.
2. **Non-stacking of Limits.**
   Regardless of the number of **insured vehicles, insureds,** policies of insurance with us, claims made or vehicles involved in the **occurrence,** the most we will pay for all damages resulting from any **occurrence** is the limit of liability shown in the Declarations subject to reduction as outlined in the next paragraph.
3. **Reduction of Amounts Payable.** Amounts payable for damages under Coverage P will be reduced by:
   a. All sums paid by or on behalf of persons or organizations who may be legally responsible for the **bodily injury** to which this coverage applies. This includes all amounts paid under the liability coverage of this or any other policy;
   b. The sum of all amounts payable under any worker's compensation, disability, or similar law;
   c. All sums paid under medical payments or death benefits coverages of any policy issued by us. Any payment under this coverage to or for an **insured** will reduce any amount that person is entitled to receive under this policy's liability coverages.
4. **Hit-and-run Accident.** At our request, the **insured** shall make available for inspection any **motor vehicle** or **trailer** which the **insured** occupied at the time of a hit-and-run accident. The **insured** must notify the police within twenty-four (24) hours of a hit-and-run accident.
5. **Arbitration.**
   a. If we and an **insured** disagree whether the **insured** is legally entitled to recover damages from the owner or driver of an **insured motor vehicle** or do not agree as to the amount of damages, either party may make a written demand for arbitration. In the event, each party will select an arbitrator. The two arbitrators will select a third. If they cannot agree upon a third arbitrator within thirty (30) days, either may request that selection be made by a judge of a court having jurisdiction. Each party will pay the expenses it incurs and bear the expenses of the third arbitrator equally.
   b. Unless both parties agree otherwise, arbitration will take place in the county in which the **insured** lives. Local rules of law as to arbitration

procedure and evidence will apply. A decision agreed to by two of the arbitrators will be binding.

6. **Trust Agreement.** If a claim or payment is made under this coverage:
   a. We will be entitled to reimbursement of payments we have made to an **insured** to be taken from the proceeds of any judgment or settlement;
   b. An **insured** will hold in trust all rights or recovery for us against any person or organization. That person will also do whatever is proper to secure those rights and do nothing after the loss to prejudice any rights of recovery;
   c. If we make the request in writing, the **insured** must take any necessary or appropriate action to recover damages from any other person or organization through any representative we designate. Any action may be taken in the **insured's** name and in the event of recovery, we will be reimbursed for any expenses, costs, and attorney fees we incur; and
   d. The **insured** must execute and deliver any document to us that may be appropriate for the purpose of securing the rights and obligations for the **insured** and for us as established by this provision.
7. **Payment of loss.** We have the option to pay any amount due under this coverage as follows:
   a. To the **insured;**
   b. If the **insured** is deceased, to the **insured's** surviving spouse; or
   c. To a person authorized by law to receive such payment, or to a person who is legally entitled to recover the damages which the payment represents.
8. **Nonbinding Judgments.** No judgment resulting from a suit brought without our written consent is binding on us, either in determining the liability of the **uninsured motor vehicle** operator or owner or the amount of damages to which the **insured** is entitled.

ENDORSEMENTS APPLICABLE TO SECTION III

Each of the following endorsements may be purchased by your payment of an additional premium. All policy provisions apply to these endorsements unless an endorsement specifically states otherwise. **An endorsement applies only when it is listed in the Declarations, and you pay this premium.**

No. 323 Drive Other Car.

Coverage N of Section III is amended to cover you while you are operating a **motor vehicle** that does not qualify as a **nonowned vehicle,** provided you have the permission of the owner of the vehicle. This endorsement does not cover a **motor vehicle:**

1. Owned in whole or in part by you or any **relative;**
2. Registered in your name or in the name of any **relative;**
3. Used in transporting persons or property for hire.

This endorsement shall not cover the owner of the **motor vehicle** you are driving.

No. 334 Emergency Road Service.

We will pay for reasonable and necessary towing and labor expense, but not to exceed $40, caused by the disablement of your **insured vehicle,** provided the expense is incurred at the place of disablement. No deductible applies to this coverage.

No. 335 Additional Living Expense.

If loss exceeds the applicable deductible to your **insured vehicle** we will pay for your reasonable and necessary additional living expense incurred as a result of the disablement of your vehicle due to loss covered under Coverages S or T. The maximum we will pay for this additional living expense is $75 per day up to a maximum of $300 per disablement. The loss must occur more than 100 miles from the place of principal garaging for this additional living expense coverage to apply. No deductible applies to this coverage.

No. 368 Car Rental Reimbursement.

If a loss exceeds the applicable deductible to the **insured vehicle** under Coverages S or T, we agree to reimburse you for:

1. The expense incurred by you for the rental fee (excluding all other charges) of a substitute automobile from a car rental agency or garage; or
2. The expense incurred by you for taxicabs during a period starting at 12:01 a.m. on the date following:
   a. The date of loss if as a direct result of this loss the **insured vehicle** cannot be operated under its own power; or
   b. If the **insured vehicle** is operable, the date you authorize repairs and deliver the vehicle to the repair shop.

   In no event, however, shall we be liable for more than $25 per day to a maximum of $500 for taxicab or for rental fees.

Regardless of the policy period, our liability for taxicab or rental fees shall end on the earliest of the following:

1. Upon completion of repair or replacement of property lost or damaged;
2. Upon such date as we make or tender settlement for the loss or damage.

This coverage shall not apply in the event of a theft of the **insured vehicle** for which reimbursement of transportation expense is provided elsewhere in this policy.

No 303 Underinsured Motorist Coverage

Coverage P is changed to include Underinsured Motorist Coverage.

We will pay damages which an **insured** is legally entitled to recover from the owner or operator of an **underinsured motor vehicle** because of **bodily injury** sustained by an **insured** and caused by an **occurrence.** The owner's or operator's liability for these damages must arise from the ownership, maintenance or use of the **underinsured motor vehicle.**

The following additional definitions apply to Coverage P:

1. **Insured** means:
   a. You and any **relative;**
   b. Anyone **occupying** an **insured vehicle;** or
   c. Anyone **occupying** a **nonowned vehicle** while operated by you or any **relative.**
2. **Underinsured motor vehicle** means a **motor vehicle** or **trailer** for which the sum of all liability bonds or policies applicable to an **occurrence** is less than the amount of damages an **insured sustains** because of **bodily injury** caused by that **occurrence.**

3. An **underinsured motor vehicle** does not include any **motor vehicle** or **trailer:**
   a. Owned or operated by a self-insured as defined by any applicable **motor vehicle** law; (Not applicable if this policy is issued in Arizona).
   b. Owned by any governmental unit or agency;
   c. Designed for use mainly off public roads while not on public roads;
   d. Used as a residence;
   e. Owned by you or any **relative,** or furnished or available for regular use by you or any **relative;**
   f. Which is an **insured vehicle;**
   g. Which is insured by a **bodily injury** liability bond or policy at the time of the **occurrence** but its limit of **bodily injury** liability is less than the minimum limit for **bodily injury** specified by the financial responsibility law of the state in which your **insured vehicle** is principally garaged.

Exclusions:

In addition to the general exclusions of Section III, the following exclusions apply to Coverage P. Coverage P does not apply to:

1. **Bodily injury** sustained by any **insured** while **occupying** a **motor vehicle** or **trailer** without the permission of the owner.
2. The direct or indirect benefit of any insurer or self-insured under any worker's compensation, disability benefits or similar law.

Conditions:

In addition to the general conditions applicable to Section III, the following conditions apply to Coverage P only.

1. **Limits of Liability.**
   Our total limit of liability Coverage P for all **bodily injury** resulting from one **occurrence** shall not exceed the applicable limit of liability stated in the Declarations.
2. **Non-stacking of Limits.**
   Regardless of the number of **insured vehicles, insureds,** policies of insurance with us, claims made or vehicles involved in the **occurrence,** the most we will pay for all damages resulting from any **occurrence** is the limit of liability shown in the Declarations subject to reduction as outlined in the next paragraph.
3. **Reduction of Amounts Payable.** Amounts payable for damages under Coverage P will be reduced by:
   a. The sum of all amounts payable under any worker's compensation, disability, or similar law;
   b. All sums paid under medical payments or death benefits coverages of any policy issued by us.

   Any payment under this coverage to or for an **insured** will reduce any amount that person is entitled to receive under this policy's liability coverages.
4. **Hit-and-run Accident.** At our request, the **insured** shall make available for inspection any **motor vehicle** or **trailer** which the **insured** occupied at the time of a hit-and-run accident. The **insured** must notify the police within twenty-four (24) hours of a hit-and-run accident.
5. **Arbitration.**

- **a.** If we and an **insured** disagree whether the **insured** is legally entitled to recover damages from the owner or driver of an **underinsured motor vehicle** or do not agree as to the amount of damages, either party may make a written demand for arbitration. In this event, each party will select an arbitrator. The two arbitrators will select a third. If they cannot agree upon a third arbitrator within thirty (30) days, either may request that selection be made by a judge of a court having jurisdiction. Each party will pay the expenses it incurs and bear the expenses of the third arbitrator equally;
- **b.** Unless both parties agree otherwise, arbitration will take place in the county in which the **insured** lives. Local rules of law as to arbitration procedure and evidence will apply. A decision agreed to by two of the arbitrators will be binding.

6. **Trust Agreement.** If a claim or payment is made under this coverage:
   - **a.** We will be entitled to reimbursement of payments we have made to an **insured** to be taken from the proceeds of any judgment or settlement;
   - **b.** An **insured** will hold in trust all rights of recovery for us against any person or organization. That person will also do whatever is proper to secure those rights and do nothing after the loss to prejudice any rights of recovery;
   - **c.** If we make the request in writing, the **insured** must take any necessary or appropriate action to recover damages from any other person or organization through any representative we designate. Any action may be taken in the **insured's** name and in the event of recovery, we will be reimbursed for any expenses, costs, and attorney fees we incur; and
   - **d.** The **insured** must execute and deliver any document to us that may be appropriate for the purpose of securing the rights and obligations for the **insured** and for us as established by this provision.
7. **Payment of Loss.** We will pay only after all liability bonds or policies applicable to the **occurrence** have been exhausted by judgments or payments. We have the option to pay any amount due under this coverage as follows:
   - **a.** To the **insured;**
   - **b.** If the **insured** is deceased, to the **insured's** surviving spouse;
   - **c.** To a person authorized by law to receive such payment, or to a person who is legally entitled to recover the damages which the payment represents.
8. **Nonbinding Judgments.** No judgment resulting from a suit brought without our written consent is binding on us, either in determining the liability of the **underinsured motor vehicle** operator or owner or the amount of damages to which the **insured** is entitled.

SECTION IV—INLAND MARINE

The coverage under this section applies as indicated by endorsements attached to and listed in the Declarations. All policy provisions apply to these endorsements unless an endorsement specifically states otherwise.

CONDITIONS APPLICABLE TO SECTION IV

1. **Your Duty after Loss.** In case of a loss to which this insurance may apply, you must see that the following duties are performed:
   a. Give written notice to us or our agent, as soon as practicable, and also give notice to the police if loss is suspected to be in violation of a law;
   b. Protect the property from further damage, make reasonable and necessary repairs required to protect the property and keep an accurate record of repair expenditures;
   c. Prepare an inventory of damaged property showing in detail the quantity, description, actual cash value and amount of loss. Attach to the inventory all bills, receipts, and related documents that substantiate the figures in the inventory;
   d. As often as we may reasonably require, exhibit the damaged property and submit to examination under oath and subscribe the same;
   e. Within sixty (60) days after our request, submit to us your signed, sworn statement of loss which sets forth the following information to the best of your knowledge and belief:
      (1) The time and cause of loss;
      (2) The interest of the **insured** and all others in the property involved and all encumbrances on the property;
      (3) Other insurance which may cover the loss;
      (4) Changes in title during the term of the policy;
      (5) Specifications of any damaged property and detailed estimates for repair of the damage;
      (6) An inventory of damaged property as described above.
2. **Loss to a Pair or Set.** In case of a loss to a pair or set, we may elect to:
   a. Repair or replace any part of or restore the pair or set to its value before the loss; or
   b. Pay the difference between the actual cash value of the property before and after the loss.
3. **Valuation.** We shall not be liable beyond the actual cash value of the property at the time of any loss or the applicable endorsement limit, whichever is less. In no event shall we be liable for more than what it would cost to repair or replace the property with material of like kind and quality.
4. **Other Insurance.** The insurance under Section IV is excess over any other valid and collectible insurance except insurance written specifically to cover as excess over the limits of liability that apply in this policy.

Special State Provision

Our state of location as stated in the Declarations will determine which of the following special provisions apply to your policy. Read the provisions following the applicable state heading to determine which paragraphs apply to you.

1. **Arizona**
   A. **Cancellation Sections I, II and IV**
   You may cancel Sections I, II and IV of this policy at any time by returning it to us or by notifying us in writing of the date cancellation takes effect. The date of cancellation must not be earlier than the date

you mail or deliver notice to us. If you cancel, the refund premium, if any, will be computed in accordance with the customary short rate tables and procedures.

We may cancel this policy only for the reasons stated in this condition by notifying you in writing of the date cancellation takes effect. This cancellation must be mailed to you at your last mailing address known by us. Proof of mailing will be sufficient proof of notice.

(1) When you have not paid the premium, whether payable to us or to our agent, we may cancel at any time by notifying you at least ten (10) days before the date cancellation takes effect.

(2) When this policy has been in effect for less than sixty (60) days and is not a renewal with us, we may cancel for any reason by notifying you at least ten (10) days before the date cancellation takes effect.

(3) When this policy has been in effect for sixty (60) days or more, or at any time if it is a renewal with us, we may cancel:

(a) If there has been a material misrepresentation of fact which if known to us would have caused us not to issue the policy, or

(b) If the risk has changed substantially since the policy was issued. This can be done by notifying you at least ten (10) days before the date cancellation takes effect.

(c) **Non-renewal.** We may elect not to renew Sections I, II and IV of this policy. We must do so by mailing written notice to you at least thirty (30) days before the expiration date of this policy. This notice will be sent to your last mailing address known by us. Proof of mailing will be sufficient proof of notice.

(4) When this policy is cancelled, the premium for the period from the date of cancellation to the expiration date will be refunded to you.

If the return premium is not refunded with the notice of cancellation of when this policy is returned to us, we will refund it within a reasonable time after the cancellation takes effect.

If we cancel, the refund premium, if any, will be computed on a pro-rata basis.

B. Cancellation Section III

You may cancel Section III of this policy by returning it to us or by written notice mailed or delivered to us. The notice must give us the date to cancel which must not be earlier than the date you mail or deliver it to us.

We may cancel by mailing a notice of cancellation or termination to you at the address shown in the Declarations or by delivery of the notice. The notice will give the date the cancellation is effective. It will be mailed to you at least ten (10) days before the cancellation effective date.

Proof of mailing a notice is proof of notice.

If you cancel, the refund of premium, if any, will be computed in accordance with customary short rate tables and procedures. If we cancel, the refund, if any, will be computed on a pro rata basis. Any unearned premium may be returned at the time of cancellation or within a reasonable time thereafter. Delay in the return of unearned premium does not effect the cancellation.

The policy will automatically terminate at the end of the policy period if you or your representative do not accept our offer to renew or continue it. Your failure to pay the required renewal or continuation premium by the renewal or continuation date means that you have declined our offer.

If you obtain other insurance on your covered auto, any similar insurance provided by this policy will terminate as to that auto on the effective date of other insurance.

After this policy has been in effect for sixty (60) days, or if it is a renewal, we will not cancel or decline renewal unless:

a. You fail to pay the premium when it is due;

b. The policy was obtained through fraudulent misrepresentation;

c. You or any other person who regularly drives the auto have:

- **(1)** Had his or her driver's license suspended or revoked during the policy period;
- **(2)** Become permanently disabled either mentally or physically, and do not submit a doctor's certificate testifying to his or her ability to drive;
- **(3)** Been convicted during the three years just before the effective date of the policy or during the policy period of:
  - **(a)** Criminal negligence resulting in death, homicide or assault in connection with the use of a motor vehicle.
  - **(b)** Driving while under the influence of alcohol or drugs.
  - **(c)** Leaving the scene of an accident.
  - **(d)** Reckless driving, or
  - **(e)** Lying to obtain a driver's license.

Even if this policy has been in effect for sixty (60) days or if it is a renewal, we retain unlimited right to cancel if:

a. This policy insures four or more autos;

b. The auto is used in the auto business.

c. The auto is available to the public for hire or is rented to others; or

d. The auto insured has a load capacity of 1,500 pounds or more.

Grace Period. A grace period of seven (7) days is allowed for the payment of premium due except the first. An initial payment on the renewal of a policy is not a first payment of premium.

If the premium due is not received by the end of the grace period, a cancellation notice will be mailed to you at the address shown in the Declarations. The cancellation will be effective on the date the notice is mailed to you.

2. New Mexico

Cancellation. You may cancel this entire policy by mailing to us written notice stating when this cancellation shall be effective. We may change or cancel this entire policy or any portion of it, by mailing it to you at the address shown in the Declarations, written notice stating when not less than ten (10) days thereafter the change or cancellation shall be effective. Payment or tender of unearned premium is not a condition of cancellation. The mailing of notice shall be sufficient proof of notice and the effective date and hour of cancellation stated in the notice shall become the end of the policy period. Delivery of this written notice, either by you or by us shall be equivalent to mailing.

If you cancel, earned premiums shall be computed according to our customary short rate table and procedure. If we cancel, earned premiums shall be computed pro rata. Premium adjustment may be made at this time or as soon after as is practical. Our check mailed or delivered shall be sufficient tender of any refund of premium.

SECTION V
YOUR PERSONAL AND/OR FARM AND RANCH UMBRELLA

QUICK REFERENCE
Beginning on Page

PERSONAL AND/OR FARM AND RANCH UMBRELLA

AGREEMENT

We provide the insurance under Section V in return for the premium and compliance with its provisions.

PART I DEFINITIONS

In this section, you and your mean the named **insured** in the Declarations and spouse if a resident of your household. We, us and our mean the Company providing this insurance. Other words are defined as follows:

1. **Aircraft** means any heavier-than-air or lighter-than-air vehicle designed to transport persons or property.
2. **Automobile** means a land motor vehicle, trailer or semi-trailer.
3. **Business** includes any trade, profession, or occupation, other than farming.
4. **Damages** means the total of:
   - **a.** **damages** you must pay (legally or by agreement with our written consent) because of **personal injury** or **property damage** covered by this section; and
   - **b.** reasonable expense you incur in the investigation, defense and settlement of a claim or suit because of **personal injury** or **property damage** covered by this policy, except salaries of your regular employees and expenses payable under the Limits of Liability.
5. **Insured** means:

   When the **insured,** as stated in the Declaration page, is an individual, the **insured** means you and the following residents of your household:
   - **a.** your relatives;
   - **b.** a person under the age of 21 in the care of you or your relatives.

   When the **insured,** as stated in the Declarations page, is a partnership, the **insured** means any partner, but only with respect to his or her liability as such.

   When the **insured,** as stated in the Declarations page, is a corporation, the **insured** means any executive officer, director or stockholder, but only while acting within the scope of his or her duties as such.

   Also, any other person or organization who is an **insured** under Sections II or III of this policy or any policy of underlying insurance stated in the Declarations, subject to all the limitations upon coverage under such section or policy other than the limits of the underlying insurer's liability; but as respects **automobiles** and **watercraft,** only as stated below:
   - **a.** a person using an **automobile** or **watercraft** (with specific permission or reasonable belief that the person has such permission) owned by, loaned to or hired for use by you or on your behalf;
   - **b.** an **insured** using other **automobiles** or **watercraft** (with specific permission of an adult member of the insured's household or reasonable belief that the person has that permission) not owned by or furnished for their regular use.

   The following are not **insured's:**
   - **a.** the owner or lessee (or their agents or employees) of an **automobile** or **watercraft** loaned to or hired for use by you;
   - **b.** any person (not the **insured**) using **automobiles** or **watercraft** while employed or engaged in the **business** of selling, servicing, repairing, maintaining, parking, docking, mooring, or storing of such **automobiles** or **watercraft,** and any person (not the **insured**) or organization as respects acts or omissions of any person employed in or any person engaged in such stated **business.**

This insurance does not apply to **personal injury** or **property damage** arising out of any corporation, partnership or joint venture, of which you are a partner or member, and which is not named in this Section as an **insured.**

6. **Mobile Equipment:** a land vehicle, including machinery attached, which is:
   - **a.** not subject to motor vehicle registration;
   - **b.** used exclusively on premises owned or rented by the **insured;**
   - **c.** designed and used principally off public roads;
   - **d.** designed and maintained for the sole purpose of affording mobility to equipment which is an integral part of or permanently attached to the vehicle;
   - **e.** a farm tractor, trailer or its equipment, or other specialized equipment such as bulldozers, graders, generators, compressors, cranes, diggers, or other similar equipment.
7. **Occurrence:** an accident including the continuous or repeated exposure to conditions, during the **policy term,** which results in **personal injury** or **property damage** neither expected nor intended by you.
8. **Personal Injury:** includes:
   - **a.** mental, or bodily injury, shock, sickness or disease;
   - **b.** injury arising out of:
     - **(1)** false arrest, detention or imprisonment, malicious prosecution;
     - **(2)** libel, slander, defamation, humiliation, or a publication or utterance in violation of a person's rights of privacy;
     - **(3)** wrongful entry or eviction, or other invasion of the right of private occupancy;
     - **(4)** racial or religious discrimination (unless coverage is prohibited by law) committed by or at your direction, but only with respect to the liability (other than fines or penalties) imposed by law.
   - **c.** the care, loss of services or death resulting from **personal injury.**
9. **Policy Term:** the number of calendar months stated in the Declarations page. It begins at 12:01 a.m. Standard time, at the place where you reside on the effective date stated in the Declarations page.
10. **Primary Insurance:** any insurance collectible by you which covers your liability for **personal injury** or **property damage.** This includes Sections II or III or any other policy described in the Declarations page.
11. **Property Damage:** physical damage to or destruction of tangible property. This includes the loss of use of that property.
12. **Professional Liability: damages** because of injury arising out of malpractice, error or mistake of you or of a person for whose acts or omissions you are legally responsible while rendering or failing to render professional services.
13. **Recreational Vehicles:** any motorized land vehicle designed for recreational use off public roads. This includes (but is not limited to) the following: a golf cart, snowmobile, trail bike, moped, dune buggy, all-terrain vehicle or motorcycle.
14. **Retained Limit:** the limit stated in the Declarations page. This limit applies if the underlying policy or policies described in the Declarations page and the amounts of any other **primary insurance** collectible by you do not provide coverage.

15. **Underlying Limit:** the total of the applicable limits of insurance of the type of policy or policies described in the Declarations page. This includes the amounts of any other insurance collectible by you.
16. Watercraft: a craft, vessel, or vehicle designed mainly for the transportation of people or property on or over water.

PART II COVERAGES

1. **Personal Liability** - we will pay **damages** for which you become legally responsible due to **personal injury** or **property damage** caused by an **occurrence.**
   This coverage applies only to damages in excess of the underlying limit or the retained limit, whichever applies.
2. **Professional Liability** - we will pay **damages** for which you become legally responsible due to malpractice, error or omission.

PART III DEFENSE OF SUITS NOT COVERED BY OTHER INSURANCE

1. We will defend any suit seeking **damages** for **personal injury** or **property damages** covered by this section which are not payable under the terms of any **primary insurance** or under the terms of the underlying policy or policies described in the Declarations page.
2. We may investigate and settle any claim or suit we feel is appropriate.
3. We will pay costs taxed against you in a suit we defend.
4. We will pay interest accruing after a judgment is entered in a suit we defend. Our duty to pay interest ends when we offer to pay that part of any judgment which does not exceed our liability limit.
5. We will pay premiums on bonds required in a suit we defend. The bond amounts shall not exceed our liability limit. We pay the cost of bail bonds required of you because of an accident or traffic violation. We are not required to apply for or furnish bonds.
6. We will pay reasonable expenses that you incur at our request in assisting us in the investigation or defense of a claim or suit. Expenses include actual loss of earnings (not other income) up to $50 a day.

We pay any such amounts incurred, other than the sums paid to actually settle **damages** claimed or sued for in addition to our liability limits, and you do not have to pay any part of them. However, you do have to promptly repay us any sums we paid to settle **damages** within your **retained limit.** If we are prevented by law or otherwise from carrying out this provision, we pay the amount incurred with our consent.

PART IV EXCLUSIONS

We do not cover:

1. **Personal injury** to a person eligible for payments voluntarily provided by you or required to be provided under a worker's compensation, non-occupational disability, or occupational disease law.
2. The ownership, maintenance, use, loading or unloading of any **aircraft** whether owned by you or not.
3. **Personal injury** to any of your employees unless such liability is covered by valid and collectible underlying employer's liability insurance as described in the schedule of underlying insurance, and then only for such hazards for which coverage is available under that policy.
4. Any claim arising out of an intentional act committed by or at your direction. This exclusion does not apply to **personal injury** resulting from a reasonable act committed to protect persons or property.
5. **Business** pursuits or **business** property that you have unless covered by valid and collectible underlying insurance, and then only for such hazards for which coverage is available under that policy.
6. **Professional liability** unless covered by valid and collectible underlying insurance described in the schedule of underlying insurance, and then only for such errors or omissions for which coverage is available under that policy.
7. The ownership, maintenance, use, loading or unloading of any **watercraft;**
   a. owned by or rented to you if the **watercraft** has inboard or inboard-outboard motor power of 50 or more horsepower or is a sailing vessel, with or without auxiliary power, 26 feet or more in overall length; or
   b. owned by or rented to you, if the **watercraft** is powered by one or more outboard motors with 50 or more horsepower.

   This exclusion does not apply:
   a. if, on the effective date of this policy, the **watercraft** is covered by **primary insurance;** or
   b. if we are informed within 30 days after acquisition and an additional premium is paid to us.
8. **Property damage** to:
   a. property that you own;
   b. any type of property that is rented to you, used or occupied by you, or in your care, custody or control.
9. **Personal injury** or **property damage** arising out of any substance released or discharged from an **aircraft** in connection with dusting, fertilizing or spraying operation. This exclusion applies if the spraying is done by you. It will also apply if it is done for you and you do not have underlying contingent crop-dusting coverage described in the Declarations of Underlying Insurance for this section.
10. Loss of use of tangible property which has not been physically injured or destroyed, resulting from:
    a. a delay in or lack of performance by you or on your behalf of any contract or agreement;
    b. the failure of your products or work performed by you or on your behalf, to meet the level of performance, quality, fitness and durability warranted or represented by you. However, this exclusion does not

apply to loss of use of other tangible property resulting from the sudden and accidental physical injury to or destruction of your products or work performed by you, or on your behalf, after such products or work have been put to use by any person or organization other than an insured.

11. **Damages** claimed for the withdrawal, inspection, repair, replacement or loss of use of your products or work completed by or for you, or for any property of which such products or work form a part, if such products, work or property are withdrawn from the market, or from use, because of any known or suspected defect or deficiency in them.
12. **Personal injury** or **property damage** arising out of the discharge, dispersal, release or escape of smoke, vapors, soot, fumes, acid, alkalis, toxic chemicals, liquids or gases, waste materials or other irritants, contaminants or pollutants into or upon land, the atmosphere or any water course or body of water.
13. **Property damage** to your products arising out of such products or any part of those products.
14. **Property damage** to work performed by you or on your behalf arising out of the work, or any portion of it, or out of materials, parts of equipment furnished in connection with them.
15. **Personal injury** or **property damage** for which an **insured** under this policy is also an **insured** under a nuclear energy liability policy or would be an **insured** but for its termination upon using up its limits of liability. A nuclear energy liability policy is a policy issued by Nuclear Energy Liability Insurance Association, Mutual Atomic Energy Liability Underwriters, Nuclear Insurance Association of Canada, or any of their successors.
16. **Personal injury** or **property damage** arising out of the ownership, maintenance, use, loading or unloading of any **automobile** or **watercraft** while being used in any:
    a. prearranged or organized racing, speed or demolition contest;
    b. any stunting activity; or
    c. in practice or preparation for such contest or activity.
17. **Personal injury** or **property damage** caused by or resulting from declared or undeclared war, civil war, insurrection, rebellion, revolution, warlike act by a military force or military personnel, destruction or seizure or use for any government purpose, and including any consequence of these. Discharge of a nuclear weapon is deemed a warlike act even if an accident.
18. **Personal injury** to any other person who qualifies as an **insured.**
19. **Personal injury** for which an **insured** person is legally entitled to recover from the owner or operator of an uninsured or underinsured **automobile.** This exclusion does not apply if uninsured or underinsured motorists coverages are in effect under your **automobile** policy for the required **underlying limits.**

PART V LIMITS OF LIABILITY

Regardless of the number of **insured,** claims or injured persons, the most we pay as **damages** resulting from one **occurence** shall not exceed the amount stated in the Declarations page, subject to the following:

1. This section pays only after the limits of the underlying insurance, and any other **primary insurance** covering the claim, have been paid by you or on your behalf.
2. If the underlying insurance terminates or the limits are less than shown in the Declarations page, we pay **damages** we would have paid if the **primary insurance** had not terminated or its limits lessened.
3. If the underlying insurer or any other primary insurer does not pay because of bankruptcy or insolvency or because you do not comply with the terms of the underlying or **primary insurance** after an **occurrence,** we pay **damages** only which exceed the required limits of underlying insurance.
4. If the underlying insurance or **primary insurance** does not cover an **occurrence** which results in **personal injury** or **property damage,** but the **occurrence** is covered by this section, we pay **damages** which exceed the **retained limit** as stated in the Declarations page.
5. If the underlying insurance or **primary insurance** is reduced or used up by payment of loss, we will pay **damages** over the lowered limits. This will apply only to those Sections and underlying policies that have an aggregate limit of liability.
6. The insurance provided by this section applies separately to each **insured;** however, this provision does not increase our liability limit for one **occurrence.**

PART VI UNDERLYING INSURANCE REQUIREMENT

This section requires that you have and maintain the types and limits of liability insurance shown in the Declarations page. This is referred to as the Maintenance of Underlying Insurance Requirement.

Failure to maintain the underlying insurance will not void the section. We will only be liable to the extent that we would have been liable if the underlying sections or policies had been maintained in force as required. You must make every effort to reinstate the aggregate limits of any underlying section or policy that has been reduced because of the payment of a claim.

PART VII WHAT TO DO IN CASE OF ACCIDENT OR LOSS

Duties after an **occurrence,** claim or suit: if an **occurrence** is likely to involve us under this section, you must promptly give written notice to advise us or our agent of:

1. how, when and where the **occurrence** took place, and
2. names and addresses of all the injured and all witnesses.

If information regarding a claim is received or legal action is begun, you must immediately send us a copy of every notice, demand, report, summons or other legal papers.

You must cooperate with us in the investigation, defense and settlement of a claim or suit.

PART VIII POLICY CONDITIONS

1. Defense settlement: Except as provided in the Defense of Suits Not Covered by Other Insurance Section, we are not required to take charge of the investigation, defense or settlement of a claim or suit. We have the right at any time to join you or your primary insurers in the investigation, defense or settlement of a claim or suit. If the **primary insurance** limit is paid, we have the option to defend a claim or suit. We may investigate and settle a claim or suit which we feel is appropriate.
2. Appeals: We may appeal a judgment in excess of the applicable **primary insurance** limit or the **retained limit.** We pay all costs, taxes, expenses and incidental interest. Our liability for **damages** does not exceed our liability limit for one **occurrence,** plus the cost and expense of the appeal.
3. Suits against us: No action may be brought against us unless the **insured** has complied with all terms of this section.
4. Other Insurance: This insurance is excess over other collectible insurance. This does not apply to insurance purchased in excess of the sum of the **primary insurance** limit and our liability limit.
5. Our right to recover: If payment is made by us, we will join the **insured** and any primary insurer in exercising the **insured's** rights to recovery against any party. The **insured** shall not prejudice such rights after loss.
6. Assignment: Your rights and duties under this section shall not be assigned without our written consent.
7. Change, Modification or Waiver of Section Terms: A waiver or change of any terms of this section must be issued by us in writing to be valid.

   If we adopt any revision of forms or endorsements during a section term which would broaden coverage under this section without additional premium, the broadened coverage will automatically apply to this section.
8. Misrepresentation, Concealment or Fraud: This entire section is void if, whether before or after a loss:
   - **a.** an **insured** has willfully concealed or misrepresented:
     - **(1)** any material fact of circumstance concerning this insurance; or
     - **(2)** an **insured's** interest in it.
   - **b.** there has been fraud or false swearing by an **insured** regarding any matter relating to this insurance or the subject of it.

   No misrepresentation or breach of affirmative warranty made by you (or on your behalf) in the negotiation of his policy affects our obligation unless:
   - **a.** we rely on it and it is either material or made with intent to deceive; or
   - **b.** the facts misrepresented or falsely warranted contribute to the loss.

   No failure of a condition prior to the loss and no breach of a promissory warranty affects our obligation under this section unless:
   - **a.** it exists at the time of the loss; and
   - **b.** it either increased the risk at the time of the loss or contributes to the loss.
9. Death of Named **Insured:** If you die while insured under this section, your protection passes to your legal representative or other persons having proper, temporary custody of covered property. However, that person or your legal representative is an **insured** only with respect to insurance

on covered property and legal liability arising out of that property. Any person who is an **insured** at the time of your death continues to be an **insured** while residing in your household.

10. Knowledge and Acts of Agents: Knowledge by our agents of any fact which breaches a condition of this section shall be our knowledge if:
   a. that fact is known to the agent at the time the section is issued or any application made; or
   b. it later becomes known to the agent in the course of his dealing as an agent with you.

   Any fact which breaches a condition of this section and is known to the agent prior to loss shall not void this section or defeat a recovery under this section in the event of loss.

11. Section Term and Territory: We cover **personal injury** and **property damage** which occurs anywhere in the world, but only if it occurs during the term of this section.

12. Premium and Renewal of Section. All premiums for this section shall be computed according to our rules, rates rating plans, premiums and minimum premiums applicable to the insurance provided you in this section. This section may be renewed for one or more terms:
   a. by mailing to you at your last known address shown in this section, a renewal premium notice for the applicable renewal term; or
   b. by issuing or offering to issue you a renewal section, certificate or other evidence of renewal at the applicable renewal premium.

   If you do not pay the premium, this section will terminate on the expiration date.

13. Cancellation:
   a. By You: You, or any other person named on the Declarations page, may cancel this section at any time by giving us written notice or returning the section to us. You must state when after that the cancellation is to be effective.
   b. By Us: We may cancel this section by written notice delivered to or mailed to you at the mailing address shown on the Declarations page. Proof of delivery or mailing is sufficient proof of notice.
   c. We refund premium for the unexpired term as follows:
      (1) if cancelled by us - on a pro-rata basis;
      (2) if cancelled by you - calculated in accordance with our short rate table.
   d. Time of Cancellation - The effective date of cancellation is the earliest of the following:
      (1) the effective date and hour of cancellation stated in any notice;
      (2) the time you surrender the section if no cancellation date was stated; or
      (3) the expiration of the term of this section.

14. Non-Renewal: We may elect not to renew or continue this section by giving written notice of our intent at least 30 days before the expiration date or anniversary. The notice may be delivered to or mailed to you at the mailing address shown on the Declarations page. Proof of mailing or delivery is sufficient proof of notice.

15. Conformity to Statute: The terms of cancellation and/or non-renewal, which are in conflict with the statutes of the state where this policy is issued, are hereby amended to conform to such statutes.

SCHEDULE OF VEHICLES

AUTOMOBILE – ADDITIONAL POLICY DECLARATIONS

POLICY NO. 2SAMPLE DOE, PERRY AND PAULINE 5/30/91

BILLING TERM 5/30/91 TO 5/30/92

LIABILITY LIMITS

B.I. 100,000 EA PER
300,000 EA OCC
P.D. 50,000 EA OCC

MEDICAL LIMITS

10,000 EA PER
50,000 EA OCC

UNINSURED MOTORIST

B.I. 15,000 EA PER
30,000 EA OCC

UNDERINSURED MOTORIST

B.I. 15,000 EA PER
30,000 EA OCC

MATERIAL DAMAGE

ITEM	YR	MAKE	TYPE	COMP	COLL	LIAB PREM	MAT DAM PREM	LIEN
01	91	CHEV	S-102X	ACV*	500 DED	710.40	533.70	00000

SERIAL NUMBER 1GC#S19Z0M123456

* ACTUAL CASH VALUE

TOTAL ANNUAL PREMIUM = 1244.10 TOTAL

* MATERIAL DAMAGE COVERAGE APPLIES ONLY TO VEHICLES SHOWN ON THE SCHEDULE OF VEHICLES INSURED FOR MATERIAL DAMAGE. NEWLY ACQUIRED VEHICLE(S) MUST BE REPORTED TO THE COMPANY OR AGENT WITHIN 30 DAYS OF ACQUISITION OR THE POLICY PERIOD, WHICHEVER IS SHORTER, IF MATERIAL DAMAGE COVERAGE IS DESIRED.

* NEWLY ACQUIRED VEHICLES COVERAGE FOR COMP. OR COLL. APPLICABLE ONLY TO VEHICLES WITH MODEL YEAR 8 YEARS OLD OR LESS FROM CURRENT CALENDAR YEAR.

COUNTRY SQUIRE DECLARATION SHEET

WESTERN AGRICULTURAL INSURANCE CO.
PO BOX 20180 PHOENIX, ARIZONA 85036

ISSUE DATE 2/01/91

DOE, PERRY & P.
10505 N. 89TH ST.
SUITE 600
SCOTTSDALE, AZ 85253

POLICY NUMBER 14311501
COUNTY 07 AGENT 468
TERM 1 YR THOMPSON, STEVEN

POLICY TERM 1/09/91 12:01 A.M. TO 1/09/92 12:01 A.M.

INSURANCE IS PROVIDED ONLY WITH RESPECT TO THOSE COVERAGES DESIGNATED BELOW BY EITHER PREMIUM OR THE WORD INCLUDED, BUT ONLY TO THE EXTENT SET FORTH IN THE SPECIFIC FORMS AND ENDORSEMENTS MADE A PART OF THE POLICY. COVERAGE IS AS PECIFIED ON ATTACHED ADDITIONAL POLICY DECLARATION SHEETS.

SECTION I – PROPERTY COVERAGE EFF 1/09/91............1,271.40
SECTION II – LIABILITY COVERAGE EFF 1/09/91 .... 180.80
SECTION III – AUTOMOBILE COVERAGE .... .00
SECTION IV – INLAND MARINE COVERAGE EFF 1/09/91 .... 36.60
SECTION V – UMBRELLA COVERAGE EFF 1/09/91........... 353.00

TOTAL ANNUAL PREMIUM 1,841.80

ENDORSEMENTS–
391 (06–90) 111 120 114 F02A
438–BFU (5–42) EM–L (10–80) 401
30 (5–42) 408 L93 L95(11/89) L9
L97(11/89) L99(11/89) L30

LEGAL LOCATION–
REFER TO SCHEDULE OF LOCATIONS L0

MORTGAGE CLAUSE– IF A MORTGAGE AND/OR LOSS PAYABLE CLAUSE(S) SHALL BE APPLICABLE.

36822 SEC I
DEER VALLEY CR UN
P.O. BOX 8000
PHOENIX, AZ 85066

THE INSURANCE AFFORDED BY THIS POLICY AS INDICATED WITHIN THIS DECLARATION SUPERSEDES AND REPLACES ALL INSURANCE PREVIOUSLY AFFORDED BY THIS POLICY. ASSIGNMENT OF THIS POLICY SHALL NOT BE VALID UNLESS WE GIVE OUR WRITTEN CONSENT.

____

COUNTERSIGNATURE *SEE ATTACHED SCHEDULE(S)*

SCHEDULE OF ADDITIONAL DWELLINGS, PERSONAL PROPERTY, AND OUTBUILDINGS

AS144 COUNTRY SQUIRE - ADDITIONAL POLICY DECLARATION

POLICY NO. 14311501 DOE, PERRY & P. 2/01/91

BILLING TERM 1/09/91 TO 1/09/92

ITEM NO.	TYPE	DESCRIPTION	DED	PERIL	INSURANCE AMOUNT	PREMIUM AMOUNT	MORT. NO.
01	F.P.P.	FARM PERSONAL PROP.	100	1-24	16,275	109.00	
01	DWELLING	GUEST HOUSE	100	25	40,000	180.00	
04	DWELLING	EMPLOYEE MOBILE	100	1-9	3,000	13.00	
02	OUTBUILDING	HAY SHED	100	1-9	3,000	17.90	
03	OUTBUILDING	PIPE BARN	100	1-9	5,000	29.90	
04	OUTBUILDING	TENNIS CRT WNDSCRN	100	1-9	1,000	6.00	
05	OUTBUILDING	TENNIS COURT FENCNG	100	1-9	4,000	23.90	
06	OUTBUILDING	TENNIS COURT LGHTNG	100	1-9	5,000	29.90	
07	OUTBUILDING	STORAGE SHED	100	1-9	8,000	58.40	
01	ELEC. MOTOR	400AMP ELEC PANEL	100	25	3,000	64.70	
02	ELEC. MOTOR	WELL PMP MTRS#M729	100	25	2,000	43.10	
TOTALS					90,275	575.80	

80 PERCENT COINSURANCE ON ALL ELEC. MOTOR ITEMS.

REFERENCE ADDITIONAL INSUREDS, ADDRESSES OR DESCRIPTIONS

(ITEM 02) '71 NATIONAL M/H, S#3856, 12' X 60'

(ITEM 03) '74 PARK MANOR M/H, S#FPA-4173-E, 14' X 70'

(ITEM 04) '72 STREAMLINE TRAVEL TRAILER, S# D25S2984, 8' X 26'

S P E C I A L L I M I T S O F L I A B I L I T Y A R E A S F O L L O W S -

- -

COV D HAY, STRAW, AND FODDER, PER STACK OR BUILDING $10,000

COV D HORSE, CATTLE, MULE OR DONKEY, PER HEAD $ 500

COV D SWINE, SHEEP, OR GOAT, PER HEAD $ 100

END 114 BORROWED EQUIPMENT - SAME AS THE FARM P.P. LIMIT

SCHEDULE OF SECTION II

COUNTRY SQUIRE - ADDITIONAL POLICY DECLARATION

POLICY NO. 14311501   DOE, PERRY & P.   2/01/91

BILLING TERM 1/09/91 TO 1/09/92

LIABILITY TERMS $300,000 BI-PD MEDICAL LIMITS 5,000 EA. PER.
EA. OCC. 25,000 EA. OCC.

ITEM	DESCRIPTION	AMT. OF INS. OR OTHER	ANNUAL PREMIUM
	LEGAL DESCRIPTION		
01	REFER TO SCHEDULE OF LOCATIONS	10 ACRES CROP	180.80
	-FOR ADDITIONAL LOCATIONS SEE SCHEDULE OF LOCATIONS		
	COV. F,G,M		INCL
		TOTAL PREMIUM	180.80

SPECIAL LIMITS OF LIABILITY ARE AS FOLLOWS

COV M DAMAGE TO PROPERTY OF OTHERS, PER OCC. $ 500

SCHEDULE OF SECTION IV

COUNTRY SQUIRE - ADDITIONAL POLICY DECLARATION AS145

POLICY NO. 14311501 DOE, PERRY & P. 2/01/91

BILLING TERM 1/09/91 TO 1/09/92

OTHER SCHEDULED PERSONAL PROPERTY.

ITEM	DESC & SERIAL NO	FORMS	DED. AMOUNT	AMOUNT OF INSURANCE	TOTAL PREMIUM
02	FEATHERED VASE	K	NIL	185	1.00
03	FISHING BOY	K	NIL	165	1.00
04	MORNING AIR	K	NIL	2,800	5.50
05	MOTHER AND COLT	K	NIL	2,500	5.00
06	FRIENDS	K	NIL	475	1.00
07	ECLIPSE	K	NIL	1,800	3.60
08	XEROX COPIER	K	NIL	750	1.50
09	TRS80 II MICRO CMPT 025717	X	NIL	1,000	9.00
10	TRS80 II DISK SYSTM 123601	X	NIL	700	6.30
11	TRS80 MDL 4 DM PRTR	X	NIL	300	2.70
*** TOTAL					36.60 ***

FORMS TABLE

K = 401
X = 408

SCHEDULE OF SECTION V—UMBRELLA

```
AS1455              COUNTRY SQUIRE -                2/01/91
               ADDITIONAL POLICY DECLARATION

POLICY 14311501      NAMED INSURED PERRY & PAULINE DOE
BILLING TERM  1/09/91 TO  1/09/92

LIABILITY LIMIT -  $2,000,000 EACH OCCURRENCE
                   $2,000,000 EACH AGGREGATE

SELF-INSURED RETENTION - $1,000

              SCHEDULE OF UNDERLYING INSURANCE

PREMISES AND OPERATIONS LIABILITY -

(X) SECTION II
( ) OTHER POLICIES -

AUTOMOBILE LIABILITY -

( ) SECTION III
(X) OTHER POLICIES -

TYPE OF
POLICY

UM / UIM LIAB
                            ANNUAL PREMIUM -    $353.00
ENDORSEMENTS - L9 L21
```

SCHEDULE OF LOCATIONS

```
   COUNTRY SQUIRE - ADDITIONAL POLICY DECLARATION
                                              AS141

POLICY NO. 14311501      DOE, PERRY & P.       2/01/91
ITEM                                        DWELLING
 NO.    LOCATION                 ACRES     TYPE    NO.

 01     S29 T6N R3E                                 02
 02     X-REF WITH ALL BUILDINGS                    01
 03     S29 T6N R3E                 10    ACRES     01
```

SCHEDULE OF COVERAGE—(A) DWELLING(S) OR (C) CONTENTS

AS144 COUNTRY SQUIRE - ADDITIONAL POLICY DECLARATION

POLICY NO. 14311501 DOE, PERRY & P. 2/01/91

BILLING TERM 1/09/91 to 1/09/92

..(COV A)....(COV B)....(COV C)..

ITEM NO.	TYPE	DWELLING	ADDL.(1) LIVING EXPENSE	PERSONAL(1) PROPERTY	DED	COV A PERIL	COV C PERIL	PREMIUM AMOUNT	MORT. NO.
01	DWELLING TERR=A	309,600	61,920	154,800	1000	25	1-18	695.60	36822
							LOAN = 149179		
TOTALS		309,600						695.60	

INFLATION GUARD - 120 - APPLIES TO DWELLING(S) -01

ENDORSEMENT 111 - APPLIES TO DWELLING(S) - 01

(1) COVERAGE APPLIES INDIVIDUALLY AND SEPARATELY TO EACH SCHEDULED ITEM.

S P E C I A L L I M I T S O F L I A B I L I T Y A R E A S F O L L O W S -

- -

REFRIGERATED PRODUCTS $500

GLOSSARY

■ **Abnormally dangerous activity**
Activity for which a defendant is strictly liable if someone is injured; characterized as an activity having a high degree of risk of serious harm that cannot be eliminated with due care and whose value is outweighed by its dangerous attributes.

■ **Absolute privilege**
Absolute defense to defamation, regardless of defendant's motives.

■ **Abuse of process**
Use of litigation devices for improper purposes.

■ **Accrual**
Time at which a statute of limitations begins to run, usually at the time the plaintiff is injured.

■ **Action in trespass (*vi et armis*)**
Early cause of action involving serious, forcible breaches of peace that evolved to encompass even minor physical contact; no showing of fault was required.

■ **Actual cash value**
Policy that pays the insured on the basis of the initial cost of the property minus any accrued depreciation.

■ **Actual cause**
Cause in fact of plaintiff's injuries.

■ **Actual malice**
Acting with knowledge of the falsity of one's statement or with reckless disregard to the truth or falsity of one's statement.

■ **Adhesion contract**
Standardized contract characterized by the unequal bargaining power of the parties and the lack of negotiation regarding the terms of the contract.

■ **Affirmative defense**
Any defense that a party asserts for which it bears the burden of proof.

■ **Alienation of affections**
Causing a plaintiff to lose affection for his or her spouse.

■ **Answer**
A pleading in which the defendant responds to the plaintiff's complaint.

■ **Appellant**
One who appeals a decision made by a lower court.

■ **Appropriation**
Use of the value of the plaintiff's name or picture for the defendant's financial gain.

■ **Assault**
Intentional causing of an apprehension of harmful or offensive contact.

■ **Assumption of risk**
Defense that the plaintiff voluntarily consented to take the chance that harm would occur if he or she engaged in certain conduct.

■ **Attractive nuisance**
Dangerous condition on the defendant's property that is likely to induce children to trespass.

■ **At-will employee**
Employee who, because of the nature

of his or her employment contract, can be discharged at any time for any reason.

Avoidable consequences rule
Obligation of a plaintiff to minimize (mitigate) her damages.

Bailee
One who is temporarily entrusted with the custody of goods.

Bailor
One who entrusts his or her goods to the temporary custody of another.

Battery
Intentional infliction of a harmful or offensive contact upon a person.

Bench trial
Trial before a judge.

Binding authority
Legal authority that a court must follow.

Breach of duty
Failure to conform to the required standard of care.

Briefing
Summarizing the key elements of a case, including the procedural history, facts, issues, legal rules, holdings, and rationale.

Burden of persuasion
Burden of proving the elements of a case by preponderance of the evidence.

Burden of production
Burden of producing sufficient evidence to avoid a directed verdict.

Case of first impression
First case heard within a particular jurisdiction regarding a specific point of law.

Challenge for cause
Request to remove a potential juror because of his or her alleged inability to decide the case impartially.

Charging the jury
Process in which the judge instructs the jury in rules of law they are to apply.

Chattels
Personal property.

Collateral source rule
Right of a plaintiff to recover twice for damages.

Comparative negligence
Defense that the plaintiff's recovery should be reduced in direct proportion to the plaintiff's percentage of contribution to his or her own injuries.

Compensatory damages
Damages designed to compensate the plaintiff; consist of both general and special damages.

Complaint
An initial pleading filed on behalf of the plaintiff whose purpose is to provide the defendant with the material elements of the plaintiff's demand..

Concurrent tortfeasors
Tortfeasors who independently cause the plaintiff injury.

Contribution
Partial reimbursement of tortfeasor who has paid more than his or her pro rata share of the damages.

Contributory negligence
Defense that the plaintiff contributed to his or her own injuries and should therefore be barred from recovery.

Conversion
Substantial interference with another's property to the extent that justice demands payment for the full value of the property.

Coordination of benefits provision
Policy provision that precludes payment to the insured if the insured has other insurance available.

Counterclaim
A claim presented by a defendant in opposition to the plaintiff's claim.

Covenant not to sue
Promise by a plaintiff not to sue a particular defendant.

Co-insurance limit
The point in a health insurance policy at which an insurer is totally responsible for payment of expenses; up to that point the insured is

responsible for a percentage of the expenses (that percentage is designated in the policy).

■ **Criminal conversation**
Having sexual intercourse with another's spouse.

■ **Crossclaim**
A claim brought by a defendant against a co-defendant in the same action.

■ **Deceit**
Common law cause of action equated with intentional misrepresentation; also referred to as fraud.

■ **Declaratory judgment action**
Action in which the court renders an opinion as to a matter of law or in reference to the rights of the parties but does not order any action to be taken.

■ **Defamation**
Statement that tends to harm the reputation of another, encompassing both libel and slander.

■ **Default judgment**
Judgment entered due to lack of opposition on behalf of opposing party.

■ **Defective warning**
Defect arising out of a manufacturer's failure to give adequate warnings or directions for use.

■ **Demand letter**
A letter detailing a client's damages and setting forth the reasons for her demand.

■ **Demurrer**
Motion for dismissal based on a defect in the form or content of a complaint.

■ **Deposition**
Oral examination of a witness under oath.

■ **Derivative claim**
Claim derived from underlying claim, e.g., loss of consortium is a derivative claim.

■ **Design defect**
Defect arising out of a manufacturer's use of an unreasonably dangerous design.

■ **Dictum**
Discussion in a court opinion not related to the issues actually before the court.

■ **Directed verdict**
Request that the case be dismissed because of the opposing party's failure to meet the requisite burden of proof.

■ **Discounting an award**
Reducing an award to its present value.

■ **Discovery**
Process that parties engage in in order to find out as much as possible about the other side's case.

■ **Discretionary function**
Act of a government employee requiring the use of judgment.

■ **Economic loss**
Diminution in the value of a product.

■ **Excess judgment**
Judgment in excess of the insured's policy limits.

■ **Express warranty**
Express representation by a seller that a product possesses certain qualities.

■ **Fair market value**
Amount property could be sold for on the open market.

■ **False imprisonment**
Intentional confinement of another.

■ **False light**
Representing the plaintiff to the public in a way that would be highly offensive to a reasonable person.

■ **Family purpose doctrine**
Doctrine that makes the owner of a car liable for the tortious acts of family members committed while driving.

■ **Fiduciary relationship**
Relationship based on trust and confidence that imposes an obligation to act in good faith; an example is the attorney-client relationship.

■ **First party coverage**
Coverage providing reimbursement to the insured for losses sustained directly by the insured.

■ **General damages**
Compensatory damages that can generally be anticipated to result from

the type of conduct the defendant engaged in.

■ **General verdict**
Verdict in which a jury decides issues of liability and damages.

■ **Governmental function**
Task typically performed by a governmental entity.

■ **Holding**
Appellate court's decision.

■ **Immunity**
Absolute defense derived from the defendant's status (e.g., a government official) or relationship to the plaintiff (e.g., spouse of the plaintiff).

■ **Implied warranty**
Representations as to a product's qualities that are implied by virtue of the product being offered for sale.

■ **Imputed negligence**
Negligence that is charged or attributed to another.

■ **Indemnification**
Total acceptance of financial responsibility by one tortfeasor for another.

■ **Independent contractor**
Someone hired to do a job who works at his own pace, in his own way, under his own supervision.

■ **Informed consent**
Knowledgeable consent based on disclosure of all relevant facts, allowing one to make an informed decision.

■ **Injurious falsehood**
False disparagement of a plaintiff's business, product, or property rights.

■ **Innuendo**
Use of extrinsic facts to convey the defamatory meaning of a statement.

■ **Intentional tort**
Tort in which the tortfeasor intends to bring about a particular consequence or knows with substantial certainty that a result will occur.

■ **Interrogatories**
Written questions submitted to the opposing party which that party must answer in writing and under oath.

■ **Intervening cause**
Act that contributes to the plaintiff's injuries but does not relieve the defendant of liability.

■ **Invitee**
Person invited by possessor of land onto her property for the purpose of conducting business.

■ **IRAC**
Steps involved in legal analysis: identifying the issue (I), identifying the applicable rules (R), applying the rules (A), and drawing a conclusion (C).

■ **JNOV (Judgment Notwithstanding the Verdict)**
Motion arguing that the verdict reached was contrary to the evidence and the law.

■ **Joint and several liability**
Liability for an entire loss if the loss is indivisible.

■ **Joint enterprise**
Two or more persons who agree to a common goal or purpose, who share a common pecuniary interest, and who have an equal right to control the direction of the enterprise.

■ **Joint tortfeasors**
Those who act together to cause the plaintiff's injury.

■ **Last clear chance doctrine**
Doctrine that allows the plaintiff to recover in a contributory negligence system despite the plaintiff's negligence.

■ **Latent defect**
Defect that is invisible or not readily discoverable.

■ **Libel**
Written defamatory statements.

■ **Licensee**
Person who has possessor's consent to be present on land.

■ **Loan value**
The amount of monies that will be loaned by an insurer to an insured based on the contractually determined value of the life insurance policy.

■ **Loss of consortium**
Loss of services, including

companionship, sex, and earnings outside of the home.

Manufacturing defect
Defect arising out of a deviation in the manufacturing process.

Motion for protective order
Motion that protects a party from having to disclose privileged information.

Motion for summary judgment
Motion requesting that the court enter a judgment on the party's behalf because there is no material fact at issue.

Motion to compel
Motion compelling the opposing party to comply with request for discovery.

Motion *in limine*
Motion to prevent evidence from being presented to the jury.

Necessity
Privilege that justifies the defendant's harming of the plaintiff's property in an effort to prevent great harm to the defendant or others.

Negligence *per se*
Presumed negligence that arises from the unexcused violation of a statute.

Nominal damages
Damages awarded when liability is shown but no actual damages are proved.

Nuisance
Substantial and unreasonable interference with a plaintiff's intent; includes public and private nuisance.

Objective Standard
Comparison of a defendant's conduct to that of a reasonable person.

Parasitic damages
Damages attached to physical injury, e.g., mental suffering.

Patent defect
Defect that is visible or readily discoverable.

Pecuniary
Monetary; that which can be valued in terms of money.

Peremptory challenge
Request to remove a potential juror for no articulated reason.

Persuasive authority
Authority that a court may consider but which it is not legally bound to follow.

Plit limits coverage
Fixed amount of coverage that is available for each individual claim with a different fixed amount for the total of all the claims (puts a cap on individual recovery).

Preexisting condition
Medical condition suffered by an insured prior to his or her application for a health insurance policy.

Present value
Current value of money that is to be paid in the future, based on the assumption that money received today is worth more than money received in the future because of the investment potential of money.

Presumed damages
Damages that ordinarily stem from a defamatory statement and that do not require the showing of actual harm.

Pretrial conference
Conference involving the judge and parties at which issues and procedures for the trial are clarified and efforts are made at settlement.

Primary coverage
Insurance carrier providing initial coverage for all damages up to the limits of the policy.

Privity
Requirement that the plaintiff must contract directly with the defendant in order to recover for losses.

Proprietary function
Function performed by the government that could just as easily be performed by a private entity.

Proximate cause
Legal cause of plaintiff's injuries; emphasis is on the concept of foreseeability.

Publication
Hearing or seeing a defamatory statement by someone other than the plaintiff.

Public figure
One who has achieved persuasive fame

or notoriety or who becomes involved in a public controversy.

■ **Public policy**
Consideration by judges of the effects of proposed legal principle on society as a whole.

■ **Punitive damages**
Damages designed to punish the defendant (also referred to as exemplary damages).

■ **Qualified privilege**
Privilege that applies only when a defendant acts on the basis of certain well-defined purposes.

■ **Reformation of a policy**
Construing a policy to provide the minimum coverage required by statute.

■ **Release**
Agreement to absolve a defendant of all liability.

■ **Replacement cost policy**
Policy that pays the insured on the basis of the cost of replacing the property at the time the loss is incurred.

■ **Request for admissions**
Request by one party asking the other party to admit certain facts.

■ **Request for medical examination**
Request that the opposing party be examined by a physician chosen by the party making the request.

■ **Request for production of documents**
Request for document in possession of the opposing party.

■ **Reservation of rights**
Decision of insurer to defend insured until it determines that it has a right to deny coverage.

■ ***Res ipsa loquitur***
Doctrine plaintiff can turn to in proving negligence when it is difficult to obtain information about the defendant's conduct.

■ ***Res judicata***
Legal principle that requires that issues litigated cannot be relitigated at a later time.

■ ***Respondeat superior***
Doctrine establishing the vicarious liability of employers for the acts of their employees.

■ **Satisfaction**
Payment of a judgment.

■ **Secondary coverage**
Insurance carrier providing coverage for damages incurred but not until the limits of the primary policy have been exhausted.

■ **Single limit coverage**
Fixed amount of coverage that is available to all those injured regardless of how great their losses arem.

■ **Slander**
Oral defamatory statements.

■ **Slander of title**
False disparagement of plaintiff's property right.

■ **Slander *per se***
Slander in which pecuniary harm can be assumed.

■ **Slippery slope argument**
Argument that once you take a first step in allowing something in one instance you are in danger of falling down the "slippery slope" into a bottomless pit of circumstances requiring comparable treatment.

■ **Special damages**
Compensatory damages specifically linked to the plaintiff.

■ **Special harm**
Harm of a pecuniary nature.

■ **Special verdict**
Verdict in which the jury is required to answer special interrogatories, which the judge must review in order to determine who the prevailing party is.

■ **Stacking of policies**
Using one or more policies to provide coverage for the same incident.

■ **Statute of limitations**
Statute that limits the time period in which a claim can be filed.

■ **Statute of repose**
Statute of limitations in products liability cases that limits the time period during which suit can be filed.

■ **Strict liability**
Liability imposed without a showing of intent or negligence.

■ **Structured settlement**
Agreement to pay damages in installments rather than a lump sum.

■ **Subjective standard**
Use of the defendant's own subjective perceptions to determine whether the defendant behaved reasonably.

■ **Subrogation**
The right of an insurer to institute suit in the name of the insured against the responsible party to collect for monies paid by the insurer to the insured.

■ **Superseding cause**
Act that contributes to the plaintiff's injuries to the extent that the defendant is relieved of liability.

■ **Survival action**
Action that survives the decedent's death.

■ **Third party coverage**
Coverage that indemnifies the insured for damages he or she caused or for which the law holds him or her responsible.

■ **Trade libel**
False disparagement of plaintiff's goods or business.

■ **Transferred intent**
Intent with respect to one person (or tort) is transferred to another person (or tort).

■ **Trespass on the case**
Early cause of action involving injuries inflicted indirectly and requiring some showing of fault.

■ **Trespass to chattels**
Intentional interference with another's use or possession of chattels.

■ **Trespass to land**
Intentionally entering or wrongfully remaining on another's land.

■ **Umbrella policy**
Policy that provides a secondary source of coverage after the deductible has been paid, usually coordinated with the limits of the underlying policy.

■ **Unavoidably unsafe products**
Products incapable of being made safe for their ordinary and intended use.

■ **Verification**
Affidavit indicating plaintiff has read the complaint and to the best of his or her knowledge believes it to be true.

■ **Vicarious liability**
Liability for the tortious acts of others.

■ ***Voir dire***
Process of jury selection involving the use of challenges for cause and peremptory challenges.

■ **Warranty of fitness for a particular purpose**
Implied warranty that goods are suitable to be used for a particular (noncustomary) purpose.

■ **Warranty of merchantability**
Implied warranty that goods are fit for the ordinary purpose for which they are used.

■ **Wrongful death action**
Action brought by third parties to recover for losses they suffered as a result of the decedent's death.

TABLE OF CASES

Underlined cases appear in the text. Cases not underlined are referred to in the text.

Real Do1 Steele

INDEX

D

J

K

L

T

U

V

W

Z